FOLKLORE
and FOLKLIFE

Edited by Richard M. Dorson

FOLKLORE
and FOLKLIFE
AN INTRODUCTION

The University of Chicago Press
Chicago and London

The University of Chicago Press, Chicago 60637
The University of Chicago Press, Ltd., London

© 1972 by The University of Chicago
All rights reserved. Published 1972
Second Impression 1973
Printed in the United States of America

International Standard Book Number: 0–226–15870–5
Library of Congress Catalog Card Number: 77–189038

CONTENTS

ILLUSTRATIONS

PREFACE
Richard M. Dorson

This volume is intended to answer the questions "What is folklore?" and "What does a folklorist do?" Anyone who teaches, studies, or does research in folklore continually faces these questions, whether at cocktail parties, where he is supposed to give a sweeping answer in thirty seconds, or from friends, relatives, colleagues, parents, and new acquaintances in almost any social situation. The harassed folklorist would like to be able to recommend a comprehensive book to his inquisitor, who indeed frequently requests the title of such a work. But no satisfactory survey of the subject in English has existed. The field is too vast and complex for any one individual to cover it in depth and until recently enough specialists have not been available to make a collaborative effort feasible for the English-speaking world.

At Indiana University a folklore department came into being in 1963, the first in the United States, and its faculty provides the nucleus for this undertaking. Seven contributors are members of the department—Dégh, Dorson, Glassie, List, Oinas, Richmond, and Roberts, and an eighth, Messenger, now of The Ohio State University, was a member at the time of writing. Other contributors who have taught as visiting professors in the Indiana University Folklore Institute are Abrahams of the University of Texas and Wildhaber of Switzerland, while Evans from northern Ireland has lectured in the geography department. Three contributors hold their doctorates in folklore from Indiana University: Dundes of the University of California at Berkeley, Georges of UCLA, and Smith of the University of Kansas, while Kealiinohomoku has taken her doctorate at Indiana University in anthropology. The folklore department of the University of Pennsylvania is represented by Yoder. European folklore scholars, in addition to Wildhaber and Evans, include Jenkins from Wales and MacDonald from Scotland, as well as Indiana's Dégh and Oinas, originally from Hungary and Estonia.

For funds to provide me with a research assistant for this and other tasks I wish to thank the Indiana University Research Committee, and for filling the assistantship so capably I am grateful to Inta Carpenter. Felix J. Oinas has kindly checked the transliteration of Russian proper names and titles throughout the volume, and Henry Glassie has given valuable aid with the illustrations.

Folklore Institute
Bloomington, Indiana

INTRODUCTION
CONCEPTS OF FOLKLORE AND FOLKLIFE STUDIES
Richard M. Dorson

Folklore emerged as a new field of learning in the nineteenth century, when antiquaries in England and philologists in Germany began to look closely at the ways of the lower classes. In 1812 the German brothers Jacob and Wilhelm Grimm commenced publishing influential volumes of oral folk narratives and interpretations of Germanic mythology. The word they used to denote this subject was *Volkskunde*. Then, on 22 August 1846, an English antiquary, William John Thoms, sent a letter to the *Athenaeum,* a magazine catering to the intellectually curious, suggesting that the new word "Folk-lore" be thenceforth adopted in place of the cumbersome phrase "popular antiquities." The term caught on and proved its value in defining a new area of knowledge and subject of inquiry, but it has also caused confusion and controversy. To the layman, and to the academic man too, folklore suggests falsity, wrongness, fantasy, and distortion. Or it may conjure up pictures of granny women spinning traditional tales in mountain cabins or gaily costumed peasants performing seasonal dances. In the present work, folklore will mean both a field of learning and the whole subject matter of that field. History as a term possesses the same ambiguity, standing for the discipline and for the content, but it does not create the same possible misunderstanding.

In recent years another term, folklife, has vied with and even threatened to dominate folklore. The supporters of folklife studies claim that folklorists are too narrowly preoccupied with verbal forms and neglect the tangible products of folk artisans. They maintain that folklife embraces the whole panorama of traditional culture, including oral folklore. Conversely, the champions of folklore stoutly maintain that their term includes traditional arts and crafts. The following chapters give equal time and space to the two terms, recognizing their nuances and their partnership.

THE FIELDS OF FOLKLORE AND FOLKLIFE STUDIES

The matters that occupy the student of folklore and folklife may be placed under four large groupings. One of these sectors is *oral literature,* sometimes called verbal art or expressive literature. Under this rubric fall spoken, sung, and voiced forms of traditional utterance that show repetitive patterns. One large subdivision is folk narrative, which in turn has its own manifold distinctions. Another major subdivision is folksong or folk poetry, with its own family of related species. Traditional tales and songs correspond to the written productions of novelists and poets, but they circulate by word of mouth and without known authorship. They may be short anecdotes and rhymes or elaborate romances and epics. Certain brief genres of oral expression are classed as proverbs and riddles. Oral literature can and frequently does enter into written literature. A new generation of African novelists educated in England strews the proverbs of their native languages throughout their fiction. What we may call folk speech embraces the local and regional turns of phrase that deviate from the standard language taught in the schools. Such archaic and dialectal words are of interest to the folklorist both in themselves as parts of daily language, and within tales, songs, and sayings. Not all oral folk expression is verbal. Yodels, hollers, cries, chants, and laments may acquire their own traditional character based on nonlexical sounds.

In direct contrast to this oral folklore is physical folklife, generally called *material culture.* Now we deal with the visible rather than the aural aspects of folk behavior that existed prior to and continue alongside mechanized industry. Material culture responds to techniques, skills, recipes, and formulas transmitted across the generations and subject to the same forces of conservative tradition and individual variation as verbal art. How men and women in tradition-oriented societies build their homes, make their clothes, prepare their food,

farm and fish, process the earth's bounty, fashion their tools and implements, and design their furniture and utensils are questions that
concern the student of material culture. In a tribal society all processes
are traditional and products handmade, although of course innovation
occurs. The folklife specialist directs his attention to the high civilizations where the phenomenon of cultural lag is evident, that is, where
the older peasant and pioneer life styles lie in the shadow of the industrial revolution. The kinds of investigations he pursues are indicated
in the journal *Folk Life,* founded by the Society for Folk Life
Studies in 1963. Here we find articles on bowl turners and spoon
carvers, a hand comber in the wool textile trade, the long-house in
Wales, the byre-and dwelling in Ireland, elver fishing in the Severn
River, methods of dyeing wool, lacemaking in the East Midlands,
quilting in the north of England, tools of the shipwright, and fashions
in horseflesh. All these matters belong to an older, submerged culture
about which surprisingly little is known and recorded.

In between oral literature and material culture lie areas of traditional life facing in both directions. One such area we may call *social
folk custom.* Here the emphasis is on group interaction rather than on
individual skills and performances. English antiquaries lumped under
"custom and usage" a great many community and family observances
connected with villages, manors, landmarks, households, churches,
holidays, and such *rites de passage* as birth, initiation, marriage, and
death. Customs of this sort include "telling the bees" of a death in the
family by draping the hives in black, or nailing up a horseshoe on
the front door to avert witchcraft, or making a wish before tasting the
first fruits of the season. These customs are often closely bound up with
deeply held folk beliefs, which in themselves constitute a folklore
genre. Some customs may be highly specific and local. For an instance,
penny loaves are given away every 11 March in Newark-upon-Trent,
in England, to whoever appears at the town hall, according to the will
of one Hercules Clay, dated 1694. Clay dreamed three nights in a row
that his house had been set afire by the parliamentary army under
Oliver Cromwell. He quitted his house, and a few hours later a fire
bomb did land on his house; in gratitude for his deliverance he made
his bequest, resulting in the custom still followed. General and special
customs usually involve a physical action (giving the food), a shared
belief (the premonitory dream), and a material object (the penny
loaf). Customs that have acquired considerable magical and sacred
potency are known as rituals.

The participation of large social units in public performances and
entertainments leads to another kind of social folk custom to which
the terms festival and celebration generally apply. Music, dance, costume, floats, and processions may all enter into festivals, which are

based on both religious and secular traditions. Certain games and recreations, or sports and pastimes as Joseph Strutt called them in his pioneering work on the subject, are learned through tradition rather than by codified rules and regulations. The difference is between baseball and what may have been a precursor, a game such as one-a-cat still played by boys: a short stick is tilted against a stone and then knocked in the air and struck with a larger stick.

The religious aspects of social folk custom cover the modes of worship that lie outside the established church. Such modes may hark back to pre-Christian times, as in the local shrines dotted around the Japanese countryside, where offerings are ritually made to unquiet spirits; or they may derive from folk reinterpretations of Christian doctrine and gospel, as in American Negro revisions of Baptist services through the incantatory sermon and congregational spiritual; or they may involve syncretism between indigenous deities and the monotheistic religions, as in the identification of African gods with Catholic saints. Throughout Latin America, the processes of reinterpretation and syncretism are especially noticeable in religious services featuring a black Christ or the crucifixion of the Virgin Mary. Folk religion overlaps at points with folk medicine in instances where a famed miracle-maker saves souls and heals bodies. Saints of the Roman Catholic and Eastern Orthodox churches are given gifts and vows in return for their curing of fatal illnesses and repairing of mangled bodies, while noted healers acquire folk sainthood and have their pictures placed on home altars alongside canonized saints. All kinds of cult leaders, prophets, faith healers, occultists, hoodoo doctors, and dealers in black and white magic cast their charismatic spells over their followers. Strictly in the realm of folk medicine fall the bloodstoppers, burn healers, wart charmers, cancer curers, and such specialists who through inherited or transferred powers can remedy ailments beyond the capacities of medical doctors. The spectrum of folk-medical practitioners extends from these users of invocations and secret charms to the herbalists and grannies employing old wives' recipes that sometimes, as in the discovery of penicillin in bread mold, have been shown to possess demonstrable curative properties.

A fourth sector of folklore and folklife may be designated the *performing folk arts.* Here we think primarily of traditional music, dance, and drama. While the renditions of a folktale or a folksong are now usually referred to as performances, they are more casual in nature than the conscious presentation of these arts by individuals or groups with folk instruments, dance costumes, and scenario props. The performing arts intersect each with the other and often appear in conjunction. Violet Alford introduces her book *Sword Dance and Drama* with a quotation from T. F. Ordish: "The shaping factor in folk

drama was the Sword dance with its circle, chorus and carefully con-
certed movements." The performing folk arts also interact with the
formal performing arts. Today the regional peasant and tribal dances,
songs, and music of Europe, the Americas, Asia, and Africa have become increasingly popular entertainment fare for urban audiences,
and consequently the performers adopt sophisticated techniques and
mannerisms. On the other side, elements of high culture continually
seep into folk repertoires.

The four divisions sketched here are not all-inclusive or mutually
exclusive. Where do we place traditional gestures, for instance? They
might be bracketed with "folk speech," as a folk communication system,
even though such placement leads to the paradox of subsuming gestures under oral folklore. How does one draw a firm line between festival and the performing arts? Should beliefs and superstitions be considered a separate entity or be incorporated with legends, customs, and
folk religion? One can quibble endlessly over these matters, and folklorists usually do. But our four groupings throw in relief the general
terrain of folklore and folklife studies.

THE SKILLS OF THE FOLKLORIST

If folklore does embody a special subject matter omitted from other
fields of learning, we should now consider the person who studies this
subject, the folklorist. Is he an independent scholar in his own right,
and is his field properly a separate discipline, or should folklore and
folklorists be entrusted to departments of English and anthropology
or whoever manifests a sympathetic interest? In most countries of Europe, folklore is indeed a recognized university discipline, with its own
chairs and research institutes. In England, in spite of an illustrious
history of private scholarship in the nineteenth century, folklore has
not achieved academic status. In Scotland and Ireland, two well-staffed
collecting and research institutes are crossing the line to faculty and
teaching responsibilities. In the United States, folklore during the
1960s gained a foothold in several universities as a graduate department leading to M.A. and Ph.D. degrees, and as an undergraduate
concentration at Harvard. In the same period the American Folklore
Society underwent a considerable transformation from a loose and
floundering organization, dependent on amateurs or academics studying folklore as a secondary interest, to a vigorous and solvent society
strongly supported by faculty members and graduate students considering themselves folklorists first and foremost. The production of
Ph.D.s in folklore by Indiana University and the University of Pennsylvania and their infusion into the American academic bloodstream
were chiefly responsible for this change. Academic folklorists have be-

come, if not a commonplace, at least more than a rarity in the university landscape. They thus begin to replace the antiquaries, the popularizers, the songbirds, and the professors of other subjects as the qualified spokesmen for folklore and folklife.

What then are the skills, perspectives, and methods that set the folklorist apart from the anthropologist, the historian, the literary critic, the sociologist, the psychologist, and the political scientist? We can enumerate a baker's dozen of these skills that the practicing folklorist must master. *Fieldwork* enables him to penetrate into alien cultures— at his back door, not necessarily in remote lands. The *use of archives*, into which the manuscript and taped results of field recordings are poured in complex systems, allows him to tap vast unpublished collections of folklore. He must also become adept in *use of the folk museum*, whose artifacts of material culture correspond to the texts and tunes in the archives. Through *mastery of bibliographic tools* he will find his way through the mountains of publications of folklore in the world's languages. Bibliographical finding aids go only so far, and the folklorist in order to identify and classify his materials must cultivate the *use of indexes*, the ingenious classificatory systems such as Stith Thompson's giant *Motif-Index of Folk Literature*, the Aarne-Thompson type-index of folktales, Archer Taylor's arrangement of English riddles, Francis James Child's canon of English and Scottish popular ballads, and similar taxonomic works. Related to indexing is the technique of *annotating*, whereby the folklorist succinctly documents the traditional pedigree of his text, much as an historical scholar footnotes a statement open to question. *Terminology* can also be considered a specialized skill, for the folklorist must employ familiar words laden with ambiguity, such as fairy tale, legend, and myth, and whole dictionaries of esoteric terms developed by foreign scholars to express the elusive and subtle concepts underlying the genres of folklore. Since he cannot rely exclusively on field data and archival resources, the folklorist must equip himself in the technique of *using printed sources*, and grapple with the difficult problems of detecting folk traditions in manifold publications and analyzing their relationship to original oral forms.

The international nature of folklore studies leads to the cultivation of still other skills by the folklorist. One such skill or technique may be termed *international communications*. The professional folklorist cannot simply plough the soil of his own environs, for the trail of the most localized item of folklore will eventually lead around the world, and the problems he confronts are also being faced, with perhaps a good deal more support, on other continents. Hence he must establish connections with the world-wide fraternity of folklorists, through participation in international organizations, conferences, and symposiums, and the cultivation of personal, professional, and institutional relationships. Also he must familiarize himself with the *history of folkloristics*, so that he knows the broad outlines of the development of the subject in different countries, each with its own illustrious personalities, nationalistic biases, and theoretical preferences.

Yet another cluster of skills involves the folklorist with other disciplines. He needs sufficient familiarity with literature to investigate *literary uses of folklore*, with anthropology to explore the *relationships of folklore to culture*, and with history to comprehend the *historical validity of oral tradition*. Other fields such as linguistics, geography, musicology, sociology, and psychology are also indicated, but the literary, anthropological, and historical approaches are primary.

It is apparent that the training of the folklorist requires considerable experience in the field, the library, the archives, the museum, and in foreign countries. Yet many persons seem to feel they can obtain the answers to "What is folklore?" and "What does a folklorist do?" in a five-minute conversation. They would not ask this question so casually of a scholar in other disciplines of the humanities or the social sciences.

CURRENT THEORIES OF FOLKLORE

So far we have been talking about the distinctive subject matter and training of the folklorist, but we have not commented on his goals and purposes. How does he envisage his particular contribution to knowledge, and what are his guiding intellectual and conceptual frameworks? We may distinguish a number of theoretical points of view that currently vie for acceptance.

HISTORICAL-GEOGRAPHICAL

By employing the so-called Finnish historical-geographical method, the comparative folklorist endeavors to reconstruct the history of a complex folktale, or occasionally a folksong or other folklore item. The method was designed to thwart rash generalizations about the origin and meaning of the folktales through a thorough and unprejudiced examination of each individual tale. This research technique is called a "method" rather than a "theory." Nevertheless, the method rests on certain theoretical assumptions, and has given rise to considerable theoretical controversy.

The Finnish method, while disclaiming dogma, has selected one of various possibilities to account for the origin and spread of oral tales. According to its premises, a tale that has been found in hundreds of oral variants must have originated in one time and one place by an act of conscious invention. Subsequently this tale must have traveled in ever-widening arcs from its point of creation. The "wave-like" diffusion of the tale will be affected by facile routes of trade and travel, and possibly by the secondary influence of manuscript and printed texts, but diffusion takes place over an expanding geographical area.

Consequently the Finnish method rejects such blanket theories of origin as polygenesis or independent invention of complex tales, dream origins, ritual origins, origins based in observation of heavenly phenomena, or in the savage mentality, or as the expression of repressed infantile fantasies. Likewise the Finnish scholars dismiss antidiffusionists who aver that tales cannot cross linguistic and cultural boundaries. The evidence of their monographic studies demonstrates that certain tales and ballads easily leap language walls, more easily even than they pass cultural frontiers. Further, the evidence indicates that the tales move from more-advanced to less-civilized peoples. With the expansion of Europe in the fifteenth and sixteenth century, European colonizers transported folktales to the continents of North and South America and Africa, but the tales of Africans and American Indians are not found among European peasants. Hence the areas of origin of the widely diffused folktales that have been intensively studied prove to be India and Western Europe, with Asia Minor and other zones of Europe as secondary centers of diffusion.

The Finnish method imposes certain arduous obligations upon the comparative folklorist. Having selected the Märchen, Sage, animal tale, or ballad for his quest, necessarily choosing one for which hundreds of variants exist, he must assemble the texts of these variants from printed collections, folklore archives, and the versions in literature. He analyzes his basic plot into traits or essential components, constructs percentage tables for the regional frequencies of occurrence of each trait, maps their geographic distribution, evaluates the early literary recordings, and judges the oldest traits of the story. Certain established principles of variation in oral transmission, such as compression, elaboration, and substitution, assist him in making this judgment. For instance, a razor appearing in "The Magic Flight" as one of the objects that grows to great size and blocks the ogre in his pursuit of the hero is obviously a later form of magic object than a stone or a twig, and represents a substitution. At the end of the painstaking inquiry the investigator presents his richly documented results. These are the hypothetical Ur-type from which all variants of the tale or ballad as originally composed have sprung; its geographical starting point; and its historical routes of travel.

The Finnish school remains today the dominant force in folklore science, but its assumptions and procedures have come under increasing attack, and its supporters have given some ground. A formidable scholar of the generation just past, the Austrian Albert Wesselski (1871–1939), contended that literary versions of a tale exercised an influence on its circulation so powerful as to invalidate any attempts to trace oral diffusion. The eminent Swedish folklorist, Carl von Sydow (1878–1952), believed that local historical and cultural factors molded an international tale into subtypes, or regional oikotypes, as he termed them, which possessed their own separate histories. A postulated Ur-form that can never be substantiated was, he felt, itself a fairy tale.

Other scholars in the forefront of Scandinavian folklore activities today, such as Reidar Christiansen of Norway and Laurits Bødker of Denmark, object to the rigidity and mechanical nature of the Finnish monographs. According to these criticisms, the Finnish method reduces tale studies to statistical abstracts, summaries, symbols, tables, and maps, ignoring aesthetic and stylistic elements and the human side of the narrator. Further, the laborious requirements of the Finnish method seem disproportionate to the results, for the task of assembling all known variants practically defies completion.

Thus a recent monograph employing the Finnish method, *The Tale of the Kind and the Unkind Girls,* by Warren Roberts (1958), assembles over nine hundred texts of Type 480 from all over the world. Yet one reviewer, Thelma James, mentions the omission of one hundred and nine Latvian examples, while the dean of comparative folktale scholars, Walter Anderson, points out gaps for Portugal, Spain (including Catalonia), Spanish America, France, Italy, Germany, Russia, the Ukraine, Greece, Hungary, Tartary, the Caucasus, Persia, and Japan. Roberts's study takes cognizance of earlier criticisms of the historical-geographical approach, and gives due attention to literary appearances and to regional subtypes. It modifies the concept of the "archetype" to mean not the one original form of the tale but the most important form influencing the versions found today in a particular area. Roberts dates the tale as arising in the Near East before the fifteenth century and entering northern Europe through a route between the Black and the Caspian seas, but he does not attempt to conjecture how the tale reached India and Japan. Before the sixteenth century a new form of the story starts traveling from the Near East, which drops the episode where the heroine encounters three talking animals, plants, or objects. A number of local formations of the Märchen are isolated, as in Turkey, where the tale is introduced by the heroine pursuing a rolling cake instead of falling into a well or being carried downstream. In its techniques, conclusions, and theoretical basis, this is a representative study of a European Märchen by the Finnish method. Such a study demonstrates that a complex folktale undergoes change and yet retains its identity as it travels from its point of origin along traceable routes across the Indo-European land mass.

To avoid the complications of literary versions and overseas migrations in reconstructing the history of a folktale, Stith Thompson chose a narrative confined to North American Indian tribes. His monograph on "The Star Husband Tale" sought to test the Finnish theory of the wave-like diffusion of tales under ideal conditions. Wesselski had charged that influential literary versions, and outstanding individual narrators, were chiefly responsible for the dissemination of traditional narratives. Using eighty-six versions, recorded from some forty Indian tribes across the continent, Thompson tentatively concluded that the basic form of the story originated in the Central Plains before the eighteenth century. In this form, two girls marry stars and then escape from the heavens. From the slight modifications it underwent in the Central Plains area, Thompson reasoned that the tale moved by diffusion from tribe to neighboring tribe, regardless of the skill of particular storytellers. One subform of the tale, found in a sweeping arc from southern Alaska to Nova Scotia, was presumably carried across Canada by travelers. True to his empirical skepticism, Thompson finds no indications of esoteric meanings, mythological or religious, in the narrative.

Here is a test case of the Finnish method undertaken by an eminent comparative folklorist, in rebuttal against criticisms of the method. The conclusions are modest. We know no more about the age of the story after the exhaustive investigation than we did before, since there is no way to date its history before the advent of the white man. The absence of written records, while permitting a clear examination of an oral tradition, prevents chronological treatment in depth by the monographer. Thompson's final conjecture that the Star Husband tale originated at the central point of its present distribution in the Great Plains area could be surmised as a matter of common sense. The study does present a simple basic form and some local variations with their presumed routes of travel, and it testifies to the coherence and tenacity of a folktale despite the mysteries and vagaries of oral wanderings. But again, since the inquiry commences with a number of closely similar variants, excluding texts remote from the central plot, the proof of oral stability is already predetermined. One persuasive result of the study is its evidence for wave-like diffusion.

Critics of the Finnish method point not only to the meagerness of conclusions but also to its limited applicability. Most monographs following its procedures deal with the complex European folktale. But the simple, single-motif tale resists this kind of analysis. Nevertheless, such a study has been made by Butler Waugh. Some ballad studies have adopted the historical-geographical approach, but the choice of ballads is restricted to those with a tight narrative structure and stanzas of incremental repetition. Ballads with these fixed formulas lend themselves very well to a statistical computation of trait changes, and so do many European Märchen with their tri-episodic plots. The most celebrated monograph of the Finnish school, *Kaiser und Abt* by Walter Anderson (1923), pursues a tale based on riddling questions; the questions may change, but the structural core of thorny questions and trick answers remains constant. These points are skillfully made by Holger Nygard in his own study, *The Ballad of Heer Halewijn* (1958).

Nygard comments on the major differences in construction between folktale and ballad that place most ballad texts outside the scope of the Finnish method. Ordinarily the traditional ballad does not rely on repetitive formulas, and again the ballad more than the tale owes a heavy debt to the stabilizing influence of literary texts. Yet Nygard goes on to say this method of dealing with the manifold variants of "Heer Halewijn," Child ballad #4, takes cognizance of historical chronology and geographical distributions. His chief modification of the Finnish method is the conducting of his inquiry within separate national-linguistic areas—Teutonic, Scandinavian, French, English. And this revision recalls the oikotypes of von Sydow.

Another and far more liberal conception of the Finnish method is advanced by the eminent American folklorist Archer Taylor, who has studied with equal authority individual tales, ballads, proverbs, and riddles. Taylor has characterized the historical-geographical approach as basically a matter of common sense, practiced by such respected folklore scholars as Child, Grundtvig, Gaston Paris, and Friedrich Ranke before the Finns. In their headnotes to texts or in longer studies they compared available variants, and on occasion sought to establish the oldest traits. The Finnish folklorists codified and sys-tematized procedures that any thorough scholar would at least initiate: the gathering together of all available evidence, and the organizing of this evidence into meaningful units.[1] One advance in folklore science whose importance the Finnish school has particularly recognized is the concept of the variant. Older folklorists employed the nearest text at hand to illustrate their discussion, not realizing that every text is a variant captured at some point in time and place, and undergoing change at every point. The instinctive search for parallels for a given text seems second nature among even the earliest folklorists, and William John Thoms, for example, the coiner of the word "folk-lore," regularly annotated items of tradition sent in to the columns of *Notes and Queries*.

In Taylor's view, the common-sense principles of the Finnish method

1. Archer Taylor, "Precursors of the Finnish Method of Folklore Study," *Modern Philology* 25 (1928) : 481–91.

can be applied to any form of folk tradition. In his own study of the proverb, "All Is Not Gold that Glitters," he has written, "Although reconstructions seem risky in the extreme, we have seen that the systematically chronological and geographical arrangement of the texts has given us new information." The vast preponderance of the current and recent examples of the proverb as Taylor found them contained the verb "glitters." But "glisters" also appeared. By assembling all the earlier texts available, Taylor was able to demonstrate that "glisters" was indeed the original form, antedating "glitters," which replaced it in the late eighteenth century, perhaps when the actor David Garrick spoke the now-current form in the prologue to a popular play by Goldsmith. Shakespeare had used "glisters" correctly, as it turns out, in *The Merchant of Venice*. Taylor concludes, "It would be difficult to find a more convincing illustration than this of the historical-geographical method."[2] The initial presumption that the form overwhelmingly reported today is the oldest or most popular form fails to stand up when tested against early usage. Since the folklorist must depend for his field materials on the collections made within the past hundred and fifty years, he must always encounter difficulties when he seeks to probe behind the nineteenth century for the history of a tradition. The historical-geographical method recognizes the problem and redresses the balance by giving weight to early documentary versions, to early traits surviving in oral tradition, and to major changes that recast the tradition.

The comparative folklorist of the Finnish school has diverted attention from philosophical and metaphysical questions of meaning to empirical questions of fact. If his quest for *Urformen* has been challenged, he has succeeded in establishing the *Normalformen*. No one can complain that this species of folklorist is unscholarly. The Finnish monograph may be described as a protracted, exhaustive, and exhausting annotation. But it ignores some of the questions that most interest scholars. Considerations of style and artistry, of the mysterious processes of creation and alterations, of the influences of national cultures, the social context, the individual genius, are out of order among percentage tables and plot summaries. Such questions have been left for the speculation of other groups of folklorists.

HISTORICAL-RECONSTRUCTIONAL

Certain scholars welcome the use of folklore and folklife materials to recapture vanished historical periods for which other evidence is scanty. Such a method, which can be called historical-reconstructional, attracted the Grimm brothers, especially Jacob, who in his encyclo-

2. Archer Taylor, "'All is Not Gold That Glitters' and Hypothetical Reconstructions," *Saga och sed* (1959), pp. 129–32.

pedic work on *Teutonic Mythology* sought to re-erect the old pantheon of German gods and goddesses now shrunk to withered specters and goblins in the popular imagination. Jacob Grimm's thesis powerfully attracted the nineteenth-century British folklorists, but after the insertion of evolutionism into scientific thought, following Darwin's publication of *The Origin of Species* in 1859, historical reconstructionism added a preamble of prehistory to its chronology and looked back to a primitive savage rather than to a civilized pagan. All the Victorians, committed as they were to the doctrine of survivals, showed interest in the historical application of folklore, but George Laurence Gomme pursued the problem most tenaciously in a series of volumes culminating in *Folklore as an Historical Science* (1908). Gomme believed it was possible to separate layers of folk traditions deposited by different races successively settling and conquering on the same terrain. For Britain he would distinguish the pre-Aryan from Aryan customs now blended in village folklore, and so reconstruct cultural institutions of the original stock.

Japanese folklorists, working in physical and intellectual isolation, did read the British folklorists and were much influenced by Gomme. The contemporary school of Japanese folklore, inspired by Kunio Yanagita, based its extensive research activities on the hypothesis of historical reconstructionism, and sought to recapitulate the ancient Japanese animistic religion. Through observation of extant harvest festivals, agricultural rituals, household magic, burial and marriage customs, and narratives of degenerated deities, Yanagita and his disciples endeavored to peel off the later historical accretions of imported Buddhism and official Shintoism to arrive at the earliest core of cosmological beliefs. All the essays in the volume *Studies in Japanese Folklore* (1963) pivot around this approach. Writing on "The Concept of *tamashii* in Japan," Narimitsu Matsudaira works back from the current notion of *kami*, or higher spirit, to a monster-ghost-glowing ball-essence conglomerate, the *tamashii*, from which it presumably derived. The *tamashii* inhabited the body of the living, and hovered for a period around his corpse. Vestiges of the *tamashii* belief still are noticeable, Matsudaira believes, in Shinto rites of food offerings at altars and ritual purification to placate raging spirits. Studies of this sort not only aimed at making the past more comprehensible, but also at explaining the irrational ideas of the present; *tamashii* explains *kami* as much as *kami* explains *tamashii*. In another essay in *Studies in Japanese Folklore*, Keigo Seki examines a folktale popular in Japan concerning the marriage of a young girl to a serpent in human disguise. She bears a son with scales on his back who grows up to become a great hero and fathers scale-bearing children. In its earliest form Seki sees the tale as an origin legend reflecting worship of the serpent as a tutelary deity. Families that believed themselves descendants of a divine serpent transmitted the legend. During successive historical periods, before, during, and after the Japanese Middle Ages, the narrative underwent changes reflecting the general shift from animistic to naturalistic beliefs in folk psychology. Thus in the Middle Ages it became attached to semihistorical figures and local shrines, and subsequently the character of the serpent lost its nimbus of divinity. Seki has in this way dissected the chronological layers in the narrative.[3]

In dealing with oral narratives, historical reconstructionists have to face a problem puzzling to many besides folklorists, namely the degree of trust that can be placed in the historical and ethnological content of narrative traditions. In a damaging review of Gomme's *Folklore as an Historical Science*, Andrew Lang pointed out that the legend of London Bridge and the treasure dreamer used by Gomme to support his thesis of the importance of London Bridge in antiquity was found in many other places. The battle over the historicity of oral tradition has raged among archeologists, anthropologists, classicists, the historians of Africa and Polynesia, students of the Icelandic sagas, biblical scholars, and indeed wherever verbally transmitted chronicles are found. The skeptics, like Lord Raglan in England and the American anthropologist Robert Lowie, reject all historical traditions as mythical or trivial, but others, like Hector and Nora Chadwick, see a kernel of historical fact in all the great folk epics. The resolution of this thorny problem lies in an analysis of each individual tradition according to certain criteria: have the tradition carriers resided continuously in the same locality, so that visible landmarks reinforce the story line? does the culture institutionalize oral historians? are the tribal traditions supported by other kinds of evidence—linguistic, ethnological, documentary—and by external traditions? If such questions can be answered affirmatively, the presumption of historical trustworthiness increases.

A new development in historical reconstruction is now emerging among American folklorists who are synthesizing folkloric and historical techniques. Since the American folk historian deals with more recent history than his European or Asian counterpart, his problems might seem smaller, but oral chronicles referring to only one past generation offer puzzles enough. In *The Saga of Coe Ridge* (1970), subtitled "A Study in Oral History," William Lynwood Montell relied primarily on reminiscences, recollections, and traditions that he recorded on tape or in notebooks to piece together the history of a Negro community established in the foothills of southern Kentucky

3. Keigo Seki, "The Spool of Thread: A Subtype of the Japanese Serpent-Bridegroom Tale," *Studies in Japanese Folklore*, edited by Richard M. Dorson (Bloomington, Indiana, 1963), pp. 267–88.

after the Civil War. By the 1960s the small community had vanished, a victim of economic and racial pressures, and Montell had to recreate its story from interviews with former residents now scattered and nearby white residents in the county. The oral data of seventeen black and twenty-two white informants proved surprisingly reliable for historical, genealogical, and ethnographic information, when corroborated by documentary sources. Coe Ridge lasted in community memory because it represented a unique Negro enclave in a white mountain area dating back to the immediate post-Civil War era. To an extent Coe Ridge had itself become legendary, as stories of crimes of passion and mysterious disappearances gathered around the settlement. As a trained folklorist Montell was able to detect the folk motifs and legend-building incidents strewn through factual episodes of slavery times, the founding of the settlement, social feuds, logging, rafting, and moonshining activities, and the economic decline of the colony. The Coetowners made heroes of slaves who escaped to freedom and their descendants who killed feuding whites. In his field plus library study Montell demonstrated the possibilities of using oral sources to reconstruct folk attitudes and events of local history.

Similar research was undertaken by Gladys-Marie Fry in reconstructing from interviews with descendants of slaves a tradition unremarked by historians of the Peculiar Institution. From her informants Fry learned about "Night Riders" or "Night Doctors" who supposedly abducted runaway slaves to sell their cadavers to medical institutions. With the bogey figure southern planters played on the supernatural fears of the slaves to keep them from escaping. Night riders, patterollers, ghosts, and Ku Klux Klan all meshed into the same technique employed by southern whites to intimidate the antebellum and postbellum Negro.[4]

These two historical monographs demonstrate the possibilities of utilizing traditional recollections to reconstruct the recent past.

IDEOLOGICAL

The ideological manipulation of folklore for purposes of *Realpolitik* in the twentieth century derives from the romantic nationalisms of the nineteenth century. In the wake of the German poet Johann Gottfried von Herder, who identified national bodies of folk poetry, scholars in one country of Europe after another searched for the soul of the people revealed in the native dialects, the folktales and folksongs carried in those dialects, the literature developing the themes of the folklore, and the history glorifying the deeds of national heroes. This impulse stirred the Grimms in Germany, Asbjörnsen and Moe

4. Gladys-Marie Fry, "The Night Riders: A Study in Techniques of the Social Control of the Negro" (Indiana University doctoral dissertation, 1967).

in Norway, Lönnrot and the Krohns in Finland, Vuk Karadžić in Serbia, Douglas Hyde in Ireland, and other illustrious scholars. As a stimulus to imaginative research and innocent national pride, this quest for a heritage had its virtues, but in extreme form it became entwined with political ideology and virulent nationalism, especially in Nazi Germany and Soviet Russia.

The first national state to make political capital of folklore studies was the National Socialist government of Hitler. During the 1930s a massive literature of folklore was published in Germany, documenting the Nazi concept of a *Herrenvolk* united by mystical bonds of blood and tongue, culture and tradition. The term Volk had ever since the days of Herder possessed a mystical aura, and it now became endowed with political meaning; the Volk was the nation. Because of Hitler's dogma of racial unity, the Nazis cast aside the concept of Hans Naumann (whose *Grundzüge der deutschen Volkskunde*, 1922, would be attacked by the Soviets on quite different grounds) that credited the origins of folklore to an *Oberschicht*, an intelligentsia, from whom the folklore trickled down to an *Unterschicht*, the peasantry. In 1929 Naumann published a modified edition. Searching for a spiritual ancestor, the Nazi folklorists bypassed the famous names of German scholarship like Grimm, Mannhardt, Köhler, and Bolte, and fastened on Wilhelm Riehl, a sociologist and travel-writer who in 1858 had written *Die Volkskunde als Wissenschaft*, "Folklore as a Science." The Nazis appreciated Riehl's recommendation that folklore, and the social sciences generally, should concentrate on things German, and apply this knowledge to practical use. Thus police science could benefit from a knowledge of popular customs and usages.

In the late 1920s folklore became a popular subject in some universities, often being an obligatory course, or an adjunct to a broader course in German *Kulturkunde* or *Landeskunde*. A weighty treatise of 1937, *Deutsche Volkskunde* by Adolf Bach, closed with the concept of a *Führerschicht* whereby Hitler, being himself so imbued with the spirit of Volk, becomes the arbiter of German folk culture. Hitler regarded the "folkish" state as the central point of his political thought. When an *Arbeitsgemeinschaft für Deutsche Volkskunde* was organized in 1937, its founders included Alfred Rosenberg, philosopher of the Nazi revolution, Walter Darré, Hitler's minister of agriculture, Baldur von Schirach, leader of the Hitler Youth Movement, and even Heinrich Himmler, Hitler's minister of internal affairs.

Soviet Russia has perceived in folklore a powerful force to advance communism. In the nineteenth century, folklore studies made signal advances in Tsarist Russia under the leadership of such scholars as A. F. Gil'ferding (1831–1872), who focused attention on the biography and personality of the individual informant. His organized field trips to Olonets province in northern Russia yielded rich harvests of *byliny*. The academic interest in the collection and analysis of folk materials continued its momentum through and beyond the October Revolution. One day in 1936, however, the Communist Party abruptly awoke to the fact that their folklore scientists were espousing anti-Marxist theory. In the view widely held by continental folklorists, and formulated most precisely by the German Hans Naumann, folklore descends from the elite to the folk, among whom it is found as a kind of *gesunkenes Kulturgut*. By swift Party decree, this thesis of origins was reversed, and the principle laid down that folklore originated as the creative expression of the working class.

There seems almost an inevitable logic that Soviet policy makers should have concentrated upon folklore. Substitute the "people" for the "folk," an equation easily made, since the Russian word *narod* is used for both. Emphasize the themes of class conflict readily available in heroic legends and songs of the daring outlaw who outwits the greedy landlord, bigoted priest, tsarist soldier, grasping mill owner. And the case for a people's folklore is launched.

When the moment of truth finally dawned on the Party nineteen years after the October Revolution, the directors of Soviet thought moved quickly to revamp the subject according to Communist doctrine. Russian folklorists had no other choice than to follow the official trends. Propp renounced formalism, Andreev the Finnish method, Žirmunskij and Sokolov the vulgar sociology of Hans Naumann. Academician Y. M. Sokolov and other folklorists now recognized their neglect of the creative factor in the poetic compositions of the working class, and their failure to perceive the true social and class nature of oral poetry and legend. In the new "folkloristics" written by Sokolov, the Marxist principles governing the study are dramatically pronounced:

(1) *Folklore is an echo of the past, but at the same time it is also the vigorous voice of the present.*

(2) *Folklore has been, and continues to be, a reflection and a weapon of class conflict.*

In other words, folklore was to take its place alongside literature, music, and the arts as a controlled expression of proletarian ideals. But the unique quality of folklore, rendering it so precious to the Soviet ideology, lay in its possession by the farm and factory workers, and not by a small intellectual elite expressing the ideals of the people. For propaganda purposes the theory that the workers not only recited but also created the lore was mandatory. The revisionist view declared that the presence of boyars and Cossacks and other aristocrats in *byliny* was due to poetic idealization. Cleverly the Party line fastened onto the creative role of folk narrator and folksinger, an emphasis in which nineteenth-century Russian folklore scholarship had indeed taken the lead. In his new look at *Russian Folklore*, Sokolov (1950) marshals quotations from Marx, Engels, Lenin, and Stalin to demonstrate their sympathies for folk productions. Thus Lenin declared that folklore must be considered from the "social-political point of view," as an aid to understanding the "hopes and expectations" of working masses in the past. The older schools of folklore are denigrated as Slavophiles, romantics, and spokesmen for "official nationalism."

Folklore is recognized as a fighting ground, not only over conflicting reactionary and socialistic interpretations, but also between classes preempting the traditions of the workers. The kulaks, or the petty bourgeoisie, or criminal elements, had in the past appropriated the people's folklore, a process explaining the appearance of similar traditions among different social classes. Consequently the *byliny*, the legends, the *skazki,* the *častuški,* the laments, must not be left to drift among the population, but should be collected and composed under proper direction, then sifted out and redistributed to the workers through all available media—radio, cinema, theater, phonograph, print. Encourage the collective-farm stations to create songs and legends glorifying the Revolutionary movement, and honor outstanding folk creators. Oral literature served not only the socialist but the nationalist cause by welding the diverse peoples of the Soviet Union into closer unity based on a common workers' lore.

At the First All-Union Congress of Soviet Writers in 1934, the writer A. M. Gorky, whose own works had drawn deeply from folklore, declared that oral poetry depended for its powerful generalizing images upon laboring activity. Examples are seen in such heroic laborers as Hercules, Prometheus, Mikula Seljaninovič, and Svjatogor. Gorky then paid tribute to an illiterate folk bard, Sulejman Stal'skij, brought from Daghestan to be honored at the congress, calling him the "Homer of the twentieth century." These state rituals marked the introduction of organized Soviet folklore.

As one of their new tasks, the folklorists searched for pre-Revolutionary evidence of proletarian attitudes revealed in folklore. Nineteenth-century folklorists who properly understood the principles of social development were now given belated recognition. I. G. Pryžov had recognized that folklore reflected the real life of the people in their struggle against the tsars, clergy, and landowners; I. A. Xudjakov had pursued the themes of social protest and class satire in popular tales and historical folksongs.

Vigorous research ferreted out pre-proletarian folklore in the manorial and possessional factories, among forced labor groups, bond servants, urban handcraftsmen, and home artisans. Interviews with old men, and digging among older collections, brought to light a protest lore of factory and mill. V. P. Birjukov's *Prerevolutionary Folklore of the Urals* (1936), proudly presented miners' songs and legends of protest against cruel foremen and mineowners. In these studies Soviet folklorists made the points that peasant and worker were closely akin, that the early factory was actually a manufactory, and that the crafts practiced on the farm were simply being moved to the city.

The prize find of Birjukov was "The Secret Tale of the Golden Commander," a legend preserved among the working class unknown to their bosses. The "Golden Commander" was the nickname of Andrej Stepanovič Plotnikov, a peasant serf who became a foundry worker, and then a bandit leader in the Urals. In 1771 he killed the cruel millowner Širjaev. But when Širjaev's niece was taken by his robber band, Plotnikov, bare-handed, slew his own commander who wished to violate her. In return she gave the Golden Commander a magic spell that opened up for him the treasures of the mountains. After his capture and execution, the Golden Commander lived on in legends modeled on the Returning Hero who waits for the moment of crisis to return and succor his people. Here are all the desired ingredients for the pre-revolutionary hero. Plotnikov is a peasant turned worker; he breathes the spirit of class insurrection, and is pure in heart. Historic fact blends with folk motifs in the legend cherished by the oppressed workers.

Collecting contemporary Soviet folklore of the proper ideological hue proves much simpler than unearthing pre-revolutionary folklore. Under the Soviet regime a new genre of popular tradition has come to the fore, the "martial revolutionary song." Older forms are adapted to revolutionary heroes. A cycle of verses celebrates Budennyj and his famous Red cavalry, and a cycle of tales glorifies the hero of the civil war, Čapaev. A master bard composing an heroic narrative about Čapaev employs traditional fairy-tale themes and structure, such as the conquest by the knight of serpents and demons. Summing up the role of folklore, Sokolov writes, ". . . what a vastly important artistic force this is in the propagandizing of the resplendent socialist culture."

Soviet ideology comes into still sharper focus when it interprets the American folklore scene. Writing in the journal *Soviet Ethnography* in 1962, L. Zemljanova stated her point of view plainly in her title, "The Struggle between the Reactionary and the Progressive Forces in Contemporary American Folkloristics" (translated into English in the *Journal of the Folklore Institute*, 1963). The progressives were those scholars "for whom folklore is the living and developing art of the broad working masses." Irwin Silber and his magazine *Sing Out!* exemplified this progressive recognition of the "class nature of folklore." In his book *Songs of the Civil War*, Silber presented texts revealing "progressive ideas of the struggle against slavery" along with songs reflecting southern conservatism that were "artificially created and employed by the reactionary forces of that time as propagandistic means in the struggle against democracy." Zemljanova's *bête noire* is Richard Dorson, who "denies the leading role of the masses in the history of society and culture" and robs the Negro of his folklore by imputing to him European sources and ignoring the Negro folk expression of protest against white racists. Dorson "employs pragmatic 'historicism' " to dethrone a true worker's hero such as Paul Bunyan and glorifies a false folk hero such as Henry Ford in order to appease the ideology of bourgeois democracy.

The arguments of Zemljanova can easily be dismissed. A substantial body of Negro protest lore does indeed exist and had Zemljanova read a bit further, she would have discovered the section of "Protest Tales" in my collection *Negro Tales from Pine Bluff, Arkansas, and Calvin, Michigan.* But much Negro folklore does not concern social protest. Paul Bunyan was promoted to national prominence by the advertising agent of a lumber company, and is a product of the bourgeois capitalism Zemljanova abhors. Henry Ford is nobody's folk hero, but rather the butt of a joke-cycle. What concerns us here is not so much Zemljanova's obvious errors but her dogmatic assumptions about folklore as an expression of the class struggle that follow so purely the dialectic of Marx and Lenin, and that she would apply to the United States, or to any country, with the same confidence as to the Soviet Union.

FUNCTIONAL

One persuasive approach to folklore studies eschews questions of origin and distribution to concentrate on the role played by folklore in a given culture. American cultural anthropologists in particular have espoused this point of view, concerned as they are with the operation and fitting together of the parts of nonliterate societies. The question they ask is how folklore—a word they avoid for synonyms like verbal art and expressive literature—contributes to the maintenance of social institutions. Simply put, how does folklore function in the culture?

Franz Boas, the father of modern American anthropology, always evinced partiality for folkloric data in his own field expeditions, in his injunctions to his students, many of whom became illustrious in their own right, and as longtime editor of the *Journal of American Folklore.* Boas himself was not so much the functionalist as some of his students, since his energies were devoted in good part to demonstrating the diffusion of oral narratives from tribe to tribe at points of culture contact, in order to refute the theory of unilinear cultural evolution and the independent invention of tales. His student and successor as editor of the *Journal of American Folklore,* Ruth Benedict, propounded one functional use of folklore in her *Zuñi Mythology* (1935), revising her master, who had claimed that tribal narratives mirrored the ethnography of the culture. She countered with illustrations to show that the folklore often violated the cultural norms as a means of gratifying fantasies and expressing the hostilities of the culturebound. Recognizing that "tales tally with, and yet do not tally with" the culture, Benedict examined the lines of divergence, such as the abandonment of babies so recurrent in the tales and yet untrue to Zuñi culture. This paradox she explains with the seminal concept that suppressed tensions in the society are released and made manifest in the oral literature. Children's resentment against their parents is the covert theme. The tales constitute a fantasy world, constructed from the cultural realities. If the taboo against intercourse with one's mother-in-law did not exist in Plains Indian culture, its violation by Coyote would not evoke laughter.

The clearest articulation of the functional thesis has come from William Bascom, a student of Melville Herskovits, who was a student of Boas. Bascom regards "verbal arts," his term for folklore, as the creative compositions of a functioning society, dynamic not static, integrated not isolated, central not peripheral components of the culture. Expanding the viewpoint of Bronislaw Malinowski in *Myth in Primitive Psychology* (1926), Bascom calls attention to various functional roles of folklore. Proverbs help settle legal decisions, riddles sharpen wits, myths validate conduct, satirical songs release pent-up hostilities. So the anthropologist searches for context as well as text. A tale is not a dictated text with interlinear translation, but a living recitation delivered to a responsive audience for such cultural purposes as reinforcement of custom and taboo, release of aggressions through fantasy, pedagogical explanations of the natural world, and application of pressures for conventional behavior.

Ethnographic examples can illustrate the cultural functioning of different folklore genres. Fieldworkers in Africa have pointed out the prevalent use of proverbs in judicial proceedings. Among the Anang in Nigeria, whom John Messenger observed, a plaintiff secured considerable sympathy in court by employing this proverb against an habitual thief: "If a dog plucks palm fruits from a cluster, he does not fear a porcupine." The saying signified that if a dog could take the fruits from an oil palm tree in spite of its sharp needles, he would have no hesitation in tackling a prickly porcupine; hence a man known to steal regularly would not hesitate to steal from his neighbor. The defendant managed to turn the sentiment rising against him in his favor by saying "A single partridge flying through the bush leaves no path." Since a covey of partridges can be trailed by the bent grass they leave on the trail, the implication is that a single, friendless individual carries little weight and will be unfairly judged. The accused was acquitted. This key role of proverbs in swaying the opinion of the justices is unrecognized by the Anang themselves, since they are so accustomed to employing proverbial phrases in daily conversation as a means to instruct the young and in the course of ritual ceremonies.[5]

Validation of belief, conduct, and ritual is another function performed by the tribal folklore, particularly by the myth narratives. Among the Dahomeans, as the Herskovitses inform us, myth-chronicles relating the history of the great families were first assembled in the early eighteenth century by King Agadja, who even had his singers versify them, and again in the later nineteenth century by King Glele. The Dahomean kings possessed their own special "Remembrancer," who recited the illustrious genealogies of the ruler before his awakening each morning. These chronicles or *hwenoho*, which were "narrated, chanted, or sung," commenced with mythical beginnings and came down to modern times, thus buttressing the historic record with divine ancestry. *Hwenoho* served as the ultimate reference on points of legal, political, social, and economic rights and status. A Remembrancer missed a praise-name at the cost of his life. The Herskovitses report the bewilderment of one Dahomean who heard the same episodes belonging to his own clan-history repeated in the *hwenoho* of another family.[6]

Tribal myths may even function as an ego-reassurance mechanism in dreams. Studying three hundred and ten dreams of a Hopi Indian, Dorothy Eggan found one-third of them to incorporate folklore characters or themes, manipulated to deal successfully with problems of the dreamer Sam in the real world. In seventy-three dreams a personalized spirit-guardian appears, known to the Hopi in a vague, unspecified form *(dumalaitaka)*. He assumes the role of a powerful friend who leads Sam to treasure, rescues him from disaster, ridicules his enemies, and in general imparts to Sam his own wisdom and strength. Sam worries because he is a poor hunter, grieves over his five babies who have died, and frets about his temporary impotence. In his dreams, Sam the hunter shoots rabbits, which change into small crying babies, and the Guide gives him pills to feed them. Three white girls bathe and greet Sam, who hesitates until ordered by his Guide to make love to them; thereupon they turn into ears of corn, and Sam

5. John Messenger, "The Role of Proverbs in a Nigerian Judicial System," *Southwestern Journal of Anthropology* 15 (1959) : 64–73.
6. Melville J. and Frances S. Herskovits, *Dahomean Narrative, a Cross-Cultural Analysis* (Evanston, Ill., 1958) .

realizes his newfound potency has magically ensured good crops for his people. The guardian thus builds Sam's confidence when he confronts the real world where he feels himself a misfit.[7]

The practice of divination among the Dahomeans, Yoruba, and Ashanti in West Africa, Brazil, and Cuba illustrates another functional use of folklore. A divination system associated with the god Ifa employs both mythical and fictional tales to provide solutions and to suggest sacrifices for clients consulting a diviner. William Bascom describes this system in his *Ifa Divination* (1969). According to the arrangement of seeds or nuts he has thrown on the ground, the diviner recites verses. Some diviners know as many as four thousand verses and all know at least a thousand. A given verse incorporates a traditional narrative, and eventually the diviner relates one applicable to the situation of his client, who identifies himself with a legendary or animal character of the tale. Thus, in a tale cited by Bascom, Leopard refuses to sacrifice one bag of cornskins and four pigeons when clearing land for a new house, and eventually loses his land and house and very life to Goat. The client readily perceives both the necessity for and the nature of the sacrifice. Divination keeps a vast stock of folktales continuously circulating among West African peoples. Diviners refuse to acknowledge the independent secular existence of folktales, all of which, they claim, were originally transmitted to the Ifa diviners by the gods. Some mythical traditions explain the origins of the Fa or Ifa divination, and so give historical sanction to the system that in turn disseminates tales. Skeptics of the Ifa system fail to realize, as Bascom points out, that clients remember the successful predictions and rationalize away or dismiss the failures. They are comforted by shifting the responsibility for their decisions to Ifa, much in the same way that American farmers in need of water have recourse to water-witches to assist them in facing an anxiety-laden dilemma, as Ray Hyman and Evon Vogt explain in their *Water-Witching U.S.A.* (1959).

In a far-removed culture area, the Polynesian, mythical traditions also support divination. William Lessa reports on the system of divination in the Carolines known as *bwe*, in which knots made from coconut or palm leafs are counted in the hand or on a mat, and the pairs of numbers resulting from two hundred and sixty-five possible combinations in the counting procedure are linked with names of mythical boatmen. These sailors were created by the god Supunemen, who taught them the divining art, which they in turn taught to single islanders. In other forms of the myth the boatmen are spirits of heaven

7. Dorothy Eggan, "The Personal Use of Myth in Dreams," *Journal of American Folklore* 68 (1955): 445–53.

or of the sea. *Bwe* diviners, whose persons are sacred and whose habits are ritually controlled, divulge information to their clients concerning hostile and malevolent supernatural beings. On islands like Yap and Truk the inhabitants consult the diviner for any major event, whether fishing or housebuilding, making a voyage, falling sick or falling in love, turning Christian or choosing allies in a World War. Danger from typhoons is particularly dreaded. Thus the *bwe* myths control the transaction of daily life by sanctioning the role of the diviners.[8]

In Europe even more than in America, the functional theory has received strong support from the new generation of folklorists. The gulf in European scholarship between anthropology and folklore is bridged by the median discipline of ethnology, the study of peasant cultures. Ethnologically minded folklorists look at the complete social setting of the folkloric item. In contrast to the Grimms, who considered the refined texts of national folktales their end product, the modern folklorist studies a community in historical depth, resides in it over protracted periods as participant-observer-collector, and gathers information on the occasions of tale-telling, audience reactions, biographies and personalities of the major and run-of-the-mill narrators, influences on the tale repertoire from popular and art literature, and the meanings and satisfactions derived by tellers and auditors from the narrative genres. Such a wealth of data is obtained that the tales themselves are crowded into the background, and may only be printed in illustrative samples. An exemplary study of this sort is Linda Dégh's *Folktales and Society: Story-Telling in a Hungarian Peasant Community* (German edition 1962, American edition 1969). Dégh provides a detailed theoretical statement of the functional position, documented from the works of eastern and western European scholars and from American anthropological folklorists. She then illustrates her platform with empirical data from the transplanted Szeklers in Kakasd, Transylvania. Dégh describes the new Hungarian research method as wishing to capture the "social function of storytelling." She speaks of the "functional approach to folkloristic phenomena" and of "The Functions of Storytelling," which changed from furnishing entertainment to expressing aspirations and hopes, as the folktale dropped from the day laborers on the estates of rich landowners to the poorest class of peasants after the breakup of the estates. Without audiences, storytelling cannot function. When fishermen in Zemplén county, Hungary, shifted to farming, after land from the manors was distributed, they ceased narrating the tales they had been wont to tell at get-togethers of fishermen. In the functional theory, the text itself

8. William A. Lessa, "Divining from Knots in the Carolines," *Journal of the Polynesian Society* 68 (1959) : 188–204.

is meaningless apart from its living presentation, or performance, to a responding audience.

Functionalism can be applied to material culture as well as to oral literature. In his monograph on *The Function of Folk Costume in Moravian Slovakia* (English translation 1971), Petr Bogatyrev categorizes magical, religious, regional and national, age-group, erotic, and everyday functions of traditional attire. The form of the costume reflects its particular function. According to Bogatyrev, "The functional method expands the subject matter of ethnography," so that village buildings, farm implements, and verbal folklore can all be examined from the functional point of view.

PSYCHOANALYTICAL

The most speculative body of current folklore theory belongs to the psychoanalytical school that memorializes Sigmund Freud. This is also the school of interpretation most abhorrent to orthodox folklorists.

Psychoanalytical readings of myths and folktales substitute sexual symbolism for the nineteenth-century symbolism of heavenly phenomena. A direct historical connection can be seen between the German celestial mythologists and the Austrian psychoanalytical folklorists, who have borrowed the method of their predecessors and simply changed the symbols. In an early work to employ the Freudian method, *Dreams and Myths*, by Karl Abraham (1913), the author hails Adalbert Kuhn as the founder of comparative mythology, and builds upon Kuhn his own interpretation of the Prometheus myth. In accord with his predilection, Kuhn saw Prometheus the fire-bringer as the lightning, supporting his view with the usual Sanskrit etymology of the nature mythologists. Abraham agreeably concedes that astronomical considerations may influence the "outer form" of myths, but asserts that several symbols often cloak the same person; Prometheus is both lightning and—again with a Sanskrit key—"borer" or "generator." Lightning brings fire to primitive man, but early man also learns to make fire by twirling a straight hard stick—the "borer"—into a soft, round, wooden disc. These are obvious genital symbols, and Abraham interprets the myth of Prometheus to proclaim "the masculine power of procreation as a principle of all life."

Where once the fairy tales and myths had portrayed a heavenly battle, the contention of sun and night, thunderstorm and morning sky, they now describe the earthly strivings of male and female. The erstwhile solar-hero—Achilles, Theseus, Perseus, Heracles—has become the phallus and the enveloping night the womb. Erich Fromm has catalogued the Freudian symbols. "The male genital is symbolized by sticks, trees, umbrellas, knives, pencils, hammers, airplanes. . . . The female genital is represented in the same manner by caves, bottles, boxes, doors, jewel cases, gardens, flowers. . . ."[9] Dreams or fairy tales about dancing, riding, climbing, and flying signify sexual enjoyment. Hair falling out symbolizes castration.

Sigmund Freud leaned heavily on myths and fairy tales, taboos and jests and superstitions to support his explorations of the subconscious mind. In the *Interpretation of Dreams* (1900) he presented his thesis that dreams express the latent repressed wishes and fears of infantile sexuality in symbolic disguises. The next step was the equation of dreams with myths and other kinds of folklore. "The dream is the myth of the individual," wrote Abraham. The same psychological mechanisms operated in dreams and myths, and were subject to the same interpretations. If the dream uncovered the infantile desires of one human being, myths revealed psychic repressions of the childhood of the race. Such mechanisms as condensation, elaboration, and substitution transformed the childish, half-forgotten sexual urges into objects and images taken from daily life. Properly understood and logically arranged, the symbol figures told a story of sexual hunger, guilt and shame. Beneath the manifest content lurks a latent fantasy of masturbation, castration, body-destruction, penis-envy, incest.

In the myth of Oedipus, Freud found a superlative illustration of the mythical narrative that exposes the dark suppressed desires and drives of children grown to adults. The boy-child loves his mother incestuously and dreams of slaying his father; in *Oedipus Rex* his wishes are grievously fulfilled. Here is the model upon which all later extensions of psychoanalytical probing into folklore are based. Yet as Abraham pointed out, the model is really too transparent. Infantile desires are not usually disclosed so nakedly. A "censor" imposed by the superego screens the brute wishes of the libidinous id, and they emerge in dreams and myths in symbolic garb. It is the business of the psychoanalytical folklorist to penetrate the veil of the censor and read the true message of the fantasy.

To this task of deciphering the latent meanings in folk custom, belief, ritual, narrative, and game the disciples of Freud have avidly turned. Their interpretations appear in such periodicals as the *Psychoanalytic Quarterly* and the *American Imago*, in monograph series, and in popular books. A look at the three most energetic analyzers of folk traditions, Jones, Fromm, and Roheim, can illustrate their methods.

Ernest Jones (1879–1959) the close friend and biographer of Freud, has shown a constant partiality toward folklore. Addressing the English Folk-Lore Society at their fiftieth anniversary congress in 1928, he

---

9. Erich Fromm, *The Forgotten Language, an Introduction to the Understanding of Dreams, Fairy Tales, and Myths* (New York, 1951), pp. 68–69.

spoke for a mutually enriching communion between "Psycho-Analysis and Folklore." Aware of his audience, Jones pressed the parallels between "survivals of life from the racial past and survivals from the individual past," a note likely to find response in the society that for so long had championed the doctrine of survivals in folklore. We may surmise that the listeners felt less sympathy for a listing of symbols in folklore indicating the female genitalia, in such objects as cups, goblets, cauldrons, caskets, the crescent moon, the opening under a leaning ladder, and the inverted horseshoe. A lengthy paper by Jones on "The Symbolic Significance of Salt in Folklore and Superstition" assembles evidence for the endowment of salt with magical properties in the folk mind, as in rituals which use salt for exorcising devils. He concludes that white, life-giving salt is a symbol for semen and "represents the male, active fertilizing principle."

In his most extensive treatise on folk beliefs, *On the Nightmare* (1959), Jones deals with medieval demons such as the vampire, werewolf, incubus, witch, and the Devil. In the terrors of the nightmare and the dreaded bogeys of goblindom, Jones perceived direct associations between the infantile fantasies projected in dreams and in folklore. The belief in bloodsucking vampires points to nocturnal emissions and a repressed oral sadism. The Devil, whose phallic symbolism is evident in his frequent identification with the snake, is a father-figure incarnating two repressed wishes, the desires of the son both to imitate and to defy his father. The witch is an exteriorization of a woman's unconscious thoughts about herself and her mother, and her ritual fornication with the Devil spells an unconscious incestuous phantasy. Repressed incestuous wishes are latent in all these beliefs, and can be attributed to the oedipal emotions fostered by a patriarchal, ascetic Church.

The German-born lecturer and author Erich Fromm, who came to the United States in 1934, has written a primer for the psychoanalytical exegesis of dreams, myths, and fairy tales entitled *The Forgotten Language*. Fromm points out the universal symbolism in such mythical relations as the story of Jonah, where Jonah, successively cradled in the ship's hold, the ocean, a deep sleep, and the belly of the whale, exemplified the foetus in the mother's womb, and the inner experience of protective isolation. Fromm seeks to demonstrate the variations and subtleties possible in the interpretation of phantasies, much in the way that the celestial mythologists of the nineteenth century wrangled with each other over whether the sun or the lightning or the aurora was the symbol intended in the myth. So Fromm adds a nuance to the Oedipus complex, bringing the full trilogy into play, and conceiving the myth-dramas as a struggle between the patriarchal tyranny of Creon and the matriarchal order represented by

Antigone and supported by Oedipus, who dies fittingly in the grove of matriarchal goddesses. In his interpretation of "Little Red Riding Cap," Fromm goes beyond the obviously Freudian reading of a maiden (the red cap is a menstrual symbol) straying from the path of virtue and being seduced by a wolf (man). The wolf is really displaying pregnancy-envy when he fills his belly (womb) with the girl and her grandmother, and is punished when Little Red Riding Hood stows stones, the symbol of sterility, in his insides. This is presented as a tale of women who hate men and sex.

Special claims of authority can be advanced by Géza Róheim (1891–1953), who commenced his career as a Hungarian collector of folklore, and studied Australian aborigines in the field before settling in the United States. Róheim has analyzed a good many myths and tales, in the psychoanalytical journals, in his study of Australian tribes of Central Australia, and in his compendious work *The Gates of the Dream* (1952). In his analyses Róheim sees the dream as precursor to rather than parallel with myth and tale, or combining with unconscious phantasies to form myths. Demon Grendel choking sleepers and drinking their blood is a nightmare episode. Odysseus rams a spit into the eye of Polyphemus while the giant sleeps, and so the sleeper's castration anxiety (blindness) is projected onto the father imago. The widely distributed fairy tale incident of the magic flight, in which the little hero fleeing from the giant throws objects in the path which swell to enormous size, Róheim interprets as a "urethral awakening dream." Since one of the objects is customarily a bottle of water that expands into a lake, Róheim brings to bear evidence from his patients who dream of bodies of water when their bladders are full and of obstacles when the bathrooms are closed. The urinary stimulus becomes a sexual one, represented in the tale by the chase.

Róheim postulates a basic dream that forms the substance of mythical tales. The dreamer falls into a lake or a hole, and this is the penis entering the vagina. Out of his body he then forms a womb, symbolized as an ocean or a lotus, and here is the origin of a creation myth such as the Earth-Diver. The deeper the dive, the greater the penis, for diving in a dream signifies an erection. Róheim believes that one person once dreamed such a dream and repeated it to others, who had themselves experienced similar dreams, and from the repetitions a myth developed.

All manner of folk materials, not simply myths and tales, yield their latent content to the psychoanalyzing folklorist. The children's game of hide-and-seek reenacts the infantile trauma of the clinging child separated from its mother, and by the reenactment softens the blow. A strange pastime of ritual insults exchanged by Negro youths, known as "the dozens," provides the taunter with an opportunity to voice repressed wishes concerning incest, homosexuality, and exhibitionism. The analysis of the Dutch folk festival of the Innocents, coming soon after Christmas, leads into the Christ figure. In the festival children play at being father and mother, and this make-believe reveals their repressed wishes to kill their parents, and so explains why they had to die. The proximity of this festival to Christmas further reveals that Christ died sacrificially to expiate the same sin of rebellion against parental authority. Now his oedipal nature becomes clearer. The father-figure of King Laius in *Oedipus Rex* is divided in the New Testament between God the Father and King Herod.[10]

Even the contemporary myth of the cowboy has been subjected to psychoanalysis. Kenneth J. Munden of the Menninger Foundation correlates the literature—including movies and television Westerns—with the psychiatric data on a cowboy patient. He finds that his patient's history conforms to the myth. The cowboy under analysis had early left home because of parental difficulties, and taken up a wandering life on the range. Coming to the city he felt lonely and insecure, and was unable to hold down a regular job. His strongest attachments were directed to his gun and to horses. Dr. Munden recommended that he return to the range. Similarly, in the myth the cowboy hero appears as a celibate nomad, challenged by his father and siblings whom he defeats and kills (removes from the scene). Always in evidence is the hero's gun (phallus), accurate, potent, deadly, everloaded. In the death ritual as filmed, hand and gun are prominently displayed, a round dark orifice is thrust at the spectator in close-up, there is an ominous silence, a sudden explosion, a slumping body—all pointing to an orgiastic climax. The mother figure emerges as the well-to-do leader of the opposition who hires the gunman but himself lacks a gun. When the herd thrashes this androgynous imago, he gratifies both oedipal emotions simultaneously. Notching the gun is a symbolic act of self-castration as atonement for killing the father. In its manifest denial of the female and mother figure, the cowboy myth represents the intense desires and attendant fears of child for mother. Millions of film and television viewers, Munden believes, watch Westerns out of a "repetition compulsion" that obliges them to reenact their childhood traumas.[11]

The most substantial recent exploration of a body of folklore from Freudian premises is the compendious *Rationale of the Dirty Joke,*

10. Hedwig Keri, "Ancient Games and Popular Games: Psychological Essay," *American Imago* 15 (1958) : 41–89; John Dollard, "The Dozens, Dialectic of Insult," *American Imago* 1 (1939) : 3–25; Richard Sterta, "A Dutch Celebration of a Festival," *American Imago* 2 (1941) : 205–8.

11. Kenneth J. Munden, "A Contribution to the Psychological Understanding of the Origin of the Cowboy and His Myth," *American Imago* 15 (1958) : 103–48.

an Analysis of Sexual Humor by Gershon Legman (1968), an authority on the pornographic literature of folklore. Stating his special debt to the third chapter of Freud's *Wit and Its Relation to the Unconscious*, titled "Hostile and Obscene Wit," Legman proceeds to analyze jokes about fornication, marriage, adultery, and the sexual misadventures of men and women in order to expose their latent content of aggression, fear, and hostility. In an earlier work with similar qualities of brilliance, ferocity, and erudition, *The Horn Book, Studies in Erotic Folklore* (1964), Legman had already attacked the prudishness of the Finnish school reflected in Thompson's Motif-Index, with its blank space at X700–799, "Humor Concerning Sex," as well as the faults of the index itself in using characters rather than actions for classification purposes. Nevertheless, Legman atttempted to fit his joke texts, as far as practical, within the existing motif-index system while preserving the logical integrity of his material.

Quite apart from its Freudian interpretations, *Rationale of the Dirty Joke* contributes to folklore research because it recognizes the joke, particularly the off-color joke, as the major folk narrative genre in contemporary society. Indeed, as Legman remarks, accurate collections of orally collected jokes are practically nonexistent in any language. He himself has not set down verbatim his hundreds of texts, but summaries serve his purpose, which is not to explore individual storytelling style but rather sociocultural codes of sexual behavior and their violations in reality and in humorous phantasy. As a comparative folklorist he ranges widely to show the longevity and diaspora of jokes, documenting specific instances and large statements, such as the assertion that western European tales and jokes entered Italy and Spain from the Middle East during the Arab conquest, and east European jokes through Turkey and Greece, mainly through written sources, some of which he identifies.

Still it is the joke analyses that count most, and these introduce the reader to a world filled with oedipal fears, anxieties, and hostilities. If a dirty joke seems to the unsuspecting listener or reader a simple transgression of anal and sexual taboos for comic effect, unraveled it turns into an exposé of homosexual drives, castration dreads, sexual inadequacies, hatred of women. Each joke teller has his favorite good ones, which lay bare his (or her) secrets. Legman relays the joke of the unhappily married, middle-aged housewife who claims she knows no jokes, then remembers one about the husband who complains that his wife keeps such a messy house that he can't even piss in the sink because of the dirty dishes. This would be her joke, no joke at bottom but a bitter truth about an empty marriage, even to the symbolism of male impotence. Mainly it is men who tell jokes exclusive of or derisive toward women. What Legman calls the "crucial neurotic mechanism in homosexuality" (p. 771) is the phantasy of the oedipal son in humiliating the father with a homosexual triumph, before the father threatens him in the same fashion, as punishment for the son's urges toward his mother. In cycle after cycle of jokes Legman calls attention to homosexual implications. The spate of brags about enormous penises concentrates on male genitalia and relieves castration worries. Stories about contests to see who has the longest penis deal with the search for the father-figure with the strongest phallic power, who is then to be either vanquished or conciliated homosexually. Meanwhile the woman is forgotten. Pictorial illustrations actually show men fencing with their penises, a theme traceable back to the scene in Pharaoh's court when Aaron's rod turns into a serpent and eats up the rods of Pharaoh's sorcerers (p. 295). A number of jokes set in urinals and bars are patently phantasies of homosexual encounters.

However one may react to Legman's exegeses, he is following a well-worn path in folklore interpretation. Like Max Müller and Andrew Lang before him, he is admittedly seeking to account for the irrationality and grossness in folktales. Müller used comparative philology and the thesis of forgetfulness in language, Lang used evolutionism and the thesis of savage survivals, and Legman uses Freudian psychoanalysis and oedipal symbolism to explain why men tell obscene tales.

C. G. Jung severed his intellectual relations with Freud in 1913, and established his own school of analytical psychology in Switzerland. Rejecting the name and the sexual symbolism of psychoanalysis, Jung and his followers group themselves under a distinct branch of psychology. From the viewpoint of folklore, however, Freudians and Jungians have much in common. Both circles regard folklore as an integral part of their discipline, and the Jung Institute in Zurich includes a training course on "Practise in the Psychological Intepretation of Fairy Tales." Both Freud and Jung interpret myths and fairy tales by the method of symbolism. The methods are not incompatible, and so ardent an exponent of Jung as Joseph Campbell includes Freudian readings in his exegesis of the world's mythology. The Freudian pairs of opposites—male-female, phallus-vagina—recur in Jung in metaphysical rather than nakedly sexual terms: consciousness-unconsciousness, life-death, God-Satan. Both schemes of interpretation employ the key concept of the unconscious.

The favorable acceptance of Jungian ideas by mythologists like Joseph Campbell and a host of literary critics is balanced by criticism and rejection from folklore-minded anthropologists for what they consider Jung's abstraction of archetypes from a cultural context. A young American folklorist with training at the Jung Institute in Zurich, Switzerland, Carlos C. Drake, in two incisive articles has pointed out errors and misunderstanding of Jung's concepts by well-known anthropologists, and sought to clarify these concepts and their usefulness for the folklorist.

One concept posits basic psychological types, the extrovert and introvert, each of which is divided into four subtypes according to thinking, feeling, intuition, and sensation. The collector may be aided in his fieldwork, Drake believes, if he knows the psychological types of his informants and of himself, so that he can relate more effectively to them, as well as better understanding their personal styles. An analysis of collectors in Freudian terms by Alan Dundes defines the anal-retentive type, who jealously guards and refuses to publish or lend what he collects, and his opposite, who prints everything in a diarrhea-like flow. There is no question that the personality and predispositions of the collector should be made known to the reader of his materials.

By the "collective unconscious" Jung had in mind a deeper layer behind the "personal unconscious" recognized by Freud. All men shared in the collective unconscious, whose contents Jung called "archetypes." But the archetypes themselves represented form rather than content. Archetypal dream images emerged from a master mold of the collective unconscious and sometimes became associated with the contents of the personal unconscious. One sees this relationship in the dual nature of mythical figures, like the Greek gods, both helpful and destructive. Jung used further terms to describe the composition of the individual: *persona*, to denote his public or professional role, and *anima* to denote his feminine principle (*animus* for the male principle in women). The *anima* mediated in archetypes between the conscious and the unconscious.

In myths and folktales, as in dreams and phantasies, Jung perceived shadow figures and situations representing the dark side of the personality. These unconscious factors could be identified by the folklorist, Drake claims, and he gives examples. Helpful witches appear in Pueblo Indian tales, but never in the culture, where the witch is commonly despised. Hence the witch is to be interpreted as a collective shadow figure, whose helpful side, revealed in the tales, provides an emotional outlet for a repressed people. In the well-known folktale of "The Brave Tailor," who swatted seven flies and placarded himself that he had killed seven (giants?) at one blow, the hero lives up to his *persona* of the victorious champion, conquers dangers from the unconscious symbolized by ogres and beasts, and wins the princess, his *anima*, in a successful resolution of his personality.[12]

12. Carlos C. Drake, "Jung and His Critics" and "Jungian Psychology and Its Use in Folklore," *Journal of American Folklore* 80 (1967): 321–33, and 82 (1969): 122–31.

Jung frequently invokes folklore in his writings. In one of his last works, Jung wrote on a modern phenomenon with folkloric implications, *Unidentified Flying Objects*. The sighting of these objects can be explained, he felt, by the congruence of deep societal anxieties with the space-conscious aspirations of our phantasies. People today, especially Americans, Jung postulated, seek liberation from their earthly confines and believe that the people of other planets want to fly to us. One of Jung's most pertinent essays for the folklorist is "On the Psychology of the Trickster Figure" in Paul Radin's *The Trickster, a Study in American Indian Mythology* (1956). Jung analyzes the trickster as God, animal, and man all in one, at once subhuman and superhuman, bestial and divine, characterized chiefly by unconsciousness and unreason. The myth of the trickster is remembered because it holds the earlier low intellectual and moral level before the more highly developed individual. Civilized man has forgotten the trickster, who reemerges when the individual is caught in the crowd. In the same volume Karl Kerényi gives a Freudian interpretation of the trickster as the phallus, while Radin combines Freudian and Jungian concepts to envisage trickster as all things to all men, interpreted anew in every generation.

Orthodox folklorists and anthropologists have reacted variously to psychoanalytical theory, ranging from disgusted rejection through cautious, partial acceptance to some instances of wholesale endorsement. They have, for instance, considered the Oedipus complex in the light of the familial structure and tribal narratives of non-Western cultures. Herskovits extends the classic theorem by pointing to factors unconsidered by Freud, such as sibling jealousy for the favor of the mother, and the father's fear of displacement by his son. Dahomean family relationships, in which the child is always dependent on the mother and little aware of his polygynous father, explain the dominance of these themes. Earlier, Malinowski had shown that among the Trobriand Islanders the father's brother who brought up the son became the object of childhood resentment. In an ingenious examination of Oedipus-type tales collected in Oceania, William Lessa points out that the plot appears within a kin group society on Ulithi atoll quite unlike the Euroamerican nuclear family. Oedipus tales thus appear in cultures lacking oedipal-complex situations, and fail to appear in Africa, China, much of Asia, North and South America, and Australia. They are therefore not a universal development from a universal complex, nor does the plot seem related to its social environment. Presumably the tale has traveled from Europe to Oceania by diffusion. This kind of rigorous empirical testing of Freudian hypotheses reveals a willingness by anthropologists to consider them seriously in the scrutiny of oral literature.

STRUCTURAL

The most influential and enticing theory to emerge in American folk-lore circles in the 1960s was structuralism. Advocates of structural analysis had advanced their proposals before the sixties, for instance, the German André Jolles in his *Einfache Formen* (1930), an attempt to establish the primary forms of folk expression, and Lord Raglan in his controversial book *The Hero* (1936), which elaborated a general pattern of episodic experiences for classical and mythological heroic narratives. Eclipsing these and other attempts at structural vivisection was the study of the Russian formalist Vladimir Propp, first published in Russian in 1928 and in English translation in 1958 as *Morphology of the Folktale*. As the reputation of Propp's work continued to grow, it was reissued in 1968 with an introduction by Alan Dundes, an apostle of the new creed, which he succinctly summarized. Dundes's own book, *The Morphology of North American Indian Folktales* (1964), applied structural analysis to a corpus of tales previously considered formless, and stated his conception of the structural theory in broad intellectual perspective. Other young folklorists of Dundes's generation in dissertations and essays have fashioned their own structural models.

Propp is the true father-figure of the new movement, and he purposely introduced his scheme to displace the taxonomy of Antti Aarne. He felt that classifying folktales by dramatis personae, as Aarne did, was misleading, for the same action in variant tales could be performed by an ogre, a dragon, the devil, a giant, or a bear. But the action remained constant, and one action episode followed another in a fixed pattern, at least in the body of Russian fairy tales from the collection of Afanas'ev that Propp analyzed. The action slots into which variable actors fit Propp called functions, and the generic actors he called the Hero and the Villain. Propp enumerated thirty-one functions, whose sequential arrangement constituted the morphology of the fairy tale. Every Russian tale in the corpus could be fitted into the one skeletal plot outline.

Propp's *Morphology* heralded a dramatic, if somewhat belated, turning point in folklore studies. Just as Stith Thompson and other Americans reacted delightedly to the sight in America, several years after its publication in Finland in 1910, of Aarne's catalog rendering an order out of the chaos of European folktales, so Alan Dundes and others responded to the delayed translation in 1958 of Propp's system. This shift from typology by content to typology by structure caught the mood of the fifties and sixties. Types and motifs reflected the vagaries of random field collecting. They stood in no essential relationship to each other. Now Propp had constructed a model and revealed the design that explained the construction of all Russian *skazki*.

This accomplishment endeared Propp to the younger American folklorists who admired the precision and data-supported generalizing of the social sciences. As Dundes recognized, the intellectual fashion had shifted in the thirties and forties from the piecemeal to the whole, from the atomistic part to the unified conception. The *avant garde* talked of pattern in culture, of the New Criticism that looked at the whole work of art, of Gestalt psychology, of linguistic structures.

In his own *Morphology*, Dundes made certain refinements of Propp's agenda. For Propp's colorless term "function" he substituted "motifeme," a coinage derived from the linguist Kenneth Pike, and he proposed "allomotif" to designate motifs occurring as part of the motifeme. In this way Dundes hoped to make a bridge from Stith Thompson's vague use of motif, so widely accepted in folklore circles, to a much more rigorous terminology based on structural models that precisely represented folklore genres.

For if structural analysis worked in one case, it could presumably work in others. It explained the Russian fairy tale, and then the North American Indian tale; its proponents argued that it could lay bare other tale repertoires and other genres, such as superstitions, games, and riddles; that it could represent the social context and the linguistic texture as well the folklore text, diagram cultural preferences, predict acculturative behavior, link genres, and sharpen functional and psychological studies. Such was the table of bountiful expectations set by the structural folklorists.

Another method of structural analysis of folklore texts based on linguistic theory is advanced by the French anthropologist Claude Lévi-Strauss. In an influential article, "The Structural Study of Myth,"[13] he proposed a wholly new direction in mythological interpretation. The older schools had always found some inferences to draw from a simplistic comparison of myths to culture: the myths either mirrored or distorted realities of the culture. But why did myths around the world show so many similar features? Lévi-Strauss believed the answer would be found in a logical structure within the human mind, even the savage mind. Taking the Oedipus myth and certain North American Indian myths for examples, he dissected them on the basis of "bundles of relations." These repeated narrative elements revealed certain common ideas, such as "the denial of the autochthonous origin of man," represented in the slaying of monsters by heroic men. Another set of elements balances this feature with the idea of "the persistence of the autochthonous origin of man," illustrated by lame men, like Oedipus himself, who emerge from the depths of the earth malformed. The Oedipus myth is trying to resolve the contradiction between the cultural belief that man is aboriginal

13. *Journal of American Folklore* 78 (1955), 428–44.

and the realization in life that he is born of man and woman. Every variant of each myth seeks to mediate between such opposing ideas. The ambivalent character of the trickster can be explained by this structure, for he mediates between pairs of extremes, whether sky and earth, wild and cultivated, male and female, good and bad.

The system of Lévi-Strauss relies on a sorting out and rearrangement of the narrative features in the myth, to reveal the inherent structure, while that of Propp follows the story line. These are the two basic kinds of structural analysis, for which Dundes proposes the terms paradigmatic and syntagmatic, since Lévi-Strauss aims at a paradigm or conceptual framework behind the myth while Propp considers the syntax, so to speak, of the tale. These and other structural expositions seek to reduce folklore genres to universal models and formulas.

ORAL-FORMULAIC

Literary students of folklore have responded with growing enthusiasm to the oral-formulaic theory of folk expression. This theory looks to the narrator and his performance for the key to the composition and structure of epic, ballad, romance, and folktale. Its chief proponents have been the assiduous Harvard scholars Milman Parry (who died prematurely in 1935), a classicist, and the Slavists Albert Lord and David Bynum. The field trips of Parry from 1933 to 1935, and of Lord in 1937, 1950, and 1951, amassed some 13,000 Slavic texts, now deposited in the Parry Collection at Harvard; a selection from Novi Pazar was published in 1954 with English translations, interview transcripts, photographs of informants, and musical notations by Béla Bartók. Parry sought to analyze the oral style of the Homeric epics through a close study of a living tradition of European heroic poetry. Explaining Parry's and his own conclusions to a conference of folklorists in 1950, Lord gave this summary statement: "In studying oral epic with a mind to distinguish it from written epic, the factors which we have found of most help thus far have been the formula, which involves a study of the line; enjambement, which involves a study of the way in which one line is linked with another; and the theme, which involves a study of the structure of the poem as a whole." This method of formulaic analysis can be applied, Lord contended, to other forms of folklore like folktales and ballads. In *The Singer of Tales* (1960) he presented a full-length study of the Homeric epics as products of oral composition in the manner and method continued by the Yugoslav folk bards. This work discusses intensively the concepts of formula and theme, and the observable process of oral heroic poetry, to demonstrate the generic unity of folk epics from classical to modern times.

The theory emerging from the meticulous recording and close analysis of Yugoslav hero-poems involves the form and style of oral literature. Because of the exigencies of oral transmission, the folk-singer and tale-teller must rely on a stock repertoire of descriptive phrases or formulas and a set metrical or episodic structure to bolster his memory and enable him to improvise each new rendition. This theory was boldly applied to the celebrated English and Scottish popular ballads by James H. Jones in 1961. The ballad-singer employed commonplaces as the epic-singer employed formulas, to enable him to "compose rather than merely transmit." In a counterstatement Albert Friedman defended memorization against improvisation, pointing to the very close likenesses in versions of Child ballads.[14]

Where Jones made sweeping claims for formulaic composition in ballads, W. Edson Richmond offers a more modest, and consequently more persuasive, claim in the case study of a Norwegian ballad. He looks at two versions of "Den utrue egtemann" ("The false knight"), which are too dissimilar to be variants from the singers' memories, but too parallel episodically to be separate song narratives.

They tell of a knight who scorns his wife to ride off and bed his mistress, returns to hear from gravediggers or litter bearers of his wife's death, and puts himself to the sword. These episodes are rife with commonplaces abounding in other Scandinavian ballads. Yet none of them match the story line of "Den utrue egtemann." Richmond decides that "One must predicate an archetype and conclude that it was reconstructed by two (or more) singers relying upon their stock-in-trade: a memory for plot and the traditional phrases and stanzas common to their particular community."[15]

The oral-formulaic theory has attracted increasing numbers of converts in various of the folklore genres. Folklorists and literary scholars have applied it to Anglo-Saxon epic poetry, to medieval romances, to Russian *byliny*, to Negro revivalist sermons. Lord himself tried it to his own satisfaction on folktales of Angola in Portuguese West Africa, in his introduction to *Umbundu,* collected by Merlin Ennis (1962). In the Angolan narratives he perceived the same techniques of oral composition, relying upon repetition of thematic units—much as the theme of repetition itself, or of frightening distraction—that he had uncovered in Yugoslav and Homeric folk epics. Further demonstra-

---

14. James H. Jones, "Commonplace and Memorization in the Oral Tradition of the English and Scottish Popular Ballads," *Journal of American Folklore* 74 (1961): 97–112, and Albert B. Friedman, "The Formulaic Improvisation Theory of Ballad —a Counterstatement," *idem* 74 (1961): 113–15.

15. W. Edson Richmond, "'Den Utrue Egtemann': A Norwegian Ballad and Formulaic Composition," *Norveg,* Folkelivsgransking 10 (1963): 62.

tions of the oral-formulaic technique and the reliance of reciters upon thematic clusters can certainly be expected.

An imaginative application of the oral-formulaic theory to a fresh body of material was undertaken by Bruce A. Rosenberg in *The Art of the American Folk Preacher* (1970). Directly acknowledging his debt to Lord and Parry, Rosenberg analyzed the texts of chanted sermons by Negro preachers that he tape-recorded in church. The "spiritual" preacher, as distinguished from the "manuscript" preacher who relies on a written-out sermon, improvises his sermon text from a repertoire of formulas, clichés, and themes in his head, although he claims to speak with the spirit of the Lord. A minority of spiritual preachers chant their sermons, in performances that arouse the congregation to enthusiastic responses, and to their recitals Rosenberg applied the oral-formulaic analysis. He found these orally delivered sermon texts to possess narrative, metrical, and rhythmic elements that were manipulated by the preacher in a manner offering fair analogy to the Yugoslav *guslar*. Both composed their recitations at each new rendition by relying on associational clusters of phrases and images, which they fitted into metrical lines. The preacher enjoyed considerable flexibility in pursuing a narrative, combined literacy with oral spontaneity, and used stall formulas to gain time to think of his next passage, all mannerisms distinguishing his techniques from that of the *guslar*. But the analogies far outweighed the differences and add another persuasive body of evidence to the proponents of oral-formulaic folklore creativity.

CROSS-CULTURAL

Prominent schools of folklore theory that came to the fore in the second half of the nineteenth century indulged in bold generalizations covering all the cultures of man. The evolutionary anthropology of Edward B. Tylor, who made considerable use of folkloric data, influenced a whole school of Victorian folklorists, led by Andrew Lang and Edwin Sidney Hartland, to accept a scheme of uniform cultural development from savagery to civilization. Folklore represented survivals of primitive beliefs held by all races of men at the lower rungs of the evolutionary ladder. In his twelve volumes of *The Golden Bough*, James G. Frazer advanced another comprehensive proposal, extended by his myth-ritual followers, namely that all myths and all folklore stemmed from ancient sacrificial fertility rituals. At one time the myths explained the rituals, but with the passing of human and animal sacrifices, the myths went their separate ways, and the rites shrank to vestigial harvest customs.

In the twentieth century, anthropologists cut these theories to ribbons. They pointed out the dangers and fallacies in superficial comparisons across cultures, and concentrated on intensive studies of single cultures. In place of a closed evolutionary scheme they asserted a pluralistic, open-ended world in which every society possessed its own unique history and values. Nationalistic folklorists responded to this premise and searched for the soul of their people in the traditions of their land.

Yet cross-cultural folklore theory has returned in the 1960s, formidably armed with all the glittering weaponry of the social sciences. Climaxing a series of preliminary papers and reports on his cantometrics project, Alan Lomax published in 1968 *Folk Song Style and Culture* under the august sponsorship of the American Association for the Advancement of Science. By cantometrics, Lomax meant a measuring system "for evoking performance style from sound recordings," but he intended to extend his investigations to other cross-cultural expressive arts, such as dance, which would be evaluated through choreometrics. He envisaged a "science of social aesthetics" that would establish "predictable and universal relationships" between the "expressive and communication processes, on the one hand, and social structure and culture pattern, on the other." Folksongs were the first cultural indicator he had examined, because world-wide recordings of folksongs were available, peoples in all cultures sang folksongs and, by their built-in redundancies, folksongs mirrored cultures. Folktales, being less redundant, could stray further from cultural norms. It was these norms, or life styles, that represented Lomax's quest.

Through the measurement of qualities in folksongs he believed he had found correlations with other parts of the culture, such as relationships between the sexes, the level of economic productivity, and motor behavior. Thus in the Sudan, where the chastity of girls is protected by a sealing of the vagina, and dire punishment, even death, is meted for transgression, the muezzin crying prayers to Allah and the shrill-voiced cafe singers express in their piercing, quivering tones the "erotic hysteria" of Sudanese women. This musical style and restrictive sexuality accompany the relatively complex irrigation cultures of the Far East. Conversely, in those gardening and peasant societies where women labor along with men and sexual relations are freer, the singing style is manifested in wide, relaxed voices. Lomax intersperses many such examples among his graphs and tables. African pygmy hunter societies rank lowest in the scale of affluent societies, but they rank highest in the synchrony of their song and dance, and this achievement reflects their total sharing of material goods and emotional stresses.

In place of the nineteenth-century cross-cultural generalizations based on evolutionary uniformity, Lomax has accepted some cultural pluralism, with its key anthropological concept that every culture contains its own inner harmonies and its own expressive style. Using sophisticated scientific precision tools, he has blocked out six world regions with their own grand styles, divisible into smaller regional units. In the end he hopes that recognition of these styles will lead to their better appreciation and preservation, through cultural feedback via the mass media, against the corrosive forces of mechanization and industrialism. This aspiration echoes the sentiments of the nineteenth-century romantics who viewed with dismay the passing of the old traditions and customs. But in every other respect *Folk Song Style and Culture* reflects the academic style of its own day. It is the production of a team of specialists in the behavioral sciences—linguistics, kinesics, ethnology, psychology, ethno-history, musicology, economics, sociology. It is funded handsomely by foundation and government grants. It has programmed "hard data" for the computer, that final arbiter of measurable knowledge. It relies on statistical tables at every step. It talks of prediction, communicative and expressive systems, data banks, and similar talismanic terms. It relies on the empirical evidence of tapes and films from the field. It embodies the creed of the social sciences, that hard-nosed scholars can predict laws of human behavior.

FOLK-CULTURAL

The point of view sponsored by the advocates of folklife studies may conveniently be labeled "folk-cultural," a favorite adjective in their vocabulary. At the present time they are hortatory rather than theoretical, ethnographic rather than philosophical. Their chief plea and plaint, whether uttered by Iorwerth Peate in Wales, founder and editor of the folklife journal *Gwerin* (the Welsh word for folk), or by Don Yoder in America, founder and editor of the magazine *Pennsylvania Folklife,* is to broaden the concerns of the folklorist so that they will embrace the tangible products of the folk, and indeed the totality of folklife.[16] Individual studies on folklife subjects deal with matters of physical description (often accompanied by photographs and sketches), historical reconstruction, and distributional analyses.

To anticipate objections that the folklife researcher is the old antiquary with a new name, Henry Glassie in his *Pattern in the Material Folk Culture of the Eastern United States* (1969) has set forth certain guidelines. "The best student of folk culture is both fieldworker and theorist, and a modern study of material culture might include the detailed description and ordering of field data, the historic-geographic connections of types, constructions and uses, as well as functional and

16. Don Yoder, "The Folklife Studies Movement," *Pennsylvania Folklife* 13 (July 1963) : 43–56.

psychological speculations" (p. 16). Glassie proposes to go beyond the discussion of the history and distribution of the object, and to probe into its emotional and cultural role in the life of its makers and users. Thorny theoretical questions that Glassie mentions during his copiously illustrated and documented treatise are the nature of folk aesthetic, the relation of folk arts to popular arts, defining regional areas of folk culture (the main burden of his study), the interaction between the movement of ideas and of objects, the satisfactions of material culture in a world of mass technology, and the development of an American folklife style. His emphasis is toward the geographer and against the historian, for spatial diversities and against chronological homogeneity.

A basis for theory is laid in a nine-hundred-page doctoral dissertation by Michael O. Jones at Indiana University (1970), "Chairmaking in Appalachia, a Case Study of Style in American Folk Art." Jones elaborates a complex theoretical model for the study of handmade items of material culture intended for utilitarian purposes. The model considers the local economics of production and distribution, the psychological types of the artists, external influences of taste and demand affecting the folk community, the ecological factors controlling the raw materials, and the traditional techniques manipulated by the artist. Jones seeks to take into account every element—historical, individual, cultural, traditional, aesthetic, economic, environmental—entering into the folk art process.

MASS-CULTURAL

Deep in the twentieth century, the battle continues between the urban, technological, mass-production and mass-consumption culture and the rural, peasant folk culture. Always the cry is that the flowers of tradition are being relentlessly crushed by the steamroller of industrial civilization. In a few more years, there will be no more folklore, and, *ergo,* no need for any folklorists.

Whether in self-defense, or with a new enlightenment, folklore scholars in the 1960s have reinterpreted the opposition between the mass and the folk cultures. They have begun to see interpenetration instead of confrontation. Ethnic and rural folk pour into the cities, adjust in varying ways to the urban tempo, and struggle to maintain their folk identities. The city is indeed increasingly a conglomeration of folk societies, as the middle classes flee town for the suburbs, and the ghetto takes over. So too do the omnivorous mass media of television, films, recordings, and radio absorb and engulf all kinds of folk themes and formulas, to spew them out to their giant audiences in a cultural feedback. A doctoral candidate in folklore at Indiana University watched and recorded television shows continually for one day from 6:15 A.M. to 1:30 A.M., and extrapolated 101 folkloric themes and items, divided among traditional music and song (27), folk belief (24), gesture (11), narratives—all jokes (10), proverbs and proverbial sayings (9), custom, signs, dance, games, and rhymes (2 each). The student, Tom Burns, realized the impossibility of identifying an item of folklore in exact correspondence on the television screen, and so worked out a scheme analyzing the components of a traditional item into text, performance style, situation, and audience. While in most cases all four elements would not be present on television shows and advertisements, one or more were recognized in each case.[17]

Mass-cultural orientation in folklore has not produced as yet a comprehensive theoretical statement, but rather points to enticing research topics. Marshall McLuhan's widely read interpretations of our present "oral-aural" culture, which he believes is displacing the literary-print culture of yesterday and reverting to the tribal culture of an earlier day, intrigues the mass-minded folklorist. The few studies yet undertaken, such as Roger Abrahams' *Deep Down in the Jungle* (1964, revised edition 1970), appraising the Negro narrative lore in a Philadelphia district, and Charles Keil's *Urban Blues* (1966), scrutinizing the mechanisms that transmute folk into mass performance in Chicago recording studios, are eclectic in their theory. They enlist psychological concepts of child development, sociological concepts of small group behavior, ethnomusicological concepts of music as social expression, literary concepts of folklore as rhetorical discourse, and folkloric concepts of the oikotype or regional genres. Abrahams explains the altered repertoire of the northern urban Negro in terms of the tough talk and aggressive style of ghetto life; Brer Rabbit is now a struggling badman. Keil generalizes beyond his precise field data on the Chicago blues singers, B. B. King and Bobby Bland, to demonstrate the process from input of country folk tradition to the output of national packaged entertainment. While the Negro subculture has changed from sleepy southern rhythms to the fast northern staccato pace, it still remains an auditory and tactile rather than a visual and literate culture. So a second step is needed, to bring the black man-of-words, hustler, and entertainer into the cultural mainstream. The sequence is often preacher, bluesman, militant, author— Malcolm X, Eldridge Cleaver, James Baldwin, Ralph Ellison. The folksinger and storyteller tailors his art to studio demands; he becomes a celebrity; he writes books translating powerful spoken words into powerful written words.

While these complementary studies have dealt with the Negro,

17. Tom Burns, "Folklore in the Mass Media: Television," *Folklore Forum* 2: 4 (July 1969) : 90–106.

other urban enclaves are beginning to receive similar attention. In fieldwork with Hungarian steelworkers and their families in East Chicago, Linda Dégh has observed the adaptation of Old Country folkways to the American urban milieu. The telephone now becomes an instrument to hold together a dispersing ethnic group, and a channel for not only communication but also performance, as housewives relate to each other gossip and scandals and alarms decked out with the formulaic patterns of the Märchen. Certain German folklorists, notably Hermann Bausinger, who wrote on *Volkskultur in der technischen Welt* (1961), have renounced the Romantic search for antiquarian survivals and embraced the phenomena of modern life. Bausinger asserts pointedly that "We no longer believe that industrialization necessarily implies the end of a specific folk culture, but rather we attempt to trace the modifications and mutations undergone by *folk culture in the industrialized and urbanized world*" (italics his).[18] This new species of folklorist differs from the sociologist in his methods and aims, and will investigate the social effects of tourism, voluntary associations, small-scale arts and crafts producers, the urban folksong revival, popular theater, mass literature, and holiday customs. He seeks to trace continuities from a living past to a vital present, and scorns relics, survivals, and archaisms. The "pure" folk art of yesterday might itself have served as a tourist attraction. The old folklore is not as old as it appears, and the new may be older than it seems.

HEMISPHERIC

The hemispheric theory of folklore, which is my own theory, divides the folklore of the Old and New Worlds for analytical purposes.[19] This theory hinges on the historical fact of colonization of the Americas late in recorded history by European maritime powers, notably Spain, France, England, and Portugal. The wholesale importation of African Negro slaves by the European colonizers added one more racial element to the population mixture. Europeans and Africans mingled with the indigenous Indians from country to country in varying degrees of interaction. Then in the nineteenth and twentieth centuries, after the colonies had established themselves as independent republics, waves of immigrants descended from the British Isles, northern and eastern Europe, and Asia to fill the still open spaces of the western hemisphere.

Clearly one cannot speak about an Old World national tradition, with its relative stability, rootedness, and long ancestry, in the same

18. Hermann Bausinger, "Folklore Research at the University of Tübingen," *Journal of the Folklore Institute* 5 (1968) : 127.
19. Richard M. Dorson, *American Folklore and the Historian* (Chicago, 1971) .

fashion as the New World blends. (Australia, also a colonized continent with separate aboriginal and settlers' traditions, belongs with the Americas in this formulation.) The question has even arisen whether one can speak at all about an American, or a United States, folklore. Yet abundant folklore in the Americas has been collected and published, although not properly studied in its own terms.

According to the hemispheric theory, the folklore of each New World country needs to be analyzed in terms of its ethnic-racial and historical ingredients. In one country the African element may be high, in another the Indian, in another the colonial German. The task for the New World folklorist is to examine closely the processes of syncretism, adaptation, acculturation, retention, accommodation, revitalization, recession, and disappearance that determine the ultimate product. Several collateral traditions, rather than one homogenized folklore, coexist. Some South American folklorists of Iberian background discuss only the imported tales of Spanish and Portuguese origin, oblivious to the Negro and the Indian.

Various processes are operating simultaneously. What might be called recession is the withdrawal of formerly active parts of folk tradition into the back of the mind, where it becomes "memory culture," to be elicited only by a chance association or a collector's prodding. Elimination refers to those portions of Old Country lore that never survive the Atlantic crossing, chiefly local legends and demonic beliefs connected with landmarks. Retention denotes the survival of Old World customs that prove to be more conservative in the Americas than in Europe, where the parent language and lore have continued to change. Generalizations about acculturation must not be applied sweepingly to all immigrant groups. Some ethnic societies prove to be much more retentive than others. The Serbs are more tenacious of their folk inheritance than the Croats, with whom they are customarily paired, because Serbians have their own mother church and their own strong sense of national history, where Croatians are Catholic and were engulfed within Austria-Hungary. Nor can one generalize about a whole ethnic group. The German immigrants range from the Old Order Amish to dispossessed liberals of the 1830 and 1848 abortive revolutions. The intensity of genres will also vary from one country to another. In the United States the festival is more commercial than folk, and not very prominent, but religious and secular folk festivals pervade Latin America.

Besides the ethnic-racial mix, the New World folklorist needs to weigh the special historical and environmental factors that have shaped traditions. The revolutions of the late eighteenth and nineteenth centuries bred national heroes and hallowed events that entered folk history. Long coastlines, towering mountain ranges, arid deserts, great lakes, and mighty rivers formed the backdrop for New World legends and exploits. Specifically American types, like the cowboys and gauchos of the plains and pampas, evolved and became the bearers and subjects of song and story. The folklorist dealing with the New World must take into account these many complex and variable strands.

CONTEXTUAL

A growing movement among energetic younger folklorists in the United States may be given the umbrella-name "contextual." While as yet they do not form a cohesive school, they do share doctoral training in folklore at the universities of Indiana and Pennsylvania in the 1960s; a leaning toward the social sciences, particularly anthropology, linguistics, and the cultural aspects of psychology and sociology; a strong preoccupation with the environment in which the folklore text is embedded; and an emphasis on theory. They object strenuously to the text being extrapolated from its context in language, behavior, communication, expression, and performance, overlapping terms they continually employ. These ideas unite such young Turks among the folklorists as Roger Abrahams, Dan Ben-Amos, Alan Dundes, Robert Georges, and Kenneth Goldstein. From linguists they have drawn the concept of verbal behavior, from anthropology of functionalism, from sociology of role-playing, from psychology of ego mechanisms, and they seek to apply these perspectives to the folklore traditions.

As yet this rising generation of folklorists has not produced the single monolithic work expressing their thought, but rather they have advanced their views in highly theoretical papers. Their rejection of the older static typology of folklore texts and stress on a three-dimensional context is seen in such phrases as "ceremonial communicative interaction of small groups";[20] "complex communicative event";[21] "texture, text, and context";[22] "cultural categories of communication";[23] "a definite realistic, artistic, and communicative process."[24]

What distinguishes this young generation of folklorists is their insistence that the folklore concept apply not to a text but to an event in time in which a tradition is performed or communicated. Hence

20. Roger Abrahams, "The Complex Relations of Simple Forms," *Genre* 2 (1969) : 105.

21. Robert A. Georges, "Toward an Understanding of Storytelling Events," *Journal of American Folklore* 82 (1969) : 317.

22. Alan Dundes, "Texture, Text, and Context," *Southern Folklore Quarterly* 28 (1964) : 251–65.

23. Dan Ben-Amos, "Analytical Categories and Ethnic Genres," *Genre* 2 (1969) : 275.

24. Dan Ben-Amos, "Toward a Definition of Folklore in Context," *Journal of American Folklore* 84 (1971) : 10.

the whole performance or communicative act must be recorded. The collector can no longer simply write down or tape-record a text, for the text is only part of each unique event. To circumvent this difficulty Goldstein proposes "The Induced Natural Context" whereby the collector organizes a riddling or tale-telling or other folkloric session that simulates a situation where he is not present.[25] In the revised edition of his *Deep Down in the Jungle* (1970), Abrahams inserts a section on his own field attitudes and relationships to give the reader a truer picture of the performance situation behind the texts. Frequently the young male black narrators shortened their "toasts" for lack of a responsive, enthusiastic audience.

Working with a Yoruba student in the United States, Dundes presents the cultural contexts of Nigerian proverbs in analytical descriptions following each text. He does this as a preferred model for proverb hunters in place of the usual lists of proverb texts from the foreign culture juxtaposed to fancied parallel proverbs from the home culture. Thus he gives the Yoruba saying "The hand of a child cannot reach the high shelf, nor can that of an older person enter a calabash," and then appends a long paragraph of contextual explanation. Yoruba society emphasizes the principle of mutual responsibility between old and young, parents and children. An uncle may ask a nephew to fetch him water several times. One day the youth asks his uncle for pineapples and is refused. Next day the nephew refuses to do an errand for his uncle. The uncle complains about this conduct to a peer, who quotes him the proverb. Now the meaning is clear from the context. Seniors and juniors must help each other.[26]

The term contextual, while it appears frequently in their writings, does not necessarily appeal to all these theorists. Abrahams speaks of a rhetorical theory of folklore, and Georges thinks of himself as a behaviorist. Indebted to Kenneth Burke's rhetorical method of examining the strategies of artistic utterances, Abrahams emphasizes the equality of "performance, item, and audience." He reaffirms the need for the folklorist to seize the "context of performance" as a means of relating folklore to the dynamics of culture.[27] Georges emphasizes that he is not making another plea to study storyteller, audience, and context along with story text, but introducing a wholly new concept, the holistic rather than atomistic study of the unique social experience

25. Kenneth E. Goldstein, "The Induced Natural Context: An Ethnographic Field Technique," in June Helm, ed., *Essays in the Verbal and Visual Arts* (Seattle and London: University of Washington Press for the American Ethnological Society, 1967), pp. 1–6.

26. Alan Dundes and E. Ojo Arewa, "Proverbs and the Ethnography of Speaking Folklore," *American Anthropologist* 66, No. 6, Part 2 (1964): 78.

27. Roger Abrahams, "Introductory Remarks to a Rhetorical Theory of Folklore," *Journal of American Folklore* 81 (1968): 143–58.

that constitutes a "storytelling event." Ben-Amos also parts company with previous scholarship to assert the social interaction of teller and tale, process and product in an artistic form. Folklore actions are distinguished from other modes of social interaction by "contextual conventions" of time, place, and company.[28]

The emergence of this sophisticated circle of youthful academic folklorists heralds a new departure in the writing of folklore books of the future. Texts and annotations will be subordinated to close analyses of group dynamics and psycho-cultural relationships. Fieldwork will become a more elaborate enterprise than the securing of verbatim texts.

What judgment can be made on these vigorously competing theories? No observer can be impartial, and I myself am committed to one of these twelve outlooks. Still some generalizations can be advanced. All these theories are strongly proclaimed, monistic in concept, and imperialistic in design, seeking to annex more and more folklore genres and culture areas. Yet they are not mutually exclusive, and an eclectic folklorist may find all of them useful at one time or another. He will at least need to be acquainted with them, if he wishes to become a knowledgeable student of folklore and folklife.

Bibliography and Selected Readings

Bascom, William. *Ifa Divination*. Bloomington: Indiana University Press, 1969. A close examination of the magico-religious divining system through which the Yoruba intercede with their deities. The diviners place great reliance on folktales in arriving at prescriptions for their clients. A good example of the American anthropological functional school.

Chadwick, Hector M., and Nora K. Chadwick. *The Growth of Literature*, 3 vols. Cambridge: Cambridge University Press, 1932–40. The Chadwicks subscribe to the theory of an Heroic Age in the history of peoples when oral legends gather around a great champion. From these legends the bards fashion romances and epics. The authors pursue this theory across the world with extensive and persuasive illustrations.

Dégh, Linda. *Folktales and Society*. Bloomington: Indiana University Press, 1969. A richly informative ethnographic study of the role of storytelling and storytellers in a Szekler community in Hungarian Transylvania. The emphasis is on the function of the tale repertoire in daily life and on the personalities of the narrators rather than on the tale texts.

28. Dan Ben-Amos, "Toward a Definition of Folklore in Context," 11.

Dorson, Richard M. *American Folklore and the Historian.* Chicago: University of Chicago Press, 1971. Essays written over a twenty-five year period contending that the study of American folklore should be pursued in the light of the special factors shaping American history.

———. *The British Folklorists, A History.* Chicago: University of Chicago Press, 1968. London: Routledge and Kegan Paul, 1968. Traces the genesis and development of the concept of folklore as a branch of learning from the national history of Camden in the sixteenth century to its flowering with the late Victorian folklorists. The history gives most space to the "Great Team" of anthropological folklorists who espoused the doctrine of survivals, i.e., folklore represents the relics of primitive thought and ritual.

———. "Current Folklore Theories." *Current Anthropology* 4 (1963): 93–112. An earlier form of the present Introduction.

———, ed. *Studies in Japanese Folklore.* Bloomington: Indiana University Press, 1963. Essays translated from the Japanese by leading folklorists in the school of Kunio Yanagita, founder of folklore studies in Japan. They employ the method of historical reconstruction to determine the original forms of animistic religious rituals surviving in contemporary Shinto ceremonies.

Finnegan, Ruth. *Oral Literature in Africa.* Oxford: Clarendon Press, 1970. The first comprehensive account of African expressive forms, rich in illustrative examples and source references, and wide-ranging in its discussion of genres from praise poems to personal names. Finnegan seeks to link oral to written literature, at the expense of folklore analysis, and emphasizes oral poetry over folk narrative.

Fontenrose, Joseph. *Python, A Study of Delphic Myth and Its Origins.* Berkeley and Los Angeles: University of California Press, 1959. A splendid comparative folklore study of the legend of the dragon-slayer as found in Greek myths and elsewhere in the ancient world.

Glassie, Henry. *Pattern in the Material Folk Culture of the Eastern United States.* Philadelphia: University of Pennsylvania Press, 1969. A pioneering volume in the folklife approach to American traditions. The author examines the regional distribution of a number of folk products, from house types to sling shots, to show how they fall into distinct subregional groupings. Densely documented and illustrated with photographs and designs.

Jacobs, Melville. *The Content and Style of an Oral Literature.* Chicago: University of Chicago Press, 1959. A psychologically oriented anthropologist attempts to bridge the culture gap between the Clackamas Chinook Indians of the Pacific Northwest and modern America by presenting their tales as dramatic performances. Jacobs fills in the texts with nuances and inferences understood by the original audience. Suggestive as a method for providing cross-cultural context.

Keil, Charles. *Urban Blues.* Chicago: University of Chicago Press, 1966. An examination of the mechanisms by which the mass media transform a rural folk performer into a recording artist and public performer. Keil uses first-hand field data from interviews with the Negro blues singers B. B. King and Bobby Bland as a basis for sophisticated generalizations employing concepts of the folklorist, ethnomusicologist, social psychologist, and anthropologist.

Legman, Gershon. *Rationale of the Dirty Joke.* New York: Grove Press, 1968. An impressive example of the psychoanalytical school of folklore interpretation. Some readers may consider the heavily Freudian interpretations of the joke texts overstrained, with the emphasis on latent homosexuality, castration fears, and phallic pride. Commendable for giving attention to the humble joke.

Lord, Albert B. *The Singer of Tales.* Cambridge, Mass.: Harvard University Press, 1960. The work that introduced the oral-formulaic theory of folk-epic composition. On the basis of field-collected South Slavic epics, Lord devised the hypothesis that the bards reconstructed their songs on each new performance from a basic stock of themes and epithets. He applied this thesis to the Homeric epics as well.

Lomax, Alan. *Folk Song Style and Culture.* Washington, D. C.: American Association for the Advancement of Science, 1968. An ambitious attempt to demonstrate correlations of culture traits with traditional singing styles throughout 56 world areas. Lomax goes against the current scholarship in seeking to establish world-wide generalizations for folk behavior. He enlists the aid of experts from computer mathematicians to ethnomusicologists to support his bold hypothesis.

Paredes, Américo, and Richard Bauman, eds. *Toward New Perspectives in Folklore. Journal of American Folklore* 84 (January-March 1971). The essays in this special issue represent, according to the editors, a new generation of folklorists with a "common commitment to illuminating the expressive behavior of man." Contributors draw from literary, anthropological, psychological, and linguistic theory, but they agree in conceptualizing folklore as event or process rather than item or product. This work reflects the present mood of younger folklore scholars in America with its emphasis on theories of communication and cultural behavior, and neglect of historical factors.

Propp, Vladimir. *Morphology of the Folktale.* Translated by Laurence Scott. Revised by Louis A. Wagner. Introduction by Alan Dundes. Bloomington, Indiana: Research Center in the Language Sciences, 1968. A structural analysis of Russian fairy tales, first published in 1928, which on its translation into English in 1958 excited Western folklorists with the possibility of classifying folktales by form rather than by content.

Radin, Paul. *The Trickster: a Study in North American Indian Mythology.* With commentaries by Karl Kerényi and C. G. Jung. New York: Philosophical Library, 1956. Pedagogically, an excellent volume to represent the psychoanalytical approach to folklore, employed on the same body of Winnebago Indian trickster tales by the classicist Kerényi, who gives a Freudian interpretation, by Jung, who departed from Freud to develop his own symbolism of the collective unconscious, and by the American anthropologist Radin, who occupies a median position.

Raglan, Lord. *The Hero: a Study in Tradition, Ritual and Drama.* London: Methuen & Co. Ltd., 1936. Orthodox folklorists of the Finnish historical-geographical school have severely criticized Raglan's thesis that the great hero-cycles of epic, saga, romance, and balladry derive from mythic narratives accompanying fertility rituals. Raglan contends that after one hundred fifty years historical tradition becomes pure fiction.

Sokolov, Y. M. *Russian Folklore.* Translated by Catherine Smith. New York: Macmillan Co., 1950. An ideological survey in depth of the genres of folk tradition found in the Soviet Union, prefaced by a lengthy essay in Marxist terms on the history of folklorists. Sokolov sees folklore as the expression of resentment and revulsion by the peasantry and proletariat toward the nobility and landowners.

I The Fields of Folklife Studies

ORAL FOLKLORE
1 FOLK NARRATIVE
Linda Dégh

Narration is ageless. The impulse to tell a story and the need to listen to it have made narrative the natural companion of man throughout the history of civilization. Stories are able to adapt themselves to any local and social climate. They are old and venerable, but they are also new and up to date. While recognizing that folk narratives contain persistent and yet continually reinterpreted ideas, the student of folklore observes folktales mainly as an art creation shaped and carried by different groups of people. He views the diverse forms of the narratives, including their content elements and structural framework, as complex wholes of an oral art. Close scrutiny of oral narrative categories followed the publication in 1929 of the famous and controversial book *Einfache Formen* by André Jolles, historian of art and literature. As the title suggests, Jolles considered oral literary forms as simple, spontaneous products originating in the spoken language, as opposed to complex, consciously created literary forms. Jolles's essay, intended as the first part of a general history of literature, opened a vista for future generations of folklorists seeking to determine the narrative genres and their interrelations. Folk narrative scholars stress the following questions: What is the message of folktales? What are the forces that create, launch, disseminate, maintain, vary, corrupt, and reinforce them? What do they mean to their performers and their audiences?

These questions had been raised and approached through different avenues by succeeding groups of scholars in various countries who have devoted themselves to the study of the folktale for a period of more than a hundred and fifty years. They amassed, classified, and preserved in well-organized archives representative bodies of their national tale stocks and undertook ambitious studies to disclose the secrets of origin, dissemination, and variation of the diverse narrative forms.[1]

Literary artists popularized folktales long before they became the focus of scholarly interest. The well-educated reader enjoyed the taste of the naïve folktale quite early. Such works as Gianbattista Basile's collection of fifty Neapolitan tales, the *Pentamerone* (1634–36), Charles Perrault's *Contes de ma Mère l'Oye* (1695–98), and the Countess d'Aulnoy's *Contes des Fées* (1697–98) gained general acclaim. Through these and similar publications and the translated editions of the great oriental storybooks, the *Panchatantra,* the *Arabian Nights,* and the adaptation of the Aesopian fables, folktales inspired both folklore and literature.

Jacob and Wilhelm Grimm, the first scholarly folktale collectors, compiled their *Kinder- und Hausmärchen* (1812–14, two volumes) both from the tellings of oral poets and from early literary collections, because "old" and "folk" were identical for them. Jacob, the scholar, wanted to print the stories as he found them, whereas Wilhelm, the literary man, displeased with the imperfect style of the collected versions, touched up the texts to make them worthy of the natural poets who created them: the Folk. The two hundred tales, stylized by Wilhelm Grimm and continuously reprinted, had a tremendous impact on the international folktale. They soon became the subject of folktale research. The *Household Tales* stimulated collectors throughout the nineteenth century. Aleksandr Nikolaevič Afanas'ev in Russia, Peter Christen Asbjörnsen in Norway, Evald Tang Christensen in Jütland, Svend Hersleb Grundtvig in Denmark, Karel Jaro-

---

1. The "simple forms" idea was expanded and reinterpreted by several scholars in an attempt to determine the genres of the folk narrative. See Walter Berendsohn, "Einfache Formen," *Handwörterbuch des deutschen Märchens,* ed. Lutz Mackensen (2 vols.; Berlin and Leipzig, 1930–40), 1: 484–98; Albert Wesselski, "Die Formen der volkstümlichen Erzählguts," *Die deutsche Volkskunde,* ed. Adolf Spamer (2 vols.; Leipzig: Bibliographisches Institut, 1935), 1: 216–48; Kurt Ranke, "Einfache Formen," *Journal of the Folklore Institute* 4 (1967): 17–31.

mír Erben in Bohemia, György Gaal in Hungary, Georg Hahn in Greece and Albania, Lazar Săineanu in Romania, Giuseppe Pitré in Sicily, and Emmanuel Cosquin in French Lotharingia followed their example and presented the first national collections of their respective countries. Only a few agreed with Jacob Grimm and insisted on the unaltered recording of the tales. John Francis Campbell's words introducing his tales of the West Highlands of Scotland (1860) express an aim that came true only in the age of the tape recorder:

> The following collection is intended to be a contribution to this new science of "Storiology." It is a museum of curious rubbish about to perish, given as it was gathered in the rough, for it seemed to me as barbarous to "polish" a genuine popular tale, as it would be to adorn the bones of a Megatherium with tinsel, or gild a rare old copper coin. On this, however, opinions vary, but I hold my own, that stories really collected can only be valuable if given unaltered ....

According to the concept of the Grimms and their disciples, folktales are the late relics of the ancient mythology of the Indo-Germans, and the myths of gods and heroes can be reconstructed from these fragmentary mosaics. According to the "heritage theory" of the Grimms, hero and magic tales were invented by the Indo-Germanic races and borrowed by others through migration and culture contact. Jacob Grimm's *Teutonic Mythology* (1835) inspired the so-called Mythologists, who saw generic relationship between language and mythology and claimed that the folktales reflected the symbolism of natural phenomena established by the myths. Max Müller (1823–1900), the most original among the Mythologists, traced the paths of the evolution of the ancient Aryan myths to verbal utterances originating in everyday experience of the primitive Aryans. Müller's mythology, most persistently propagated by his disciple, the Italian Angelo de Gubernatis (1840–1913), centered on solar symbolism, while others, like Adalbert Kuhn (1812–1881) and Wilhelm Schwarz (1821–1899), emphasized the forces of nature, and so were called "meteorologists" by their challengers.

When Edward B. Tylor (1832–1917), founder of the British school of anthropology, pointed out the survivals of "savage" myths in modern folk society and described their stages of evolution, the study of folktales acquired an ethnological foundation. It was Andrew Lang (1844–1912) who applied Tylor's ideas to narrative research. He compared motifs of European tales with Aryan and classical myth motifs and traced them back to primitive peoples, suggesting that the tales originated in the customs and beliefs of prehistoric man. Several of Lang's associates worked out special fairy tale monographs. Marian Roalfe Cox's *Cinderella* (1893), Edward Clodd's *Tom Tit Tot*

(1898), and Edwin S. Hartland's *The Legend of Perseus* (1894–96) deserve special mention. Another work by Hartland, *The Science of Fairy Tales* (1891), deals with tale incidents, actors, and storytellers.

Theodor Benfey (1809–1881), the father of historical-comparative folktale research, came from the same German school as Müller and also specialized in Sanskrit. While Müller exploited the Vedas, Benfey scrutinized the *Panchatantra,* a fifth-century Indic literary tale and fable collection, and related oral tales to literary origins. In 1859, in a six-hundred-page introduction to his translation of this work, Benfey analyzed the variants of each story. Except for the animal tales of Greek extraction, Benfey related all magic tales to Indic-Buddhistic educational literature. According to his migration theory, tales invaded Europe through the Arab conquest in Spain and the influx of Levantine traders into the Byzantine Empire, affecting mainly literary media. A third impulse came through the Mongolian invasion that helped import oral tales into eastern Europe.

The Indic origin theory stimulated heated discussions. Supporters and challengers both sought evidence through the study of parallels. The most powerful disputant, Joseph Bédier, analyzed *Les Fabliaux* (1893), suggested that the similarities concerned only general features, and voted rather for the polygenetic than for monogenetic origin of the tales. In retrospect, we might say that Benfey's merit was to prove that tales do migrate, that they are disseminated by people, and that oral tradition is certainly not void of literary impulses.

The inquiry into the origin and diffusion of the tales was further elaborated by Russian scholars of epic poetry and later by Finnish scholars of the *Kalevala,* the national epic of the Finns. Julius Krohn (1835–1888) and his son Kaarle (1863–1933) contended that folklore forms might well be spread from one definite center but that, nevertheless, tale variants reflect independent creative processes wherever and whenever they are found. Kaarle Krohn's methodology and theory were incorporated into his *Die folkloristische Arbeitsmethode* (1926) that became a guide for the adherents of the historical-geographical school. Tale type monographs sorted out the variants according to their chronological and geographical distribution, seeking to reconstruct the place of origin and route of travel of a hypothetical archetype. A number of these monographs have appeared in the prestigious *Folklore Fellows Communications* issued from Helsinki. Some outstanding ones are *The Tale of the Two Travelers or the Blinded Man* by the Norwegian, Reidar Christiansen (1916), *Kaiser und Abt* by the Estonian, Walter Anderson (1923), *The Black Ox* by the American, Archer Taylor (1927), and *Die zwei Brüder* by the German Kurt Ranke (1934). To furnish the necessary amount of international versions, folklorists constructed convenient indexes and variant classifications. The first tale type catalog by the Finn Antti Aarne (1867–1925) was issued in 1910 and expanded in the 1928 and 1961 editions by the American Stith Thompson to embrace all available national catalogs and archive materials. Thompson's six-volume *Motif-Index of Folk Literature*, first issued in the 1930s and reissued in expanded form in the 1950s, incorporates and classifies narrative units of stories. The compilation of variants to the Grimm tales in five volumes (1918–32) with other important materials on the history of the folktale, by Johannes Bolte and Georg Polívka, is an indispensable reference work for comparativists.

Although the historical-geographical school was most influential over a long period of time, many folklorists questioned the validity of the results reached by using text abstracts without consideration of their cultural environment. A former disciple of Krohn, Carl Wilhelm von Sydow (1878–1949) from Sweden, was the first to criticize the theoretical basis of this school. He did not believe in the study of single tale types but rather in the investigation of type families within regional ethnic formations that he called "oikotypes." Sydow saw a major contribution to the maintenance and spread of the tales by the "bearers of tradition" and incorporated his conceptions in a volume of *Selected Papers on Folklore* (1948). Other Swedes, Anna Birgitta Rooth in *The Cinderella Cycle* (1951) and Jan-Öjvind Swahn in *The Tale of Cupid and Psyche* (1955), demonstrated and developed further ideas of Sydow.[2]

Interest in individual performers among the nineteenth-century *byliny* collectors impressed the proponents of a new Russian school of folktale specialists, who switched the interest from the tale texts to the creativity of the storytellers. Mark Asadowskij's portrait of the personality of an illiterate Siberian narrator, Natalja Ossipowna Winokurowa, in *Eine sibirische Märchenerzählerin,* appeared in the *Folklore Fellows Communications* in 1928 and inspired a new trend in European folktale studies. During the thirties and forties such scholars as Friedrich Ranke, Julius Schwietering, and Gottfried Henssen in Germany and Gyula Ortutay in Hungary established schools for the study of the role of personality and society in folktale performance. They made known outstanding storytellers and their communities. Some are Henssen's Egbert Gerrits, the Dutch hired man, Ortutay's Michael Fedics, the illiterate Hungarian sharecropper, Carl-Herman Tillhagen's Dimitri Taikon, the Swedish Gypsy tinker, and

2. Juha Pentikäinen, "Grenzprobleme zwischen Memorat und Sage," *Temenos* 3 (1968): 137–67, is the most recent and fullest discussion of Sydow's narrative categories.

Peig Sayers, an exceptionally fine Irish storyteller discovered by the fieldworkers of the Irish Folklore Commission. Since the end of World War II, research methods have been considerably refined. Scholars of today employ the principles of cultural anthropology based on scrupulous ethnographic fieldwork. Local collections are no longer limited to the recording of texts but include the totality of the cultural context, performance of the narrators, and the response of the audiences. A fairly complete survey of the accomplishments of this trend is given in Linda Dégh's *Folktales and Society* (1969).

Other modern directions in folktale research may be briefly mentioned. Among the many approaches to the folktale in its literary relationships, there is a growing interest in the exploration of early written and printed sources, as represented by the work of German folklorists Lutz Röhrich and Elfriede Moser-Rath. A recent contribution to the study of the interrelation between oral and literary narratives, in the path of Albert Wesselski (1878–1941), is Joseph Szövérffy's volume on the sources of Irish folk narratives. The impact of printed matter on contemporary stories is being dealt with by Hermann Bausinger and Siegfried Neumann in Germany. The leading expert on the style and the form of the folktale is the Swiss Max Lüthi. Many psychologists and psychoanalysts of the school of Freud and Jung utilized folk narrative texts for their own purposes. Several among them wrote books that are worthy of mention, such as the study of the Märchen as connected with the phantasies of children by Charlotte Bühler and Josephine Bilz of Germany, and the interpretation of Märchen symbolism by the Jungian Hedvig von Beit of Switzerland. Unfortunately, no folklorist since Ludwig Laistner's *Der Rätzel des Sphynx* (1889) has made use of the teachings of psychology in oral narrative studies. One of the most intriguing new directions is morphological tale analysis, a technique adapted from structural linguistics and structural anthropology. The followers of Vladimir Propp's 1928 study of the Russian fairy tales, and the disciples of the myth model of Claude Lévi-Strauss are increasing in the United States and, more recently, in European countries. Russian folktale experts, on the other hand, updated the ideas of Aleksandr Veselovskij (1833–1906) and through the guidelines of Viktor Žirmunskij plan a cross-cultural typological study of the folktale as it emerged and developed historically.

BASIC FORMS OF NARRATION

Folk narrative encompasses all genres of oral literature in prose. Since the historic statement of Jacob Grimm, "das Märchen ist poetischer, die Sage historischer" (*Deutsche Sagen,* 1816), folklorists have accepted the distinction between the magic tale (Märchen) and the legend. The two forms correspond to primary attitudes in human culture and by their very nature merge and blend into each other; the magic tale expresses the escape from reality, and the legend faces the facts of reality.

The radical changes in folk culture following World War II made it clear to folklorists that they must devise a more elaborate distinction of the genres.[3] Since for more than a hundred years folklore theory was tailored to fit the study of the Märchen, other categories were neglected. As industrial expansion and urbanization lessen the disparity between villagers and city dwellers, even in the more isolated peripheries of the Western world, non-Märchen narratives take the place of the moribund fairy tale. Folk narrative scholars realize that they either have to become antiquarians searching for the vestiges of the magical tale in manuscript archives or in the deficient memory of inactive storytellers, alienated survivors of the "temps perdu," or that they have to accept the facts of modern life and observe the shift of the genres. A new assessment is in progress on the basis of new collections and field observation.

Because of their oral existence, narrative genres float in an unlimited number of variants around a limited number of plots. Hence a perfect classification based on form, content, and function would hardly be possible. All categories have then to remain abstractions from real life, for the convenience of scholarly study. The form, contents, and function of the stories belonging to different genres are always variable. Identical stories can be found within different genres. They may be shaped into fictitious, credible, revered, or ridiculed treatments. What is a tale for one culture may be an origin legend for another; a twist in a tragic story for one can render it extremely funny for another. The change of characters—mortal, divine, supernatural or animal—may move the same plot into a different genre category. As the meaning of the plot changes, so does the form. A simple plot may become complex or it may be expanded or reduced to a succinct relation or even a formless fragment. Folk narratives are subject to such essential changes not only when they adjust to different cultures and epochs but also when they follow internal changes within the same culture. Rooted in their social environment, stories are extremely sensitive to group and individual attitudes; the greater their popularity, the greater their inconsistency. They have no "final" form: They stiffen and freeze when they are no longer told, as if they were written on paper. As long as they are told, they vary, merge, and

3. Hermann Bausinger, *Formen der "Volkspoesie"* (Berlin, 1968); Roger D. Abrahams, "The Complex Relations of Simple Forms," *Genre* 2 (1969): 104–28.

blend; a change in their social value often results in a switch into another genre. Keeping this in mind, we will for practical purposes divide the narrative genres into tale genres, legend genres, and true experience stories.

TALE GENRES

The folktale embodies the highly polished, artistic story genres that have a relatively consistent, finished form. Their origin, goals, and themes, on the other hand, are diverse. Like novels and short stories, their sophisticated counterparts, folktales are told primarily for entertainment although they may have secondary purposes. They are believed to be fictitious, and are cited as lies by storytellers and commentators, who mean that tales are the creation of human phantasy. "Let's lie" urged an Irish storyteller on a competitor, and a Russian storyteller boasted that he was a renowned liar who could fill three sacks with lies. The tale, whether composed of one or many episodes, is always a well-proportioned whole. It is fashioned from stable formulas commonly known to the tellers who adjust them to a basic outline kept together by a frame. This outline—the skeleton of the tale as well as the formulas—is shared by the bearers of a tale tradition. Putting the outline into words and embellishing it by the combination of the available formulas is the creative act of individual narrators. The stable formulas, known as the "building blocks" of the tale, are quite diverse in their quality and narrative value. Yet they all affect the composition and structure of the tale.

(1) *Types* and *motifs* are the formulas chiefly recognized as elements of the content. The Finnish scholar Antti Aarne succeeded in establishing a system for the classification of the international folktale in 1910 in his *Verzeichnis der Märchentypen*. The revised edition of this work by Stith Thompson in 1928 specified the "narrative elements" or motifs within the tale types. As Thompson made clear in his introduction to his *Motif-Index of Folk Literature* (1st ed., 1932–36), motifs are the smallest firm units within narrative folklore, the "details out of which full-fledged narratives are composed." They "may be centered on a certain type of character in a tale, sometimes on an action, sometimes on attendant circumstances of the action." Further terms for narrative units of the tale, recognized since Aarne and his teacher Kaarle Krohn pointed out the multiple ways of tale variation, are the *incident*, the *episode*, and the *motif sequence*, which connote frequent motif clusters. Such clusters create links between seemingly independent tale types.

(2) The *framework* of the tale comprises the introduction and the conclusion as well as the formulaic interjections used by the narrator. These elements are directly related to the telling situation. They

prepare the atmosphere for the acceptance and enjoyment of the tale action, and by providing a happy ending guide the audience back to everyday reality. Frame sequences vary in size and tone according to the tale they adorn. They range from the simple "Once upon a time" and "They lived happily ever after" to the Irish "runs," the Turkish "tekerleme," the insertion of tales of lying, and the rhythmic recital of funny absurdities of different kinds. The formulaic *initial situations* that launch the story action are fewer in number than the tale types and link different tales into related groups.

Personal intrusions by the teller form a third formulaic bridge between the reality of the performance scene and the fantasy of the told narrative. He interjects comments at turning points of the story, announces and highlights thrilling episodes, and makes smart allusions to the rewards he deserves, all in the tradition of medieval court entertainers.

(3) Patterned *figures of speech* are commonly employed in the schematic description of heroes and anti-heroes, scenes of beauty and horror, climaxes and turning points of the narrative. The opposites of good (beautiful) and evil (ugly) are depicted in extreme colors: sparkling, metallic radiance represents fairyland, kingdoms, and riches, whereas dark and bleak hues signify dangerous avenues of the unknown, the site of evil, poverty, or just dull, everyday· village life.

(4) *Formulaic verbal sequences* include recurrent *monologues* of the principal actor preceding essential endeavors and dramatical *dialogues* between the actors in key situations. Heroes turn foes into friends by using the right formulas, and attain their goals by addressing helpers in the right manner; bogeymen engage in stereotyped dialogues with their victims and victor. Numskulls in humorous tales often display their stupidity through dialogue, which renders unnecessary any explanation on the part of the narrator.

(5) *Repetition* of certain passages, sequences, or the whole narrative adventure is essential to the tale structure itself, and also provides a thread for the narrator in his composition techniques as he puts flesh on the tale skeleton. There is a ruling order of tri-episodic action-repetition throughout the story. How this works is best exemplified by complex tale forms although it is present in simple forms as well. Each test in a complex tale is described as a forthcoming event when first told, in the form of advice from the hero's helper. The test is recounted again as it happens, by the narrator, and yet again for the third time when the hero repeats it at the tale's end, exposing the villain. All three versions in this case are identical. As the tale adventure moves toward its climax, the action falls into a progressive trichotomy, in which the repeated parts remain essentially unaltered but the hardships of the tests are increased. Heroes repeat

actions and tests three times, twice failing, finally succeeding. The hero and his failing shadows (two brothers or two companions) may be one and the same. Or the hero may succeed each time in three increasingly difficult tasks. Other minor, subordinated triple episodes embellish and emphasize the prose rhythm of the tale and serve as artistic detours before the happy conclusion.

All these features make the tale a well-balanced, perfectly tailored, and logical construction. Actors and actions are represented symbolically rather than as flesh and blood characters. They have their proper place, and the tale events follow smoothly, almost automatically, in their assigned sequence. No matter how self-contained they may be, tale incidents are symbiotic, they make sense only as they are juxtaposed; hence a tale always has to be recited from the beginning to the end. The clarity of the style and the structure reflects the objectivity of the genre. A given tale tells about extreme cruelty, suffering, torturous death, wonders never heard of, impossible human acts, and superhuman adventures. Yet none of these elements calls for compassion because order is restored and justice is done to satisfy the tale audience which seeks vicarious enjoyment of fictitious horror, tragedy, comedy, and romance. The audience's familiarity with the tale, and its desire to hear it repeatedly, are factors contributing both to the formulaic structure of the folktale and to its entertainment value.

Complex Tales

(1) *The Märchen or Magic Tale (Types 300–749)*. Märchen, the diminutive form of the old German "mär" meaning a short story, is the technical term for what was earlier and is still called, in the English-speaking world, the magic tale, the fairy tale, or sometimes the hero tale. The word was adapted from the *Kinder- und Hausmärchen* of the brothers Wilhelm and Jacob Grimm (1812), the first storybook published for scholarly purposes. The Grimms and later German folktale scholars used the word as an umbrella for all kinds of folktales.

The types of the Märchen have always been in the center of scholarly inquiry. Their attraction has not faded, nor has the enigma of their nature been solved after more than one hundred and fifty years. The Aarne-Thompson typology orders the types according to their supernatural focus:

Supernatural Adversaries—Supernatural or Enchanted Husband (Wife) or Other Relative—Supernatural Tasks—Supernatural Helpers—Magic Objects—Supernatural Power and Knowledge.

These headings show that the Märchen themes center on man's fascination with supernatural adventures. They tell about an ordinary human being's encounter with the suprahuman world and his becoming endowed with qualities that enable him to perform supernatural acts. The Märchen is, in fact, an adventure story with a single hero. The hero, as Kurt Ranke puts it, "is a traveler between the worlds."[4] The hero's (or heroine's) career starts, as everyone else's, in the dull and miserable world of reality. Then, all of a sudden, the supernatural world involves him and challenges the mortal, who undertakes his long voyage to happiness. He enters the magic forest, guided by supernatural helpers, and defeats evil powers beyond the boundaries of man's universe. Crossing several borders of the Beyond, performing impossible tasks, the hero is slandered, banished, tortured, trapped, betrayed. He suffers death by extreme cruelty but is always brought to life again. Suffering turns him into a real hero: as often as he is devoured, cut up, swallowed, or turned into a beast, so does he become stronger and handsomer and more worthy of the prize he seeks. His ascent from rags to riches ends with the beautiful heroine's hand, a kingdom, and marriage. The final act of the Märchen brings the hero back to the human world; he metes out justice, punishes the evil, rewards the good.

What is the true meaning of this sketchy outline common to the magic tales? Is it all symbolic? Is it a fantastic reflection of reality? Does it originate in dream images? Is its childish world of enchantment the vehicle of our hidden desires and aggression through which the subconscious mind can express itself, eluding social censorship? Or is the magic tale the medium of wish fulfillment, giving satisfaction and redress for social injustice to the underprivileged? Is it pure poetry? Is it a storehouse of survivals of an ancient religion and ancient society? Folklorists have raised all these questions. As they consider the actions, the actors, the climate, and the scenes of this intricate genre, it becomes clear that the Märchen is all this and much more. Observing it as an entity in itself, we have to disregard the original qualities of its constituent elements, whatever they may have been. The Märchen has to be understood as it stands before us.

We now know that the magic tale is a precious document of human history. Like the zone-rings in a very old tree trunk, important events in the cultural evolution of man can be traced through a Märchen. A relative chronology might be set up by scrutinizing the Märchen motifs in one and the same narrative. The oldest layer and also the most impressive for modern man is the reflection of a strange world. It is ruled by a primitive belief in pan-animism; all animals, natural forces, and objects in the universe are humanized.

4. Kurt Ranke, "Betrachtungen zum Wesen und zur Funktion der Märchens," *Studium Generale* 11 (1958) : 649.

People are attached with strong ties to these phenomena, which can be viewed as totemistic. Men may assume the shapes of animals, plants, or objects, which can possess supernatural power and knowledge. Neither in time nor in space is there a limitation to human life. The young hero exits from the narrow limits of his home village and travels the magic number (usually seven or nine) of layers to the other world—above the earth, to the center of the earth, or beyond the glass mountain and fiery ocean to the end of the world. Crossing seven times seven borders in seven times seven years, the hero never grows old, nor do any of the tale characters. The tale world is full of supernatural spirits, vegetation demons, guardians of nature, revenants, and ancestors whose benevolence or malevolence depends on the hero's conduct. And there are the evil demons, giants, witches, monsters, and dragons whose destruction is the object of heroic tales. Beside early mythical motifs, the tale also preserves traces of religious and social institutions of ancient society that affect the attitudes of the tale characters. Exploratory sea voyages, with the experience of daring travelers exploring the dangerous waters of an unknown world, exerted a remarkable impact on the world concept of the tale, setting borders between the known (human) and the unknown (superhuman, immortal) ocean.

The mythical Märchen-universe as briefly pictured here presents an atmosphere of the age of feudalism. It is a world of heroic virtues in which people acquire power by their good sword. Petty monarchs rule the world; they live at a day's horseback-ride from each other and can easily be upset by a valiant challenger. If one king declares war and attacks a neighboring ruler, both mobilize their warriors and the two armies meet at a designated place, the "battlefield" where king fights against king, soldier against soldier, crossing swords in single combat. The royal entourage, the architecture of the palace, the garb of heroes and heroines, often skilfully depicted by storybook illustrators, evoke the spirit of the Middle Ages. The "king" lives in a luxurious castle wrapped in radiant gold, in accordance with the hyperbolical tale-style, but he hires the swineherd himself and counts the pigs daily before the hero can drive them to the pasture. Relationship between master and servants is as patriarchal as in feudal courts. The king attends church service with his family on Sundays, while the princesses rivet their eyes on the hero sitting at the rear. The mores of the magic tale recall the dominance of the medieval church. Pious, God-fearing heroes personify Christian virtues: innocence, constancy, righteousness, fidelity. Their physical beauty is the God-given reflection of their spiritual beauty. The superimposition of Christian religion on the spirit world of the magic tale is shown by the introduction of the devil and his associates among the hero's adversaries, and of the saints and God among the hero's helpers.

Besides prehistoric totemism and medieval feudalism, a third layer discernible in the Märchen originates in the real life of the tale-tellers. Motifs from real life serve to connect phantasy with reality and to bring the anachronistic world of the tales up-to-date. The Märchen developed and maintained great popularity in rural Europe for many centuries but began to decline in the age of the industrial revolution. By the third decade of the twentieth century the magic tale vanished from most of the western European countries, and the large scale urbanization after World War II narrowed its chances of survival even in the marginal areas of southern and eastern Europe. All Märchen texts we know as authentic are recorded since the 1930s. They all show a natural adjustment to the milieu of the teller and audience. The home village of the tale hero resembles the village of the narrator, the characters are patterned after stereotypes known to everyone. Even the imaginary characters of the wonder world do not differ in their way of life from the life of a farmer. The king is presented as a well-to-do farmer with much land and cattle. The dragon does not differ much from an ordinary but vicious human being—he marries girls, has a normal family life, eats at the table, smokes cigars, and so forth. The hero or heroine is often the child of poor people who obtains a job in a household doing the chores common to peasant boys and girls: cleaning rooms and stables, helping in the kitchen, tending the geese and the turkeys, grazing the horses. Even the impossible tasks to be performed function as ability tests in farming. In a Märchen the hero is required to sow wheat during the night, grow and harvest it by morning, and make fresh bread for the king's breakfast. Another test is to keep a herd of sheep on the pasture, and yet another is to clean out the manure in the stable of the magic horse.

In a still more important process of acclimatization the magic tale absorbs local folk beliefs. Such beliefs, enjoying full credit in the community, bring the strange Märchen-world closer to the people. The real and supernatural characters (milk witches, revenants, wise women, water dragons) and the variety of magic practices (healing, incantation, and similar rites of everyday life in a rural community) remain mostly on the surface layer (indicated above as *framework*) and depend on the skill and interest of individual narrators. Their role is extremely important in keeping the tales realistic. It might be noted, on the other hand, that modern technological inventions—trains, cars, telephones, the telegraph, for example—represent a different dimension of magic experience and exert a minor effect on the Märchen. Judging from its world view, the magic tale seems to have crystallized some time in the early Middle Ages.

(2) *The Religious Tale (Types 750–849).* The religious tale is distinguished as a category in the Aarne-Thompson index because it deals with Christian virtues and has a close relationship with Christian legend. Its personnel are divided between vicious and virtuous human beings and supernatural characters. The Lord, the Savior, and the Saints of Heaven are opposed to the dark powers, Lucifer and his evil team in Hell. In other respects the tales in this group are less homogeneous than the Märchen. They differ in size and complexity; some contain one episode and some reach the length of the most intricate magic tale. None are as cohesive as a Märchen. Were it not for the characters of Heaven and Hell, many religious tales would equally well fit into other categories: anecdotes, jokes, riddle-tales, explanatory legends, or regular Märchen. In the Aarne-Thompson catalog the religious stories are divided into four topical groups:

God Repays and Punishes—Truth Comes to Light—The Man in Heaven—The Man Promised to the Devil.

If the origins of the magic tale are hard to trace because its tracks, leading back to the mythical cogitation of early man, have been covered by different cultural processes, the formation of religious tales seems to be quite well documented. Contrary to the oral, popular background of the Märchen, religious tales originate in medieval literature. The medieval Church, adapting oriental, religious, and didactic literary sources, used moral stories for religious education. Preachers dispensed these narratives from the pulpit and churchgoers enjoyed the stories that enlivened the sermons. The literary *exemplum mirabilis*, the saints' legends and other moral stories exemplifying the teachings of the Church, had been reinforced continually from the tenth century. Translated and adapted from the written Latin into the vernacular languages of Europe, religious themes poured into oral tradition and were easily modified to the standards of folk piety. Departing from the dogmatic spirit and moralizing style of the literary religious tale, the folk religious tale humanizes the dwellers of Heaven and Hell and wraps morality in delightful colors.

Some typical themes will illustrate the diversity of religious tales. A whole cycle of popular stories (most of them listed under Types 750, 751, 752, 774A-P, and 791) revolves about Jesus Christ and Saint Peter as traveling companions. They tell how the wanderers happen to witness scenes of human life and encounter persons in distress, suffering injustice, and mistreated by other people. The wanderers help the devout and hospitable poor and punish the sacrilegious, haughty rich. Sometimes a parallel narrative features the antagonism between the Divine and the human personages represented by Christ and Saint Peter. In a humorous twist, Saint Peter tries to imitate and surpass his Master and fails. He is foolish, gluttonous, talkative, and a braggart who, like the dupe in situation comedies, is always beaten up at the end. The aim of this profane cycle is more anecdotal than religious and didactic, as indeed are almost all stories about the mortal (shoemaker, soldier, smith, and so on) in Heaven (Types 800–809). Among the complex Märchen-like tales in this group, that of the Penitent Sinner (Type 756A, B, C) is noteworthy. It follows the outline of a hero tale, although its roots are in the medieval vision-literature that deals with the hero's voyage to Hell and his liberation of poor souls. In another group of religious tales a clever mortal outwits the Devil who tries to capture souls.

(3) *The Romantic Tale or Novella (Types 850–999)*. This category includes complex tales of diverse nature having in common their realistic tendency. The novella has the same composition as the magic tale but the fantastic element plays a lesser role. Heroes and heroines tend to be simple people rather than royalty and are often identified by individual names. Likewise, the story told in a novella takes place in the real world at a definite time and location. Heroes do not seek their luck beyond human limitations although their lust for adventure or their evil fate may take them far from their homeland. Except for Divinity and Devil, the representatives of superhuman power in novella belong to this world. Antagonists are not demons and monsters but rather ruthless human characters whose cruelty has always a human motive.

Themes of the novella are more adventurous, pathetic, and sentimental than wondrous. There is more emphasis on human qualities like cleverness, wit, wisdom, trickery, endurance, and patience than on heroism. The Aarne-Thompson index divides its topics as follows:

The Princess's Hand is Won—The Heroine Marries the Prince—Fidelity and Innocence—The Shrewish Wife Reformed—The Good Precepts—Clever Acts and Words—Tales of Fate—Robbers and Murderers.

Novellas dwell on riddle-solving ability and witty replies to tricky questions to reach a desired goal. Contestants for the hand of the Princess have to solve her riddles (Type 851) or make her laugh or find out her hidden marks (Type 850). A clever peasant girl marries a lord whom she baffles with smart talk (Type 875); a king rewards a poor youth for answering his riddles and outsmarting courtiers (Types 922–927), and a suitor wins a girl by telling lies her father cannot believe (Type 852). Another set of tales is about clever thieves tested in their trade (Type 950). Other stories feature the clever girl who tricks the suitor who tries to seduce her (Type 879) and the proud, haughty, shrewish girl who is reformed by her suitor (Type 900). Wisdom is the central motif of stories in which the hero earns good advice in return for his good services and through which he achieves happiness.

Aside from such amusing stories, another group of romantic tales depicts the slandered, banished, innocent woman who suffers patiently until her innocence is proven or takes revenge disguised as a soldier (Type 883, 884). The somber message communicated through the tales proves that no one can escape destiny, that everyone's fate is predestined: some become rich, happy, and powerful no matter what evil forces work against them (Types 930, 938), others die no matter how well protected they are (Type 934) or commit the horrible sin of incest (Types 931, 933) in spite of all precautions.

The sources of romantic tales are literary. Popular tradition absorbed Indic, Persian, and Arabic story collections as well as biblical, classical, Greco-Roman, and medieval romance literature with court epics and Renaissance storybooks. Therefore, not only the philosophy and religious ideals of Buddhism, Islam, Judaism, and Christianity are reflected in the novella, but also the topography of the world as it was perceived by different cultures. Meanwhile, folk tradition was continually influenced and reaffirmed by popular chapbook editions until the late nineteenth century, a process assuring a relative consistency to the novella.

Simple Tales

(1) *The Animal Tale (Types 1–299).* The animal tale is, as a rule, a short narrative that contains the adventures of the animal that is its principal character. While almost all of the actors are animals, they act as human beings and their world is analogous to the human world. The style and structure of the plots are a simple parallelism of thesis and antithesis: a smart or a stupid trickster tries to cheat another animal and succeeds or is caught in his own trap. The mono-episodic and independent stories become easily linked to each other, whereby clusters and even whole cycles tend to develop around certain animal heroes and their antagonists such as the fox versus wolf and bear, rabbit versus fox, and gazelle versus leopard. The Aarne-Thompson index classifies animal tales according to the species of animals:

Wild Animals—Wild Animals and Domestic Animals—Man and Wild Animals—Domestic Animals—Birds—Fish—Other Animals and Objects.

This division allows repeated listing of the same tale types, since the actors can belong in several categories. Animal tales may share identical plots with etiological legends or with anecdotes about human actors. Animal tales in whole or in part are used as Märchen episodes as well.

In Western folk societies, animal tales are generally told for the entertainment of small children. Considering their origins, in creation myths and culture legends on the one hand and literary fables on the other, they properly belong with didactic tales. The Buddhistic Indic fable collections, like the Jatakas and the *Pantchatantra,* and the classical Greco-Roman Aesopian fable with its highly moralistic-educational purpose, were widely popularized through medieval exemplum collections. Animal tales continued to appear in the jest and fable books through the Renaissance and the age of humanism, but in most countries they exercised a lesser impact on oral tradition than romances or anecdotes. The French beast epic, *Roman de Renart,* seems to have been more influential, especially in northeast Europe. Genuine folkloric animal tales are relatively smaller in number than other kinds. A rich cluster developed in the Russian-Baltic area around the Fox cycle and in the southern United States, among American Negroes, by the adaptation of both European and African traditions embodied in the Brer Rabbit tales.

(2) *Jokes and Anecdotes (Types 1200–1999).* This large group of humorous narratives is called "Jests and anecdotes" by Thompson. These three terms—joke, jest, anecdote—are used more or less interchangeably, replacing Aarne's original term *Schwank.*

The *Joke (Witz* in German), defined by the philosopher Kuno Fischer as "a playful judgment," is always short, built on a double meaning of words, and therefore not open and obvious to everyone.[5] Its source of humor is in the speech itself, not the narrative, explanatory portion, which is kept to a minimum, serving only to enhance the sudden surprise of the punch line. The joke is an extremely succinct, polished form. Counting on general familiarity of the audience with the topic, it limits itself to a dramatic dialogue or even to a question and answer sequence. In this respect, it approaches related speech forms such as riddles or Wellerisms. Although jokes tend to come in series (sick jokes, elephant jokes, shaggy dog stories), they center on real or imaginary personalities (Graf Bobby, Klein Erna, Polack) and react immediately to worldwide and local events. The patterns are as old as those of the Schwank. Like the Schwank, the joke deals with universal themes of uncommon occurrences in commonplace situations; it does not elaborate on the context, it is flexible, and it travels speedily across borders. Adjusting to modern requirements, joke tellers have no stable repertoire; they owe their popularity rather to an ability to pick up current jokes and to tell them well. They do not necessarily perform for an audience; more often they crack jokes alternately with others at occasional get-togethers or casually for any individual.

5. This definition was further elaborated by Sigmund Freud in his *Jokes and Their Relation to the Unconscious* (New York, 1963) in the fullest theoretical discussion of the genre.

The *Anecdote* characterizes a person, a memorable event, or a place through a representative personal episode. As a brief and funny experience story it resembles a Schwank not fully developed; indeed, it can be viewed as a Schwank-episode.

The literary anecdote is printed and the folk anecdote is oral, but both revolve about historical personalities and local happenings. Because of its gossip-like formlessness, the quality of the anecdote as a folk narrative is seldom recognized. All kinds of more or less realistic comical episodes about memorable witty sayings, stupidities, travel, war, work, adventures, lucky accidents, lies, and so on circulate in anecdotal form. If the joke is a condensed and crystallized derivation of the Schwank, the anecdote is, indeed, its rudimentary, fragmentary form. None of the three genres has been adequately studied as yet. The Schwank, at least, has been classified and typified and a wealth of collections is at the disposal of interested folklorists.

In spite of its artistry, variety, and age, folklorists until recently have neglected the most elaborate genre of the humorous narrative, the *Schwank*. This is a relatively long, well-structured, realistic narrative without fantastic or miraculous motifs. Its humor is obvious and easy to comprehend and the action is funny in itself without a punch line. The themes, though universal, are always localized in villages and small towns, the actors being peasants, small craftsmen, soldiers, itinerants, and members of religious orders. Schwank tellers usually develop their own repertoire of specific stories that they tell upon the request of their audiences.

The topical groups of the Aarne-Thompson tale-type index on the Schwank are the more meaningful because the Schwank usually involves comic situations and characters.

Numskull Stories—Stories about Married Couples—Stories about a Woman (Girl) Stories about a Man (Boy)—The Clever Man—Lucky Accidents—The Stupid Man—Jokes About Parsons and Religious Orders—Anecdotes about Other Groups of People—Tales of Lying.

The target of the Schwank is human frailty. Its aim is not simply to make people laugh by telling an hilarious story about ridiculous characters or about clever tricksters who make others look ridiculous. The Schwank is also highly didactic, trying to reform people of bad habits by magnifying them or to express disapproval by scoffing at persons of bad conduct. It is dramatic in its rendition with minimum epic and maximum dialogue presentation, accompanied with gestures and body and facial movements imitating the ludicrous actors. The mono-episodic stories tend to cumulate and form a complex of similar adventures.

The comedy characters belong to the universe of the traditional small community. One group are common folk characters who display their stupidity in every possible situation. The Schwank pillories the lazy, unclean, talkative, sleepy, uncouth, marriageable girl; the old maid who makes a fool of herself in trying to capture a husband; the greedy, stingy, tipsy, gossipy wife who does not know how to cook, spin, or launder; the dull-witted, gullible boy; the simpleton husband of the adulterous wife. Another group of stories pokes fun at the upper classes as viewed by the folk community: woman-chasing parsons and friars; ignorant preachers, doctors, judges, teachers, and lawyers; craftsmen outwitted by clever peasant women and poor men. Folklorists emphasize the anticlerical tendency and social criticism expressed by these tales. A third group of stories deals with a clever person (boy, girl, young woman) who dupes a member of the upper classes.

Numskull stories (1200–1349) form a specific narrative group that mocks the stupid acts of a whole community. This technique brings the numskull stories close to the anecdote. They are brief, often reduced to a simile or a proverbial saying. They are variable, and tend to cluster around localities presumably settled by silly people. Since the publication of the late-sixteenth-century German collection of stories mocking the citizens of Schilda, variants of numskull tales have been uncovered around the world.

The *Tales of Lying* (1875–1999) seem to be closer to formula tales than to the Schwank, as they often occur in the introductory and closing portion of the Märchen. The telling itself is rhythmical and rapid, stressing the virtuoso accumulation of absurdities rather than the content. They are recited in the first person. Although the catalog does not list many types of the lying tale, they are extremely popular and even today new varieties tend to develop. Besides the hunting stories in the Type Index, the adventures of soldiers, sailors, travelers, and fishermen and other sportsmen might easily be added. A remarkable new crop has developed in the Anglo-American tradition of the New World. The *Tall Tale*, as this subvariant is known, flourished in America and still continues to bear new fruits. The Baron von Münchausen (1720–1797), hunter, soldier, and famous raconteur, allowed his facetious stories to be taken down and published in English by R. E. Raspe as early as 1785 (Types 1889 A-P), and they soon became popular and even influenced Indian myths. American pioneers developed new Münchausen-like heroes, and the unexplored land offered sufficiently remarkable natural phenomena to boast about.

(3) *Formula Tales (Types 2000–2399).* This group includes playful, witty, gamelike forms with a brief narrative core. The single motif

can be used for the introduction and the conclusion of a complex tale, for children's entertainment, or for a humorous trick of refusal to tell a tale. As with certain lying tales (Types 1875–1886), the narrator of the formula tales does not demand attention to and concern for the content but rather expects emotional response to the stylistic devices he employs.

The most elaborate of all is the *cumulative tale* (2000–2199), also called *Kettenmärchen* or *chain tale*. It has a definite narrative core that must be repeated exactly, as each new actor, whether object or person, enters the tale. The action may be launched at a wedding, through the death of an animal, by the eating of an object, or by the refusal of an actor to do a bidden deed. Some of the widely known types are "Death of the Little Hen" (2022), "The Old Woman and her Pig" (2030) and "The House that Jack Built" (2035).

The *Catch tale* (2200–2249) is a traditional child teaser that forces the listener to interject a question that is rebuffed by an obvious or a ridiculous answer. Other kinds of formula tales include the *Endless tale* (Type 2300), in which an introductory action of a prospective complex tale is repeated until the audience gets tired of it and realizes the trick, and the *Clock tale* (Type 2320), a form of endless tale that always returns clockwise to the point of departure.

Formula tales belong within the compass of the folktale and offer variable elements that skilled storytellers can adapt to given situations. They are as old as the oldest of international folktales.

LEGEND GENRES

In the Preface to the second edition of his *Deutsche Mythologie* (1844), Jacob Grimm declared: "The fairy-tale (Märchen) is with good reason distinguished from the legend, though by turns they play into one another. Looser, less fettered than legend, the fairy-tale lacks that local habitation, which hampers the legend, but makes it the more homelike. The fairy-tale flies, the legend walks, knocks at your door; the one can draw freely out of the fullness of poetry, the other has almost the authority of history. As the fairy-tale stands related to the legend, so does legend to history, and (we may add) so does history to real life."

Although it was published more than one hundred and twenty years ago, we still feel that the essential features of the legend are pointed out in this comparative definition. Subsequent generations of legend experts, impelled by the diverse interests of different folklore schools, have collected, archived, published, classified, and studied hundreds of thousands of legend texts and still have added little to this concise statement. Folklorists still view the legend by contrast with the more familiar Märchen: what is *unlike* the Märchen is the legend.

Why is it so hard to describe the legend? Grimm's definition includes only certain important aspects: the legend is related to the Märchen; it is localized, down-to-earth, and has historic validity. Additional statements emphasize certain attributes of the legend: it is didactic (Theodor Benfey), it is the archive of the prehistory of a people (Reinhold Köhler), it is a "dramatized superstition" (Karl Wehrmann), it belongs to the "naïve uncritical learning of the folk in relating an extraordinary experience or event believed to be true" (Friedrich Ranke). To be sure, these rather haphazard characterizations do not attempt to describe the generic form, style, meaning, or function of the legend. The legend does not have a polished style, its frame and form do not coordinate narrative elements into a logical chain. Hence, the legend is extremely variable, reacting sensitively to local and immediate needs that modify and reformulate both the narratives and the messages they communicate. The legend, above all, is more local than the tale, more likely to develop local patterns in spite of its tendency to migrate and spread cross-culturally. It ranges from the simple communication of belief through various levels to the most intricate, multi-episodic narrative.

The only classification that focuses on finished legend types is Reidar Christiansen's *The Migratory Legends*. In this scheme, Christiansen continues the Aarne-Thompson numbers from 3000 on and constructs type outlines based on the listed versions of Norwegian variants.

Scrutinizing the form of the legend, one must agree with Leopold Schmidt who feels the legend has only content and no fixed form at all and depends on the nature of the message it communicates. The reason for telling a legend is basically not to entertain but to educate people, to inform them about an important fact, to arm them against danger within their own cultural environment. Therefore, as Matthias Zender expresses it, understanding of the legend is possible if one views it through the general living conditions, belief, and ideology of a culture. By the same token, Max Lüthi contends that, unlike the tale centering on a glorious hero who seeks adventures, the legend deals with experiences an ordinary man has to face passively. The tale-hero rises above the events he stimulates, the man in the legend remains helpless before the events he encounters. The legend happening starts without warning in man's own familiar environs and neither removes him from them nor changes his life conditions. The legend stops as abruptly as it begins. While the folktale hero is blindly guided by advice and tasks, the man in the legend acts according to his own initiative and satisfies his hunger for acquiring knowledge about the unknown.

The aim of the legend then is to answer an unuttered question about man's microcosmos. What is it? Why is it so? What can be done about it? The legend explains an extraordinary phenomenon or a memorable event, it communicates traditional learning and knowledge to the young and the uninitiated, it advises people how to act in critical situations and warns them against doing the wrong thing. This educational essence is dramatized by an example that is the narrative content of the legend. The story does not have to be recited in full from the beginning to the end, for its components are traditionally known in the given community. Hence the fragmentary and unfinished form of the legend narrative. It seems to be a segment or an episode of a nonexistent, longer autobiographical narrative, of which only some facts remain stable.

What are the facts upon which the legend is built that renders the story credible and the message acceptable? There are two kinds of so-called reality factors. One is a verifiable fact commonly known to be true, for it has been experienced or preserved in memory, and may also be supported by physical evidence, by an object that commémorates a past event. The other kind is an illusion, commonly believed to be true. The unassailable fact of the memory of the Turkish invasion among the peoples of east-central Europe, the hoofmark of a horse on a rock where the Serbian hero Marko Kraljević rested before he fooled his pursuers, a bullet hole in the wall, a war memorial, and a weeping willow's bent branches are all equal proofs of a legend. By the same token, the vision and hallucination of a lonely stroller at night encountering stray animals, the belief in supernatural agencies, the proximity of semi-real witches, who can tie and undo and milk dry the cow and kill with evil eye, are valid evidences giving credence to a legend. By stating that a legend is believed to be true we do not mean to say that each individual in a community necessarily has to believe in the legend he tells or hears. People's attitudes may vary in this respect, even in backward communities. The acceptance of the validity of the legend is expressed by its convincing style. Claim for belief lies in the style of the legend, in the way it is structured, in its painstaking precision to present witnesses and evidence. If there is artistry in the way a legend is told, it is in the skilful formulation of convincing statements.

The manner of telling a legend is conversational. Common talk about everyday matters of general interest, in the evenings, during leisure time, while engaged in cooperative manual work or while attending social get-togethers, may end with legend-telling. An illness magically caused in animals or people, a casual question about a local hero, the sight of a strange reflection of the moon, may launch a single legend that is followed by others. General talk follows, with the participation of all those who have information on the topic. Sometimes the community pieces the story together and there is no dividing line between audience and teller. They make no effort to elaborate and polish the story. In many instances, the more factual the legend is, the more communal and the less polished is the telling.

Here is an example of a legend told by girls at gossipfests that has no single full variant. This legend is widely popular throughout the United States:[6]

> Two coeds spend a vacation in an empty college dormitory. An escaped sex maniac with an ax is reported at large. When one of the girls leaves the room for some reason, the other girl bolts the door and goes to sleep. She awakes in the middle of the night to hear a scratching noise at the door. Frightened out of her wits, she waits until morning, when the sound stops. She calls for help; the other girl is found outside the door with an ax buried in her head. Her fingernails are worn away from the effort of scratching for help.

Parts of this arbitrary outline occur in varied tellings. Sometimes the episode is given in the first person as the teller's experience. There are well-elaborated, dramatic versions and there are dry, factual accounts; there are essential deviations from the main plot, and there are mere references to the tragedy. One such reference spread as the result of a rumor in the fall of 1968 about a prophecy attributed to Jean Dixon, the famous Washington clairvoyant, concerning the mass murder of girls in college dorms. One cannot know whether a legend will develop or the spreading rumors will fade away, to be replaced by others.

In spite of its fragmentary style, the legend has a well-recognizable structure. An introduction presents evidence needed to assure the credibility of the story, such as the exact hour, day, season, and year, and a description of the scene of the event. The narrator names the dramatis personae and makes sure that everyone knows them. Often he does this in lively dialogue with others who share knowledge of the story. If the story is an experience of the teller, he does everything possible to convince the audience of his trustworthiness. If he refers to a relative or a neighbor, from whom he has heard the account, he insists that but for these decent, God-fearing people, he never would have believed such things could happen. The concluding part usually repeats the essential admonition of the narrative and again names the source.

6. This and similar folk legends are discussed in Linda Dégh, "The Roommate's Death and Related Dormitory Stories in Formation," *Indiana Folklore* 2 (1969): 55–74.

Folklorists in the wake of the Grimm brothers distinguished three kinds of legends: local, etiological, and historical. In view of the role legends play in society, this distinction does not always make sense. All three elements can be present in the same story, which may be attached to a certain locality, may mention an historical character, and may conclude by explaining a natural phenomenon. An example is the migratory Kyffhauser legend about King Friedrich the Redbeard who sleeps with his warriors in a cave of striking formation, awaiting the day when his people need him. The hero is awakened by the bagpipe music of a shepherd boy and rewards the intruder.

In 1963 an international committee drew up four tentative categories of legends based on available collections:[7]

(1) *Etiological and Eschatological Legends.* These include explanatory stories about the creation of the world, the origin of things, striking natural phenomena, unusual geological formations, and the nature of plants and animals closely observed by man in his small universe. This material is usually considered as folk-wisdom accumulated by oral transmission through many generations.

(2) *Historical Legends and Legends of the History of Civilization.* Local historical accounts are incorporated in narratives based on a segment of national history. Each locality develops its own body of folk history, composed partly of local events passed down in family tradition as home educational matter and partly of written sources absorbed from schoolbooks, chapbooks, and newspapers and like sources. Among the historical legends, two kinds are the most popular: stories about national and social heroes (e.g., righteous rulers and outlaws), and stories about events that affected the life of local communities, such as enemy attack, cruel lords, or the Black Plague. Other kinds include stories about the names of places, rivers, and hills and the origins of prehistoric ruins and mounds.

(3) *Supernatural Beings and Forces or Mythical Legends.* In the main, the source of belief-legends is local folk belief, based on folk piety and Christianized nature worship. These legends are concerned with supernatural beings, persons with supernatural knowledge and power, ancestors and revenants, white and black magic, and the protection and destruction of family and property.

(4) *Religious Legends or Myths of Gods and Heroes.* The Christian legend, the only legend form that originates in literature, is newly added to folk legendry by scholars on the grounds of having been folklorized and absorbed into folk culture. Pre-Christian beliefs infiltrated the stories about saints, martyrs, and miracles stimulated by the

7. Wayland D. Hand, "Status of European and American Legend Study," *Current Anthropology* 6 (1965) : 439–46.

early Christian church. By the sixteenth century, the Catholic hierarchy banned legend recitals at the shrines of its saints and thereby unwittingly encouraged Christian miracles to pour into folk tradition.

These four categories include an enormous storehouse of traditional wisdom and knowledge. Viewed as educational materials in folk society, one can compare them to the mythology and legendry of preliterate people. As origin and genealogical legends teach tribal history, so do historical legends in folk culture teach about the past. The myth passed on to the initiated young adults incorporates tribal religion, while the belief legend instructs about folk religion. The authority of oral history and folk religion remains on the folk level and is necessarily peripheral because of the authoritative education fostered by the established church and the compulsory school system. Besides, the belief legends of a community never do comprise a systematic folk religion. Historical legends are even scantier. The meager accounts of local history can never be as relevant to daily needs as the pressing matters treated by magic.

Legends do not seem to wither under the impact of urban life. On the contrary, they appear to be the hardiest of folk narrative forms, not only in adjusting easily to modern conditions but by generating new types based on the most up-to-date issues of contemporary life. The legends of today do not belong solely to the backward, uneducated layers of the population. They capitalize on pervasive beliefs, on the search for the unknown, on the extraordinary and unusual, and hold the interest of men of all classes.

TRUE EXPERIENCE STORIES

A work session of the International Society of Folk Narrative Research, meeting in Liblice, Czechoslovakia, in 1966, devoted special consideration to the so-called mixed forms or transition forms of the folk narrative.[8] As Kurt Ranke observed, mixed forms are becoming increasingly important for the student of tales in our day. He stated that there are Märchen-Schwänke and Schwank-legends, and animal stories that may be turned into fables, etiological legends, or jokes. A parable may be downgraded and turned into a joke by one people who misunderstand its meaning, and a legend may be promoted into a Märchen during its long journey across cultures.[9] These statements of Ranke are generally recognized today. How genre blends are formed is hard to determine. We know of simple combinations of two genres, sometimes when one is inserted into another and sometimes when one devours another. We are no longer so concerned with functional changes produced by traditional folk communities or with

8. *Fabula, Journal of Folktale Studies* 9 (1967).
9. Kurt Ranke, "Kategorienprobleme der Volksprosa," *Fabula* 9 (1967) : 4–12.

ethnic changes due to the diffusion of narratives—it is rather with the
degenerative and regenerative process that occurs as genres lose their
old meaning and are reformulated to fit new social settings. In the
industrial community many of the traditional forms have survived
because they are given a new meaning. The legends and the jokes
that enjoy the greatest popularity in industrial society react sensitively to individual attitudes toward belief and humor; variants of the
same story may now be a legend, now a joke. As folklorists leave
behind the old confines of traditional society and pursue folk narrative as it steps out of the straitjacket of genre categories, they realize
how narration can be an immediate reflection of culture. Modern
life changes the picture all around; folklorists scrutinize new sources
and new processes such as the reduction, replacement, and the reinforcement of old forms. And here we arrive at the problem of "true
stories."

Jolles, Wesselski, von Sydow, and other theoreticians of the past
have recognized the informal and spontaneous stories growing out of
everyday experiences in all types of communities. Their modern suc-
cessors, Hermann Bausinger and Siegfried Neumann, see three basic
attitudes expressed by the Märchen, the Schwank, and the legend.[10]
Bausinger distinguishes three categories of current narratives: (1)
happy occurrences (replacement for the Märchen); (2) merry occurrences (replacement for the Schwank); and (3) sinister occurrences
(replacement for the belief legend).

No matter how loose the structure and how flexible the framework
of these everyday stories, they follow the trend of the more established
genres. They use such devices as threefold repetition, dramatized
dialogues, and endings signaled with a bang. These true stories grow
out of reminiscences of the past, and events, hearsay, rumor, gossip,
and personal experiences of the present. They may be told in the first
or the third person. In examining their contents one can see why the
true story easily assumes the role of traditional narration. Stories of
luck deal with romantic love (poor girl marries the boss), big win-
nings (at races, cards, lottery, bingo), narrow escapes from grave danger, or intrigues with a happy ending. Horror stories rationalize the
mythical elements of the belief legend, in touching on crime, mass
murder, suicide, disaster, and fateful and mysterious tragedies. Humorous stories bear a strong resemblance to improvised anecdotes but
are usually narrower, centering on one comic incident.

Simple, everyday stories can be classified according to their topics.
Since very little planned research has been done in this field, we can

10. Hermann Bausinger, "Strukturen des alltäglichen Erzählens, *Fabula* 1 (1958):
239-54.

only briefly refer to the themes already explored or currently under investigation.

(1) *Labor Reminiscences.*[11] The experiences of men and women while at work include stories about the nature of their occupations, success and failure in professional and social roles, and the human relations established on the job. Many studies have been published about the reminiscences of such workingmen as seamen, fishermen, miners, stonecutters, huntsmen, soldiers, navvies, and sharecroppers who leave their homes temporarily and upon return find interested audiences for their experiences.

(2) *Autobiographical Stories.* Many traditional narrators display ability to incorporate intricate novellas into their life history. The Blasket Island storyteller of Ireland, Peig Sayers, recounted *An Old Woman's Reflections* (London, 1962), and W. H. Barrett, a laborer from the Norfolk-Cambridgeshire borderland in England, filled three volumes with his pungent recollections. Besides the old-time village chroniclers and diary writers, folklorists today seek the personal experience stories of raconteurs whose lives have changed from a rural to an urban style, as they move from traditional isolation into a pluralistic environment. Among the outstanding personalities who switched from traditional storytelling to the creative reflection of new experiences is Marem'jana Golubkova, once an illiterate Russian ritual singer, who wrote down her experiences of the two worlds in which she had lived. The Hungarian Julia Tóth, a kitchen helper in a new industrial center, was well liked for her Märchen on the farm where she was born as the daughter of a sharecropper and in the village where she lived as the wife of a well-to-do farmer. When fate left her a widow, she moved to the city with her children and became an accomplished entertainer. She stopped telling old stories and made up new ones for her audience of construction workers, shaping exciting narratives of her childhood adventures, fears, pain, and love affairs.[12] Among experienced storytellers, women favor the themes of first love, marriage ritual, intimate sexual relationships, child-rearing, family life, and grievances and injustices, whereas men prefer telling of "heroic" deeds, how they challenged and eventually beat up their bosses and how they excelled in military service. Obscene, humorous, and horror stories are less subject to improvisation. They continue a more established tradition, but are greatly influenced by mass media.

(3) *Emigrant and Immigrant Epics.* The narratives told by up-

11. Siegfried Neumann, "Arbeitserinnerungen als Erzählungsinhalt," *Arbeit und Volksleben*, ed. Gerhard Heilfurth and Ingeborg Weber-Kellermann (Göttingen, 1967), pp. 274–84.

12. Ilona S. Dobos, "Über die Dichtungsart der 'wahren' Geschichten," *Ethnographia* 75 (1964): 198–217.

rooted and relocated people in their new community of compatriots contain both labor reminiscences and life stories. Nevertheless, they have different emphases and a much greater significance for the group than old and still-repeated tales and legends. Immigrant colonies in the United States relate special narratives of their exodus and careers. Within this general type, each individual has his own, continuously repeated life story, beginning with the memory of the Old Country, a dramatic performance that remains always relevant to the community. Everyone's story has similar facts, yet everyone's story is unique.[13]

Since folk literature depends on its own cultural climate, modern folk stories are influenced by the most important features of modern life, mobility and mass communications. Easy travel opportunities and immediate information on world affairs have made folk communities more cosmopolitan than ethnic. Ubiquitous reading matter in the form of novels, magazines, and newspapers, and audio-visual media of radio, TV, and movies, one-dimensional like the Märchen, have to be considered as important sources of folk narration. The retelling and the passing on of the plots of novels, movies, and television shows deserve the attention of the folk narrative scholar.

Bibliography and Selected Readings

Reference Works

Aarne, Antti, and Stith Thompson. *The Types of the Folk-Tale; a Classification and Bibliography.* Folklore Fellows Communications, 184. Helsinki, 1961. The standard typology of European traditional narratives.

Bolte, Johannes, and Georg Polívka. *Anmerkungen zu den Kinder- und Hausmärchen der Brüder Grimm.* Leipzig, 1913–32. Vols. 1-3 contain parallels to the two hundred Grimm tales. In vols. 4 and 5 different scholars discuss different historic and functional aspects of the folktale. Bibliographies are divided according to culture areas.

Christiansen, Reidar Th. *The Migratory Legends.* Folklore Fellows Communications, 175. Helsinki, 1958. A proposed list of types with a systematic catalogue of the Norwegian variants.

Mackensen, Lutz, ed. *Handwörterbuch des deutschen Märchens.* 2 vols. Berlin and Leipzig, 1930–40. Includes excellent articles on the Märchen from A. to G., but supplementary volumes were never completed.

Megas, Georgios A., ed. *IVth International Congress for Folk-Narrative Research in Athens. Lectures and Reports.* Athens, 1965. The seventy-six papers delivered at the Athens congress cover a great variety of topics and represent various trends in folk narrative scholarship.

13. Richard M. Dorson, "Is There a Folk in the City?" *Journal of American Folklore* 83 (1970): 185–216 discusses extensively the problem of immigrant narratives.

Petzold, Leander, ed. *Vergleichende Sagenforschung*. Darmstadt, 1969. A resourceful compendium encompassing the most relevant studies in the folk legend from 1925 to this day.

Ranke, Kurt, ed. *Fabula. Journal of Folktale Studies*. 1957 to date. The official journal of the International Society of Folk Narrative Research.

———. *Internationaler Kongress der Volkserzählungsforscher in Kiel und Kopenhagen. Vorträge und Referate*. Berlin: Walter de Gruyter, 1961. This volume contains fifty-eight papers given by folktale scholars from around the world at the 1959 meeting of the International Society of Folk Narrative Research.

Thompson, Stith. *The Folktale*. New York: Holt, Rinehart and Winston, 1946. Primarily a study of the European folktale with some reference to folktales in primitive cultures, based on the international folktale index.

General Works

Anderson, Walter. *Kaiser und Abt. Die Geschichte eines Schwankes*. Folklore Fellows Communications, 42. Helsinki, 1923. A classic and model study in which the great, flamboyant adherent of the historic-geographical school outlines his ideas on the stabilization of folk narratives in oral tradition.

Asadowskij, Mark. *Eine sibirische Märchenerzählerin*. Folklore Fellows Communications, 68. Helsinki, 1926. This influential and concise personality description is based on the author's field research in the Wercholensk region in 1915.

Bausinger, Hermann. *Formen der "Volkspoesie."* Berlin: E. Schmidt, 1968. This detailed description of the folklore genres is originally meant for the student of literature but its modern aspects are suggestive to folklorists.

Bühler, Charlotte, and Josephine Bilz. *Das Märchen und die Phantasie des Kindes*. München, 1958. The important study of Bühler, originally published in 1918, was supplemented by Bilz's study on tale events related to maturation processes.

Crowley, Daniel J. *I Could Talk Old-Story Good: Creativity in Bahamian Folklore*. Berkeley and Los Angeles: University of California Press, 1966. Deals with the technique of the telling and the style of tales distinguished as "old stories" in a particular region. With sample texts.

Dégh, Linda. *Folktales and Society: Story-Telling in a Hungarian Peasant Community*. Bloomington: Indiana University Press, 1969. A complex study of narrators, performance and audience participation based on the example of a relocated Hungarian community. With an extensive bibliography.

Finnegan, Ruth. *Limba Stories and Story-Telling*. Oxford: Clarendon Press, 1967. A collection of tales and an important study of narration among the Limba, a group of 200,000 people in northern Sierra Leone.

Hand, Wayland D., ed. *American Folk Legend, a Symposium*. Berkeley and Los Angeles: University of California Press, 1971. Fourteen folklorists examine the concept of legend for the United States.

Henssen, Gottfried. *Überlieferung und Persönlichkeit: Erzählungen und Lieder des Egbert Gerrits.* Münster i. Westf., Aschendorff, 1951. The repertoire of texts with a study of the life and function of the narrator.

Jolles, André. *Einfache Formen. Legende, Sage, Mythe, Rätsel, Spruch, Kasus, Memorabile, Märchen, Witz.* 3d ed. Tübingen: M. Niemeyer, 1965. A classic description of oral narrative genres.

Krohn, Kaarle. *Die folkloristische Arbeitsmethode.* Oslo, 1926. Translated as *Folklore Methodology* by Roger L. Welsch. Austin and London: published for the American Folklore Society by the University of Texas Press, 1971. Theoretical and methodological outline of the Finnish historic-geographic method of folklore.

Lüthi, Max. *Volksmärchen und Volkssage. Zwei Grundformen Erzählender Dichtung.* 2d. ed. Bern and Munich: Francke, 1966. The most representative book on the form and style of the folktale and the folk legend viewed by a literary scholar.

Meletinskij, E. M. *Geroj volšebnoj skazki.* Moscow, 1958. This Soviet work deals with tale episodes that can be viewed cross-culturally as they evolved at different stages of social history.

Ortutay, Gyula. *Fedics Mihály mesél* (M. F. Tells Tales). Budapest, 1940. Contains forty tales and a study of the personality and style of the eighty-six-year-old narrator. It became a model for the study of creativity in folktales.

Ranke, Kurt. *Die zwei Brüder. Eine Studie zur vergleichenden Märchenforschung.* Folklore Fellows Communications, 114. Helsinki, 1934. An exhaustive study of one of the best known dragon-killing hero tales. (Types 300 and 303.)

Röhrich, Lutz. *Märchen und Wirklichkeit.* 2d enlarged ed. Wiesbaden: F. Steiner, 1964. Discusses different aspects of reality manifested in folk narratives. The source materials of the author are mainly the texts of the Grimm Brothers and those in the series *Märchen der Weltliteratur.*

Sydow, Carl Wilhelm von. *Selected Papers on Folklore. Published on the Occasion of His 70th Birthday.* Copenhagen: Rosenkilde and Bagger, 1948. Ten of the author's most influential essays are reprinted in this volume. It also contains a list of his books and articles.

Taylor, Archer. *The Black Ox.* A Study in the History of a Folktale. Folklore Fellows Communications, 70. Helsinki, 1927. Short and impressive analysis of Motifs D2121.8 and D2122.3.

von Beit, Hedwig. *Das Märchen. Sein Ort in der geistigen Entwicklung.* Bern and München: Francke, 1965. As in her voluminous book on the symbolism of the Märchen, the author sorts out tale incidents and interprets them as reflections of different stages of human development.

Žirmunskij, Viktor. *Skazanie ob Alpamyše i bogatyrskaja skazka.* Moscow, 1960. A stimulating experiment to establish typological relationships between hero tales and heroic epics.

Collections

Dorson, Richard M., ed. *Folktales of the World.* Chicago: University of Chicago Press, 1963–. Tale repertoires of specific countries are assembled by leading scholars. Each volume contains explanatory notes and a bibliography and a Foreword by the general editor and an Introduction by the volume editor that discuss the history of folktale research in the country and features of the national tale corpus.

Grimm, Jacob and Wilhelm. *Household Tales.* Translated and edited by Margaret Hunt. 2 vols. Introduction by Andrew Lang. London, 1884. The dated but classic collection, with Lang's treatise on survivals in folktales, and a valuable history of interest in folktales in the second volume.

2 NARRATIVE FOLK POETRY
W. Edson Richmond

Most literary genres are easily identifiable in terms of structure: everyone recognizes a novel when he sees it; almost everyone recognizes a poem by its appearance on a printed page if in no other way. But folk poetry is different, for it is defined not only in terms of form but also in terms of its manner of transmission. Thus a narrative folk poem is not only a poem that tells a story; it is also a poem that, no matter how it was composed, has been transmitted primarily by word of mouth and changed in the process. Therefore, without additional, extraneous information, no one can distinguish a narrative folk poem from any other sort of narrative poem. One must know something about its history: how it first came to be written down (if indeed it ever appears in writing), how it came to its singer or narrator, and whether or not it exists in other forms. Identification of a poem as a folk poem is impossible without at least this information, for it is quite possible for a sophisticated poet to imitate the characteristics of folk poetry with success, and, indeed, many poets such as Herder, Percy, Scott, and Runeberg, to name only a few, have done so.

But the oral tradition that is the incubator of folk poetry is not maintained by the singing, dancing throng of the romantics nor even the somewhat less ecstatic masses of peasant or proletariat conceived by twentieth-century visionaries. Folk poetry is transmitted and re-created by popular virtuosi. Only where such virtuosi still exist is folk poetry a living tradition, and there is absolutely no evidence to support any imaginative postulate of a culture in which Everyman is a singer-composer. At most one can say he accepts or rejects the materials offered for his appreciation. There is, on the other hand, considerable evidence to support the hypothesis that when popular virtuosi go out of fashion, when their function is replaced by some other medium, especially a medium over which Everyman has little control, folk poetry deteriorates, fades away, and becomes, at best, an imperfectly remembered survival. Such is the situation in America, Europe, and much of western Asia today.

The songs that have survived in these cultures, however, the songs perpetuated by virtuosi subject to restrictions of popular criticism, show certain common characteristics. If not peculiar to narrative folk poetry alone, they are nevertheless constant: narrative folk songs concentrate on a single episode, develop their stories dramatically, and are impersonal in their approach to their subject matter. This is true no matter whether the narrative folk poem is a Yugoslav oral epic, a Russian *bylina,* a Scandinavian or English ballad, or any of a number of particular types of folk poem.

Note, for example, "Brown Robyn's Confession" (Child 57A), a Scottish ballad first collected in the early years of the nineteenth century:

> 1. It fell upon a Wodensday
>   Brown Robyn's men went to sea,
>   But they saw neither moon nor sun,
>   Nor starlight wi their ee.
>
> 2. 'We'll cast kevels us amang,
>   See wha the unhappy man may be';
>   The Kevel fell on Brown Robyn,
>   The master-man was he.
>
> 3. 'It is nae wonder,' said Brown Robyn,
>   'Altho I dinna thrive,
>   For wi my mither I had twa bairns,
>   And wi my sister five.
>
> 4. 'But tie me to a plank o wude,
>   And throw me in the sea;
>   And if I sink, ye may bid me sink,
>   But if I swim, just lat me bee.'

5. They've tyed him to a plank o wude,
     And thrown him in the sea;
   He didna sink, tho they bade him sink,
     He swimd, and they bade let him bee.

6. He hadna been into the sea
     An hour but barely three,
   Till by it came our Blessed Lady,
     Her dear young son her wi.

7. 'Will ye gang to your men again,
     Or will ye gang wi me?
   Will ye gang to the high heavens,
     Wi my dear son and me?'

8. 'I winna gang to my men again,
     For they would be feared at mee;
   But I woud gang to the high heavens,
     Wi thy dear son and thee.'

9. 'It's for nae honour ye did to me, Brown Robyn,
     It's for nae guid ye did to mee;
   But a' is for your fair confession
     You've made upon the sea.'

This ballad, which is known also in Denmark, Norway, and Sweden and has Russian parallels as well, concisely illustrates each of the principal characteristics of narrative folk poetry. Beginning *in medias res,* it concentrates intensely on a single episode: the earthly punishment and spiritual redemption of its protagonist whose sole action of concern to us is his confessed sin. Similarly, its plot is developed dramatically both in the sense that the principal action is revealed by dialogue rather than epic narration and in the fact that the poem is scenic, shifting its action from shipboard to the wastes of the sea with but the barest implication of transition in stanzas five and six. And, finally, the poem is impersonal. Here there are no intrusive comments by author or singer. If we condemn Brown Robyn out of repugnance for his sin or feel relieved because of his salvation, we do so out of our own emotional response to the narrative, not because the composer, in the manner of an eighteenth-century novelist, instructs us in the proprieties.

The bulk of narrative folk poetry could be analyzed in the same way, though there are minor deviations from these general principles according to the exact type of poem being examined. Oral epics, for example, rely less upon dialogue than upon episodic, scenic development for their dramatic effect. Moreover, it should also be pointed out that an equally important attribute of all narrative folk poetry is its phraseology. This is characterized by repetition, which is sometimes apparent in a single poem, as stanza five of "Brown Robyn's Confession" repeats in action the directions given in stanza four, and stanza eight replies to the questions asked in stanza seven in nearly identical words. But more often one must be familiar with an entire corpus of folk poetry in order to recognize its repetitious nature.

Indeed, repetition is not only the hallmark of folk poetry, it is the very sum and substance of its being. The poet who addresses an academically trained audience must exhibit originality, especially in detail and expression; no matter how old his wine, he must pour it into new bottles. The poet who addresses the non-academically trained, however, has another problem: no matter how new his wine, he must package it in the old, familiar bottles. Similar events demand similar expression, even to identical or nearly identical wording. Brown Robyn exhorts his men to let the sea have its way with him with the words:

> 'And if I sink, ye may bid me sink,
> But if I swim, just let me bee.'

Similarly, Willie's lady in "The White Fisher" (Child 264A), in order to test the fidelity of her husband and his devotion to their son, orders that her babe be thrown in the sea, and

> 'Gin he sink, ye'll let him sink,
> Gin he swim, ye'll let him swim.'

Nor does one have to be familiar with the Scandinavian languages to see the similarity between stanza nine of the Norwegian version of "Dalebu Jonson" (Landstad XXIV)

> Aa Dalebu Saðlar sin gangare grá
> sá riðer han seg til kongens garð,

with stanza three of the Norwegian "Knut liten og Sylvelin" (Landstad XXVII)

> Knut liten han saðlar sin gangare grá
> sá riðer han seg til Sylvelins garð.

and with stanza one of another Norwegian ballad, "Herre Per og stolt Margit" (Landstad LXXIV)

> Herre Per saðlar út gangaren grá,
> sá riðer han seg til stolt Margits gárð.

where little is changed except the names.

No matter where one looks in narrative folk poetry, such formulas appear and reappear. If the ballad protagonist finds news disappointing, it may well be said of him, as it is of Sir Patrick Spens:

> The first line that Sir Patrick red,
> A loud lauch lauched he;
> The next line that Sir Patrick red
> The teir blinded 'his ee.
> (Child 58 A, stanza 4)

and of Mary Hamilton,

> When she gaed up the Cannogate,
> She laughed loud laughters three;
> But when she came down the Cannogate
> The tear blinded her ee.
> (Child 173A, stanza 8)

as well as of Johnie Scot,

> The first look that Johnny lookd,
> A loud laughter gae he;
> But the next look that Johnny gae
> The tear blinded his ee.
> (Child 99B, stanza 12)

and many others. Little imagination is required to convert such a formula to:

> O the firsten step she steppit,
> she steppit on a stane;
> But the neisten step she steppit,
> she met him Lamkin.
> (Child 93A, stanza 18)

The protagonist who must depart in haste may well instruct his groom:

> 'O saddle me the black, the black,
> Or saddle me the brown;
> O saddle me the swiftest steed
> That ever rade frae a town.'

Lord William says such words to his page in "Lady Maisry" (Child 65A, stanza 25), Fair Isabell to her page in "The Lass of Roch Royal" (Child 76A, stanza 3), the Lord of Primrose to his servant in "Lord Lovel" (Child 75I, stanza 10), and, among many others, Lord Barnard to his page in "Little Musgrave and Lady Barnard" (Child 81I, stanza 7). Indeed, it is not especially remarkable to find a narrative folksong text in which every stanza has its parallel in some other song.

Poetry composed in such a manner is not apt to be subtle. Consequently, the phraseology of narrative folk poetry is characterized not only by repetition, but also by exaggerated statement, even at the expense of common sense and pragmatism. As commonplace a stanza in ballads as any of those quoted above is:

> The horse Fair Annet rade upon,
>   He amblit like the wind;
> Wi siller he was shod before,
>   Wi burning gowd behind.
>   (Child 73A, stanza 16)

Yet any of the folk among whom ballads circulated would be well aware not only of the economic foolishness but also of the physical impracticality of shoeing horses with gold and silver. The same folk would be equally well aware of the improbability, and perhaps even of the grisly humor, to be seen in stanza fifty of Child's B text of "The Hunting of the Cheviot" (Child 162) :

> For Witherington needs must I wayle
>   as one in dolefull dumpes,
> For when his leggs were smitten of,
>   he fought upon his stumpes.

But the world of narrative folk poetry is a world of vivid contrasts. Superlatives are the order of the day.

Poetry of this sort, dramatic, impersonal poetry marked by intense concentration, repetition, and exaggerated statement, appears to have been popular in the European, western Asiatic, and Mediterranean areas at least as early as the ninth century B.C., at one time in its history serving as the model, if not the prototype, for such sophisticated poems as *The Iliad* and *The Odyssey*. Each culture in which such poetry has lived, however, has produced its own prosodic patterns, and these, in turn, have undergone their own evolution. At any given time and in any given place, moreover, the prosodic patterns of narrative folk poetry appear to be more limited than those of art poetry or even than those of non-narrative folk poetry. In some cultures, narrative folk poems are constructed of individual verse lines, or half-lines, each independent of all of the others but held together internally by some such linguistic device as the regular spacing of long syllables or the alternation of stressed and unstressed syllables with, perhaps, the additional device of patterning the stressed syllables according to their initial sounds. In other cultures, individual verse lines may be arranged in clusters and linked to each other by rhyme or assonance. Such patterns are governed to a large extent by the structure of the language in which the poem is composed. Consequently, as languages change, so do the possible poetic structures, especially in folk poetry that closely reflects common speech patterns.

To illustrate all of these patterns is impossible, not only because of lack of space here but also because the English language does not easily lend itself to illustrations of quantitative verse. Early English popular verse was, however, alliterative. The significant prosodic element was the verse line, which was identified by four stressed syllables alliterating according to a pattern set by the first stressed syllable in the second half of the line, the unstressed syllables counting for nothing:

> Swýlce ða gebróðor ‖ bégen íǽtsomne,
> Cýning and᾽ǽðeling, ‖ ᾽cýððe sóhton,
> Wésseaxna lánd, ‖ wíges hŕemge.
> ("The Battle of Brunanburh,"
> lines 57–59)

In time, however, as English evolved from a synthetic to an analytic language, such patterns became cumbersome and artificial, and they were replaced by end rhyme and a nearly natural alternation of stressed and unstressed syllables. Though it was a process of slow and gradual evolution, the result was eventually what is today known as the "ballad stanza," a quatrain rhyming *abcb* and having four stresses in the first line, three in the second, four in the third, and three in the fourth:

> 'Hŏw dáur yŏu pú m̃y flówer mădám?
> Hŏw dáur yĕ bréak m̃y trée?
> Hŏw dáur yĕ cóme tŏ Chártĕr's h'a,
> Wĭthóut thĕ leáve ŏf m'e?'
> ("Tam Lin", Child 39E, stanza 4)

It will be noted that the ballad stanza, like the Old English alliterative line, is constructed with little regard for unstressed syllables, but the very nature of the English language tends toward an alternation of stressed and unstressed syllables, producing what is frequently called the "ballad lilt," well-illustrated in the stanza from "Tam Lin" quoted above. But stanzas as regular as these are rare. Almost as common are quatrains built entirely of four stress lines:

> 'Ŏ prómiše m̃e nów, Clérk Cŏlvíll,
> Oŕ ĭt wĭll cóst yĕ múcklĕ stŕife,
> Rĭde néver bý thĕ Wélls of Sláne,
> Ĭf yé wăd líve ańd bróok yŏur lífe.'
> (Child 42B, stanza 2)

And many of the earliest ballads appear to be rhymed couplets with four stresses in each line:

> 'Thŏu aŕt oĕr yóung ă máid,' quŏth h'e,
> Maŕriĕd wĭth m̃e thăt thŏu wóuldst bé.'
> (Child 2B, stanza 5)

though such stanzas are frequently interspersed with refrain lines giving the effect of a quatrain rhyming *abab*:

Shé săt down bĕlów ă thórn,
Fińe flówĕŕs iń tȟe válȳĕy
Ańd thére sȟe hás hĕr sẃeet băbe bórn.
Ańd tȟe gŕeen lĕaves thĕy gŕŏw ráŕĕly.
(Child 20B, stanza 1 and refrain)

Variations of these patterns are infinite, governed, in all probability, not only by the skill of the composer but also by the demands of the tune, and they are always variations of the basic, recognizable pattern.

Finally, it should be pointed out that refrains also, while generally following the patterns of basic ballad stanzas, vary to some degree from each other. In some instances, the last line of a narrative stanza is repeated either exactly or with slight verbal changes that contribute to the sense of the stanza. In other instances a single additional line is appended, the so-called ballad burden, which, since it often has nothing to do with the narrative, often degenerates into nonsense syllables. In yet other instances, as in the last example quoted above from "The Cruel Mother," refrain lines alternate with narrative verse lines. The most common type, however, is the "carol" refrain, a completely separate stanza sung or recited in the manner of a chorus after each stanza of the narrative. But refrains are by no means a constant of narrative folk poetry, and, despite theories to the contrary, they seem to be a rather late contribution to the genre.

Stanzaic, narrative folk poetry of this sort is common in northwestern Europe, the British Isles, and, of course, North America. Such poetry became possible in England shortly after the Norman conquest when the structure of the English language changed and the influence of French poetic forms percolated down to the people, but the earliest indisputable example of this poetic structure is found in "Judas," a late-thirteenth-century poem for which there is no proof of oral tradition. Very probably the form enjoyed some popularity during the next century, but there is no further concrete evidence of its existence until the middle of the fifteenth century when the ballad of "Robin Hood and the Monk" was written down. From that time on, however, the genre apparently grew in popularity, reaching such a peak in the seventeenth century that it became a model for literary hacks, then slowly declined to its present state of survival. On the Continent ballads both appeared and achieved popularity somewhat earlier, and it is interesting to note that in Denmark a manuscript anthology of ballads and related materials entitled *Hjertebogen* was compiled by a royal chef, one Albert Muus, as early as 1553–55, and Anders Sorensen Vedel published what is perhaps the earliest printed collection of texts, *It Hundrede udvaalde Danske Viser,* in 1591, a volume that went through eight reprintings in the seventeenth century.

Strangely, although the folksong stanza here described appears to have originated in France, it was never popularly adopted in central and southern Europe, western Asia, or the Near East. In these areas, narrative folk poetry is basically strophic, and the over-all structure is reminiscent of the epic, albeit an epic having the characteristics of concentration and scenic construction, or of the romance, albeit a romance lacking in extraneous details.

Whether strophic or stanzaic, however, narrative folk poetry always deals with materials of dramatic and local significance. The king who serves as the protagonist of a narrative folksong is a man who happens to be a king; similarly, events sufficient to reduce great nations to shambles are in narrative folksongs described in terms of their effects upon narrowly circumscribed communities. This narrowing of focus can be most economically illustrated by quoting again from balladry:

> Queen Jane was in labour full six weeks and more,
>   And the women were weary, and fain would give oer:
> 'O women, O women, as women ye be,
>   Rip open my two sides, and save my baby!'
>
> 'O royal Queen Jane, that thing may not be;
>   We'll send for King Henry to come unto thee.'
> King Henry came to her, and sate on her bed:
>   'What ails my dear lady, her eyes look so red?'
>
> 'O royal King Henry, do one thing for me:
>   Rip open my two sides, and save my baby!'
> 'O royal Queen Jane, that thing will not do,
>   If I lose your fair body, I'll lose your baby too.'
>
> She wept and she waild, and she wrung her hands sore;
>   O the flour of England must flurish no more!
> She wept and she waild till she fell in a swoond,
>   They opened her two sides, and the baby was found.
>
> The baby was christened with joy and much mirth,
>   Whilst poor Queen Jane's body lay cold under earth:
> There was ringing and singing and mourning all day,
>   The princess Eliz[abeth] went weeping away.
>
> The trumpets in mourning so sadly did sound
>   And the pikes and the muskets did trail on the ground.
>   .   .   .   .
>   .   .   .   .
>
> (Child 170 A)

Some semblance of the royal nature of Henry VIII and his English queen, Jane Seymour, penetrates the confusion of historical fact on which this version of the ballad is based. Unlike art poetry, ballads and other narrative folk poems have no authorized text: each version, each singing or recitation, is as valid as any other, and the concept of such poetry is similar to that of a phoneme and its related allophones. In other words, when one speaks of a specific narrative folk poem, he is speaking of an idea that is factually represented by a number of different forms. Thus, as the controlling facts of history and legend faded from the memory of the folk, "The Death of Queen Jane" developed many new versions until only the basic narrative core remained:

> 'Ye midwives and women-kind do one thing for me;
> Send for my mother, to come and see me.'
>
> Her mother was sent for, who came speedilie:
> 'O Jeanie, Queen Jeanie, are ye gaun to dee?'
>
> 'O mother, dear mother, do one thing for me;
> O send for King Henry to come and see me.'
>
> King Henry was sent for, who came speedilee:
> 'O Jeanie, Queen Jeanie, are ye gaun to dee?'
>
> 'King Henry, King Henry, do one thing for me;
> O send for a doctor, to come and see me.'
>
> The doctor was sent for, who came speedilie:
> 'O Jeanie, Queen Jeanie, are ye gaun to dee?'
>
> 'O doctor, oh doctor, do one thing for me;
> Open my left side, and let my babe free.'
>
> He opened her left side, and then all was o'er,
> And the best flower in England will flourish no more.
>
> (Child 170 E)

In the same way that Henry VIII and Jane Seymour are here reduced to their common humanity and the subsequent events of international significance that resulted from the death of Queen Jane are ignored, so also the focus in all narrative folk poetry is on the individual and the immediate event. Great leaders though they may have been, Marko Kraljević in the Yugoslav oral epics, Marsk Stig Andersson in Scandinavian ballads, and the Cid of the Spanish *romancero* differ in no significant way from such lesser known and perhaps fictional folksong protagonists as Johnie Cock, Hobie Noble, and little Musgrave. Consequently, the subject matter of narrative folk poetry encompasses the entire range of human experience as exhibited by specific example.

It was, perhaps, this universal humanity of spirit that first led scholars to the serious study of narrative folk poetry. As has already been noted, collections of related materials were made in Denmark as early as the middle of the sixteenth century only shortly before Sir Philip Sidney was to write, with qualified enthusiasm, of English historical ballads, but not until the middle of the eighteenth century was the study of folk poetry to come into existence in any true sense. At that time, nourished by the same spirit which gave rise to romantic nationalism, folksong scholarship took root and has continued to grow to the present day, though some of its most showy blooms have faded overnight, especially when transplanted in alien soil. There is, unfortunately, space here for a discussion of only a select few, though these derive from the original ground-stock.

To some degree the lines followed by even the most recent students of narrative folk poetry were sketched out in the latter half of the eighteenth century when Bishop Thomas Percy quarreled with Joseph Ritson about how ballads were created and about how they should be presented to the public. Percy's *Reliques of Ancient English Poetry,* first published in 1765, was intended primarily as a poetic anthology for the edification of a literate public. Condescending in his attitude toward his materials, many of which derived from a mid-seventeenth-century folio manuscript discovered in the house of a friend, Bishop Percy buffed, polished, and augmented the poems that he edited until they were appropriate to the taste of his age. With this practice Joseph Ritson had little sympathy, though he was otherwise as egregiously mistaken in his attitude as the man he condemned, for he felt that printed texts were received texts to be treated as authoritative. Neither man seemed aware of the processes of oral tradition; each believed in individual authorship, a concept to which their very influential successor, Sir Walter Scott, also adhered in his *Minstrelsy of the Scottish Border* (1802–03).

Scott, however, was strongly influenced as well by ideas then developing on the Continent. Familiarity with the works of Johann Gottfried von Herder and other German romantics augmented his already developed sense of nationalism. While as an author he sympathized with Percy's desire to amuse an educated audience, as a romantic nationalist he delighted in the bluntness of the texts that he collected and he paid lip service, at least, to the exacting standards of Ritson.

Out of this confusion grew some of the great collections in Europe. Pastor M. B. Landstad of Norway, relying heavily upon materials actually collected from oral transmission by both himself and associates, published an extensive collection of moderately revised texts in 1853, the same year in which appeared the first volume of Svend Grundtvig's *Danmarks gamle Folkeviser,* one of the world's truly great ballad collections. But while Landstad was to polish his texts, Grundtvig adhered to the principle of publishing everything exactly as he found it. Grundtvig, moreover, supplied exhaustive introductions for each ballad, tracing the history of its narrative and showing its relationship to parallel song and prose traditions. *Danmarks gamle Folkeviser* became a model for ballad editing; it set a pattern followed to the present day.

It was this pattern that was picked up by Francis James Child, the first and greatest of the American ballad editors. During the middle decades of the nineteenth century, Professor Child instituted an extensive search for manuscript copies of popular ballads in Great Britain while at the same time he culled the printed editions published by Percy, Scott, and their followers. The result was an eight-volume work entitled *English and Scottish Ballads* published in the British Poets Series in 1847–59 and addressed to a literary audience. Limitations of both space and time made this a selective edition, but Professor Child adhered to the Ritsonian principle of publishing unaltered texts while at the same time printing only those texts that he felt to be complete. It was on this foundation that Child built his *magnum opus, The English and Scottish Popular Ballads* (1882–98). These five massive volumes, patterned after the works of Svend Grundtvig, contain the texts of 305 distinct ballad types, divided into versions and variants with extensive head- and footnotes. Significantly, something less than one-half of the ballad types show positive evidence of oral tradition, for Child intended the volumes to be definitive and thus included not only items he knew to be ballads but also many he intuitively felt to be ballads. The result, for better or worse, was an established canon of English and Scottish balladry that has affected every subsequent ballad editor.

Unfortunately, Professor Child died before he was able to see his last volume through the press, and his projected general introduction was never written. Many scholars rushed to fill the gap, the most influential of whom was Francis B. Gummere, a onetime student of Child's who vigorously promulgated the theory of "communal origins." This theory, best expressed in his *The Popular Ballad* (1907), insists that ballads as a genre (though not the individual ballads that we now know) originated as the instinctive reaction of a homogeneous community to an event of local and dramatic significance. Ballads were thus defined in terms of theoretical origins, and extant texts were looked upon primarily as vestiges of ancient popular poetry. So influential were Professor Gummere's ideas that no modern scholar has been able to ignore them, and such masterpieces of logical refutation as Louise Pound's *Poetic Origins and the Ballad* (1921), while they have buried the theory, have been unable to lay its ghost.

Percy, Ritson, Scott, Child, and Gummere all conceived of the ballad as literature, and they seemed scarcely aware that they were songs as well. The situation in Europe was hardly different, though many Scandinavian nineteenth-century editions contained musical notation as a kind of afterthought. In the English-speaking world it remained for Cecil Sharp to insist upon the importance of tunes. A professional musician and indefatigable collector, Sharp built upon the literary tradition as represented by Child on the one hand and a musical tradition, perhaps best represented by W. Christie's *Traditional Ballad Airs* (1876–78), on the other hand. In his *English Folk Song: Some Conclusions* (1907) he clearly indicates the need for studying texts and tunes conjointly and the equally important need for specific attention to oral tradition. Two present-day works, Bertrand H. Bronson's *The Traditional Tunes of the Child Ballads* (1959 *et seq.*) and Claude M. Simpson's *The British Broadside Ballad and its Music* (1966) now make such study feasible.

It should finally be noted that the researches made by the late Milman Parry and Albert B. Lord into the nature of Yugoslav oral epics have made a significant contribution to our understanding of narrative folk poetry in general. Their description of the processes of oral composition, best expressed in Lord's *The Singer of Tales* (1960), does much to explain many of the peculiarities of folk poetry, be it recited or sung, makes necessary a reevaluation of all previous theories, and opens many fruitful areas of investigation.

Bibliography and Selected Readings

Editions

Bronson, Bertrand H. *The Traditional Tunes of the Child Ballads.* 4 vols. Princeton: Princeton University Press, 1959–70. Prints and analyzes all known tunes for the ballads found in the Child collection, treating them in much the same manner as Child treats texts.

Child, Francis J. *The English and Scottish Popular Ballads.* 5 vols. Boston: Houghton Mifflin, 1882–98; reprinted by Dover, 1965. The basic collection of ballads in the English language; for comments, see especially p. 96 above.

Grundtvig, Svend, *et al. Danmarks gamle Folkeviser.* 10 vols. Copenhagen: Carlsbergfond, 1953–; reprinted by Universitete-Jubilæets Samfund, 1966–67. The prototype for modern ballad editing; for comments see especially pp. 95–96 above.

Landstad, M. B. *Norske Folkeviser.* Christiania (Oslo) : Chr. Tönsberg, 1853.

Leach, MacEdward. *The Ballad Book.* New York: Harper, 1955. A one-volume edition of ballads selected from Great Britain, North America, and Scandinavia, this is an excellent introduction to the genre.

History, Criticism, and Analysis

Entwistle, W. J. *European Balladry*. Oxford: Clarendon Press, 1939. An exhaustive survey-description of the narrative folksongs of Europe that describes much that lies outside the strict bounds of balladry.

Gerould, Gordon H. *The Ballad of Tradition*. Oxford: Clarendon Press, 1932. The basic introduction to the study of ballads, this book defines the genre and exhaustively surveys the known examples. Though still basic, it is out of date.

Hodgart, M. J. C. *The Ballads*. London: Hutchinson's University Library, 1950. A British supplement to Gerould's book.

Hustvedt, S. B. *Ballad Books and Ballad Men*. Cambridge, Mass.: Harvard University Press, 1930. History of ballad scholarship in Great Britain, Scandinavia, and North America, more detailed than Wilgus but ending where the latter begins.

Jones, James H. "Commonplace and Memorization in the Oral Tradition of the English and Scottish Popular Ballads." *Journal of American Folklore* 74 (1961): 97–112. An application of the theory of formulaic composition to ballads.

Sharp, Cecil. *English Folk Song: Some Conclusions*. 4th rev. ed. Belmont, California: Wadsworth Publishing Co., 1965. For comments, see p. 97 above.

Steenstrup, J. C. H. R. *The Medieval Popular Ballad*. Translated by E. G. Cox. Boston: Ginn and Company, 1914. The Scandinavian equivalent of Gerould and Hodgart; valuable introduction to the European point of view.

Wilgus, D. K. *Anglo-American Folksong Scholarship Since 1898*. New Brunswick, N. J.: Rutgers University Press, 1959. Survey of the Anglo-American folksong scholarship since Child; should be read in conjunction with Hustvedt.

3 FOLK EPIC
Felix J. Oinas

Folk (or oral) epic songs are narrative poems in formulaic and ornamental style dealing with the adventures of extraordinary people. They
are traditional, that is, handed down by word of mouth, as distinguished from literary epics, attributed to definite authors. The long
epics, such as the Old English *Beowulf*, the medieval German *Nibe-
lungenlied* and the medieval French *Chanson de Roland,* also should
be excluded from the term folk epic, since their development involves
both oral and literary versions. In Europe, the folk epic in its purest
form appears among the Slavs (especially Russians, Yugoslavs, and
Bulgarians) and the Balto-Finns (especially Finns and Karelians). In
this survey, we are going to give examples from the Slavic and Finnish-
Karelian (here called simply Finnish) epics.

The collection and study of folk epics on a large scale began in
eastern Europe during the last century. Much collecting in Finland
was done in the 1820s and '30s by Elias Lönnrot, who combined the
songs about Finnish heroes into the epic *Kalevala*. The best and most
complete epic songs were found in northern Finnish Karelia and in

Russian Karelia. The merit of gathering a large collection of epic songs and other folklore in Yugoslavia belongs to Vuk Karadžić, who began his work in the 1820s. Yugoslav epics are best preserved in Serbia, Montenegro, and parts of Dalmatia.

In Russia, the epic songs were thought to have almost died out around the middle of the last century until P. N. Rybnikov and A. F. Gil'ferding (in 1860 and 1871, respectively) found the tradition still flourishing in Karelia—around Lake Onega and to the north of it. This discovery was so surprising and sensational to the educated world that, like Macpherson's poems of Ossian in England, it aroused some skepticism. Later collectors have added to the important Russian epic areas the region of the White Sea and of the rivers (Pinega, Mezen', and Pečora) flowing to the north.

A look at the map shows that all these epic areas are situated on the periphery of Finland and the Slavic countries, far away from the cultural centers. In these areas life continued in the same primitive, patriarchal way through centuries and thus secured the favorable conditions for the preservation of the epic tradition.

The beginnings of the folk epic go back to times immemorial. The creation of the oldest Finnish epic songs has been placed in the middle Iron Age (400–800 A.D.) or the beginning of the Viking era (800–1050 A.D.). A number of these songs have the sea as their milieu and share the fishermen's sphere of interest. They were evidently created in the coastal areas of western Finland.[1]

The Russian heroic epic, called *byliny* (sing. *bylina*), goes back as far as the dawn of Russian history, but is probably much older. A considerable body of the *byliny* deals with the Tartar invasion (first half of the thirteenth century), the most fateful event in Russian history. It is probable that the earlier skirmishes between the Russians and their neighbors (such as Pechenegs and Polovtsians) were reinterpreted in *byliny* as fights with Tartars.

It is thought that the Yugoslav folk epic emerged in the early Middle Ages, although nothing of this early form has been preserved. Scholars have assumed that the battle of Kosovo (1389), in which the Serbian state was crushed by the Turks, changed this epic completely. The fight against the Turks remained the primary theme of the Yugoslav epic until the beginning of the last century.

As for the creation and dissemination of folk epic songs, the Soviet theories have found general acceptance among the Slavs. According to former theories, advanced by Vsevolod Miller around the turn of the century and shared by other representatives of the historical

1. Martti Haavio, *Väinämöinen: Eternal Sage* (Folklore Fellows Communications, 144; Helsinki, 1952), pp. 62–63, 80–81.

school, the Russian *byliny* originated in the higher classes—among the singers of the princes' retinue. It was assumed that later on the *byliny* was taken over by the *skomoroxi*, professional singers of the lower classes, in whose hands they received their final form. The *skomoroxi*, because of their persecution by the government in the seventeenth century, moved to the peripheral areas of Russia, especially to the north. There the peasants took over the *byliny* from the *skomoroxi*, developing them further and adding features from their typical peasant setting.

This theory of the creation and transfer of the *byliny* had general currency in the Soviet Union up to the mid-thirties, when the government and party decided to bring it in line with Soviet doctrine. A wide folkloristic discussion was started about the character and origin of the epic. It resulted in a basic change in the attitude toward *byliny*, denying their aristocratic origin and insisting upon their "genuine nationalism." After this change of policy, the folklorists had to denounce their former ideas as erroneous and to search for proof of the vital role that the peasants and working people had in the origin of *byliny*.

This Soviet theory was transplanted to Yugoslavia. There, too, the former ideas about the military aristocracy as the creator of the folk epic were condemned and the new theory about the peasantry as the seedbed of the epic was proclaimed as the only valid one. Though it is true that the peasantry has preserved the songs, altered them, and created some new ones on the existing models, it is doubtful that they were responsible for their original composition. Ultimately these songs must have been the work of professional singers, in the same way that the western European epic was the creation of minstrels and troubadours.

The folk epic can be divided into the following categories: shamanistic, heroic, romantic, and historic. The shamanistic epic deals with deeds that are not heroic in the real sense, but are accomplished by magical, *non*-human means. The Finnish-Karelian epic is basically shamanistic. Two of its leading figures, Väinämöinen and Lemminkäinen, are magicians. To build a boat Väinämöinen needs not special skill but magic words. In case he does not know all the words in the spell, he goes for them to the other world or enters a shaman, Antero Vipunen, who has been dead for a long time. He descends into Vipunen's stomach through his mouth and roams around there. Väinämöinen and Lemminkäinen are noted for their ability to sing, that is, for the use of charms. Väinämöinen sings the young braggart Joukahainen into the swamp, from which he cannot escape without the former's help. When Väinämöinen sings, to the accompaniment of his miraculous *kantele* (a stringed instrument), then all nature, the animals, and fairies come to listen to him. Lemminkäinen sings the participants in the Päivölä festivities into gold and silver garments, except for a loathsome cattle herder; in retaliation, the herder kills him.

The Russian epic hero Volx (or Vol'ga) Vseslav'evič is close to the shamanistic Finnish heroes. He can change himself into a pike, a falcon, and a wolf in order to procure food for himself and his retinue. In the shape of various animals, he destroys the Indian tsar's horses and ruins his weapons. Finally he, together with his retinue, smashes the tsar's army.

The heroic epic presents acts of prowess and courage of which no ordinary human beings are capable. These acts are directed against the internal and external enemies of the country. The Russian *byliny* hero Il'ja Muromec kills Nightingale the Robber, a monstrous combination of a bird and of a human, who controls a highway and does not let anyone pass:

> Nightingale whistles like a nightingale,
> He shrieks, the wretch, like a wild beast:
> The dark forests bow to the earth,
> All the herbage and grass withers up,
> The azure flowers wilt,
> Every mortal creature falls dead.[2]

Il'ja also fights and kills the Great Idol, who is two *sažen's* (1 sažen' = 7 feet) tall, eats three cows at one meal, and keeps a king as his cook. Dobrynja Nikitič slays a formidable dragon with twelve jaws who used to fly to the Russian land to kidnap and kill people. The fight lasts for three days, during which Dobrynja is encouraged from heaven not to cease fighting. Aleša Popovič kills Tugarin, the dragon's son, who is three sažen's tall and is carried to Prince Vladimir's feast by thirty plus thirty heroes. Even Tugarin's horse is frightening: it is a ferocious wild beast, from whose jaws pour flames and from whose ears issue columns of smoke.

The Russian *byliny* show clearly a striving for powerful effects. The singer endeavors to produce an effect of surprise and amazement in his listeners. This is done by the constant use of contrasts. At the beginning of the *bylina*, the hero is underestimated and the enemy is overestimated; the latter is shown as having invincible strength and power. All are afraid of the enemy and depressed by his violence, until at the end the hero conquers him with utmost ease.[3]

---

2. N. Kershaw Chadwick, *Russian Heroic Poetry* (New York, 1964), p. 67.
3. A. P. Skaftymov, *Poètika i genezis bylin* (Moscow and Saratov, 1924), pp. 46–61.

The heroes of Yugoslav epic songs are not inferior to the Russian ones in their prowess. In the song "The Marriage of Dušan" the young Miloš Vojinović slays a king's champion in single combat, overcomes the three-headed Vojvoda Balačko, and destroys his Latin (i.e., Catholic) escort. The prisoner Jurišić Janko goes alone, on a poor nag and with a blunt sword, against the sultan's elite troop of two hundred *janizaries* (soldiers in the sultan's guard), kills half of them, and drives the other half back to the sultan. Prince Marko's feats are innumerable. He frees thirty Serbian women prisoners from the vizier Gološan and his three hundred Turks. He alone overcomes General Vuča's son and his army of three hundred horsemen and General Vuča himself together with his one thousand horsemen, ties the general and his son together, and takes them to his city to prison. He even overpowers a mountain spirit (*vila*), whom he compels to revivify Vojvoda Miloš, whom she had killed. The terror that Marko's mere presence instills is demonstrated by the fact that the knees of Ljutica Bogdan, who terrorizes his neighborhood, begin to shake when his eyes meet those of Marko. And the daughter-in-law of General Vuča, when noticing Marko in the field near their castle, begins to shiver in fear and shivers for three years as if in fever.

The romantic epics include poems of love and adventure and not of heroic feats. The Finnish songs centered around Kaukamoinen and Ahti Saarelainen ("man of the Island") are filled with the adventurous spirit of the Viking age. Kaukamoinen (sometimes also called Lemminkäinen in the songs) is the Finnish Don Juan. He uses his sword too readily and has love affairs with scores of women. When the situation becomes unbearable and dangerous, he, in a cowardly fashion, disappears from the scene. Ahti Saarelainen is so eager to fight that he abandons his young wife after she breaks a promise to him and—together with his war-loving comrade—sets out for war. Lönnrot in the *Kalevala* has attributed the adventures of Kaukamoinen and Ahti to Lemminkäinen and has thus created a complex figure.

Čurilo Plenkovič is a typical ladies' man in Russian *byliny*. Renowned for his yellow curls and good looks, he arouses the interest of Vladimir's wife Apraksija, who wants to have him as her chamberlain; he ends his life in bed with a married woman whose enraged husband kills him. The song "Aleša and Dobrynja" tells of Aleša's attempt to marry Dobrynja's wife during Dobrynja's extended absence. The attempt fails due to Dobrynja's unexpected return on the wedding day. In the epic song about Nightingale Budimirovič the amorous interest is reversed; after Nightingale, a rich foreign merchant, has built a palace in Kiev, Prince Vladimir's niece Zabava Putjatična offers him her hand. Likewise, Marinka, a witch, uses every means to win Dobrynja as her husband, but is finally killed by him. Also the songs of Sadko can be included in the romantic epics. Sadko, a poor *gusli*-player in Novgorod, so fascinates the water king of Lake Il'men' with his playing that he is rewarded with a fish with golden gills. Later he spends several years in the kingdom of the tsar of the sea, entertaining the tsar with his music, before he succeeds in returning to his native city.

The historical songs deal with various historical events and figures. They show the impressions made by some event or person and the feelings they released. Thus, they are not history, but a contemporary poetical reaction to a historical event or character.[4]

In Russia, the historical songs arose only in the sixteenth century as a result of a new attitude toward historical personages. At that time is was no longer possible to describe the heroes as superhuman beings whose deeds were on a level at which ordinary laws no longer applied.[5] The historical songs concentrate on some popular tsars, such as Ivan the Terrible and Peter the Great. They describe anecdotal happenings, such as how a bold soldier prevented the execution of soldiers by Ivan the Terrible in the mining galleries under Kazan' and how a young dragoon defeated Peter the Great in a wrestling match. A number of historical songs are connected with some events of great historical importance, for instance the conquest of Siberia (with Ermak Timofeevič as the central figure), the turbulent years of the Time of Troubles (with False Dmitrij as the main hero), and the peasant movements led by Stepan Razin and Emeljan Pugačev.

The Yugoslav epic songs from the sixteenth century on can also be termed historical. Then the decline of the Osmanli Empire became apparent, thus giving greater freedom of action to the local Turkish officials in Serbia and resulting in the oppression and mistreatment of the Christian population. The activity of the fighters within the country (the so-called *hajduks*) and of those from abroad (the so-called *uskoks*) against the Turks increased. This was reflected in the epic songs; instead of the songs with Marko as their main hero, the *hajduk* and *uskok* songs with their fearless leaders and their joy in heroic adventure became predominant. The incidents describing the revenge meted out to the Turkish oppressors are, in general, close to historical truth.

The chief characters of the folk epic are no ordinary men. The central figures of the Finnish epic songs, Väinämöinen and Ilmarinen, are cultural heroes. Väinämöinen was one of the builders of the cosmos at primeval times, and his belt, bastshoes (birch-bark shoes), and scythe are still to be seen in the starred sky. As a shaman, he is a

4. Carl Stief, *Studies in the Russian Historical Song* (Copenhagen, 1953), p. 262.
5. Stief, p. 265.

mighty sage and the spiritual leader of his tribe. It is possible that the songs of Väinämöinen are based on the legends about a shaman who actually did live and was held in high esteem by his tribe. Ilmarinen is a smith-demiurge, the northern relative of Hephaestus, who made the stars in the sky and even forged the whole celestial vault. He is the first one to strike a fire spark and, together with Väinämöinen, to bring fire to the people. Ilmarinen forges the *Sampo*, the miraculous mill that ceaselessly grinds out grain, salt, and money, which—as to its origin—is considered to be a replica of the world pillar supporting the sky.[6]

The chief figures of the Russian and Yugoslav epics display prowess to the highest degree. The Russian *bylina* hero Il'ja Muromec is adorned with the ideal features of an epic hero; he is brave, an unselfish servant of his country, the defender of orphans, widows, and the poor. He says of himself:

> I am going to serve for the Christian faith,
> And for the Russian land,
> And for the capital city of Kiev,
> And for the widows, orphans and the poor.[7]

Dobrynja Nikitič, in addition to being very brave, is an ideal knightly diplomat. He has courteous manners and clever speech. Prince Vladimir uses him whenever he has to send an envoy on a diplomatic or other mission. The character of Aleša Popovič is more complex. He is, on the one hand, very bold and adroit, but on the other is endowed with traits of jealousy, greed, and arrogance. These negative features may have been attributed to him because of his origin as a priest's son (Popovič, "priest's son").

While Il'ja's and Aleša's figures were evidently not modeled after any historical persons, Dobrynja may have had connections with Vladimir's uncle, Dobrynja; some of the latter's roles (Prince Vladimir's matchmaker for Rogned' and his helper in the Christianization of Rus') coincide with those of the *bylina* hero.

Prince Marko is a many-sided figure in the Yugoslav folk epic. The question about the relationship between Prince Marko the epic hero and the historical Prince Marko, the ruler of a small principality in Serbia (1371–95), has not yet been solved. The historical Marko was an insignificant ruler, an obedient servant of his suzerain, the Turkish sultan, and died while fighting the Christians. The epic retains the historical truth of Marko's recognition of the sultan's authority, but

6. Haavio, pp. 206–36; Lauri Honko, "Finnische Mythologie," H. W. Haussig, ed., *Wörterbuch der Mythologie* 2: *Das alte Europa* (Stuttgart, n.d.), pp. 360–61, 309–11.

7. A. M. Astaxova, ed., *Il'ja Muromec* (Moscow and Leningrad, 1958), p. 395.

shows him as the fiercest fighter against the Turks, of whom even the sultan himself is afraid. His "sword was sharp and his hand self-willed," prepared for any exploit. He was ready to enter the most fearful conflict even unarmed. His immense physical strength was coupled with his wit. He had also some negative traits; he was quick-tempered, wilful, and given to drink.[8]

Other older heroes of the Yugoslav epic are sketched with a few strokes. Miloš Obilić, the slayer of the sultan Murat, is a fearless, perfect knight. Vojvoda Momčilo's main characteristic is his great physical and moral strength. The Jugović brothers are a moving symbol of heroic resignation to death in the fight against the enemy, as are also King Lazar and Stevan Musić and many others.[9]

The characters in historical songs are closer to ordinary human beings. Russian historical songs show the rulers and rebels in a rather neutral light. Only the figures of some simple people who appear as rulers' partners in the songs get some tint of glorification. Yugoslav historical songs somewhat remind one of the heroic songs in that they endeavor to show the hajduk and uskok leaders as fearless and brave fighters against the wilfulness of the Turks.

The length of epic songs varies. Finnish epic songs are rather short, averaging from 50 to 400 lines. Russian songs are from 100 or fewer lines to 1,000 lines and over. The average length of Yugoslav epic songs is 300-500 lines, although songs of 800-1,000 and even over 2,000 lines are no rarity. The longest Yugoslav epic songs recorded run over 13,000 lines.

The songs deal usually with one event, seldom with more. There have been tendencies to combine songs having a central theme or about a certain hero into a single epic. In Finland, songs about the Sampo, the miraculous mill, were brought together in the far-distant past to form a close-knit sequence. They tell how the Sampo was promised to Pohjola and was forged; and how it was stolen and of the adventures following it. The most ancient episode in the cycle was the theft of the Sampo, an episode created under the influence of the Scandinavian fornaldar sagas describing journeys to mythical Norðbotton.[10]

In Russia and in Yugoslavia, similar attempts to unite songs about individual heroes or themes into cycles were made in more recent times. It has been pointed out, justly, that such cycles compiled by

8. Vojislav Djurić, "Prince Marko in Epic Poetry," Journal of the Folklore Institute 3 (The Hague, 1966), 315–24.

9. Djurić, pp. 324–30.

10. Matti Kuusi, Sampo-eepos: Typologinen analyysi (Mémoires de la Société Finno-ougrienne 96; Helsinki, 1949), pp. 311–56; Martti Haavio, Kirjokansi: Suomen kansan kertomarunoutta (Porvoo and Helsinki, 1952), pp. 280–94.

merely stringing independent songs together cannot be called long epics; individual songs will assume their independent existence again as easily as they were joined together.

A step in the development of the long epic, although still at an initial stage, may be cited in heroic songs from Krajina in northwestern Bosnia. This epic is characterized by the broadening of the epic songs cross-wise, rather than length-wise, that is, building up the main narrative parts of the song rather than stringing the songs mechanically one after another. The action in the Krajina epic is developing toward double-strandedness: it takes place, for example, in both the hero's and the enemy's camps. Characteristic also is the so-called center: a person, having occupied a central position, gives an account of everything that is going on in range of his vision.[11]

The folk epic adheres to a grandiose "epic ceremonialism"—the repetitions, traditional formulas, detailed descriptions of actions, ornamental adjectives, and similes, for the purpose of retardation, that is, slowing down the action for artistic purposes.

There are a great many different kinds of repetition in folk epic, which can be divided into two basic types: the so-called nucleus repetition and the frame repetition. The first type is characterized by the repetition of the nucleus of the motif without changing it. In the second type, the nucleus of the motif is changed.

Nucleus repetition appears, for example, in the Serbian "Song of Baghdad." Here the sultan tells his pashas and viziers to have imperial tents carried forth to the open plain, to set up the imperial cauldrons and to place shining salvers beside them in order to prepare to welcome the Bosnians. Then, repeating every detail in the same words, the song tells that the sultan's orders are being carried out.

Frame repetition can be illustrated with an example from the Finnish song "The Wooing Contest." Ilmarinen's sister sees Väinämöinen sailing on the sea and asks him where he is going. Väinämöinen tells her that he is going to fish for salmon. The girl calls him a liar, since he has no nets in his boat. When the girl asks Väinämöinen the same question the second time, he answers that he is going to hunt geese. The girl again calls him a liar, since he has no dog or bow with him. When the girl inquires about his destination for the third time, Väinämöinen has to admit that he is going to woo the maiden of Pohjola. In this example, the same motif is used, with some modifications, three times. It appears that frame repetition is especially suited for epic retardation.

11. A. Schmaus, "Episierungsprozesse im Bereich der slavischen Volksdichtung," *Münchener Beiträge zur Slavenkunde: Festgabe für Paul Diels* (Veröffentlichungen des Osteuropa-Institutes München 4, 1953), pp. 303–20.

The study of the types of repetition can reveal the approximate time of the creation of the songs, since certain repetition types have been fashionable at certain times. A subtype of the frame repetition (the so-called dialogue form), characteristic of a number of Finnish epic songs and almost lacking in the Slavic songs, may have been introduced in the Viking era.[12]

The folk epics rely strongly on the use of traditional formulas (*loci communes*) that describe certain situations with the same, or almost the same, words. The formulas often begin the song, or appear in transitional places that connect two episodes of the action. One of the customary devices for beginning a Russian or Yugoslav epic song is the description of a feast or of the knights' riding out to encounter adventures. A typical feast is described in a Russian epic as follows:

> In the glorious city of Kiev,
> By gracious Prince Vladimir,
> A splendid, honourable feast was given
> For the company of princes and boyars,
> For powerful, mighty heroes,
> For all the bold fighting-women.
> The white day drew to evening,
> And the prince was making exceeding merry.[13]

The Russian *byliny* also apply traditional formulas to describe the hero's getting up in the morning, his arrival at the prince's court and entrance into the palace, his hunting, the horse's leap, and other acts. In Yugoslav epic formulas are used furthermore for the receipt of a written message, the greeting of two heroes, and for various stages of single combat. Such seemingly unimportant actions as arrivals and departures, the hero's rising, dressing, and taking up arms are specially liked by the audience. The singers who do not use them are occasionally encouraged by the audience to do so—perhaps by shouting to them: "Do decorate the man and the horse—you need not pay for it!" Although trivial in themselves, such descriptions keep the narrative going and help to create a world of its own.[14]

There is the trend in the epics to use constant epithets, that is to qualify a certain noun with a certain adjective. In Russian *byliny* a horse is called "good" and a field "open." A birch tree, day, swan,

12. Matti Kuusi, "Über Wiederholungstypen in der Volksepik," *Studia Fennica* 4 (Helsinki, 1952), 77 ff.; Milman Parry, coll., and Albert B. Lord, ed., *Serbocroatian Heroic Songs* 1: *Novi Pazar: English Translations* (Cambridge and Belgrade, 1954), pp. 79–80.
13. Chadwick, p. 92.
14. C. M. Bowra, *Heroic Poetry* (London, 1964), pp. 197–214; Maximilian Braun, *Das serbokroatische Heldenlied* (Opera slavica 1; Göttingen, 1961), pp. 62–72.

and tent are invariably "white," a table and gate are "high," a sun and gold are "red," a wolf and goose "gray," and the steppe, road, and yard "broad." In Yugoslav epics the day is "white," the sky "clear," and the earth "black." The courts are always "white," the castles and towers "white" or "slender," the towns and sheep "white" or "brilliant white."

Epithets are used if the typical quality of certain beings or things is to be emphasized. If, however, a nontypical characterization is intended, the constant epithets are replaced by individual epithets. For instance, a peasant girl in Russian *byliny* is normally referred to as "beautiful." When Prince Vladimir intends to get married, a suitable candidate is described to him in special terms, avoiding the epithet "beautiful."[15]

Comparisons are occasionally used in the epic songs. The Great Idol is described in a Russian *bylina* as having "Great eyes, like bowls, a great hand, like a rake." Of someone's moustache it is said in the Yugoslav epic: "He looked as if he had a black lamb between his teeth," or "The breast armor shines through the moustache as the moon through the pine forest." Typical of the Slavic epics are the so-called negative comparisons, e.g., in Russian:

> It's not thunder rolling, it's not rumble rumbling,
> It's Il'ja who is speaking to his father.

In Serbo-Croatian:

> Loud a grey-blue cuckoo-bird lamented
> On the hillock over Bijeljina;
> 'Twas no grey-blue cuckoo that lamented,
> But the mother of Orugdžic Meho.[16]

The historical epic songs use ornamentation and retardation much more sparingly than the heroic songs; therefore they are shorter and their pace is much quicker. They also avoid detailed descriptions of situations. It is their task not to paint pictures from the heroic world but to relate recent events.[17]

The singers do not learn songs by heart, but remember only the most characteristic turns of the song. They use a special technique of composition that makes rapid composing possible. The basis of this technique is the so-called formula ("a group of words that is regu-

15. P. D. Uxov, "Postojannye èpitety v bylinax kak sredstvo tipizacii i sozdanija obraza," V. V. Vinogradov *et al.*, eds., *Osnovnye problemy èposa vostočnyx slavjan* (Moscow, 1958), pp. 161–68.

16. Bowra, pp. 266–70.

17. Stief, p. 262.

larly employed under the same metrical conditions to express a given essential idea"), the key words of which can be replaced by others. The presentation of an epic song involves the process of constant substitution.[18]

The east European folk epic, like the epic in general, is composed not in stanzas but in single lines. The meter of the epic songs of individual nationalities varies. The line of Finnish epic songs is made up of four trochaic feet, that is, of eight syllables altogether. The quantity rules require that a short first syllable of a word not be used in the ictus position, and the long first syllable not be used in the non-ictus position. The Russian *bylina* verse is characterized by the presence of three or four dominant stresses, whereas the number of unstressed syllables is unimportant. The length of a *bylina* verse varies from eight syllables to as high as fourteen or fifteen. There is a tendency to end the verse with a dactylic cadence. The Yugoslav epic makes use of the ten-syllable trochaic lines (*deseterac*), with a caesura after the first four syllables. In former times, the so-called *bugarštica* verse of longer lines (14-18 syllables) was also used. The question of the relative chronology of the *deseterac* and *bugarštica* has not yet been solved.

Folk epic is chanted, usually to the accompaniment of some stringed instrument. In Finland and Karelia, epic songs were sung by men and women. There are data, primarily in older sources, about the singing of two men, while a third man accompanied them with the kantele. The singers were sitting and had their right hands joined. One of them, the fore-singer, sang until the third or the fourth foot of the line, when the other, the after-singer, joined him; they sang the line to the end. Then the after-singer repeated most of the line alone and was joined in the last foot by the fore-singer. The fore-singer sang the next line, and they alternated in this manner. The specific position taken by the singers and their cooperation may be a vestige of shaman activity. The fore-singer corresponded to the shaman and the after-singer to the shaman's helper. The function of the shaman's helper was to bring the shaman back from his trance.[19] Recent research has revealed that singing by one man or one woman has also been generally practiced in Karelia since olden times. Some songs belonged primarily to the repertoire of men singers and others to women singers; they were sung in gatherings of either sex.[20]

Singing epic songs in Finland and Karelia was in former times not

---

18. Albert B. Lord, *The Singer of Tales* (Cambridge, Mass., 1960), pp. 30–67.
19. Haavio, *Väinämöinen*, p. 132.
20. Leea Virtanen, *Kalevalainen laulutapa Karjalassa* (Suomi 113:1; Helsinki, 1968), pp. 39–41, 49–51.

a leisurely pastime, not art for art's sake, but an act of magical significance. These songs contained most sacred and powerful knowledge that could be used to influence man's life. Songs sung in connection with the spring and fall sowing were aimed at promoting the fertility of the fields, and those sung while hunting and fishing were aimed at increasing the game and catch.

Among the Slavs (except the Macedonians), epic songs were sung by an individual singer. In Russia, the oldest instrument used for the accompaniment was the *gusli*, an instrument originally of five to seven strings, later of about thirty strings. Afterward its place was taken by the balalaika—a stringed instrument with a triangular body. In some areas the balalaikas were used up to recent times, in others (Olonec) they went out of use some time ago. Only one or two monotonous tunes were known to the *bylina* singers.

The Russian epic songs were sung by both men and women. It is true that the women preferred to sing the so-called *byliny* ballads, ballads in bylina style, in which the women functioned prominently. There were places in Russia where the *byliny* were sung by men only when they were away from home for extended periods of time for fishing. Thus the women had no opportunity of hearing and learning them.

In Yugoslavia, the folk epic is sung by men to the *gusle*, an ancient violin-like instrument with one string, seldom with two strings. Very widespread there is also the singing of epic songs without any accompanying instrument, especially during travel and work.

The folk epic, which has inspired the Finns and Slavs for about a millennium or more, is now in its last gasp. The Finnish-Karelian epic songs suffered a decisive blow after the Winter War in 1940 and after the second World War, due to the extensive resettlement of the people from the areas incorporated into Russia. Similarly, in Russia, the introduction of the Soviet system in 1917 with its fundamental changes in the way of life of the people strongly accelerated the disappearance of the folk epic. In the 1930s and '40s, attempts were made in Russia to replace the "old songs" (*stariny*), as people used to call *byliny* and historical songs, with the so-called new songs (*noviny*). The latter eulogized the deeds of Soviet political and military leaders in the old, traditional form of *byliny*. The "new songs," however, did not gain currency among the singers and, right after the death of Stalin, they were discouraged as "not genuine folklore." The folk epic tradition is perhaps strongest in Yugoslavia, its last stronghold, where the partisan movement during the second World War was responsible for its revival.

Bibliography and Selected Readings

General

Bowra, C. M. *Heroic Poetry.* London: Macmillan and Co., 1964. The best and most comprehensive general survey of heroic epics. Analyzing the representative epics all over the world, the work purports to "provide a kind of anatomy of heroic poetry."

Chadwick, Hector M., and Nora K. Chadwick. *The Growth of Literature.* 3 vols. Cambridge: Cambridge University Press, 1932–40. Reprinted 1968. Although this work is a general survey of heroic folk literature in a number of countries, it concentrates especially on the epic and establishes some of its main characteristics. Considerably outdated.

Lord, Albert B. *The Singer of Tales.* Cambridge, Mass.: Harvard University Press, 1960. A significant study of the art of oral composition. The author (following Milman Parry) first establishes the principles of the oral ‘composition as used by the Yugoslav *guslars* and then applies this evidence to *The Iliad* and *The Odyssey* and several western European epics to prove their popular origin.

Vries, Jan de. *Heroic Song and Heroic Legend.* New York: Oxford University Press, 1963; Oxford Paperback, No. 69. The best general introduction to heroic epic. Gives surveys of several European and Asian epics and traces the underlying patterns of society and of the heroic life.

Žirmunskij, V. "Èpos slavjanskix narodov v sravnitel'no-istoričeskom osveš-čenii" [The Epic of the Slavic Peoples in the Comparative-Historical Interpretation]. *Narodnyj geroičeskij èpos.* Moscow and Leningrad: Gosudarstvennoe izdatel'stvo xudožestvennoj literatury, 1962. Pp. 75–194. A stimulating comparative discussion of epic songs. Similarities between Slavic and other epic songs are shown as being typological rather than genetic. The work is available also in German translation: Viktor Schirmunski, *Vergleichende Epenforschung* [The Comparative Study of the Epic]. I. Berlin: Akademie-Verlag, 1961.

Finnish Epic

Haavio, Martti. *Kirjokansi: Suomen kansan kertomarunoutta* [The Patterned Cover: Epic Poetry of the Finnish People]. Porvoo and Helsinki: Werner Söderström, 1952. A comprehensive anthology of Finnish epic songs for the general public. The song texts are slightly modified to comply with the normal structural pattern as established by the editor. Though the selection has primarily esthetic goals, the comments attached contain results of scholarly research on each song.

———. *Väinämöinen: Eternal Sage.* Folklore Fellows Communications, 144. Helsinki: Suomalainen Tiedeakatemia, 1952. A penetrating study of the central figure of the old songs of the Finnish people. Analyzing the more important songs of Väinämöinen and the milieu reflected in them, and making use of extensive comparative material from all over the world, Haavio modifies considerably the concept of Väinämöinen that had prevailed.

Krohn, Kaarle. *Kalevalastudien* [Kalevala Studies], 1–4. Folklore Fellows Communications, 53, 67, 71, 72, 75, 76. Helsinki: Suomalainen Tiedeakatemia, 1924–28. Contains the sum total of Kaarle Krohn's studies on ancient Finnish folk poetry. Although Krohn's underlying theory of the historicity of the Kalevala songs has been refuted by later scholars, the work has still preserved its value as the most detailed over-all study on the Finnish epic.

Kuusi, Matti. *Sampo-eepos: Typologinen analyysi* [The Sampo Epic: A Typological Analysis], Mémoires de la Société Finno-ougrienne, 96. Helsinki: Suomalais-ugrilainen Seura, 1949. A meticulous typological study of five songs, the so-called *Sampo* epic, that constitute the epic kernel of the *Kalevala*. Applying primarily an analysis of style and using data on the history of colonization, the author establishes the mutual relations between these songs and their chronology.

———. "Varhaiskalevalainen runous" and "Sydänkalevalainen epiikka ja lyriikka" ["The Early Kalevala Poetry" and "The Peak Period of the Kalevala Epics and Lyrics"]. Matti Kuusi, ed., *Suomen kirjallisuus*: 1: *Kirjoittamaton kirjallisuus*. Helsinki: Suomalaisen Kirjallisuuden Seura and Otava, 1963. Pp. 129–272. A good up-to-date survey of Finnish epic and lyric songs, presented against the broad Finno-Ugric and Baltic background.

Russian Epic

Astaxova, A. M. *Byliny: Itogi i problemy izučenija* [Byliny: The Results and the Problems of Their Study]. Moscow and Leningrad: Nauka, 1966. A critical discussion of studies on *byliny* published primarily in the Soviet Unon.

———. *Russkij bylinnyj èpos na severe* [The Russian Bylina Epic in the North]. Petrozavodsk: Gosudarstvennoe izdatel'stvo Karelo-Finskoj SSR, 1948. An important work on Russian *byliny*. Unlike the leading pre-revolutionary folklorists, Astaxova studies the *byliny* not as archaic, stagnant phenomena but as living processes. Analyzing the *bylina* tradition of the last one hundred fifty years, she establishes basic laws pertaining to the creative process of the folk epic and considers the significance of the environment and the influence of written literature on the *byliny*.

Chadwick, Nora K. *Russian Heroic Poetry*. New York: Russell and Russell, 1964. A collection of Russian *byliny* and historical songs, in English translation, first published in 1932. The introduction and headnotes are partly outdated.

Propp, V. Ja. *Russkij geroičeskij èpos* [The Russian Heroic Epic]. 2nd ed; Moscow: Gosudarstvennoe izdatel'stvo xudožestvennoj literatury, 1958. In this work Propp, following Belinskij, endeavors to formulate the basic idea of each *bylina,* contending that the idea of a *bylina* expresses the ideals of the corresponding epoch. Numerous assertions are disputable.

Skaftymov, A. P. *Poètika i genezis bylin: Očerki* [The Poetics and Genesis of Byliny: Essays]. Moscow and Saratov: Knigoizdatel'stvo V. Z. Jaksanova, 1924. A formalistic study that emphasizes the significance of the investigation of *bylina* structure over that of ideology. The central portion was republished in Skaftymov's *Stat'i o russkoj literature*. Saratov: Saratovskoe knižnoe izdatel'stvo, 1958. Pp. 3–76.

Sokolov, Y. M. "The Byliny" and "Historical Songs." *Russian Folklore*. Hatboro, Pa.: Folklore Associates, 1966. Pp. 291–370. Good general surveys of *byliny* and historical songs, with useful bibliographies.

Stief, Carl. *Studies in the Russian Historical Song*. Copenhagen: Rosenkilde and Bagger, 1953. A collection of important essays on Russian historical songs.

Trautmann, Reinhold. *Die Volksdichtung der Grossrussen* 1: *Das Heldenlied (Die Byline)* [The Folk Poetry of the Great Russians, 1: The Heroic Song (The Bylina)]. Heidelberg: Carl Winter, 1935. A comprehensive, though somewhat outdated, survey of Russian *byliny*. While the first part deals with *bylina* genre in general, the second gives German translations (slightly abbreviated) and comments on individual *byliny*. Trautmann tends to assign a later origin to a number of *byliny* than do the majority of *bylina* scholars.

Yugoslav Epic

Braun, Maximilian. *Das serbokroatische Heldenlied* [The Serbo-Croatian Heroic Song]. Opera slavica, 1; Göttingen: Vandenhoeck and Ruprecht, 1961. The best survey of the Yugoslav heroic epic. The first part gives the general background and characteristics of the heroic epic, and the second discusses themes and individual songs.

Burkhart, Dagmar. *Untersuchungen zur Stratigraphie und Chronologie der südslavischen Volksepik* [Studies of the Stratigraphy and Chronology of the South Slavic Folk Epic]. Slavistische Beiträge, 33; Munich: Otto Sagner, 1968. The work concentrates on the epic songs of the Macedonian and West Bulgarian region, supposedly the most archaic in the entire South Slavic area. Two themes—the dragon fight and heroic wooing—are examined in detail.

Maretić, Tomo. *Naša narodna epika* [Our Folk Epic]. 2d ed. Belgrade: Nolit, 1966. First published in 1909, this work surveys the Yugoslav epic in the framework of philology. Though partly antiquated, it is still one of the most important sources for the identification of historical personages appearing in epic songs.

Murko, Matija. *Tragom srpsko-hrvatske narodne epike* [In the Footsteps of the Serbocroatian Folk Epic] 1–2. Djela Jugoslavenske akademije znanosti i umjetnosti, 41–42; Zagreb: Jugoslavenska akademija znanosti i umjetnosti, 1951. A report of Murko's field trips in Yugoslavia from 1930 to 1932, supplemented with factual material drawn from literature. It gives a broad picture of the state of Yugoslav epic between the two World Wars. Concentrates especially on the singers.

Nazečić, Salko. *Iz naše narodne epike* [About Our Folk Epic]. Sarajevo: Svjetlost, 1959. A study of history and folklore—of the *hajduks'* fights in the neighborhood of Dubrovnik and of the folksongs about them.

Abundant examples of the process of dehistoricization of later songs and of the trend toward the idealization of *hajduks* as time goes on.

Parry, Milman, coll., and Albert B. Lord, ed. *Serbocroatian Heroic Songs* 1: *Novi Pazar: English Translations.* Cambridge and Belgrade: Harvard University Press and the Serbian Academy of Sciences, 1954. ———. *Srpskohrvatske junacke pjesme* 2: *Novi Pazar: Srpskohrvatski tekstovi* [Serbocroatian Heroic Songs, 2: *Novi Pazar: Serbocroatian Texts*]. Belgrade and Cambridge: Srpska akademija nauka and Harvard University Press, 1953. The first two volumes of a promised monumental series of Serbo-Croatian heroic songs. The second volume contains the original Serbian texts of thirty-two songs recorded in Novi Pazar (Serbia), and the first volume the English translations. The collection is arranged as a field report grouped according to the singers. Each section begins with a conversation between the recorder and the singer, which is followed by the song texts.

Schmaus, A. *Studije o krajinskoj epici* [Studies on the Krajina Epic]. Rad Jugoslavenske akademije znanosti i umjetnosti, 297; Zagreb: Jugoslavenska akademija znanosti i umjetnosti, 1953. A detailed study of the incipient structural transformation of the epic of Krajina (northwestern Bosnia). A condensed version of this work with some additions was published in German under the title "Episierungsprozesse im Bereich der slavischen Volksdichtung" ["The Processes of Epic Development in the Area of Slavic Folk Song"] in *Münchener Beiträge zur Slavenkunde: Festgabe für Paul Diels*. Veröffentlichungen des Osteuropa-Institutes München, IV; Munich: Isar Verlag, 1953, pp. 294–320.

4 PROVERBS AND PROVERBIAL EXPRESSIONS
Roger D. Abrahams

Proverbs are one of the most easily observed and collected genres of traditional expression, yet one of the least understood. This misunderstanding is due, perhaps, to their very familiarity; we tend to take more note of things exotic or unusual, and proverbs have remained a part of the verbal resources of sophisticated Western cultures long after larger oral genres either have been forgotten or have developed into the complex forms of "modern" literature.

This misunderstanding is in some degree due to the long history of proverb collections in print. In fact, many of the earliest and most popular of books were collections of proverbs, the most notable being Erasmus's bestseller of the early Renaissance, the *Copia*. Such works may have been occasioned in part by the apprehension concerning the loss of the oral arts (in this case, oratory) attendant upon technological innovations like the printing press. But the compilers of these encyclopedic works were recognizing some of the most important attributes of the print medium—its usefulness in ordering a wide range of materials in a permanent manner—and were therefore

using proverbs as they did other data, as information to be encyclo-
pedically handled. But these collections were more than encyclo-
pedias of *sententiae*. They were also educationally useful in two ways:
as repositories of wisdom to be learned by the young courtier, and
(most important) as devices to be learned and used by fledgling
orators.[1]

Almost immediately, belletrists saw more to proverbs than just useful oral devices, however. As early as 1546 John Heywood's *A Dialogue
of Proverbs* developed a witty poetic tradition of devising whole
poems and songs from these sayings, a tradition drawn upon for hundreds of years by many poets, serious and popular, including Gilbert
and Sullivan and many American minstrel performers. More importantly, from the proverb developed the tradition of the literary epi-
gram, the occasional short verse in which the same kind of moral
point is made, but because of the change in the medium, from a face-
to-face to a reading experience, its application to a situation had to
be indicated either in a title or within the verse. This was almost
surely the most important influence on the development of the heroic
couplet, which has in turn provided a number of proverbs in oral
currency—like Pope's "To err is human, to forgive divine."

Given this beginning to the history of proverb-collecting, it is
hardly surprising that it was carried on primarily in encyclopedic
form and with a great deal of borrowing from one compilation to the
next. No amount of novelty was necessarily called for, nor any reference to the actual oral currency of the *sententiae* reported. Rather, the
books continued to act as reference works for those who wanted to
appear wise in public statements; wisdom and wit are therefore
stressed in these works, and sayings are added from a wide variety of
traditions throughout the world.

With the development of the folklore movement in the nineteenth
century, another kind of collection came into existence in addition to
these reference works of wisdom. Growing out of comparative philological study, with its strong focus on rural (archaic) dialects, the
study of proverbs, or paroemiology, came to be recognized as one of
the most conservative features of such talk, and therefore texts were
widely collected and included in most of the tremendous number of
dialect dictionaries that emerged during that century. Eventually
whole works were given over to the genre, such as the books on Scottish proverbs by Hislop and Henderson, the English volumes by
Wright and Lean, and, in this century in the United States, the dictionaries (made up of materials culled primarily from past litera-

1. For a discussion of these usages see Walter J. Ong, S. J., "Oral Residue in
Tudor Prose Style," *PMLA* 80 (1965) : 145–54.

tures) of Tilley, Taylor and Whiting, Jente, Arora, Brunvand, and others.

In spite of the tremendous number of texts that have been assembled, we still know little of why and how people use proverbs, or anything of the range of social uses and cultural situations in which they are encountered. Taylor's *The Proverb* remains the best introduction to the subject (and a very good one indeed), but primarily it surveys the different types of English-language proverbs and proverbial phrases encountered in the literature. One must therefore go to the ethnographic reporting of Firth, Herzog, Messenger, Seitel, and Arewa and Dundes[2] to derive insight into the actual patterns of use of proverbs. This type of reportage is crucial to an understanding of proverbs because these studies are carried on within societies in which proverbs are used in the educational and juridical systems of the groups described rather than as argument-markers and intensifiers of conversation as they are commonly used throughout Europe. That is, proverbs must be studied within groups which use them if we are to understand why so many diverse peoples have been attracted to such sententious inventions. There are, however, certain remarks that can be made about proverbs in general simply because they are sententious, witty, and used to embody wisdom.

Proverbs are short and witty traditional expressions that arise as part of everyday discourse as well as in the more highly structured situations of education and judicial proceedings. Each proverb is a full statement of an approach to a recurrent problem. It presents a point of view and a strategy that is self-sufficient, needing nothing more than an event of communication to bring it into play. (For a fuller discussion of proverb strategy see my "Introductory Remarks To a Rhetorical Theory of Folklore.")[3] Proverbs take a personal circumstance and embody it in impersonal and witty form. Proverbs are nearly always stated in the form of a single sentence. They are among the shortest forms of traditional expression that call attention to themselves as formal artistic entities. As artful, and therefore artificial and witty, items of discourse, proverbs use all of the devices we commonly associate with poetry in English: meter, binary construction and balanced phrasing, rhyme, assonance and alliteration, conciseness, metaphor, and occasional inverted word order and unusual construction.

2. E. Ojo Arewa and Alan Dundes, "Proverbs and the Ethnography of Speaking," *American Anthropologist* 66 (1964) : 70–85; Raymond Firth, "Proverbs in Native Life," *Folk-Lore* 37 (1926) : 134–53, 245–70; George Herzog, *Jabo Proverbs from Liberia,* London, 1936; John C. Messenger, "The Role of Proverbs in a Nigerian Judicial System," *Southwestern Journal of Anthropology* 15 (1959) : 64–73; Peter Seitel, "Proverbs: A Social Use of Metaphor," *Genre* 2 (1969) : 143–61.

3. *Journal of American Folklore* 81 (1968) : 143–58.

It is primarily the pronounced effect of balance that produces the witty effect of the proverb, and this balance arises most notably from a binary (two-part) composition. The proverb is generally a sentence that is perceptibly broken in the middle. (The break is called a *caesura.*)

A stitch in time/saves nine.

The length of the sentence generally conforms to the common length of a line of folk verse. In English, this means not a set number of syllables but rather a line of four stresses (a measurement usually called *isochronic*) broken into two parts, each involving one primary (') and one secondary (") stress. Each part is commonly called a *dipod* (literally "two feet").

      "   '   "   '
A rolling stone/gathers no moss.
/_____ (dipod) _____/ /___ (dipod) _____/

This two-part effect is often underscored by having the two dipods rhyme:

An apple a day/keeps the doctor away.

Occasionally a proverb will develop these techniques into a longer pronouncement, encompassing two or more lines.

A dog, a woman, a walnut tree—
The more you beat 'em, the better they be.

This unusual saying illustrates some of the other poetic techniques noted, specifically the use of alliteration (". . . *b*eat them, *b*etter they *b*e.") and the uncommon final grammatical construction.

Many of the most widely known and interesting proverbs tell a condensed story; these items often function metaphorically when used in a conversational context. That is, in the proverb "People who live in glass houses should not throw stones" we are given an image suggestive of a story, but the comparing effect of the metaphor is not present. Yet when this proverb is used it does imply that the person in the glass house is to be compared to the one to whom the saying is directed.

Up to now we have been looking at proverbs primarily on the level of language—in terms of ordered sounds and rhythms. We have seen that the most salient features of this genre revolve around its concise binary construction. This principle also operates in the area of meaning. A proverb is a description made up of two or more elements, and these elements often conform to the two parts of the balanced structure. These two or more elements are usually tied together either by a verb of equivalence or a verb of causation. And the relationship between the elements may be rendered positively or negatively. Thus, there are four common types of proverbs.

> 1) positive equivalence
>   Time is money.
> 2) negative equivalence
>   Money isn't everything.
> 3) positive causational
>   Haste makes waste.
> 4) negative causational
>   Two wrongs don't make a right.[4]

These four types may be compounded by the addition of modifiers. Further, not all proverbs fully state their descriptive proposition; one element may simply be implied.

The binary construction of proverbs has been emphasized because the clear relationship of the two parts is one of the primary means by which the strategy of clarification is put into effect. Proverbs are descriptions that propose an attitude or a mode of action in relation to a recurrent social situation. They attempt to persuade by clarifying the situation, by giving it a name, thus indicating that the problem has arisen before and that past practice has come up with a workable solution. The appearance of clarification is produced by casting the proverb in witty form, and the most apparent form of the wit is the effect of balance. As opposed to riddles (which are also descriptions) in which the elements of the description are not cast in an easily understood relationship, the two or more parts of the proverbial description are immediately and observably related. And the feeling of relationship is commonly provided by the equational or causational verb between the two elements. This provides a sense of verbal stability that seems to be transferred to the social situation that is being named and commented upon by the proverb.

This does not mean that all proverbs attempt to produce an action immediately. Many proverbs rather attempt to produce an attitude toward a situation that may well call for inaction and resignation. This is the usual use for proverbs like "Such is life" and "Don't cry over spilt milk." We can distinguish two kinds of occasions, then, in which proverbs attack ethical problems: one, in which a proverb is used to direct future activity; and two, in which a proverb is invoked to alter an attitude toward something that has already occurred. In either case, the proverb places the problem situation in a recognizable category by providing a solution in traditional witty terms.

---

4. This typology was worked out in discussions with Alan Dundes and derives in part (as does some of the following argument) from Dundes and Georges's study of the structure of true riddles, noted in the chapter on riddling.

Proverbs work, in other words, because they *seem* to embody the wisdom of the past. "Seem" is emphasized because it is the appearance of collective wisdom that is the most important of the persuasive characteristics of proverbs. Proverbs work because they make the problem seem less personal, by showing that situations like this have occurred before. This impersonalization is achieved not only by the casting of the description in witty and traditional terms, but by using what seems to be an objective frame of reference. This appearance of objectivity is achieved by the use of abstract terms ("*Honesty* is the best *policy*," "Neither a *borrower* nor a *lender* be") or by illustrative concretions ("While the cat's away, the mice will play;" "A new broom sweeps clean"). When abstractions are used, the argument is overtly didactic; concrete illustrations argue more obliquely. When a personal pronoun is used, as in "You can't get blood out of a turnip" or "You can lead a horse to water but you can't make him drink," the pronoun is essentially translatable to the impersonal "one."

Perhaps the more interesting of the depersonalizing effects is the use of concrete illustrations. Often these seem to tell a capsule story ("A drowning man will catch at any straw"). There are certain proverbs that actually refer to a traditional story without telling it. They rely on the knowledge of the story by the hearer ("He's just crying 'Wolf' "; "That's only sour grapes"). Such proverbs add a dramatic dimension to their repertoire of effects.

This dramatic projection is also utilized by that special type of proverb called the *Wellerism* (after Dickens's Sam Weller who often used the form). The proverb or cliché is imputed to have been uttered by a specified speaker. The most common Wellerisms in contemporary English parlance are versions of " 'I see,' said the blind man as he picked up his hammer and saw," and " 'There's no disputing taste,' said the old woman as she kissed the cow." This dialog-proverb form is really a joking device in English, but in many African and New World Negro groups Wellerisms are used for less jocular purposes. West Indians, for instance, have many proverbs like "Jack-spanner [wasp] say 'Me wais' so small, but I make the biggest man bawl,' " and "Crapeau [frog] say, 'Wha' fun to you is deat' to me.' " Such Wellerisms are structurally different from the "I see" type. In the jocular type the speaker is announced after the saying, and before in the "serious" part. The speaker provides the occasion of the humorous invention in the former, but in the latter he provides a short-hand stock characterization (the wasp as the conventional "little-big man").

The two types differ mostly in how they affect the proverb proper. The serious type intensifies the wit and the impersonality of the proverb; the joking sort resuscitates a cliché that otherwise might seem too "corny" to introduce into conversation. The latter, then, exist in a milieu that has become somewhat antagonistic to the use of proverbs, an attitude widely observable in sophisticated cultures. It is strongly felt in many groups today that those who use proverbs do so because of an inability to converse effectively in any other way. This attitude goes back at least to Shakespeare's day, for he put effusions of proverbs into the dialog of fatuous comic characters such as Polonius (in his farewell speech to Laertes) and Jaques ("All the world's a stage . . .").

But as the Wellerism shows, we have found self-conscious ways of resuscitating proverbs so that we may continue to use this technique of persuasion. There have been other humorous conventions developed to keep sayings alive, such as the "echo proverbs" as Frances Barbour calls them. This calls for the addition of a qualifying or "echo" line to a proverb to turn it into a joke.

> An apple a day keeps the doctor away;
> An onion a day keeps everyone away.

There is some question as to whether such inventions should be called proverbs since their strategy seems to differ so completely from that of clarification.

The study of proverbs has been severely complicated by the grouping of conventional conversational devices that share almost nothing but their brevity and their traditional currency. Almost certainly this complication is due to the fact that proverb dictionaries were written not for the purpose of defining this genre but for storing any device useful in developing oratory techniques. Thus these compendia contained not only true proverbs but hyperbolizing devices, such as traditional exaggerations, that were useful in ornamenting extemporized formal speech.

Conversation rather than oration is the most common milieu for both proverbs and conventional intensifiers. While proverbs are often used to flavor conversation or oration, they are self-contained units; they have a moral weight of their own and an argument that is virtually self-sufficient. On the other hand, the formulaic intensifiers exist for no other reason than to decorate speech. These are devices of hyperbole; they take an ongoing argument and lend it wit and color. As noted, these conventional exaggerations are often called proverbial, but they are like proverbs only insofar as they are conventional and commonly arise in conversational contexts. They are really the most formulaic elements of folk speech.

There are a number of formulas observable in English parlance. The most common of these are proverbial similes—"as right as rain," "as sly as a fox"—and comparisons—"like a bat out of hell," "like a madman on the loose." Given their hyperbolic status, such sayings are subject to expansion, given the proper context. Thus, the widely observed "slow as molasses in January" in tall-tale telling and anecdotal situations often becomes "slow as molasses in January running uphill . . . backward."

The more modifiers added, the more vivid the picture created. Images are even more elaborate and humorous in another formulaic type, ones that begin "He's so ——— that ———." Though most of these are simply colorful, as in "She's so ugly her face would stop a clock," some suggest an anecdotal (usually numskull) situation: "He's so dumb he couldn't pour piss out of a boot even if the instructions were printed on the heel."

Beside these formulaic intensifiers there is a multitude of other adjectival phrases that are sometimes referred to as proverbial. These phrases are like the other intensifiers in their use of conventional images to produce colorful effects. Phrases of folk speech of this sort include "a snake in the grass," "a chip off the old block," "blow your own trumpet," "a bad egg" and "bury the hatchet." But, as noted for the other intensifying devices, their rhetorical function is quite unlike that of true proverbs.

Bibliography and Selected Readings

Arewa, E. Ojo, and Alan Dundes. "Proverbs and the Ethnography of Speaking." *American Anthropologist* 66 (1964) : No. 6, Part 2, 70–85. Discusses proverbs as communication and stresses the need to study the function of proverbs in a given society. Includes texts and explanations of function in the society of twelve Yoruba proverbs. Contains a short bibliography.

Bohn, Henry George. *A Handbook of Proverbs.* London, 1855. Important nineteenth-century collection, still widely cited as a reference work. Contains English and non-English proverbs. There is an alphabetical listing of the proverbs, and a reprint of Fuller's *Worthies of England,* but otherwise few notes.

Bonser, Wilfrid, and T. A. Stevens. *Proverb Literature.* London, 1930. A bibliography of works relating to the proverb. Most material deals with European proverbs, but other areas are included. Works are arranged alphabetically under topographical divisions. There are over 4,000 entries and an index.

Brunvand, Jan H. *Dictionary of Proverbs and Proverbial Phrases from Books Published by Indiana Authors before 1890.* Indiana University Folklore Series, No. 15. Bloomington: Indiana University Press, 1961. A collection of proverbial material excerpted from ninety-five books. R. E. Banta's bibliography of Indiana writers served as a guide. The introduction attempts to identify general sources for the material. Contains about 1,500 items.

Firth, Raymond. "Proverbs in Native Life, with Special Reference to those of the Maori." *Folk-Lore* 37 (1926) : 134–53, 245–70. Contains native texts of approximately fifty Maori proverbs and explains their functions in Maori society. Examines economic proverbs in relation to moral concepts and origins of the proverbs.

Hazlitt, William Carew. *English Proverbs and Proverbial Phases.* London, 1882. Hazlitt includes in the several thousand entries only true proverbs, and arranges them in alphabetical order. The introduction gives a good discussion of earlier proverb literature. Contains notes regarding origin, history, and meaning.

Herzog, George. *Jabo Proverbs from Liberia.* London, 1936. A collection of nearly five hundred proverbs and proverbial sayings from the Jabo tribe of Eastern Liberia. Includes a short phonetic key to the Jabo language, a fifteen-page introduction and a comparison of Jabo and Kru proverbs. The native text is given, followed by a literal translation, a translation into coherent English, and where available, an explanation of the meaning and function of the proverb in Jabo society.

Hulme, Frederick Edward. *Proverb Lore.* London, 1902. A comprehensive study dealing with definition, historical aspect, structure, and the "power" of proverbs as a form of speech. Notes early collectors and users of proverbs from Solomon through Erasmus and Shakespeare to Franklin.

Krappe, Alexander H. "Proverbs." *The Science of Folklore.* New York: W. W. Norton, 1964. A good short introduction to the proverb form, dealing with the problems of definition, origin, and the presence of contradictory proverbs in a given society.

Lean, Vincent Stuckey. *Lean's Collectanea.* 4 vols. Bristol and London, 1902. A vast compilation of miscellanies including proverbs, similes, archaic expressions, aphorisms, common beliefs, and local and domestic sayings. British material predominates, but some continental European items are included.

Messenger, John. "The Role of Proverbs in a Nigerian Judicial System." *Southwestern Journal of Anthropology* 15 (1959) : 64–73. Gives examples of proverbs used as legal arguments in trial proceedings among the Anang Ibibio.

Marvin, Dwight Edwards. *The Antiquity of Proverbs.* New York and London, 1922. An intelligent introduction written for the general reader. The author discusses the long history of proverbs, their former importance as constituting a living ethic, methods by which proverbs become traditional, and reasons for change and for decline of usage. Contains detailed treatments of several proverbs, including the meaning (as understood by the author), a history, and a list of variants and related proverbs.

Partridge, Eric. *A Dictionary of Clichés.* London: George Routledge, 1940. Attempts to distinguish between proverbs and clichés. Origins are researched. Pleasant reading.

Proverbium. 1965–. A bulletin issued in serial numbers by the Finnish Literature Society, Helsinki, devoted to articles, notes, and reports on research in proverb scholarship, in English, French, German, and Russian.

Randolph, Vance, and George P. Wilson. *Down in the Holler: A Gallery of Ozark Folk Speech.* Norman: University of Oklahoma Press, 1953. The chapter on "Wisecracks and Sayings" is one of the best treatments of proverbial material in print. The sayings are presented with indications of usage and social context; origin is explained in some cases. Attempts at explanation of meaning are given for readers who are not hill folk.

Roback, Abraham Aaron. *A Dictionary of Ethnophaulisms.* Cambridge: Sci-Art Publishers, 1944. A dictionary of slang and proverbial phrases that utilize national stereotypes for their metaphors or that are used to characterize national or racial "types." A study of the folklore of prejudice follows the collection. Includes a bibliography, index and register of personal names.

Seitel, Peter. "Proverbs: A Social Use of Metaphor." *Genre* 2 (1969) : 143–61. An application of the ethnography-of-speaking concept to proverb analysis.

Smith, William George, and Janet E. Heseltine, eds. *Oxford Dictionary of English Proverbs.* Oxford: Clarendon Press, 1948. A vast compilation of proverbial material from English literary sources, ranging from poetic and dramatic works to actual proverb collections. The proverbs are arranged alphabetically with variants listed chronologically under each heading. Probably the most useful collection of English language proverbs and proverbial phrases.

Stevenson, Burton Egbert. *The Home Book of Proverbs, Maxims, and Familiar Phrases.* New York: Macmillan, 1948. A 2,957-page collection containing entries from international sources. Entries are arranged by subject headings, sources are given, variations are listed chronologically. Includes an index.

Taylor, Archer, and B. J. Whiting. *A Dictionary of American Proverbs and Proverbial Phrases, 1820–1880.* Cambridge, Mass.: Harvard University Press, Belknap Press, 1958. A major compendium compiled from literary sources published between the dates given in the title. The editors point out difficulties encountered when dealing with proverbs, especially that of definition. Key words are listed alphabetically; proverbs using a key word are arranged under it and are numbered. The literary source of each is cited.

——. "Proverb." *Standard Dictionary of Folklore, Mythology and Legend.* Edited by Maria Leach. 2 vols. New York: Funk and Wagnalls, 1950. Clearly the best published short introduction to proverbs. Defines proverb, explains types of proverb structure, compares proverbs to clichés, toasts, and *blason populaire.*

——. *The Proverb and Index to "The Proverb."* Hatboro, Pa.: Folklore Associates; Copenhagen: Rosenkilde and Bagger, 1962. The most valuable study of the proverb genre in English. Four major sections take up origins, content, style, and, lastly, proverbial phrases, comparisons, and Wellerisms. Taylor includes proverbs of many European languages. The index section lists, according to languages, all the proverbs and proverbial expressions in the book. References to sources and parallel material are given.

——. *Proverbial Comparisons and Similes from California.* University of California Publications Folklore Series, No. 3. Berkeley and Los Angeles: University of California Press, 1954. An important collection of proverbial comparisons in English, consisting of about one thousand entries, carefully cross-referenced. Copious notes give references to other collections and a variety of literary works.

——. "Proverbial Phrases." *Standard Dictionary of Folklore, Mythology and Legend.* Edited by Maria Leach. 2 vols. New York: Funk and Wagnalls, 1950. Distinguishes proverbial phrases from proverbs, discusses allusions in several common English proverbial phrases, notes the difficulty of distinguishing between proverbial expressions and idioms.

——. "Wellerisms." *Standard Dictionary of Folklore, Mythology and Legend.* Edited by Maria Leach. 2 vols. New York: Funk and Wagnalls, 1950. Definition by discussion of examples. Divides Wellerisms into three classes, those quoting familiar proverbs, those using a generalized figure as the speaker, and those using a specific figure as a speaker. Discusses original forms.

Tilley, Morris Palmer. *A Dictionary of the Proverbs in England in the Sixteenth and Seventeenth Centuries: A Collection of the Proverbs Found in English Literature and the Dictionaries of the Period.* Ann Arbor: University of Michigan Press, 1950. Compilation of proverbs drawn from hundreds of printed sources, including Shakespeare. The several thousand entries are alphabetically arranged. Sources are listed and cross-references to related proverbs are given.

Whiting, B. J. "The Nature of the Proverb." *Harvard University Studies and Notes in Philology and Literature* 14 (1932) : 273–307. An excellent treatment of the definition and the history of attempts at definition of the proverb from Aristotle to the present. States that we must make distinctions between proverbs, proverbial phrases, and *sententiae.*

——. "The Origin of the Proverb." *Harvard University Studies and Notes in Philology and Literature* 13 (1931) : 47–80. Whiting believes that to study the proverb-making process we must examine proverbs in present-day "primitive" societies. Existence and importance of proverbs in a variety of these societies, mostly African, are noted. Whiting assumes that earlier stages of our own civilization can be seen in "primitive" cultures.

5 RIDDLES
Roger D. Abrahams and
Alan Dundes

Before attempting a brief survey of riddle forms, Anglo-American riddle forms in particular, it might be well to indicate some of the sources of riddle scholarship. Two useful bibliographies are Archer Taylor, *A Bibliography of Riddles* (1939), and Aldo Santi, *Bibliografia delle Enigmistica* (1952). The riddle is one of the best-attested ancient folklore genres with numerous examples in Greek, Latin, Hebrew, and Sanskrit traditions. (Examples and important collections are discussed in J. B. Friedreich, *Geschichte des Rätsels* [1860], and Archer Taylor, *The Literary Riddle Before 1600* [1948].) Indicative of the early interest in the riddle are Aristotle's comments on the relationship between riddle and metaphor, e.g., in *The Rhetoric,* Book III, Chapter 2 and *The Poetics,* XXII.

Since the beginnings of folkloristics in the nineteenth century, riddle studies have generally followed the main direction of folklore scholarship. Comparative investigations were encouraged by Karl Müllenhoff in 1855 and Gaston Paris in 1877, but may have reached their high point with Antti Aarne's remarkable comparative studies of individual riddles (1918–20), inasmuch as there have been relatively few thorough studies of single riddles since Aarne's work (but see Kozumplik's 1941 essay). An innovation in riddle classification was made by Argentinian folklorist Robert Lehmann-Nitsche, who in his 1911 collection *Adivinanzas rioplatenses* made the nature of the comparison (e.g., comparisons to animals, to plants, and so on) the basis of the classification rather than the nature of the solutions or answers. Lehmann-Nitsche's system was used by the Swedish folklorist von Sydow in 1915 and later by Archer Taylor in his superb collection *English Riddles from Oral Tradition* (1951).

The modern analysis of the stylistic features of the riddle may be said to have started with the 1899 dissertation by Robert Petsch, *Neue Beiträge zur Kenntnis des Volksrätsels*. Other formalistic studies have continued to the present time.

The European-literary approach to riddles has tended to emphasize questions of origins, diffusion, classification, and form. An excellent introduction to this approach is Mathilde Hain, *Rätsel* (1966), while Laurits Bødker, *The Nordic Riddle: Terminology and Bibliography* (1964), demonstrates the great concern with genre and subgenre definition. Generally speaking, the functions of riddles are rarely considered, and it is principally to the contributions of anthropologists that anyone seriously interested in riddle context and use must turn. Representative of this scholarship is Donn V. Hart, *Riddles in Filipino Folklore: An Anthropological Analysis* (1964).

It is tempting to restrict a survey of riddles to "true riddles," that is, enigmatic questions in the form of descriptions whose referent must be guessed. From a Western literary point of view, these are the most interesting for they employ witty devices in order to confuse. They compare disparate traits discontinuously and call for a flash of recognition when the referent of the description is given and continuity is established. But in communities in which riddling is actively practiced, all sorts of enigmatic questions are posed. We will describe the more common types in English, since a number of the most important types found internationally have been reported in this language.

Riddles are questions that are framed with the purpose of confusing or testing the wits of those who do not know the answer. They are commonly called forth during "riddling sessions"—special occasions during which such witty devices may be used in a properly playful contest situation. Georges and Dundes (see bibliography) point to the most important technique of confusion in the construction of riddles when they emphasize the importance of establishing internal contradictions or "oppositions" within the riddling description. Abrahams, in a further study (see bibliography), demonstrates that opposition is only the most salient of four techniques by which the image (or *Gestalt*) presented in the riddle-question is impaired and therefore is, in most cases, undecipherable. These techniques are:

1. opposition—*Gestalt* is impaired because the component parts of the presented image do not harmonize.
2. incomplete detail—not enough information is given for proper *Gestalt* to be made (i.e., for the parts to fit together).
3. too much detail—the important traits are buried in the midst of inconsequential detail, thus "scrambling" *Gestalt*.
4. false *Gestalt*—details are provided that lead to an ability to discern a referent, and thus call for an answer, but the answer is wrong. This answer is often an embarrassing, obscene reference. This technique is most common in catch riddles.

DESCRIPTIVE RIDDLES

Archer Taylor's compendium, *English Riddles from Oral Tradition*, contains the major kinds of "true riddles," enigmatic questions in descriptive form. It includes the poetic, metaphoric riddles that are the most attractive and historically interesting in the language.

> White bird featherless
> Flew from Paradise,
> Perched upon the castle wall;
> Up came Lord John landless,
> Took it up handless,
> And rode away horseless
> To the King's white hall.
> ——Snow (ER 368) [1]

Taylor's classic compilation also includes other riddles that describe objects or actions in literal terms by selecting salient traits. These mainly rely on an incomplete *Gestalt* to confuse, though they may also have internal opposition, such as in this riddle:

> A house full, a yard full,
> Couldn't catch a bowl full.
> ——Smoke (ER 1643a)

A great majority of texts in Taylor's compilation depict a static image

1. Numbers refer to those assigned by Archer Taylor in *English Riddles from Oral Tradition* (Berkeley and Los Angeles: University of California Press, 1951). For an international comparative study of this riddle see Antti Aarne, *Vergleichende Rätselforschungen* (Folklore Fellows Communications, 26–28, Helsinki, 1918–20), and Archer Taylor, "'Vogel federlos' Once More," *Hessische Blätter für Volkskunde* 49/50 (1958):277–94.

—an animal, object, or person—and, by describing selected features, permit the riddlee to attempt to guess what it is:

> In spring I am gay,
> In handsome array;
> In summer more clothing I wear;
> When colder it grows,
> I fling off my clothes;
> And in winter I quite naked appear.
> ——Tree (ER 587*b*)

One special sort of riddle, some examples of which Taylor provides, departs from this technique slightly. Here, rather than having the described object stationary, it is delineated by its changing conditions. This may be, like the last example, simply a temporal progression, but in others the description is made not in terms of what it looks like but what is done to it.

> I went to the wood and got it,
> I sat me down and looked at it;
> The more I looked at it, the less I liked it,
> And I brought it home because I couldn't help it.
> ——Thorn (ER 1634*a*)

> The man who made it didn't need it, the man that sold it didn't want it, the man that used it didn't know.
> ——Coffin (ER 1429*f*)

Similarly, something may be described in terms of how a variety of actors stand in relation to it.

> What the king seldom sees,
> What God never sees,
> We see every day.
> What that now?
> ——An equal (ER 1716)

There are a number of riddles, some of which are included by Taylor, that describe a scene and a series of actions within it. The actions make these riddles significantly different from other types because they add many elements to the description and all of the referents must be guessed. These descriptions become enigmatic and yet capable of being solved because most of the action is expressed literally; the enigmatic quality of the riddle is in the substitution of names for the actors.[2]

2. Archer Taylor, "An Annotated Collection of Mongolian Riddles," *Transactions of the American Philosophical Society*, N. S. Vol. 44, Part 3 (1954) : 408–10.

One type of the substitution riddle substitutes queer words for the actors to be guessed.

> As I went up the Humble Jumble Jiny
> There I met Higma Dignee
> Eating up my Yakum Piny.
> If I'd a had my Handsome Kansom
> I'd a paid the Higma Dignee
> For eating up my Yakum Piny.
> ——Humble Jumble Jiny = hill; Higma Dignee = fox;
> Yakum Piny = goose; Handsome Kansom = gun.

Another sort uses a part for whole substitution. Frequently it is a distinctive physical feature that serves as the *pars pro toto*.

> Two-legs sat upon three-legs,
> One-leg knocked two-legs off three-legs,
> Two-legs hit four-legs with three-legs.
> ——A man was sitting on a three-legged stool
> milking a cow. The cow kicked him, and
> he hit her with a stool.   (ER 462*c*)

> Blackey went into blackey, blackey came out of
> blackey, and blackey left whitey in blackey.
> A black hen went in a black stump and laid
> a white egg.   (ER 867)

One type of riddle not included by Taylor in his dictionary is the so-called neck-riddle. These are riddles that in northern European and some African traditions are generally framed by the story of the man who saved his neck by the exercise of his wit, by propounding a riddle his executioner could not answer. (For a survey of these stories in English see bibliographical entry under Norton.) Not all neck riddles result in the saving of riddlers. In southern European tradition, for example, a "neck type" task is more commonly used in the same dramatic situations as impossible tests (cf. Aarne-Thompson 927). The essential characteristic of this type is that the riddle must be based on some experience that only the riddler has undergone or witnessed. The most common of these in the United States concerns a "Mr. Horn" who cooks a goat and climbs a tree to eat it, where he is then sighted.

> Horn ate horn up a white oak tree.
> You guess this riddle and you can hang me.

In diction and technique of confusion, these riddles are close to many of those that Taylor includes. In most cases, they are not intended to be told as riddles but as elements in stories and therefore must be considered separately. In their technique of confusion, they use a number of kinds of oppositions and cleverly selected traits. The major confusing element is that only the fictional riddler can possibly know the answer because of the private nature of the subject of the riddle. This aspect is unique in riddling.

The biblical riddle is another special type that shows a close relation to those in Taylor, especially in regard to its manner of description. The uniqueness of the referent of the biblical riddle is a biblical character (often an animal associated with a certain personage) and the description refers to his special traits as he is depicted. Thus, the ability to answer is, in part, dependent on knowing the Bible well. But many of the devices of confusion of the descriptive riddle are used. These riddles may vary from short, paradoxical questions such as:

> Who was born before his father and died before
> his mother?
>
> > ——Abel

to long enigmatic descriptions of the character's life:

> God made Adam out of dust,
> But thought best to make me first;
> So I was made before man,
> To our God's most holy plan;
> My body God did make complete,
> But without arms or legs or feet;
> My ways and acts he did control,
> And to my body gave no soul.
>
> A living being I became
> And Adam gave to me a name;
> I from his presence then withdrew,
> And more of Adam never knew;
> I did my maker's law obey,
> Nor from it ever went astray;
> Thousands of miles I go in fear,
> And seldom on the earth appear.
>
> For purpose wise, which God did see,
> He put a living soul in me;
> A soul from me, my God did claim,
> And took from me that soul again;
> For when from me that soul had fled,
> I was the same as when first made;
> And without hands or feet or soul,
> I travel on from pole to pole.
>
> > ——The whale that swallowed Jonah

An enigmatic type of description rare in English is the dialogue riddle. Such riddles give a dialogue and ask us to identify the speakers.[3]

> Crooked and straight, which way are you going?
> Croptail every year, what makes you care?
> ——Meadow to a brook and the brook's reply.

Finally, there are a number of descriptions whose referents are
words and letters as orthographic rather than linguistic entities. In
some, the fact that the orthographic object is being described is not
made clear, and this is the main source of its confusion.

> The beginning of every end,
> The end of every place,
> The beginning of eternity,
> The end of time and space.
> ——Letter E

One special kind sometimes called "charades" establishes by convention that a word is being described, as it must break up the word into
syllables and give a description of each. This is primarily a literary
form of riddle.

> A bottle [nec] is my first, and I have nine.
> My second is a sailor [tar], bold and jolly.
> My first and second have been deemed divine [nectar].
> Not to take ease within [in] my third is folly
> What am I?
> ——Nectarine

Certain charades confound the confusion by offering two orthog-
raphies, the usual and the one provided by numerals, both Roman
and Arabic, in their descriptions.

> Fifty is my first, nothing is my second,
> Five just makes my third, my fourth's a vowel reckoned;
> Now, to fill my whole, put all my parts together;
> I dies if I get cold, but never fear cold weather.
> ——L-O-V-E

Closely related to these are the unusual descriptions of the orthog-
raphy of words in terms of their geometric shape.

> Three-fourths of a cross, and a circle complete,
> A rectangle where two semi-circles meet,
> Two semi-circles and a circle complete.
> ——Tobacco

3. Archer Taylor, "Riddles in Dialogue," *Proceedings of the American Philosophical Society* 97 (1953) : 61–68.

A type of description that is not verbal and yet is otherwise firmly in the riddle mold is the visual riddle. These include two types. One is done by gesture: The Riddler pulls back the corners of his eyes and asks who he is. The answer: A girl whose pony-tail is pulled too tight. The other is presented as a rough sketch (sometimes called a "Droodle") :

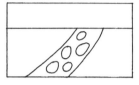

——A giraffe as seen through a half-open window

JOKING QUESTIONS

A joking question is an enigma in which the question simply functions as a set-up for a punch-line.

There are a number of joking questions that parallel riddling techniques but demand a description in the answer. These joking questions may be termed "reverse riddles." For instance, the dialogue riddle has its counterpart in the question "What did the —— say to the ——?" Whereas in the dialogue riddle we are given the dialogue and asked for the speakers, here we are given the speakers and asked for the dialogue. Similarly, the metaphoric riddle describes an object in terms suggesting something else, thus making an implicit comparison between the apparent referent and the real one; in the many joking questions that begin "What is the difference between —— and ——?" and "How (when, why) is —— like ——?" we are given the comparison explicitly and asked to provide the description of common traits.

Though a great many joking questions work like reverse riddles, giving the referent and asking for the description, by no means all do. In some, a *cause* is given, and the answer is an *effect*.

> What happens to little girls who swallow bullets?
> ——Their hair grows out in bangs.

In others, an effect is given and the answer is a cause.

> Why does a freight car need no locomotive?
> ——Because the freight makes the car-go.

Note, however, that both are causal in form rather than descriptive. The riddlee is asked for cause or effect; he is *not* asked to guess the referent of pure description.

It is clear that these joking questions, because they are impossible to answer, need to use few methods of confusion beyond the simple phrasing of the question. Therefore they are most easily distinguished by the ways in which the question is phrased. They tend to be formulaic in construction and to run in cycles (such as the Elephant, Grape, and Polack series of the sixties, or the earlier moron jokes.) Some of the more common formulas, other than the comparative and the dialogue riddles mentioned above, are: "If —— then ——?"; "When is a —— not a ——?"; "What time is it when ——?"; "What is the definition of ——?" or the closely related "What is the height of ——?" and "Which is more ——?". A great many joking questions are simply parodies of wisdom questions, and thus begin with any of the interrogative pronouns.

WISDOM QUESTIONS

As in joking questions, the wisdom question cannot be answered from the content of the question. The answer must be known already. Unlike any other kind of enigmatic question, there is no display of wit or cunning in a wisdom question. Consequently, from the point of view of the rhetoric of the riddle, they are of little interest.

It does seem necessary to point out, however, certain types of wisdom questions because they do enter into riddling sessions and are parodied in certain joking questions. Most wisdom questions call upon the knowledge of memorized facts in some special field, such as geography or physics or literature or from some esoteric work like the Bible, or even baseball. Some of them may have a slight twist to them because of phrasing: "How many outs in an inning of baseball?" Answer: Six.

Such questions may, in certain cases, involve a special kind of wisdom, that of the learned response. The answers to such questions are either doctrinaire (as in the catechetical question) or are arbitrary and poetic in their answers. We see this in the questions in the song "Riddles Wisely Expounded" (Child 1) where such questions are asked as "What is whiter than the milk?" (snow) and "What is softer than the silk?" (down). Certainly there are many other things whiter than milk and softer than silk, but these are the approved responses. Not many of this type of question emerge in riddling sessions; two that are fairly common are: "What is blacker than a crow?" (his feathers) and "What is not now and never shall be?" (a mouse nesting in a cat's ear).

PUZZLES

Puzzles concentrate upon the riddlee more than any other kind of enigmatic question. He not only serves as a reflector for the wit of the riddler, but also must attempt to come up with an answer. Accordingly, it takes more time to solve puzzles than to answer riddles. Probably because of this fact, few puzzles are found in riddling sessions; when one emerges it tends to elicit other puzzles. The puzzle is so confusing on its very face, in other words, that it does not need the riddling context to heighten its confusion.

Perhaps the most common puzzle type asks for the use of some kind of special knowledge (as in the wisdom question) in the logical process by which the answer is arrived at. Many call for simple arithmetic knowledge, much as the ubiquitous "If a chicken and a half could lay an egg and a half in a day and a half, how long would it take five chickens to lay five eggs?" (One day). Closely related to these puzzles are ones that call for a knowledge of currency value.

> How can you change a dollar into exactly
> fifty coins?
> ——Forty pennies, eight nickels, two dimes

An interesting group emphasizes the confusing aspects of family relationships.

> Brothers and sisters have I none,
> But that man's father is my father's son.
> Who is he?
> ——His son

This last puzzle is often found in a narrative frame, such as the neck-riddle story.

Puzzles may be divided conveniently, as with riddles and reverse riddles, between those that describe a situation in which a problem exists and ask for its solution, and those that not only give the situation but also provide the answer, the problem then being to decide how the answer was arrived at. The coin puzzle is an example of the reverse puzzle since we know that some combination of coins makes a total of fifty possible, the problem being which coins? On the other hand, the genealogical puzzle gives the process (the relationships) and asks for a solution and therefore might be termed a true puzzle. The analogy between these two types and the riddle, reverse-riddle situation can only be carried so far, since reverse riddles are *not* riddles, but both types of puzzles *are* puzzles.

The range of these puzzles includes one that places a person in the midst of a problem situation:

A man wished to travel through a jungle inhabited by two tribes—the Full Bloods (who always speak the truth) and the Half Bloods (who always speak in opposites.) Our man needed a truthful guide for his trip through the jungle, so when he saw three jungle inhabitants, he asked the first one, "Are you a Full Blood or a Half Blood? The native answered, "Oogley oomba." "He said he was a Half Blood," said the second native. "No, he didn't. He said he was a Full Blood," said the third native. From just this conversation the man was able to determine at least *one* Full Blood. Who and how?

The third one, at least, was a Full Blood and telling the truth; for the only answer the first one could have given, regardless of whether he was Half Blood or Full Blood, is "Full Blood."

Closely related is the "Solomonic" type of story that places the solution in the hands of a wise man.

Two horses are in a race. The winner will get $5,000, but the winner will be the one who crosses the finish line last. Before they get to the finish line, the two jockeys stop and ponder this problem. While they are pondering, they meet a wise man, and they ask him what to do. When he tells them, they jump on their horses and race away as fast as they can travel. What does he tell them?

———Change horses

The most extended form of those puzzles that give the answer and ask for a description of the solution process is the "detective story" type, described earlier. In these we are only given the end of a story (generally a murder) and are asked to find out what went before. These are sometimes so difficult that they cannot be answered unless the riddler helps the riddlee by allowing him to ask questions that can be answered "Yes" or "No."

A man standing behind a counter reads in the newspaper that some woman has been killed in Switzerland in a fall down a mountain. He immediately calls up the police and tells them to arrest the husband. Why?
———He is an airline agent. The week before he had sold this man tickets to Switzerland, one one-way and one round-trip.

This kind of solution-giving is found in many visual puzzles, such as the match tricks where you are asked to make a certain seemingly impossible figure with a limited number of matches. You know that it can be done; thus in a sense you are given the solution, and asked to figure out the process of solution only.

PARODY RIDDLES

The analysis of riddles must take into account the total range of items that arise in riddling sessions. It is toward this end that we have made this survey. But we have only begun to take into account the relationships between different riddle types (for instance, in the discussion of riddles and reverse riddles, and the two types of puzzles.)

Riddles are by their very nature conventional, as are all genres of oral literature. These conventions are important because they provide the framework by which they are recognized and remembered. Each riddle announces itself as being of a certain type by its conventional phrasing. This conventional frame creates a pattern of expectation on the part of the hearers, allowing them to hazard a guess at the answer, since the range of possible answers is limited by the riddle's conventional mode of proposition. Further, a riddle of one type when proposed in a riddling session will tend to elicit others in the same class often using the same formula. But these conventions, in keeping with the intent of the riddler to confuse the riddlees, may be used to set up the pattern of expectation and then to frustrate it.

One of the most common ways in which this frustration is engineered is in the use of "catch-riddles." These are commonly phrased as if they were true riddles—i.e., they are in descriptive form. But whereas most true riddles seem to defy decoding, it appears to be possible to guess the referent of the catch. But, as with all catches, the ease of guessing is simply a device to get the other person to make a move that places him in a vulnerable and often embarrassing situation. For instance, a riddler may propose the following: "What has four legs, a wagging tail, and barks?" On the face of it, this calls for a flash of triumph from the riddlee, for in the emotionally charged riddling session he is glad to be able to solve one. Therefore, he commonly hastens to answer "A dog." To which the riddler is then able to say, "Oh, you've heard that one," thereby making a statement about the simplemindedness of the riddlee.

Catch-riddles more usually frustrate expectations by appearing to refer to one object when they actually refer to another. This type commonly turns on an obscene referent that the riddle seems to describe: What is it that sticks out of your pajamas in the morning, strong enough to hold up a hat? The apparent referent, the penis, when enunciated is then answerable by the real referent, the head; there is then a clear imputation of "dirty-mindedness" to the riddlee. (Catch-riddles are related to catch tales, for which see Aarne-Thompson 2200–2249.)

This frustration of expectation is not unique to the catch. For each type of riddle, there seems to be a parody of that type. The major confusing element of such parodies is in the use and then frustration of the pattern. One of the most common ways in which descriptive riddles are parodied is to introduce an element of nonsense. It is assumed when a description is given that it will add up to a referent that is a real, observable, part of everyday life. By introducing the element of nonsense, the true riddle is turned upside-down and made into the set-up for a nonsensical punch-line, thus coming close to the traditional joking question. This formula appears in the numerous recent joke-riddle cycles, like those concerned with elephants.[4]

> What is big, gray, lives in trees and is dangerous?
> ——Elephant

It is this parodic technique that breaks down the stabilizing force of riddling conventions, thus contributing to the atmosphere of creative confusion. Any type of enigmatic question can be parodied. For instance, the following is a parody puzzle:

A batter in a baseball game is at the plate.
No one is on base.
The pitcher throws a baseball, and the batter hits it over the left field fence. He carefully lays the bat down, runs to first and touches the base, runs to second and touches the base, runs to third and touches the base, runs home and touches the base.
The catcher asks the umpire for another ball, tags the batter, and the umpire calls him out. Why?

When the riddlee can't establish why in the usual manner of solving the puzzle, he "gives up." The answer given is "He didn't touch second base," and the riddlee usually replies "But you said he did!" to which the riddler responds "I lied."

For parody riddles like this to work there must be established the conventional statement of puzzle-riddles that may then be used in order to frustrate expectations. This technique must then be added to the central devices of riddling, that contest of confusing and witty questions. These conventions allow for riddles to give the impression of being of a class of non-understandable speech acts that seem capable of being understood. Furthermore, they provide the model for the creation of new riddles. But, as noted, these compositions may utilize formulas to frustrate expectations just as clearly as they are used to fulfill them.

Bibliography and Selected Readings

Aarne, Antti. *Vergleichende Rätselforschungen.* Folklore Fellows Communications, 26–28. Helsinki, 1918–20. Valuable comparative studies of various individual riddles.

4. For further consideration of this cycle see Roger D. Abrahams and Alan Dundes, "On Elephantasy and Elephanticide," *The Psychoanalytic Review* 56 (1969) : 225–41.

Abrahams, Roger D. "Introductory Remarks to a Rhetorical Theory of Folklore." *Journal of American Folklore* 81 (1968) : 143–58. A discussion of the strategy of folklore performances with special reference to riddles.

Bascom, William R. "Literary Style in Yoruba Riddles." *Journal of American Folklore* 62 (1949) : 1–16. A study of Yoruba riddle stylistic formulas.

Beuchat, P. D. "Riddles in Bantu." *African Studies* 16 (1957) : 133–49. A comparative study of Bantu riddle linguistic features.

Blacking, John. "The Social Value of Venda Riddles." *African Studies* 20 (1961) : 1–32. A collection of 313 Venda riddles prefaced by an excellent ethnographic discussion of riddle context.

Bødker, Laurits, *et al. The Nordic Riddle: Terminology and Bibliography.* Copenhagen: Rosenkilde and Bagger, 1964. A list of all the terms for riddles and related forms in English, German, and the Scandinavian languages wth some attempt to show correspondences and analogous forms.

Georges, Robert A., and Alan Dundes. "Toward a Structural Definition of the Riddle." *Journal of American Folklore* 76 (1963) : 111–18. An attempt to delineate the morphological characteristics of English riddles.

Goldstein, Kenneth S. "Riddling Traditions in Northeastern Scotland." *Journal of American Folklore* 76 (1963) : 330–36. One of the few studies of riddling in a European context.

Hain, Mathilde. *Rätsel.* Stuttgart: J. B. Metzler, 1966. A thorough survey of the German riddle with comprehensive bibliographical references.

Hamnett, Ian. "Ambiguity, Classification and Change: The Function of Riddles." *Man,* N.S. 2 (1967) : 379–92. A sophisticated consideration of riddles as vehicles for the expression of native cognitive categories.

Hart, Donn V. *Riddles in Filipino Folklore.* Syracuse: Syracuse University Press, 1964. A collection of 909 riddles prefaced by several valuable survey chapters including one devoted to "The Functions of Riddles."

Kozumplik, William A. "Seven and Nine Holes in Man." *Southern Folklore Quarterly* 4 (1941) : 1–24. An extended comparative study of a single traditional riddle.

Lehmann-Nitsche, Robert. *Folklore Argentino, I, Adivinanzas rioplatenses.* Buenos Aires, 1911. A collection of riddles perhaps best known for its novel classification scheme.

Müllenhoff, Karl. "Nordische, englische und deutsche Rätsel." *Zeitschrift für deutsche Mythologie* 3 (1855) : 1–20. An early attempt to compare riddle cognates.

Norton, F. J. "Prisoner Who Saved His Neck with a Riddle." *Folklore* 52 (1941) : 27–57. A fine survey of the neck-riddle.

Paris, Gaston. "Preface" to Eugène Rolland, *Devinettes et énigmes populaires de la France.* Paris, 1877. Pp. 1-xvi. A scholarly comparative consideration of specific riddles.

Petsch, Robert. *Das deutsche Volksrätsel.* Grundriss der deutschen Volkskunde. Strassburg, 1917. An excellent survey that has now been partly superseded by Hain's work.

————. *Neue Beiträge zur Kenntnis des Volksrätsels.* Palaestra IV. Berlin, 1899. One of the most extensive investigations ever undertaken of the stylistic features of riddles.

Santi, Aldo. *Bibliografia delle Enigmistica.* Firenze: Sansoni, 1952. The most recent comprehensive worldwide survey of riddle collections.

Scott, Charles T. *Persian and Arabic Riddles: A Language-Centered Approach to Genre Definition.* Bloomington: Indiana University Press, 1965. An unsuccessful but nonetheless important attempt to isolate linguistic features of riddles sufficient to define the riddle as a folkloristic genre.

Taylor, Archer. *A Bibliography of Riddles.* Folklore Fellows Communications, 126. Helsinki, 1939. A valuable bibliography compiled by the leading scholar in riddle studies.

————. "An Annotated Collection of Mongolian Riddles." *Transactions of the American Philosophical Society,* N.S. 44 (1954) : 321–425. An excellent collection of texts with model annotative headnotes.

————. *English Riddles from Oral Tradition.* Berkeley and Los Angeles: University of California Press, 1951. One of the finest collections of riddles in any language. Many of the headnotes read like miniature monographs. A *vade mecum* for the student of Anglo-American riddles.

————. *The Literary Riddle Before 1600.* Berkeley and Los Angeles: University of California Press, 1948. A prime source for early riddle scholarship.

————. "The Riddle." *California Folklore Quarterly* 2 (1943) : 129–47. One of a number of invaluable surveys of the riddle genre published by Professor Taylor.

————. "Riddles in Dialogue." *Proceedings of the American Philosophical Society* 97 (1953) : 61–68. The best available survey of this particular riddle form.

————. "The Varieties of Riddles." In Thomas A. Kirby and Henry Bosley Woolf, eds., *Philologica: The Malone Anniversary Studies.* Baltimore: Johns Hopkins Press, 1949. Pp. 1–8. Another useful survey.

Tupper, Frederic, Jr. "The Comparative Study of Riddles." *Modern Language Notes* 18 (1903) : 1–8. A discussion of the relationship between folk riddles and literary riddles as well as a brief consideration of several widely distributed riddles.

Williams, Thomas Rhys. "The Form and Function of Tambunan Dusun Riddles." *Journal of American Folklore* 76 (1963) : 95–110. An attempt to show the inadequacy of the European notion of riddling as a leisure activity by using data from the Dusun of North Borneo.

von Sydow, C. W. "Om Gåtor och Gåtsystematik." *Folkminnen och Folktankar* 2 (1915) : 65–80. An attempt to test the utility of the riddle classification scheme proposed by Lehmann-Nitsche.

6 FOLK SPEECH
W. Edson Richmond

No one learns his native language in a formal school. He learns by a kind of linguistic osmosis, absorbing vocabulary and language patterns from his family, his friends, and his associates who, in turn, are conditioned by their own cultural milieu. Formal schooling, if it is a part of one's environment, then modifies this already absorbed material, not only in classes devoted to the study of language but also by familiarizing the speaker with a kind of ideal and standardized language deemed especially appropriate of expression within his particular speech community. This standardized form is usually conservative, often rigidly restrictive, and frequently highly artificial. In a culture such as that found in North America that strongly emphasizes formal schooling, such a standardized mode of speech rapidly becomes the norm, strengthened by its use on radio and television and in newspapers, magazines, and books. Its influence thus snowballs, quickly encompassing regional and social variants and so absorbing them into the whole that they soon lose their individuality.

Nevertheless, even in North America and other cultural areas stressing schooling and literacy, pockets of linguistic individualism continue to exist. To these deviations from the accepted, academic linguistic norm the word *dialect* is frequently applied, though there is considerable disagreement as to the precise meaning of the word itself. It is common, for example, even for scholars to speak of the Norwegian, Danish, and Swedish languages while at the same time speaking of the Zurich and Tyrolean dialects of German; yet Norwegian, Danish, and Swedish differ from each other no more than the speech patterns of Zurich and the Tyrol differ from those of Berlin and Hamburg. Most commonly, however, the word *dialect* is used to refer to a specific form of an accepted language—of the Telemark dialect of Norwegian, the Neapolitan dialect of Italian, the Cockney dialect of British English, and the New England dialect of American English, for example.

One dialect may differ from other dialects within a given language in its vocabulary, pronunciation, and grammar. This difference is most often brought about by geographical peculiarities, though it is sometimes affected by social conditions as well. Norwegians living in Telemark and Americans living in the southern Appalachians are geographically isolated from the mainstream of normative speech patterns; Cockneys living in London are socially isolated from the mainstream of Received Standard British speech. The result is a distinctive and recognizable form of language peculiar to the geographic area or the social group that employs it. The New England American will employ "tonic" and "frappe" for what the bulk of Americans refer to as "soda pop" and a "milk shake"; the British Cockney will employ the same degree of aspiration for words beginning with a vowel whether they are spelled initially with an "h" or not, thus seeming to add an "h" where none appears and to drop it when it does appear; and the southern American contributes to the grammar of English by creating a plural second personal pronoun, "you-all," where his countrymen in general fail to distinguish between a singular and plural "you."

Nor is there anything abnormal about a dialect in this sense. The one irrefutable law of linguistics is that languages change. It has been said that the speech patterns of the southern Appalachian region of the United States are "Elizabethan English, pure and undefiled." This is utter nonsense. The speech of a southern mountaineer is as different from that of a sixteenth-century Londoner as is the speech of a proper Bostonian or an improper Chicagoan—it simply differs in different ways, having retained some sixteenth-century features lost in other American dialects and having lost some of the sixteenth-century characteristics retained in other parts of the country. The result is a distinctive form of American English, in some ways archaic and in other ways further along its evolutionary path than its sister dialects.

The speech patterns of the southern mountaineer have developed differently from those of other Americans because the mountaineer has lived in a relatively homogeneous community isolated from the mainstream of American speech and education. His is a geographical dialect. But, as Henry Cecil Wyld has pointed out, "Everyone who does not speak a regional dialect speaks a class dialect."

A class dialect differs from a regional dialect because it is dependent upon social and economic factors for its evolution and continuance rather than upon geographical factors. In England this is more obvious than in the United States, for Received Standard British is a semi-artificial class dialect that is taught and perpetuated by the British public school system that caters to a select portion of the population, the rest of whom attend county schools. The bulk of the English people speak a Modified Received Standard that clearly distinguishes them from those who have attended public schools and is frequently strongly marked by their regional dialects. In addition, a relatively small number of English people who have had little exposure to formal schooling or who, for one reason or another, have rejected formal schooling (it little profits the trade unionist at the local level to appear overly educated), speak what is presumably a form of their regional dialect unmodified by formal education. Moreover, it is extremely difficult in England for one to change his social position, either up or down, without a concomitant shift in dialect, for one's position on the social scale is as clearly revealed by his pronunciation, his vocabulary, and his grammar as by his place of residence, his manner of dress, or his occupation.

In the United States and Canada, the situation is not quite so drastic in spite of a pervasive belief that grammatical correctness is devoutly to be desired though almost impossible to attain. Indeed, pronunciation, the true shibboleth of British class dialects, is relatively insignificant as a social marker in North America except in East coast urban areas and parts of Ontario. One need merely compare the speech patterns of four recent presidents of the United States to see how little regional pronunciation affects social advancement. Two of these men, Harry S. Truman and Dwight D. Eisenhower, spoke what is commonly, though a little loosely, called General American only slightly modified by regional peculiarities in pronunciation. The speech patterns of the other two, John F. Kennedy and Lyndon B. Johnson, were strongly marked by regional peculiarities in pronunciation conditioned even further by the types of schools that each attended. Though from the point of view of a school ma'am the speech of the first two men exhibited occasional lexical and grammatical infelicities, it was primarily their political opponents who seized upon these as an excuse to criticize the men; the bulk of the American populace who were conscious of the "errors" saw them as evidence of the men's humanity and identification with the common man. But of even greater significance is the fact that none of these men found it necessary to change his normal speech patterns in order to achieve political and social success.

Nevertheless, recognizable class dialects do exist in the United States and Canada, even if they are socially less restrictive than those of England and other western European countries. Indeed, standards of correctness in North America are regional rather than national, and, informally at least, the field workers for *The Linguistic Atlas of the United States and Canada* recognize three levels of speech within each major regional dialect area: Cultivated Speech, Common Speech, and Folk Speech, though from a strictly scientific point of view these terms leave much to be desired. It is generally assumed today that within the United States alone there are at least seven principal regional dialect areas: Eastern New England, New York City, East Midland, Inland Northern, West Midland, South Midland, and Southern. Thus, on the surface at least, it would appear that the United States exhibits at least twenty-one dialects, since there are three varieties of each regional dialect. But even this is an oversimplification, for within each region there may be more than one kind of Common Speech and Folk Speech.

We are not here concerned with cultivated speech, that is, the speech patterns of the highly educated, but rather with folk speech, the speech patterns that develop independently of formal schooling and are characteristic of, but by no means entirely limited to, the older and relatively uneducated group within any regional dialect area.

In Europe, both dialect studies and studies of Folk Speech are generally limited to analysis and description of the speech patterns of older people living in isolated, rural areas. The field workers for such seminal works as the *Atlas linguistique de la France,* edited by Jules Gilliéron and Edmond Edmont, and the *Sprach- und Sachatlas Italiens und der Südschweiz,* edited by K. Jaberg and J. Jud, were instructed to seek out good, natural speakers of the regional dialect— by which was meant older speakers little contaminated by education. The methods developed for these atlases were accepted with surprisingly few modifications even by the early editors of *The Linguistic Atlas of the United States and Canada.* Only in quite recent years have dialectologists shifted to a wider base. Today, however, as can be seen in the *Österreichische Volkskundeatlas,* edited by Ernst Burgstaller and Adolf Helbok, in *An Introduction to a Survey of Scottish Dialects* by Angus McIntosh, in the surveys of Swedish dialects conducted by the *Landsmals- och Folkminnes-arkivet i Uppsala* under the direction of Dag Strömbäck, and especially in the work preparatory for a *Dictionary of American Regional English* conducted by the American Dialect Society under the direction of Frederic G. Cassidy, it is not only the speech of the older inhabitants of rural areas that is subject to investigation but rather that of all speakers, old and young, rural and urban, educated and uneducated alike. It is now recognized that the lines between Cultivated, Common, and Folk Speech cannot be sharply drawn and that those who commonly employ Cultivated and Common speech patterns use their regional dialect on occasion and are seldom confused by local patterns of Folk Speech even if they only infrequently or never use them.

Nowhere is this more evident than in the area of taboo speech. Few indeed are the speakers of English, be they British or American, male or female, educated or illiterate, who are unfamiliar with the so-called four-letter words referring to body organs, sexual intercourse, and other bodily functions. These words are a fundamental part of the English vocabulary. Though once essential for the expression of certain ideas, they were replaced in nearly all strata of society by substitute, and often learned, words, and went underground where they continued as a living but entirely oral segment of the language. This restriction to oral circulation is characteristic of Folk Speech in general. Within the total vocabulary of every speaker there is a large number of words that he never writes and seldom uses in formal situations, though he is not ashamed of them as he might be of the taboo words that he knows. They are simply words that seem more at home in the family kitchen than in the living rooms of friends. Often, though they may be recognized by all speakers of a given language and even form a part of their passive vocabulary, their extensive use is limited to a particular regional dialect. The word *parlor* is a good example. Still widely used in eastern New England, this word has a delicately archaic flavor in the rest of the United States where it has been replaced in both Cultivated and Common Speech with *living room,* a term that supplanted the once equally ubiquitous terms *sitting room* and *front room.* Similarly, the general term *porch* is known and used by all Americans, though to many such words as *piazza, veranda,* and *stoop* come quite naturally in familiar situations, while to still others these words do not appear to be synonyms at all but to refer to distinct types of house appendages.

The distinction between the terms mentioned above is primarily a distinction between an active and a passive vocabulary. Most speakers of English recognize all of the terms, even though each might habitually choose a particular one. But there are also many words employed in Cultivated and Common Speech for which there are regional synonyms unknown outside of relatively restricted areas. All Americans, and perhaps all speakers of English, would know what to expect should they be offered *cottage cheese* but confused if offered *Dutch cheese* in New England, *smearcase* in West Virginia, Pennsylvania, and Ohio, or *pot cheese* in the New York City area where these are the colloquial terms. In like manner, the word *chipmunk* is known to all speakers of English, but the animal is called by other names as well. It is known as a *ground squirrel* in parts of Pennsylvania and the south Atlantic states, as a *ground hackie* in southeastern Pennsylvania and northern Delaware, as a *chickery* in northern Maryland, and as a *grinnie* in southeastern Ohio and southwestern Pennsylvania. Similarly, the insect generally known as *dragonfly* throughout North America is called a *darning needle* almost exclusively in New England, the state of New York, and eastern New Jersey, a *spindle* in a few isolated areas in the last-named state, and a *mosquito hawk,* a *snake feeder, snake doctor,* or *snake waiter* throughout the South.

At times such regional and social variation can be most confusing. The word *cottage,* for example, has a generally accepted denotation throughout the English-speaking world. It usually refers to a small house, often one used primarily for vacations. In southern New Hampshire, however, the word is used to designate a seashore vacation residence, no matter how grand. Moreover, any other vacation home, be it a one-room hut entirely lacking in facilities or a fourteen-room mansion with sunken baths, is called a *camp.* It can be most disconcerting to the midwesterner invited to spend a few days at a camp on the shores of Lake Winnepesaukee to find himself in an environment where dressing for dinner would be *de rigeur* were it not for the fact that *dinner* is served at noon and *supper* in the evening.

Such differences between Folk Speech on the one hand and Cultivated and Common Speech on the other are by no means limited to vocabulary alone. There are significant grammatical, idiomatic, and phonetic differences as well.

To describe the grammar of a language is to describe the devices that that language employs to show the relationship of one word to another within a given statement. The English language employs two principal devices for this purpose: word order and formal modification. Since word order is the more significant of these two devices in modern English, it can be varied only slightly without seriously interfering with communication; but formal modification is a relic of earlier stages of the language and subject to considerable variation without causing significant confusion. If the word order for such a sentence as "The dog bit the man" is changed to "The dog the man bit," the statement becomes ambiguous, to say the very least, but no one is confused if one says "Give the book to *whomever* wants it" instead of "to *whoever* wants it," which is the preferred form. Changes in word form in order to indicate case are no longer major factors in the English grammatical system. They are important socially, but not linguistically.

As a result, the grammatical differences between Folk Speech and Cultivated/Common Speech appear primarily in the area of word form and to some slight degree in idiom (which is frequently more closely related to vocabulary than it is to grammar). As has already been noted, Cultivated and Common speakers in the southern part of the United States have created a special second-person plural pronoun, "you-all." Folk speakers, too, have felt the need to distinguish between singular and plural when speaking to others. Thus the nominative and objective cases of the pronoun *you* in modern American English can be charted thus:

Northern	*Singular*	*Plural*
cultivated and common	you	you
folk	you	youse
Southern		
cultivated and common	you	you-all
folk	you	you'ns

Folk Speech also employs a number of grammatical constructions frowned upon by cultivated speakers. Some of these, such as the use of the double negative as in "he ain't got none," the use of prepositions to end sentences with, and the use of *them* as a demonstrative adjective as in "them books," have a long history in the English language. Others, such as the use of *anymore* in positive constructions ("When I come to New York anymore, I stay in a hotel") are relatively recent contributions to the language. For centuries grammatical constructions of this sort have been condemned as vulgarisms, illiteracies, and as substandard speech. As a result, they have been insufficiently studied even though they are basic to an understanding of the growth of the language.

On the borderline between grammar and vocabulary are those set expressions found in every language that are frequently called idioms. Whether one habitually says "four forty-five," "a quarter of," "a quarter to," "a quarter till," or "fifteen to/till/of five" seems to be dependent primarily upon regional preferences and appears to be a lexical rather than a grammatical problem. The same may be said for such expressions as "clearing," "clearing up," "to clear off," or "to clear up," but there are other idiomatic expressions that clearly involve grammatical problems and equally clearly reflect social distinctions. Throughout the United States and Canada, most speakers of Cultivated and of Common Speech say "I want to get on" or "off" a bus or merry-go-round, but in Pennsylvania and the eastern borders of the Middle West folk speakers content themselves with "I want on" or "I want off." This construction may be the result of a strong German influence, for in the same areas one encounters the Folk expression "the oranges are all" where Cultivated Common speakers would say "the oranges are all gone," and both of these sentences resemble similar grammatical constructions in German. Similarly, the phrase "to redd up" and "to redd off," common in the Folk Speech of Pennsylvania and Ohio, apparently show German influence, though such a statement as "I'd just as lief redd up after him as anyone" suggests the possibility of a purely English development merely strengthened by analogy with German, for *redd* in the sense of "to tidy up" can be traced to Old English *hreddan*, "to put in order," and *lief* to Middle English *lef*, Old English *leof*, which in adverbial constructions meant "gladly."

Folk speech may also be contrasted with Cultivated and Common speech in its pronunciation. One cannot travel anywhere in the English-speaking world without becoming aware of what are popularly called regional accents, and there are comparable differences in pronunciation found in all living languages. Though in England, as has been indicated previously, Cultivated speakers adopt a special set of phones distinct from those of their native region, in North America both Cultivated and Common speakers tend to retain the phonetic patterns common to their places of residence. Thus, no matter what their social status or educational level, natives of eastern New England pronounce the words *path*, *bath*, and *half* with a low central vowel (/paθ, baθ, haf/) instead of with the low front vowel '(/pæθ, bæθ, hæf/) common to the northern midlands. Similarly, all natives of the so-called Deep South not only omit postvocalic *r*'s when they are final or precede words beginning with a consonant (as do most New Englanders also), they omit the postvocalic *r* generally. Such distinctions are legion and too complex to go into here, and, in addition, there is an overlay of folk pronunciation that transcends regional dialect boundaries. Most frequently this folk pronunciation reflects normal phonetic evolution, while Cultivated and Common pronunciation is frequently affected by certain extraneous factors such as spelling. For example, the word *creek* which Cultivated and Common speakers rhyme with *leak* is pronounced by Folk speakers to rhyme with *lick*, which it would have rhymed with on all levels of speech had it not been for the influence of the way the word is spelled.

There are thousands of such words in English. Though it is rapidly becoming a relic, it is characteristic of American folk speech that *deaf* is pronounced to rhyme with *leaf.* Similarly a relic, though very much alive, is the pronunciation of the word *creature* when it refers to cattle, though not when it refers to human beings, as if it rhymed with *sitter.* Of a slightly different nature are the words *Detroit* and *elm.* Among Folk speakers the place-name follows the usual pattern of stress or emphasis on the first syllable, a characteristic of English and other Germanic languages; thus the word is pronounced *De*troit and no longer resembles its French source in any way except spelling. It is also characteristic of Germanic languages that *m*'s and *n*'s that follow certain resonants take on the quality of syllables; thus, among Folk speakers the word *elm* is often pronounced as if it rhymed with *antebellum* and *prune* and *June* as if they rhymed with *ruin.* Finally, it should be pointed out that some of the pronunciation patterns of Folk speakers are by no means universal, though they frequently overlap the boundaries of recognized regional dialects. The word *rinse,* for example, is pronounced as if it rhymed with *pinch* or *wrench* by Folk speakers on the western edges of the New England dialect area, on the eastern edges of the northern and southern Midland areas, and on the northern edge of the southern dialect area.

In addition to regional and class dialects there are also innumerable specialized vocabularies to be found in all languages. Frequently referred to as cant, argot, and jargon—slang is something else again and it will be discussed later—these are, strictly speaking, not dialects, for they follow the same patterns of pronunciation and grammar as does the language of which they are a part. They are merely groups of words employed by particular segments of society, sometimes in a deliberate attempt to conceal meaning, at other times because of the need to express particular ideas. The pages of *American Speech* and some issues of the *Publications of the American Dialect Society* are packed with lists of such words, ranging from the vocabularies of college students through those of specialized technical workers to those of criminals. It is customary, for example, for college students throughout the United States to speak of a "hay" course, implying that it is so easy that it would be impossible to "flunk" it no matter how often one "cut" it in order to attend a "boress" (bull session). More confusing is the language of pickpockets who call themselves "cannons," sometimes working as a "single cannon" and sometimes with a "class mob" and classifying their "marks" as "eggs" (men under thirty), "bates" (men over forty), and "pappies" (elderly men).

Language of this sort is closely allied to slang. Indeed, slang often derives from such specialized vocabularies, but it is appropriately so called only when it ceases to be the property of a particular group and passes into general circulation. Even here it is dangerous to give examples, for today's slang may well be tomorrow's standard speech or may be so outdated as to sound foolish and artificial. Words such as *cab, mob, bus,* and *quiz,* all eighteenth-century contributions to the English language, were condemned as slang as late as the early years of the twentieth century; yet they are an accepted part of cultivated speech today. Such expressions as "Twenty-three skidoo" and "Oh, you kid" are meaningless to anyone born after the first World War; yet they were an essential part of "smart" conversation in the early 1900s. Nevertheless, some slang words maintain a tenuous existence, never attaining respectability but never quite dying. Such has been the fate of such words as *floozy* and *flapper, gizmo* and *guts.*

It should be obvious by now that Folk Speech is the foundation on which all language is based. Speakers of Cultivated, and even of Common, speech are inhibited by rules frequently based more on misconception than on actuality, though often the rules of prescriptive grammarians are justified in terms of logic. But living languages are seldom entirely logical, and Folk Speech is, in a sense, the result of doing what comes naturally. Nowhere is this more obvious than in the processes commonly known as "folk" or "popular etymology." This process, which is the result of applying false logic to puzzling linguistic situations, has contributed greatly to the vocabulary of the English language, having given us, among thousands of others, such disparate words as *bridegroom, hiccough,* and *sparrow grass.*

The first two examples, both of which exist on all levels of speech, are a result of phonetic analogy, and, in the first instance, the disappearance of a word from common usage. Old English, that is, the form of the English language that existed up to about the year 1100, had two words, *bryd* (bride) and *guma* (man), which in Middle English—the name given to the form that the English language took between 1100 and 1500—were combined as *bridegome,* that is, the male equivalent of *bride.* For various complex reasons, the word *guma* fell into disuse and finally disappeared, and in time, because of its phonetic similarity to this word, the word *groom* was substituted for the lost word *guma.* The result was a new word, familiar in both of its parts, but hardly flattering to either bride or groom. In a similar manner, *helpmate* derives from the earlier *helpmeet,* itself the result of a misunderstanding of a phrase from Genesis: "an help meet for him" in which two words were misunderstood and compounded. Logic, even though false, and phonetic analogy also play a part in the development of modern *cold slaw* from older *cole slaw,* the English attempt to pronounce Dutch *koolsla* (*kool,* "cabbage," and *sla,* "salad").

A slightly different process is involved in the development of the word *hiccough,* which today is often pronounced to rhyme with *cough,* though the word was originally pronounced in English to rhyme with *cup.* First created as a word imitative of the sound it labeled, and thus pronounced *hiccup,* the word was later subject to logical analysis and written as *hiccough.* Later, as a result of its spelling, the pronunciation of the word was changed.

Sometimes such creations never go beyond Folk Speech. In its original Greek form, the word that became *asparagus* in Early Modern English meant simply "sprout," though it was often applied specifically to the same plant that we now know. The phonetic similarity of the final portion of the word to the well-known English word *grass,* when coupled with the fact that it was green and growing, developed the apparently more meaningful form *aspergrass.* But this, too, seemed nonsensical, and the process of phonetic analogy again came into effect. The result was the substitution of the logically foolish but phonetically similar *sparrow* for *asper* and the creation of the name *sparrow grass,* which at least had the virtue of consisting of two meaningful elements. Though this form achieved wide circulation in English among the speakers of everyday language and even served as the basis for certain *ex post facto* explanations of the word (sparrows were said to be especially fond of this kind of grass!), it was seldom written and seems now to be disappearing from the language.

Obviously, the study of dialects and Folk Speech in all of their aspects is no job for the untrained amateur. To properly collect and analyze such materials requires training in the techniques and methods of descriptive linguistics, in phonetics and phonemics, and in lexicography. In addition, it requires a fine ear for the nuances of grammatical patterns and the subtleties of sound, and, just as importantly, sufficient knowledge of standard speech to recognize those items that are peculiar to a particular region or a particular social class. Nevertheless, the groundwork for such studies has been done by *The Linguistic Atlas of the United States and Canada* and by the directors of the proposed *Dictionary of American Regional English.* One who is sufficiently interested to spend two or three months learning how to use a phonetic alphabet and who carefully studies the methodology described in the books of Hans Kurath in the bibliography that follows can produce truly valuable and significant work.

Bibliography and Selected Readings

Journals

American Speech. Though semi-popular in its style, this journal offers a good introduction to the problems and methodology of language analysis. Its articles are often amusingly written.

Publications of the American Dialect Society (PADS). A serial publication rather than a typical magazine, *PADS* publishes everything from word lists to monographs on such topics as place-names, bilingualism, and zoosemiotics. The quality is varied.

Linguistic Atlases

Gilliéron, Jules, and Edmond Edmont. *Atlas linguistique de la France*. 35 parts. Paris, 1902–10. Seminal linguistic atlas.

Kurath, Hans, et al. *Linguistic Atlas of New England*. 3 vols. Providence, R. I., 1939–43. Patterned in its general principles on Gilliéron and Edmont, this is the earliest significant scientific analysis of American dialects.

Books and Articles

Burling, Robbins. *Man's Many Voices: Language in its Cultural Context*. New York: Holt, Rinehart and Winston, 1970. An introduction to the study of the relationship between language and culture, this book ranges over many of the languages of the world and is espec:ally concerned with speech patterns that have not been influenced very much by education.

Estrich, Robert M., and Hans Sperber. *Three Keys to Language*. New York: Rinehart, 1952. Analyzes the conflict between "natural" speech habits and social taboos upon language; the point of departure is the English language.

Kurath, Hans. *Handbook of the Linguistic Geography of New England*. Providence, R. I., 1939. An interpretation of *Linguistic Atlas of New England* and a model example of dialect analysis; its principal emphasis is upon the speech patterns of the old and uneducated.

———. *A Word Geography of Eastern United States*. Ann Arbor: University of Michigan Press, 1949. Similar to *Handbook of the Linguistic Geography of New England,* this book covers the same linguistic items and describes the dialects of the states bordering the Atlantic ocean and their immediate neighbors.

Labov, William. *The Social Stratification of English in New York City*. Washington, D.C.: Center for Applied Linguistics, 1966. A microscopic examination of the sociolinguistics of New York City, this book not only details all of the elements that distinguish a dialect but also suggests the causes and effects of such distinguishing elements; not for the beginner.

Maurer, David W. *Whiz Mob: A Correlation of the Technical Argot of Pickpockets with their Behavior Patterns*. Gainesville, Fla.: American Dialect Society, *PADS*, 1955. A model study of a professional argot that reveals much of the psychology of linguistic invention.

McAtee, W. L. *Studies in the Vocabularies of Hoosier Authors: Edward Eggleston (1837–1902)*. Chapel Hill, N. C.: printed by the compiler, 1961. Written by an amateur linguist, this book gives special insight into the peculiarities of dialect writing in the nineteenth century and the bases on which the modern dialects of Indiana are built.

McDavid, Raven I., Jr. "Folk Speech." In *Our Living Traditions*. Ed. by Tristram Potter Coffin. New York: Basic Books, 1968. Pp. 228–37. A definition of "folk speech" with special references to its dialectal peculiarities, this is an article intended for a nonspecialized but intelligent audience.

McIntosh, Angus. *An Introduction to a Survey of Scottish Dialects.* Edinburgh, New York: Nelson, 1952.

Mencken, H. L. *The American Language: The Fourth Edition and the Two Supplements.* Abridged and edited in one volume by Raven I. McDavid, Jr. New York: Knopf, 1963. Like the three volumes it abridges, this book is informative, scholarly, and witty and it is invaluable for the scholar and amateur alike.

Orton, Harold, and Wilfrid J. Halliday. *Survey of English Dialects.* 2 vols. Leeds: E. J. Arnold, 1962.

Wyld, Henry Cecil. *A History of Modern Colloquial English.* 3d ed. New York, 1937. This is a thorough study of modern noncultivated English speech, its origins and characteristics. Now slightly out of date.

SOCIAL FOLK CUSTOM

7 FESTIVALS AND CELEBRATIONS

Robert Jerome Smith

Most, if not all, of the societies of the world periodically set aside portions of time for celebration. These are moments of special significance to the group or community. They may be moments of transition, from one season to another or from one stage of life to another; they may be anniversaries of historical events, of the legendary day of the birth or death of a hero or a god; or symbolic reenactments of events in the life of a religious leader or the founder of a society. They may be moments set aside to honor some living person or some group, or occasions for communal work, with feasting and play added.

These recurring moments of special significance, with the celebrations that fill them, are called festivals, and their study has long been a major occupation of British and continental folklorists. In the British Isles, descriptions of local festivals appear in county histories from the seventeenth century onward. In the eighteenth century, such periodicals as the *Gentleman's Magazine* devoted space in almost every issue to the description of one local festival or another, along with comments by scholars on classical or pagan parallels to the modern rustic festival behavior. Later, continual references to festivals could be found in *Notes and Queries*, in the journal and other publications of The Folklore Society, and in the works of such county collectors as William Henderson[1] and Charlotte Sophie Burne.[2]

Thus, the antiquarian influence within the British folklore movement contributed a wealth of data and description to the study of the festival. Another movement, originating on the continent and brought to England in the second half of the nineteenth century, contributed the theoretical frameworks for its study. The various students of mythology, beginning with Jacob Grimm, continuing through Max Müller, Andrew Lang, Wilhelm Mannhardt, and James Frazer, continually turned to modern folk festivals to obtain clues as to the belief and ritual of early man. These folklorists speculated that modern festivals were survivals of ancient community magical ritual whose purpose was to make the days grow longer, to expel winter, to appease gods of the fields, forests, and skies, and most especially, to promote fertility. Festival activities were thus construed as symbolic representations of situations the participants would like to occur. Thus, feasting was a fertility rite, a prayer for abundance; sexual license during the festival was a magical ritual to ensure an abundant harvest, and so forth. On the basis of this sort of hypothesis, whole systems were built in explanation of the nature of the primitive mind, the relation of myth to ritual, and the nature of the festival itself.

These conclusions were speculative, based on often tenuous formal similarities between festival behaviors. Further, they were speculations about origins, rather than about festivals as occasions and forms of behavior that persist through time. Looking at festivals as they exist, one readily sees that they include ceremonial acts, but not all of the behavior in the course of a festival is ceremonial. It may include actions prescribed by law or by the rules of some organization, although not all festival behavior is so prescribed. Above all, one sees that much of the celebration may be directed toward an individual or event honored by the occasion, but by no means does all festival behavior have such a direct symbolic connection. A revealing clue to the persistence of the festival is the fact that a great number of festivals continue to flourish, maintaining essentially the same form, long after their original meaning has been forgotten. This clue should suggest to the investigator that the enduring significance of the festival lies less in its avowed purpose or meaning than in the fact of celebration itself.

1. *Notes on the Folklore of Northern Scotland and the Borders* (London, 1866) .
2. *Shropshire Folklore* (London, 1883) .

SEASONAL FESTIVALS

Given the universality of festivals, it would seem that people need periodic times of escape from work, times in which they can be joyous together. Especially in northern countries, the changing of the seasons provides such spaced occasions. In winter, the nights are long and the days are cold; but then in March days of good weather begin to appear. The snows melt, and buds appear on the trees. In April, the ground is clear, and by May the leaves have come out and flowers are blooming. In Europe, festivals have been celebrated in these months since long before the Christian era, festivals that survive even now as (for example) Carnival and May Day. While often the festivals have included such ceremonies as the burning of an effigy called Winter and the bringing in of a representation of Spring, they have also been strongly associated with unrestrained revelry, with gluttonous eating, violent contests and games, with the playing of pranks, and dancing and masquerade. It is these festive practices that show the stronger tendency to remain constant through time and space, while the ceremonial aspects are subject to great variation. In the Middle Ages, Spanish officials were hard-pressed to curb the exuberance of Shrovetide festivals; their efforts are largely ineffective even today. Among university students of the United States, Spring Holiday (descended from pre-Christian fertility rites?) has become a festival of pilgrimage to Florida, to Bacchanalian revels on the beach.

Summer comes, and the summer solstice. Much has been written about the festivals on the longest and shortest days of the year as being instances of widespread sun-worship, but the case seems to be that generally the midwinter and midsummer festivals were only about the time of the solstice. Whatever the "original" significance, Midsummer and Midwinter were and continue to be occasions for important festivals. Midsummer in much of Northern Europe is associated with going out into the country, gathering flowers and tree branches, and decorating houses, inside and out. Even more widespread on this day is the custom of lighting bonfires and torches. Again, whether the lighting of these fires was originally done as some kind of solar ceremony, or as rites of purification, or for some other reason (it has even been suggested that this was simply a traditional time for burning accumulated rubbish), the practice lives merrily on with no serious magical connotations.

Autumn comes, and the harvest. Through the cold months to come, farmers will be living off stored food, the result of this year's work. At harvest time the food is all there before them, and it is a natural time for a feast, and, perhaps, a thanksgiving.

Then come the cold days, and the first frosts; it is time to bring the cattle down from the mountains and the forests. Since the winter fodder will not be enough to feed all the animals, in the middle of November a number of them are slaughtered and a feast is held. This feast, accompanied by observances in honor of the dead, was the New Year's festival of pre-Christian Germans and Celts: the festival of Yule, as the Scandinavians called it.

CHRISTIAN CALENDAR FESTIVALS

With the rapid spread of Christianity throughout Europe, seasonal celebrations became more complicated. The pagans were willing to accept the Christian dogma, but were reluctant to give up their festivals. The Christian solution was to superimpose Christian meanings onto the old festivals. In 601 A.D., Pope Gregory expressed a policy that had already been pursued by the church for a great many years:

Let the shrines of idols by no means be destroyed, but let the idols which are in them be destroyed. Let water be consecrated and sprinkled in these temples; let altars be erected, and relics laid upon them, because if these same temples are well built it is necessary that they should be converted from the worship of evil spirits to the service of the true God, so that the people, not seeing their own temples destroyed, may displace error from their hearts, and recognise and adore the true God, meeting in the familiar way at the accustomed places. And because they are wont to sacrifice many oxen to devils, some celebration should be given in exchange for this, as that on the day of dedication, or the nativity of the martyrs whose relics are there deposited, they should build houses out of tree branches round the churches which used to serve as temples, and should celebrate a religious feast, and no longer offer beasts to the devils, but kill cattle, and worship God by their feasting, and give thanks to the donor for their abundance; so that while they still keep outward pleasures, they may more readily receive the spiritual joys.[3]

In the spirit of this policy, the unknown day of the birth of Christ was set, for ceremonial purposes, at the twenty-fifth of December, approximately the time of the winter solstice. It quickly displaced such festivals as the Teutonic Yuletide and the Roman Saturnalia and Kalends, taking unto itself as it went many of their attributes, including the Yule log and Paschal candles, feasting, visiting, and decorating with evergreen.

Carnival took a certain respectability as the last days before Lent. May Day activities were carried on during the Day of the Cross: now Christians trooped out into the country as before, to sing, to dance, to adorn themselves with flowers—and to decorate the crosses in the

3. Cited in Mary Hamilton, *Greek Saints and their Festivals* (Edinburgh and London, 1910), p. 5.

surrounding hills. Midsummer became Saint John's Day, and its celebration lived on virtually unchanged except in name. The old Celtic
New Year's festival of Samhain became All Saints (1 November), but
pagan witches continued to ride on its eve. The ancient use of this
occasion to commemorate the dead was given new charter by the
establishment of the festival of All Souls (2 November), on the eve
of which, it was believed, the dead returned, looking for food and
companionship. Even today in much of Europe and the Americas,
villagers observe this festival by baking special food for the dead,
staying off the streets (but leaving their doors ajar so the dead can
enter), and going to the graveyard to eat and drink with the dead
and decorate their graves.

Through the same policy, local gods were replaced by patron saints,
who were considered to take a special interest in the community and
with whom, therefore, the community identified itself. In many
villages, towns, and even nations, the annual festival to the patron is
the most elaborate and most significant of all the festivals of the year.
Legends grow up that tell of the origin of the image, which prove that
the image was determined to remain in this particular locality and
no other. Other legends validating the miraculous (often even living)
nature of the image are developed, along with hundreds of memorats
attesting to specific miracles the image has performed. The saint, then,
is the protector of the community, and all the members of that community are united in their allegiance to him. His festival tends to
become a civic as well as a religious occasion, and is generally a time
for homecomings, feasting, dancing, and other public expressions of
communal satisfaction and good will.

A secular equivalent of the patronal festival is the national celebration in many modern countries, such as the Fourth of July in the
United States and May Day in Russia. These celebrations, however,
tend to be organized institutionally. For the people, the occasion is
mainly one of respite from work (a holiday) and of opportunity for
witnessing a spectacle (a military parade or a fireworks display). In
the United States, there are no national holidays *per se*; all such days
of rest are proclaimed by the individual states. Nevertheless, there
are a few holidays that are observed in almost all the states: New
Year's Day, Washington's Birthday, Good Friday, Memorial Day,
Labor Day, Thanksgiving, and Christmas. Four of these days were
celebrated long before the republic came into being; they are the ones
that are still most popularly celebrated. Of the others, Washington's
Birthday and Labor Day are celebrated by hardly anyone, while Independence Day, once heartily celebrated with community picnics,
parades, band concerts, patriotic speeches, toasts, games, and dancing,
has become, in much of the United States, simply an occasion for

eating watermelon and exploding fireworks. Indeed, even on the most important of our festivals, communities very seldom assemble together to celebrate. Instead, millions of people go into their living rooms at the same time to watch a football game on television or to see "A Christmas Carol" performed. Can we say that they are watching it together? They are having a common, but not a shared, experience. At any rate, there is a strong tendency for community festivals to become transformed into holidays in which spectacles are witnessed.

All the festivals referred to above can be thought of as general participation festivals, which are characterized by large-group celebration. One has a right to take part simply by virtue of being a member of a community; indeed, it is often a man's participation that confirms him as a member. The celebration is generally (though not always) institutionally sanctioned, and celebrated annually on a fixed date.

LIMITED PARTICIPATION FESTIVALS

The act of celebration is not limited only to communities; smaller, more exclusive groups also have their festivals. Occupational groups, as of craftsmen or fishermen, have their celebrations, often on the day of the saint who has been designated their special protector: Saints Crispin and Crespinian (25 October) for cobblers, Saint Peter (29 June) for fishermen, Saint Morand (3 June) for vine-growers. The university, that most traditional of institutions, will celebrate its Founder's Day, Commencement Day, and, above all, Homecoming, with traditional ceremonies, while within its walls fraternities and sororities continue to reenact annually their tribal seasonal festivals of initiation and fertility. The Masons and the Elks, the Country Club and the Explorer's Club will all have their periodic celebrations. Theoretically every new type of group a society can devise or a classifier can discern creates the possibility of a new class of limited participation festival.

Within this class of festival lies a subclass that is living and growing luxuriantly: the businessman's or scholar's convention. More or less peculiar to our time, the convention yet would seem to have its behavioral roots in the oldest of traditions. Achievements of the past year are summed up, those for the new year are projected. The old leader is deposed, a new one is inaugurated. There is a formal reading of papers (= Scriptures?), and there is festive interaction in bars, hotel rooms, and whatever other entertaining places the conventioneers may discover. In other words, the group periodically comes together to interact ceremonially and festively.

Of the class of limited participation festivals, by far the largest number is that of genetic kinship groups, in which participation is limited mainly to members of a nuclear or extended family. Most of these celebrations are associated with formalized transitions of individuals from one stage of life to another, and thus are occasional, not periodic. One's life, in most cultures of the world, is not only a simple biological progression from birth to death but also a social movement from one status and role to another. The occasion for passing from one such stage to another is marked by special ceremonies and festivities, by "rites of passage." In most cases, each of these celebrations will be directed toward any given individual only once in his life, but he will participate in such celebrations any number of times.

The moments considered as critical in a person's life vary immensely from culture to culture. In some societies the child's first haircut is a time for celebration, in others, the first cutting of the fingernails, in others, the first communion. The forms for celebration also vary widely until the only constant that remains is the fact of occasional celebration. In the United States, a child is born, and the father hands out cigars (a symbol of his proven virility?). The mother's hospital room is filled with flowers, and visitors parade in to pronounce ritualistic benedictions ("He looks just like his father").

In a few days the Catholic family may congregate for toasts, fellowship, and a meal on the occasion of the baby's formally receiving his name and his godparents. The child grows, and at a certain age (about the time of puberty) is admitted to adulthood with a rite and a feast. The Bar Mitzvah is a good example of this moment. The coming-out party, in which a girl is formally presented to society, is another.

A young man asks a young woman to marry him; she says yes, and then he must engage her father in a peculiar ritual (in the study, behind closed doors, with the father feigning reluctance). Then the parents meet, with a formal meal and toasts to the young couple, everyone sizing up everyone else, in discreet reminiscence of the older, franker custom of an economic accounting between the parents before the match was approved.

The marriage date is set, and friends start giving "showers" for the bride-to-be. Gifts are given, refreshments are taken, and games are played (whoever crosses her legs must pay a forfeit). The groom is given a bachelor party on the eve of the wedding. His friends get him as drunk as they can, console him for the awful thing that is about to happen to him, and make ribald references to his coming honeymoon.

The wedding takes place, generally in the morning, and involves costumes particular to the occasion, and a ring, and something old, something new, something borrowed, something blue, and a bouquet tossed to the bridesmaids, and rice and tin cans and a reception with a wedding cake, and the bride and groom sneaking away while the guests go on celebrating without them.

The couple usually observe their anniversaries privately, until, if they have been able to stay together that long, the whole family joins in celebrating their twenty-fifth and fiftieth anniversaries.

The final transitional rite is that of the funeral, with its rigidly stereotyped gestures of respect and mourning for the deceased. In a good number of societies (including Ireland and Andean South America) these behaviors are accompanied by such reintegrative practices as getting drunk, singing, and telling funny stories. Life must go on.

The only periodic family festival is the annual celebration of an individual's birthday, at which time family and friends come together to reassure him of the affection and esteem in which they hold him.

In addition to the above festivals, there may be celebrations accompanying communal work: barn-raising, seeding, road-construction and maintenance, nut-gathering, roundups, and hunting expeditions. Rodeos and fairs constitute another special class of community celebration.

In the villages of Mediterranean and South American countries, most, if not all, of the several classes of festival are still regularly observed. An individual will take part every year in the birthday celebrations of his family and friends, will participate in their "rites of passage," will celebrate the patronal festival of his town (and perhaps also of his region and his country), will celebrate the occasions of Carnival, seeding time, Holy Week and Easter, Corpus Christi, Saint John's Eve, Harvest, All Hallow's and All Souls, and Christmas, as well as that of his occupational patron, and of the annual fair. Festivals, then, play no small part in his life.

FUNCTIONS OF THE FESTIVAL

As may well be supposed, festivals, which involve a great expenditure of energy by the entire community, have a number of very important functions, which can be either positive or disruptive. Economically, they can provide occasion for redistribution of wealth; witness Christmas in the United States. Many people save their money all year in "Christmas Clubs" (providing banks with additional investment capital), in order to have enough money in December to make the gifts expected of them. For many businesses, Christmas sales make the difference between profit and loss for the year. Negatively, festivals may hurt the economy by taking people away from work. In many parts of Peru, the people used to celebrate Carnival for two weeks, no less, until the government forbade its celebration on working days, on the grounds that it was crippling to commerce and industry. In many countries of Central and South America, the "cargo" system, whereby once a man has adequate economic resources he is expected to bear the costs of the patronal festival, effectively works to keep any individual from accumulating much wealth; indeed, it sometimes bankrupts him.

State festivals have long been used for political purposes. The ruler's birthday has for centuries been celebrated in countries throughout the world, and the practice has been adapted by modern countries to promote patriotism, to generate intense feelings of devotion to the democratic, or communistic, or socialistic way of life.

These functions, important though they are, must be regarded as secondary; they are not sufficient in themselves to explain the prevalence and persistence of festivals. The ritualistic and ceremonial functions of the festival—to bring prosperity or (more concretely) rain, to foretell and influence the course of the coming year, to honor someone or something—all are obviously important in themselves, but are also inadequate as explanation of the function of the festival as a whole, since such ceremonials can, and do, exist independently.

Rather, the central function of the festival seems to be to give occasion for men to rejoice together—to interact in an ambience of acceptance and conviviality. In the case of general participation festivals, the festival is often the *only* occasion in which the members of a community come together. On this occasion, they interact; the interaction is satisfying, therefore likely to be repeated. The satisfaction creates a bond between the participants; they have had pleasure in each other's company. They identify with each other; in a general participation festival the individual relates to, and identifies himself with, the community. Thus, the festival is a prime device for promoting social cohesion, for integrating individuals into a society or group and maintaining them as members through shared, recurrent, positively reinforcing performance. It is, indeed, "the most concrete expression of collective emotions and loyalties."[4]

It would seem to follow that with the diminution of festivals would also occur a corresponding lessening of identification of the individual with his society (which is not to say that one causes the other). Note, for example, the decline of Independence Day celebrations and also of patriotism; on the other hand, the flourishing of university Homecomings and also of alumni associations. Homecomings maintain the individual's identification with his extended family and alma

4. Robert Briffault, "Festivals," *Encyclopaedia of the Social Sciences* (New York, 1931), 6: 201.

mater; presumably, such identification is less among those who do not participate.

Occasional, limited-participation festivals, especially those associated with the "rites of passage," have other functions. The celebrations performed when a person comes of age, and when he is betrothed and married, mark the occasion of the assigning of a new role to the individual. From this moment he can no longer behave in the old way; he must behave in the new. Much of the joking and crying associated with weddings are traditional ways of communicating the significance of the occasion. At the same time, these celebrations function to honor the individual and confirm his membership in the group.

The prime function of the festival is to provide occasion and form for positive group interaction, which is a necessary condition for the continued existence of the group. We have talked of festivals primarily in terms of occasion; now it is necessary to view them as providers of form.

THE STRUCTURE OF THE FESTIVAL

The festival cannot be defined as a particular kind of behavior, as can song or storytelling; rather it is a set of traditional behaviors. Indeed, the festival itself is often the context for the other genres of folklore. The festival is often the only occasion of the year in which the inhabitants of a region wear their traditional dress; it is often validated by an origin legend and traditional recitations of miracles or great events of the past; festival behavior may include the decorating and carrying in procession of an image, and popular devotions to that image. It will almost certainly include a feast (put together with traditional recipes) and drink (drunk in a ceremonial way, with traditional toasts and manners of tossing it down). There will be proverbs and sayings associated with the festival. Celebrants may sing and dance to traditional music played on handcrafted instruments. Beliefs and corresponding memorats that prescribe correct behavior may abound.

In a word, the festival may be considered a major class of folklore, one that may include within itself almost all the others as subclasses. A festival gives a unified context for the description and definition of the genres that occur within it, providing a basis for inter-genre comparison. A complex entity, a structural whole, the festival cannot be understood without an understanding of the interrelation of its components.

Unfortunately, most of the past scholarship touching on festivals has been not of the festivals themselves in all their complexity, but of the components, taken out of context. Thus, students of comparative religion have taken the ritualistic or ceremonial elements out of many festivals and made lists of them (e.g., Saint John's bonfires, Carrying out of Winter, Christmas trees), fitting them together to support theories. Meanwhile, folklorists have evolved what may be considered a subgenre in its own right: Calendar Customs. Here, individual practices associated with festivals are listed, as in an archive, according to the day or the occasion with which they are associated. The result is a jumble of unrelated, generally quaint, behaviors. Many articles have been published on such subjects as Holy Week processions, Nativity Plays, caroling, and Easter eggs, with little or no indication given that these occur or exist as integral parts of festivals. Consequently, our knowledge of both the festivals and these components is incomplete.

To give a few examples: Our idea of the nature of the folk religion of an area will be far different if we extract from the festival only the popular devotions—the candle-burning, making of vows, giving of ex-votos, carrying the image in procession—without considering the behavior the people indulge in between these practices—the drinking, dancing, game-playing and love-making. What are the motivations for and the uses of dance, song, and music? The Peruvian *Marinera* is danced as a courtship ritual; it is also danced before the altar in honor of the patron saint. It is often danced in both sacred and secular contexts in the same festival by the same dancers. Music, words, and movement remain constant, yet the significance changes according to the place of the behavior in the festival. One cannot necessarily infer meaning or function from content or form. Likewise, the typical costume of a region may, as in most of Spain, be worn only during regional festivals. Why are they worn then? Because wearing of the costume is one of the means that the festival provides for the individual's identifying himself as a "member" of the region. Not to realize the part played by costume in the festival can lead to two common errors: to believe that the "typical" garb described is the everyday dress of the inhabitants of the region; or to conclude that this is "not really" the regional garb, but only a fossil preserved by tradition and sentimentality.

This is not to say that subclasses of festival behavior should never be taken out of context, but only that there are few questions, outside of certain problems of structure and content, that can be answered by reference to these behaviors in isolation. To be sure, in the course of time many festivals disappear altogether, leaving only disconnected activities associated with a certain day: fireworks on the Fourth of July, pancakes at Shrovetide. These calendar customs may now exist quite independently of any festival.

If the festival must be analyzed as a complex, integral whole, upon what principles can such an analysis be organized? One promising way is to try to determine how each kind of behavior contributes to the function of the festival as a whole. It may be assumed that festival behavior, being voluntary, and being repeated by the individuals of a community year after year through centuries, is rewarding to the performer; further, it may be assumed that the reward is not in the cognitive domain but rather in the affective (one does not go to a festival to learn anything new). That is, the interaction of individuals is of the kind that generates a positive emotional response or expresses a positive emotional condition. The traditional forms of festival behavior can be seen as affective symbols, which function to express and generate not concepts but desired emotions. The festival is a shared sequence of emotional experiences based on symbolic interaction.

We have seen above how the wearing of a traditional costume may be an expression of belonging. Allegiance, subservience, and devotion all have their conventionalized expression, most notably in the participation in processions or parades, the carrying of an image or a flag, and the singing of an anthem or hymn. Acts generative of feelings of contentment and well-being are among the most typical of festival behaviors, most usually taking the form of eating and drinking, often to excess.

The sum total of all these behaviors is the festival. Abstracting from the concrete behaviors and their results, one can often make a rough distinction between three large classes of festival: those expressive mainly of devotion, loyalty, allegiance—such as patriotic celebrations, Holy Week processions, and many urban religious festivals; those expressive of joy—Carnival and New Year's are good examples of this class; and those in which the two above classes are brought together, as in the Mediterranean patronal festival, in which there are prayers, but there is also drunkenness; fulfillment of vows, but also music and dance; pious legends and stories that are not so pious; songs to the Virgin and also to faithless women.

The festival, in short, is an extremely complex and important social phenomenon that needs, and merits, close inquiry and analysis. Yet it is a neglected area of folklore study; most significant studies of the festival in the United States and Great Britain in the last thirty years have been made by anthropologists and students of comparative religion, and even these studies are only of aspects of the festival. It seems ironic that folklorists should forfeit by neglect the very genre that includes within it most of the other folklore genres, and so gives them coherence.

The student might do well at this point to take a look at his own life and the part festivals have played and continue to play in it. New Year's, Valentine's Day, Spring Vacation, Memorial Day, Independence Day, Halloween, Thanksgiving, along with birthdays, weddings, and funerals, and Junior Proms, and Moratorium Days, and marches on Washington, and Spring Flings and Candlings and rock festivals—these have been and continue to be significant occasions for most of us. They have affected the form and substance of our lives. In our celebration of them each of us participates, at one level of abstraction or another, in folk traditions that span the world and time.

Bibliography and Selected Readings

Barnouw, Victor. "The Changing Character of a Hindu Festival." *American Anthropologist* 56 (1954) : 74–86. The classic problems of cultural persistence and change are put into a festival context.

Briffault, Robert. "Festivals." *Encyclopaedia of the Social Sciences.* New York: The Macmillan Company, 1931, 6: 198–201. A brief, well-written survey of festival types, mainly in terms of origins. See also the related topics listed at the end of the article.

Dobbyns, Henry F. "The Religious Festival." Ph.D. dissertation, Cornell, 1960. An excellent comparative work that classifies festivals primarily in terms of their participants.

"Festivals and Fasts." *Encyclopaedia of Religion and Ethics.* New York: Charles Scribner's Sons, 1961, 5: 835–94. An extensive overview of the main feast days of many of the world's religions, giving essential information on the liturgical norms around which folk practices tend to cluster.

James, E. O. *Seasonal Feasts and Festivals.* London: Thames and Hudson, 1961. Though the work concentrates mainly on calendar celebrations of the ancient world, it also throws in two interesting chapters on folk festivals and folk drama.

McNeill, Florence. *The Silver Bough.* Glasgow: Maclellan, 1957. "A four-volume study of the national and local festivals of Scotland."

MacNeill, Maire. *The Festival of Lughnasa.* Oxford: Oxford University Press, 1962. Derived mainly from archival sources, this diachronic study of an old Irish festival is one of the best of its kind.

O'Sullivan, Sean. *A Handbook of Irish Folklore.* Dublin: Educational Company of Ireland, Ltd., for the Folklore of Ireland Society, 1942. Contains a long section on "Festivals of the Year" that well illustrates the direction of interest of Irish folklorists by the kinds of questions they ask.

Powdermaker, Hortense. "Feasts in New Ireland; the Social Foundation of Eating." *American Anthropologist* 34 (1932) : 236–47. An interesting study of one of the prime components of the festival.

Shoemaker, Alfred L. *Eastertide in Pennsylvania.* Kutztown, Penn.: Pennsylvania Folklife Society, 1959. An excellent example of the way many American students of folklife approach the festival.

Turner, Victor W. *The Ritual Process.* Chicago: Aldine Publishing Co., 1969. A mine of fertile ideas about relationships between festivals and social needs and problems.

Van Gennep, Arnold. *Manuel de folklore français contemporain.* Paris: A. Picard, 1, pts. 1–5, 1943–51; 3, 1937. In six volumes, this is probably the most comprehensive regional study of festivals ever published. Vol. 3 presents the questionnaires that were used, affording a useful handbook to the student of festivals.

———. *The Rites of Passage.* Trans. M. B. Vizedom and G. L. Caffee. London: Routledge and Paul, 1960. First published in 1909 and never superseded, this is still the best general study of transition rites, though there are a number of excellent works on the sociology of marriage and death.

Von Sydow, Carl Wilhelm. "The Mannhardtian Theories about the Last Sheaf and the Fertility Demons from a Modern Critical Point of View." In his *Selected Papers on Folklore,* ed. Laurits Bødker, pp. 89–105. Copenhagen: Rosenkilde and Bagger, 1948. A disciplined, common-sense antidote to the theories of Sir James Frazer, which are still cited all too often by students of myth and ritual.

Wright, A. R., and T. E. Lones, eds. *British Calendar Customs.* 3 vols. London: W. Glaisher, Ltd., for the Folk-Lore Society, 1936–40. Essentially a bound archive, full of bits and pieces of customs associated with the days of the year.

8 RECREATIONS AND GAMES
Robert A. Georges

Play is a form of expressive behavior common among all human beings and manifested overtly in all cultures. Like art, language, and religion, play is a complex phenomenon that cannot be defined succinctly. Several characteristics, however, can readily be isolated. First, play is voluntary in that it does not directly satisfy biological needs associated with survival. In addition, because it does not result in the production of wealth or goods, play can be said to be nonproductive in any tangible sense, even though it may contribute substantially to the physical, social, and psychological growth and development of the individual. Thus, a person learns to play ball because he sees others doing it and because he thinks it will be enjoyable. He is not forced to participate, nor does he expect any reward for having done so. Another characteristic of play is that it is separated from reality in time and space; therefore, its goals and sources of motivation are intrinsic. Children playing "house," for example, establish their own imaginary roles and realm; what they do and what they work toward are determined within the context of this microcosm. The cessation of such a play activity, either voluntarily or because of outside intrusion, brings to an end the temporal and spatial detachment from reality.

As long as there is no competitive interaction, the pastime can be called a nongame or, for convenience here, recreation. Games, however, differ from other play activities in that they involve competition between at least two persons. Explicit or implicit rules, which specify the kind of human interaction permissible and which the players are familiar with before the activity begins, are also required, as is a specific method for determining the winner (s) and loser (s). In "Musical Chairs," for example, the players know (1) that there will always be one less chair than needed; (2) that they are in competition with other players to find an empty chair when the music stops; (3) that the one who fails to find an unoccupied chair will be eliminated from the game; and (4) that there can be only one winner, the person who is left after all others have been eliminated. It is this awareness of the game as a system and the ability of the participants to discover, in turn, the subsystems within that system that differentiates games from other play activities of both humans and other animals.[1]

Early investigators were not concerned with the nature of play. Instead, they concentrated on the history and distribution of specific recreations and games. Joseph Strutt, a pioneer in the field, was interested in the leisure-time activities of his countrymen because he thought they could provide some insight into the English national character. "In order to form a just estimation of the character of any particular people," Strutt wrote in the introduction to his monumental study *The Sports and Pastimes of the People of England* (1801), "it is absolutely necessary to investigate the sports and pastimes generally prevalent among them." Strutt adds that "when we follow them into their retirements, where no disguise is necessary, we are most likely to see them in their true state, and may best judge of their national disposition."

Others shared Strutt's interest, and the number of collections of national games and recreations multiplied rapidly in Europe during the remainder of the nineteenth century. Among the first of these were compilations of games and rhymes from Scotland (1842) and England (1842, 1849) by Robert Chambers and J. O. Halliwell re-

---

1. These general characteristics of play and games have been noted in a number of investigations, including Johan Huizinga, *Homo Ludens* (London, 1949; first published in 1944 in German); Jean Piaget, *Play, Dreams and Imitation in Childhood*, trans. C. Gattegno and F. M. Hodgson (London, 1951); and Roger Caillois, *Man, Play, and Games*, trans. Meyer Barash (Glencoe, Ill., 1961).

spectively[2] and an extensive collection of German children's games, *Alemannisches Kinderlied und Kinderspiel aus der Schweiz* (1857), by Ernst L. Rochholz. It was during the last quarter of the century, however, that the scholarly output reached its peak. Seminal and definitive studies were published during this period for such countries as Germany, Russia, Hungary, Norway, and Denmark.[3] In the year 1883 alone, an impressive Sicilian collection by the Italian folklorist Giuseppe Pitré appeared in print, as did the pioneering work on the games and songs of France by Eugène Rolland and the major study *Games and Songs of American Children* by William W. Newell.[4] Lady Alice B. Gomme's *Traditional Games of England, Scotland, and Ireland*, the standard work for Great Britain and still recognized by many as a model collection because of its comprehensiveness, was published in two volumes in 1894 and 1898. During the same period, Stewart Culin, an American anthropologist, turned his attention to the traditional pastimes of more exotic cultures, publishing valuable texts from Hawaii, Korea, and the Philippines by the end of the century[5] and completing his definitive study *Games of the North American Indians* in 1907. Special mention must also be made of the eight-volume collection *Kinderspel en Kinderlust in Zuid-Nederland* (1902–8) by Alfons de Cock and Isidor Teirlinck, the most exhaustive compilation ever assembled for a single nation.

Like folklorists generally during the nineteenth and early twentieth century, these early investigators of traditional recreations and games had as their primary objectives to gather and edit texts and to provide distributional and historical descriptions. They paid little attention to theoretical matters, except to comment on the origins of traditional pastimes in general or to speculate occasionally about the probable source of specific games (e.g., that "London Bridge" may

2. Robert Chambers, *Popular Rhymes of Scotland* (Edinburgh, 1842); James O. Halliwell, *The Nursery Rhymes of England* (London, 1842) and *Popular Rhymes and Nursery Tales* (London, 1849).

3. Friedrich Zimmer, *Volkstümliche Spiellieder und Liederspiele* (Quedlinburg, 1879); E. A. Pokrovskij, *Dĕtskie igry* (Moscow, 1895); Aron Kiss, *Magyar gyermekjátékgyüjtemény* (Budapest, 1891); Bernt Stφylen, *Norske Barnerim og Leikar* (Kristiania, 1899); and E. T. Kristiansen, *Danske Börnerim, Remser og Lege* (Århus, 1896).

4. Giuseppi Pitré, *Giuochi fanciulleschi siciliani*, in *Biblioteca delle tradizioni popolari siciliane* 13 (1883); and Eugène Rolland, *Rimes et jeux de l'enfance* (Paris, 1883). Newell's collection was enlarged and reissued in 1903, and that revision is now available in a Dover paperback edition (New York, 1963).

5. "Hawaiian Games," *American Anthropologist*, n. s., 1 (1899): 201–47; "Philippine Games," *American Anthropologist*, n. s., 2 (1900): 643–56; and *Korean Games, with Notes on the Corresponding Games of China and Japan* (Philadelphia, 1895; reissued as *Games of the Orient: Korea, China, Japan* [Rutland, Vt., 1958]).

have had its roots in the practice of foundation sacrifice or that "Hop-scotch" may have developed from classical myths of the labyrinth).[6] Their productivity, however, and the scope of their work have never been equaled.

Since the early 1900s, folklore scholars have devoted comparatively little attention to traditional pastimes. No classification systems have been prepared for games and recreations as they have for folk narra-tive, and no new theories of play have been advanced by folklorists. Furthermore, while innumerable articles on the subject have been published in the scholarly journals, book-length studies have ap-peared only sporadically. Most of these, moreover, merely follow the precedent set by earlier writers in that they are collections rather than analytical works. This is true of the publications of Paul G. Brewster, the leading American authority on games and one of the most prolific writers on the subject. Brewster's standard work, *American Nonsing-ing Games* (1953), and his studies of European, Asian, and African games[7] provide excellent texts and extensive comparative and histo-rical notes, but offer no innovations in methodology or analytical techniques. The same thing can be said for such works as those on Jamaican games by Martha Warren Beckwith (1922), Danish games by S. T. Thyregod (1931), and singing games from Tobago and Trinidad by J. D. Elder (1965).[8]

Several other studies provide some commentary on the context and function of selected recreations and games. Works by Wolford (1916), Botkin (1937), and Warnick (1942) illustrate the historical develop-ment and social significance of the American play-party, a short-lived diversion that drew on folksongs and games for its subject matter.[9] Thomas W. Talley's *Negro Folk Rhymes* (1922), the only book-length study of the rich vein of rhyme, game, riddle, and speech of the American Negro, provides extensive, though frequently tenuous,

6. For representative comments of this sort see Newell (1963 reprint edition), pp. 210–11, 254; and Gomme, 1 (1894), 226–27, 346–50.

7. Representative publications by Brewster are the following: "Some Games from Other Lands," *Southern Folklore Quarterly* 7 (1943): 109–17; "Three Russian Games and Their Western (and Other) Parallels," *Southern Folklore Quarterly* 23 (1959): 126–31; *Games and Sports in Shakespeare,* Folklore Fellows Communi-cations, 177 (*Helsinki,* 1959); and (with Thomas A. Sebeok) *Studies in Cheremis: Games,* Indiana University Folklore Series, No. 11 (Bloomington, Ind., 1958).

8. Martha Warren Beckwith, *Folk-Games of Jamaica,* Publications of the Folk-Lore Foundation, 1 (1922); S. T. Thrygod, *Danmarks Sanglege* (Copenhagen, 1931); and J. D. Elder, *Song Games from Trinidad and Tobago.* Publications of the American Folklore Society, Bibliographical and Special Series, 16 (1965).

9. Leah Jackson Wolford, *The Play-Party in Indiana,* Indiana Historical Col-lections, 4 (1916); Benjamin A. Botkin, *The American Play-Party Song,* The Uni-versity Studies of the University of Nebraska, 37 (1937); and Florence Warnick, *Play Party Songs in Western Maryland* (Washington, D. C., 1942).

interpretations of his data. Particularly significant is the work of the English folklorists Peter and Iona Opie, whose book *The Lore and Language of Schoolchildren* (1959) includes myriad texts and functional analyses of jokes, juvenile rites, pranks, and nicknames as well as children's games and calendar customs. But even these works devote a disproportionate amount of space to compilations of texts.

New directions for research on traditional pastimes are implicit in recent work in the other social sciences, notably in psychology, sociology, and anthropology. Although the full significance of these studies has yet to be assessed, some of the findings have already been applied to play, particularly by Johan Huizinga, Jean Piaget, Erik Erikson, Roger Caillois, Brian Sutton-Smith, and John M. Roberts. Piaget and Erikson have limited their research to the play activities of children, Sutton-Smith and Roberts have examined games of all kinds cross-culturally, and Huizinga and Caillois write about play generally.[10] We shall draw on the tentative findings of these investigators in the discussion of the nature of traditional pastimes which follows.

As has been pointed out repeatedly above, students of traditional recreations and games have devoted the bulk of their time to recording, editing, and annotating texts. But each investigator has also had to cope with the problem of the nature of traditional pastimes, if for no other reason than to find a suitable classification system for his material. Perusal of any standard collection reveals the difficulties inherent in such a task. Games, for example, are sometimes grouped along configurational lines (bridge, circle, and line games), frequently according to the nature of the activity involved (chasing, guessing, and hiding games), often on the basis of the sex of the players (games of little girls, boys' games), and occasionally according to the type of equipment used (specialized versus readily available objects).

That the investigators themselves are frequently unhappy with such overlapping and inconsistent categories is readily apparent. Brewster, for example, notes in his introduction to the games that he edited for *The Frank C. Brown Collection of North Carolina Folklore*: "The system of classification which I finally adopted is of my own devising, and I anticipate criticism of it by admitting that it is not without flaws. However, it is the best that several hours of trial and error and general puzzlement could evolve." Sutton-Smith makes a similar admission in his study *The Games of New Zealand Children* (1959), adding that the reason for the difficulty in classifying games is "be-

10. Representative works by these investigators are given in n. 1, above, and in notes 13, 16, 19, 27, and 30, which follow.

cause games are complex group behaviors deriving their nature from many sources."[11]

Sutton-Smith's explanation is indeed valid, not only for games, but for play in general. For this reason, it is wise to eschew classification systems *per se* and to concentrate instead on the kinds of behavior inherent in play activities. Keeping in mind the general characteristics of play and games mentioned earlier, we can examine traditional recreations and games within the context of four "models," each of which is based upon the principal kind of behavior necessary to achieve the ultimate goal or objective of the play activity.

The first model can be exemplified by the nongames (recreations) "Kings of Spain" and "Old Witch." A typical variant of the former is the following text from North Carolina:

> The girls seat themselves in a row. The boys advance toward them singing:
>   "We are three fine kings of Spain
>   We've come to court your daughter Jane."
>   "My daughter Jane she's far too young
>   To be courted by your lyin' tongue."
>   "Be she young or be she old
>   Her beauty's fair, she must be sold."
>   "Go back, go back, you Spanish king,
>   And choose the fairest in the ring."
> The girl chosen takes his hand, and they promenade around the two groups. The game continues until all the boys and girls are matched, and they then play some game that requires partners.[12]

"Old Witch" ("Molly Bright," "Chickamy, Chickamy, Craney Crow") is more involved. Each participant is assigned to a specific role: that of mother, child, or witch. The mother leaves her children in order to run an errand and warns them not to let the old witch in. They do, and the witch carries them off one by one. After the last child has been abducted, the mother is invited to the witch's house, where each of the stolen children is served to her as a delectable dish. Through prescribed ruses, the mother rescues all of her children, they return home, and the action usually ends. In some variants, however, the witch is pursued, caught, and punished, while in others it is the witch who must chase and tag someone to become her successor, thus injecting an element of chance and perhaps even fear into the action.

Both "Kings of Spain" and "Old Witch" are, in essence, miniature

---

11. Brian Sutton-Smith, *The Games of New Zealand Children* (Berkeley and Los Angeles, 1959), p. 7.

12. Paul G. Brewster, ed., "Children's Games and Rhymes," in *The Frank C. Brown Collection of North Carolina Folklore* 1 (Durham, N. C., 1952): 93.

play-dramas in which the players act out assigned parts. While the dramatization focuses on courting and mate selection in the former and on the abduction and rescue of children in the latter, the primary demands of each play activity are on role-playing and imitation. These recreations (nongames), then, can be regarded as models of mimicry in which the imitation of social roles and human activity is an end in itself.[13]

Since play activities that are models of mimicry are imitative rather than competitive, it is not surprising to discover that they are particularly popular among preschool and primary school children. Furthermore, as Piaget and Erikson have noted, such pastimes are probably mandatory in the normal process of socialization, for it is largely through them that the child first learns to imitate reality objectively.[14] Thus, whether he is simulating everyday activities (e.g., washing clothes, sweeping the house, going to church in "Here We Go Round the Mulberry Bush"), projecting himself into familiar social roles (e.g., the farmer, his wife, their child in "The Farmer in the Dell"), or dramatizing incomprehensible transitional stages in life (e.g., death and burial in "Jenny Jones"), the child is learning to deal with realistic experience through planning and experimentation.

Turning now to the second model, we will once again find it advantageous to begin with two examples, both of which have long histories and considerable geographical distribution. The first of these, "Prison Base" ("Bars," "Prisoner's Bars"), dates back to at least the thirteenth century. A representative description of this game is the following one provided by Brewster:

Two leaders are chosen. These choose alternately their followers from all those playing. Each group selects a base some fifty yards from that of its opponent, and each dares the other. Any member of either side tapped by someone belonging to the opposite side must stand in prison, a ring marked on the ground a few yards behind the base. He may be won back if one of his own side dares to run in and tap him. The game ends when all members of one side have been caught.[15]

Quite similar to "Prison Base" is the game "How Many Miles to Babylon" ("Marlybright," "Molly Bright," "King and Queen of Cantelon"), which appears to have enjoyed a continuous dissemination since Elizabethan times. In this game there are two groups of players

13. The term *mimicry* is also used by Caillois (pp. 19–23), but in a different context.

14. Piaget, pp. 142–46; Erik Erikson, *Childhood and Society* (New York, 1950), pp. 182–218.

15. Brewster, *The Frank C. Brown Collection*, p. 73.

who stand at opposite ends of a designated play area. The central person, usually referred to as "the witch," positions himself midway between them. The game begins with a dialogue between the two groups, most often similar to this text given by Newell:

> "Marlow, marlow, marlow bright,
> How many miles to Babylon?"
> "Threescore and ten."
> "Can I get there by candlelight?"
> "Yes, if your legs are as long as light,
> But take care of the old gray witch by
>   the road-side."[16]

The players then run from one side of the play area to the other while the person who is "it" tries to catch as many as he can. All who are caught must assist the "witch," and the game continues until there is a single uncaptured person remaining. He is declared the winner and may also be designated to be the "witch" for the next game.

The characteristics that differentiate the second model from the first are readily apparent in "Prison Base" and "How Many Miles to Babylon." Both are competitive, and each has a set of rules that must be followed. Thus, they are both games; and like all games, their ultimate objective is to determine the winner(s) and loser(s). As was noted above, however, it is not the *objective* of the play activity that distinguishes one model from another, but rather the principal kind of behavior necessary to achieve that goal or objective. For this second model, it is physical skill and dexterity that receive the greatest emphasis. The running, chasing, and tagging that are required in these games are physical acts; and it is the player who is most skillful and dexterous who wins the game. Such games as "Prison Base" and "How Many Miles to Babylon," then, can be regarded as models of achievement in which success is determined by physical skill and dexterity.[17]

The competition in games that follow this model may be among individuals, as is the case in "Hopscotch," "Jacks," and "Marbles"; between teams or packs (e.g., "Anthony Over," "Capture the Flag"); or between an individual and a pack, as in various games of "Tag." In all cases, however, it is the physical ability of the individual players, taken either singly or collectively, that is prized.

16. Newell (1963 reprint edition), p. 153.

17. Sutton-Smith, Roberts, and others also discuss games of physical skill, but for them the term tends to be used as a class or category of games rather than as a model of behavior. See, for example, John M. Roberts, Malcolm J. Arth, and Robert B. Bush, "Games in Culture," *American Anthropologist,* n. s., 61 (1959): 597–605; and Brian Sutton-Smith and John M. Roberts, "Rubrics of Competitive Behavior," *Journal of Genetic Psychology* 105 (1964): 13–37.

Preliminary cross-cultural surveys conducted by anthropologists indicate that games emphasizing physical skill and dexterity have a near-universal ethnographic distribution.[18] In addition, studies of child development have stressed the significance of such activities in the growth of motor coordination and manipulative skill.[19] There is also evidence available that suggests that a close correlation exists in a given culture between child-training practices and the number and kinds of games stressing physical skill.[20] There can be little doubt that games of all kinds emphasizing skill and dexterity provide the most important key to our understanding of why people play.

To exemplify the third of our four models, we shall utilize the game "Hare and Hounds." The following variants, cited by Strutt (1801), Lady Gomme (1894), and Brewster (1953) respectively, indicate how little this traditional game has changed through time.

I. In this game one of the boys is permitted to run out, and having law given to him, that is, being permitted to go to a certain distance from his comrades before they pursue him, their object is to take him if possible before he can return home. We have the following speech from an idle boy in an old comedy, written towards the close of the sixteenth century,

> And also when we play and hunt the fox,
> I outrun all the boys in the schoole.[21]

II. A boys' game. One boy is chosen as the Hare. He carries with him a bag filled with strips of paper. The rest of the boys are the Hounds. The Hare has a certain time (say fifteen minutes) allowed him for a start, and he goes across country, scattering some paper on his way in order to deceive his pursuers, but must keep up the continuity of his paper track-signs. The Hounds follow him and try to catch him before he gets home, which is a place agreed upon beforehand.[22]

III. The "fox" is allowed a few minutes (or a few yards) start, and then the "dogs" start in pursuit of him. Like a real fox, the former uses every possible trick to throw his pursuers off his trail, doubling on his tracks, hiding until they have passed him, etc.[23]

In "Hare and Hounds," as in other games, there is competition (in this case, between an individual and a pack), and the primary objective of each side is to win (i.e., the "hare" by avoiding capture, the "hounds" by catching their victim). Once again, however, it is the

18. Roberts, Arth, and Bush, pp. 603–4.
19. Piaget, pp. 142–46.
20. John M. Roberts and Brian Sutton-Smith, "Child Training and Game Involvement," *Ethnology* 1 (1962) : 174, 180.
21. Strutt, "Hunt the Fox," p. 284.
22. Gomme, "Hare and Hounds," 1: 191.
23. Brewster, "Fox," in *American Nonsinging Games*, p. 77.

method of achieving this objective rather than the objective itself that is important. The texts cited above are instructive on this point: the "hare" attempts "to deceive his pursuers" (text II), and he "uses every possible trick to throw his pursuers off his trail" (text III). The "hare" is thus a strategist, and his would-be captors as well rely upon strategy to find him. Both the pursuer and the pursued have a number of courses of action open to them, and both must make choices among alternatives. They do so, though, only after they have analyzed the probable choices of the others in alternative situations. In other words, each can see himself in a "reciprocal perspective,"[24] thus enabling the participants to play the game from both sides, as it were. "Hare and Hounds," then, can be considered a model of achievement in which success is determined by strategy.[25]

The kind of strategy necessary is determined, for the most part, by the nature of the competition. In "Noughts and Crosses" or "Tic-Tac-Toe," for example, the two players can be considered equals: each tries to get three X's or three O's in a row before the other does. In the game "Steps" or "May I?" on the other hand, the central person is in a dominant position, for it is he who has control over the actions of the other players. Since he specifies the number and kind of steps each game participant may take (e.g., "three giant steps," "five baby steps"), he can, and frequently does, show partiality. The other players, being in a subordinate position, cannot rely upon counter-strategy except, perhaps, through silent protest when they deliberately refrain from asking "May I?"

The similarity between games emphasizing strategy and actual life situations is obvious. The student who writes an examination paper in which he presents the kinds of information that he thinks the professor will be most impressed with is following this model of behavior. The same can be said for the young child who knows precisely what to do to get attention or the army general who plots a military offensive. As is true for traditional recreations and games patterned on the first two models, those that emphasize achievement through successful strategy are undoubtedly preparatory for or reflective of realistic human behavior.[26]

24. This term is used in a discussion of games of strategy in Omar K. Moore and Alan R. Anderson, "The Structure of Personality," in *Motivation and Social Interaction,* ed. O. J. Harvey (New York, 1963), p. 179.

25. For additional discussion of the role of strategy in games see Roberts, Arth, and Bush, pp. 600–601; Moore and Anderson, pp. 178–82; and Sutton-Smith and Roberts, "Rubrics of Competitive Behavior" and "Child Training and Game Involvement," passim.

26. Roberts, Arth, and Bush postulate that a relationship probably exists between social complexity (e.g., political organization) and the presence of games of strategy (pp. 600–601), which may prove to be a significant discovery if proved and demonstrated specifically.

The final model with which we shall be concerned can be illustrated by a number of well-known traditional pastimes for which brief descriptions will suffice. First, there is the guessing game "Odd or Even," in which one player must indicate whether he thinks the number of counters (e.g., stones, marbles) clenched in the hand of another player is odd or even. Another example is counting out, the practice frequently utilized to determine which player will be "it" for a given game (e.g., "Eenie, meenie, miney, moe," "One potato, two potato," "Onery, twoery, ickery, Ann").[27] Finally, there is "Spin the Bottle," in which one player spins a bottle and kisses the person at whom the bottle points when it stops.

Although these play activities differ considerably from each other in content, they exhibit a number of important similarities. There is, first of all, no causal relationship between the actions of the participants and the results. The outcome in every instance is thus determined by chance. Furthermore, the ratio between the probability for and the probability against any given outcome (i.e., the *odds*) is usually known. (In "Odd or Even," mentioned above, for example, the chances for the guesser's being correct are fifty-fifty; in counting out and "Spin the Bottle," on the other hand, the odds are dependent upon the number of participants.) A final similarity is that the player's role is passive rather than active at the point at which the outcome is being decided. These pastimes, then, can be regarded as models of probability in which the outcome is determined by chance.[28]

Traditional recreations and games following this model frequently require the player(s) to guess the whereabouts of a given object (e.g., of the button in "Button, Button" or the thimble in "Hide the Thimble") or the identity of an unseen object or person (e.g., in "Punchboard," a player who has been punched in the back while his eyes were covered must identify the person who has punched him). In other pastimes, such as traditional games of dice, the player(s) merely interprets a sign, such as the number that appears on the dice, and accepts the consequences of it. Despite these differences, each of these play activities is a probability model, and the players are willing to submit to chance.

Each of the four models described above provides a useful context within which to examine traditional recreations and games. It is only

27. Over eight hundred counting-out rhymes from both preliterate and literate societies are presented in Henry C. Bolton, *The Counting-Out Rhymes of Children: Their Antiquity, Origin, and Wide Distribution* (London, 1888).

28. For further discussion of the element of chance in many games see Anderson and Moore, pp. 176–78; John M. Roberts and Brian Sutton-Smith, "Cross-Cultural Correlates of Games of Chance," *Behavior Science Notes* 3 (1966): 131–44; and Caillois and Huizinga, *passim*.

when they are considered together, however, that the full significance of such a context can be recognized. First, all are models of behavior rather than classes or types of play activities. Because of this, none is mutually exclusive. That is, a game or recreation in which one kind of behavior is emphasized will usually require, to lesser degrees, the other kinds of behavior as well. Although strategy is the principal method of winning in "Hare and Hounds," for instance, both the "hare" and the "hounds" are normally required to depend upon physical skill at some point in the game; and some element of chance is also usually operative. Similarly, in "Hide and Seek," a game in which physical skill is necessary for success, those hiding utilize strategy to find safe hiding places; and the seeker, familiar with the area in which the game is being played, is aware of the most likely hiding places, thus illustrating his reliance upon strategy as well.

Another significant thing about these models is that they are useful for both traditional and nontraditional games and recreations. The implications of this are important for a number of reasons: (1) it indicates that, from a behavioral point of view, there is no difference between traditional and nontraditional play activities; (2) it also makes clear the fact that what distinguishes traditional games and recreations from all others is really the method of transmitting rules; and (3) it emphasizes the fact that traditional pastimes are not merely quaint and curious survivals from past ages, but that they are vital, functioning, and meaningful systems of behavior that are as important to our understanding of human play as are spontaneous play activities and organized athletics. The intriguing questions for the folklorist, then, are, first, why have men of different cultures and different eras found certain traditional games and recreations to be satisfying, useful, and meaningful; and second, what relationships exist between traditional play activities and other forms of expressive behavior that are traditional?

While it is impossible to answer these two questions satisfactorily until much more research has been completed, certain observations can be made that perhaps point toward the answers. To give but one example in response to the first question, there is in many traditional recreations and games a direct correlation between the language of a text and the actions of the players. Thus, in "Sally Waters," the actions of the person in the center of a ring are performed in accordance with instructions recited or sung by the other participants:

> Little Sally Waters,
> Sitting in the sun,
> Crying and weeping,
> For a young man,
> Rise, Sally, rise,

> Dry your weeping eyes,
> Fly to the East,
> Fly to the West,
> Fly to the one you love best.[29]

One does not learn the text of "Sally Waters" and then add movement to it; he learns the rhyme (song) and the actions simultaneously. The language and the actions, therefore, constitute an inseparable whole. When verses are omitted, forgotten, or changed, as they frequently are in the normal process of oral transmission, the accompanying actions are also modified. Thus, Lady Gomme was able to classify "Sally Waters" as a marriage game because thirty-three of the forty-eight variants that she gathered included verses about the actual wedding of Sally and her chosen mate.[30] But texts recorded in more recent years make no mention of the marriage; consequently, no wedding ceremony is acted out either. What is suggested by the popularity of "Sally Waters" and similar traditional pastimes (e.g., "London Bridge," "Here Come Three Dukes A-Riding," and most play-parties) is that words accompanied by movement and movement accompanied by words may have special appeal to human beings. And since it is always more difficult to make up a new pattern of verse and action than it is to learn one already familiar to other members of one's culture, this may well be the reason for the dissemination of such pastimes across cultures and through time.

The second of the two questions raised above—what relationships exist between traditional play activities and other traditional forms of expressive behavior—has already been explored by several investigators. Sutton-Smith, Roberts, and Kendon have pointed out the significance of the role of strategy in both games and folktales;[31] and Dundes, working within a formal rather than a behavioral context, has noted the similarity between the structures of games and folktales.[32] There also appears to be a tantalizing similarity between the behavior of persons asking and answering riddles and our third and fourth model respectively: the riddler is, in fact, a strategist, while the answerer is a fortunist. These are preliminary observations only, however; but they are suggestive enough to stimulate further analytical work in the field.

It should be apparent from this discussion that traditional recreations and games are among the most complex forms of expressive

29. Newell (1963 reprint edition), p. 70.
30. Gomme (1898), 2: 149–79.
31. John M. Roberts, Brian Sutton-Smith, and Adam Kendon, "A Strategy in Folktales and Games," *Journal of Social Psychology* 61 (1963): 185–99.
32. Alan Dundes, "On Game Morphology: A Study of the Structure of Non-Verbal Folklore," *New York Folklore Quarterly* 20 (1964): 276–88.

behavior that folklorists study. Like other items of folklore, some traditional pastimes are short-lived, while others, such as "Odd or Even" and "How Many Horns Has the Buck," date back to ancient Greek and Roman times. Furthermore, game preferences change, and the number and kinds of traditional play activities vary from age group to age group and culture to culture.[33] But whether games and recreations are ancient or recent, widely disseminated or culture-bound, traditionally learned or formally taught, their functions remain the same, for all are forms of play. Perhaps future research on play will prove that Johan Huizinga was close to the truth when he postulated in the foreword to his classic study *Homo Ludens* (1949) that "civilization arises and unfolds in and as play."

Bibliography and Selected Readings

Bett, Henry. *The Games of Children: Their Origin and History.* London, 1929. The thesis of this work is that most children's games are of great antiquity and that many of them are derived from ritualistic practices common in pagan times and among primitive peoples. The history and geographical distribution of individual games (e.g., "London Bridge," "Oats and Beans and Barley Grow") are discussed, as are the kinds of beliefs and concepts that are implicit in these play activities.

Brewster, Paul G. *American Nonsinging Games.* Norman, Okla.: University of Oklahoma Press, 1953. An anthology of game descriptions and the linguistic texts and formulas employed in playing them, this work focuses upon play activities reported from the United States that are normally unaccompanied by singing. Extensive historical and comparative notes are included.

———, ed. "Children's Games and Rhymes," in *The Frank C. Brown Collection of North Carolina Folklore* 1: 31–219. Durham, N. C.: Duke University Press, 1952. A collection of game descriptions and rhymes reported from oral tradition in North Carolina, this essay includes comparative notes that provide potential insights into the historical development and geographical distribution of many children's play activities.

Caillois, Roger. *Man, Play, and Games.* Translated by Meyer Barash. Glencoe, Ill.: Free Press of Glencoe, 1961. This work is concerned with the

---

33. For discussion of this point see Leah R. C. Yoffie, "Three Generations of Children's Singing Games in St. Louis," *Journal of American Folklore* 60 (1947): 1–51; and Brian Sutton-Smith and B. G. Rosenberg, "Sixty Years of Historical Change in the Game Preferences of American Children," *Journal of American Folklore* 74 (1961): 17–46.

concepts of play and games and attempts to provide concise characterizations of the nature of these concepts. The author discusses the inferences that can be drawn about the functions of play and games in society.

Cox, John H. "Singing Games." *Southern Folklore Quarterly* 6 (1942) : 183–261. This collection of descriptions and linguistic texts of forty singing games (most of them recorded in West Virginia) includes musicological transcriptions as well as comparative notes to other American and British game collections.

Culin, Stewart. *Games of the North American Indians.* 24th Annual Report, Bureau of American Ethnology. Washington, D. C., 1907. This anthology of game descriptions reported by ethnologists in native North America is the only work of its kind available for the play activities of North American Indians.

Eckenstein, Lina. *Comparative Studies in Nursery Rhymes.* London, 1906. A study in the origins, history, and dissemination of rhymes commonly attributed to children, which includes discussions of the probable sources of many nursery rhymes in broadsides and romantic ballads, choral dances of the past, and popular songs. The author demonstrates that the comparative study of rhyme texts often enables one to determine the probable meaning and symbolic significance of obscure words and images.

Enäjärvi-Haavio, Elsa. *The Game of Rich and Poor: A Comparative Study in Traditional Singing Games.* Folklore Fellows Communications, 100. Helsinki, 1932. Following a brief discussion of the history of game research, the author characterizes singing games as epic, lyric, and dramatic. "The Game of Rich and Poor," a dramatic singing game, is then examined and analyzed in detail in an attempt to determine its possible original source and routes of disseminaton. The Finnish or historic-geographic method of research is employed.

Erikson, Erik. *Childhood and Society.* New York: Norton, 1950. A cross-cultural study of child-training practices and of the role of children in different societies. Erikson examines the role of play in the physiological, psychological, and social development of the child, challenging numerous, widely-held assumptions about the nature and social significance of play activities.

Georges, Robert A. "The Relevance of Models for Analyses of Traditional Play Activities." *Southern Folklore Quarterly* 23 (1969) : 1–23. The thesis of this essay is that traditional play activities are complex social events, the multiple aspects of which can best be comprehended in terms of analytical models suggested by behavioral research findings. Three illustrative models relevant to the analysis of traditional play are presented, discussed, and exemplified.

Gomme, Lady Alice B. *The Traditional Games of England, Scotland, and Ireland.* 2 vols. London, 1894, 1898. This standard work on traditional games in the British Isles includes descriptions of games and game rules, organized in dictionary form according to the most commonly used names of the play activities included. Variant descriptions and notes document changes in the nature of these games that have occurred through time.

Huizinga, Johan. *Homo Ludens: A Study of the Play-Element in Culture.* London: Routledge and Kegan Paul, 1949. In this theoretical discussion of the nature of play and its role in cultural development, the author emphasizes the multiple aspects of play behaviors. "In its more developed forms," he asserts, "it is saturated with rhythm and harmony, the noblest gifts of aesthetic perception known to man."

Maclagan, Robert C. *The Games & Diversions of Argyleshire.* Publications of the Folk-Lore Society, 47. London, 1901. A collection of descriptions of the traditional games and pastimes in one specific area, sampling diverse play and recreational activities. Additions to the work can be found in *Folk-Lore* 16 (1905): 77–97, 192–221, and 340–49; and in *Folk-Lore* 17 (1906): 93–106, and 210–29.

Newell, William W. *Games and Songs of American Children.* New York, 1883. The pioneering work on American children's songs and games. Texts of songs and rhymes and brief descriptions of games reported from the United States. Notes and comparative references provide insights into the possible origin and historical development of many of the play activities, emphasizing their genetic relationships with the play activities of the British Isles and continental Europe.

Northall, G. F. *English Folk-Rhymes.* London, 1892. A collection of folk rhyme texts that includes a description of counting-out rhymes and games as well.

Opie, Peter and Iona. *Children's Games in Street and Playground.* Oxford: Clarendon Press, 1969. Based on information collected during the 1950s and 1960s, this work concerns games that children of six to twelve "make up" and play without adult supervision. Most of the over 10,000 informants were from metropolitan areas of England and Scotland. Includes descriptions, diagrams, plates, and distribution maps.

———. *The Lore and Language of Schoolchildren.* Oxford: Clarendon Press, 1959. Children's seasonal customs, rituals, rhymes, riddles, and chants are included in this discussion of the play behavior and linguistic games observed and recorded in England, Scotland, and Wales during the decade of the 1950s. Historical and comparative notes are provided throughout the volume.

———. *The Oxford Dictionary of Nursery Rhymes.* Oxford: Clarendon Press, 1951. More than five hundred rhymes and songs are included in this basic reference work. Historical and comparative notes offer insights into the development and diffusion of individual rhymes and songs in time and space.

Roberts, John M.; Malcolm J. Arth; and Robert R. Bush. "Games in Culture." *American Anthropologist,* n.s., 61 (1959): 597–605. After attempting to clarify the meaning of the term *games,* the authors of this essay propose a classification scheme for games based upon the principal means of determining game outcomes and discuss the frequency of occurrence of each of these game types in fifty societies.

Strutt, Joseph. *The Sports and Pastimes of the People of England.* London, 1801. A pioneering work on the subject of games and recreations. Strutt gives an extensive sampling of these activities and suggests the significance that studies of such pastimes might have in historical and cultural research. With color reproductions from earlier books and manuscripts.

Sutton-Smith, Brian. *The Games of New Zealand Children.* University of California Folklore Studies 12. Berkeley and Los Angeles: University of California Press, 1959. Comparative and historical notes suggest the relationships between New Zealand games and those reported from other parts of the world, particularly from Europe.

Tylor, Edward B. "Remarks on the Geographical Distribution of Games." *Journal of the Anthropological Institute of Great Britain and Ireland* 9 (1880) : 23–30. The author stresses the significance of comparative game research for insights into the movement of peoples and culture contacts throughout the world.

Wolford, Leah Jackson. *The Play-Party in Indiana.* Indiana Historical Collections 6 (1916) ; edited and revised by W. Edson Richmond and William Tillson and reissued as *Leah Jackson Wolford's The Play-Party in Indiana.* Indiana Historical Society Publications 20. Indianapolis, 1959. A collection of texts and descriptions of play-parties commonly engaged in by residents of the state of Indiana, with musicological examples, notes, and bibliographical entries.

9 FOLK MEDICINE
Don Yoder

FOLK MEDICINE AND MODERN MEDICINE

Folk medicine is related to three other levels or types of medicine practiced in the world. At the other end of the medical spectrum stands scientific, academic, or "modern" medicine, with which it has coexisted in increasingly uneasy tension since the eighteenth century. Folk medicine is related derivatively to the academic medicine of earlier generations. Certain ideas that were once circulating in academic medical circles and are now discarded have become part and parcel of the folk-medical viewpoint. Examples are the doctrine of "signatures," the seventeenth-century idea of "sympathy," and from earlier cultural strata astrology and the doctrine of the four humors. It is true that these have long ago been scrapped by science, but they provide us with instructive examples that folk medicine, like certain other aspects of folk-culture, has many *gesunkenes Kulturgut* items in its repertory. At the same time, there is much evidence that some medical practice went in the other direction, making modern medicine in part a derivative of primitive and folk medicine.

The other levels of medicine to which folk medicine has a relation are primitive medicine, with which it shares common elements of materia medica, techniques, and worldview, and popular medicine. While folk medicine and primitive medicine share worldview and magical techniques, they differ in social context, the classical primitive medicine (difficult to locate in the twentieth century) being the only type of medicine found natively in the culture, while folk medicine (representing the "little culture") shares the ground with and exists in tension with the higher forms of medicine (representing the "large culture"). Popular medicine is in a sense folk medicine gone commercial, the patent medicines and techniques of which it consists being frequently derived from the folk-medical repertory.

Of folk medicine there are essentially two varieties, two branches: (1) natural folk medicine, and (2) magico-religious folk medicine. The first of these represents one of man's earliest reactions to his natural environment, and involves the seeking of cures for his ills in the herbs, plants, minerals, and animal substances of nature. Natural medicine, which is sometimes called "rational" folk medicine, and sometimes "herbal" folk medicine because of the predominance of herbs in its materia medica, is shared with primitive cultures, and in some cases some of its many effective cures have made their way into scientific medicine. The second branch of folk medicine is the magico-religious variety, sometimes called "occult" folk medicine, which attempts to use charms, holy words, and holy actions to cure disease. This type commonly involves a complicated, prescientific worldview that we will describe in detail later.

Folk medicine, like folklore, has outgrown its strict identification with peasant cultures. Its clientele is drawn from a wide variety of groups and individuals. In the 1930s, writing of Franconia in central Germany, the medical historian Büttner described the clientele of the folk-medical practitioners as generally the older generation of the peasantry, plus the working classes and petty bourgeois of the cities. Folk-medical ideas of the older traditional sort were to be met most frequently in the mountainous areas that had little communication with the outside world, more in Catholic than in Protestant circles, and more among women than among men. The middle classes and working classes of the cities had turned away from folk medicine to the empirical and rational viewpoints, and now normally went first to the physician and only secondarily to the practical healers, the naturopaths, the quacks, and the magicians. Even among the classes with more formal education, the women especially patronized occult medicine, astrology, pseudo-radiology, and other modern cultic forms of popular medicine. In other words, a great many representatives of different classes and educational strata patronize nonscientific medicine.[1]

Writing of the situation in the United States in mid-twentieth century, Wayland Hand points out that "superstition is not the preserve of the unlettered only, but is a state or a way of looking at things that may befall even the most sophisticated members of society. Professional people of all kinds, no less than tradesmen, are prone to many of the same popular conceits and mental errors to which, for want of formal education, members of the humbler classes have fallen heir."[2] He cites Eugen Mogk's formula that every *Kulturmensch* has within him the rudiments of a *Naturmensch*.[3] And Richard Weiss, who wrestled with this basic question of definition, finally defined "folk" not in terms of class or cultural level in society but as a way of thinking within the individual, always combined today with other levels and types of thinking.[4]

Perhaps this gives us insight toward a simpler, more workable definition of folk medicine for the present time. Hanns Otto Münsterer's useful admonition points in this direction: "We must therefore resolve to describe folk medicine from the widest possible standpoint, as whatever ideas of combatting and preventing disease exist among the people apart from the formal system of scientific medicine."[5] The editors of the recent *Wörterbuch der deutschen Volkskunde* come to the same conclusion, urging scholars to underplay the linear historical viewpoint of *gesunkenes Kulturgut* and stress the place of folk medicine in the folk-cultural milieu.

The first question should not be, What did the people receive from above in the course of history, but rather: What viewpoints about sickness and health do the people possess on the ground of their own thinking? The answer to this question shows us that folk medicine has grown organically out of the whole of folk belief and custom, thought, life and speech. Medicine is older than doctors. Hence the definition: Folk medicine is the sub-

1. Ludwig Büttner, *Frankische Volksmedizin: Ein Beitrag zur Volkskunde Ostfrankens* (Erlangen, 1935), p. 14.
2. Wayland D. Hand, ed., *Popular Beliefs and Superstitions from North Carolina, The Frank C. Brown Collection of North Carolina Folklore* 6 (Durham, N.C., 1961), Introduction, pp. xix–xx.
3. Eugen Mogk, "Wesen und Aufgaben der Volkskunde," *Mitteldeutsche Blätter für Volkskunde* 1 (1926): 17–24.
4. Richard Weiss, *Volkskunde der Schweiz* (Erlenbach-Zurich, 1946), pp. 6–9.
5. Hanns O. Münsterer, "Grundlagen, Gültigkeit und Grenzen der volksmedizinischen Heilverfahren," *Bayerisches Jahrbuch für Volkskunde* 1 (1950), 9–20; reprinted in Elfriede Grabner, ed., *Volksmedizin: Probleme und Forschungsgeschichte* (Darmstadt, 1967), pp. 289–314.

stance of all the traditional viewpoints on sickness and the healing methods applied against disease which exist among the people.[6]

FOLK-MEDICAL RESEARCH IN EUROPE AND THE UNITED STATES

The history of the study of folk medicine has followed the same general pattern as other aspects of folk culture, first the literary or philological approach, followed by the sociological and functional approach. Pioneer European folklorists, fascinated with the philological aspects of folklore, collected charms in the nineteenth century, stressing their antiquity and their value for linguistic research. Ancient finds were made—in Germany the Merseburg formulas, in England the Anglo-Saxon leechdoms—and the horizon of folk medicine was pushed back to the early Middle Ages. At the same time the classical scholar became interested in the medical systems of classical antiquity, and the comparative religionist in the medical materials in the Vedas, which provided parallels from across the roof of the world to ancient European tribal forms of medicine.

The charm-collectors not only scoured medieval literature but also began to collect and analyze the manuscript charm-books that exist all over Europe, the *Zauberbücher*, or *Svartböcker*, which provided them with over-all glimpses of the practice of the folk-healer, the conditions he attempted to cure, and the immediate documentary background of the living charms of the current practitioners who were found to exist in every area of Europe in the nineteenth century. Among the great European collections are Dr. A. Christian Bang's *Norske Hexeformularer og Magiske Opskrifter* (Kristiania, 1901–12) ; and F. Ohrt's collection of Danish formulae, *Danmarks Trylleformler* (Copenhagen and Christiania, 1917). The largest collection of Germanic charms was the Adolf Spamer Collection, now housed in the Institut für deutsche Volkskunde, Deutsche Akademie der Wissenschaften, at the Humboldt-University in Berlin. This collection, now containing over 25,000 separate items, was built up largely by Spamer himself in forty years of collecting in every area of Germany.[7] Spamer's analysis of the major motifs in this unique corpus of material was edited by Dr. Johanna Jaenecke-Nickel, Spamer's successor at the institute, in the volume, *Romanusbüchlein: Historisch-philologischer Kommentar zu einem deutschen Zauberbuch* (Berlin, 1958).

6. Oswald A. Erich and Richard Beitl, eds., *Wörterbuch der deutschen Volkskunde*, 2d ed. (Stuttgart, 1955), "Volksmedizin," p. 823.
7. See the report of the holdings of the Institut für deutsche Volkskunde, by Johanna Jaenecke-Nickel, in *Current Anthropology* 4 (October, 1963) : 370–71.

The publication of national charm collections is still continuing, the most recent example from western Europe being Dr. Jozef van Haver's *Nederlandse Incantatieliteratuur: Een Gecommentarieerd Compendium van Nederlandse Bezwerings-formules* (Gent, 1964).

In addition to the national collections, there were, again, following a major trend in folklore in the nineteenth and early twentieth century, comparative studies of folk medicine. The largest of these, still of basic use, is the two-volume work by the Viennese physicians Oskar von Hovorka and Adolf Kronfeld, *Vergleichende Volksmedizin: Eine Darstellung volksmedizinischer Sitten und Gebräuche, Anschauungen und Heilfaktoren, des Aberglaubens und der Zaubermedizin* (Stuttgart, 1908). Volume I is essentially a dictionary, from *Aal* to *Zwiebel*; Volume II is an analysis of all the branches of medicine from obstetrics to dermatology, with discussion of the folk cures and treatments comparatively from around the world and historically from antiquity to the present. Its Pan-European viewpoint is especially valuable, with useful comparative materials from the Germanic, Slavic, and Mediterranean culture areas.

But the great comparative product of European scholarship is the ten-volume *Handwörterbuch des deutschen Aberglaubens* (Berlin, 1927–42), edited by the Swiss scholars Hanns Bächtold-Stäubli and Eduard Hoffmann-Krayer with the assistance of the widest possible network of academic collaborators.

European studies of magic, from Frazer to Malinowski, have also widened our understanding of folk medicine in many directions. Particularly useful has been the definition of types of magic—imitative, contagious, homeopathic, sympathetic—and the analysis of the theory of magic in primitive and folk culture. A volume by Irmgard Hampp, *Beschwörung, Segen, Gebet: Untersuchungen zum Zauberspruch aus dem Bereich der Volksheilkunde* (Stuttgart, 1961) analyzes the close relation between conjuration, blessing, and prayer, which exist together in most folk-religious milieux. And the magnificent volume on amulets by Liselotte Hansmann and Lenz Kriss-Rettenbeck, *Amulett und Talisman: Erscheinungsform und Geschichte* (Munich, 1966), widely illustrated from every cultural level and geographical area, speaks authoritatively on fetish magic and its usage.

Recently there has been a stepping up of scholarly interest in folk medicine in Europe. Of the more recent studies to come out of this European academic activity, the two most valuable volumes are the symposium on folk medicine edited by Carl-Herman Tillhagen, *Papers on Folk-Medicine given at an Inter-Nordic Symposium at Nordiska Museet, Stockholm 8–10 May 1961* (Stockholm, [1963]); and the extremely useful reader on folk-medical research edited by Elfriede Grabner, *Volksmedizin: Probleme und Forschungsgeschichte*

(Darmstadt, 1967), in the series *Wege der Forschung*, Vol. 63. As an English-language introduction to the problems involved in the study of folk medicine, the symposium is my choice for student use and should help to stimulate similar research in the United States.

The Scandinavian symposium grew out of the work of Carl-Herman Tillhagen, director of the Section on Folk Belief at Nordiska Museet, who earlier had produced what undoubtedly is the best single regional treatment of European folk medicine since World War II, *Folklig Läkekonst* (Stockholm, 1958). The symposium centered on the topic of the relationship between scientific and folk-medical traditions. A distinguished panel of twenty scholars from Sweden, Norway, Denmark, and Finland represented the disciplines of medicine, history of medicine, veterinary science, cultural anthropology, history of religions, and ethnography. The papers include analyses of the humoral-pathological system in folk-medicine, medical magic in Linnaeus' dietetics, the personality and work of the "wise woman" as healer, the question of the effectiveness of folk medicine, rational folk medicine, Lapp medicine, and other topics. We will discuss several of these contributions during the course of this chapter.

Elfriede Grabner, specialist in folk medical research at the Steirisches Volskundemuseum in Graz and the author of several dozens of basic articles on problems of folk medicine, has reprinted twenty-two selections from 1913–64, including the major essays on basic folk-medical theory and practice, including those by Jungbauer, Marzell, Diepgen, and Münsterer, and others. Specialized treatments deal with folk-medical dentistry, ethnobotany in the light of modern antibiotic research, astrology and medicine, healing gestures in folk medicine, humoral-pathological theory in folk medicine, and other subjects. Three of the selections deal with Slovene and Serbo-Croatian folk-medical practices. Two essays (Weiser-Aall and Honko) are reprinted from Tillhagen. On the development of scholarly theories about the nature of folk medicine and its relation to academic medicine, this book is the indispensable introduction.

In the United States the gathering of folk-medical materials has been more sporadic. There was a flurry of interest around the turn of the century, when the *Journal of American Folklore* published many articles of folk-medical collectanea. A few statewide collections have been made, the best of which is the two-volume work by Wayland D. Hand in *The Frank C. Brown Collection of North Carolina Folklore*, Volumes 6–7, *Popular Beliefs and Superstitions from North Carolina* (Durham, North Carolina: Duke University Press, 1961–64). Hand has collated each item with all the major printed comparative studies from the United States, providing American scholars with the best comparative materials yet available on folk medicine and the related areas of witchcraft and weather lore. His introduction to

Volume 6 offers a valuable survey of American research in these areas and points out the basic reason for the differential in European and American research:

Whereas European workers have been able to consider superstitions and folk beliefs as part of broad ethnological studies by country, region, or special occupational or ethnic groups, American folklorists have not been in any such enviable position. In default of full ethnological data, and in fear of losing what precious relics of folk life still remain, they have concentrated on the breadth of their collecting, not on its depth, nor on the meaning and connections of the material collected.[8]

Various ethnic and regional treatments have appeared in article or monograph form. Two of the most extensive studies deal with the Pennsylvania Germans, David E. Lick and Thomas R. Brendle's *Plant Names and Plant Lore Among the Pennsylvania Germans,* Proceedings of the Pennsylvania German Society, vol. 33 (1923), and Thomas R. Brendle and Claude W. Unger's *Folk Medicine of the Pennsylvania Germans: The Non-Occult Cures,* Proceedings of the Pennsylvania German Society, vol. 45 (1935). For the Southwest Spanish cultural area there have been many useful treatments, including Wilson M. Hudson (ed.), *The Healer of Los Olmos and Other Mexican Lore* (Austin, Texas 1951). For Negro healing practices, "cunjuring" and "hoodoo," there is the pioneer work by Newell Niles Puckett, *Folk Beliefs of the Southern Negro* (Durham, North Carolina, 1926). Puckett's work stressed the acculturated character of Negro folk belief, with some Africanisms persisting, although his estimate was that four or five beliefs recorded among American Negroes were actually European in origin.

The most extensive research project in American folk-medical research is the "Dictionary of American Popular Beliefs and Superstitions," edited by Wayland D. Hand at the University of California, Los Angeles, on the plan and scale of the European *Handwörterbuch des deutschen Aberglaubens.* State research committees have been set up to gather regional materials for the work, so that it has become a national project.

THE TWO VARIETIES OF FOLK MEDICINE

Let us look first at natural, rational, or herbal healing, and secondly, at magico-religious healing.

NATURAL FOLK MEDICINE

Natural or herbal folk medicine is undoubtedly as ancient as occult folk medicine and has been as widely practiced in the United States as in Europe. This type of healing in its commonest form is

8. Hand, p. xxxiv.

old-fashioned, domestic, household medicine, the kind our mothers and grandmothers normally practiced on the farms and in the villages of America, and in some cases in the cities. "Home remedies" were passed down from generation to generation. Herbs that were thought to give them special curative ability were gathered in woodland and field, in the Fall or on certain days of the church year, and the women planted herb gardens that were used for medical much more than for culinary purposes.

A large part of this branch of folk medicine was herbal, its materia medica drawn from the plants of woodland and field. "God Almighty never put us here without a remedy for every ailment," exclaimed one of Vance Randolph's informants in the Ozarks. "Out in the woods there's plants that will cure all kinds of sickness, and all we got to do is hunt for 'em."[9] In one of the best introductions to natural folk medicine in the United States, Vance Randolph describes the use in Missouri and Arkansas of such herbs as mullein, horehound, horse-mint, slippery-elm bark, spice-bush, dogbane, and sassafras. Almost every wild plant and many domestic plants had their curative uses. Most widespread were the decoctions or "teas" made from the various mints and wild plants and barks. Even tobacco had its medicinal value:

Tobacco is used in other ways by the yarb doctors and granny-women. I have seen severe abdominal pain, later diagnosed as appendicitis and cured by surgery, apparently relieved at once with a poultice of tobacco leaves soaked in hot water. The tobacco poultice is very generally used for cuts, stings, bites, bruises, and even bullet wounds. A poultice of tobacco leaves is often applied to "draw the pizen" out of a boil or a risin'.[10]

In addition to the women of the average American household who gathered and cultivated herbs, there were sometimes herbal specialists in the community, usually men, the "yarb doctors" of the Ozarks, who gathered herbs widely, professionally, one may say. Sometimes, too, special occupational classes, like shepherds, had herbal as well as magical cures for their animals and their colleagues.

Herbs were not the only source of the materia medica of the natural healer. Minerals and animal substances were widely used, including such things as clay, mud, animal organs, and even human urine and excrement. There was even a time when the latter departments of natural medicine were dignified by being raised into a sort of scientific medical fad—in the late seventeenth century when the German doctor

9. Vance Randolph, *Ozark Superstitions* (New York, 1964), p. 93. See his entire chapter, "Mountain Medicine," pp. 92–120.

10. Ibid., pp. 98–99. See also Katharine T. Kell, "Tobacco in Folk Cures in Western Society," *Journal of American Folklore* 78 (April-June, 1965): 99–114.

Paullini issued his now amusing *Dreckapotheke* or "Pharmacy of Filth."[11]

In many cases herbs and other rational cures were overlaid with magical ritual either in the preparation or in the healing technique. In most cases, as Hultkrantz points out in his recent study of healing methods among the Lapps, healers and clientele made no definite distinction between rational medicine and the irrational type.[12] Rational medicine may be "strengthened" by a magic spell and thus be drawn into the irrational zone. Examples of this process are found on a worldwide basis. Sympathetic prescriptions are followed in gathering herbs, bark, and roots. Leaves plucked upward from a plant have efficacy as an emetic; downward, as an enema. Randolph has described this belief in the Ozark regional setting:

> In scraping bark from a tree or shrub, the direction in which it is cut may make a vast difference as medicine. Peach-tree bark, for example, if the tree is shaved upward, is supposed to prevent vomiting, or to stop a diarrhea. But if the bark is scraped downward, the tea made from it is regarded as a violent purgative. In general, the old-timers say that if the pain is in the lower part of the body, it is best to scrape the bark downward, to drive the disease into the legs and out at the toes. If the bark in such a case were stripped upward, it might force the pizen up into the patient's heart, lungs, or head, and kill him instantly.[13]

The time of year in which the herb is picked and dried also was prescribed by folk-medical tradition. In some cases the plants had to be chosen in connection with some religious holiday in the church year, or again, in connection with the zodiacal positions or the "phases" of the moon. Not all of these prescriptions were nonsense from the scientific standpoint. As an example borne out by modern medicine, recent botanical studies have shown that the time when plants are picked does in some cases affect their medicinal efficacy.

Despite the derogatory terms for this type of medicine—"old wives' medicine" and *"Dreckapotheke"* being two favorite ascriptions—did any of the old traditional remedies have an efficacy? On just this point Lauri Honko warns us that we cannot understand folk or

11. Paullini's book had the title: *Neu-vermehrte, heylsame Dreckapotheke, wie nämlich mit Kot und Urin fast alle, auch die schwerste, giftigste Krankheiten u. bezauberte Schäden vom Haupte bis zu den Füssen innerlich und ausserlich glücklich curieret worden; Mit allerhand raren, so wohl nutz- als ergötzlichen Historien . . . von Christian Franz Paullini* (Frankfurt a. M., 1696). For his ideas, called "Paullinism" in medical history, see Erich-Beitl, p. 142.

12. Åke Hultkrantz, "The Healing Methods of the Lapps: Some aspects from the point of view of comparative religion," in *Papers on Folk-Medicine*, edited by Carl-Herman Tillhagen (Stockholm, 1963), p. 168.

13. Randolph, p. 95.

primitive medicine solely from the viewpoint of modern medicine, but must

> ...look upon this art from the point of view of its cultural background and its function in an authentic milieu. Problems then arising thus acquire medicinal interest, not only folkloristic. One can ask in all seriousness: was the primitive art of medicine really effective in its own environment? Were the primitive healers able to treat successfully the same diseases as modern man suffers from and as are now treated by entirely different methods? Are there any special diseases or groups of diseases for which the popular methods were particularly suitable?[14]

The first factor in the success of folk medicine, as Honko sees it, was the use of "objectively effective medicines"—estimated at possible 25 percent of the entire primitive pharmacopoeia. Examples: salicyl, aspirin, cocillana, cocaine, quinine, ephedrine, cascara. Second, effective folk techniques included compresses, scarification, hot baths and the sauna, primitive surgery, and even vaccination. On the other hand, these "natural" cures were rarely used without magical spells or rites to accompany them, and in the resultant "cures" there was no attempt made to differentiate the material and spiritual effects. Also, the primitive pharmacopoeia was in some cases harmful to the patient.

The great "herbals" of Elizabethan England and Renaissance Europe in a sense standardized the herb lore of the Middle Ages. In addition, other printed sources, like the colonial almanacs, made much of herbal remedies. Pastor Stoy's cure for rabies, a famous colonial remedy from the Pennsylvania German country, involves the use of pimpernel ·(Anagallis arvensis L.) and was widely reprinted in broadside form and presumably used.[15]

In a study of "Rational Folk-Medicine" in the Scandinavian countries, Olav Bø points out the neglect that this type of medicine has suffered from researchers, most of whom have concentrated on the more spectacular magical variety. Bø points to a wide variety of healers who used rational techniques, from bonde-dokter (peasant doctors) to medisinkoner (medicine women), the latter presumably so named because "they always provided their patients with medicine, herb concoctions they had prepared themselves." Bø's study is important for giving us historical guidelines on the types of medicine operative in peasant Norway in the nineteenth century. The years

14. Lauri Honko, "On the Effectivity of Folk-Medicine," in Tillhagen, *Papers,* pp. 132–142.
15. For Stoy see David E. Lick and Thomas R. Brendle, *Plant Names and Plant Lore among the Pennsylvania Germans,* The Pennsylvania German Society, Proceedings and Addresses, 33, 3 (1923) : 189–92.

around 1850, he points out, formed a dividing line between scientific medicine and folk medicine.

Not until that time was there any real progress in learned medicine and only then did the first trained doctors go out into the country districts to act as district physicians. But their practices were few and far between on account of the great distances in sparsely-populated Norway, so a long time passed before any real order with regard to health matters was established. Apart from this the doctors demanded cash payment, too much in the people's opinion, and they turned therefore to those whom they knew both could and would help without demanding payment. It was typical of many of the good local-doctors that they regarded their work as a Samaritan occupation and were not in it for profit. If they were paid, it was usually in kind, but this only applied to doctors who were themselves so poor that they had to be paid.

These lay practitioners were normally called "doctors." It was not until later that the Enlightenment word "quacks" (*Kvaksalvar*) was introduced, along with education, legislation, and medical usage. This was the derogatory expression of modern medicine for the popular forms, whether magic or rational.[16]

MAGICO-RELIGIOUS FOLK MEDICINE

An historical perspective on magico-religious healing in Western civilization can be provided by the following analysis. The principles of religious healing, rooted in antiquity, were channeled into Christianity, where healings in the name of the deity were permitted, and with the growth of the cult of the saints, a special category of saint arose, the healing saint. The powers of the healing saints could be tapped through prayer or even through contact with their material relics, tombs, holy places, chapels, and shrines. Miraculous intervention in healing was an important belief in the Middle Ages. In both Eastern Christendom and Roman Catholicism healing shrines and healing saints were recognized, and in most cases the people's drive toward connecting faith and healing was diverted into ecclesiastical, church-sanctioned channels.[17] Through its systems of blessings, benedictions, and its wide use of sacramentals (essentially expressing the belief in the holiness of material objects) the medieval Church

16. Olav Bø, "Rational Folk-Medicine," in Tillhagen, *Papers*, pp. 143–53.
17. A vast literature has appeared on healing shrines and healing saints in Europe. Among the foremost tillers of this field is Rudolf Kriss, whose *Volkskundliches aus altbayrischen Gnadenstätten* (Augsburg, 1930) has been followed by a distinguished series of volumes dealing with the pilgrimage system and the folk-cultural practices associated with it for eastern as well as western Europe; for comparative materials on Islamic cultures see Rudolf Kriss and Hubert Kriss-Heinrich, *Volksglaube im Bereich des Islam*, 2 vols. (Wiesbaden, 1960, 1962).

ministered to and encouraged the principles that we consider basic to folk medicine of the magico-religious sort: the ideas of the availability of supernatural powers for healing, and the mediation of that power through material objects as well as human healers.[18]

A radical change was initiated at the time of the Reformation. Saints in the Catholic sense, healing and non-healing, were exscinded from the Protestant worldview. In the process folk healing as such was driven underground, falling completely into the hands of lay practitioners, and within the purview of the church only formal churchly prayers for the sick were permitted. Hence all over Protestant Europe folk healing was driven underground, while it continued to be permitted, even blessed, in Catholic cultures. In the four hundred years since the Reformation, there has been a gradual restoration, so to speak, of magic healing apart from the churches, in such forms as conjuration, *Belezen, Brauchen,* powwowing—there are words for this phenomenon in all European cultures. Since belief in the possibility of healing through faith and prayer is a widespread human hope, this idea has occasionally emerged above ground and crept back into official Protestantism, first among the sects and cults, and now in the twentieth century among the churches. Two examples of faith healing becoming official in organized Protestantism are (1) the Pentecostal sects, which practice healing officially, gearing it into the worship services of the group; and (2) Christian Science, which teaches faith healing on a sophisticated, philosophical level.

It is unofficial religious healing, the type not connected with the churches, that we wish to analyze. In the United States the commonest word for this type of folk healing is "powwowing," which, according to the historical dictionaries of the English language, passed over into English usage from the Algonquin languages of New England in the first half of the seventeenth century. Other English words for "powwow" are to "charm," to "conjure" (Southern and Negro usage), to "try for" (central Pennsylvania and western Maryland), and to "use" (a direct "translation" of the German dialect word *brauche* reported from the Carolinas). The term "power doctor," used in the Ozarks and elsewhere,[19] appears to be a variant of the older term "powwow doctor," a change undoubtedly involving folk-etymology.

Powwowing is magico-religious healing, on the folk-cultural or

18. Adolph Franz, *Die kirchlichen Benediktionen im Mittelalter,* 2 vols. (Freiburg im Breisgau, 1909), is essential as background for understanding the medieval prayers and blessings for healing and protection that were sanctioned by the Roman Catholic Church.

19. See Randolph, chap. 7, "The Power Doctors," pp. 121–61, one of the best American analyses of the work and context of the magic healer studied in a regional setting.

traditional level, using words, charms, amulets, and physical manipulations in the attempt to heal the ills of man and beast.[20] It is based on the primitive worldview of the unity of all things, heaven, earth, man, animal, and nature. Within this unity there is a dualism between evil powers, concentrated in the Devil and his voluntary servitors the witches, and good powers, concentrated in God, the Trinity, the saints, and the powwower who is the channel for healing power from source to patient. Disease is believed to be demonic, "sent" by evil forces into the person or animal, hence it has to be removed by a "counterspell," which can be provided by ritual, written charms involving holy words, or prepared amulets. In most cases the powwower attempts to heal by ritual and spoken word; in cases of severe demonic action, he relies on paper amulets with elaborate occult texts or simple occult formulas such as the *SATOR*-formula, which he gives, usually for a fee that is understood rather than demanded, to his patient. The matter of fees is a touchy one, since set fees can bring arrests on the charge of practicing medicine without a license. Several of the powwowers from whom I have recorded in Pennsylvania never actually took money from the patient's hand, but suggested that they put it on the table, thus avoiding actual transfer of currency.

American folk-medical techniques of a magical character are discussed in a series of recent articles by Wayland D. Hand. In primitive as well as folk medicine, one of the commonest methods of ridding a person of disease is through transference of the disease, either by direct transfer or by way of an intermediary person or thing, into another person, an animal, a plant, or an object. The transference can be accomplished through contact or it can take place symbolically, as for example, "selling" a wart. One of the commonest examples of the "direct" method is the transfer of disease to trees or shrubs by means of plugging, wedging, or nailing. The practice and the idea behind it is connected with the transference of evil in general, to which so much attention has been paid, from biblical scapegoats to contemporary psychiatric transference.[21]

Folk diagnosis is kept to a minimum. While there are many folk names for diseases or conditions, generally it is conditions rather than

20. The description is based on my own researches into Pennsylvania German powwowing or *Braucherei*. On this subject see the standard volume, Thomas R. Brendle and Claude W. Unger, *Folk Medicine of the Pennsylvania Germans: The Non-Occult Cures*, Proceedings of the Pennsylvania German Society, vol. 45 (1935) ; also Don Yoder, "Official Religion versus Folk Religion," *Pennsylvania Folklife* 15 (Winter 1965–66) : 36–52; Don Yoder, "Twenty Questions on Powwowing," *Pennsylvania Folklife* 15 (Summer 1966) : 38–40.

21. Wayland D. Hand, "The Magical Transference of Disease," *Folklore Studies in Honor of Arthur Palmer Hudson, North Carolina Folklore* 13 (1965) : 83–109.

precisely defined ailments that are recognized and "treated." In speaking of folk dermatology, Büttner makes the comment, "The folk do not differentiate these sicknesses. They name them according to the symptoms and rarely according to the etiology, which they do not know."[22] As we have pointed out, folk etiology ascribes sickness to supernatural or irrational causation. The ascriptions range from witchcraft to the predestinarian idea that "God causes sickness." Puckett's study of Negro medicine makes the statement that the first thing the conjure-doctor has to do "is to diagnose the case, tell the person whether he is conjured or not, or in Negro parlance, to find out who 'layed de trick.' " The "trick" (charm) has to be found and destroyed and the patient cured. If the patient wishes, the trick must also be turned back upon the one who set it.[23]

Of course folk medicine includes veterinary practice. This was, in fact, one of the larger branches of the art. More difficult than treating human beings, since the patient was incapable of self-diagnosis, it was of utmost importance on the rural scene. According to a German folk-medical historian, the livestock were the living capital of the peasants, who sometimes, it was rumored, paid more attention to the health of their stock than to that of their families. They also believed that animals, being without a soul, were more vulnerable to influence from witchcraft than persons, and misfortune in the stables was usually attributed to witchwork (*Unglück im Stall ist Hexenwerk* . . .).[24] Elaborate rituals involving stall and stable as well as farmhouse and farmyard protected the animals on the farm. Special church-sponsored blessings were carried through under the aegis of the ancient medieval protector-saints, Saint Leonard for horses, Saint Patrick for cattle. Protection was furnished the cattle of the alpine pastures by the chanting of the *Alpsegen*, unforgettable to those who have heard it.[25] As these examples show, folk medicine and folk religion often overlap.

THE FOLK-MEDICAL PRACTITIONER AND THE PATIENT

In general, the research that has been done on the sociological background of the practitioner of magico-religious healing shows us that, like the primitive "shaman," the powwower and the conjurer, even in the most ordinary of American rural communities, were set apart and recognized by at least some members of the community as having

22. Büttner, p. 39.
23. Newbell Niles Puckett, *Folk Beliefs of the Southern Negro* (Chapel Hill, N.C., 1926) , p. 207.
24. Walther Zimmermann, *Badische Volksheilkunde* (Karlsruhe, 1927) , p. 94.
25. For the *Alpsegen, Betruf, Alpruf* and related practices see Weiss, pp. 223, 228, 231, 274–75.

supernatural powers.[26] They were, if we may be permitted the term, a kind of folk-clergy, recognized as having "God-given" powers of healing. From my own researches into Pennsylvania's powwowing tradition, I have found that there was a kind of hierarchy of personnel, all of whom were powwowers of different sorts and status. The commonest type was the completely respectable "unprofessional" powwower—the grandmother, for example, who could "blow burns" and "stop blood" and powwow for a few ailments, along with being an expert brewer of folk teas and stirrer of folk salves and embrocations. The professional powwower, while recognized by the community, was in a sense withdrawn from the community, not a completely "respectable" member of society. In fact he often lived apart literally—in Europe as a shepherd, in Pennsylvania as a hermit or hill country healer on the back roads. Professional powwowers, especially those who achieved the status of "witch doctors" (*Hexedokter*), who specialized in counter-charms against witchcraft that in their elaboration and in their claims approached witchcraft itself, were actually feared and avoided by the community, resorted to only for healing or countering the spells of the neighborhood witch. Among southern Negroes, Puckett observes that "in almost all cases the conjure-doctor is a peculiar individual, set aside because of his very peculiarity for dealings with the supernatural."[27] Sometimes he was physically marked, queer, misshapen. In all of this we see the "outsider" character of the charismatic leader whose charisma disturbs as well as integrates the believing community.

In recent years much has been written on the role of the magico-religious healer, the shaman, the medicine-man, the powwower—as primitive psychiatrist. In his paper on the effectiveness of folk medicine, cited above in connection with natural medicine, Lauri Honko deals at length with the folk healer as a psychotherapist.

One cannot doubt that the primitive doctor has equally good, if not better qualifications to act as a psychotherapeutic practitioner than the modern psychiatrist. No scientific criticism shakes his visionary confidence in

26. In addition to the works on shamanism by Eliade and others, and basic anthropological analyses such as A. Irving Hallowell's *The Conjuror in Salteaux Society* (Philadelphia, 1944), the principal work on the role of the magic healer in folk culture would appear to have been done in Scandinavia in the twentieth century. Carl-Herman Tillhagen's *Folklig Läkekonst* (Stockholm, 1958) contains detailed analysis of the role of the folk healer in European society. A thorough treatment using American materials is William Madsen, *The Mexican-Americans of South Texas* (New York, 1964), especially chaps. 10–11, "Curers and Physicians" and "Folk Psychotherapy". Other volumes in the same series, the Holt, Rinehart and Winston Case Studies in Cultural Anthropology, also have useful materials on traditional medical practices and practitioners.

27. Puckett, p. 206.

the effectivity of his actions. He is not content only to activate the faith of the patient, but also instills into the whole group a certain conviction of the success of his treatment, awakens the collective faith and promotes the integration of the group. The system of social values as a whole supports his activities, the myths, the religious dogmas, the group feeling of solidarity and the patterns of role-behavior. The modern doctor can nowhere near satisfy the primitive need for motivation of the modern man, or in other words answer the question: why must I be the one to suffer?

In a sense the primitive healer is successful because he treats the community along with the patient. The patient is an integral part of the folk community; the loss of life and the loss of work at crucial times during the year are losses to the community—a disturbance of the normal rhythm of life. The community enterprise, the community itself is endangered, and the practitioner must reunite the broken community. However permanent the recovery of the patient, "the ritual-mechanism was more or less infallible in dispersing the clouds of uncertainty and fear of the mystery of disease. With the aid of ritual, the crisis which had overtaken the group was overcome and normal order was restored. . . . This social reintegration is in fact one of the most important functions of the healing rites, and it is here that they diverge most sharply from the modern art of medicine."[28]

Practitioners of magico-religious medicine normally learned their trade either directly from older practitioners or indirectly from books. If from older practitioners, the usual system in some cultures was to alternate the sexes, a man teaching a woman, and vice versa. Sometimes in recording folk-medical materials from an informant, this sex alternation stands in the way, the informant refusing to recite a charm or describe a technique to a person of the same sex. "I would lose my power," is the usual explanation.

The printed charm books of Europe and the United States are extensive. Most of those in current circulation arose in the eighteenth century and, like earlier mystical and prophetic literature, following the biblical precedent, were ascribed falsely to earlier authorship. Moses, Solomon, Albertus Magnus, and Romanus were among the most popular pseudepigraphic ascriptions. For example, in France the commonest books are called *Le grand Albert, Le petit Albert, L'Albert moderne, Clavicules de Salomon,* and so on.[29] In German-

---

28. Honko, pp. 140–41. On this subject see also Ari Kiev, *Magic, Faith, and Healing: Studies in Primitive Psychiatry Today* (Glencoe, Illinois, 1964) ; and Jerome D. Frank, *Persuasion and Healing: A Comparative Study of Psychotherapy* (New York, 1963) .

29. Arnold van Gennep, *Manuel de folklore français contemporain,* 4: 560 ff.

speaking countries, the most popular folk-medical book was *Romanus,* the first-known edition of which appeared in 1788; others were *Albertus Magnus, or Egyptian Secrets,* and the pseudo-cabbalistic *Sixth and Seventh Books of Moses.* All of these German volumes made their way to America, beginning with German editions in Pennsylvania in the nineteenth century. While "powwowing" had been practiced generally in the colonies, the art was standardized and formalized by the Pennsylvania Germans, whose charm corpus was put into print in 1820 by a German emigrant named Johann Georg Hohman in the volume *Der lang verborgene Freund.* Of this curious book, which is the American equivalent of the Romanus book and in fact is pirated in large part from Romanus with some additions from other sources, there are two English translations, both done in Pennsylvania before the Civil War. The first, still in print and available under or over many book counters in the United States, is called *The Long Lost Friend,* and appeared for the first time in Harrisburg, Pennsylvania, in 1846. The second translation, *The Long Hidden Friend,* published at Carlisle, Pennsylvania, in 1863, was reprinted in annotated form in 1904 in the *Journal of American Folklore* and is thus readily available to our readers.[30] This Hohman powwow book is without doubt the most influential conjuring book in the United States; its influence extends to the Negro, the Cajun in Louisiana, the hill man in the Ozarks, and other groups.

Like those used in Europe, the American powwow charms are primitive in text but set in a Christian frame. Most charms, to be effective, must end in the "three highest names"—the trinitarian formula. Christological symbols (the blood of Jesus, the cross of Jesus, the "five wounds" of Jesus, all of which have salvational significance in the official religion) frequently appear. The Virgin Mary and the saints (Peter, Lawrence, Caspar, Melchior, Balthasar), the four Evangelists, and the three Archangels make a post-Reformation appearance in many charms. Primitive aspects of the formulae include the fact that to be effective a charm must use the name (usually the baptized name) of the patient. The frequent use of the number *three* has of course both Christian and primitive undertones. The references to the "three holy drops of blood," "three holy wells," "three lilies on Christ's grave," "three worms," "three false tongues," "three holy tongues," and the poetry of the charms provide living American parallels to the Welsh triads and other medieval folk-poetry of the Middle Ages.

30. Carleton F. Brown, "The Long Hidden Friend," *Journal of American Folklore* 17 (April-June 1904) : 89–152.

An example is here given from the corpus of Pennsylvania German magic formulae. For the skin inflammation called erysipelas (wild-fire) the following charm is used:

> *Wildfeier, flieh, flieh, flieh!*
> *Der rode Fadem jagt dich hie, hie, hie!*
> (Erysipelas, fly, fly, fly!
> The red string chases you away, away, away!)
>
> † † †

Note that the disease, conceived animistically, is addressed directly in the charm. While repeating the charm three times, the powwower three times "measures" the patient with a red woolen string (red is the color of the ailment). The disease is symbolically "collected" into the string, which is then "smoked" (lighted to smolder) above the kitchen stove, and slowly turned to ashes. When the string has turned completely to ash, it is brushed into the fire. The belief is that as the string disappears, so the disease disappears. The primitive ideas of transference and vicarious destruction of the disease are clearly seen in this example. The three crosses represent the Christian framework into which the primitive text is set. They signify the Trinitarian formula, since charms normally end with the words: "God the Father, God the Son, and God the Holy Ghost, help to this [here the patient is named]. Amen."

At the present time in the United States a variety of folk-medical practices still exist for study. In most communities there is a kind of hierarchy of medical practice, from scientific medicine to the crudest types of folk practice.

Attitudes of the patient toward his illness and toward the various levels of medicine that exist together in many communities are expressed in a recent study made during three months' fieldwork in a Bohemian speech community in Iowa.[31] "Older Bouhimis (at least) are likely to take pain as the result of some minor injury. They do not consider themselves to be ill until they are unable to walk around." When one is sick, the treatment followed is likely to be as follows:

1. Ignore it—it may get better.
2. Try some home remedy or a patent medicine.
3. Make an appointment for chiropractic treatment.
4. Consult a medical doctor, all else having failed.

In rural Iowa the chiropractor seems now to be filling the role of folk practitioner. There are several reasons for this change of roles. Home

---

31. Edward Kibbe and Thomas McCorkle, *Culture and Medical Behavior in a Bohemian Speech Community in Iowa*, 3d ed. (Iowa City, 1959), pp. 26–27. I have also used Thomas McCorkle, *An Abbreviated Statement on Folk Practices in Rural Iowa* (Iowa City, Iowa, 1960), pp. 4–5.

remedies, while still used by some people, are now too difficult to make for oneself; medical doctors are too expensive; hence one turns to the chiropractor who charges more modest fees. Second, rural Iowans prefer chiropractors because they rarely advise bed rest. Third, the farmer likes the chiropractor's "simple, mechanistic theory of disease and therapy," for they believe that pain is normally the result of some injury rather than "disease," although some still feel that accidental injuries are punishments for wrongdoing. Hence chiropractors are consulted "not only in cases involving muscular and other aches and pains, but also for the treatment of respiratory troubles and conditions described as 'nervousness,' a category that may include psychiatric disorders."

The same claims were made for the Iowa Amish, in a study emanating from the same source.

> Like other rural Iowa populations encountered so far, the Amish exhibit a distinct predilection for availing themselves of chiropractic treatment. Strongly influenced by non-medical health education literature, they make a theoretical distinction between chiropractors, who are used for the treatment of nameless pains and chronic disorders, and who are said to treat the "causes" of illness; and medical doctors, who are said to be pre-eminent in the handling of broken bones and performing surgery, and are said only to treat the "effects."[32]

A similar study of the Pennsylvania Amish, by John A. Hostetler, dealing with the persistence of folk medicine in the Amish community, points out that "certain types of illnesses are taken to the physician and other types to the folk practitioner. The selective principle would appear to operate in this way: critical incapacitating malfunctions are taken to the scientifically trained practitioner, while chronic non-incapacitating ailments are treated by the folk practitioner and by traditional means."[33]

These are some of the areas of investigation in which the folk-cultural scholar obviously needs the help of the medical sociologist.

FOLK MEDICINE IN THE TWENTIETH CENTURY

It always comes as a shock to learn that folk medicine, like witchcraft, astrology, and other ancient aspects of folk belief, is actually still very much around. With the great advances of modern science in the seventeenth century and the basic shift in worldview brought by

32. Jochem von Heeringen and Thomas McCorkle, *Culture and Medical Behavior of the Old Order Amish of Johnson County, Iowa* (Iowa City, Iowa, 1958), pp. 27–28.
33. John A. Hostetler, "Folk and Scientific Medicine in Amish Society," *Human Organization* 22 (Winter 1963–64): 269–75.

the Enlightenment, the educated classes tended to drop these aspects of culture, but they continued on popular and folk levels. As European scholarship has been pointing out for decades, "folk" attitudes often persist in an individual alongside "modern" educated attitudes.

In the twentieth century, in fact, there would seem to have been an increase in irrational-medical attitudes and practice, particularly on the popular level of middle-class and mass levels of culture, where astrology, horoscopes, health food fads, Indian healers, blessed handkerchiefs, chain letters, faith healers, rub doctors, blow doctors, and other related phenomena assault us from newspaper, radio, and TV screen. Undoubtedly as in the Hellenistic era, the breakup of the standard religions and the resultant "loss of nerve," to use Gilbert Murray's phrase, have caused a backwash of parareligious activities and institutions to flow back into Western civilization as substitutes for organized religion. One of the oldest of these substitutes is astrology, which as "Chaldean science" had invaded the Hellenistic world 2,500 years ago and has been waiting in the wings ever since.[34] The astrological worldview, that the heavens and earth are intimately connected in mutual influences, has always been an important ingredient in most European folk worldviews. Today it is seized upon by culturally and spiritually rootless urbanites, without the folk-cultural matrix in which it was once functional, as one version of our century's widespread fatalism.

Another sign of the times is the stepping up of the "fortune teller" as medical practitioner, especially in the pseudo-folk forms of "Indian healer" and "Indian Reader." In the post-World War II era these have spread into many areas, mostly within and on the fringes of urban settlement. A recent study of this type of healer pointed out that the same persons who normally form the clientele of native magical healers are turning also to Indian healers. The background of the Indian healers, despite their appeal to the American Indian as symbol, appears to be Mediterranean, and is probably related to the Puerto Rican invasion of the Eastern United States since 1950.[35]

Since World War II, also, there has been significant growth of "faith healing" under the aegis of the established, organized religions of the United States. No longer leaving it to the Pentecostal and other healing sects, such groups as the Episcopalians and the United Church of Christ have become concerned to bring religious healing "back where it belongs," i.e., in the hands of the ordained clergy

34. See Franz Cumont, *Astrology and Religion among the Greeks and Romans* (New York, 1960), originally published in 1912; see also Louis MacNeice, *Astrology* (Garden City, N. Y., 1964).

35. George Peterson, III, "Indian Readers and Healers by Prayer: A Field Report," *Pennsylvania Folklife* 16 (Fall 1966): 2–7.

and under the control of the institutional church. The Episcopal Church has been the leader in this movement, with weekly "healing missions" in selected churches in American metropolitan areas (for example, Saint Stephen's Episcopal Church in Philadelphia and the Order of Saint Luke the Physician, which is a national organization involving those Episcopalian priests who are practicing religious healing). At the same time, seminary education is including studies of the relation of religion to medicine, and offering widened programs in pastoral counseling, the native ecclesiastical form of psychotherapy. The significance of these movements is that they are attempting to return religious healing, for those who want it, to organized religion, where it had existed as a normal and permitted phase of religion until Protestantism exscinded it from its world of possibilities, driving it underground in the European Protestant cultures.

Certain new trends in science are also, at last, recognizing the serious study of folk medicine. It is no longer viewed as the "curiosity show" of peasant credulity, smeared with the Enlightenment labels of "superstition" and "quack medicine," but is now taken seriously, and placed, not against the background of bourgeois culture, but in its own proper folk-cultural matrix where its functions and reciprocal relations with the entire culture are obvious. If the religious values in occult folk medicine are being absorbed in the ecclesiastical movements discussed above, its psychological value is being recognized in psychosomatic medicine, community medicine, and psychiatry. In the newer field of parapsychology, European scholars are also investigating a great many subjects of interest to folk-cultural scholars, including extrasensory perception, telekinesis, witchcraft, stigmaticism, and religious healing, and American parapsychologists are beginning to follow their example.[36]

It is strange how wider cultural movements have always determined a generation's academic approach to folk-cultural phenomena. Enlightenment "rationalism" and its nineteenth-century offspring "scientism" made mock of folk medicine. Even the biblical healing episodes, which were both analogues to and in some cases precedents for folk-medical healings, were discarded in the eighteenth and nineteenth centuries, then cautiously taken back in the twentieth century, to be explained by psychological, anthropological, psychiatrical, and Jungian approaches.[37] Even the Mesmers, the Swedenborgs, and the

36. Utrecht and Zurich have been European centers for parapsychological studies. Cf. especially the work of Professor W. H. C. Tenhaeff, Professor of Parapsychology and director of the Parapsychological Institute at the University of Utrecht, *Aussergewöhnliche Heilkräfte: Magnetiseure, Sensitive, Gesundbeter* (Olten and Freiburg in Breisgau, 1957).

37. Cf. Don Hargrave Gross, "A Jungian Analysis of New Testament Exorcism," Ph. D. dissertation, Harvard University, 1963.

Jung-Stillings—Enlightenment Age antiheroes, so to speak, whose ideas formed counter-currents to the dominant rationalism of the era—are receiving respectful attention at the present time.

Folk medicine, especially when labeled "superstition," is one of those areas of folk culture on which ingroup attitudes can be touchy. Vance Randolph includes the cautionary statement:

> Many of the civic boosters in the Ozark area are sensitive about their hillbilly background and regard anybody who mentions the old customs or folk beliefs in the light of a public enemy. This sentiment is reflected in the Ozark newspapers, particularly in the smaller cities.[38]

Andrew Pearce, writing in the first volume of the *Caribbean Quarterly,* is equally frank about Caribbean sensitivities:

> We are most grateful to our contributors, and it is fitting to remind them that the dominant theme of these articles may be regretted by considerable numbers of West Indians who may feel that they have illuminated those dark corners of West Indian life which were best forgotten, i.e., "bad" English and French, crude superstitions, a past linked with Africa, and charismatic leadership. These doubters pose the question whether an attempt to reassess the achievements of the "common man" in the West Indies during the past 120 years is compatible with a relentless drive towards enlightenment and progress in science, technique and politics. To this we must answer that progress is not merely compatible with a study of the backward past, but that our thinking and planning for tomorrow will lead us astray if it is not based on a realistic study of yesterday. Enlightenment is not the process of "keeping things dark."[39]

The signs everywhere seem to be pointing to the need for reexamining our folk-medical heritage. We can profitably close with a favorite statement of mine. Ruth Benedict makes clear the value of investigating folk belief and folk custom in these words: "More than any other body of material it makes vivid the recency and the precariousness of those rationalistic attitudes of the modern urban educated groups which are often identified with human nature."[40]

Bibliography and Selected Readings

Blum, Richard H. and Eva. *Health and Healing in Rural Greece.* Stanford, California: Stanford University Press; London: Oxford University Press, 1965. Chaps. 11 and 12 deal with folk healing and folk healers.

---

38. Randolph, p. 7.
39. Andrew Pearce, Editorial Note, *Caribbean Quarterly* 1:3.
40. Ruth Benedict, "Folklore," *Encyclopedia of the Social Sciences* 6:288.

Bouteillier, Marcelle. *Médecine populaire d'hier et d'aujourdhui*. Paris: Editions G.-P. Maisonneuve et Larose, 1966. The most basic recent study of French traditional medical practices and ideas, by the director of the section of folk belief at the Musée de l'Homme. Particularly good are the materials on the range of healers in French society, based on years of fieldwork and questionnaire analysis.

Brendle, Thomas R., and Claude W. Unger. *Folk Medicine of the Pennsylvania Germans: The Non-Occult Cures*. Proceedings of the Pennsylvania German Society, 45. Norristown, Pennsylvania, 1935. So far this is the most detailed analysis of the theory of disease and the charm corpus of any of the older ethnic cultures of the United States.

Clark, Margaret. *Health in the Mexican-American Culture: A Community Study*. Berkeley and Los Angeles: University of California Press, 1959. This is a study based on intensive fieldwork in the Mexican-American community of San Jose, California.

Cockayne, Oswald. *Leechdoms, Wortcunning, and Starcraft of Early England*. 3 vols. London, 1864–66. Chronicles and Memorials of Great Britain and Ireland During the Middle Ages, No. 35. Textual studies of the magical charm corpus and related aspects of folk belief from Anglo-Saxon England.

Davidson, Thomas. "Animal Treatment in Eighteenth-Century Scotland." *Scottish Studies* 4 (1960) : 134–49. Discusses the full range of folk-medical veterinary practice from charms to curing-stones.

Frank, Jerome D. *Persuasion and Healing: A Comparative Study of Psychotherapy*. Baltimore: Johns Hopkins Press, 1961; New York: Schocken Books, 1963. Provides comparative treatment of modern psychotherapy, primitive healing, religious healing of the Lourdes type, religious revivalism, and Communist thought reform.

Hand, Wayland D. *Popular Beliefs and Superstitions from North Carolina*. The Frank C. Brown Collection of North Carolina Folklore, vols. 6–7. Durham, North Carolina: Duke University Press, 1961, 1964. The best American regional collection of traditional beliefs, including those dealing with medicine, carefully annotated from a wide variety of collections of similar materials from every ethnic and regional culture of the United States.

Howells, William. *The Heathens: Primitive Man and His Religion*. Garden City, New York: Doubleday Anchor Books, 1962. Despite its unfortunate title, this is an extremely useful introduction to concepts of magical healing. See especially chap. 5, "Magic, Black and White," and chap. 6, "Disease and Medicine." A volume in the Natural History Library, sponsored by the American Museum of Natural History.

Jones, Glyn Penrhyn. "Folk Medicine in Eighteenth-Century Wales." *Folk Life* 7 (1969) : 60–74. Offers a full discussion of the range of practitioners of community medicine from apothecaries and apothecary-surgeons through magicians, wizards, and medical astrologers, to country parsons who practiced medicine in their parishes. Also treated are the use of healing stones, herbal medicine, cupping, and household remedies in general.

Kemp, Patience. *Healing Ritual: The Technique and Tradition of the Southern Slavs.* London: Faber and Faber, 1935. One of the few good treatments in English of traditional medicine in the Slavic cultures; based on fieldwork in Yugoslavia.

Kiev, Ari, ed. *Magic, Faith and Healing*: *Studies in Primitive Psychiatry Today.* New York: The Free Press of Glencoe, 1964. Anthropological symposium with materials from many cultures. See particularly the editor's introductory essay, "The Study of Folk Psychiatry," pp. 3–35.

Lessa, William A., and Evon Z. Vogt. *Reader in Comparative Religion*: *An Anthropological Approach.* Evanston, Illinois: Row, Peterson and Company, 1958; 2d ed., enlarged and revised, New York: Harper and Row, 1965. A useful collection of essays by the key contributors to the development of comparative religion studies on the subject of magic and related beliefs. See especially chap. 6, "Magic, Witchcraft, and Divination," and chap. 7, "The Magical Transference of Disease."

Madsen, William. *The Mexican-Americans of South Texas.* New York: Holt, Rinehart and Winston, 1964. This volume, in the series Case Studies in Cultural Anthropology, is the most concise analysis of the theory and practice of traditional medicine among the Southwest Spanish groups yet available. See especially chap. 7, "Religion"; chap. 8, "Sickness and Health"; chap. 9, "Witchcraft"; chap. 10, "Curers and Physicians"; and chap. 11, "Folk Psychotherapy."

Middleton, John, ed. *Magic, Witchcraft, and Curing.* Garden City, New York: The Natural History Press, 1967. This volume, in the series American Museum Sourcebooks in Anthropology, gathers together a variety of ethnographic reports and theoretical discussions on magic, sorcery, shamanism, and their relation to healing, mostly in primitive settings.

Preisendanz, Karl L. *Papyri Graecae Magicae.* Leipzig, Berlin: Trubner, 1928–31. The standard textual study of the basic body of magical formulae from the Hellenistic world, echoes and analogues of which appear everywhere in the folk-medical practice of medieval and modern Europe.

Sigerist, Henry E. *A History of Medicine.* 1. *Primitive and Archaic Medicine.* New York: Oxford University Press, 1951. Among the many histories of medicine in English, this work is the best introduction to the initial stages of medical belief and practice, with examples from many cultures.

Tillhagen, Carl-Herman, ed. *Papers on Folk-Medicine given at an Inter-Nordic Symposium at Nordiska Museet, Stockholm 8–10 May 1961.* Stockholm, 1963. Reprinted from *Arv*: *Journal of Scandinavian Folklore* 18–19 (1962–63) : 159–362. The best regional approach in English to research problems, typology, and theory of traditional medicine.

Tillich, Paul. "The Relation of Religion and Healing." *The Review of Religion* 10 (May 1946) : 348–84. The basic theological approach, starting with the fundamental connection in all the ancient religions between religion and health. Religion (essentially salvation) symbolically restores the broken unity of both cosmos and individual.

Wallace, Anthony F. C. *Religion: An Anthropological View.* New York: Random House, 1966. Contains several theoretical sections on religion and magic; see especially "Ritual as Therapy and Anti-Therapy," pp. 113–26.

Weatherhead, Leslie D. *Psychology, Religion and Healing.* 2d ed. London: Hodder and Stoughton, Ltd., 1952. Discusses all the "non-physical methods of healing" and the principles underlying them. Includes detailed analysis of the healing practices of the organized healing cults within Protestantism.

Williams, Phyllis H. *South Italian Folkways in Europe and America.* New Haven: Yale University Press, 1938. Reissued New York: Russell and Russell, 1969. Especially good on the evil eye and the magical remedies used to counteract its spell.

10 FOLK RELIGION
John C. Messenger

All known societies, past and present, have possessed religions, and elaborate cave burials made by Neanderthal Man reveal that as long as 150,000 years ago our ancestors may have worshiped the supernatural. During the past century, different groups of scholars have studied religions in different ways. Archeologists and historians have examined the religions of extinct peoples as manifested in their artifacts and written records. Sociologists have studied organized religious groups—ecclesiae, denominations, and sects—of civilized peoples. Folklorists have recorded folk or peasant religions and the orally transmitted superstitions or popular beliefs of civilized peoples. And cultural and social anthropologists have studied the religions of primitive peoples. This division of scholarly labor, however, has not been clear-cut, for folklorists have always been interested in certain aspects of civilized sects and in primitive religions, while anthropologists in recent decades have increasingly turned their attention to folk religions. Whereas folklorists have done a vast amount of research in Europe and the United States, cultural anthropologists have concentrated their studies of folk peoples in Latin America and Asia. European social anthropologists, who might have interested themselves in their own peasant traditions, have instead studied primitive societies, especially those in the colonial territories of their respective nations.

Although the religions of many primitive peoples have been rather fully documented by anthropologists, there are few major works dealing with particular folk religions; the religions of peasant societies have usually been treated as a single component of their total lore or culture. Nor has a body of popular beliefs of a civilized society ever been adequately described in an important study. To give the reader some idea of the scope of popular beliefs in the United States, I quote the main topics considered in a course on American folk religion at the University of Pennsylvania: Celtic and Germanic religions and their survivals, Mediterranean religions and their survivals, religion and healing, witchcraft, West Indian Voodoo and American Negro folk belief, folk religion in the church year (Christmas, Easter, planting, and harvesting rituals), and religious folk costume, folksong, and folk art.

Primitive, folk, and civilized religions number more than 5,000 in the world today, and each is a composite of varying beliefs, behavior, specialists, and groups. Religious beliefs, to be so defined, must involve supernatural entities toward which sacred attitudes are directed by groups of people. These qualifications rule out as religions all nontheistic belief systems, such as communism and psychoanalysis, as well as individual belief systems. Every religion recognizes several or all of the following entities: one or more deities, spirits and demons, personal and impersonal power, one or more souls, ghosts, fate, luck, magic, and witches. In addition, each religion attaches religious significance to certain objects and places, such as the insignia of a priest or the mountain abode of a deity.

The sacred and the profane (or secular) are attitudes expressed by all peoples toward the supernatural and natural worlds. Although the two worlds everywhere are differentiated, the province of the supernatural tends to be expanded in primitive and folk societies, where such intellectual forces as philosophical rationalism and science have as yet made little impact. Sacred attitudes usually are described as subjective feelings of awe, wonder, reverence, and the like evoked by supernatural symbols, but the *Outline of Cultural Materials* of the Human Relations Area Files systematically delineates a number of "religious experiences" that make up the sacred: "oppressive fear of malevolent higher powers, overwhelming awe of divine might, luxurious sense of dependence upon a benevolent and all-knowing superior, reassuring feeling of security through conformity, prideful conviction of right, grateful release from the burdens of a guilty conscience, groveling humility of self-abnegation, ecstatic release of inner power, mystic sense of identification with or absorption in the divine essence, esthetic thrill in religious art, music, or ceremonial."[1]

Also listed in the outline, and linked to appropriate experiences, are basic "religious practices" or acts of behavior: propitiation, purification, expiation, avoidance, taboo, asceticism, orgies, revelation, divination, ritual, and magic. Each practice is further subdivided; thus, for instance, propitiation subsumes obeisance, laudation, prayer, sacrifice, vows, endowing of shrines, among others.[2] These acts are engaged in by both specialists and laymen. In most primitive groups, the only specialists are workers of magic and diviners of many sorts —known as shamans when they combine the arts of magic and prognostication. But in folk and civilized societies, priests serve as functionaries in various ecclesiae, denominations, and sects. Priests are sometimes found in primitive societies, where they are usually heads of political and kinship groups and conduct rituals on behalf of their followers; and, in some civilized societies, priests perform as workers of magic and diviners as well as clergy.

An ingenious classification of religious phenomena and the religions of the world is found in Anthony F. C. Wallace's *Religion: An Anthropological View* and will be utilized in this chapter. Given the "supernatural premise" that spiritual beings exist, the author conceptualizes religion as a series of building blocks. Forming the base are thirteen "minimal categories of religious behavior," recognized by social scientists, theologians, and laymen alike. These acts of behavior are combined into various sequences called "rituals" and their rationalization by "beliefs," which include cosmological conceptions and values expressed in myths and legends. At the apex of the structure is the organization of the various rituals into complexes called "cult institutions." Thus, Wallace defines the religion of a society as a conglomeration of rituals and beliefs whose components are integrated at the level of cult institutions.[3] Later, he adds another conceptual building block—the "functions of religion"—by examining the intentions of performers of particular rituals: to control nature, to make people sick or well, to organize human behavior, to remit psychopathology, and to revitalize society.[4] His thirteen categories of behavior in large measure parallel those of the *Outline of Cultural*

1. George P. Murdock et al., *Outline of Cultural Materials* (New Haven, Conn.: Human Relations Area Files, Inc., 1950) , p. 127.

2. Ibid., pp. 127–29.

3. Anthony F. C. Wallace, *Religion: An Anthropological View* (New York: Random House, 1966) , pp. 52–101.

4. Ibid., pp. 167–215.

Materials and include prayer, music, physiological exercise, exhortation, reciting the code, imitating things, touching things, not touching things, feasts, sacrifice, congregating, inspiration, and the use of symbolic objects.

In primitive and peasant societies, myths and legends are part of oral tradition and specify the supernatural entities believed to exist, describe the origins of things, explain the nature of reality, and assert the proper organization of values. These narratives become codified in the scriptures and auxiliary texts of civilized peoples and, over time, come to form consistent, logically integrated, closed systems of thought that explain all phenomena of the universe. Primitive belief systems, on the other hand, are inconsistent and poorly integrated; this is so because of the lack of writing and the absence of theologians and apologists whose task it would be to render the systems closed and rigid in order to cope with heresies and antagonistic doctrines put forth by philosophy, science, and competing religions.

Wallace describes four kinds of cult institutions: individualistic, whose rituals are performed by laymen; shamanic, whose rituals are performed by workers of magic and diviners for laymen; communal, whose rituals are performed by lay officials who act as priests for particular groups at prescribed times; and ecclesiastical, whose rituals are performed by a professional clergy organized into a bureaucracy. Examples of these cult institutions in our own society, in the above order, are the luck cult, the fortune-teller cult, the patriotic association cult, and the denomination cult. In the town where he lived as a youth, Wallace discovers four major cult institutions, which he labels "denominational congregations," "religio-political," "superstitious," and "children's." The last two are individualistic and embrace rituals and beliefs concerning luck, magic, witchcraft, Halloween, and the Santa Claus aspect of Christmas. The religio-political cult is a nondenominational, theistic faith used to sanction political, military, and other secular institutions; it finds expression on such holidays as the Fourth of July and Labor Day.

According to the relative presence or absence of these cult institutions, four types of religions can be distinguished. The shamanic possesses only individualistic and shamanic cult institutions. The communal possesses individualistic, shamanic, and communal cult institutions. The Olympian possesses all four kinds of cult institutions and is polytheistic. And the monotheistic also possesses all four kinds but accepts one deity (or recognizes that other supernatural entities are subordinate to, or are alternative manifestations of, a single supreme deity). Theoretically, societies having only individualistic cult institutions should once have existed, but there are no surviving examples. A map of the world drawn by Wallace shows that shamanic religions are found today among the Eskimos, the northern Athapascan and Algonkian hunters, the Paleo-Siberians, the central Asiatic steppe and forest tribes, the Lapps, the Andaman Islanders, the Semang of Malaya, and the African pygmies. American Indian societies, other than those in the far north and in Middle America, have communal religions, as do Australian and Oceanian societies and African societies outside of Central and North Africa. Olympian religions characterize Middle American, Central African, and East Asian peoples on the margins of India and China. The monotheistic religions are the Hindu-Buddhist, Judaeo-Christian, Islamic, and Chinese and their offshoots.

Monotheistic religions that exist today have long histories marked by changes in rituals and beliefs. Since most of them are proselytizing, especially the Judaeo-Christian and Islamic faiths, they have imposed themselves on other religions and have attempted to obliterate them, usually without complete success. Thus, where monotheistic religions are dominant now, their followers cling to rituals and beliefs of religions that have been replaced and of those practiced at earlier stages in their own histories. Added to these are invented and diffused forms from whatever source deemed unacceptable by the present orthodoxies. According to Wallace's classification of cult institutions and religions, it is apparent that folklorists and anthropologists who have studied religions in the United States and Europe have concentrated on individualistic, shamanic, and communal cult institutions of the past and present. These are supported in oral tradition and coexist or have become reinterpreted with Judaeo-Christian cult institutions. On the one hand, these cult institutions are manifested in the superstitions and certain sect practices of civilized Americans and Europeans and, on the other hand, in the religious systems of folk enclaves in the Western world, which compose an amalgam of old and new elements.

At this point, let us examine a folk religion of Ireland, long studied by Irish and Continental folklorists and by the author and his wife. It is part of a tradition that has left an indelible imprint on popular beliefs in the United States.

The collection of folklore concerning the supernatural in Ireland commenced in the early part of the last century and was spurred on by the Gaelic Revival that produced such notable writer-folklorists as William Butler Yeats, Lady Gregory, Douglas Hyde, and John Millington Synge. The scientific recording of folk beliefs was institutionalized in the Republic by the formation, first, of the Folklore of Ireland Society in 1926, then the Irish Folklore Institute in 1930, and, finally, the Irish Folklore Commission in 1936. Commission collectors have recorded vast amounts of oral data from the length and breadth of Ireland, in Gaelic and in English, guided by Seán Ó Súilleabháin's *A Handbook of Irish Folklore* (1963). Among other important works dealing with folk religion are E. Estyn Evans's *Irish Heritage* (1942) and *Irish Folk Ways* (1957), Kevin Danaher's *In Ireland Long Ago* (1962) and *Irish Country People* (1966), Maire MacNeill's *The Festival of Lughnasa* (1962) and Seán Ó Súilleabháin's *Irish Wake Amusements* (1967). The major cultural anthropological studies are those of Conrad Arensberg, *The Irish Countryman* (1937), and Arensberg and Solon T. Kimball, *Family and Community in Ireland* (1968). These authors were members of the Harvard University anthropological survey team that worked in Ireland between 1932 and 1934.

Ireland is composed of many regional folk subcultures, one of which embraces the Aran Islands of film and literary fame. In these three islands lying across the mouth of Galway Bay is found one of the most traditional folk societies of Europe, where countless customs once practiced throughout Ireland and the rest of the Celtic world still survive. The prehistory and history of Aran are dramatically recorded in a multitude of monuments and artifacts of stone and metal, including Mesolithic ax-heads, Neolithic kitchen middens, Copper-Bronze Age gallery grave tombs and burial mounds of earth and stone, Celtic forts of the Iron Age, medieval Christian monasteries, churches, cemeteries, corbelled stone houses, and holy wells, as well as a three-story tower house built by the political overlords of the islands—the O'Briens of County Clare. From 1586 until 1886, Aran was owned by a succession of absentee Anglo-Irish landlords, who were largely responsible for conditions of poverty and servitude among the population.

The islanders qualify as folk in almost every respect, according to folkloristic and anthropological definition. The society has maintained its stability for at least three centuries; there is a strong bond between the peasants and their land, and agriculture (and once fishing) provides them with the major source of their livelihood. Production is mainly for subsistence and is carried on with a simple technology, which includes the digging stick, spade, and scythe. The people participate in a money economy, but barter is still practiced; a low standard of living prevails, and the birth rate is high; the family is of central importance, and marriage figures prominently as a provision of economic welfare. The islands are integrated into the county and national governments and are subject to their laws; the peasants have long been exposed to urban influences, have borrowed cultural forms from other rural areas on the mainland, and have integrated them into a fairly stable system. And, finally, the experience of living under English rule for several hundred years has created in the islanders an attitude of dependence upon yet hostility toward the government that continues to this day. The only conditions in Aran that run counter to those found in most other folk societies are a low death rate and illiteracy rate and bilateral rather than unilineal descent.

Christianity came to Aran in the closing decades of the fifth century, when St. Enda with numerous disciples settled among the indigenous Celts. During the sixty years that he remained there, he founded ten monasteries and thirteen churches. Aran became one of the famous monastic centers of Ireland in the centuries that followed; over a hundred saints lived there or visited, among them Columbkille, Kieran, Brendan, Gobnet, Finnian, Kevan, Fursa, and Brecan. Late in the Middle Ages, the islands became a place of pilgrimage for Christians from all over Europe and attracted a multitude of ascetics. The peasants today are very conscious of this venerable tradition and profess to be devout Catholics. In defending their way of life against those who denigrate their poverty and folk retentions, they stress the sanctity of Aran and the strength of Catholic belief with its concomitant morality; they are boastful of the fact that crime is rare and police are not stationed in the two small islands.

More important than the formal political system of which Aran is a part are the local informal system—which includes the parish priest, curates, headmasters, and a self-appointed "king" in one of the islands—and social control techniques of gossip, ridicule, and opprobrium. Priests dominate the informal system, and anticlerical sentiment (seldom manifested in overt acts) is as strong as or stronger than its antigovernment counterpart. In the past, the amount of influence exerted by clerics has varied; some have been concerned mostly with fulfilling their spiritual responsibilities, while others, by sermon, threat, and even physical action, have curtailed such activities as courting, dancing, visiting, gossiping, and drinking. In addition to interfering in secular affairs, priests have been accused of living too "comfortably," being away from the islands too often, "extorting" money and services from the people in lieu of seeking archdiocesan support, and acting in an overly aloof and supercilious manner. Many folk assert that the clergy have employed informers, allocated indulgences, withheld the sacraments, and placed curses ("reading the Bible at") in their efforts to regulate Aran life.

It is widely believed in Ireland, because of the writings of nativists, that the Catholicism of the islanders embodies an ideal unattained on the mainland, where the faith is thought to set an example for all Christendom. In actual fact, the peasants' worship is obsessively oriented toward salvation in the next world with a corresponding preoccupation with sin in this world. There is a marked tendency toward polytheism in the manner in which they relate to the Blessed Virgin and certain Irish saints, who are thought to possess power and to act independently of God. Rituals and sacred objects, Christian as well as indigenous, often are employed to serve magical ends; and many rituals and beliefs that the islanders hold to be orthodox Catholic are in reality idiosyncratic to Aran or to Ireland. Christian morality in its "outward manifestations" is realized to a remarkable degree, as we have seen; but it is less a product of the emphasis placed on good works as a means of gaining salvation than of the techniques of social control exercised by priests, based on an overwhelming fear of damnation. Widespread mental illness, alcoholism, and the exaggerated use of mechanisms of adjustment also are linked with this fear.

The folk religion of Aran exhibits a wide array of retentions and reinterpretations, of which only those most deeply and widely held will be discussed. It is difficult to determine the age of retentions, since they represent survivals from Celtic and even pre-Celtic times, from medieval Christianity, and from other bodies of tradition of the past, all of which have been subject to constant change and interplay over the last four millennia. To compound the problem, Celtic and medieval cult institutions are known only in their broadest features due to a paucity of trustworthy historical information and widespread revisionism of early nativists. Irish scholars label as pagan unorthodox rituals and beliefs of any sort from any age, and many of these have become reinterpreted with those of Christianity. Reinterpretation is a universal phenomenon of acculturation, or culture contact, in which borrowed elements are interpreted by the members of a society according to traditional standards and indigenous elements according to borrowed standards. First retentions, and then reinterpretations, of religion in Aran will be taken up in the following pages.

Non-Christian ecclesiastical and communal cult institutions evidently disappeared long ago from the islands. The three surviving shamanic cult institutions—workers of magic with herbal, bone-setting, and animal medicine skills—have become extinct in this century. Some elders claim, and early writings on Aran appear to support their view, that once both workers of good and evil magic and diviners flourished there, but now retentions of rituals and beliefs are totally individualistic. The youth of the islands overtly disallow the existence of other than church-approved supernatural entities. One vigorous disclaimer of paganism, however, occasionally is visited by the ghost of his father, who urges the continuation of a family feud. But the elders cling tenaciously to the old ways about which they are extremely secretive for fear of being ridiculed by outsiders and their more skeptical neighbors. As late as 1963, there were two renowned storytellers, one a *sgealai* and the other a *seanchai,* on the small Aran island, both of whom had large repertoires of prose narratives concerning the pagan supernatural in which they believed implicitly. Stories told by the *seanchai* of changelings, fairy ships, ghosts, the pookah, and other spiritual beings in Aran are reported by Messenger.[5]

Celtic deities no longer exist in Aran lore, although some might regard the semideification of the Blessed Virgin, Saint Patrick, Saint Enda, and Saint Brigid as a form of reinterpretation. Certainly the culture heroes of the Iron Age, such as Cuchulainn, Finn, and Oisin, still figure prominently in legends, and the forts and other monuments and some of the geographical features (for instance, glacial boulders) of Aran are explained by the actions of Celtic heroes. A few fortunate fishermen have sighted to the west the afterworld of the Celts in the form of the Isle of the Blest, or the Land of Youth, either low-lying on the horizon when it has risen from the sea or in the ocean deep with the spires of its buildings near the surface and their bells tolling. A widely read book written in 1962, P. A. O Siochain's *Aran: Islands of Legend,* claims that the Aran Islands are the easternmost extension of what was legendary Hy-Brasil, linked to the lost continent of Atlantis, both now sunk beneath the sea, where highly civilized Celts once lived.

Beliefs concerning spirits in human form and animal spirits, or demons, are dominant among Aran retentions, and few indeed are the peasants who have not had at least one experience with these beings. Local spirits include mermaids, the trooping fairies, and the leprechaun, *fear dearg,* and banshee among the solitary fairies. Foremost of the demons are pookahs, water steeds, and *spiorad mara.* Personal confrontations with spirits often are described by men in the pubs, and their mention of the nude mermaids who frequent certain locations along the coastline always embarrasses the sexually puritanical folk. Trooping fairies, who spend most of their time feasting, singing, dancing, fighting, and making love, are feared because they will on occasion steal the souls of humans and leave in their stead changelings, who sicken and eventually perish. The solitary fairies are mostly harmless if spoken of and treated well; the leprechaun is a cobbler and hoarder of treasure, and the *fear dearg* a perpetrator of bizarre practical jokes. Affiliated only with particular families, the banshee announces impending death with its keening wails. An aged Aran man was seriously ill on the night that the author and his wife sponsored a dancing party, and a young man leaving the party three hours after midnight played his accordion as he walked to his home near that of the sick person. On learning of this event, the nurse shortly after dawn hurried to her patient to assure him that the wails he might have heard came from the instrument of the inexpert youth and not from the family banshee; at this news his life was prolonged three weeks, when the banshee at last cried and was heard by those at his deathbed.

The pookah of Aran lives in a Copper-Bronze Age burial mound contiguous to the beach and common land of the small island. During the day it will twist the limbs of unwary individuals who choose to fall asleep on the mound, and at night it will occasionally race across the sands of beach and common land, altering its size from that of a small dog to that of a bull, and frightening those who might pass on a nearby trail. Water steeds and *spiorad mara* are sea creatures; the former has the shape of a horse with a fish tail like the mermaid, while the latter is a seaweed-covered hulk with huge, glaring eyes. When in Norway, the author and his wife purchased as a good luck charm a foot-high statue of a troll made of moss with large glass eyes. It was hung from the wall of their kitchen in Aran and invariably aroused excitement among the fishermen, who thought that it closely resembled the *spiorad mara*. One islander reasoned that this being must inhabit all of the northern seas and probably causes equal consternation to Scottish and Scandinavian seafarers. The Celts believed in the metempsychosis of human souls into animals, as well as their transmigration to the Isle of the Blest, and in Aran some seals are thought to be the repositories of souls. They look and act like humans and attach themselves to fishermen who have aided or harmed them, following their canoes for miles and even coming far up on the beach in relentless pursuit of those whom they dislike.

Although specialists who can foretell the future using various methods of divination are rare in Aran, everyone has access to an ancient corpus of omens. Likewise, with the disappearance of workers of magic, everyone is acquainted with magical procedures many centuries old. Sorcery appears not to be practiced as an individualistic, cult institution today. Most magic involves the use of charms and incantations to ward off evil powers, and indigenous and Christian objects and utterances are believed to be equally efficacious in coping with Druidic and Satanic forces. At one time, hag witches lived in Aran and employed animal familiars to pilfer milk, and with their supernatural cousins, the trooping fairies, they substituted changelings for souls. Several peasants, it is said, possess scars of the fire into which they were cast in order to regain their souls stolen by witches. The only form of witchcraft practiced now is the casting of the evil eye, and several islanders, suitably ostracized, are purported to be able to do evil by the act of complimenting their intended victims.

Especially feared are the compliments of one man who, when very young, caused a newly assigned curate on his first walk of the small island to fall and break a leg when he expressed admiration for the vigorous stride of the priest. Compliments rarely are paid by the folk, and, when proffered, "God bless" is appended; the same magical incantation is directed by those near him toward one who sneezes successively, in this case to prevent his soul from being stolen by hag or fairies.

Other beliefs of significance in Aran are: the existence of fairy ships that not only appear and disappear instantaneously in nearby waters but have crossed the islands and created certain valleys and crevices; the presence of evil in people of swarthy skin and black hair; the ability of certain inanimate objects to move by their own volition; the capacity of befriended animals to take on the illnesses of their human benefactors; the intrinsic value of "natural foods" and other materials impinging on the human body; and the ascription of mental illness to attacks by malevolent beings. Mental disorders also are attributed to inheritance, the menopause in women, God's punishment for sinning, and the perversity of the Devil. A temporary curate in 1960 was a man of dark skin and hair, and he was feared and mistrusted by many islanders for his appearance, even though "a man of the cloth, chosen by God Almighty."

The church in the early Middle Ages urged systematic reinterpretation of Christian and pagan cult institutions as a means of gaining converts. (In 601 Pope Gregory I urged it in a letter to priests attempting to convert the Britons.) This policy is attested to in Aran by Christian cemeteries located on the site of or next to earlier cemeteries, Christian church buildings incorporating Druidic temples, and Celtic sacred wells being appropriated by Christian worshippers. The fact that a sanctified medieval graveyard overlies the Copper-Bronze Age burial mound in which the pookah of Aran resides has not hampered its nocturnal wanderings. Few peasants will molest the ruins of the past because of their belief that trooping fairies or souls of the dead, which may live within, will be annoyed and seek revenge.

Both misinterpretation of Catholic doctrine and reinterpretation mark beliefs in Aran about purgatory. On the one hand, it is asserted that only the souls of saints go directly to heaven following death, and that all other souls either go to hell to await the last judgment or to purgatory to endure temporal punishment for sins previously forgiven before entering heaven. On the other hand, an exception is made of the person who sees an eel or small fish in a holy well; in magical fashion his soul too goes to heaven immediately on death. Furthermore, it is widely held that souls of the dead in purgatory can visit the world as ghosts or "shades" and do penance by laboring at tasks near their former homes. Purgatory thus embraces the earth as well as a spiritual locus, and just as most folk have had contact with spirits, they also have seen ghosts at work—carrying seaweed, planting gardens, and fishing from canoes. Sometimes a shade is recognized as a relative or acquaintance, and always the work that he has done at night is undone by dawn. Heaven and the Isle of the Blest are syncretized by a few elders, and souls from there in youthful guise occasionally travel eastward across the Atlantic to visit Aran.

Christianity touches on the evil eye in more ways than providing the incantation "God bless," which automatically opposes God's power to that of the witch. It is thought by many islanders that the human body is inhabited by both God and the Devil; God rests on the right side and urges the person to do good deeds, while the Devil rests on the left and tempts the person to commit sins. In most individuals, God dominates their bodies, but in the case of one with the evil eye the Devil has somehow gained ascendancy and transmits his destructive power through the left eye of his carrier. As a result, the witch of this genre is known not only through the after-effects of his compliments, but by a disfigurement of some sort in or near his left eye.

Much has been written about the reinterpretation of Celtic festivals and Christian feast days in Ireland and elsewhere in Europe, so mention will be made of only the four major Celtic festivals as they are observed in Aran. Before Christianity came to hold sway in Ireland, the Celts celebrated *Imbolc* on the first of February, *Bealtaine* on the first of May, *Lughnasa* on the first of August, and *Samhain* on the first of November. Imbolc heralded the coming of spring with the lactation of ewes, while at Bealtaine cattle were driven to open grazing after passing between bonfires as a magical precaution to protect them from disease and to ensure their fertility. The harvest commenced with Lughnasa, and the grazing season ended and the new year was ushered in with Samhain. Aran peasants now celebrate Saint Brigid's Day on the first of February. A cross, which embodies both Celtic and Christian symbols, is woven in each cottage in honor of the saint; it is first placed above the front door where it serves as a protective charm, and then thrust into the inside thatching of the roof (providing, incidentally, a means whereby houses can be dated). This day still is regarded as the first of the spring season, and planting starts soon afterward. Bealtaine is remembered by placing flowers on the altars of the medieval churches on the first of May, but the bonfires that once were lighted at this time now are lighted on Saint John's Eve on the twenty-fourth of June. Until the introduction of "early potatoes" into Aran, harvesting began on the first of August, but now Lughnasa is no longer observed. Samhain has become All

Souls' Day, when the graves of the dead are visited in the cemeteries. Trails are deserted on Allhallows' Eve because of the ancient belief that malignant entities are abroad seeking innocent victims.

The tenacity of retentions and reinterpretations is now a source of irritation to most of the clergy and prompts sermons of denunciation and instruction. But it is claimed that exorcism has been resorted to from time to time by certain priests within the past century, to banish disruptive pagan forces designated by them as "works of the Devil." Some islanders express skepticism about both Christian doctrine and folk beliefs, but none are dissenters. Frequently the author and his wife were proselytized by the peasants (and even by two priests), who wished the outsiders to join them in heaven where only Catholic souls reside. Several close friends predicted an eventual reunion in heaven, because religions are like canoes that set out for Doolin (a nearby port on the mainland) on separate courses, yet all reach the same destination. Always the author and his wife were cautioned not to disclose this personal view to the curate.

Bibliography and Selected Readings

Banton, Michael, ed. *Anthropological Approaches to the Study of Religion.* London: Tavistock Publications, 1966. The essays by Clifford Geertz, on religion as a cultural system, and Melford Spiro, on problems of definition and explanation in religion, are outstanding anthropological statements on contemporary religious theory. The other three essays, narrower in scope and more descriptive, are case studies of African peoples by social anthropologists.

Eliade, Mircea. *Pattern in Comparative Religion.* New York: Sheed and Ward, 1949. The author introduces the reader to the "labyrinthine complexity of religious data, their basic patterns, and the varieties of cultures they reflect," by examining various hierophancies—of sky, waters, earth, and stones. The first and the last three chapters deal with sacred time, the morphology and function of myths, and the structure of symbols. In some ways, this is a modern, compressed *The Golden Bough,* with its wealth of comparative materials; but it eschews evolutionary theory, and its sources are more dependable.

Frazer, James G. *The Golden Bough.* London: Macmillan, 1911–15. A famous classic of comparative religion, this grandiose work contains in its twelve volumes a wealth of data on classical and modern civilized religions and on folk and primitive religions. It is much criticized by social scientists today for its outmoded evolutionary theories and its dependence on often questionable source materials.

Geertz, Clifford. *The Religion of Java.* Glencoe, Ill.: The Free Press, 1960. The author describes the "true folk tradition" of the island of Java—a "balanced integration" of "animistic," Hindu, and Muslim forms—from three perspectives: *abangan,* that of the peasant, which stresses animistic elements; *santri,* that of the traders, which stresses Muslim elements; and *prijaji,* that of the government bureaucrats, which stresses Hindu elements. Geertz analyzes each subtradition as to its religious orientation, value system, and political alignment.

Harper, Edward B., ed. *Religion in South Asia.* Seattle: University of Washington Press, 1965. Eight chapters deal with Indian religion and the ninth with Ceylonese. Most of the contributors are anthropologists whose work has focused on the Little Tradition—"Popular Hinduism"—but the Great Tradition also is dealt with, as is the "common belief and action system participated in by Hindu and non-Hindu personnel alike within the dominant civilization."

Herskovits, Melville J. *Trinidad Village.* New York: Knopf, 1947. Herskovits has written extensively on the retention of African religious patterns and reinterpretation of African and Christian forms among New World black folk. This book is based on the third research project conducted in the New World by the author (preceded by research in Dutch Guiana and Haiti); and four of the eleven chapters deal with folk religion. In addition, one of the appendixes concerns "Shango worship," a cult of West African derivation, later studied by numerous social scientists.

Hori, Ichori. *Japanese Folk Religion.* Chicago: University of Chicago Press, 1968. Hori delineates the major features of Japanese folk religion, many of which are retentions from early phases of Japanese history. He shows how this religion resembles many archaic and primitive ones in other parts of the world, and how it has greatly influenced political and economic events in the past. In the final chapter, the author considers the survival of shamanism today.

Leslie, Charles, ed. *Anthropology of Folk Religion.* New York: Knopf, Vintage Books, 1960. Nine anthropologists write of folk and primitive religions in Africa, India, the South Pacific, and the New World.

Lessa, William A., and Evon Z. Vogt, eds. *Reader in Comparative Religion.* New York: Harper and Row, 1965. This is probably the best and most widely used textbook of readings in comparative religion. It contains eighty-two essays by prominent social scientists concerning the origin and development of religion, the functions of religion, religious beliefs and practices, religious specialists and groups, dynamics of religion, and new methods of analysis. With an annotated bibliography of forty-eight monographs on non-Western religious systems and a general bibliography.

Marriott, McKim, ed. *Village India: Studies in the Little Community.* Chicago: University of Chicago Press, 1955. Eight Indian communities are described by eminent anthropologists. Most of the essays look at the Great and Little Traditions. The greatest amount of data on folk religion is found in Marriott's own "Little Communities in an Indigenous Civilization" (reprinted in *Anthropology of Folk Religion,* listed above) and "The World and the World View of the *Kota,*" by David G. Mandelbaum.

Metraux, Alfred. *Voodoo in Haiti.* New York: Oxford University Press, 1959. The African-derived cults of the folk of Haiti are the subject of this important study. The author takes up the origin and history of Voodoo, the social framework of the cults, beliefs and rituals, magic and sorcery, and the relationship of Voodoo and Christianity. Illustrated with excellent photographs. Included is a glossary of Voodoo terms.

Nilsson, Martin P. *Greek Popular Religion.* New York: Columbia University Press, 1940. The lectures that comprise this volume, delivered by a noted philologist-archeologist-historian, deal with Greek popular religion of the Hellenic period, which had its roots in beliefs and practices of Doric, Achaean, Minoan, and primitive precursors. This work goes far beyond describing the syncretistic religion of the folk; it is a rather full account of Greek peasant culture as it was 2,500 years ago, since neglected by historians preoccupied with urban civilization.

Norbeck, Edward. *Religion in Primitive Society.* New York: Harper & Brothers, 1961. This volume is probably the best of the recently published textbooks on primitive religion by a single author. It covers most of the field, includes much data of a comparative nature on folk and civilized religions, has a good bibliography, and is written in a very readable style.

Redfield, Robert. *Tepoztlán: A Mexican Village.* Chicago: University of Chicago Press, 1930. This work and the two following are distinguished studies of acculturation among Mexican Indians of five communities. The fusion of Spanish Catholic and Mayan and Aztecan elements, which constitutes the religion of these folk, is the central concern of all three books. In his 1941 volume, Redfield discusses at length his concept of the folk society (later to become the little community), which he conceived of in the 1930s and which later exerted a profound influence on the social sciences. Many of the attributes of the ideal folk culture are religious ones.

———. *The Folk Culture of Yucatan.* Chicago: University of Chicago Press, 1941.

———, and Alfonso Villa Rojas. *Chan Kom: A Maya Village.* Washington: Carnegie Institution of Washington, Pub. No. 448, 1934.

Spiro, Melford E. *Symposium on New Approaches to the Study of Religion.* Seattle: University of Washington Press, 1964. Ten essays on primitive and folk religions written by anthropologists. Among the outstanding articles are those by Igor Kopytoff on "Classifications of Religious Movements: Analytical and Synthetic" and by the editor on "Religion and the Irrational."

Wallace, Anthony F. C. *Religion: An Anthropological View.* New York: Random House, 1966. Latest of the textbooks on primitive religion, this work is notable for its classification of religious phenomena and the

religions of the world, its discussion of the universal functions of religion, and its emphasis on recent research and methods of analysis in
the anthropology of religion.

Yinger, J. Milton, ed. *Religion, Society, and the Individual.* New York:
Macmillan, 1957. The sociology of religion focuses on civilized religions
and their groupings, and of the several textbooks in this field Yinger's
is outstanding. It includes a lengthy essay by the author followed by
thirty-nine essays by eminent social scientists, mostly sociologists. There
are more data pertaining to folk and primitive peoples in this work
than in any other such textbook, and a strong emphasis on the impact
of religion on institutions and personality.

MATERIAL CULTURE
11 FOLK CRAFTS
Warren E. Roberts

In dealing in limited space with a topic as broad as folk crafts, one can only generalize and enumerate the various crafts. The first consideration must be: what are folk crafts? Here the element of tradition is of primary importance, and one can say generally that folk crafts are traditional crafts. It is, indeed, in the crafts that one can observe with special clarity the operation of tradition. Until relatively recent times, craft techniques and designs were passed down within one family for many generations or were transmitted by the apprentice system wherein a boy learning the craft served for as long as seven years under a master craftsman. Only fairly recently has the older, traditional system of transmitting the skills and knowledge of a craft been partially supplanted by formalized training in schools and by printed manuals and books.

The strong traditional element in the crafts is also apparent in the great antiquity of many crafts. The making of pottery, for example, is immensely old and has changed little over the centuries, while the flint knappers of England who in mid-twentieth century were still producing shaped flints were using a craft technique of unknown antiquity. Tradition usually has a geographical as well as an historical spread; that is, while an element of folklore is passed from one generation to the next within any given area, it also usually spreads from one part of the world to another. So it is with the crafts, some of which are of worldwide diffusion. The expansion of European culture has made it difficult to ascertain distribution patterns. Thus pottery was made in most parts of the world prior to the spread of European culture, and the production of flint knives and arrowheads was also practiced all around the world in prehistoric times. While it is certainly impossible to prove in every case, folklorists are convinced that most folklore elements that are widely distributed were not invented independently in many parts of the world but were invented or created at one time and in one place and hence spread by the migrations of people or were passed from one group to the next over a long period of time.

Certain general requirements will determine when a craft is a folk craft. The element of tradition is more important than the element of age. Every craft item that is old is not necessarily a product of a folk craft. It would be incorrect to consider such famous eighteenth-century cabinetmakers as Chippendale as folk craftsmen. At the same time, many traditional crafts still flourish today. While there is, obviously, a strong correlation between antiquity and folk crafts, one cannot assume that everything old is folk while everything new is non-folk. In order to be considered a folk craft, too, a craft must have been in fairly general use and not restricted only to the upper layers of society where learned, academic, or sophisticated modes of transmission exist. The craft of the goldsmith, therefore, probably lies outside the realm of folk crafts. Although there are strong traditional elements in goldsmithing, the goldsmith catered to the very wealthy and drew his designs often from printed rather than traditional sources. Finally, crafts in which primarily one man creates and designs the finished product have a better claim to consideration as folk crafts than those processes involving mass production, with one man repeating a single operation over and over making only one small part, or with machines doing most of the work.

Another, broader question involves the distinction, if any, between a craft, an art, and an occupation. Although there is much confusion in terms (for example, the term "manual arts"), in general practice the so-called fine arts are distinguished from the crafts. Hence painting and sculpture when traditional are considered as folk art rather than folk craft. Moreover, occupations such as mining and logging are usually not deemed crafts, for the miner, for example, simply produces the metals with which the blacksmith and the tinsmith work while the craftsman produces the finished product. Moreover, the craft demands, on the whole, a greater degree of training and skill than does the occupation.

Although much has been written on folk crafts in certain European countries, especially in Scandinavia, relatively little has been written of a scholarly nature in Great Britain and the United States. A number of popular works, especially "how-to-do-it" books for hobbyists, have been published over the years. In Great Britain earlier works dealt with the history either of crafts in general or of a particular craft, while only a few, such as Norman Wymer's *English Country Crafts* (1946), attempted to describe on the basis of fieldwork the traditional crafts still practiced. In the last decade there have appeared a number of important works, most of them by members of the Society for Folk Life Studies, organized in 1962. Two books by J. Geraint Jenkins illustrate two primary research methods in folklife research. *The English Farm Wagon* (1961) is an exemplary survey of a single topic based in large part upon questionnaires and fieldwork. *Traditional Country Craftsmen* (1965) covers a number of crafts and is based almost exclusively on fieldwork. In the United States even less has been done. Excluding the "how-to-do-it" books, scholarly American works on folk crafts have mostly emphasized the history of crafts, especially in the seventeenth and eighteenth century, as does Carl Bridenbaugh's *The Colonial Craftsman* (1950), Henry C. Mercer's *Ancient Carpenters' Tools* (1929), and a number of brief articles by various authors in the journal *Pennsylvania Folklife*.

In times past, prior to the Industrial Revolution, folk crafts played an immensely important role in traditional society, for practically everything the individual could not produce for himself was produced by craftsmen living in his own locality. It would be fair to say that the folk society of Europe was characterized by the extended family unit, the self-sufficient farm, and traditional crafts. Stores or shops as we know them today hardly existed in the countryside in earlier times, and if a farmer needed an item that could not be produced on the farm, he went directly to the craftsman to obtain the item or the craftsman came to the farm to produce it. Traveling peddlers did bring craft products to farms, but poor roads made it difficult for them to carry around large or heavy items in any quantity. Occasionally farmers traveled to nearby towns to sell or barter their excess produce and to purchase ready-made items, and in many areas fairs at which craftsmen set up their booths and sold their wares were a regular event eagerly looked forward to.

In the majority of cases, there was close personal contact between the craftsman and his customer. The visit of the farmer to the craftsman to order or pick up an item was a social event as well as a business matter. In many areas, too, craft shops such as the smithy served as social centers where men tended to gather to discuss news and local events and to tell stories. In those instances where craftsmen traveled from farm to farm, they also lived with the family during their stay and were a valuable source of news, stories, and the like. In many areas, for instance, a weaver went to a farm when the wife had accumulated a sufficient quantity of thread that she had spun herself. There, on his own portable loom or on the loom already at the farmhouse, the weaver wove cloth for all the family's needs or wove certain specialized fabrics requiring more skill than the average farmwife possessed. In the same way, the shoemaker often journeyed from farm to farm making shoes for the entire family from the store of leather that had been accumulating since his last visit. Under such circumstances the craftsman and his customer usually developed a special relationship. The craftsman knew his customer and the family needs, while the customer bartered produce of various kinds to suit the needs of the craftsman and his family. The customer received craft items made specifically to suit his special needs and could be sure of receiving serviceable and reliable items, for often his family had known the craftsman's family for several generations, while the craftsman, on the other hand, was eager to produce satisfactory items, for he knew his customers and was anxious to serve them again. A scythe handle, for example, had to be made to match the height and arm length of its user. Small wonder, then, that craftsmen often played important and influential roles in the rural societies of earlier times.

Before we enumerate the various folk crafts, some general statements should be made. The first involves the Industrial Revolution, its effects upon the crafts in general, and the plight of the craftsman at the present day. As manufactured goods began to flood the countryside in the eighteenth and nineteenth century, the craftsman was, of course, immediately affected. When it became possible to buy factory-made goods at a price lower than the craftsman could make and sell his products, most people, of course, began buying the cheaper goods. Unable to sell his products at a decent price, the craftsman, by and large, ceased being a maker and became a repairer of manufactured objects. The watchmaker, for example, no longer actually made watches but repaired factory-made watches, while the shoemaker rarely made shoes but repaired worn factory-made shoes. The date at which factory-made goods supplanted those made by the craftsman differs from place to place and from craft to craft. In most areas in the United States, it was not the progress of manufacturing but the progress of transportation that determined whether a craftsman could still receive a decent return for his work. As long as transportation costs were high, the purchaser who lived some distance from a factory could often buy an item made locally by a craftsman more cheaply than the manufactured item. During the second half of the nineteenth century, cheap and efficient transportation spelled doom for the age-old system of craft production wherein the craftsman produced items as needed for his own neighbors. At this time, too, factory-made items often had a certain glamor or prestige that handmade items lacked, so that the purchaser was happy to pay extra for the factory-made item. Now, however, in many instances the handmade item commands a higher price.

In proof that ancient traditions and ways of life are tenacious and cannot be destroyed overnight by changing economic situations, the folk crafts still survive in contemporary society in the United States. In some areas, remote from contemporary urban society, some crafts survive with something approaching their original vigor. Two examples will indicate their diversity. In the southern mountain regions, chairmakers are still producing and selling their distinctive chairs of traditional design because the customer can barter produce for a chair rather than paying cash, and because the raw materials used for the chairs are plentiful and cheap. No better-paying jobs being available, the craftsman continues with his craft and lives on an income pitifully small by standards of other parts of America. Among the Amish, who are surrounded by and yet apart from contemporary society because they have chosen to cling to the old ways of life for religious reasons, many crafts such as blacksmithing survive. The Amish cannot purchase factory-made items in the old-fashioned designs they demand, and they refuse to make use of motor-driven tools and other mechanical equipment. The well-known Amish buggy is a case in point. Because there is no large demand for it, local carriage-makers, wheelwrights, blacksmiths, and harness-makers find employment producing a limited number of vehicles that a factory would find unprofitable to make.

Second, some craftsmen still flourish in areas where they repair factory-made items, although not all crafts survive in this way. Weavers, for example, do not mend torn or worn-out cloth (the specialists who re-weave cigarette burns in garments use entirely different equipment and techniques) but survive in other ways, and basketmakers do not customarily mend worn-out or broken baskets. To survive by doing repairs, many crafts have had to change their operations. The cabinetmaker in most areas usually does more refinishing of furniture and reupholstering than anything else, while the blacksmith generally spends much of his time welding with modern equipment and tools.

Craftsmen also manage to survive for various special economic and technological reasons. It is economically feasible for some weavers in southern Indiana to weave rag rugs at their looms because the raw materials—rags—cost little or nothing and hence they can sell their rugs at a price comparing favorably with even the cheapest factory-made rugs. From the technological standpoint, some crafts manage to survive because machines have never been developed that can do the work of the hand craftsman. No machine presently makes baskets, so basketmakers still flourish in some parts of the United States even though factory-made containers of paper or plastic have largely replaced baskets and even though foreign baskets can be imported and sold more cheaply than the local basketmaker's product.

A fourth reason the crafts survive today in many areas is that a hand-made item has, for many purchasers, a prestige or glamor that factory-produced items cannot match, quite apart from the question of better workmanship. As a result, craft shops flourish in districts where there are many tourists and where craftsmen can find a market for their products. Craft production of this type does not always represent any noteworthy tradition, for in some cases the craftsmen have learned their craft in schools or in some other formalized way and the items they produce sometimes do not follow traditional designs. A number of organizations and foundations have stimulated craft production of this sort, finding or training craftsmen, supplying designs, and arranging for marketing.[1]

Certain crafts exist today in yet a fifth way, for pottery-making, weaving, silversmithing, and several other crafts have been elevated to the status of fine arts and are taught in art schools. Here again, while the techniques are undoubtedly mainly traditional, emphasis is upon creativity in design rather than upon the observance of tradition.

Finally, in the United States today many crafts are practiced as hobbies because many individuals find great personal satisfaction in making useful or decorative items for their own use or for their friends. Numerous books on weaving, furniture-making, tinsmithing, and the like explain the rudiments of these crafts and supply designs for the hobbyist to follow. While crafts pursued as hobbies testify to the vitality of the crafts and to the important social role they once

1. At Berea College in Kentucky, for instance, the teaching of crafts is emphasized. While many traditional designs from the surrounding areas are used, some copies of eighteenth-century New England furniture are produced. Henry Glassie cites the case of southern mountain craftsmen making Dutch colonial chairs and Tyrolean baskets following designs introduced to them from urban sources. See his *Pattern in the Material Folk Culture of the Eastern United States* (Philadelphia, 1969), p. 1.

11–1. Howard F. Dautrich, a contemporary folk craftsman. Like many modern craftsman, Mr. Dautrich has adapted a traditionally learned craft to shifting times. He continues to employ techniques he learned as a youthful apprentice to an elderly Pennsylvania German tinsmith, but as a competitive sheet metal worker he has innovated with timesaving methods and tools. The forms he produces include traditional items such as kitchenware, which is sold to Amish and Mennonite farm folk, as well as novel items designed to appeal to the antiquarian tastes of tourists. The photograph was taken in the shop at his home near Reading, Berks County, Pennsylvania, in April 1967 by Henry Glassie.

played in providing an outlet for individual talent and creativity, the element of tradition is largely lacking when designs and techniques are learned mainly from books, so that we would not be justified in considering hobbies as folk crafts.

Another point on the crafts in general concerns the individual—the farmer—as his own craftsman. For practically every craft to be enumerated below there were specialized craftsmen, such as blacksmiths, coopers, wheelwrights, and so on, but many farmers had the ability and the tools to carry on to some extent these specialized crafts themselves (Fig. 11–2). The situation varied a great deal from individual to individual, but many farmers could make simple items from metal, wood, and leather, or repair broken or worn items without requiring the services of a specialized craftsman, and it is likely that a farmer with the tools and a special ability in a craft such as blacksmithing would assist his neighbors even though it remained a sideline with him and he never became a specialist. At the same time, craftsmen were also usually part-time farmers who had some land on which they grew crops and raised animals, devoting time to their own farm when they could. Hence it is difficult to draw a hard and fast line between the farmer and the specialized craftsman. The specialized craftsman, however, devoted much more time to his craft and derived a significant amount of his income from it in comparison to the average farmer.

The list of different crafts to be given below is not exhaustive but suggestive. It might prove impossible to list every specialized craft that ever flourished in Great Britain and the United States, to say nothing of other countries, but we mention most of the crafts widely practiced over a long period of time, with their common names based upon American usage. (Variant names for different crafts, especially as they relate to family names, is an interesting topic, but beyond our present scope.) The crafts are arranged loosely according to the main material with which the craftsman worked, such as wood or metal. If he used more than one material—for instance, a clockmaker can make clocks with both wood and metal parts—a decision was made on the basis of what seemed the more important. The crafts covered are those that flourished during the eighteenth century and continued on at least into the nineteenth century in the United States.

Throughout history, wood has proved to be an immensely important raw material for mankind. Light in weight, durable, easily worked, elastic, smooth to touch, capable of absorbing shock, and possessing many other useful qualities, wood has served man in an astonishingly wide variety of ways. Since woods possess different qualities, craftsmen have needed to know what wood is best for which use and how best to work with different woods. Hence we begin our listing of crafts

11–2. A farm blacksmith shop. The shop is located on the farm of Homer Martin, north of Alpharetta, Fulton County, Georgia. When it was extensively photographed in November 1966, this small shop (it measures only 8 1/2 by 17 feet) was no longer in use; it was, however, in perfect condition, with its forge at one end, a work bench at the other, and an anvil in the doorway, and Mr. Martin, who is pictured at the anvil, was genially available for interview. Mr. Martin used the shop primarily to repair his own farm equipment, although he also did some blacksmithing—sharpening plowshares mostly—for his neighbors. Fieldwork and artwork by Henry Glassie.

with those primarily utilizing wood. The cabinetmaker or joiner comes immediately to mind. While some cabinetmakers who catered to the wealthy drew some of their designs from printed sources such as the famous design book of Chippendale, most cabinetmakers relied heavily upon traditional designs. Designs and a sense of proper proportion were part of the lore transmitted from one generation of craftsmen to the next, and one can discover many furniture designs or types made by a number of cabinetmakers over a period of at least one century over a wide geographical area. While a country cabinetmaker usually fashioned all sorts of furniture and made complete pieces, other craftsmen who also worked on furniture are sometimes separately identified. Chairmaking in many areas was a distinct craft, for in making chairs somewhat different techniques are used than in making case pieces such as a chest of drawers. Turning is important in making the round legs and other parts of chairs, and whereas the builder of a chest of drawers works almost exclusively with right angles, the chairmaker seldom uses right angles, for in order to be comfortable the back of a chair, for example, cannot be at a right angle to the seat. Country chairmakers usually employed a few designs, the most common being the Windsor chair and the slat-back chair. Turning was often a separate craft, for turners made on their lathes many other items such as turned wooden bowls and wooden buttons in addition to chair parts. The woodcarver was sometimes called upon to use his talents in the decoration of furniture; in seaports he was likely to carve ships' figureheads, in cities to make carved shop signs, including cigar store Indians.

The carpenter, either house carpenter or ship's carpenter, represents a craft working with wood still very much alive although considerably changed by the developments growing out of the Industrial Revolution. Prior to the nineteenth century, the carpenter and the cabinetmaker used very much the same techniques, for both joined pieces of wood, whether delicate table parts or huge barn timbers, with the mortise and tenon joint, in which a protruding member on one piece of wood (the tenon) fits into a matching cavity (the mortise) in the other. The development of cheap nails largely put an end to this technique in carpentry, in the United States at any rate. Modern, power-driven saws have likewise supplanted the age-old technique of shaping wood in the direction of the grain by splitting and hewing, while other technological developments have radically changed the craft of the carpenter in other ways.

Before the nineteenth century, when containers were made by hand, the cooper together with the basketmaker were important craftsmen in the town. Great quantities of barrels in many sizes were needed for the storage and transportation of solids and liquids. In some areas a distinction was made between the tight cooper who made barrels to contain liquid and the slack cooper who made barrels for solids. From staves held together by hoops the cooper made many other containers, both large and small, bearing names now largely forgotten—piggin, noggin, and firkin. Emerson's line, "The meal's in the firkin, the milk's in the pan," preserves one of these terms.

It is probably simplest to place under the heading of wainwright all crafts devoted to making such wheeled vehicles as carriages and wagons. One of the best books available in English on any craft, *The English Farm Wagon* by J. Geraint Jenkins, shows the wide variety of vehicles of traditional design that were developed in response to special needs and the differing requirements of varying terrain in many localities. Often farm wagons as well as carriages were painted in traditional colors and with traditional designs. Closely allied with the wainwright was the wheelwright, who also worked closely with the blacksmith, for an important step in making one type of wheel involved heating an iron tire of the correct size until it expanded. Then it was slipped over the wooden wheel and immediately doused with water so that it contracted and forced the wooden parts of the wheel almost inseparably together. The interdependence of many crafts is shown also in the fact that the blacksmith supplied the wainwright with many iron fittings, hinges, and similar parts needed for the vehicles.

Until the twentieth century many utensils and containers used in the kitchen, dairy, and dining room were made of wood rather than pottery or metal. These wooden bowls, churns, spoons, trenchers, and mugs are generally classified together as treenware. Some of these were made of staves and hoops by the cooper, and some were turned on a lathe by the turner, but many were carved or chiseled from different kinds of wood by the treenware-maker or by the farmer himself during the long winter evenings. Nearly unbreakable and easily cleaned, such treenware had many practical advantages.

The agricultural implement-maker of the past produced such items as rakes, grain cradles, and grain scoops. Many implements made largely of iron at the present, such as rakes and spades, were once made either entirely of wood as in the case of rakes or mainly of wood and shod with iron as in the case of spades. Makers of ax handles, scythe snaths, and the like can also be placed in this category, although often the individual farmer kept a pattern for the utensil handle that best suited his personal requirements and made his own handles from ash, hickory, or other suitable woods.

Other craftsmen who worked mainly with wood include the millwright, who constructed the gears, wheels, and shafts for water and wind mills; the fiddle-maker, who shaped other musical instruments besides fiddles; and the clock-maker who, in the early era of factory production, used many wooden parts in the works of his clocks.

A number of other crafts used metals of various kinds. Certainly the most common of the metal-working crafts was blacksmithing, and the smithy was a familiar feature in small communities and towns, whether or not it stood "under the spreading chestnut tree." The knowledge of how to work with iron, transmitted from one generation to another, was, of course, of crucial importance to the progress of civilization, for with tools and implements of iron farmers could raise more foodstuffs and build a greater variety of structures. Items of iron made by the blacksmith were important to many other crafts, for not only did the blacksmith make many of the tools that the carpenter, for instance, used in his work, but also the blacksmith provided the iron nails and hinges that the carpenter needed in building a house. In the twentieth century blacksmiths were largely occupied in shoeing horses, but in earlier times horseshoeing was done by another craftsman, the farrier, who depended upon the blacksmith to supply the necessary shoes and hence worked in close connection with him. When factories began to supply more and more ready-made iron items, many blacksmiths gradually assumed the role of farrier.

Another metalworker especially important during the pioneer periods in various parts of the United States was the gunsmith. The famous Kentucky rifles, actually made mostly in Pennsylvania, played a key role in the period of expansion when the pioneer was forced to contend with Indians and to secure a large part of his food supply from wild game. Guns have generally been regarded as decorative as well as purely utilitarian objects, and the gunsmith chose beautifully grained wood for gun stocks and also used metal inlays and engraving for decoration.

The pewterer, the tinsmith, and the coppersmith all made items that were used in the farm dairy and kitchen and at the dining table. Many families owned a certain number of pewter plates and bowls, and even spoons were often made of pewter. The metal is relatively soft, of course, but if a pewter item were damaged it could be returned to the pewterer who would melt it and recast it. Pewter buttons were also frequently used in an earlier age. The tinsmith made a wide variety of pots, pans, and other containers as well as funnels, strainers, lanterns, and the like (Fig. 11–1). In the eighteenth century, painted tinware, called tôle, in the form of trays and coffee pots became popular. The coppersmith supplied the large copper kettles essential to such diverse household tasks as cheese and apple-butter making. In many places traveling tinkers repaired worn or damaged household wares.

Other craftsmen working in metal include the locksmith, the cutler, the sawsmith, and the bell maker. Certain metal crafts that catered to the wealthy and flourished in the large urban centers should probably be considered outside the realm of folk crafts. These are goldsmithing and silversmithing.

A number of crafts that used mainly various vegetable fibers can be considered together. Basketmakers wove containers of many sizes and shapes for a wide variety of uses (Fig. 11–3). They also employed raw materials of many kinds depending, of course, on what raw materials were available. Varieties of willow especially suitable for basketry were cultivated in some areas, while in other areas certain kinds of wood, especially ash, were used that separate into long thin strips when pounded along the grain. Tree bark of various kinds and straw and grasses were sometimes used to weave baskets, and a special technique of braiding straw and grass and building up a container from such coils was also practiced. Weaving chair seats of fiber would seem to be closely connected with basket-weaving. Certainly the same materials and techniques are used in each craft. Chair seats woven from wild rushes were common where rushes were available in sufficient quantities, though basketmakers did not make much use of rushes.

Ropemakers also used many kinds of fibers, though hemp was the mainstay of those craftsmen in seaports who supplied the great quantities of rope needed aboard sailing vessels. In the countryside, however, ropes were often made from straw, flax fibers too coarse for textiles, bark, animal sinews, leather, and other substances.

Although they used other substances as well, both broom-makers and thatchers made extensive use of straw. Special varieties were cultivated to supply the straw used in these crafts, but brooms were also made from twigs and reed was often used for thatched roofs. Thatching seems to have been used very little in the United States, for the abundance of suitable kinds of wood for splitting shingles made shingle roofs common as early as the seventeenth century, and their popularity has continued in most parts of the country into modern times.

Wherever suitable clays could be found, potters supplied local needs; the countryside used to be dotted with small potteries operated often by a single family. Brick and tile makers also worked where suitable clay was available, though often brick for a house was made right on the site where a house was built, using the clay excavated when the cellar was dug. Clay pipes were also made by specialists.

Wherever suitable stone could be found, masons also were in demand. Masonry can be of many types. A structure, be it a building, a chimney, a foundation for a building, or a fence, can be made of stones that are gathered and used in their natural shape (field stone, for example) or artificially shaped pieces of stone quarried from the ground or brick. The masonry can either be fitted together without mortar (dry laid), or mortar of various kinds can be used. In many areas these various kinds of masonry are found side by side. Stone fences or walls of field stone laid without mortar, for example, may surround fields, while foundations of houses may be made of field stone laid in mortar and chimneys may be made of shaped stones or bricks laid in mortar. Of these various techniques, the naturally occurring stone laid without mortar must be the most ancient, but it is still being used at the present time.

Another use of stone in building was made where naturally occurring slate made slate roofs possible. Stone was useful in other ways, for grindstones, whetstones, millstones, and gravestones, while containers were often made from soft, easily worked soapstone.

Leather was another raw material for several crafts. The tanner had to work with the animal hides before they could be used in many ways, though rawhide was often used in small quantities for light ropes and cords. Tanned leather was essential for the shoemaker who, as mentioned previously, sometimes traveled from farm to farm making shoes for the entire family from the store of tanned leather that had accumulated since his last visit. The harnessmaker and the saddler also required tanned leather. Frequently leather garments were worn, and some craftsmen, such as blacksmiths, required leather aprons, and these, as well as leather gloves, were supplied by the glover.

A few other crafts associated with other raw materials may be mentioned briefly. Glassblowers were very uncommon outside large urban areas because their products were both fragile and expensive and because glassblowers worked in groups rather than singly. A large furnace was needed to produce the molten glass, and it was not feasible for a single craftsman to maintain such a furnace for his own use. A group of men working together needed to be near a city to find a large enough market for their products. Animal horn was another substance used by occasional craftsmen to produce horn combs and spoons, while powder horns were, of course, also made from animal horns.

Other crafts practiced not by specialized craftsmen but by practically every farmer and his wife need separate treatment. Although not often recognized as crafts, the daily tasks of the farmer may be called subsistence crafts and the daily work of the farmer's wife may be considered household crafts. Both may be treated briefly here because

11–3. Joseph Westfall, of near Higbee, Missouri, one of the few basketmakers who still uses traditional techniques and designs in making baskets of hand-riven white oak. Photograph by Howard Marshall, 1969.

of their importance and because they do not fall under other categories.

The subsistence crafts of the farmer cover a wide range of activities and each activity required considerable skill and a sound knowledge of the traditional lore associated with it. In addition to raising crops, most farms carried on dairying, animal husbandry, and poultry raising. Fruit was grown, the different kinds depending to some extent on the locality, though the apple was probably most important. Berries also were cultivated. Practically every farm had a number of beehives. In most of the eastern United States this source of sweetening was supplemented by maple sugar and by sorghum syrup. Other subsistence crafts were practiced on the average farm, but those mentioned will give some notion of the wide variety of basic crafts.

Where the natural environment made it possible, fishing, hunting, and trapping were also practiced. Under fishing would come such matters as the making of nets and their use, eel-spearing, ice-fishing, and the like. Trapping involves a great deal of lore concerning different kinds of snares and traps, while under the general topic of hunting and trapping may be listed all sorts of subjects connected with survival in the woods such as the construction of temporary shelters, the kindling of fires, the use of pack-baskets, the making and use of snowshoes, and the training of hunting dogs. It is in this sphere of human activity that much research remains to be done on the relationships between the white man and the American Indian. While the European settler borrowed a great deal from the Indian in the New World, the question of how much he brought from the Old World, how his importations were modified, and what, if any, the Indian borrowed of woodland lore from the white man has never been adequately explored.

If the farmer practiced many crafts in the course of his daily tasks, so also did the farmwife in her daily duties. In preparing foods she drew heavily upon traditional recipes and techniques. In addition, the preservation of foods was mainly her work. In the long history of human life, the discoveries of various ways to preserve foods take on great significance. In a northern climate, foods are abundant at harvest time but scarce at other times of the year, especially in the winter. Great effort was devoted to preserving foods when they were abundant so they would last throughout the year. Methods of preservation include drying of fruits and meats, smoking of meats, conserving of fruits and berries with sugar, pickling of meats and vegetables, spicing as in the making of sausages, and storing root crops in cool root cellars or straw-lined trenches in the ground. Cheese-making may be considered here too, for when milk is plentiful during the summer months cheeses are made to be eaten during the winter. Cider-making and vinegar-making are also ways of preserving apple products past the harvest time.

Another group of crafts practiced in practically every farmhouse are those devoted to producing textiles. In an earlier era, practically all textiles used in the home were produced in the home, and it was a rare occasion when a piece of cloth was purchased. The textiles in common use were linen and wool. Practically every farmer kept enough sheep to provide the wool for his family, while flax also was grown practically everywhere in the eastern United States. The first step in producing cloth was preparing the fiber, shearing the sheep, washing the wool and carding and combing it, or retting, swingling, and combing the flax. Next came spinning the fiber into thread, a time-consuming process. A spinning wheel or two, a smaller one for flax and a larger one for wool, stood in practically every farmhouse, and the women members of the family spent so much time in spinning that the distaff became the symbol for women. Weaving also required much time, and in larger houses a special room was allocated to the loom so that it could be used over a period of time. In most households, however, the loom was set up for shorter periods and then dismantled and stored. In some areas, as previously noted, professional weavers traveled from farm to farm weaving patterns too complicated for the average farmwife or bringing with him to be set up a large loom capable of producing wider webs of cloth than the family looms could produce. Dyeing was another important step in producing cloth. The cloth could be dyed after it was woven, or the thread could be dyed before weaving began so that a colored pattern was produced in the weaving. Most dyestuffs were grown on the farm or gathered in field and forest, and there were many traditional recipes for preparing batches of dye. Various nuts, for instance, produced different shades of brown, while the indigo plant was often cultivated for the sake of the blue dye it produced. Many garments were knitted rather than woven from wool, and fulling was a step in the production of woolen cloth in which moisture, heat, and pressure were used to shrink and thicken the cloth.

A certain number of textile crafts are practiced largely for decorative purposes. These include embroidery, crewel work, needle-point, and crocheting. Girls also made samplers that involved intricate decorative needlework. While it is true that these decorative techniques were frequently used by the young ladies of well-to-do families and were taught in schools, they were also traditional and practiced in leisure hours by most women.

A final group of textile crafts may be termed "salvage" crafts. These include quilting, hooking rugs, braiding rugs, and weaving rag rugs.

Sound portions of garments outgrown or worn beyond patching and scraps of leftover material were used in all these crafts. There are several different kinds of quilting, but a common one, the patchwork quilt, involved a pattern of usually different colored pieces of cloth of different sizes sewn together. Not only is the technique of quilting traditional, but designs of great variety, often with colorful names, were also passed from one quilter to the next. In hooking, braiding, and weaving rugs, pieces of cloth useless for other purposes are cut into long, narrow strips. For hooked rugs these strips are worked through a coarsely woven piece of cloth leaving loops protruding. For hooked rugs also traditional patterns are widely known and used. In braided rugs, the strips are braided into coils that are sewn together while for a woven rag rug the strips are woven on a loom very much as any cloth is woven.

Other household crafts include such tasks as brewing, soapmaking, and candlemaking. Prior to the religious revivals of the late eighteenth and nineteenth century ale was brewed in many households and drunk at home as well as at inns and taverns. Wines and cordials such as elderberry wine and dandelion wine were often homemade. Whiskey was also distilled, and eighteenth and early-nineteenth-century American records and travelers' accounts testify to the large quantities that were consumed. Soap was made at home from animal fats treated with lye obtained from wood ash. Candles were also made from animal fats as well as from waxes including that obtained from the bayberry. Candles were made either by dipping lengths of string into molten fat or wax or by using candle molds. All in all, the household of an earlier era was a busy place. The farmer and his wife must have gained considerable personal satisfaction from supplying the needs of their families by their own hands, guided by their inherited knowledge of necessary techniques and patterns.

Bibliography and Selected Readings

United States

Bridenbaugh, Carl. *The Colonial Craftsman*. New York: New York University Press, 1950. Chicago: The University of Chicago Press, 1961. Included as the best example of a number of works by historians on early crafts and industries. The craftsman, his social position, and the role of specific craftsmen in historical events are the themes of this book rather than the traditional aspects of craft techniques and products or the crafts in traditional culture.

Eaton, Allen H. *Handicrafts of the Southern Highlands*. New York: Russell Sage Foundation, 1937. Although designed primarily to encourage the revival of handicrafts as "leisure-time occupation" and "therapy for grown-ups," this work does give the best available survey of surviving traditional crafts in that area in the United States that is probably the richest in such survivals.

――――. *Handicrafts of New England.* New York: Harper, 1949. The companion volume to the above work for another rich area.

Glassie, Henry. *Pattern in the Material Folk Culture of Eastern United States.* Philadelphia: University of Pennsylvania Press, 1969. While emphasizing architecture, much material on folk crafts is included in an attempt to block out tradition areas. The method used is that of the cultural geographer rather than the folk atlas technique. The book incorporates the best available bibliography on folk crafts in the eastern United States but is difficult to use since the bibliographical section of the book is arranged alphabetically by author.

Kettel, Russell H. *The Pine Furniture of Early New England.* Garden City, New York, 1929. The best available work on furniture of traditional design made both by traditionally trained craftsmen and by nonspecialists for their own use. Lavishly illustrated.

Kovel, Ralph and Terry. *American Country Furniture, 1780–1875.* New York: Crown, 1965. The Kovels use the term "country furniture" in the antique dealer's sense, i.e., in contrast to the high-style furniture made for the wealthy in the cities. Although the book contains a number of examples of relatively late, factory-made pieces, nonetheless it does contain a fair number of examples of traditional designs.

Lord, Priscilla S., and Daniel J. Foley. *The Folk Arts and Crafts of New England.* Philadelphia: Chilton Books, 1965. Although poorly written and superficial, this work does bring together photographs covering a number of traditional crafts and is a useful supplement to Eaton, above.

Mercer, Henry C. *Ancient Carpenters' Tools.* Doylestown, Pa.: The Bucks County Historical Society, 1929, 1960. The best American book in the field of folk crafts. Mercer, a self-trained scholar, used all the techniques of the comparative folklorist: distribution and historical studies, functional concepts, extensive fieldwork.

Needham, Walter, and Barrows Mussey. *A Book of Country Things.* Brattleboro, Vt.: Stephen Green Press, 1965. Of special interest to the folklorist in that Mussey tape-recorded Needham's reminiscences about his grandfather and what he taught him. The recordings appear to be reproduced with substantial authenticity. Good coverage of the crafts practiced on the farm in the nineteenth century.

van Wagenen, Jared. *The Golden Age of Homespun.* Ithaca, N. Y.: Cornell University Press, 1953. Covering upstate New York, this book is the best general American survey of the nineteenth century crafts of the countryside including professional craftsmen, crafts carried on in the home, and subsistence crafts.

Great Britain

Evans, E. Estyn. *Irish Folk Ways.* London: Routledge and Kegan Paul, 1957. Describes and illustrates many aspects of material culture and traditional crafts, in such chapters as "Furniture and Fittings," "Hearth and Home," and "Home-Made Things."

Grant, Isabel F. *Highland Folk Ways*. London: Routledge and Kegan Paul, 1961. Contains discussions of Highland weavers, spinners, tinkers, woodworkers, and other craftsmen, with many text figures.

Jenkins, J. Geraint. *The English Farm Wagon*. Lingfield, Surrey: Oakwood Press, 1961. A model work, sponsored by the Museum of English Rural Life. Applies the methods developed by Scandinavian scholars to English material.

———. *Traditional Country Craftsmen*. London: Routledge and Kegan Paul, 1965. The best survey in English on crafts that still flourish today.

12 FOLK ART
Henry Glassie

The artifact, the object of material culture such as the crucifix or plow, simultaneously gives pleasure and serves some practical social or economic end. If a pleasure-giving function predominates, the artifact is called art; if a practical function predominates, it is called craft. These simplifications are less important than the complicated truth that all artifacts have more than one function, whether a single function is clearly dominant or not. The interior of a house is designed primarily to be used, and its function may be classed primarily as economic; its exterior is designed primarily to be seen, and its function may be classed as primarily aesthetic. The artifact is art to the extent that it is an expression of an intention to give and take pleasure, and it is folk art to the extent that the intention was esoteric and traditional. The artistic nature of a folk artifact is generally subordinate to its utilitarian nature so that most folk art exists within the immediate context of folk craft. The problem of folk art (as opposed to folk craft) scholarship, then, lies less in identifying specific forms and technics than it does in identifying the characteristics of

the traditional aesthetic philosophy that governs the selection, production, treatment, and use of forms.

A HISTORY OF THE AWARENESS OF FOLK ART

Young William Morris saw the skies and streams running black.
Agriculture had given way to industry: the cities, packed with rural
immigrants, were becoming slums, shunned by middle-class subur-
banites. Each Sunday found fewer people in church; each day found
a bellicose government more committed to an anti-Russian stance.
They were times of prosperity and intolerance. William Morris hated
the times: he looked at the sky blanked with soot; he looked into
the milky faces of the workers, locked into a mechanical routine; he
saw the waste of labor and life, and looked for an alternative. In
1853, Morris, a child of romanticism who was reading Scott's Waverley
novels by the age of four, began his studies at Oxford where he
quickly became part of a brotherhood of artists who were comforted
in mutual conversation on neomonastic possibilities and socialism, on
the decline of art and being. In that year, John Ruskin published the
second volume of *The Stones of Venice* and its chapter "The Nature
of Gothic" provided Morris with the idea he needed to organize
conversation into concept and action. Medieval Gothic art, Ruskin
wrote, is seen as savage, but unlike the great styles that came before
and after, it was not based on slavery: imperfect, it was noble and
moral. The artist was laborer, the laborer artist, and the lesson holds
for the present:

If you will make a man of the working creature, you cannot make him a
tool. Let him but begin to imagine, to think, to try to do anything worth
doing; and the engine-turned precision is lost at once. Out come all his
roughness, all his dulness, all his incapability...; but out comes the whole
majesty of him also....It would be well if all of us were good handicrafts-
men in some kind, and the dishonour of manual labour done away with
altogether....There should be less pride felt in peculiarity of employment,
and more in excellence of achievement. And yet more, in each several profession, no master should be too proud to do its hardest work. The painter
should grind his own colours; the architect work in the mason's yard with
his men....[1]

The Middle Ages provided the alternative. Morris's friends, the
painters of the Pre-Raphaelite Brotherhood, leapt the worldly and
rationalistic High Renaissance to find stimulus in the spiritual intensity of Botticelli and Fra Angelico. Like his contemporaries who were
similarly infused with the new romantic spirit and spent their leisure

1. John Ruskin, *The Stones of Venice* (London: Smith, Elder, 1853) 2: 162, 169.

in the collection of ballads and Märchen, Morris became aware of the aesthetic energies of the Middle Ages found in works by the likes of Chaucer and the architect of Amiens cathedral—an awareness followed by the recognition of the local survival of humble medieval monuments and a hazy comprehension of the (somewhat degenerated) persistence of medieval sensibilities and talents among rural folksingers and craftsmen. In the same half decade that the Chaucerian scholar, Francis James Child, published *English and Scottish Popular Ballads* in the British Poets Series and that the analytical 1856 edition of the Grimms' *Kinder- und Hausmärchen* appeared, Morris and Company opened its doors. The craftsmen at The Company labored tediously by hand to produce works in the modern medieval taste: stained glass and oak furniture, embroidery, wallpaper, metalwork, tiles, carpets, jewelry, and tapestries. Morris called himself a designer, but his gentle upbringing did not keep him from the loom and dye vat; often mistaken for a laborer, Topsy Morris was the kind of artist Ruskin called for. His involvement with medieval art led him to study as well as practice; he was both a weaver and a museum consultant on antique textiles. In 1879, when the movement for folk museums was gaining momentum on the Continent,[2] William Morris founded the Society for the Protection of Ancient Buildings in England.

Whether composing poetry in the style of the ballad or marching in a Socialist demonstration, translating Icelandic sagas, complaining about urban sprawl, or designing the Kelmscott Chaucer, Morris provides us with an exquisite exemplar of the Victorian intellectual's rearview medievalism.[3] Product and producer of romantic radicalism, Morris was but one among many advocates of medieval revival (and he was no more influential than his friends John Ruskin and Dante Gabriel Rossetti), but more than any other he originated and stimulated the interest in "the lesser arts," in folk craft and art. Morris's scholarly inclinations limited the freedom of his creative practice, but his ambiguity of role allowed others, stimulated by the Arts and Crafts Movement that flowed from his genius, to move in either an artistic or a scholastic direction. On the Continent, the progressive artists rejected the Arts and Crafts historicism, but accepted its em-

2. Holger Rasmussen, ed., *Dansk Folkemuseum and Frilandsmuseet* (Copenhagen: Nationalmuseet, 1966), pp. 7–11.
3. For Morris, his friends and times, these readily available books are valuable: Paul Thompson, *The Work of William Morris* (New York: Viking, 1967); Asa Briggs, ed., *William Morris: Selected Writings and Designs* (Baltimore: Penguin, 1962); William Gaunt, *The Pre-Raphaelite Dream* (New York: Schocken, 1966); Robert Furneaux Jordan, *Victorian Architecture* (Baltimore: Penguin, 1966); John Gloag, *Victorian Taste* (London: Adam and Charles Black, 1962).

phasis on craft and naturalistic decoration; as a result Art Nouveau is the only movement in Western art since before the Renaissance noted as much for its furniture and jewelry as for its painting and sculpture. The serious interests of the personalities of the Arts and Crafts Movement were compatible with other antiquarian aspects of the romantic nationalism of the period. In different Western countries collectors rummaged through the countryside, and the museum became a repository for collections of old folk artifacts, a source for revivalistic designers, an escape for careworn workers and, on the Continent and especially in Scandinavia where the folk museum idea was born, a center for research on the history of artifacts. Before the end of the nineteenth century, nationalistic pride in old things as mirrors of a country's development had jelled and become the dominant motive for the collection, preservation, and reproduction of folk artifacts. In the late 1880s, at the time that the American Folklore Society was founded, the American authors of popular books on architectural design, though still inveighing against the old-fashioned "barnesque style of Architecture" and still recommending elaborately ornate English, French, and Swiss folkishly romantic designs, were beginning to accept the "Colonial"—American romantic—as an important modern style.[4]

The interest in the folk artifact developed apace with romantic nationalism, receiving official sanction in the 1930s—in Nazi Germany and Depression America. While Thomas Hart Benton[5] and Ben Shahn were celebrating folklife in paint and the WPA was funding ballad collectors, artifacts were being assembled for the Rural Arts Exhibition held at the Department of Agriculture in 1937. The interest of the governmental handicrafters was more in therapeutic and economically rehabilitory utilization than in scholarship, and, like the English Arts and Crafts Movement, it involved the invention, diffusion, and alteration—"improvement"—of crafts as well as their preservation; still, the exhibit was a major impetus for the spread of interest to contemporary craft. At the same time that the New Deal's "rural-handicraft movement" was endeavoring to democratize the concept of art, exhibiting new quilts and baskets as if they were Old Masters,[6] others were hunting for lower class art that paralleled that

4. For examples: *Palliser's New Cottage Homes and Details* (New York: Palliser, Palliser, 1887), p. 1, pls. 7, 39; *Shoppell's Modern Houses* 1: 1 (January 1886): especially 1–2, 30, 63, 64.

5. Michael Owen Jones treats Benton briefly in "Two directions for Folkloristics in the Study of American Art," *Southern Folklore Quarterly* 32 (September 1968): 249–59.

6. For the exhibit: Allen Eaton and Lucinda Crile, *Rural Handicrafts in the United States*, Miscellaneous Publication, 610 (Washington: U.S.D.A. and Russell Sage Foundation, 1946), pp. 8–21. Eaton wrote two major books on crafts, each

of the wealthy—in short, for paintings and sculpture. Serious American collectors had been producing books on the "decorative arts," such as furniture and silver, since the turn of the century, but it took the egalitarian thirties to produce the seminal book on American "folk art": Holger Cahill's *American Folk Art: The Art of the Common Man in America, 1750–1900.*[7]

There are now many museum exhibits and many big books devoted to "folk art." There is material to study, but no theories have been developed to enable that study. Neither the Congrès international des arts populaires, held at Prague in 1928, nor the symposium on folk art in *Antiques* magazine in 1950 came near a satisfactory definition of folk art. One of the most knowledgeable scholars on folk art, Robert Wildhaber, director of the Museum für Volkerkunde und Schweizerisches Museum für Volkskunde, could state recently that for the field of folk art (unlike many other areas of folk cultural research) "a definitive scientific study still remains to be written."[8] The concepts useful in determining what folk art is do exist, but they exist outside the thinking of the compilers of most folk art collections. They exist in writings on art by art critics and historians, aesthetic philosophers, and artists; they exist in writings on the means and manners of cultural expression by folklorists, anthropologists, and linguists.

It would be easy to dismiss the writings of "folk art" collectors with exactly the adjectives they apply to the materials they study: naïve, provincial, primitive, crude, unsophisticated, nonacademic.[9] Some of their notions must be discarded because "folk" is not one "style" of art, folk art is not confined to a certain historical period, folk art is not inevitably rural, and the subjective evaluation of an alien academic is of no worth in a scientific study. If, however, we assume a compassionate, cultural-relativist posture, we will discover in the vague writings on "folk art," and its conceptual companion "country furniture,"[10] a set of notions that are consistent with more rigorous thinking.

---

including information on both folk and revivalistic crafts: *Handicrafts of the Southern Highlands* (New York: Russell Sage Foundation, 1937) ; *Handicrafts of New England* (New York: Harper and Brothers, 1949) .

7. (New York: Museum of Modern Art and W. W. Norton, 1932.)

8. In H. J. Hansen, ed., *European Folk Art in Europe and the Americas* (New York and Toronto: McGraw-Hill, 1968) , p. 7.

9. These are the adjectives of most of the contributors to "What is American Folk Art? A Symposium," *Antiques* 57 (May 1950) : 355–62.

10. The results of "Country Furniture: A Symposium," *Antiques* 93 (March 1968) : 342–77, were similar to those of the earlier symposium on "folk art." Another statement produced at the same time is Eric de Jonge's "Country Furniture, So-Called," *The Delaware Antiques Show* (Wilmington: Wilmington Medical Center, 1968) , pp. 75–85.

Both of the words, folk and art, have been mistreated. The adjective "folk" when applied to an object provides specific information about the source of the ideas that were used to produce the object. Saying of an object that it is "art" provides information about the intentions of its producer. In order to expose the meaning behind the assertion that an object is "folk art" the words will be treated serially below.

ART THAT IS FOLK

The ideas that the artist puts into action to create an object can be classified by the relationships they bear to the cultural norm that receives overt and massive support from the agents for economic, religious, and political stability. With regard to this public culture, some of the ideas in the artist's mind may be considered conservative, some normative, some progressive—or, in the usual terms of the folklorist, folk, popular, and elite (or academic). If the idea was, when expressed, conservative, the resultant object—the song or story or sculpture—can be called folk. Saying that a thing is "folk," then, implies that the idea of which it was an expression was old within the culture of its producer and that it differed from comparable, contemporaneous ideas explicitly advocated as the popular culture of the dominant society. That means that the folk object is like the elite object but unlike the popular object in depending for its existence upon local or individual patronage (although the time depth of the networks linking localities can enable a folk idea to achieve numerical dominance). It means also and most significantly that the folk object, unlike the popular and elite object, is not part of rapidly changing fashions; the establishment of the folk nature of an idea is the demonstration of its persistence through time. The artist may or may not be aware of the fact that his idea is folk; his conservatism might be self-consciously archaic and nativistic, or it might be the only way he knows: the folk artist's usual answer to an inquiry about the logic of his *métier* is, "Well, how else would you do it?"

The division of culture into folk (conservative), popular (normative), and elite (progressive) is often treated as if it carried socioeconomical validity. Although considered to be "levels of society," these abstract distinctions are most useful when thought of as opposing forces having simultaneous existence in the mind of every individual, though one or another of the modes of thinking may predominate in certain individuals or in the groups they combine to form.

Against this background, we may examine the "folk art" collectors' adjective, "naïve." In getting at their meaning it is useful to recognize that their studies have been tempered by historical concepts of

connoisseurship and style. By style they mean a subjectively determined assemblage of artistic features that fits into a chronological
sequence, or, more or less, the elite and popular aesthetic of a distinct
period. The works displayed in a "folk art" gallery are called "naïve"
because (1) they do not fit into a "style"; (2) they represent a single "style" incompletely; (3) they represent a mixture of "styles";
(4) they represent an apparent imperfection of execution within a
"style."

These distinct connotations of "naïve" provide a series of possible
relationships between folk and nonfolk impulses. The first case is the
object produced out of ideas that are unrelated to those of the contemporary popular and elite dominant cultures. These ideas may
have originated in primitive, nonliterate cultures. Primitive art was
once easily separable from western folk or elite art; today most art is
produced within the socioeconomic frame of the West and phenomena like African airport sculpture and modern Navaho rugs are folk
art. Of the ideas within Western folk art, some are of such ancient
origin—an antiquity provable via archeology—that there is no way to
relate them except within the folk tradition, while others are ideas
of elite origin and popular dissemination that thrive within the folk
tradition, although they are outmoded and have lost their mass
support.

The action of the Western folk artist usually results in a new artifact that closely resembles an old one, since the artist who deviates
from known and accepted sources can jeopardize his status.[11] While
the elite artist may be willing to risk his standing to appear ahead of
his times, it is only a rare folk artist who strives for innovation; his
replication is an affirmation of a tradition. This does not mean that
the folk artist is an exacting copyist or that there is no margin for
variation within folk tradition. From his perceptions of a number
of similar artifacts, the folk artist abstracts a structural concept that
is a minimal description of the form of an object, containing a specific relationship of components without which the object would not
be the object—without which a bench would not be a bench. From
his perceptions he abstracts, as well, a small set of rules that define
the limits within which he can modify the concept according to his
taste and talent and the taste and pocketbook of his client. The long
benches in the kitchens and on the porches of Pennsylvania German
farmhouses, for example, are basically the same, except that there is
a traditional tolerance for the elaboration of the ornamentation of
the legs, the fronts of which vary from straight to complex combina-

11. Cf. H. G. Barnett, *Innovation: The Basis of Cultural Change* (New York
and Toronto: McGraw-Hill, 1953), pp. 318–21.

tions of C-scrolls (Fig. 12–1). The mental process of abstraction not
only enables variation within a tradition, it facilitates creativity. When
a new idea is presented to the artist he does not have to reject or
accept it completely. Through the process called *bricolage* by Claude
Lévi-Strauss,[12] the new idea is broken down and compared with old
ones and a composite idea is developed to suit the artist's psychobio-
logical nature and his social and physical environment. The novel
synthetic idea may be a compromise of fashionable and unfashionable
ideas; its result may be seen by the folklorist as partially folk and by
the art historian as an incomplete expression of a "style" or as a
mixture of "styles." In mid-eighteenth-century Lancashire, for example, a common piece of furniture was an oak settle with up-to-date
"Queen Anne" cabriole legs and padded seat and outmoded "Jaco-
bean" arms and wainscot back.[13] A horizontal line imagined through
the settle would separate it neatly into its seventeenth-century upper
half and eighteenth-century lower half. Since pieces of the kind were
made later than the date of origin of their newest elements, their
older elements were out of style and traditional—they were folk. While
the settle is a simple example, the mental dynamics of *bricolage* allowed for very complicated syntheses of old and new ideas.

Most of the "naïve" paintings hanging in "folk art" galleries are
there because the curator considers them to be "untrained" but "expressive" attempts at illusionistic representation. Generally the curator distinguishes only between academic and nonacademic art;[14] "folk
art" becomes then a category for art works that are substandard but
charming. These "folk paintings" are either good expressions of a
popular style that has limited appeal to the modern curator because
it lacks elite analogues, or poor expressions of a popular style that
are appealing because of an accidental similarity to modern art, or
they may even be folk art.

Huck Finn at the Grangerfords' provides the modern reader with
a flood-lit view into the home of a mid-nineteenth-century carrier ·of
the popular culture. Huck was impressed with the mass-produced
hardware and clock, but the art in the neoclassical-maudlin mode
gave him "the fan-tods." One picture was of "a woman in a slim
black dress, belted small under the arm-pits . . . and she was leaning

12. Claude Lévi-Strauss, *The Savage Mind* (Chicago: University of Chicago
Press, 1969), pp. 16–22.
13. Arthur Hayden, *Chats on Cottage and Farmhouse Furniture* (London:
Ernest Benn, 1950, reprint of 1912), pp. 107, 109–10, 131.
14. More sophisticated art historians carefully distinguish between folk art,
popular ("amateur") art, and fine art; see E. P. Richardson, *A Short History of
Painting in America* (New York: Thomas Y. Crowell, 1963), pp. 4–6; James
Thomas Flexner, *Nineteenth Century American Painting* (New York: G. P. Put-
nam's Sons, 1970), chap. 6.

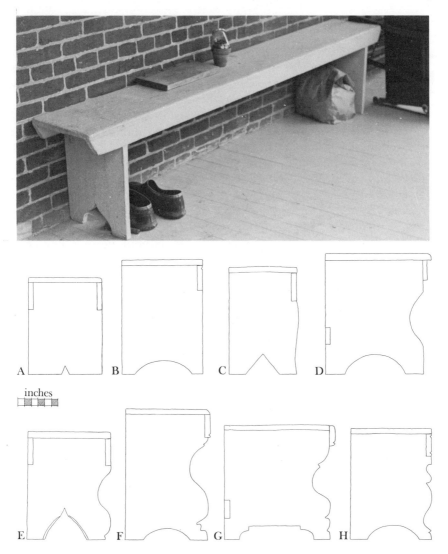

12–1. Pennsylvania German bench. The photograph shows the bench on the side porch of a farmhouse, east of Palm in Lehigh County, Pennsylvania. A through H are end views of benches of this type: A) near Emmitsburg, Frederick County, Maryland; B) north of Bermudian, York County, Pennsylvania; C) at West End, Bedford County, Pennsylvania; D) near Lebanon, Lebanon County, Pennsylvania; E) near Littleton, Adams County, Pennsylvania; F) north of Lancaster, Lancaster County, Pennsylvania; G) north of Bermudian, York County, Pennsylvania; H) east of Palm in Lehigh County, Pennsylvania. All of these benches were photographed and measured in the spring of 1967. All of the photographs and drawings accompanying this chapter are by the author; unidentified artifacts are in his collection.

pensive on a tombstone on her right elbow, under a weeping willow, and her other hand hanging down her side holding a white handkerchief and a reticule. . . ."[15] Such pictures were painted and stitched by girls under the watchful scowl of a teacher. Schoolgirl exercises of the sort are found in most "folk art" collections,[16] although they are clearly examples of popular rather than folk art.

The gallery's walls are lined with portrait and genre scene, landscape and still life. Utilizing the same kind of thinking that generated the communal theory of ballad origins, the "folk art" curator occasionally supposes that the untutored geniuses of his imagination independently invented the varieties of realistic painting. It took centuries of labor by the best of Western minds to isolate landscape and still life as distinct pictorial types, and, as the critic Clement Greenberg has pointed out, "it is highly unlikely that a 'naïve' artist would have ventured upon pure landscape or still life without being encouraged by precedents."[17] The precedent for the naïve painter was the same as that for the sophisticated painter; they had the same sources, produced the same popular art. The difference was that naïve painters were people who, in Joyce Cary's term, had difficulty closing the mind-body gap[18]—they were children or adults of limited talent. Most of the naïve paintings produced by middle-class daubers in the late eighteenth and early nineteenth century in Latin America[19] as well as in Europe and the United States were the same kind of Sunday painting that is popular among today's hobbyists. They copied land-

15. Mark Twain, *Adventures of Huckleberry Finn* (New York: Charles L. Webster, 1885), chap. 17.

16. Holger Cahill, *American Folk Art*, pp. 11, 18, pls. 79–108; Agnes Halsey Jones and Louis C. Jones, *New-Found Folk Art of the Young Republic* (Cooperstown: New York State Historical Association, 1960), pp. 7–8, 16, fig. 17; Peter C. Welsh, *American Folk Art: The Art and Spirit of a People* (Washington: Smithsonian Institution, 1965), figs. 1, 9, 21; Mary Black and Jean Lipman, *American Folk Painting* (New York: Clarkson N. Potter, 1966), pp. 99–100, 119, 121–23. Nina Fletcher Little intelligently avoids the adjective "folk" in *Country Art in New England: 1790–1840* (Sturbridge: Old Sturbridge Village, 1965), pp. 22, 34–35, though she allows it in *American Folk Art from the Abby Aldrich Rockefeller Folk Art Collection* (Williamsburg: Colonial Williamsburg, 1966), pp. 10, 16–17. Works of art such as these, of course, deserve preservation and study; calling them "folk," which relates them automatically to cultural expressions like fraktur, however, confuses the issue beyond the possibility of meaningful communication.

17. Clement Greenberg, *Art and Culture: Critical Essays* (Boston: Beacon Press, 1969), p. 130. This essay, "Primitive Painting," pp. 129–32, as well as his opening piece, "Avant-Garde and Kitsch," pp. 3–21, show that, while his terminology is unfamiliar to the social scientist, he distinguishes between three kinds of art—folk, kitsch, avant-garde—in a way similar to the folklorist.

18. Joyce Cary, *Art and Reality: Ways of the Creative Process* (Garden City: Doubleday, 1958), pp. 41–43.

19. Leopoldo Castedo, *A History of Latin American Art and Architecture*, Phyllis Freeman, trans. and ed. (New York and Washington: Frederick A. Praeger, 1969), chap. 16.

scapes from books like *Views in America, Great Britain, Switzerland, Turkey, Italy, The Holy Land, Etc.*,[20] and simply did not copy them very well. Their portraits and especially their genre representations of workaday life are valuable records, often, of folk behavior but no more valuable than the popular genre paintings of more talented people, like William Sidney Mount in America or William Powell Frith in England, from whom the genre concept came to the naïve painter. Whether naïve or sophisticated in execution, a mid-nineteenth-century genre painting or a mid-eighteenth-century Chippendale highboy is part of the mainstream aesthetic and can be considered folk only if we class clumsy renditions of the latest hit tunes as folksongs—and we do not.

In his third discourse, Sir Joshua Reynolds marshaled ancient authority to define the artist as the person who corrects the imperfections in nature.[21] Figurative folk art is not crude popular art; it is the improvement of reality. It is the result of drawing the real world or the illusionistic popular artwork through a traditional filter that improves the figure, that is, renders it more in keeping with the folk aesthetic philosophy held by the artist and his audience. The most significant attribute of the filter is that it yields works that are impressionistically low in specific information and that can be, therefore (as an individual folktale, ballad, or artwork would be), repeatedly experienced by the same audience. The walls of houses in southern Sweden were decorated in the eighteenth and nineteenth century with paintings[22] compatible with the aesthetic that scholars are accustomed to find in the ballad (Fig. 12–2). The painted people, like the protagonists in a ballad, are minimally identified as individuals (most have the same face) and are unemotional (the faces have the same expression). The characters are ambiguously familiar: their dress is anachronistically modern and local, but they are engaged in foreign activities of biblical or historical origin; farmers do not sing about the agricultural round, and it is a city person, not a peasant from Småland or Halland, who wants a landscape or a painting of farming. The ballad does not limit the imagination by supplying psychological motivations or descriptive details, and the singer does not histri-

20. (New York: J. Milton Emerson, 1852)—a book consisting entirely of advertisements and scenic engravings, mostly of pictures by W. H. Bartlett, whose illustrations were widely reproduced as homemade paintings.

21. Sir Joshua Reynolds, *Discourses on Art* (London: Collier-Macmillan, 1969, based on 1797 ed.), pp. 42–52.

22. A good early study of the paintings is Sigurd Erixon, "Schwedische Bauern-Malereien," in *Vom Wesen der Volkskunst, Jahrbuch für historische Volkskunde* 2 (Berlin: Herbert Stubenrauch, 1926): 110–25. An easily accessible source is: Iona Plath, *The Decorative Arts of Sweden* (New York: Dover, 1966, reprint of 1948), chap. 7.

onically highlight the ballad's drama; similarly, the Swedish folk painter does not dictate the audience's perceptions and reactions with illusionary space. The artist's unmodeled figures exist flatly without a hint at the third dimension; they are quietly focused with only the amount of action and setting absolutely required for identification; they do not tell a story so much as refer to a known story. The ballad and the paintings exhibit the traditional horror of the vacuum; the ballad when heard presents no aural lacunae, and in the Swedish paintings the blank spaces are similarly stopped with spots and dots and flowers. The ballad is an oral expression, the wall painting a material expression of the same folk aesthetic.

The selection and treatment of the content in the Swedish wall paintings was conditioned by the filter that had been developed to make the naturalistic art of the post-Renaissance period suit folk taste. The formalistic aspects of the filter caused a drive to frontality and symmetry. These characteristics can be found in the Swedish paintings, but the filter's best test came during Spanish colonialism. In the areas into which the Spanish religious adventurers introduced ecstatic baroque art—the Philippines, the Caribbean, Central and Latin America, and the southwestern United States—the folk carvers stilled the supercharged gesticulations of the baroque into symmetry. The image faces forward, the nose of its face perpendicular to its shoulders. It was designed to be viewed from the front— a two-dimensional denial of its three-dimensional actuality. Passionate realism had given way to geometric design. But the design was not mere decoration. The religious power of baroque sculpture was clearly signified by the actions of the figures, but, as with African sculpture, the Spanish colonial *bulto* was not manifestly potent. In Africa, the power may be conserved tensely inside the figure,[23] but in Western religious folk art power is brought to the placid figure by the believer. The power of the polychromed wooden saint is apparent only when the carving stands as an icon within its sacred context, when a human being is using it as a mediator with God. Superficial realism had given way to transcendent symbolism (Fig. 12–3).

The symbolizing nature of the folk filter led to the establishment and repetition of conventional designs. Just as people were drawn from the front, tulips were drawn from the side, sunflowers from the top, and four-legged beasts from the side, spread into a flying gallop. A characteristic motif in Europe and European America was the angel reduced to its cherubic essence: a winged head. The expressionless

---

23. See Robert Plant Armstrong's stimulating essay, *Forms and Processes of African Sculpture* (Austin: African and Afro-American Research Institute of the University of Texas, 1970), pp. 17–21.

12–2. Swedish folk painting. This painted wall hanging is from Småland and dates to about 1770. Clockwise from the upper left panel it depicts the three kings, the adoration, the nativity, the crucifixion, and the annunciation. It is taken from plate 16 of *Vom Wesen der Volkskunst*.

visage faces forward; on each side is a wing of equal size. The motif is a characteristic piece of Western folk design: a bilaterally symmetrical whole, composed of three distinct units, the outside two being mirror images of each other, the central one—the focus of attention—being different but internally symmetrical (Fig. 12–4).

Figurative paintings and sculpture that postdate the Renaissance and seem to be naïve may be stabs at realism that failed, or they may be the products of an aesthetic flourishing outside the mimetic progression. Given their cultural milieux and the intentions of their artists, they may be bad or they may be good, and it is not always possible to tell which is which from the work alone. But representational folk art is not a failure at illusionary art; it is, like European fine art before Giotto and after Cézanne, like most primitive art,[24] abstract. The beginning of Renaissance art was marked by a move from convention to realism. Folk art is characterized constantly by moves from realism to convention.

FOLK CULTURE THAT IS ART

The person with an idea to express can choose from among communicating media with different potentials for permanence and semantic clarity. Bodily action leaves a gesture, a word, or an artifact in the air. These media affect different sets of senses. Any medium, affecting any sense, can be the conveyer of an aesthetic, and art, therefore, can be either gestural or verbal or material, although art is generally considered to be only those parts of an event that the anthropologist has termed material culture: the artist produces a material object that is perceived visually. Other kinds of sensory perception, though often ignored, are important in material folk culture, especially taste and smell, in the case of the folk art that is food, and touch. The academic critic may restrict his appreciation to observation, but the folk critic wishes to "feel of it," to gauge the artifact's surface and balance with his hands. It is the peculiar property of material culture that its expressions can be touched and that exactly the same object—not merely a representation of it as in a recording of a tale—can be repeatedly reexperienced.

The artifact produced out of the maker's aesthetic, out of, essentially, his desire to please himself and his audience, is art. With centuries of art criticism behind us, it is often surprising that the folk artist has no articulation for his aesthetic other than production. But as recently as the sixteenth century, the aesthetic vocabulary was quite limited. By reading the words of Giorgio Vasari, the painter and

24. Raymond Firth, *Elements of Social Organization* (Boston: Beacon Press, 1963), pp. 163, 173–75.

12–3. Puerto Rican *santo*. This sculpture, monumental in spite of its 5¾–
inch height, represents the Virgin. It dates to about the middle of the nineteenth century and has been attributed to a carver named Pedro Ramas.

friend of Michelangelo who spent his leisure writing the biographies of artists, and examining the works he admired, his aesthetic can be understood, but nowhere in his *Vite,* first published in 1550, can one find that aesthetic rigorously and lucidly outlined. Similarly, the folk aesthetic can rarely be elicited directly; analysis of artifacts, behavioral observation, and ethnoscientific questioning are the means for its determination. Modern Papago Indian potters were shown alien kinds of pottery; quietly they listened to suggestions for innovation; then, silently they continued to make pottery of the old kind, thus materially stating their taste.[25] Bernie Wise, a lower Potomac waterman and old-time market hunter, could readily separate good duck decoys from bad, good workboats from bad, but only rarely did he bother with verbalized rationalizations for his selections.[26] Cruising through the harbor of River Springs, Bernie easily classified the workboats docked there. Most were old and accepted types of craft used in tonging for oysters and trot-lining for crabs. There were also two new types, both combinations of a bow from one tradition and a stern from another. One of these, the "flare-bow"—its bow copied from a police boat that had come from up the Chesapeake Bay—had proved popular and its maker, Perry Gibson, was kept busy supplying the demand for boats of the kind. The other boat with its "dory bow" and "box stern" looked "pretty funny" to Bernie; he grinned, nearly chuckling, and said that he did not guess there would ever be another like it. Bernie Wise and his friends have an aesthetic. The lack of an aesthetic vocabulary does not prevent aesthetic operation.

The modern designer,[27] anticipated by John Ruskin,[28] recognizes the simultaneity of the artifact's aesthetic and practical functioning. Like the industrial engineer, the folk artist often denies his aesthetic, defending his choices and actions solely on the basis of utility. Though he lavished great care on the form and finish of the baskets he made, John O. Livingston, a proud central Pennsylvania craftsman, discussed their virtues only in terms of their strength and use-

25. Bernard L. Fontana, William J. Robinson, Charles W. Cormack, and Ernest E. Leavitt, Jr., *Papago Indian Pottery* (Seattle: University of Washington Press, 1962), pp. 81–83.

26. Bernie Wise lives in the vicinity of River Springs, Saint Mary's County, Maryland. I have enjoyed talking with him many times; the interviews discussed here took place in May of 1969. An outstanding local historical book, full of folklife data (including good information on boat types) for this area, is Edwin W. Beitzell's *Life on the Potomac River* (Abel, Md.: Edwin W. Beitzell, 1968).

27. David Pye, *The Nature of Design* (New York: Reinhold, 1967), p. 21; Richard S. Latham, "The Artifact as Cultural Cipher," in Laurence B. Holland, ed., *Who Designs America?* (Garden City: Doubleday, 1966), pp. 261–62; James Marston Fitch, "The Future of Architecture," *The Journal of Aesthetic Education* 4:1 (January 1970): 102–3.

28. John Ruskin, *Lectures On Art* (New York: John Wiley, 1888), lecture 4.

A

A) From the hood of a mid-eighteenth-century Friesland clock or *Stoelklok*; this type of Dutch peasant clock can be found in W. Lüpkes, *Ostfiresische Volkskunde* (Emden: W. Schwalbe, 1925), p. 143; E. J. Tyler, "Clockmaking in Holland," *Bulletin of the National Association of Watch and Clock Collectors* 4:6 (December 1950): 241–47.

B

B) From the front panel of a chest from Breton, dating to the first half of the seventeenth century, after J. Stany-Gauthier, *Meubles et Ensembles Bretons* (Paris: Charles Massin, n.d.), pl. 16.

C

C) From the gravestone of Rebeckah James, who died in 1730, located in Newport, Rhode Island (July 1967).

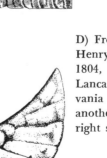

D

D) From the gravestone of Henry Naugel, who died in 1804, located in Brickerville, Lancaster County, Pennsylvania (December 1968). For another example see the lower right section of 12–2.

fulness.[29] But man does not make an artifact without applying or communicating his aesthetic; there is no artifact totally lacking in art. In working to establish valid distinctions among artifacts, the art historian George Kubler identified the useless object—the thing that is not a tool—as the work of art.[30] Useless objects—objects of art—do, however, fit into large structures as components in objects combining aesthetic and practical functions: a painting, itself "useless," is hung on the walls of a house, a useful tool in environmental modification, or in a museum, a useful educational tool.

In folk tradition there are few material objects that can be legitimately separated from their contexts as objects of art, and the only common one is the garden, the product of the aesthetic application of the farmer's tools, techniques, and expertise. The medieval philosopher, for whom art was not a reality independent of other realities, viewed the garden as the supreme worldly delight; for Dante it was the pinnacle of Purgatory. Francis Bacon wrote, "God Almighty first planted a garden. And indeed it is the purest of human pleasures."[31] The dooryard's traditional plots of flowers, whose existence is owed alone to the desire to participate in the creation of beauty and live in its presence, are folk art. But they exist not in a vacuum, but as the decorative elements in traditional landscaping plans—plans that include the location of the woodshed and dungheap as well as the flower garden.

The garden decorates the land as the painting decorates the wall. The art historian has often made the error of equating art and decorative ornament,[32] and most writers on folk art consider art to be the independently movable ornament, such as a framed painting, or the conceptually separable surface ornament of a tool, such as a painting on the sides of a cart, and they have generally failed to recognize art unless there is an obviously applied decoration. However, some, like Herbert Cescinsky, an unacknowledged disciple of Morris and one of the earliest serious students of furniture, have been aware that a utilitarian artifact, "destitute of ornament," can still be artistic in "shape, proportion or otherwise."[33]

29. John O. Livingston, maker of white oak baskets, was seventy-six when I visited him several times in April and May of 1967 at his home near Mount Pleasant, northeast of Dillsburg, York County, Pennsylvania.

30. George Kubler, *The Shape of Time: Remarks on the History of Things* (New Haven: Yale University Press, 1967), pp. 14–16.

31. Francis Bacon, "Of Gardens," *Essays* (London: J. M. Dent, 1947, based on the 1625 ed.), p. 137.

32. Cf. Herbert Read, *Art and Industry* (Bloomington: Indiana University Press, 1964), pp. 22–23.

33. Herbert Cescinsky, *English Furniture from Gothic to Sheraton* (Garden City, New York, 1937; 1st ed., 1929), p. 1. His dedication and preface are vintage Ruskin and Morris: "There is no greater pleasure, to my mind, than in the

On a utilitarian object, the most obvious art is the applied ornament. Folk ornamentation may be classified into human and animal forms, vegetable forms, geometric (nonnaturalistic) forms, and surface treatment. These kinds of ornament are listed in the order in which they are most obviously distinct from utilitarian intent. This is the reverse order of their commonness as folk decoration, and it is the chronological order in which Western artists isolated them for representation and appreciation. The landscape developed as an independent pictorial type long after the portrayal of the human being, and only very recently have artists created works from which all figures have been eliminated, leaving only a solid color or the texture of the surface. In the mid-sixties in New York, Ad Rinehart explored the minimal limits of art with his rollered black canvases.[34] Many folk cultures have no tradition of human representation, fewer lack naturalistic designs of any sort (consider the Oriental rug), fewer still have no kind of nonnaturalistic geometric decorative design, and there are no folk cultures that lack traditional proclivities for surface treatment, for certain colors or textures. The stern Old Order Amish who express a rejection of decoration are attentive to surfaces. The women wear dresses without "patterns" but they may be bright blue or purple. The expensive suits of the men have been reduced to the flat black of an Ad Rinehart painting.[35]

The degree of ornamentation varies from culture to culture. In some folk cultures, such as the Irish, the aesthetic drive is channeled more through oral than material media and there is little ornamental folk art. In other folk cultures, especially those that thrived in the glow of baroque high art in Holland, Scandinavia, France, and Germany, the amount of ornamental elaboration is great. Most of the folk cultures of North America are closer to the Irish than the Central European pattern.

In most of Western folk decoration there are two major laws operative: the dominance of form, and the desire for repetition. In some fine art, such as Gothic architecture, impressionist painting, or progressive

---

appreciation of fine things, necessarily made in an age when time was of little account, and when the craftsman gloried in his work. Modern conditions have killed all this; the refuge is only in the past."

34. Ad Rinehart, "Writings," in Gregory Battcock, ed., *The New Art* (New York: E. P. Dutton, 1966), pp. 199–209.

35. For Amish dress: Elmer Lewis Smith, *The Amish People* (New York: Exposition, 1958), pp. 164–71; Calvin George Bachman, *The Old Order Amish of Lancaster County* (Lancaster: Pennsylvania German Society, 1961), pp. 89–95; John A. Hostetler, *Amish Society* (Baltimore: Johns Hopkins University Press, 1963), pp. 134–38, 236–41, 311. The Amish plainness is well set in historic and cultural context by Don Yoder in his "Sectarian Costume Research in the United States" in Austin and Alta Fife and Henry Glassie, eds., *Forms Upon the Frontier* (Logan: Utah State University Press, 1969), pp. 41–75.

jazz, basic forms are confused under decoration, but no matter how many curls or swirls the folksinger employs, the skeleton of the melody remains apparent, and the basic form of folk artifacts is never obscured by ornamentation. Rather, ornament serves frequently to reinforce the visual effect of form; its elements may be outlined or their shapes echoed in lines drawn on them. The interior decoration of the usual room in an American folk house, for instance, consists of the color of the walls, the shapes of which, determined by openings, are outlined in woodwork, the edges being emphasized with a beaded moulding. The ornamental turning on the usual folk chair is restricted to its peripheries: the tops and bottoms of its posts. Over-all patterns are generally bound to formal areas of the object: each drawer of a bureau, each panel of a chest, is likely to have a self-contained ornament.

Folk ornamentation is repetitive, and repetitive in the ways Paul Klee described as simplest in his *Pedagogical Sketchbook*.[36] Western folk ornamentation almost never reaches the sophistication of the nonsymmetrical balance of elite art, or the rhythmic complexity of much of primitive art.[37] Often it consists of the continual repetition of the same motif, d: dddd. Most folk thinking involves the possibilities of binary sets. The ornamentation might consist of pairs of the same motif, dd: dd dd dd. The motif might be mirrored to form a symmetrical whole: db: db db db or dddbbb. A second motif might be introduced to form a pair, de: de de. But the thinking only rarely becomes so complex as to include three different motifs: d e r. Triplets usually involve the repetition of the same motif—d: ddd ddd— or the insertion of a different motif in the center—ded or dbd—but most usually the tripartite motif consists of the symmetrical pair—db —separated by a second element that is bilaterally symmetrical, so that the resulting unit still exhibits symmetrical halves: dAb: dAb dAb or dddAbbb. Through the utilization of different patterns in a single artifact, a complex, over-all design can be accomplished, but the thinking in the design of folk ornamentation (or in the performance of folksong or tale) does not often go beyond repetition, with bilateral symmetry being a special case of repetition. And it does not often go beyond variation in terms of the number two, with three being a special case of two when two of the three elements form a pair. Within folk cultures naturalistic and asymmetrical forms, such as the human body, were accepted, but they were geometrically re-

36. Paul Klee, *Pedagogical Sketchbook*, Sibyl Moholy-Nagy, trans. (New York and Washington: Frederick A. Praeger, 1965; first pub., 1925), especially pp. 22–23.
37. In *Primitive Art* (New York: Dover, 1955, reprint of 1927), chap. 2, especially pp. 40–54, Franz Boas describes these patterns.

worked so they could be used within the decorative tradition of binary repetitiveness.

The artist's idea, his plan for production, includes an invariable structure. The components that the structure serves to organize are nonessential—removable—or they are essential—those that, if removed, would cause the structure's destruction. A person's choice and handling of the components in a structure is his style and his product is art at least insofar as his feeling for beauty determines his style. Given the same structure and the same components, an artist can create a symmetrical or an asymmetrical artifact; the folk artist typically chooses the former, and his choice is the mobilization of his aesthetic. His artifact can be art, in part, even without decoration, although the art in simple forms is often difficult to see. If one were to look at traditional American jugs, the artistic nature of the decorated jug would prove obvious: a jug might have applied modeling, incising, painting, or a special glaze. If such ornamentation were the jug's only art, then the basic jug forms, given the identity of clays, techniques, volume, and use, would be the same, but they are not. There are distinct, contemporaneous preferences for very different basic forms that can be explained only on the basis of a folk aesthetic (Fig. 12–5).

In arranging an artifact's essential components (the elements of its basic shape), the folk artist works with the same laws that he employs in working with the nonessential components (ornamentation). In especially complex forms, such as the town, the symmetry may be confined to individual elements rather than to the entire form, but the ideal in even complicated Western folk designs was to form a symmetrical whole through the repetition of individually symmetrical units.

Any folk artifact could be chosen to illustrate the operation of the mechanics of the Western folk aesthetic. The façades of most Anglo-American folk house and barn types (Fig. 12–6) are examples of the bilaterally symmetrical tripartite design—dAb—that is found in innumerable decorative motifs—the angelic head with wings, for example (Fig. 12–4). The house front has three elements, the central one of which differs (it has a door) from the identical side elements that have one or two windows aligned per floor. In selective and adaptive response to the nineteenth-century introduction of the Gothic and Italianate architectural styles—confusingly asymmetrical in grander examples, though available, too, in easier to swallow, more symmetrical versions[38]—a folk Victorian decorative repertoire was de-

38. See John Maas's interesting *The Gingerbread Age* (New York: Bramhall House, 1957), especially chaps. 3–6.

veloped: the Gothic tower was reduced to a gable and added at the top of the façade's central element. Italianate brackets were lined repetitiously under the eaves, marking a natural joint in the form. Carpenter Gothic gingerbread—the rococo scroll-sawed answer to the gentry's gargoyles—was complexly curvaceous, but it was composed of symmetrical elements, symmetrically applied to places, the corners and tops and bottoms of porches mostly, where they did not disguise the house's basic form (Fig. 12–6F) —its floorplan and façade, both possible to represent formulaically as dAb.[39]

Most folk artifacts are basically utilitarian in nature. They are also artistic, but usually artistic only to a degree that does not hinder their practical effect. The Kentucky rifle was often carved and inlaid;[40] to its maker, its user, and its modern collector it was beautiful, but it was mainly a tool for the acquisition of protein: it could be beautiful, but it had to kill. If writers on the subject have overemphasized the artistic nature of utilitarian objects, they have also overemphasized the utilitarian nature of aesthetic objects. The folk artist is regularly denied his aesthetic on the assumption that his products served some specific, often magical, purpose. If the ornament of artifacts is isolated, some of it can be seen as directly and some of it as indirectly operational. Johnnie Brendel, whose granddad was a painter of "hex signs" on Pennsylvania barns, laughs at those who have accepted the piece of urban apocrypha, perpetrated by pop writers, that the "hex signs"—John and his Pennsylvania German neighbors call them "barn stars" or "barn flowers"—are apotropaic.[41] He can gloss the colors in the dominant local design, the "Cocalico star": the green is the early fields, the yellow the ripe grain, and the white signifies

39. All of the central hall house types—Georgian, Georgian I, and dogtrot houses —and the New England central chimney houses and their derivatives, and the English, Dutch, northern basement, Pennsylvania, double-crib, single-crib, and transverse-crib barns; that is, all of the common barn types and most of the common house types of the eastern United States can be represented in plan and façade by dAb. In house types there are several exceptions, though many of these are fragmentary representations—dA—or examples of the simplified db pattern, in which there is no element to mark the separation of mirrored halves (as in the Pennsylvania farmhouse, the double-pen houses and Creole houses of the south). These types are pictured and described in Henry Glassie, *Pattern in the Material Folk Culture of the Eastern United States* (Philadelphia: University of Pennsylvania Press, 1969).

40. For the art of the Kentucky rifle see: John G. W. Dillin, *The Kentucky Rifle* (York: George Shumway, Trimmer, 1959; 1st ed., 1924); Henry J. Kauffman, *The Pennsylvania-Kentucky Rifle* (Harrisburg: Stackpole, 1960); Joe Kindig, Jr., *Thoughts on the Kentucky Rifle in its Golden Age* (York: Trimmer, 1960).

41. John B. Brendel is the recipient of generations of Pennsylvania Dutch wisdom. A middle-aged highway worker, he lives in Reinholds, Lancaster County, Pennsylvania, where I visited him regularly between 1967 and 1970. John talked often and perceptively about folk belief and barn stars; he told me about the pentangle or "hexafoos" on the evening of 4 May 1967.

12–5. Profiles of American jugs:
A is from northern New Jersey.

B and C are from south central Pennsylvania.

D is from Massachusetts.

E, F, and G are from southeastern Pennsylvania. D through G are from the private collection of E. Francis La Fond of Mechanicsburg, Pennsylvania.

the purity of the Virgin. But while the Cocalico star (like all conventions) might be considered vaguely good luck, it is painted high on the barn to beautify it. This does not mean that the barn, thus aesthetically embellished, was left vulnerable to witches and lightning, for Bible verses were secreted within, and a tiny, five-pointed star—exactly the pentangle that Sir Gawain wore on his shield when he sallied off to keep his appointment with the Green Knight[42]—was scratched in a continuous line on beams, on trough and manger, on plow or harrow. The pentangle is an operational design, considered to have direct influence in the world of confusing cause and effect. Biblical scenes on Swedish walls and Spanish-American *santos*,[43] like most representational folk art, are part of a sacred system. They are examples of informational art designed partially to affect behavior and facilitate control over events; they are indirectly operational. The art of the folk artifact when isolated—the shape of a jug, the shallow carving on a chest—is mostly abstract, and it exists as a result of a response to a culturally nurtured impulse that is, while weaker, as real and as basic to man as hunger.[44] Most folk art, though subdued by utilitarian ends and restricted narrowly by tradition, exists to allow man to explore his innovative nature. It exists to delight.

CONCLUSIONS

William Morris's quarrels with the art of his era came out of his recognition of the rationalistic fragmentation of the aesthetic experience: art had lost its place in life. In the setting of Morris's observation, two major conclusions about folk art can be offered, one on the relationship of art to other aspects of culture, the other on the relationship of art to the individual's psychology.

In the fifteenth century, Brunelleschi raised the dome of Santa Maria del Fiore into the Florentine sky and declared the separation of architect and builder. By the next century, artists like Raphael and Brueghel had separated painting from its dependence on religious function. Since the Renaissance, a spiral of self-consciousness, energized by the interaction of critic and practitioner, has left the artist and his work utterly isolated; the modern artist can state that "the new art outstrips life and shuts the door on 'practical utility'."[45] But

42. The digression on the pentangle takes place early in the tale; in Gordon Hall Gerould's translation in *Beowulf and Sir Gawain and the Green Knight* (New York: Ronald Press, 1935), it comes at pp. 148–50.

43. See José E. Espinosa, *Saints in the Valleys* (Albuquerque: University of New Mexico Press, 1967).

44. See B. F. Skinner, "Creating the Creative Artist," in Edward F. Fry, ed., *On the Future of Art* (New York: Viking, 1970), pp. 61–75.

45. Kasimir Malevich, "Suprematism," in Robert L. Herbert, ed., *Modern Artists on Art* (Englewood Cliffs, N. J.: Prentice-Hall, 1964), p. 97.

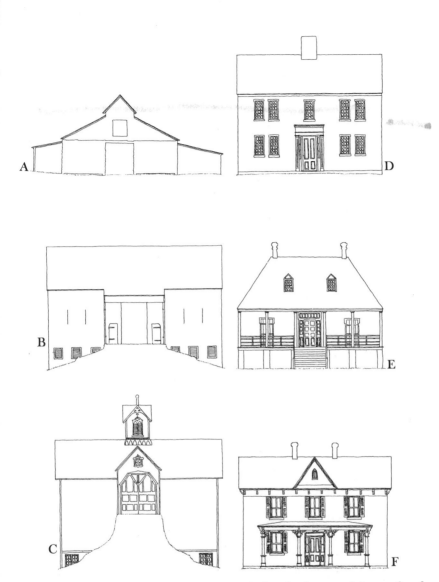

12–6. Bilaterally symmetrical, tripartite design in barn and house façades: A) saddle-notched log transverse-crib barn, located between Bismarck and Point Cedar, Hot Springs County, Arkansas (March 1964); B) stone Pennsylvania bank barn, south of Cavetown, Washington County, Maryland (July 1963); C) frame, three-level, northern basement barn with Victorian trim, near Meridale, Delaware County, New York (July 1962); D) frame, central chimney, saltbox plan house with a symmetrical gable, in Hampden, Hampden County, Massachusetts (October 1964); E) frame, Georgian plan, raised house, west of Lutcher, Saint James Parish, Louisiana (September 1967); F) frame, central hall I house with Victorian trim, in Lebanon Church, Shenandoah County, Virginia (March 1969).

the artifacts of folk art exist as complementary syntheses of the practical and aesthetic. Even things for which no practical use is envisioned are often designed as if they were utilitarian objects; the sgraffito plates of England, Germany, and Pennsylvania provide an example.[46] The folk artist is sensitive to his audience's needs and pleasures. The artist and his client collaborate, mutually influencing each other's decisions, sharing an unspoken aesthetic, discussing artifacts from the angle of practicality. In folk culture, art and labor are blended in the way William Morris wished them to be.

As part of his romantic legacy, the folklorist often imputes to the singer or tale teller the kind of expressive and variable, free flowing and organic aesthetic that William Morris ascribed to the medieval craftsman. But Western folk art, whether oral or material, is characterized by repetition, by forms that are composed of repeated motifs, by forms that exhibit over-all symmetry, by forms that are memorized and repeated. Repetition proves the absence of mistake and presence of control—control over perception and expression, control over concept, technique, and material. As Herbert Read has pointed out, symmetry as a proof of mastery has characterized Western artistic consciousness since Neolithic times.[47]

If folk art seems dead, it need only be realized that the engineer who denies art has internalized the repetitive-symmetrical aesthetic and when he creates a "purely functional" object he usually activates not the organic functionalist philosophy but the same traditional aesthetic as did his great-grandfather, the house carpenter or wheelwright. An automobile need not be bilaterally symmetrical, like a wagon, or a horse, when viewed from the front; an office building's façade need not be composed of repetitive units of equal size. But if they were not, the designer and his audience would think they looked odd or were the result of a mistake (a lack of control). The artifact of the modern engineer or the puttering do-it-yourselfer might not be folk from the standpoint of its dominant practical intent or the discrete elements of its form or its technological processing, but from the standpoint of the aesthetics of its design it probably is. So, if folk art seems dead, search your room for artifacts that do not seem to be artistic but that, nonetheless, exhibit the repetitive and symmetrical aesthetic (there are probably none that do not). Their

46. For sgraffito see L. M. Solon, *The Art of the Old English Potter* (New York: D. Appleton, 1886), pp. 82–83; Edwin Atlee Barber, *Tulip Ware of the Pennsylvania-German Potters* (Philadelphia: Philadelphia Museum and School of Industrial Art, 1903; reprinted by Dover, 1970); John Spargo, *Early American Pottery and China* (Garden City: Garden City, 1926), chap. 6; Erich Meyer-Heisig, *Deutsche Bauerntöpferei* (Munich: Prestel, 1955).

47. Herbert Read, *Icon and Idea* (New York: Schocken, 1967), chap. 2.

designer will defend their symmetry on solely practical grounds, but the appearance they presented to him and his client, whose unverbalized aesthetic is folk, was a major cause for their existing in the shape they do.

If folk art seems insignificant, ponder the reinforcing effect on the Western child raised in an immediate environment where most things —the furniture, the windows and doors, the houses along the street— are symmetrical. He will grow into a man who will place great value on repetition, control, equilibrium. He will, as farmer or city planner, try to draw nature into symmetry. He will, as scientist, try to draw empirical data into symmetrical models. He will, as old-time craftsman or industrial engineer, create objects that are apparently artless but that are actually—as if Mondrian and Klee never existed—products of the traditional repetitive-symmetrical aesthetic.

Bibliography and Selected Readings

Analysis

Boas, Franz, *Primitive Art*. New York: Dover, 1955, reprint of 1927. Although Boas's patterns do not hold precisely for Western folk art, they are suggestive and often applicable. Further, the aesthetic he outlines has been carried into non-Western folk art.

Deetz, James, *Invitation to Archaeology*. Garden City: Natural History Press, 1967. A concise and clear introduction to the analysis of material culture.

Norberg-Schulz, Christian, *Intentions in Architecture*. Cambridge: Massachusetts Institute of Technology Press, 1968. A complicated but invaluable exegesis of architecture with natural implications for the study of all artifacts.

"What is Folk Art? A Symposium." *Antiques* 57 (1950): 355–62. The symposium's dozen contributions illustrate the varieties of thought on "folk art." It forms the theoretical setting for the major collections of American "folk art" listed in note 16.

Analytical Collections

Espinosa, José E., *Saints in the Valleys: Christian Sacred Images in the History, Life and Folk Art of Spanish New Mexico*. Albuquerque: University of New Mexico Press, 1967. A scholarly historical study of New Mexican *bultos* and *retablos* as artworks and as religious icons; it includes an excellent bibliography.

Hansen, H. J., ed., *European Folk Art in Europe and the Americas*. New York and Toronto: McGraw-Hill, 1967. With contributions by many noted scholars, this beautifully illustrated volume provides a consistent survey of Western folk art.

Ludwig, Allen I., *Graven Images: New England Stonecarving and its Symbols, 1650–1815*. Middletown, Conn.: Wesleyan University Press, 1966. Though lacking in the quantitative controls for which the social scientist might wish, Ludwig's study of the forms and meanings of Yankee gravestone art is no less than superb.

Shelley, Donald A., *The Fraktur-Writings or Illuminated Manuscripts of the Pennsylvania Germans*. Pennsylvania German Folklore Society, 23 (1958–59). Allentown: Pennsylvania German Folklore Society, 1961. A solid, art-historical approach to fraktur, which includes an extensive bibliography on folk art in general.

Collections

Grancsay, Stephen V., *American Engraved Powder Horns: A Study Based on the J. H. Grenville Gilbert Collection*. Philadelphia: Ray Riling Arms Books Co., 1965; reprint of 1946. The value of this book, which is primarily a descriptive catalogue, comes from the extensiveness of the collection itself and the rigor of the collection's curator: the check list, indexes, and bibliography are exemplary.

Luther, Clair Franklin, *The Hadley Chest*. Hartford: Case, Lockwood and Brainard, 1935. Art historians like Charles Montgomery have produced excellent studies of fine furniture, but most books on folk furniture are hodgepodges of poorly identified artifacts. Luther's book, while analytically sketchy, includes a photograph and description of every known example of a highly decorated type of chest; it could form the basis of an excellent study of folk ornamentation.

13 FOLK ARCHITECTURE
Warren E. Roberts

Folk architecture may be said to be traditional architecture. It is concerned with all traditional aspects of building; the shapes, sizes, and layouts of buildings of all kinds, such as dwellings, barns, sheds, and craft shops; the materials used and the tools and techniques of building; the sites chosen and the placement of various buildings on the site; and the use to which buildings and various parts of buildings were put.

For many centuries in western Europe and in North America academic architecture and folk architecture have existed side by side, though on a quantitative basis it must be realized that folk architecture was much more significant than academic architecture. Moreover, since the Industrial Revolution, and especially in the twentieth century, what may be termed "popular architecture" has become increasingly important. Academic architecture is building that is closely connected with academically trained architects. Such buildings are designed primarily to impress the beholder and please the wealthy classes who can afford to hire architects to design and workmen to build their houses. It is academic architecture that has been most studied in the past, for architectural historians, being of the academy themselves, have concentrated upon the imposing buildings of the past and have largely ignored the "unplanned" structures of the common people, and most books dealing with architecture are devoted to public buildings and the mansions and fine dwellings of the wealthy. Moreover, when conscious attempts are made to preserve older buildings, it is generally examples of academic architecture that are chosen; examples of folk architecture are destroyed with abandon for the most part or are allowed to tumble, rot, or burn down. Popular architecture is a product of relatively recent times made possible by the Industrial Revolution. Building materials and even entire buildings are mass-produced in factories, and building plans are distributed by popular magazines, trade publications, and governmental agencies. In folk architecture, on the other hand, traditional plans are followed in that the owner or builder (who may be the same person) follows a design or plan with which he is familiar either in that it is the prevailing pattern in the area in which he lives or it is one employed by his forebears, while the materials, tools, and building techniques are traditional. Even today, many nonurban buildings not used for dwellings, i.e., barns, sheds, smokehouses, and the like, follow traditional designs and techniques, as do many dwelling houses. While fashion prevails in the realm of academic and popular architecture in the large urban centers and styles change in buildings almost as rapidly as in automobiles, in the countryside tradition holds sway and old familiar designs persist.

While it is true that there has been a reciprocal influence between folk architecture on the one hand and academic and popular architecture on the other, that traditional elements may be found in academic and popular architecture, and that traditional materials, tools, and techniques may be used in academic and popular architecture, nonetheless this survey will concentrate upon folk architecture, on which there has been relatively little written, and neglect academic and popular architecture on which many books and articles have been written.

In some ways, parallels may be drawn with other, nonmaterial forms. We have art songs cultivated by academically trained musicians, popular songs mass-produced and disseminated by the mass media, and folksongs learned and performed in traditional ways. At the same time, just as a folktale is a basic narrative pattern created by some unknown storyteller of the past and endlessly recreated by other storytellers, always with some variation, greater or less, and persisting for long periods of time, passed from one generation to the next while spreading over large areas, undergoing changes and developing special local forms when adapting to a new environment, so, too, a traditional house plan must have been created at some time in the past, perhaps by evolving out of an earlier plan, but it has persisted over a long period of time and developed innumerable variations. There are, of course, major differences between items of oral and material folklore; for example, a song or tale lives only in performance and in the mind of the performer or listener. It may die and be lost unless recorded, while most individual versions are unrecorded. A house, once built, lasts, however, and usually for a long period of time.

Generally speaking, folk architecture has been studied most extensively in the past in Scandinavia and northern Europe. Since World War II much work has been done in other European countries. The study of folk architecture is closely tied to the establishment and growth of folk or open-air museums such as Skansen, outside Stockholm (the oldest and largest folk museums are in Scandinavia). In Great Britain, excellent research has been carried out for some time in Wales where there is a Welsh Folk Museum at Cardiff (see Peate in bibliography). More recently, attention has been paid the subject in England, Scotland, and northern Ireland where folk museums are developing. In Ireland, outstanding work has resulted in publications, though no large-scale, open-air museum exists. In the United States, with the exception of work by occasional isolated individuals, most research has been carried out by cultural geographers such as Fred Kniffen and his pupils, for cultural geographers deal with the relationship between man and his physical environment and buildings are an important part of this relationship. Unfortunately, folklorists in the United States and Great Britain have neglected architecture as well as all other forms of material folklore and the folklore journals are almost completely bare of articles on these subjects. The British Society for Folk Life Studies with its journal *Folk Life* and the Pennsylvania Folklife Society with *Pennsylvania Folklife* are helping to fill a major void by promoting studies of folk architecture.

If in Great Britain and the United States folk architecture has not been studied very extensively in the past, it is not for lack of good reasons. By and large, the house or barn that a man builds during his lifetime may be considered his major tangible accomplishment; certainly it is his most readily observed and most obvious. Architecture is, therefore, a major key to the understanding of such subjects as cultural differences, the relationship between the individual and society, the diffusion of culture, the persistence of cultural traits, and the adaptation of culture to new environments or the lack of it. Moreover, the study of folk architecture may lead to purely pragmatic results. By and large, folk architecture is severely functional, and functional patterns that have developed and persisted for long periods of time should not be ignored by building planners. Further, folk architecture generally makes wise use of locally available building materials. Don Blair, writing on the traditional architecture of New Harmony, Indiana, asserts: "Here were built livable houses, economical to maintain, well insulated, centrally heated . . . functional and pleasing in design, fire resistant, weather and storm proofed, termite proof, and with many other advantages."[1] Certainly, the average suburban American homeowner today, plagued by repair bills and maintenance problems, could wish that his architect-designed or mass-produced "ranch house" had incorporated some of these features.

Such topics as building techniques, functional considerations, building sites, and the choice of materials must be slighted here. No satisfactory general classification for folk architecture has been developed. It is customary, however, to divide buildings into general categories by their function; i.e., dwelling houses, barns, sheds, smokehouses, stables, and the like. It must be pointed out, however, that the same construction techniques and the same materials may be used in buildings whose functions are very different, so that one may find log houses and log barns built in very nearly the same way (see Fig. 13–2), while houses, barns, and sheds may be built of stone and roofed with wooden shingles. Moreover, such distinctive features as the gambrel roof (see below, Fig. 13–1) may be used on barns and mills as well as on houses. Since most of the literature deals with dwelling houses, it is this subject that I shall concentrate upon, picking out two topics for special comment, frame house types in the northeastern United States and log buildings in the Midwest.

Of all parts of the United States, it is probably in New England that more frame houses of traditional types are preserved, and it is certainly true that more published information is available from this area than elsewhere. In this area, frame buildings of the one-and-a-half story type were frequently built, and three clear types may be described. A one-and-a-half story house is one in which there is less floor space available on the second floor, customarily used for bedrooms, than there is on the first, devoted to living and dining rooms, the kitchen, and the like. There are several reasons why this pattern should have proved so popular. A building that had approximately the same number of rooms and the same amount of floor space on one floor would require a much larger foundation and much more roof. When heating was done mostly with fireplaces, the one-story house required two or more chimneys; fireplaces on the second floor of a one-and-a-half story house could use the same chimney stack

1. Don Blair, *Harmonist Construction,* Indiana Historical Society Publications 23:2 (Indianapolis, 1964) : 81–82.

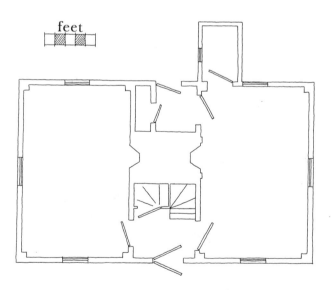

13–1. Central chimney house with a gambrel roof. This house, its two-room, central chimney plan being a conceptual transplant from southeastern England, is located at 43 Warner Street in Newport, Rhode Island (July 1967). Fieldwork and artwork by Henry Glassie.

serving the first floor, and, in addition, heat rising from the first floor helped to warm the second. At the same time, a one-and-a-half story house was more common than a two-story house because most families needed less space for bedrooms than for other rooms.

Of three one-and-a-half story types, the so-called Cape Cod house seems to have been most frequently built. It must be stressed that this house type is in no way peculiar to Cape Cod; the term, however, has been so frequently used in the United States that it is best to use it here. In the Cape Cod type of house the roof begins, front and rear, at the first floor line. The front door is generally in the center of the façade and the chimney in the center of the house, in the New England area at least. Houses of this sort, of course, are not an American invention but were first built following European, especially British, patterns. They were built during the early decades of the seventeenth century and are still being built today wherever folk architecture still holds sway. Academic and popular architecture in the twentieth century have also copied the Cape Cod style extensively. The type is found all over the eastern United States. In the South, however, most examples have a chimney at the end of the house, and sometimes chimneys at each end, rather than a central chimney. Dormer windows in the roof seem also to be more frequent in the South, perhaps because of the need for more ventilation in the warmer climate, though dormers have been added to many northern examples during the nineteenth and twentieth centuries. In floor plan, the Cape Cod house is basically two rectangular rooms joined together end to end; it is two rooms wide and one room deep.

The second one-and-a-half story frame type is the gambrel roof house (see Fig. 13–1). This type resembles the Cape Cod house in many respects except that the roof has a double pitch, steeper at the eaves and flatter at the ridge. The advantages of the gambrel roof are immediately apparent; more usable space is available on the second floor because of the steep pitch of the lower half of the roof, that extends the area in which a person can stand upright. Again, most New England houses of this type have a central chimney and the front door in the center of the façade while southern examples frequently have end chimneys. Houses of this type are often called "Dutch colonial," the inference being that the gambrel roof is of Dutch origin. Although there probably has been a strong Dutch influence on gambrel roof houses in the United States, the gambrel roof is fairly common in England, though used on utilitarian buildings such as barns and mills there. An English source for the gambrel roof, then, cannot be discounted, and the wide distribution of this type of roof in the eastern United States plus the early date—before

1650—of some examples bespeak an English derivation. The gambrel roof itself is often found on other structures besides one-and-a-half story houses: two-story houses, barns, and mills, for example. One can say that the one-and-a-half story gambrel roof house is a traditional house type that has persisted in the United States for at least two centuries and has a wide distribution.

The final one-and-a-half story frame house type to be discussed here is one variously called the saltbox or lean-to type. Since the term "lean-to" appears in early records and has been used by a number of architectural historians, I will use it here. The lean-to house is two stories high in the front and one story high in the rear, with a long, sweeping roof at the rear. The lean-to house may be built in this form from the very beginning, or may be the result of later additions. Either one is obviously a traditional building pattern, but the integral lean-to is the clearest type. New England lean-tos usually also have a central chimney and a centered front door. The advantages of the lean-to type over the other one-and-a-half story types is that it is possible to have a number of windows on the second floor without resorting to dormers that, while picturesque, complicate the building of the roof and are a potential source of roof leaks. Lean-to houses are found in England, where the term "cat-slide roof" seems to be used, and integral lean-tos were being built in New England well before 1700. Most New England examples date from the eighteenth century, but integral lean-tos were being built according to traditional patterns in southern Indiana and elsewhere in the Midwest as late as 1900. Most Indiana lean-to houses have a central chimney like New England houses, but the majority of them have two front doors side by side even though the houses are single-family dwellings. Many smaller dwellings in the Midwest and elsewhere use two front doors, however, so that this is a traditional architectural pattern.

Log buildings are so well known in the United States and so often associated with pioneer living that it is often assumed that the first settlers to reach these shores constructed log cabins as soon as they landed. Such, however, does not seem to have been the case. Although the early history of horizontal log construction in the United States is not at all clear, it seems reasonably well established that the early British, Dutch, and French settlers, unfamiliar with log construction, as soon as possible built the frame houses with which they were familiar. Indeed, this is what the folklorist who is continually aware of the persistence of traditional patterns would expect. The concept of log building was probably introduced into this country by the Swedish and German immigrants who knew it in their homelands. It was not until the eighteenth century, however, that the use of horizontal logs was taken over by Americans of British ancestry, but once it was taken over it became the customary way of building in frontier areas and developed distinctive American types.

There are many good reasons why log buildings, once the concept became established, should have become so prevalent during the pioneer period in most of the forest areas in the United States. First of all, a log building, relatively simple to construct in comparison with a frame or masonry building, is durable, easy to maintain, and, thanks to the thickness of the walls, warm in winter. The raw materials in forested areas were everywhere at hand; indeed, the first major task a pioneer had was to clear enough trees from the land to plant crops. Logs, therefore, were a hindrance to him, something to be got rid of, and most pioneers had to resort to huge bonfires to help clear their lands. A log building can be put up almost without nails or other hardware, for the weight of the logs as they rest on one another plus the way they are notched together make it unnecessary to nail the logs together. Wooden pegs, or trunnels, were also used extensively where nails would be used today. Special carpenter's tools also were unnecessary in constructing a simple log building, and a pioneer moving into a new area could ill-afford to bring large quantities of specialized tools and nails with him. Because of the difficulties of transportation and the scarcity of blacksmiths, hardware of this sort was in short supply and very expensive in newly settled regions. Finally, the specialized skills of a house carpenter were unnecessary in the construction of a simple log building, and any man capable of surviving under frontier conditions had the skills needed for log construction.

Although log buildings are rightly associated with the pioneer period, in many forested parts of the United States they have been built right down to the present day, not as a self-conscious imitation of old things but in a truly traditional way. The depression years of the 1930s in some areas in southern Indiana, for instance, saw a resurgence of log buildings because logs were readily available and a log building costs practically nothing except for labor. Clearly, then, log buildings represent an outstanding type of folk architecture in the United States because of their wide geographical distribution and their long time span.

Buildings of many kinds were constructed of logs: houses, barns, smokehouses, corn cribs, and sheds. Because a large number of diagrams would be required I will not go into detail concerning the floor plans and other features of log buildings, although some building techniques can be discussed. What may be called the perimeter foundation, in which stone is laid completely around the base of the house, seems to have been most common in northern parts of the

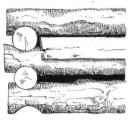

13–2. Horizontal log corner-timbering:
A) Saddle-notching; from a corncrib located south of Bardstown, Nelson County, Kentucky (August 1969).

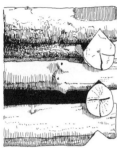

B) Saddle-V-notching; from a four-crib barn located west of Hayesville, Clay County, North Carolina (July 1964).

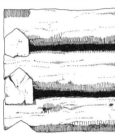

C) V-notching; from a bank barn located between Saxton and Riddlesburg, Bedford County, Pennsylvania (September 1968).

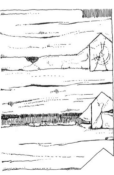

D) V-notching; from a cabin located northeast of Minford, Scioto County, Ohio (June 1969).

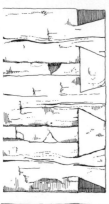

E) Dovetail corner-timbering; from a continental central chimney house located south of Cocalico, Lancaster County, Pennsylvania (October 1967).

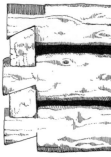

F) Half-dovetail corner-timbering; from a double-crib barn located near Harrisburg, Sevier County, Tennessee (May 1964).

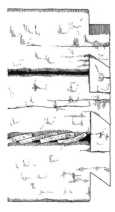

G) Half-dovetail corner-timbering; from a dogtrot house located west of Russellville, Franklin County, Alabama (December 1962).

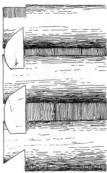

H) Half-dovetail corner-timbering; from a saddlebag house located east of Philadelphia, Neshoba County, Mississippi (November 1963).

I) Diamond-notching; from a cabin located in Calvary Community, Halifax County, Virginia (July 1963).

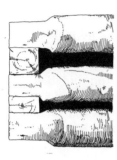

J) Square-notching; from a tobacco barn located north of Marshall, Madison County, North Carolina (June 1963).

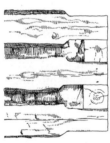

K) Square-notching; from a cabin located northwest of Chesterfield Court House, Chesterfield County, Virginia (September 1967).

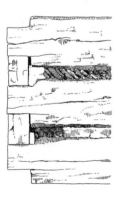

L) Square-notching; from a central hall I house located north of McDaniels, Breckenridge County, Kentucky (August 1963). Field and artwork by Henry Glassie.

country. In southern regions, however, it seems to have been more common to set stone pillars at each corner of the building and to set the sills on them. Sometimes the spaces in between the cornerstones were filled in with loose rocks to keep animals out, but not as a form of support. The sills were generally of timbers hewn square on four sides and of sufficient size to support enormous weights. Floor joists of smaller logs hewn flat on the tops rested on these sills and supported the floors, though, according to travelers' reports, many log buildings in pioneer days had only dirt floors. Then the logs themselves were added to form the walls. In early times, when haste was a primary concern, the logs were often left in the round, and in later times this was also done in simple buildings. It was much more common, however, to hew the logs when a more finished or permanent type of structure was planned. Depending to some extent upon the locality and the type of tree available, the logs could either be hewn square or could be hewn flat on two sides with the top and bottom left unhewn, even with the bark on. When a timber of this sort is hewn from a large tree, it may reach dimensions of two feet or more in width and only six inches in thickness. In such cases it is something of a misnomer to speak of a "log" house, because the timbers in question much more resemble huge planks.

In practically all American log buildings, interstices, often several inches in width, are left between the logs. These interstices are filled with "chinking," usually consisting of stones or pieces of wood laid between the logs with clay or mortar plastered over them. Only very rarely are logs fitted together so closely that no chinking is needed, and then usually in such buildings as jails. In barns and other outbuildings the interstices are often unchinked providing ventilation and light without need of windows. The logs are joined at the corners in a variety of ways, but in the most carefully constructed buildings in such a way that rainwater cannot penetrate the joints and cause the logs to rot (see Fig. 13–2). In many instances, the log walls of houses were covered on the outside with clapboards as soon as the house was built, though restored or reproduced log houses usually leave the logs exposed. At ceiling-height, joists, usually timbers hewn on all four sides, are set into the logs, and boards that at once provide the floor for the second story and the ceiling for the first are laid on top of them. Frequently, two or more logs are used in the walls above the ceiling joists, giving a second story with very little head room at the sides toward the eaves, though in some regions log houses a full two stories in height are not uncommon. The top log, or plate, upon which the rafters rest is frequently hewn square and is of approximately the same size as the sills. The walls at the gable ends are usually not of log but of vertical timbers, or studs, to which clapboards

13–3. The Cox-Linscomb log house in Green County, Beech Creek Township, Indiana. The house dates from about 1840. While the walls were once covered with clapboard siding, it has mostly fallen off. Photograph by Warren Roberts, 1965.

are nailed. For the roof, boards are nailed to the rafters and shingles fastened to the boards.

Most older log houses have fireplaces, though houses built toward the end of the nineteenth century may have only a stove and a small chimney. When present, the fireplace is most often in the outside wall at one of the gable ends of the house. While, according to travelers' reports, chimneys in early periods were often made of wood covered with clay, most log buildings surviving today have masonry fireplaces and chimneys.

Bibliography and Selected Readings

United States

Blair, Don. *Harmonist Construction*. Indiana Historical Society Publications, 23:2. Indianapolis, 1964. A brief survey of the frame houses built in the early nineteenth century in New Harmony, Indiana, by the Rappites, this work is among the best descriptions of traditional building techniques and patterns. Well-illustrated.

Briggs, M. S. *The Homes of the Pilgrim Fathers in England and America 1620–1685*. London, 1932. An important attempt to trace the survival of traditional English building practices in America. Briggs deals mainly with wooden buildings and stresses especially the use of wooden clapboards as exterior siding on walls.

Erixon, Sigurd. "Är den nordamerikanska timringstekniken överförd från Sverige?" *Folk-Liv* 19 (1955) : 56–68. Deals with the sources of log building techniques and patterns in the United States. Useful bibliographical references in notes.

Kaufman, H. J. "Literature on Log Architecture: A Survey." *The Pennsylvania Dutchman* 7 (1955) : 30–34.

Kelly, J. F. *The Early Domestic Architecture of Connecticut*. New Haven: Yale University Press, 1924. Although not dealing exclusively with folk architecture, nonetheless Kelly treats traditional building techniques and many traditional designs for frame houses. The work is especially useful for the full treatment of interior and exterior details.

Kniffen, Fred. "Folk Housing: Key to Diffusion." *Annals of the Association of American Geographers* 55 (1965) : 549–77. In addition to being an excellent survey of folk architecture in the eastern United States, this work is important in showing why students of settlement geography have done far more research in the United States on folk architecture than any other group of scholars.

———, and Henry Glassie. "Building in Wood in the Eastern United States: A Time-Place Perspective." *The Geographical Review* 56 (1966) : 40–66. The first in a projected series of articles. "We propose to consider, in order, methods of building construction, types of buildings, fences and fencing practices, field forms, agricultural practices, and other aspects of settlements" (pp. 40–41).

Long, Amos, Jr. "Pennsylvania Summer-Houses and Summer-Kitchens." *Pennsylvania Folklife* 15 (1965) : 10–19. One of a series of articles by the same author in this journal, important in dealing with a neglected subject, namely, the persistent tradition in design and construction of outbuildings of various kinds.

Shoemaker, A. L., ed. *The Pennsylvania Barn*. Kutztown, Pa.: Pennsylvania Folklife Society, 1955. Reprinted essays by several scholars on various aspects of construction and design of Pennsylvania barns.

Shurtleff, H. R. *The Log Cabin Myth*. Cambridge, Mass.: Harvard University Press, 1939. Devoted to exploding the "myth" that the Pilgrim Fathers built log cabins (see Erixon, above), this work is one of the few dealing with log buildings in the United States and can still be consulted profitably though it is out of date.

Great Britain and Ireland

Barley, M. V. *The English Farmhouse and Cottage*. London: Routledge and Kegan Paul, 1961.

Brunskill, R. W. *Illustrated Handbook of Vernacular Architecture* (New York: Universe Books, 1971). The key to a major research project in folk architecture and allied subjects undertaken by the Vernacular Architecture Group. This book supplies examples of many architectural features to guide the recorder. A number of regional surveys have already been made, though many are as yet unpublished. See Wood-Jones.

Campbell, Åke. "Notes on the Irish House, I, II." *Folk-Liv* 1 (1937) : 207–34; 2 (1938) : 173–96. A useful survey of traditional Irish house types by one of the greatest Swedish students of folklife.

Evans, E. Estyn. *Irish Folk Ways*. London: Routledge and Kegan Paul, 1957. See particularly chap. 3, "The Thatched House."

Gailey, Alan. "The Peasant Houses of the South-west Highlands of Scotland: Distribution, Parallels and Evolution." *Gwerin* 3 (1960–2) : 227–42. Useful survey with many references in footnotes. Refers to author's PhD thesis, Glasgow University, 1961, on settlement patterns in the southwest Highlands.

Grant, Isabel F. *Highland Folk Ways*. London: Routledge and Kegan Paul, 1961. See particularly chap. 7, "The Homes of the People."

Peate, I. C. *The Welsh House: A Study in Folk Culture*. London, 1940. An outstanding work by the dean of folklife studies in Wales.

Wood-Jones, R. B. *Traditional Domestic Architecture in the Banbury Region*. Manchester: Manchester University Press, 1963. This survey is based upon a study of over eleven hundred structures. See the review by I. C. Peate in *Folk Life* 3 (1965) : 107–9.

14 FOLK COSTUME
Don Yoder

WHAT IS FOLK COSTUME?

Folk costume is the visible, outward badge of folk-group identity, worn consciously to express that identity. In the peasant cultures of Europe, identity was determined geographically, and the local costumes expressed locality, region, or province. In the United States, where the peasant culture concept does not fit the historical situation, the term folk costume can be used to describe the dress of all traditional regional, ethnic, occupational, and sectarian groups, from the Allegheny frontiersman to the Cajun, and from the cowboy to the Amishman. In every case the costume is distinct and identifiable; it identifies the wearer to the outside world as well as to his own community; it is prescribed by the community and its form is dictated by the community's tradition. For the majority of Americans, the old geographical differentiation of dress has been supplanted by temporal differentiation, since today international fashion determines the styles followed by most Americans and most Europeans.[1]

1. Ruth Benedict, "Dress," *Encyclopedia of the Social Sciences*, 5: 235–38.

European scholars have normally defined folk costume as peasant costume. Within European scholarship there is a range of definition. A typical narrow-gauge definition is the following: "Folk costume in the present context means the dress of the rural population in the time before the changing of the dress custom in the nineteenth century, which at that juncture erased the difference between town and country, between higher and lower estates." This peasant costume "was the subject of a set of rules, in every detail prescribing the correct costume for every situation likely to be encountered by a member of the old village community in the course of the year and a whole life."[2] Richard Weiss, the foremost Swiss folklife scholar of the twentieth century, taking as he does the functionalist approach to folk-culture, gives us a broad-gauge definition, that folk costume is what people wear in relation to their community life as a whole. Furthermore, he insists that scholars study not merely *what* is worn but *how* it is worn. He points out that, in the twentieth century, the Swiss farmer may wear factory-made clothing, but he adapts it to his own ideas—omitting trouser cuffs as "dirt-catchers," preferring suspenders to the now commoner belt, and wearing his hat in his own special way—and literally wearing it everywhere but in church and in bed. Hence, while rural clothing is no longer homespun or even home-tailored, it is folk-cultural in the sense of its use and function within the folk community.[3]

My own attempt at summarizing the functionalist viewpoint on folk costume results in the following definition: "Folk costume is that form of dress which (1) outwardly symbolizes the identity of a folk community and (2) expresses the individual's manifold relationships to and within that community." Such a definition applies to European peasant costume as well as to its nearest American equivalents, the traditional regional, occupational, ethnic, and sectarian forms of American dress. A simpler definition, emphasizing the local variation of folk costume, could describe folk costume as "the dialect of dress," i.e., the analogue in the world of dress to dialect in the linguistic world. Folk dress and dialect are both local and regional, but both are related to larger cultural entities, in one case literary or national language, and in the other, international fashion.

Despite attempts to divide "costume" and "dress" in definition, "costume" for festival or ceremonial apparel and "dress" for ordinary wear,[4] in this essay we shall use costume, dress, apparel, garb, and

2. Peter Michelsen and Holger Rasmussen, *Danish Peasant Culture* (Copenhagen, 1955), p. 47.
3. Richard Weiss, *Volkskunde der Schweiz* (Erlenbach-Zurich, 1946), pp. 140–41.
4. Hilaire and Meyer Hiler, "Costumes and Ideologies," *Bibliography of Costume* (New York, 1939), p. xiii.

clothing as synonymous. The German word *Tracht* and the Spanish *traje* suggest etymologically at its broadest the total range of what is worn; the English word "costume" derives from the same Latin root, *consuetudo*, as "custom." In fact, Riehl suggested that folk costume, like custom, grows up gradually according to the needs of a folk community. "It has therefore the same ideal value as custom, indeed it is itself only an expression of custom."[5]

European scholars, with their ethnographic or folklife orientation, have paid much more attention to costume history than have American folklorists. Even so, European costume historians have traced in more detail the history of fashion and the dress of the upper classes. The reason seems to have been the practical one, that more examples of court and upper-middle-class costume have been preserved. These were the classes, too, whose dress has been most fully recorded in the iconography of costume. When in the twentieth century European folklife scholars did turn to traditional peasant costume, they studied its every aspect, and their best costume histories provide both a framework and a methodology for similar studies elsewhere. And not least of all, they provide American scholars with warnings both against overvaluing "the beautiful old folk costumes" of the relict areas (the popular romantic approach) and undervaluing the study of what farmers and working classes wore generally.

In our age of mass culture, where costume is determined by international style changes, it is instructive to look at the difference between traditional peasant costume and present-day dress habits. Dress is still very much the badge of group identity. If we study "American dress" in the past half century, we are tempted to the conclusion that everyday dress, as adapted to the lives of average middle-class Americans, and as mirrored in the snapshot albums, which prove that the Kennedys and the Eisenhowers dressed just like the humbler Joneses, is in a very real sense the functional equivalent, in our mass culture, of the earlier peasant dress of Europe, and is just as related to "tradition" and to "community."[6] The historical difference is that, since the breakdown of the class structure in the wake of the French Revolution, urban and rural, upper- and lower-class dress are merged into general patterns. The "community" is larger, that of international

5. Wilhelm Heinrich Riehl, *Die Pfälzer* (1857), pp. 219 ff., quoted in Ursula Ewig and Anneliese Born, *Die Frauentracht der Breidenbacher Grundes* (Marburg, 1964), p. 16. I am indebted to Dr. Ewig's perspective here as well as for several later quotations from older German works.

6. As an example of what can be done with this approach to costume research see Walter Hävernick, "Kinderkleidung und Gruppengeistigkeit in volkskundlicher Sicht. I. Der Matrosenanzug der Hamburger Jungen 1900–1920," *Beiträge zur Deutschen Volks- und Altertumskunde* 4 (1959): 37–61; and Part II: "Kleidung und Kleidersitte höheren Schüler in Hamburg 1921 bis 1939," ibid. 6 (1962): 21–64.

fashion, but the "tradition," in the sense of dress adherence, is just as rigid. The average American conforms as rigidly to the temporal changes in international style as his peasant ancestor conformed to the geographical differentiation of dress. Even the nonconformists, our analogues to the earlier sectarian groups, use costume as badges identifying their nonconformity, whether they are students, the "younger generation," hippies, yippies, beatniks, Black Muslims, or Afro-Americans.

In the United States, therefore, we have available for research the whole spectrum of what the American farmer and his craftsman and working-class counterparts have worn traditionally in the various regions that make up our cultural map—the costumes that identified them as farmers, lumbermen, watermen, or cowboys, just as the European costumes identified their wearers as peasants, drovers, chimney sweeps, Hamburger Zimmerleute, and other group representatives. Taking the broader view, we can study across the board all American traditional regional, occupational, ethnic, and sectarian costume. And for the broadest possible approach, perhaps we shall have to dig out those snapshot albums.

COSTUME AS A RESEARCH AREA IN EUROPE

Since European scholarship has produced most of the description and theoretical framework for the study of costume, we must first look at the results of costume research as a research field in Europe.

First of all, there has been systematic collecting of folk costumes in every area of Europe. Every major folk museum and almost every local Heimatmuseum has a collection of regional dress, some on display, but most of it, museum-fashion, stored for study. Two of the largest collections are the Netherlands Costume Collection at the Netherlands Open Air Museum at Arnhem and the Von Geramb Collection of Styrian Folk Costume in the Styrian Folk Museum in Graz. Eastern Europe has many extensive costume collections in its chain of ethnographic museums. The folk-cultural institutes all over Europe have studied dress as part of folk-culture, and much information has been gathered together via questionnaires, some of which has been analyzed and published in connection with regional or national folk-culture atlases. Also prints and photographs have been gathered and studied in the attempt to focus on the wider iconography of costume. The archeologist has aided the folk costume scholar with discoveries and analyses of prehistoric and early medieval costumes, particularly those preserved in the peat bogs of Denmark. The historian of fashion has added culture-historical depth to costume scholarship and produced an impressive literature, much of which is valuable as background for folk costume research.

What have been the results of this concentrated approach to European costume history?

When peasant costume was "discovered" in the Romantic Era, along with folksong, it was believed to have been a "survival," unchanged from earlier, primitive eras. As scholars began to study costume scientifically in the late nineteenth century, under the influence of evolutionary historiography, art historians and culture historians suggested that the main element of costume had been change, and that the structure of the folk costumes, which they analyzed piece by piece, was essentially a peasant-level copy of the changing fashions worn by the upper-class world. Hottenroth proved the historical dependence of folk costume on fashion in his huge, meticulously documented volumes, and other historically oriented volumes followed.[7] Naumann's theories of *gesunkenes Kulturgut* and *primitiver Gemeinschaftsgeist* used folk costume as a chief example of cultural items descending from the upper to lower levels of culture. Folk costume was to Naumann only "repetition and late echo of earlier fashionable costume."[8]

The reaction to these genetic theories led costume research in two directions. First, further research revealed, in addition to the obvious high fashion influences in the folk costumes, certain basic "primitive" forms and patterns of clothing, especially in work clothing (e.g., the clothing of hunters, fishermen, shepherds), which had continued in use in various European folk-cultural matrices since prehistoric times. Archeology, with the Danish bog burials and the costume remnants from the *Völkerwanderung* era, helped the folk-culture scholar to this insight, which was developed in Haberlandt, Hanika, Schier, and von Geramb.[9] In addition, changing the historical direction, some aspects of costume were studied as *gestiegenes Kulturgut*, as having moved from peasant level to fashion level—for examples, the apron, the *Haube*, the dirndl dress, and the *Lederhosen*.

While piece-by-piece historical analysis of folk costumes has in a sense reached a stalemate, the functionalist approach, using sociological and psychological methodology, has provided new directions. Viewing the costumes as wholes, and setting them against their func-

---

7. Friedrich Hottenroth, *Handbuch der deutschen Tracht* (Stuttgart, 1896); *Deutsche Volkstrachten—städtische und ländliche—vom 16. Jahrhundert an bis zum Anfange des Jahrhunderts*, 3 vols. (Frankfurt-am-Main, 1898, 1900, 1902).

8. Hans Naumann, *Grundzüge der deutschen Volkskunde* (Leipzig, 1922); *Primitive Gemeinschaftskultur: Beiträge zur Volkskunde und Mythologie* (Jena, 1921).

9. Michael and Arthur Haberlandt, *Die Völker Europas und ihre volkstümliche Kultur* (Stuttgart, 1928); Joseph Hanika, *Sudetendeutsche Volkstrachten* (Reichenberg, 1937); Bruno Schier, "Vorgeschichtliche Elemente in der europäischen Volkstrachten," in *Tracht und Schmuck der Germanen in Geschichte und Gegenwart*, edited by Ernst-Otto Thiele (Berlin, 1938), pp. 1–17; and Konrad Mautner and Viktor von Geramb, *Steirisches Trachtenbuch*, 2 vols. (Graz, 1932, 1940).

tional background in the total life of the folk-community, the focus is thus shifted from the origin of costume to the basic social and psychological significance of costume in the folk-cultural matrix. The sociological approach has enlightened us on the social meaning of costume as symbol; the psychological approach, involving as it does the reactions of the wearer of the costume to what is worn, has led to important conclusions on the "life laws" of folk costume, its rationale in the ingroup, and on the reasons for the decline of the costumes in the twentieth century. This community-focused costume research is well illustrated in the work of the contemporary German scholars Mathilde-Hain[10] and Martha Bringemeier.[11]

COSTUME AND FASHION

Costume or dress is what is worn generally; fashion is that changing element of style that is dictated from an urban center and spreads, in the manner of mobile culture,[12] to the susceptible classes in the area. Fashion or high fashion, the changing world of style that seems to follow certain historical fluctuations,[13] circulates first among the upper classes—in Europe, the nobility and the middle classes—and eventually affects the more conservative rural population. This would seem to be one of the general laws of costume discovered by the leading folk costume scholars of Europe—that the upper level at least partially determines the lower, or heavily influences its development. While in the eighteenth and nineteenth centuries, Paris and London fashions were copied immediately by the upper classes, certain elements in the

10. The work of Dr. Mathilde Hain, professor of Folk-Cultural Studies at the University of Frankfurt, includes her doctoral dissertation, done under Professor Julius Schwietering at Marburg, *Das Lebensbild eines oberhessischen Trachtendorfes. Von bäuerlicher Tracht und Gemeinschaft* (Marburg, 1936); the magnificent picture volume, in the series *Trachtenleben in Deutschland,* Wolf Lücking and Mathilde Hain (Berlin, 1959); and the essay that I consider the best single short introduction to costume research in Europe, "Die Volkstrachten," in Wolfgang Stammler ed., *Deutsche Philologie im Aufriss* (Berlin: E. Schmidt), 2d ed., 3 (1962), cols. 2,885–2,900.

11. Dr. Martha Bringemeier, retired professor of Folk-Cultural Studies at the University of Münster, has produced a distinguished bibliography in costume history, including the articles "Die Abendmahlskleidung der Frauen und Mädchen in der Schaumburger und Mindener Tracht," *Rheinisch-Westphälische Zeitschrift für Volkskunde* 1 (1954): 65–91; "Die Hosenmode der Frau," ibid. 10: 1–4 (1963): 134–66. The second edition of Franz Jostes, *Westfälisches Trachtenbuch* (Münster, 1961), which she edited and enlarged, has made available that standard work from 1905; and her text to Wolf Lücking and Martha Bringemeier, *Trachtenleben in Deutschland,* 1: *Schaumburg-Lippe* (Berlin, 1958) is equally distinguished.

12. Sigurd Erixon, "An Introduction to Folklife Research or Nordic Ethnology," *Folk-Liv* 14–15 (1950–51): 5–15.

13. Alfred L. Kroeber, "On the Principle of Order in Civilization as Exemplified by Changes in Fashion," *American Anthropologist* 21 (1919): 235–63; also Agnes Brooks Young, *Recurring Cycles of Fashion, 1760–1937* (New York, 1937).

fashion changes eventually registered themselves in the folk costume. In the eighteenth century, certain elements of the rococo court-costume of Versailles finally appeared in the costume of peasant women, and in the nineteenth century the Empire mode was likewise mirrored in folk-level dress.[14] Even American Quakeresses adopted the Empire dress, with its high waist and puffed sleeves, and continued to wear it long after it had been replaced by other styles in the high fashion world.[15]

This leads us to the second general rule of costume dynamics. Once adopted in the folk-cultural matrix, these adaptations of European fashion often lasted longer in rural areas through cultural lag based on rural conservatism. Thus when rococo and Empire had been replaced by Biedermeier and Victorian in high culture, the earlier styles continued among the peasantry. For example, in men's dress, military styles of the seventeenth and eighteenth centuries had a formative influence on peasant costume. In eighteenth- and nineteenth-century Sweden and Germany the peasant's cocked hat (*Dreimaster*), boots, and long, close-fitting Louis XIV *Leibrock* (*justaucorps*) all betrayed military influence. Even the military colors, the reds and blues, are said to have come into rural costume at that time, to be replaced by Victorian black in the mid-nineteenth century.

In general, this view of the relation of peasant to upper-class costume fits in with the widely held theory of the noncreativity of folk-culture, modified to suggest that the creativity consisted in the selection and synthesis, which after all did produce visibly different, often strikingly different, ensembles across a geographical area. Adolf Bach suggests that the selectivity was conditioned by peasant practicality. The "solid" peasantry adopted only those costume elements that met practical needs, never taking over, for example, in the rococo era, the perukes and powder and beauty marks of the rococo beauty or, in the Gothic period, the "mouse-tale shoes" (*Mäuseschwänze, Schnabelschuhe*). The peasant wanted something cheap and durable; he was not actually interested in fashion as such.[16]

14. Julie Heierli, *Die Volkstrachten der Schweiz,* 5 vols. (Erlenbach-Zurich, 1922–28), contains many plates and much discussion illustrating the influence of high fashion on regional Swiss folk dress in the eighteenth and nineteenth centuries.

15. The principal historian of American Quaker costume has written, "It may be set down as a safe rule, in seeking for a Quaker style or custom at any given time, to take the worldly fashion or habit of the period preceding. When the mode changes, and a style is dropped, the Quaker will be found just ready to adopt it, having by this time become habituated to its use" (Amelia Mott Gummere, *The Quaker: A Study in Costume* [Philadelphia, 1901], p. 183).

16. Adolf Bach, *Deutsche Volkskunde,* 3d ed. (Heidelberg, 1960), p. 464, citing Rudolf Helm, *Die bäuerlichen Männertrachten der Germanischen Nationalmuseums zu Nürnberg* (1932).

The different rate of adjustment to changes in urban dress on the part of rural men and women has many basic causes. Jostes suggests that the tailors who made men's clothing in the nineteenth century had to travel two years abroad as apprentices, and had to learn the latest styles of European fashion to compete in the urban milieu. When they settled down in the villages they naturally made men's clothing that showed at least partial adaptation of current styles. On the other hand, women's dress in the rural villages was made by local seamstresses who may never have traveled in the outside world. Then, too, men were more mobile than the stay-at-home village women—it was normally the men who went to the cities, to market, on business.[17] A Franconian historian writing in 1913 reported that no *Grünröcke* (farmers in green *Kittel*) came into town any more. The boys used to run behind them shouting "Quack! quack!" and they were also ridiculed as *Laubfrösche* (tree frogs) because of the color of their clothing. This deeply insulted the peasants.[18] Finally, it became too embarrassing for the farmers to wear "costume" on visits to the modern cities. Even country girls who customarily wore peasant dress in the village in secret kept "modern" hats for trips to the city.

COSTUME AND COMMUNITY

Folk costume is one of the symbols of folk community, and one of the variables of a culture. As a symbol it expresses the basic needs as well as the basic structure of a folk community, and as a variable it becomes, like regional architecture, a means of identifying the local, the vernacular. In all the historic culture areas of Europe there were once regional costumes, which followed cultural, confessional, and sometimes political boundaries. These regional costumes, which we think of today as rural, were once centered in the cities that were capitals of the regions.[19] In small areas today archaic costumes sometimes still continue to demarcate older, obsolete political boundaries, particularly those where confession was involved.[20]

17. Franz Jostes, *Westfälisches Trachtenbuch: Volksleben und Volkskultur in Westfalen*, 2d ed. edited and enlarged by Martha Bringemeier (Münster, Westfalen, 1961) , pp. 108–9.

18. Otto Langguth, "Unsere Volkstrachten," *Jahresbericht des historischen Vereins Alt-Wertheim* (1913) : 37–56.

19. For studies of urban dress in its relation to the rural folk dress of the nearby areas see, for example, Franz Joachim Behnisch, *Die Tracht Nürnbergs und seines Umlandes vom 16. bis zur Mitte des 19. Jahrhunderts* (Nürnberg, 1963) , a dissertation done at the University of Würzburg in 1962.

20. For the survival of older political boundaries as cultural boundaries see Philip L. Wagner and Marvin W. Mikesell, eds., *Readings in Cultural Geography* (Chicago, 1962) , pp. 55–56; also, in particular, Richard Weiss, "Cultural Boundaries and the Ethnographic Map," ibid., pp. 62–74. See also Richard Weiss's posthumously published essay, "Die Brüning-Napf-Reuss-Linie als Kulturgrenze

14–1. Nineteenth-century American farm dress. This illustration, entitled "The Luncheon," is taken from Sereno Edwards Todd, *Todd's Country Homes and How to Save Money. A Practical Book by a Practical Man* (Philadelphia: J. C. McCurdy, 1877), facing p. 194. Photograph: Henry Glassie.

When folk costume has achieved regional differences, have these differences developed from isolation, cultural lag, or from conscious attempts to express locality and community? The answers differ from area to area, and not all the questions have found definitive answers. Some relict areas have preserved archaic costumes, while other nearby rural or village areas display urban dress. In some cases, as we have pointed out above, rural populations wear urban, factory-made clothing, but they wear it in ways that still express folk-cultural needs, and adapt the costume selectively to their own ideas.

More recent scholarship has found firmer footing when it analyzes the social role of costume within the folk community. Within a traditionalist rural village community in central Europe, there is a spectrum of differentiation within the local costume. Costume differentiates the person who wears it in relation to the following factors: (1) sex, (2) age, (3) social status, (4) occupation, (5) work/leisure, and (6) confession. Let us look at these areas in detail.

In any traditional community the basic point of differentiation is sex. In contrast to the present-day erasing of the differences between male and female dress, melting them into a kind of androgynous costume,[21] folk costume rigidly separated the sexes. So great was the fear of the reversal of the sexes that only during the spiritual anarchy of carnival time, when the sacred year stood still and in the primitive sense the spirits were abroad, could men dress as women and women as men in an almost ritualized transvestitism. Remnants of this practice appear in certain Protestant folk cultures in the United States of the past century, in the "mumming" and "fantastical" parades of rural as well as urban America and in the Pennsylvania German custom of "Belsnickling." Other than this, men's costumes, like men's work patterns and men's roles in general, were sharply differentiated from those of women in the folk-cultural setting.

Dress also obviously varies according to one's age. From infancy to old age there is a variety of costumes that the individual wears successively. In the second half of the spectrum, from middle to old age, there is usually a growing conservative trend in dress. While in contemporary urban society, the "modern" woman (and some of the men) hope to defy time, refusing to submit to age, in traditional folk-culture areas of Europe old people were not afraid to look old and dressed the part of Grandfather or Grandmother without benefit of beauty parlor and cosmetic camouflage.

---

zwischen Ost- und Westschweiz auf volkskundlichen Karten," *Schweizerisches Archiv für Volkskunde* 58 (1962) : 201–31; also Richard Weiss, "Sprachgrenzen und Konfessionsgrenzen als Kulturgrenzen," *Laos* 1 (1951) : 96–110.

21. Martha Bringemeier, "Die Hosenmode der Frau, *"Rheinisch-Westphälische Zeitschrift für Volkskunde* 10: 1–4 (1963) : 154–66.

Status in the folk community involves several relations, one of which, the married status, is basic. In many European folk-cultures, women's dress was especially differentiated to signalize marriage. Even in villages where the dress of the unmarried girl and the married woman were almost uniform, there would be subtle variation—a telltale change of color in the *Haube*, the flowered pattern of the apron, or some other detail, as for instance, hair down for the unmarried girl, hair up and under the *Haube* for the married—that would define the difference.

The fourth area of difference in the folk costumes within a community is that of workday and festival costume. Just as the life of the community moved forward in a rhythm of alternation between the work days and the festivals, so the costumes symbolized the alternation. While everyday dress was utilitarian and sometimes, although not always, drab and nondecorative, for festival costumes decoration was allowed, even encouraged. The underlying differentiation of work and worship undoubtedly prompted this attitude. If worship is the "celebration of life,"[22] in the sense that man dramatizes the wholeness of life in his festival moods, then festival dress in European folk-cultures symbolizes this celebration. The fantastic elaboration and variation of the festival costumes of Europe also illustrate Huizinga's "play element" in relation to human life,[23] or perhaps to self-decoration that man shares with the primates.[24]

But in some folk-cultural settings the adult wore a somber formal costume for church, or more especially for communion, a costume in which he expected to be buried, suggesting not primarily joyous celebration and elaboration of the joy element in life but rather the *memento mori* that is found so frequently in Western European religion.[25]

Festival dress and everyday dress were also related structurally. Many elements of the festival dress have "graduated," in a manner of speaking, or have been "promoted" from work dress to festival status. One of these is the apron, which in festival form continued to be worn as part of the public dress of women well into the nineteenth century. Theories of the origin of the apron range from the suggestion that it was woman's original dress, a repetition and late echo of the pristine figleaf, to a festive ornament with possible symbolic meaning,

22. Von Ogden Vogt, *Art & Religion* (New Haven, 1929).

23. Johan Huizinga, *Homo Ludens,* any edition, for analysis of clothing as ornament before and after the French Revolution.

24. Ruth Benedict, "Dress," *Encyclopedia of the Social Sciences* 5: 235–38; also Mary E. Roach, *Dress, Adornment and the Social Order* (New York, 1965).

25. Martha Bringemeier, "Die Abendmahlskleidung der Frauen." See n. 11.

with the midpoint reached in the work apron which had functional meaning.[26]

Occupational dress is another differentiating area of folk costume. Within the folk community there are many specialized forms of work dress. Special craftsmen traditionally had some aspects of dress that set them apart—the leather aprons of the cobblers and blacksmiths, the specific dress of the miller, the butcher, the baker, and, if not the candlestick maker, other village specialists. Analogues of these craftsmen's costumes, from another level of culture, still may be observed in modern society, including judges' wigs and gowns in England and academic gowns and pulpit robes in the United States.[27] These suggest status as well as role.

It is important, then, that we see dress in relation to the folk community as a whole. Richard Weiss has expressed this in relation to the rites of passage:

The most important steps or stages of the individual biography become therefore community affairs, because they are construed as transitions from one group of the village community into another group. Birth is the passage into the community of the living, which is followed by entrance into the Christian community; then comes the passage from childhood into the group of single youth, which today is connected with the end of schooling, confirmation, earlier with entrance into active citizenship and military duty; the highly significant passage of marriage is next, with entrance into the married group, which in original folklife was strongly divided from the unmarried; the most significant and most mysterious passage is that into the mighty community of the dead. With this last passage the circle of individual presence is closed and rounds itself out, to begin anew in the reborn grandchild (Middle High German *enenkel–kleinen ahn, grossväterchen*) and to add a new member to the chain.[28]

Connecting the rites of passage to costume, a Swedish scholar has recently pointed out that the tendency to concretize abstract concepts in primitive thinking gave costume a strong symbolic value in connection with these great milestones in the life cycle.[29] This symbolization through costume produced the baptismal and sponsor costumes, the confirmation dress, the wedding garments, the shroud—all of them

26. For the "history" of the apron see H. Mützel, *Vom Lendenschurz zur Modetracht* (1925); and Ruth Klein, *Lexikon der Mode* (Baden-Baden, 1950), pp. 337 ff. For the significance of the apron in folk-culture see the *Handwörterbuch des deutschen Aberglaubens* 7, cols. 1,364–78.

27. America's attempts to develop "diplomatic dress" in the early Republic are detailed in Robert Ralph Davis, Jr., "Diplomatic Plumage: American Court Dress in the Early National Period," *American Quarterly* 20 (Summer 1968): 164–79.

28. Weiss, *Volkskunde der Schweiz*, p. 174.

29. Anna-Maja Nylen, "Kleidung," in *Schwedische Volkskunde* (Stockholm, 1961), p. 364.

14–2. Costume of the Mexican *Vaquero*. This is taken from Frederick Remington's "A Rodeo at Los Ojos," *Harper's New Monthly Magazine* 88:526 (March 1894) : 520. Photograph: Henry Glassie.

outer signs for the stages through which man passes in life and of his connection at each stage with his community. The criss-cross of community relationships in the clothing rituals of the rite of baptism is accented in the following passage from a Danish source:

At the baptism the godmother was the most important person—next to the child, of course. As a rule the mother did not attend the church ceremony. The godmother had to provide the christening clothes, and some much favoured godmothers laid in a stock of these which they used for all their godchildren. However, it was also common practice to hire the christening clothes from the wife of the parson or from the midwife. The godmother was usually an unmarried relative, but sometimes a married woman stood sponsor. If she was herself with child she had to wear two aprons during the christening ceremony, otherwise the child she sponsored would take the strength and happiness out of her foetus. The baptism was a very solemn affair requiring the finest clothes.[30]

In folk culture the focus is of course not on the individual but upon the community. This is one of the unwritten laws of folk costume, that the individual is not completely free to express his individuality in his dress, but rather his dress must indicate his conforming participation in his age, sex, and status groups within the unified community. In a very real sense the purpose of folk costume within the folk community is to deindividualize the individual.

This unity of the folk community, and the submergence of individual to community values, was once very graphically displayed to me. In Lancaster County, Pennsylvania, one summer Sunday, I was invited to visit the services of the Old Order Mennonites in the hill country back of Ephrata. Since the services did not begin until eight-thirty, I got there at eight, parked my car (the only one in the meetinghouse grove that morning), and waited until the congregation gathered from their farms in horse-drawn carriages, from a radius up to five miles distant. The fathers hitched their horses in the horse sheds that surrounded the grove on several sides, and the families separated, the young boys and girls seeking out their counterparts, while the married women, the young married men, and finally the older men and the older women formed separate groups. When it came time to begin the service, the age and sex groups entered the meetinghouse, from the young boys to the elders and ministers, who

30. Ellen Andersen, *Folk Costumes in Denmark: Pictures and Descriptions of Local Dresses in the National Museum* (Copenhagen, 1952), p. 5. Ellen Andersen's larger work, *Danske Bónders Klaededragt* (Copenhagen: Carit Andersens Forlag, 1960), is in my opinion the model European study of traditional rural dress, discussing historical, regional, and topical elements, superbly illustrated with photographs, genre paintings, and sketches. The volume contains an English summary, pp. 469–99.

were the last to enter, and after hanging their broad-brimmed hats on hooks above the foresinger's table, all sat down and sang the first German hymn. In the meetinghouse, a strict separation of men and women was kept, and within the separation the age groups seemed to be seated together. In other words, in the folk community as well as in the church there are age and sex divisions that are traditionally recognized—divisions long since given up in our modern urban society. The individual is subsumed under the folk community, and even in the church this structure of the folk community is symbolized. Families do not sit together as in a contemporary church or synagogue, but individuals in the church family sit in their appropriate age and sex category.

Another American religious group that operated to divide its age and sex groups, folk-cultural fashion, by costume differentiation, were the colonial Moravians. Count Zinzendorf divided his congregations into the "choir" system, or classes according to age and sex. The "choirs" were those of the children, the older girls, the single sisters, the married sisters and brethren, the widows and widowers, and the older boys and single brethren. Each of these had its own dormitory and duties, separated from the other choirs, with stated meetings of its own, although all the choirs assembled together for general church occasions. The sisters wore a uniform costume of gray or brown, and white ,for special festivals. While the sisters' costume was uniform from the girls' choir to the widows' choir, and all wore the *Schnebelhaube* or cornered cap, the color of the cap-ribbon, by which the cap was tied under the chin, designated to which choir the wearer belonged. Thus the children's caps had red ribbons; those of the older girls, light red; those of the single sisters, pink; those of the married sisters, blue; and the widows wore a white bow.

These ribbon bows were of great importance, and had quite a ritual of their own. The older girls, who wore the light red ribbons, were invested with the pink bow of the single sisters by the Deaconess of that choir in the solitude of her room upon the occasion of their entrance into that choir. When a single sister entered into the happy state of matrimony, she went to the ceremony wearing her cap tied with its pink bow. Immediately after the pastor's wife, who was always Deaconess of the married sisters, took charge of the bride, retired with her to the vestry, and invested her with the dignity of the blue bow. After which they rejoined the company, and all repaired to the place where the feast was spread.

"And," the same historian continues, "when the sad occasion came to wear the white bow of widowhood, it was the Deaconess of the widows who put the symbolic ribbon in its place, a mournful privilege requiring much gentleness, and consideration, but also with a solemn joy; for the Moravian belief is that there is no 'death'; it is 'being called home,' and so it was spoken of."[31]

The white of widowhood in this case is related to white as the earlier mourning color, a matter on which European scholarship has put much attention. Hottenroth with his culture-historical approach sees the origin of white mourning in the French court ceremonial of the fifteenth century; Zelenin suggests a racial theory, attributing its European use to East Slavic custom; while Mathilde Hain makes the reasonable suggestion that perhaps the white mourning comes from a still more primitive culture level, where white, as the natural color of wool and linen, became the symbol of death.[32] For these, but perhaps also for other reasons, some fanatically "plain" Quakers in the eighteenth century, in Ireland and the American colonies, refused to dress in dyed garments while living, for dyeing of garments, said John Woolman, led to hypocrisy since the dyeing enabled the wearer to "hide the dirt in the cloth."[33]

COSTUME RESEARCH IN THE UNITED STATES

Costume research in the United States, which compared to Europe is only in its rudimentary stages, can profitably look at historical, regional, ethnic, occupational, and sectarian costumes.

Of historical costumes two are of particular importance, colonial costume and frontier costume. Colonial costume research is important as showing the naturalization here of European styles as well as costumes. The field is a rich one, and while in some cases romanticists have carried their claims for separate ethnic costumes too far (I doubt, for instance, that there ever was an American "Huguenot" costume, as some costume historians have claimed), we do have New England, Holland Dutch, Pennsylvania German, southern Atlantic, southwest Spanish, and backcountry costume to study in early American historical documentation.

31. Elizabeth Lehman Myers, *A Century of Moravian Sisters: A Record of Christian Community Life* (New York, 1918), pp. 37–38. A similar hierarchy is reported from Hessen, where in certain costume areas red is permitted only for the youth and the unmarried, blue and green are the colors for married people, with gray and black for the aged (Mathilde Hain, "Die Volkstrachten," in *Deutsche Philologie im Aufriss* 3, Wolfgang Stammler, ed., 2d ed., col. 2,890).

32. Mathilde Hain, "Die Volkstrachten," *Deutsche Philologie im Aufriss* 3, Wolfgang Stammler, ed., 2d ed., cols. 2,892–93.

33. John Woolman, *A Journal of the Life, Gospel Labours and Christian Experiences, of that Faithful Minister of Jesus Christ, John Woolman* (Philadelphia, 1873), pp. 205–6. There were so many colonial Friends who held similar views that they were called "White Quakers." A sect known as the Nicholites on the Eastern Shore also dressed in white; see Kenneth Lang Carroll, *Joseph Nichols and the Nicholites: A Look at the "New Quakers" of Maryland, Delaware, North and South Carolina* (Easton, Maryland, 1962).

The backwoods or Appalachian frontier costume is interesting for its partial adaptation of Indian elements. One of the first native historians describes for us the dress on the Appalachian frontier:

The hunting shirt was universally worn. This was a kind of loose frock, reaching half way down the thighs, with large sleeves open before, and so wide as to lap over a foot or more when belted. The cap was large, and sometimes handsomely fringed with a ravelled piece of cloth of a different color from that of the hunting shirt itself. The bosom of this dress served as a wallet to hold a chunk of bread, cakes, jerk, tow for wiping the barrel of the rifle, or any other necessity for the hunter or warrior. The belt, which was always tied behind, answered several purposes, besides that of holding the dress together. In cold weather the mittens, and sometimes the bullet-bag, occupied the front part of it. From the right side was suspended the tomahawk and to the left the scalping knife in its leathern sheath. The hunting shirt was generally made of linsey, sometimes of coarse linen, and a few of dressed deer skins. These last were very cold and uncomfortable in wet weather. The shirt and jacket were of the common fashion. A pair of drawers or breeches and leggings were the dress of the thighs and legs: a pair of moccasins answered for the feet much better than shoes. These were made of dressed deer skin. They were mostly made of a single piece with a gathering seam along the top of the foot, and another from the bottom of the heel, without gathers as high as the ankle joint or a little higher. Flaps were left on each side to reach some distance up the legs. These were nicely adapted to the ankles and lower part of the leg by thongs of deer skin, so that no dust, gravel or snow could get within the moccasin.[34]

Doddridge also tells us that during the latter years of the Indian war "our young men became more enamored of the Indian dress throughout, with the exception of the matchcoat." The young frontiersman even adopted the Indian breech clout, and "instead of being abashed by this nudity was proud of his Indianlike dress. In some few instances I have seen them go into places of public worship in this dress. Their appearance, however, did not add much to the devotion of the young ladies."[35]

Despite the case for such Indian elements of costume as the hunting shirt, the moccasin, and the snowshoe, which earlier historians played up in their frontier school historiography, later analysis, especially that by scholars working on acculturation theory, has shown that at least some of the elements adopted by the frontiersmen

---

34. Joseph Doddridge, *Notes on the Settlement and Indian Wars of the Western Parts of Virginia and Pennsylvania from 1763 to 1783, inclusive, together with a Review of the State of Society and Manners of the First Settlers of the Western Country,* 3d ed. (Pittsburgh, 1912), pp. 91–92. The first edition of this invaluable work appeared at Shepherdstown, [West] Virginia, in 1824.

35. Ibid., pp. 92–93. For comparative materials see Elizabeth W. Loosley, "Early Canadian Costume," *Canadian Historical Review* 23 (1942): 349–62.

had originals or analogues in European dress. A. Irving Hallowell, in analyzing Indian influences on early American culture, writes of the moccasin:

> The history of the humble moccasin is less well known than corn, and presents special problems of its own. For here, too, although we need to consider the frontier situation and the conditions under which direct borrowing occurred, there are considerations other than purely pragmatic ones to be evaluated. Among them is the fact that the moccasin was a fitted type of footgear belonging to the same area of tailored clothing in the Northern Hemisphere from which Europeans came. Perhaps this fact is related to the later transformation of the moccasin into the commercialized moccasin-type shoe in present-day American culture.[36]

He also points out the delightful fact that in the 1880s, when the ancestors of the present commercially produced "moccasins" (now called "loafers") appeared in trade catalogues, they were known as "wigwam slippers."

The hunting shirt bears a distinct resemblance to the work smock of the English countryman,[37] the *Kittel* of the European peasant. Wilmer Atkinson, editor of the influential *Farm Journal* from its foundation in 1877, wrote of the hunting shirt in his autobiography:

> We workers around the stables and in the fields used to wear hunting shirts to keep us clean. We did this always when we milked. This was a garment, I believe, that did not differ from the one worn by the Continental soldiers in the Revolutionary army at the beginning of the war.

And in his reformist and editorial capacity he added, "Why present-day farmers should ever allow this garment to go into the discard I am unable to say."[38]

These relations of Indian hunting shirt, countryman's smock, European peasant *Kittel*, American drover's smock, and the ubiquitous nineteenth-century work-jacket called the "wammus"[39] deserve thorough researching. Especially important will be the sorting out of the relative influence of traditional European and Indian elements.

The simplicities and egalitarianism of the Age of Homespun broke up when class lines began to form again. Thurlow Weed, looking

36. A. Irving Hallowell, "The Impact of the American Indian on American Culture," *American Anthropologist* 59 (April, 1957): 206.

37. For the smock in England see Anne Buck, "The Countryman's Smock," *Folk Life* 1 (1963): 16–33.

38. Wilmer Atkinson, *An Autobiography* (Philadelphia, 1920), pp. 53–54.

39. The "wammus" was a work jacket. The word, which was still used in some parts of the country in the early twentieth century, is related to both German *Wams* and Dutch *Wammes*; for the Dutch background see E. C. Llewellyn, *The Influences of Low Dutch on the English Vocabulary* (London, 1936), Publications of the Philological Society, 12.

back on his boyhood on the upper Susquehanna frontier in New York shortly after 1800, has given us a graphic picture of the tensions over style in a frontier community:

> During my residence there, Mr. Wattles [a sub land agent] moved in[to] the neighborhood. They were, for that region, rather "stylish" people, and became obnoxious to a good deal of remark. One thing that excited especial indignation was, that persons going to the house were asked to clean their shoes at the door, a scraper having been placed there for that purpose. A maiden lady (Miss Theodosia Wattles) rendered herself especially obnoxious to the spinster neighbors, by "dressing up" week-day afternoons. They all agreed in saying she was a "proud, stuck-up thing." In those days, "go-to-meeting clothes" were reserved for Sundays.[40]

There is a great deal of social history wrapped up in the still extant American expression "dressed up," or "all dressed up," which implies that one's normal state of dress is work dress or everyday dress.

As the "frontier experience" continued in American history on successive frontiers almost to the end of the nineteenth century, there were of course many successive frontier costumes. The Indian-influenced dress of the old Appalachian frontier was only one of these. To contemporary television audiences, "frontier" means that never-never land of the TV Western, which has achieved a stylized version of Rocky Mountain frontier dress of the period 1865–1900. This dress ranks in authenticity with the use in Westerns of anachronistic twentieth-century limp-covered Holy Bibles, crosses on nineteenth-century sectarian churches, and other anachronisms too numerous to mention.

Speaking of anachronisms, eastern seaboard towns of colonial foundation have been invaded recently by a stylized "Pioneer Day" costume donned by local residents on town anniversary celebrations. In connection with these celebrations, local men vie in growing Civil War beards and show their interest in authentic historic costume by wearing string ties and little stiff-crowned hats. The beard-growing fraternity (nonconformists are fined) is referred to in the advertisements as "Brothers of the Brush." The women compete with the men by wearing long dresses (from assorted historical periods) and uniform flowered sunbonnets (strictly nontraditional for formal nineteenth-century dress). Tableaux of these costumed "pioneers" ride triumphantly through town on flowery floats and after the anniversary the beards quickly disappear. The point is that these stylized Western costumes have little or nothing to do with the Eastern areas, or they are anachronisms in terms of the colonial or early nineteenth-century

40. Letter of the Hon. Thurlow Weed, 1858, in H. C. Goodwin, *Pioneer History; or, Cortland County and the Border Wars of New York. From the Earliest Period to the Present Time* (New York, 1859), p. 242.

foundations of the towns involved. All this costumed fakelore, comparable to the postcard "national costume" of Wales,[41] is sponsored by tourism and occasionally engineered by commercial outfits who painlessly plan everything for the natives from the advertising to the string ties.

Regional costumes of the American past include French-Canadian and Cajun, New England, Holland Dutch, Pennsylvania German, southern, southwestern, and others. Most of these have now only historical importance, as the carrying groups either merged with the general population (Holland Dutch) or became Americanized in costume and fashion (Pennsylvania German). But in colonial travel accounts regional differences were noted, as for instance the Polish traveler who in 1798 described the "German" costume of the old ladies of Frederick, Maryland. "Though even the oldest inhabitant was born in America," he tells us, "nevertheless by dress and way of life it is easy to recognize them as Germans and even to place them as Germans of the sixteenth century. Old women, with coifs tied under their chins, wear on top of them large white hats without crowns like huge flat plates. The men have long, wide linen trousers."[42]

Most of these regional or regional ethnic costumes were defunct by the 1820s, and were for the most part replaced by general dress styles. The nearest thing to an American folk dress in the mid-nineteenth century was farm dress. By the 1820s an identifiable "American farmer" costume had developed—broad-brimmed hat, long trousers with suspenders, white shirt, work-vest, and heavy work-shoes. This outfit appears in the prints of the pre-Civil War era. Its place was taken after the Civil War by the familiar "bib overalls," which were made of differing materials until in the twentieth century blue denim came into style. Blue denim is now old-fashioned for farm use in many areas (but de rigeur, by way of Jimmy Dean, in both the college and the hippie crowd). At the time the overalls were introduced, conservative older farmers (the writer's Pennsylvania German grandfather among them) refused to submit to the new style, preferring to wear the nineteenth-century work costume into the twentieth century. Today another stage has been reached in farm dress with a new synthesis. Today most American farmers, except in Appalachia and the Deep South, wear proletarian dress of matching green or gray shirt-

41. For the curious story of the partly artificial, partly commercially inspired development of a Welsh concept of "national costume" see the important article by Francis G. Payne, "Welsh Peasant Costume," *Folk Life* 2 (1964) : 42–57.

42. Julian Ursyn Niemcewicz, *Under Their Vine and Fig Tree: Travels Through America in 1797–1799, 1805 with some further account of life in New Jersey*, trans. and ed. by Metchie J. E. Budka (Elizabeth, N. J., 1965) , p. 112; see also fig. 48.

and-trouser ensembles and yellow engineer's boots, which can scarcely be distinguished from urban factory workers or gasoline station attendants.

In the nineteenth century this American pre-overall farm dress was used to satirize the farmer on the American stage. It was in this period that city people spoke of "countrified" dress and manners, and referred to farmers as "hayseeds," "rubes," and "country jakes." If the stage character had a twang accent as well as countrified clothing, he was a satire on the New England farmer, as New England was the popular-culture symbol for American rurality in general in the Currier and Ives age. This satirization of the American farmer through his less-than-fashionable dress continued into the twentieth century—witness the long series of humorous covers on the *Saturday Evening Post,* the *Country Gentleman,* and other family magazines in the period 1900–25.

One of the hardiest of regional costume patterns, in fact one of the only identifiably regional American costumes of the present, is the southwestern costume, worn by Texans and other residents of the southwestern plains and Rocky Mountain states. As the "cowboy" costume it is occupational as well as regional.[43] It consists in one of the standard versions of "Texan" hats—lighter in color and broader of brim than current fashion-level hats—decorated cowboy boots, tight pants, and denim jackets. Texan hats, of course, are also worn with standard business suits as the one element identifying the wearer as Texan.

Of the other occupational costumes in American history, we need specific studies of the dress of lumberjacks, sailors and boatmen, such as the Jersey and Chesapeake "watermen." In addition to detailed study of farm dress in every American region, we are wanting studies of the dress of special tradesmen, such as butchers, bakers, millers, carpenters and others. Even the long history of ministerial dress in this country deserves investigation.

Ethnic costumes deserve study too. In most cases the ethnic costumes of the late-nineteenth- and early-twentieth-century emigrants from southern and eastern Europe were not transplanted, except for their recent revival among folk dance groups. With these emigrants, even though uprooted, in Oscar Handlin's phrase, from peasant

---

43. The relation of the cowboy's costume and equipment to the work dress of the Spanish colonial *vaquero* is an important area of folk costume research in the United States. On this problem see Jose R. Benitez, *El Traje y El Adorno en Mexico, 1500–1910* (Guadalajara, 1946); and Jo Mora, *Californios: The Saga of the Hard-Riding Vaqueros, America's First Cowboys* (Garden City, N. Y., 1949). For the related Gaucho tradition in South America see the recent study of René Burri and Jose Luis Lanuza, *The Gaucho* (New York, 1968).

matrices in Europe, their clothing was the first element of their culture that changed markedly.[44] Using Richard Weiss's rule that peasant use modifies even ready-made clothing, some characteristic dress habits developed. A recent study of an Italian-American community (1890–1915) pointed out that "regardless of season, they [the men] wore large-brimmed hats or caps of all shapes, short-collared shirts usually buttoned at the neck and often at the sleeves. They often wore wide suspenders and some wore both belts and suspenders." Like the Swiss peasant already referred to, "the men were rarely seen outside and often inside the house without a cap or hat." Peasant frugality still regulated clothing consumption:

Men's clothing was generally purchased at nearby stores, or it was tailor-made. Women's dress was made by an Italian seamstress or else by the women themselves. It was generally agreed that clothing was only purchased when necessary, i.e., when the material could not support patching or when the newer clothes became so worn that they could not be used for dress and so were used for work.

Some Italian elements continued. Women wore woolen shawls as a head and shoulder covering, "generally knitted at home or brought from Italy." Babies were wrapped in swaddling—remaining "rolled like a 'papoose' until he or she was a year old in order to be sure the spine developed correctly." Little boys were dressed in skirts "until they were accustomed to using the toilet." New clothes were bought for weddings and other important celebrations. An Italian old-country touch was seen in the Delabole Band, which wore hats with large black plumes that set off their bright red and black uniforms. The women and one of the men wore gold earrings. Cosmetics were not worn by the mothers, and "young girls could expect a beating for wearing them." The women generally wore their long hair braided or in knobs, while the men "invariably wore moustaches but seldom a beard." As soon as a baby girl was born it was customary to pierce its ears, the mother or the midwife performing the operation. The investigator was able to find little "status difference with regard to dress in the early settlement." "Indeed," he writes, "pretensions to superiority wittingly or unwittingly made were topics of local gossip and scorn."[45]

Sectarian costume in the United States has many analogies with European peasant costume. Since I have treated this subject in great

---

44. Philip M. Rose, *The Italians in America* (New York: George H. Doran Company, 1922), p. 65, from Emily Fogg Meade, "The Italian on the Land," *U.S. Bulletin of Labor*, 1907, pp. 507 ff.

45. Clement Valletta, "Italian Immigrant Life in Northampton County, Pennsylvania, 1890–1915, Part II," *Pennsylvania Folklife* 15 (Autumn 1965): 43–44.

14–3. A Hasidic Jew wearing the traditional garb from eastern Europe walking in the Williamsburg section of Brooklyn, now a common sight since the post-World War II immigration to New York. Photograph by Jerome Mintz, 1967.

detail elsewhere,[46] I shall here summarize briefly its significance for the United States. Religious groups, very often combined with ethnic group status, whether vicinally segregated from the larger society or living within that society, form distinct communities analogous to traditional peasant communities of Europe. As in peasant culture, costumes are worn as symbols—to designate, first, the community member in his rejection of the outside world, second, to deindividualize that individual within the community, and third, to designate the individual's status within the community. Whether we are dealing with the habits of the Roman Catholic monastic communities, the archaic eastern European costumes of the Hasidic Jews of Williamsburg and elsewhere, or the dress of the "plain" sects (Mennonites, Amish, Brethren) in Pennsylvania German culture, sectarian costumes illustrate the functionalist rationale for all traditional costumes that we have outlined above. While some of these garbs may not immediately appear related to the "folk" category of costume, all of them are prescribed by the community and their forms are determined by the traditions of that community. In some cases, perhaps only one element of differentiation marks the wearer as sectarian, as for example the "Pentecostal hairdo" that I am told by the staff of the Norse Folk Museum at Oslo in Norway can be traced to the invasion of American Pentecostal sects in the nineteenth century. The same sort of minimal "badge" is found among the Seventh Day Adventists in Germany, according to a recent study of the sect from the folk-cultural standpoint.[47] Sectarian costume in the United States is a fruitful topic for research.

COSTUME AND FOLKLIFE STUDIES

In summary, costume is one of our most important indicators and symbols of folk community. In teaching, we can use traditional costume as a departure point for discussing the structure of the folk society, for relating the little society to the larger world of fashion outside, and for considering the impact of religion on individual and community life.

We have left until last the relation of clothing to the work patterns of the community, from the preparation of garments from flax and wool culture to the finished product. The manufacture of clothing

46. "Sectarian Costume Research in the United States," a paper delivered at the 1968 Folklife Conference at Utah State University, Logan, appears in the symposium *Forms upon the Frontier* (Logan, Utah, 1969). See also "Plain Dutch and Gay Dutch: Two Worlds in the Dutch Country," *The Pennsylvania Dutchman* 8 (Summer 1956) : 34–55.

47. Irmgard Simon, *Die Gemeinschaft der Siebenten-Tags-Adventisten in volkskundlicher Sicht* (Münster/Westfalen, 1965).

14–4. American women's sectarian dress of the nineteenth century:
A) Quaker: this engraving represents the Quaker minister Rachel Hicks, of Long Island. Photograph: Don Yoder.

B) Shaker: this illustration, entitled "Sisters in Everyday Costume," comes from "The Shakers," *Harper's New Monthly Magazine* 15:86 (July 1857) : 170. Photograph: Henry Glassie.

C) Dunker: this depiction of "A Dunker Sister" is taken from Nelson Lloyd, "Among the Dunkers," *Scribner's Magazine* 30:5 (November 1901) : 515. Photograph: Henry Glassie.

gives us insight into large areas of the material culture of a folk community, such as the technology involved in the spinning and weaving processes, and the tools of this technology: the flax break, the heckle, the carding comb, the spinning wheel, the reel, the loom, the fulling mill, and the woolen mill. In textile research (design, woodblock printing, watering, dyeing) folk costume research shades over into the decorative arts. Wool-culture and flax-culture branch into ecology and cultural geography, and we can study their historical impact on specific regions such as Wales, Scotland, and Ireland.

The study of costume as personal adornment gets us into basic human drives and wider anthropological studies. Most of the courses taught thus far in the folk arts include costume as one of the arts, and properly so. Costume and religion are related at many points in the old traditional cultures. Costume and recreation are related too in such institutions in Europe as the *Spinnstube*, and the American frontier "waulking frolic" or "kicking match," when woolen cloth was put through a primitive fulling process, before the advent of the fulling mill.

For the twentieth-century American, there is also perhaps another basic value in costume research. It teaches us something of the formative pioneer period of our country's history, that age when clothing as well as every other aspect of material culture was produced within the community, the age that uses costume as its symbol—the Age of Homespun.

Finally, the study of costume can give us, like all historical studies, wider perspectives on present-day phenomena that have appeared in Europe and the United States and are often misunderstood. Dress as a symbol of nonconformity has appeared often before in history; we have had "Beatle" haircuts before; men's costumes and ornaments have in other ages and other cultural matrices matched some of the mod and hippy costumes of today. In the first part of the nineteenth century, for example, European and American males, in making a valiant protest against the drab masculine dress that threatened to become normal in the wake of the French Revolution, created the "Dandy" or "Macaroni" dress, which scandalized the middle classes and the proper element. Like most historical waves of fashion, it left its eventual mark on men's clothing. The cape overcoat of the Philadelphia "Dandy" of 1820 is still worn today. In somewhat plainer cut, it is the cape overcoat worn by the older patriarchs of the most conservative costume group in the United States, the Old Order Amish.

Today the Age of Homespun seems very remote. With the fundamental changes in life and living that the twentieth century has made normal in every area of the civilized world, there is today little room for the traditional in dress. Where it still exists, folk costume in the narrow, academic sense of the word has become more old-fashioned, more out of place than it was before the First World War, in those days when the town boys mocked the green-coated farmers as they strode into the Franconian towns. The modern forces of urbanization, commercialization, and rationalization have on the one hand dissolved the very sense of folk community, and on the other have forced the individual to submit to general styles as represented in ready-made clothing. All this is symbolized in the proletarianizing of rural dress—a worldwide phenomenon of the present century.

An earlier European historian of folk costume, in reviewing the decline of the folk costume world at the turn of our century, put it this way, and we will close with his words:

> The last short hour of the peasant costumes cannot now be very far away. Let us hope that when they are gone, the essence will not have perished with the shell, the meaning of the life they symbolized with the symbol of that life.[48]

Bibliography and Selected Readings

Benedict, Ruth. "Dress." *Encyclopedia of the Social Sciences* 5: 235–38.

Buck, Anne. "The Countryman's Smock." *Folk Life* 1 (1963) : 16–34. Typology and history of the embroidered smock-frock in rural England, worn by farmers, wagoners, shepherds, and others for work and holiday, and its structural relation to the shirt. Photographs and pattern drawings.

Cordry, Donald and Dorothy. *Mexican Indian Costumes.* Austin: University of Texas Press, 1968. Analysis of Mexican dress from pre-Columbian times to the present, presented with superb photography, and basic analysis of textiles, patterns, and structure of individual costume items. The finest costume study to come thus far from American scholarship.

Craig, Hazel Thompson. *Clothing: A Comprehensive Study.* Philadelphia: J. B. Lippincott Company, 1968. A textbook for classes in home economics, presenting basic materials for beginners, on the origin and evolution of clothing (chaps. 1–3), fashion and the garment industry (chaps. 4–7), and the social and psychological aspects of clothing (chaps. 8–11). Well-illustrated.

Crawley, A. E. "Dress." *Encyclopedia of Religion and Ethics* 5: 40–72.

Cunningham, Phillis, and C. Willett. *Handbook of English Costume in the Eighteenth Century.* Philadelphia: Dufour Editions, 1957. One of a series, projected in England by Faber and Faber, treating the centuries since the sixteenth. The evidence analyzed is from actual garments in

48. Paraphrased from Jostes, *Westfälisches Trachtenbuch*, p. 167.

museums and private collections, portraiture, literary references, private accounts, letters, diaries, and periodicals.

———, and Catherine Lucas. *Occupational Costume in England from the Eleventh Century to 1914*. London: Black, 1967. A basic, well-illustrated treatment of work dress, a subject neglected in many costume surveys.

Earle, Alice Morse. *Two Centuries of Costume in America MDCXX– MDCCCXX*. 2 vols. in one. New York: Macmillan Company, 1910. Chatty historical essays, documented within the text, dealing with most phases of American dress.

Gummere, Amelia Mott. *The Quaker: A Study in Costume*. Philadelphia: Ferris and Leach, 1901. The best study of sectarian costume in England and the United States.

Hain, Mathilde. *Das Lebensbild eines oberhessischen Trachtendorfes. Von bäuerlicher Tracht und Gemeinschaft*. Marburg, 1936. This book, which applied the sociological method to folk costume in Hessian rural communities, shifted the direction of German folk costume research from the earlier culture-history orientation to the community-based approach.

Hiler, Hilaire and Meyer. *Bibliography of Costume: A Dictionary Catalog of About Eight Thousand Books and Periodicals*. Ed. by Helen Grant Cushing. New York: H. W. Wilson Company, 1939. One of the most useful bibliographies in English on costume research, preceded by an essay on "Costumes and Ideologies."

Hottenroth, Friedrich. *Handbuch der deutschen Tracht*. Stuttgart, 1896. This lengthy treatment of all levels and types of German costume from the Middle Ages to the nineteenth century is essentially oriented to the older cultural or art history approach that viewed folk costumes as ensembles of historical relics.

Kiener, Franz. *Kleidung, Mode und Mensch: Versuch einer psychologischen Deutung*. Munich-Basel: Ernst Reinhardt Verlag, 1956. Includes chapters on nudity, shame, and morality; protective clothing; clothing as ornament; the psychology of colors, forms, and materials; and discussion of the psychology of individual clothing items.

Kybalova, Ludmila; Olga Herbenova; and Milena Lamarova. *The Pictorial Encyclopedia of Fashion*. Translated by Claudia Rosoux. New York: Crown Publishers, 1968. The best recent one-volume historical survey of clothing in the Western world, from ancient Egypt to the twentieth century. Technically perfect illustrations reproduced from every possible historical source illuminate a sound text that offers a chronological periodization plus a series of topical chapters on everything from beards and hair styles to liturgical vestments.

Loosley, Elizabeth W. "Early Canadian Costume." *Canadian Historical Review* 23 (1942): 349–62. Materials for comparative study of the pioneer period costumes of Canada and the United States.

Lucas, Anthony T. "Cloth Finishing in Ireland." *Folk Life* 6 (1968): 18–67. Historical, technological, and ethnographic data on the fulling process, by the director of the National Museum of Ireland; illustrated.

McClintock, H. F. *Old Irish & Highland Dress and That of the Isle of Man.* 2d and enlarged ed. Dundalk: Dundalgan Press (W. Tempest), Ltd., 1950. Model study based on historical descriptions and pictorial sources. See also the same author's *Old Highland Dress and Tartans.* Dundalk, 1949.

Payne, F. G. "Welsh Peasant Costume." *Folk Life* 2 (1964) : 42–57. An important study analyzing the place romanticism and tourism had in creating the so-called national costume of Wales.

Richardson, Jane, and A. L. Kroeber. *Three Centuries of Women's Dress Fashions: A Quantitative Analysis.* Berkeley and Los Angeles: University of California Press, 1940. *Anthropological Records* 5: 111–153. Valuable for its scientific investigation of the "fashion cycle" theory, which involves the alternation of the "bell," "back fullness," and "tubular" styles in women's fashion from the eighteenth to the twentieth centuries.

Roach, Mary Ellen, and Joanne Eicher. *Dress, Adornment and the Social Order.* New York: Wiley and Sons, Inc., 1965. Competent introduction to the sociology of dress.

Rubens, Alfred. *A History of Jewish Costume.* New York: Funk and Wagnalls, 1967. A comprehensive survey of Jewish dress, secular, religious, and symbolic, from earliest times to the present. Beautifully illustrated.

Sapir, Edward. "Fashion." *Encyclopedia of the Social Sciences* 6: 139–44.

Vincent, John Martin. *Costume and Conduct in the Laws of Basel, Bern, and Zurich 1370–1800.* Baltimore: Johns Hopkins Press, 1935. The only good study in English of European sumptuary laws in relation to dress.

Yoder, Don. "Sectarian Costume Research in the United States." In *Forms upon the Frontier: Folklife and Folk Arts of the United States,* edited by Austin and Alta Fife and Henry H. Glassie, pp. 41–75. Logan: Utah State University Press, 1969. An analysis of the place of sectarian costume in Hasidic Judaism, Roman Catholic monastic orders, and Protestant "plain" sects, summarizing research on the subject and offering theories of the origin of sectarian dress.

15 FOLK COOKERY
Don Yoder

INTRODUCTION: FOOD IN FOLK CULTURE

Folk cookery can be readily defined as traditional domestic cookery marked by regional variation. As everyday, domestic, family cookery based on regional tradition, it is obviously the opposite of the commercial, institutional, and scientific-nutritional versions of cookery. Diffused regionally into folk-cultural "provinces," it varies from both national and international cuisines. The study of folk cookery includes the study of the foods themselves, their morphology, their preparation, their preservation, their social and psychological functions, and their ramifications into all other aspects of folk-culture. For the total cookery complex, including attitudes, taboos, and meal systems—the whole range of cookery and food habits in a society—Honigman's term "foodways" has become useful.[1]

Folk cookery as a research field within the discipline of folklife studies, an area of such obvious and basic relevance for everyday life,

---

1. John J. Honigman, *Foodways in a Muskeg Community* (Ottawa, 1961).

has been strangely neglected in the United States. Folklorists have scarcely touched it except for "collecting" a few miscellaneous recipes in connection with other fieldwork. Historians have scarcely looked at it either, except for the discussion of pioneer and frontier cookery in our older county histories and descriptions of middle-class table manners by social historians. Home economists have touched it only tangentially, counting calories and pursuing invisible vitamins, for their task has been that of the reformer and diet-prescriber and traditional foods and foodways have been for them only evidence of the unprogressive past. The most valuable work in folk cookery done thus far has been that of our cultural anthropologists, who, however, have normally concentrated on areas outside the United States.

European folk-cultural scholarship, on the other hand, has recognized the basic place of cookery in folklife. Starting from their regionally oriented bases, European scholars of the present century have produced impressive studies on folk foods, folk methods of food preparation, the use of foods in the home, the storage of food products, the names of dishes, the meal system—every phase of the relation of food to folk culture. Europe's folklife scholars have studied their national and regional cuisines through two methods, the ethnographic and the historical. As part of the national folk-cultural atlas programs that are sponsored by many European nations, the ethnographer, through questionnaire and interview programs carried on intensively over a period of decades, has determined the traditional aspects of cookery in the region under study. The historian, through investigation of the vast historical source materials that exist in Europe from the Middle Ages to the present, culls and collates references to food and foodways. From this joint ethnographic and historical research have come archives, atlases, and research monographs on many specific food subjects.

Of cross-cultural studies dealing with European and American cuisines, the first volume of *Ethnologia Scandinavica* (1971), which is devoted entirely to folk cookery, stands in the first rank and will be useful in courses dealing with the subject. The volume, in German and English, includes the papers read at the First International Symposium on Ethnological Food Research, convened at the University of Lund in August 1970 with scholars representing the Scandinavian countries, Germany, Austria, Yugoslavia, Poland, Hungary, Czechoslovakia, Bulgaria, Scotland, Ireland, France, and the United States. The papers present a wide variety of subjects, from methodological problems of foodways research and types of source materials available for their study, to analyses of the relationships of biology and culture in the problem of hunger, studies of kitchen utensils, food habits, food complexes and individual food elements, and economic treatment of food distribution and changes in food consumption patterns. The symposium grew out of the researches of Professor Bringéus of the University of Lund, and represents an important advance in scholarship on food and foodways.[2]

A few samples of the best European historical scholarship on the subject of cookery follow: J. C. Drummond and Anne Wilbraham, *The Englishman's Food: A History of Five Centuries of English Diet* (London, 1939); L. Burema, *De Voeding in Nederland van de Middeleeuwen tot de Twintigste Eeuw* (Assen, 1953); Albert Hauser, *Vom Essen und Trinken im alten Zürich: Tafelsitten, Kochkunst und Lebenshaltung vom Mittelalter bis in die Neuzeit* (Zurich, 1961); Maria Dembinska, *Konsumpcja Zymnosciowa w Polsce Sredniowiecznej* [Food Consumption in Medieval Poland] (Wroclaw-Warsawa-Krakow, 1963); and Nils-Arvid Bringéus, *Mat och Miljö: En bok om svenska kostvanor* (Lund, 1970). Several of these works cover the national areas involved from the Middle Ages to the present day, include folk cookery as well as the cookery of all national classes and groups, and use the insights of the several disciplines dealing with food and foodways.

Of the recent European studies, the most important national survey, for its combination of historical, ethnographic, and cartographic approaches, is that by Günter Wiegelmann, *Alltags- und Festspeisen: Wandel und gegenwärtige Stellung* (Marburg, 1967). Professor Wiegelmann, who has recently accepted the chair of folk-cultural studies at the University of Münster, is Germany's leading authority on folk cookery and one of Europe's leading authorities on the subject. His book is based on the materials in the *Atlas der deutschen Volkskunde* (1930–1935) and deals with four historical periods in German foodways: (1) *1500–1680*, the post-medieval period, when medieval eating habits were still in evidence; (2) *1680–1770*, the era of the appearance of new foods among the upper classes, the potato, coffee, tea, rice, and sugar, for example; (3) *1770–1850*, the era that saw the general adoption of the new foods by the country population; and (4) *1850 to the present*, the age of world trade and technical food production. The book includes twenty-six detailed diffusion maps on folk cookery, dealing with such subjects as eating out of a

2. A good introduction to the world of Swedish folkways research is furnished by Nils-Arvid Bringéus, *Mat och Miljö: En bok om svenska kostvanor* (Lund: Gleerups, 1970), Vol. 1 of the Ethnological Handbook series edited by Bringéus and Rehnberg. The book includes historical and analytical essays on a wide variety of topics. The essays are by the major Swedish scholars who have worked on the subject of Swedish diet and are all thoroughly documented as well as illustrated. The book concludes with an extensive bibliography of Swedish folk cookery research.

common dish, potato dishes served on weekdays and festival days, wedding meals, the raising of millet and its use in cuisine, the influence of coffee on folk cuisine, the influence of foreign foods such as English pudding and goulash on German folk cuisine, the names of meals and the meal system, sour dishes, salads, and so on. A fully annotated text analyzes the diffusion problems presented by the maps, and a thoroughgoing bibliography (pp. 245–61) completes the book's major reference value.

The American scholarly world has not yet produced any books on American traditional cookery that can rank in thoroughness and authoritativeness with the European examples I have named, unless it is Richard Osborn Cummings, *The American and His Food: A History of Food Habits in the United States* (Chicago, 1940). The only national survey since Cummings, *The American Heritage Cookbook and Illustrated History of American Eating & Drinking* (New York, 1964), was planned as a commercial rather than an academic book, and unfortunately lacks the usual scholarly apparatus, notes and bibliography. Of the many Latin American studies, the most complete national survey deals with Brazil, Luis da Camara Cascudo's *Historia de Alimentação no Brasil* (São Paolo, 1967), vol. 1. This volume deals with the acculturation of the three major strands in the Brazilian diet, the native Indian, African, and Portuguese foods.

It is to the European studies, then, that we must look for guidance. They show us that among the historical determinants of cookery and foodways are environment and climate; settlement history and ethnic demography; changes due to urbanization and innovations in technology; economic history; sociological factors; and religion. Considering the reaction of man to his basic natural environment, the study of folk cookery covers such subjects as the influence of environment on cuisine, seasonal foods, and local crops and local foods of the various cultural landscapes studied by cultural geographers and ecologists. The economic historian adds aspects of food distribution, in such phases as marketing, droving, and shipping, which affect the local economy and the local foodways. The agrarian historian and the historian of technology study changes in rural technology and have contributed much pertinent data on the resulting changes in foodways.[3]

3. Two studies in folk cookery, using European as well as American perspectives, are being done at present at the University of Pennsylvania under my direction. These are doctoral dissertations by Jay A. Anderson, on "Yeoman Foodways in Stuart England" (1971), and by Eleanor F. Reishtein, on "Historical Bibliography of American Regional Cookery." I am indebted to Dr. Anderson and Mrs. Reishtein for several helpful suggestions and bibliographical items in the preparation of this paper.

In our teaching we can therefore use folk cookery as a key element in folk culture, ramifying as it does into many aspects of the entire structure. The folklorist can join the historian of religion and the anthropologist in studying the relation of sacred and secular cookery, the folklore of food taboos, the psychology of foodways, and, in the wider folklife context, can profitably exchange research data with the other sociohistorical sciences mentioned above.

RESEARCH PROBLEMS IN AMERICAN FOLK COOKERY

The student of American folk cookery has two major directions to pursue: (1) the regional variation of American domestic cookery, which deserves recording, historically and ethnographically, on the scale that European folklife research has set; and (2) the comparative study of the relation of American to European folk patterns of cookery.

While Americans today seem to be developing an eclectic "American" cookery that rises above the regions, in the past our cookery, like our speech patterns and our architecture, was divided into regional versions. Examples, which we will draw upon in our discussion, are the New England, the Southern, the Appalachian, the Pennsylvania German, and the Southwest Spanish cuisines.

All of these American regional cultures shared basic foods, but because of differing ethnic backgrounds and climatic conditions, they put them to different use. All areas used, for example, that greatest of American Indian gifts to the European settler, maize, grown in Indian fashion and formalized into foods that were borrowed from Indian culture (mush, hominy, johnny cake) but were also American adaptations, a shifting key, so to speak, of basic European foods.[4] Thus, colonial Americans from the British Isles translated their basic oats or wheaten porridge into the equivalent dish made of maize— and called it "hasty pudding" in New England (because it took so long to stir it correctly for supper), "suppawn" in New York state,

4. For Indian influences on frontier cookery see Roger Williams, *A Key into the Language of America. . .*(London, 1643), reprinted in *Collections of the Rhode-Island Historical Society* 1 (1827); John Josselyn, *New-England's Rarities...* (Boston, 1865); Fulmer Mood, "John Winthrop, Jr., on Indian Corn," *New England Quarterly* 10 (1937): 121–33; Clark Wissler, "Aboriginal Maize Culture as a Typical Culture-Complex," *American Journal of Sociology* 21 (1916): 656–60; A. Irving Hallowell, "The Impact of the American Indian on American Culture," *American Anthropologist* 59 (April, 1957): 201–17; and Louise O. Bercaw, *et al.*, *Corn in the Development of the Americas: A Selected and Annotated Bibliography* (Washington, D.C., 1940), U. S. Department of Agriculture, Bureau of Agricultural Economics, Agricultural Economics Bibliographies No. 87.

and "mush" in Pennsylvania and elsewhere.[5] Mush became an almost daily staple in pioneer times. It remained a favorite food on many American rural tables into the present century, and, judging from supermarket shelves, has even recently made a comeback into respectability. In the South the second maize product, hominy—corn grains from which the hulls have been soaked in a solution of lye—has remained as popular, so popular in fact that, as "grits," it is still served in restaurants with most cooked breakfasts as a "side dish," *caveat viator,* whether one orders it or not. Early America's dependence on cornmeal was sung by one of the first of our native poets, Joel Barlow, in the amusing work, "The Hasty Pudding," in 1796.[6]

Another example of a dish with European roots as well as American regional variation is the pie. The round fruit pie, which has been the all-time favorite American dessert, has a long and complicated history. American housewives exercised their ingenuity on this essentially English dish and came up with an immense stock of variations. The foremost novelist of New England life, Harriet Beecher Stowe, in describing the orgy of pie-baking that preceded the principal New England holiday, Thanksgiving, leaves us in no doubt as to the importance of pie:

The pie is an English institution, which, planted on American soil, forthwith ran rampant and burst forth into an untold variety of genera and species. Not merely the old traditional mince pie, but a thousand strictly American seedlings from that main stock, evinced the power of American housewives to adapt old institutions to new uses. Pumpkin pies, cranberry pies, huckleberry pies, cherry pies, green-currant pies, peach, pear, and plum pies, custard pies, apple pies, Marlborough-pudding pies,—pies with top crusts, and pies without,—pies adorned with all sorts of fanciful flutings and architectural strips laid across and around, and otherwise varied, attested to the boundless fertility of the feminine mind, when once let loose in a given direction.

She describes the mixing, rolling, tasting, and professional consulting

5. For a relatively complete cultural history of this basic frontier food see Don Yoder, "Pennsylvanians Called It Mush," *Pennsylvania Folklife* 13 (Winter 1962–63) : 27–[49], which uses ethnographic as well as historical materials on the backgrounds, preparation, use, vocabulary, and social customs associated with the dish.
6. Joel Barlow, *The Hasty Pudding: A Poem in Three Cantos. Written at Chambery, in Savoy, 1793. Omne tulit punctum qui miscuit utile dulci. He makes a good breakfast who mixes pudding with molasses* (New Haven: printed by Tiebout & O'Brien, 1796) . The poem first appeared in the *New York Magazine* (January 1796) : 41–49. It was often reprinted in the nineteenth century; one of the most attractive editions appeared in *Harper's New Monthly Magazine* (July 1856) with some amusing engravings of Indian girls stirring huge mush pots, Barlow sniffing a mush bowl for inspiration for his poetry, and a husking bee that ended in a "mush party." Basic Americana.

that went on between her mother and grandmother, and Aunt Lois and Aunt Keziah. Even the oven is described in detail:

In the corner of the great kitchen, during all those days, the jolly old oven roared and crackled in great volcanic billows of flame, snapping and gurgling as if the old fellow entered with joyful sympathy into the frolic of the hour; and then, his great heart being once warmed up, he brooded over successive generations of pies and cakes, which went in raw and came out cooked, till butteries and dressers and shelves and pantries were literally crowded with a jostling abundance.

Since not all of this pre-Thanksgiving pie crop would be consumed at the holiday tables, we are treated finally to this description of the original "deep-freeze" arrangement:

A great cold northern chamber, where the sun never shone, and where in winter the snow sifted in at the window-cracks, and ice and frost reigned in undisputed sway, was fitted up to be the storehouse of these surplus treasures. There, frozen solid, and thus well preserved in their icy fetters, they formed a great repository for all the winter months; and the pies baked at Thanksgiving often came out fresh and good with the violets of April.[7]

The pie as such, baked in a round pie shell with or without a top crust, is an English contribution to American culture. There are several analogues on the Continent, from the *pizza* to the *Kuchen*. The German *Kuchen* consisted of a thick dough base, usually rectangular rather than round, into which slices of fruit or vegetables were stuck before baking. The *Kuchen* tradition was brought to the American Colonies by the Pennsylvania Germans, among whom we hear of *Hutzelbrot* (plum bread) and *Zwiwwelkuche* (onion pie). But they also adopted the round English pie from their neighbors, calling it *"boi"* (as in the word *Schnitzboi*, dried apple pie), presumably because their neighbors pronounced it, dialect-fashion, "poy" rather than "pie."

The "pie" and the "Kuchen" existed in tension with each other for two centuries until the pie vanquished its more homely central European rival. The pastry department of Pennsylvania Dutch cookery, a veritable *Teigkultur,* is rich, literally and figuratively, with complexes of dishes centering around the noodle, the filled noodle, the dumpling, the half-moon pie (a giant cousin of ravioli, filled with fruit or corn), the vegetable pie, and the ubiquitous stew called "pot-pie." Apart from the borrowings from the British Isles, this heavy dough culture betrays the ethnic origins of the people in south Germany and Switzerland, where *Mehlspeisen* are the characteristic food.[8]

7. Harriet Beecher Stowe, *Oldtown Folks* (Boston, 1869), pp. 340, 341–42.
8. For Pennsylvania Dutch cookery see Ann Hark and Preston A. Barba, *Pennsyl-*

Pennsylvania is a representative area for comparative folk cookery research because of the mixed ethnic components of the population, the acculturation that took place between Continental and British Isles emigrants beginning in the eighteenth century, and the linkage of upstate (rural) Pennsylvania and Philadelphia (urban) foodways through the farmers' market system.[9] In a sense the Philadelphia versions of the staple foods—for example, "scrapple"[10] instead of up-country "panhaas"—became known commercially as a symbol of regional cookery, just as Philadelphia's "mummers parade" has become a folk-cultural symbol of Pennsylvania, supplanting the countless rural and village mummers' parades that used to be a part of the upstate culture until the period of World War I. The same problem exists for the cuisines of Boston, Baltimore, Charleston, and New Orleans. In each case, folk foods of the region have become standardized and commercialized in the principal cities, in a sense providing culinary symbols for present-day regionalism.

As is the case with Europe, the United States provides the student with important relict areas where earlier foodways have been preserved in the face of contemporary social change. The principal of these is Appalachia. Appalachian cookery contains elements from several cultural areas, settled as it was from both the Middle States and the Tidewater and Piedmont South. As a depressed area, it has also preserved into the twentieth century many aspects of American frontier cooking, both as to monotony of cuisine and the simplicity of food preparation. A well-known account from the 1920s describes mountain cookery as follows:

---

vania Dutch Cookery: A Regional Cookbook (Allentown, Pennsylvania, 1950), which is the best historically oriented regional cookbook issued in the United States. For historical and ethnographic details on two Pennsylvania German specialties, sauerkraut and schnitz (dried apples), see Don Yoder, "Sauerkraut in the Pennsylvania Folk-Culture," *Pennsylvania Folklife* 12 (Summer 1961) : 56–69; and "Schnitz in the Pennsylvania Folk-Culture," *Pennsylvania Folklife* 12 (Fall 1961) : 44–53.

9. John F. Watson, *Annals of Philadelphia* (Philadelphia, 1830) is delightful reading on the culinary relation of Philadelphia and upstate Pennsylvania. While Watson does not enlighten us on the scrapple-panhaas problem, he does inform us that the Quakers made "Poprobin Soup," which appears from its description to have been what the Pennsylvania Germans call "Rivvel Soup," a milk soup with addition of dough scraps rubbed with the hand into balls, "rivvels" in Pennsylvania Dutch dialect. For fuller discussion of urban-rural culinary relationships in Pennsylvania see Don Yoder, "'Historical Sources for American Foodways Research and Plans for an American Foodways Archive," *Ethnologia Scandinavica* 1 (1971) : 41–55.

10. On scrapple, there is the famous Philadelphia joke, usually told on the Prince of Wales, later Edward VII, who reported after his visit to Philadelphia that he "had met members of a large family named Scrapple, and enjoyed for breakfast a new dish called Biddle."

The average cooking is bad and renders the food unwholesome. The frying pan is the most common weapon, though a stew-pot is a close second. In combination with the poor cooking, the restricted diet is responsible for a depleted physical condition. The range of foodstuffs is far too narrow for good health. "Bread" and "meat" are the staples of diet. This means corn and pork. The poorest renter or squatter plans to "raise me a crap" or to "raise me some bread" by which is always meant corn. And usually he slaughters a hog or two for his "meat." This, salted and sometimes smoked, provides the necessary supply of bacon, "ham-meat," and lard. A family with a supply of bread and meat faces the winter without anxiety. At least they will not starve. If further provender can be laid up, so much the better. They may "hole up" in the garden a pyramid of potatoes, another of cabbage, and another of turnips, and dig them out when the larder runs low.[11]

But even these frontier amenities had their analogues, and in most cases precedents, among the peasant cultures of Europe. The extreme monotony of peasant cuisine is discussed in a recent history of Scottish agriculture:

The diet of the tenants was a monotonous one, inadequate in quality and quantity. Oatmeal of the poorest quality was the staple food. It was taken in the form of porridge eaten with thin milk or ale, as a kind of paste called *sowens,* and as bread in the form of thin, toasted cakes. The food was rendered insipid by the frequent absence of salt, the salt tax making that commodity a luxury. Oatmeal and pease-meal provided a dish called brose, made by pouring over it water in which greens had been boiled and stirring the mixture to consistency; and *kail,* or broth made from cabbage leaves, thickened with coarse barley or groats of oats, was in daily use. This diet was sometimes flavoured with a piece of salt meat but as a rule flesh meat, apart from special occasions such as a christening or a wedding, came the way of the ordinary peasant only when an animal died of starvation or disease, or a crock ewe was slaughtered; though the better-class farmer at the end of autumn killed and salted one or two animals for winter fare. A little dirty butter, an occasional egg—though both hens and eggs were kept primarily to pay the rent—a 'black pudding' made by bleeding the cows and boiling the blood mixed with oatmeal, and cheese of a poor quality from the mixture of the milk of ewes and cows eked out this scanty subsistence. Tenants living on the banks of a Highland stream had always the chance of supplementing their usual fare with a salmon, and seafish and shellfish were part of the diet of those who lived on the coast. In poorer parts of the country the food was even more scanty. In the Orkneys the daily fare consisted of a "morning piece" of half a bannock of bread made from bere mixed with seeds of all kinds of weeds. The breakfast was porridge made from the meal of the native black oats and seeds of wild plants. Fish, with nettle broth occasionally, thickened with a little meal, formed the main re-

11. James Watt Raine, *The Land of Saddle-Bags: A Study of the Mountain People of Appalachia* (New York, 1924), pp. 211–12.

past. The water in which the fish or crustacea had been boiled also served to boil the cabbage for dinner. The scourings of the pots and platters were mixed with the following morning's porridge. Salt water supplied the only seasoning. *Reuthie* bread, made from the seeds of wild mustard, filled the gap between the exhaustion of the old crop and the appearance of the new grain.[12]

It is no wonder that under such circumstances undernourishment led to ill-health; also, one can explain and understand the reverence our ancestors had for food, the "holy daily bread," which has come down to the present generation, even in affluent America, in parental admonitions to "finish your plate." Wasting food in the rural context was sinful, and the prohibition of it carried with it conscious or unconscious memories of the ancient "hunger times" that had so often afflicted rural populations in Europe.

In these days of higher and higher American living standards, and year-round supplies of frozen summer foods, the study of the cookery habits of the past can help us to understand poverty and the prudential reasons for the waste-not, want-not philosophy of our forefathers. Even in peasant areas where food was relatively abundant, if monotonous, there were times in the year when certain types of foods were in low stock. E. Estyn Evans tells us that "in Ulster the name given to July was 'the blue month' because it was a time of scarcity between the old potatoes and the new crop, but generally speaking milk products were consumed during the summer months."[13] An historian of New York rural life gives us a similar term:

My own mother, within my memory but before every country store had fresh vegetables all winter, used to speak of the "six-weeks' want," meaning the early spring period when the old vegetables and apples were gone and nothing new was available. No wonder the housewife scoured the spring fields for something green to cook. Pot herbs were a change and probably they corrected certain vitamin deficiencies, but after all they were mainly water and their caloric value low. Again, these familiar greens were commonly plants of old fields and gardens and probably would not be available to the pioneer homemaker.[14]

Viewed historically, each regional and national cuisine is a culinary hybrid, with an elaborate stratigraphy of diverse historical layers combined into a usable and evidently satisfying structure. American

12. James E. Handley, *Scottish Farming in the Eighteenth Century* (London, 1953), pp. 78–80, omitting footnoting.
13. E. Estyn Evans, *Irish Heritage: The Landscape, the People and Their Work* (Dundalk, 1949), p. 77.
14. Jared van Wagenen, Jr., *The Golden Age of Homespun* (New York, 1963), pp. 98–99.

folk cookery, like European, has preserved some ancient methods of food preparation, such as pickling, souring, drying, and smoking, all of which have lengthy European histories and which in fact are identified with different historical strata of European civilization. Gösta Berg's study of Swedish folk cookery has shown that, historically speaking, Swedish peasant cookery recapitulates the stages of Swedish civilization.[15] The common methods of preserving food in northern Sweden (souring and drying) belong to an older cultural epoch than the "newer" methods of salting and smoking that are diffused over southern and middle Sweden. The northern Swedish methods link Swedish cuisine with Arctic Asia and primitive man, the middle and southern Swedish methods show relations to Denmark, Germany, and central Europe.

Among early American foodways the souring and fermenting methods of preserving foods are of particular interest. We can study these methods in a great many folk food products, from sauerkraut to vinegar itself. Most interesting, however, are the milk products, or byproducts, that were soured and used widely by many cultures. The names given them—"bonny clabber" and "thick milk" in early America, *dicke Milch* in German-speaking areas, *langmjölk in* Sweden— show their wide use in peasant cultures. In some cases the tastes for these foods, acquired by necessity from primitive food preservation facilities, have lingered on. In the twentieth century we have witnessed the return to our tables of certain sophisticated versions of these ancient and simple folk foods that our ancestors made in many divergent European cultures. Yogurt, sour cream, and buttermilk are all "in" as health and gourmet foods today. Yogurt in particular—an almost exact equivalent of the thickened sour milk dishes of peasant Europe—has made a spectacular return to respectability via Central Asia and Paris.

Another recent phenomenon related to folk cookery is the decline of regional cooking at home in favor of eclectic "American" cuisine and the rise of regional restaurants. From the Spanish-Mexican culture area,[16] the great American Southwest, where Mexican foods are still functional both in the home and the local restaurant, "Mexican" restaurants have recently invaded the North and East, for instance in Chicago, Washington, and New York. As such they are symbolic

15. Gösta Berg, *Rökt skinka, torkade gäddor och surströmming, Svenska Kulturbilder* 6: 11–12 (Stockholm, 1932), analyzed in Brita Egardt, "Kost," *Schwedische Volkskunde* (Stockholm, 1961), pp. 376–78. The original essay has been reprinted in Nils-Arvid Bringéus, *Mat och Miljö* (Lund, 1970), pp. 161–76.
16. See the early scholarly work on this culture's folk foods by John Gregory Bourke, "The Folk-Foods of the Rio Grande Valley and of Northern Mexico," *Journal of American Folklore* 8 (1895): 41–71.

of our hybrid and interethnic twentieth-century American culture. If American regional restaurants are now offering a few good (and relatively authentic, if standardized) regional dishes or combinations of dishes, one can also sample regional dishes at the lunch counters of those common denominators of American popular culture, the 5-and-10 cent stores. In New Mexico one sees tamales and tortillas in Woolworth's, in Slavic neighborhoods one can sample pirogies and stuffed cabbage—in addition to the standard hamburgers, the bacon, lettuce, and tomato sandwiches, the canned soups, and the bakery pies. A recent development is the commercial chains of snack shops for specialty foods: "Taco House," "Pancake House," "Kentucky Fried Chicken" establishments, and now finally, returned from Germany where it was originally developed to bring American fried chicken to Europe, the Wienerwald restaurant.

American cookery today is eclectic or hybrid in a national sense. It shows deeply the effects of urbanization and food-processing technology, as well as an interest in selected foods from American ethnic cultures (pizza, bagels) and from world cuisine (smörgasbord, chow mein, sukiyaki, shishkebab). In this present state of eclectic variety, how do we study American folk cookery?

To use the two-pronged European folklife technique, we can approach American cookery (1) ethnographically, and (2) historically. Fortunately, enough of the regional specialties are still known and prepared by at least the older cooks who have not yet submitted to the TV dinner approach to family cooking that the questionnaire and direct interview methods can be used with profit in the subject of American cooking.[17] Even if the informant no longer prepares regional specialties, he can usually offer information on the change in foodways during his lifetime. One can often still record from older persons in the more tradition-oriented areas fond memories of food, food preparation, and the psychological and sociological aspects of foodways. For example, one area of research that can be assigned to students for questionnaires and interviews is the meal system in the folk culture under study. This involves (1) the number of meals per day, (2) the names given to the daily meals, (3) the foods served at these meals, and (4) food specialties served on specific days of the week.

The common three-meals-per-day system of most American homes contrasts with the earlier rural custom of five meals per day, at least

17. Thus far there have been three formal American questionnaires on the subject of cookery: (1) Bruce Buckley's Questionnaire on Rural Foods, Cooperstown Graduate Program, Cooperstown, N.Y.; (2) Norbert Riedl's Questionnaire on Tennessee Folk-Culture, University of Tennessee, Knoxville; and (3) Don Yoder's series of Folk-Cultural Questionnaires published in *Pennsylvania Folklife*.

in the summer, when men were working in the fields. Between early breakfast on the farm (6:00 or 7:00 A.M.) and "dinner" announced by bell, horn, or voice (at 12:00 M.), there was usually a mid-morning snack, around 9:00 or 10:00—carried to the men working in the harvest fields, as shown in the Brueghel paintings of harvesting in the Netherlands in the sixteenth century. European scholars have investigated thoroughly the *Zehnerbrot* or *Neunerbrot, Vorjausen* or *Halbmittag,* as German peasants called it, and analyzed the relation of the meal system of an area to the group's general sense of time.[18] An afternoon snack (compare the German *Vesperbrot*) balanced the morning snack, thus accounting for five meals a day. Americans traveling in Europe are often surprised by the formality of the survival of the five-meals-per-day arrangement, dramatized in the British Isles by the almost religious ritual of "elevenses" in the morning and the "teas" of late afternoon between the larger meals of breakfast, luncheon, and dinner. In a sense the urban American office "coffee-break" is restoring a five-meals-a-day rhythm to our eating habits.

What foods were served at the various meals? This depends on the area one is studying and the time-period involved. Breakfast is a fascinating research area in folk cookery because of the vast change that has taken place in the American breakfast in the past seventy-five years. Travel in Europe informs Americans that there is still a basic difference between the "Continental" (bread and coffee) breakfast and the "English" (or "meat") breakfast. The American breakfast, being essentially a meat breakfast, is derived from the English breakfast, and continued for generations because of the heavy work involved on American farms. After the Civil War, with the various food reforms, we have the "breakfast cereal" fad introduced, so that by 1900 some Americans *combined* the heavy cooked meat breakfast with the cereal reforms—a combination we still find reflected on restaurant menus, with the skimpy glass of juice added later, as a health-fad afterthought of the 1920s.

Recorded comments on such changes in meal patterns can and need to be sought out as basic historical documentation for American folk-cookery research. Farm periodicals are a particularly good source of such documentation, since the editors, because of their interest in "progressive" farming and living, are quite conscious of traditional ways. As an example of the value of this type of dated documentation, an editorial entitled "A Choice of Breakfasts" appeared in *The Country Gentleman,* 3 January 1907.

18. See Dietmar Wünschmann, *Die Tageszeiten: Ihre Bezeichnung im Deutschen* (Marburg, 1966), chap. 5.

The hearty meat breakfast, though still the usual thing, is not so much a matter of course in American families as it once was. Perhaps the various "breakfast foods" have done more than anything else to change our habits in this respect. These patented cereal preparations, many of them specially manufactured to be eaten without additional cooking, are generally believed to offer a wholesome economy in both labor and money. Their vogue and the resulting rich returns from their sale are attested by the constant production of new variations, each liberally and expensively advertised. As a partial substitute for a meat diet, there is much to be said in their favor. If, as some assert, much meat in the diet causes excessive stimulation of the nerves, the over-nervous American does well to be content with a cereal breakfast. Even a gritty cracker and a bunch of grapes or an apple will serve the turn of some of these enthusiasts for the new health, but most of us demand a hot breakfast, at least, especially in cold weather.

As a sample of the hot breakfast, the author recommended for Sunday breakfast: coffee, rolls, farina, stewed apricots, panned oysters, rice griddle cakes, and clover honey. This she calls "a light, delicate breakfast." For a winter Monday breakfast her recommendation is: coffee, oatmeal, Grape Nuts, apple sauce, pork chops, potato balls, fried parsnips, and buckwheat cakes with syrup. As to the latter, the early American favorite that travelers referred to as "the ubiquitous buckwheat cake," the editor has this to say:

Rye drop cakes, whole wheat gems, muffins, or corn bread will be preferred in place of the buckwheat cakes in many families. But there are still plenty of farmers' homes in which buckwheat pancakes at this season of the year is considered quite indispensable as an adjunct of a good breakfast. In a perfectly light, sweet batter, raised with yeast, and with pure, delicious maple syrup to adorn it, it is to be admitted that few things suit a cold morning better.

THE FUNCTION OF FOLK COOKERY

Folk cookery of course represents more than a mere primitive satisfying of elemental needs. Like all aspects of folk culture it was related, integrally and functionally, to all other phases of the culture, and in its elaboration became, like dress and architecture, a work of art. Let us look at two directions into which folk cookery ramifies, (1) religion, and (2) material culture.

The connection of folk cookery with religion includes positive elements (e.g., festival cookery), and negative elements (e.g., food taboos). The subject of festival cookery has occupied much European attention, with emphasis especially upon Christmas cookery, Easter breads, the Easter egg with its symbolic decoration and social function, wedding meals, and carnival cookery. In America the New England festival of Thanksgiving, Christmas traditions, Easter, and other festivals of the year have evoked monographs and articles from the various folk-cultural regions and ethnic enclaves. Even political festivals like Election Day produced in New England recipes for "Election Cake," along with election sermons; and the American camp-meetings—the true "festivals of democracy" as the French traveler Chevalier called them in the 1830s[19]—produced some cookery of their own, as evidenced by the recipes for "Camp-Meeting Cake" that appeared in nineteenth-century newspapers.

America's ethnic and sectarian communities have also produced some cookery associated with their temporal festivals. Accounts of early American Quakerism abound in descriptions of yearly meeting hospitality, when country Quakers partook of the bounty of the urban Friends during "yearly meeting week," and even Quaker "quarterly meeting meals" were memorable. While frontier Methodists lived on the meager side, as the journals of the circuit-riders testify, at a quarterly meeting in Wyoming Valley in 1809 the hostess served "half a barrel of potpie," with "other things on the same scale," as a prelude to the singing, the praying, and the shouting.[20] And the "love feasts" and "watch nights" of the pietist sects form a cookery spectrum from the full broth-and-bread meals of the Dunkards through the ecclesiastical coffee-breaks of the Moravians to the austere bread-and-water diet of Methodists, who were permitted only spiritual inebriation.[21]

Of the urban ethnic groups, American Judaism has reproduced in this country, sometimes in factory-made, "kosher" form, many of the traditional festival dishes of European Judaism. One of the earliest general American cookbooks to contain a section on Jewish cookery was *Jennie June's American Cookery Book . . . by Mrs. J. C. Croly (Jennie June), Author of "Talks on Women's Topics,"* etc. (New York: American News Co., 1874, c. 1866), "Dedicated to the Young Housekeepers of America." Jennie June's section on "Jewish Receipts," described as "all original and reliable" and "the contribu-

19. Michael Chevalier, *Society, Manners and Politics in the United States: Being a Series of Letters from North America* (Boston, 1839), p. 317.

20. George Peck, *Early Methodism Within the Bounds of the Old Genesee Conference* (New York, 1860), p. 167. Peck also refers to coon's flesh (pp. 308–9), not a favorite dish with the preachers; "slap-jack coffee," made of charred buckwheat bread (p. 149), and "sorrel pie" (p. 323). My favorite quotation from the book is Marmaduke Pearce's lament over the frontier food and living conditions that he had to put up with while preaching on the Holland Purchase Circuit in 1811. Looking back on it in 1850, he wrote: "...O the cold houses, the snow, the mud, the sage tea, the baked beans! These things, the recollection of them, is like 'the music of Carol, pleasant and mournful to the soul'" (p. 344).

21. Don Yoder, "Love Feasts," *The Dutchman* 7 (Spring 1956): 34–37. For the Dunkard Love Feast, often described by nineteenth-century travelers, see Moritz Busch, *Wanderungen zwischen Hudson und Mississippi, 1851 und 1852* (Stuttgart, 1854); and Phebe Earle Gibbons, "The Dunker Love-Feast," in *"Pennsylvania Dutch," and Other Essays* (Philadelphia, 1872), pp. 109–38.

tion of a superior Jewish housekeeper in New York," included the following: White Stewed Fish, Brown Fricassee Chicken, A Good Pudding, Purim Fritters, Codfish Fritters, Lemon Pudding, A Richer Lemon Pudding—1, Lemon Pudding—2, Apple Pudding, Albert Sandwiches, Meringues, Bread and Butter Pudding, Sally Lunn (2), Cup Cake, Hickory Nut Cake, Marmalade, Orgent, CocoaNut Pudding, Sweet Crackers, Almond Pudding, Lemon Dumplings, Light Pudding, Tomatoes for Winter Use, and Pickled Cucumbers.[22] In the past half-century, the Jewish Delicatessen-restaurant in metropolitan areas has been the channel through which eastern European specialties, such as lox, bagels, and borsch, have found their way into American menus.

Religion has also exercised a negative role in American foodways, particularly in what we may as well refer to as American "drink-ways." American drinking habits within the family, in large areas of our population, are different from drinking habits in most European cultures. Taboos on liquor are usually, but wrongly, blamed on Puritanism. The split did not appear until the nineteenth century when the American temperance movement, one of the most curious examples of religious taboo in history, invaded most of the Protestant churches, which at that time set the dominant cultural tone in America. The temperance movement is, folk-culturally speaking, a kind of watershed in America in regard to domestic life. Actually it was a middle-class wedge separating the upper and lower classes, both of which continued the earlier general drinking habits of colonial America.[23] Hence one has to divide American folk-cultures, at least those under Protestant influence, into "pre-temperance" and "post-temperance" eras. In the colonial era, wine, beer, and hard liquor flowed freely as part of family entertaining as well as at larger social gatherings, e.g., baptisms, weddings, and funerals, where the folk community gathered.[24] After temperance reform, drinking, like some older folk-cultural amusements and recreations, was made a sin.

While certain classes in American society continued to "drink," and the colonial "tavern" in turn became the nineteenth-century

22. According to Arnold Whitaker Oxford, *English Cookery Books to the Year 1850* (London, 1913), the first British Jewish cookbook appeared in 1846: *The Jewish Manual: or, Practical Information in Jewish and Modern Cookery, With a Collection of Valuable Recipes* & *Hints Relating to the Toilette. Edited by a Lady* (London, 1846).

23. For the temperance movement see Joseph R. Gusfield, *Symbolic Crusade: Status Politics and the American Temperance Movement* (Urbana, Illinois, 1963); and David Joshua Pittman and Charles R. Snyder, eds., *Society, Culture, and Drinking Patterns* (New York, 1962).

24. For drinking habits in the early republic see Alice Felt Tyler, *Freedom's Ferment* (Minneapolis, 1944), pp. 308–12; also Clifton J. Furness, *The Life and Times of the Late Demon Rum* (New York, 1965).

"saloon" and the twentieth-century "bar," nondrinking Americans had to find their substitutes in the "temperance houses," "sarsaparilla stands," and "cake and mead houses" run by genteel ladies in nineteenth-century villages, and eventually in their twentieth-century counterparts, the "corner drug store" and the "Coke counter."

In addition to the basic temperance taboo, food faddism inspired by religion has had a long history in the United States. Yankees and Yorkers, Quakers and other nineteenth-century nonconformists and reformers often pressed their hardheaded logical versions of Protestantism into extremist measures. Vegetarianism, nature foods, graham bread, and the breakfast cereal movement all came out of the Protestant reformist mentality, first in New England, and in Philadelphia and the "burned over district" of New York State, and later centered in the national headquarters of the Seventh Day Adventists—Battle Creek, Michigan—where the Kelloggs, Posts, and others attempted to apply reform principles, based on their religious ideas, to American eating habits.[25] The best history of this welter of reformist activity is Gerald Carson's *Cornflake Crusade* (New York: Rinehart & Company, Inc., 1957).

Perhaps functionally these food fads operate, as Richard Weiss hints, as unofficial Protestant substitutes for the Catholic sacramentals, which were among the medieval buffers against insecurity. In the last century Protestant cultures have developed unchurchly, pseudo-scientific, even magical means of controlling life, "from vitaminized bread and toothpaste to books on life-technique (think positively—live longer!)."[26] These rituals serve the faddist Protestant in much the same way that earlier folk-religious practices served the peasant.

FOLK COOKERY AND MATERIAL CULTURE

The study of folk cookery takes the student into many areas of folk-culture. The whole subject of food preparation, preservation, and storage, along with the actual cooking methods used and the consumption of food, is related to complexes of material objects, which should be viewed against the total culture.

Consider that most researched area of food, the history of the "daily bread" that our cultural forefathers in Europe counted their basic food.[27] In our bread cultures, the production, milling, and stor-

25. See *Seventh-Day Adventist Encyclopedia* 10 (Washington, D.C., 1966) for detailed biographies of the Kelloggs and discussion of Adventist "Health Evangelism."
26. Richard Weiss, "Grundzüge einer protestantischen Volkskultur," *Schweizerisches Archiv für Volkskunde* 61 (1965) : 77–78.
27. Of the many fine treatments of bread-making and bake ovens in Europe, cf. Åke Campbell, *Det svenska Brödet* (Stockholm, 1936) ; Hans Miese, *So backt der*

age of grain and the baking and storage of breadstuffs involve specific architectural structures (mills, granaries, corncribs, storage houses, and bake ovens) and specific tools (querns or handmills, hominy blocks, husking pegs, flails, rolling pins, dough-trays, bread baskets, peels) —the list is almost endless.

Of these the *bake oven*, its types and uses, can here provide us with valuable examples of how to study the material aspects of folk cookery. Today, except for adventurous younger housewives and a few traditional bread-baking groups, "bought bread" or "baker's bread" is found on American tables and even the memory of homemade bread is lost. In early America, before the days of the kitchen range, bread was baked by three different techniques: before the open fire, in the form of johnny cake, in the coals in a Dutch oven, or in a bake oven. The johnny-cake style of baking was not necessarily, as is often thought, an adaptation to the American frontier; it was a primitive baking method much and widely practiced in Europe. In his descriptions of the Irish peasant economy, E. Estyn Evans has discussed fireside breadbaking methods, which, like other aspects of Irish peasant life, belong to Europe's "Atlantic province" of folk-cultural phenomena. Ovens are essentially central European; hearth cookery is found around the Atlantic edge of Europe.

To understand the fireside appliances and methods of cooking certain facts should be borne in mind—the absence of the brick oven, the use of turf, a slow-burning fuel admirable for stewing and for things requiring a steady heat, and the universal preference for "thin-bread," or "bread in cakes," as English observers call it. Once more we have to remind ourselves that parallels to surviving habits can be found 40 centuries back, for pottery baking slabs are known from Neolithic western Europe and of course oatcakes are best baked in this way.[28]

Bake ovens were of two sorts. In New England and the South they were often built into the inside kitchen wall, in or beside the huge kitchen fireplace. In Pennsylvania, following European precedent, they were built as separate, freestanding buildings in the yard, with the oven openings protected from the weather by a shed roof. The

Bauer sein Brot: ein volkskundlicher Beitrag zum bäuerlichen Brotbacken und zur Entwicklung von Backöfen und Backhäusern (Bielefeld, 1959) ; Martha Bringemeier, *Vom Brotbacken in früherer Zeit* (Münster/Westfalen, 1961) ; Jozef Weyns, *Bakhuis en broodbakken in Vlaanderen* (Sint Martens-Latem, 1963) ; and Kustaa Vilkuna, "Brodet och bakningens historia in Finland," *Folk-Liv* 9 (1945) : 17–56.

28. E. Estyn Evans, *Irish Heritage* (Dundalk, 1949) , p. 73. For the flat bread made by open-hearth cookery see also Caoimhín Ó Danachair, "Bread," *Ulster Folklife* 4 (1958) : 29–32; O. Rhiner, *Dünne, Wähe, Kuchen, Fladen, Zelten. Die Wortgeographie des Flachkuchens mit Belag und ihre volkskundlichen Hintergründe in der deutschen Schweiz* (Frauenfeld, 1958) ; and A. Wurmbach, "Kuchen—Fladen—Torte," *Zeitschrift für Volkskunde* 56 (1960) : 20–40.

obvious rationale of the outdoor bake oven was threefold: (1) to
protect the house from fire, (2) to remove the elaborate baking process as well as the additional heat from the busy kitchen area, and
(3) to increase the size of the baking area.

The outdoor bake oven seems to have been a central European
institution. From what we now know of their geographical diffusion
in the United States, the center of outdoor bake oven use was originally in the Middle States, principally in the Pennsylvania German
culture area, although analogues are found in French Canada, Cajun
Louisiana, and in the Indian pueblos of the Southwest.[29] At any rate,
New Englanders and southerners did not originally have outdoor
bake ovens. This is brought out amusingly in Henry Ward Beecher's
novel, *Norwood* (1868), in which a New England soldier, wounded
at Gettysburg, is billeted on a Pennsylvania Quaker farm. While the
soldier lies recuperating in the farmhouse his New England girl
friend, who has come to nurse him, is shown the farm by the farmer's
daughter Martha.

"What is that?" said Rose, pointing to a queer stack of bricks under a
tile shed close by the house.
"That is our oven," said Martha.
"What—out of doors? We build ours into the kitchen chimney."
"It is the way of our fathers. The other perhaps is more convenient."[30]

Research into the bake oven should be of immediate concern.
Pennsylvania's bake ovens began to fall into disuse in the first decades
of the twentieth century, and already the great majority of them have
fallen in or have been removed. One can scarcely drive anywhere in
Pennsylvania Dutch country today without seeing a bake oven in
process of removal. Since there were several types, including the
"squirrel-tail" bake oven (so-called because of the S-shaped flue),
they need to be photographed, measured, and carefully described. A
prime need is a diffusion map of the outdoor bake oven, since it
spread widely from eastern Pennsylvania.

We need studies not only of the permanent bake oven but also of
the summer or temporary bake oven (the "mud oven") and the
community or village bake oven. The latter is reported from a few
mine patches in Pennsylvania's coal regions, presumably repristinated
here as an institution remembered from the Slavic homelands of
nineteenth-century emigrants in the mining counties. We need to

29. The best treatment thus far of the outdoor oven in any geographical or
ethnic context in the United States is Fred Kniffen, "The Outdoor Oven in
Louisiana," *Louisiana History* 1 (1960) : 25–35, which includes basic bibliography.
30. Henry Ward Beecher, *Norwood: or, Village Life in New England* (New York,
1868) , p. 533.

collect memories of how the bake oven fire was made, what "oven wood" was used, how one knew when the oven was hot enough to bake and not too hot to burn. Fortunately, although the bake ovens are in disuse, thousands of persons can still provide the ethnographer with first-hand information on the basic uses of the bake oven.

Cookery's connections with American folk architecture are also easily seen in the whole area of food storage. The granaries in the barns, the corncribs once found on most American farms, the attic storage of grain and herbs, the vaulted cellars underneath house or barn, the smokehouses and ham closets, the springhouses or dairies for the storage of milk and dairy products—all deserve study as to type, construction, function, and diffusion. The excellent European historical and ethnographic researches on *Haus, Hof, Scheune,* and *Speicher* can be matched eventually, in the United States.[31]

When historical sources are abstracted for this purpose, nineteenth-century novels in particular contain interesting and usable material. Harriet Beecher Stowe, in describing the parson's farmhouse at Poganuc, speaks in detail of the house as an instrument for food storage:

> The parsonage had also the advantage of three garrets—splendid ground for little people. There was first the garret over the kitchen, the floors of which in the fall were covered with stores of yellow pumpkins, fragrant heaps of quinces, and less fragrant spread of onions. There were bins of shelled corn and of oats, and, as in every other garret in the house, there were also barrels of old sermons and old family papers. But most stimulating to the imagination of all the features of this place was the smoke-house, which was a wide, deep chasm made in the kitchen chimney, where the Parson's hams and dried beef were cured. Its door, which opened into this garret, glistened with condensed creosote, a rumbling sound was heard there, and loud crackling reverberated within.[32]

The juvenile heroine of the book, Dolly Cushing, would sometimes open this door and "peer in fearfully as long as her eyes could bear the smoke," and think with a shudder of the passage in *Pilgrim's Progress* that describes a "by-way to Hell," a door opening into a hillside from which came smoke and "a rumbling noise as of fire and a cry of some tormented, and . . . the scent of brimstone." Garret

---

31. The best introduction to American farm building types, based on wide comparative fieldwork in North and South, is Henry Glassie, *Pattern in the Material Folk Culture of the Eastern United States* (Philadelphia, 1969), No. 1, University of Pennsylvania Monographs in Folklore and Folklife. This basic work is profusely illustrated with photographs and architectural drawings and contains the best bibliography thus far on American folk architecture.

32. Harriet Beecher Stowe, *Poganuc People: Their Loves and Lives* (New York, 1878), pp. 167–68. Subsequent quotation p. 176.

Number Two was the large central garret over the main part of the house, where in addition to old spinning wheels and other disused furniture, "and more barrels of sermons," there were "vast heaps of golden corn on the cob, spread upon sheets." This was the favorite rainy-day play garret of the parsonage children. Garret Number Three was Father's study with its Puritan theological library.

But the mysterious areas of the parsonage were not exhausted with its three garrets. Under the whole house in all its divisions spread a great cavernous cellar, where were murky rooms and dark passages explored only by the light of candles. There were rows of bins, in which were stored the apples of every name and race harvested in autumn from the family orchard: Pearmains, Greenings, Seek-no-furthers, Bristers, Pippins, Golden Sweets, and other forgotten kinds, had each its separate bin, to which the children at all times had free access. There, too, was a long row of cider barrels, from whence, in the hour of their early sweetness, Dolly had delighted to suck the cider through straws for that purpose carefully selected and provided.

The American farmhouse kitchen is a subject long overdue for basic research. Here we need to study the layout of the kitchen, which in many farmhouses was also the dining room. The furniture and appliances that were in the kitchen deserve study, and here memory of living persons can help, as well as research into inventories and other historical documents. Functionally the farmhouse kitchen was "the" room of the house, where life and much domestic work centered around the hearth or, later, the kitchen stove. This centralizing of family life in the kitchen had significance for many other areas of life. Since in early American farmhouses the kitchen was sometimes the only heated room and occupied by the family every evening, courting couples were forced to court in the girl's bedroom, thus continuing the "bundling" system that had such long European roots. The American kitchen also restored the family, and the mourning community to normalcy after a funeral, when the "funeral dinner" or "funeral feast"[33]—subject of many ministerial jeremiads in the nineteenth century—united them all in the continued pursuit and celebration of life.

Another indication of the basic ramifications of kitchen life and foodways into religion and folk religion is the fact that in the kitchen the father, or some other older member of the family, served in a sense as family priest, in saying the table graces or blessings at the beginning and often at the end of a meal. In Protestant areas formal family worship, Bible reading and hymn singing, sometimes accom-

---

33. For the funeral meal in Europe see A. Freybe, *Das alte deutsche Leichen-mahl in seiner Art und Entartung* (Gütersloh, 1909); also Arnold van Gennep, *Manuel de folklore français contemporain* 2 (Paris, 1946): 773–91.

panied or preceded the meal. This sense of the holiness of everyday food and the holiness of eating together was earlier expressed in the orientation of the kitchen. In the Catholic farming areas of central Europe the *Kultecke* or devotional corner often has a well-defined relation to the table where the family eats.[34] All this can help the student to understand the meaning of life in the peasant or folk-cultural setting, a life that was linked in countless beliefs and practices to the spiritual world.

TRADITIONAL COOKERY IN THE TWENTIETH CENTURY

The revolutionary technological changes of the twentieth century, following the Industrial Revolution, have radically changed cookery and food preparation as well as every phase of everyday living. All of the recent ethnographic studies of European and American communities make much of these changes, as in this observation from Cape Breton Island, Nova Scotia:

Cookery—the woman's art—has undergone a great change since first the Highland women set up homes on these shores. The traditional diet of the Highlander in Scotland at the time of the emigrations is said to have consisted of fish and boiled potatoes. In the New World the immigrants amplified this diet considerably, although it is still limited by the refrigerating problem. In the heat of summer, fish, cured or freshly caught, is still the mainstay; but in the winter, when provisions can be preserved by freezing, meat makes its appearance. The repertoire of the menu has been enlarged, moreover, by the increased quantity of fruit and vegetables once unknown in the Highlands which are now available in the New World. Some traditional Highland dishes remain to lend individuality to the Gael's table, such as porridge and oat bread. Others have unaccountably become very rare, such as the meat sausage known as *iosban,* or the oatmeal sausage known as *marag gheal,* or the blood sausage known as *marag dhubh.* The art of preparing home-made cheese is almost forgotten; although, in a few exceptional districts such as Mabou, sufficient quantities of a firm, whitish cheese are produced by home manufacture to sell in the local stores.[35]

Nova Scotians jokingly sum up the radical alterations in the old way of life through which they have lived in an oft-quoted saying, "When I was a boy, I was brought up on porridge and the Bible. But now, all I see is corn-flakes and Eaton's catalogue."[36] That is, ready-made

---

34. For the European peasant sense of holy space within his own farmhouse see Gustav Ränk, *Die heilige Hinterecke im Hauskult der Völker Nordosteuropas und Nordasiens* (Helsinki, 1949), *Folklore Fellows Communications* 137.

35. Charles W. Dunn, *Highland Settler: A Portrait of the Scottish Gael in Nova Scotia* (Toronto, 1953), p. 156.

36. Ibid., pp. 115–16.

"cold" cereals have taken the place of the home-preparation of "hot" cereal, thus sparing the housewife the labor of preparing breakfast, and whatever else she needs for the household she orders from the mail-order catalogue.

Whether we are better off with our "enriched" bread and our often flavorless frozen foods is a question that the historian and the folklife scholar as well as the nutritionist and public health official can help to answer. An Illinois social historian, in recording the change of Midwestern farm diet from "home-baked bread, meat, potatoes and pie" to "baker's bread, fresh meat, salads, vegetables and fruit from Florida and California," concludes that the farmer "lives no better, as far as food is concerned than his forbears, perhaps not as well in some respects, but he too craves variety, or at least novelty, and must pay with the profits of his own labor for baking, mending, repairs and laundry once done by the farm women."[37] In some areas, such as Appalachia, and in Switzerland's more backward alpine villages, the old ways of the twentieth century are not quite as wholesome as the romanticists have maintained. Richard Weiss, in one of his last essays, published posthumously, points to loss as well as gain:

Our city population is, in contradistinction, today healthy compared with those many residents of mountain valleys. Even the urban relationships with the surrounding world are in many respects hygienically better. In the city it is no longer the case that a great part of the families, as in Canton Wallis, sleep crowded together into one room, often in one chamber with trundle beds, which is at the same time general living room and bedroom and can scarcely be aired out. In addition there is the fact that where the ancient traditional economy of self-provision decays, a one-sided and unsound food system results, in which fruits and vegetables from the earlier system are lacking. Where the home-baked black bread is replaced by white baker's bread and the fresh milk by a coffee-like drink, deficiency illnesses take the upper hand. That tooth decay has gained ground in exact relationship to the decline of home bread production, is statistically documented for the Goms, the Upper Rhone Valley.[38]

Yet perhaps in the basic area of human nutrition it all balances out. The old foodways were not so bad after all, the newer ones are not perfect either. That would seem to be the conclusion of Richard Cummings in his basic history of American food viewed from the nutritionist's standpoint: "While Americans in the early nineteenth century knew no set principles of balanced diet, they appear, without conscious design, to have maintained food habits which cannot be

---

37. Earnest Elmo Calkins, *They Broke the Prairies* (New York, 1939), pp. 17–18.
38. Richard Weiss, "Alpiner Mensch und alpines Leben in der Krise der Gegenwart," *Schweizerisches Archiv für Volkskunde* 58 (1962): 241–42.

definitively termed unhealthful."[39] Perhaps we could close with a paraphrase of a famous statement about religion—"Each nation, each culture, and each generation, creates for itself the cuisine it deserves."

Bibliography and Selected Readings

The American Heritage Cookbook and Illustrated History of American Eating & Drinking. New York: American Heritage Publishing Company, Inc., 1964. A readable, popular collection of essays on various regional and ethnic cuisines of the United States, magnificently illustrated from historical sources.

Arnow, Harriette Simpson. *Seedtime on the Cumberland.* New York: Macmillan Company, 1960. This book, an historical study of the Cumberland Valley area of Kentucky and Tennessee, describes the entire food economy of pioneer Appalachia (chap. 14, "Around the Family Hearth," pp. 387–425).

Brothwell, Don and Patricia. *Food in Antiquity: A Survey of the Diet of Early Peoples.* New York: Frederick A. Praeger, 1969. Vol. 66 in the useful series "Ancient Peoples and Places," published in England by Thames and Hudson. Bibliography, pp. 193–200.

Burnett, John. *Plenty and Want: A Social History of Diet in England from 1815 to the Present Day.* London: Thomas Nelson, 1966; Pelican Books, 1968. Analysis of the changes in diet in rural and industrial England, fully documented with many hitherto unpublished source materials.

Coffin, Robert P. Tristram. *Mainstays of Maine.* New York: Macmillan Company, 1944. Evocative essays by the poet and littérateur on New England foods and their social setting.

Cummings, Richard Osborn. *The American and His Food: A History of Food Habits in the United States.* Chicago: University of Chicago Press, 1940. The only recommendable general scholarly historical and nutritional study of the American diet.

Drummond, J. C., and Anne Wilbraham. *The Englishman's Food: A History of Five Centuries of English Diet.* London: Jonathan Cape, 1939. The best single treatment of the changes in English diet, individual foods, meal systems, and food habits from the Middle Ages to the present.

Eckstein, Friedrich. "Speise." *Handwörterbuch des deutschen Aberglaubens* 8: cols. 156–234. Definitive article on the ramifications of diet into folk belief and folk custom.

Eidlitz, Kerstin. *Food and Emergency Food in the Circumpolar Area.* Studia Ethnographica Upsaliensia 32. Uppsala, 1969. Historical and dietetic study of the relationships of arctic and subarctic ecologies, economies,

---

39. Richard Osborn Cummings, *The American and His Food: A History of Food Habits in the United States* (Chicago, 1940), p. 229.

and food systems. Emphasis is upon alternatives to traditional western diet in a world threatened by hunger.

Gottschalk, A. *Histoire de l'alimentation et de la gastronomie depuis la préhistoire jusqu'à nos jours.* 2 vols. Paris, 1948. Standard European survey of diet and food preparation, on all levels of culture.

Honigman, John H. *Foodways in a Muskeg Community: An Anthropological Report on the Attawapiskat Indians.* Ottawa: Northern Co-ordination and Research Center, 1961. A model North American ethnography of food habits, based on fieldwork in a Canadian Indian community.

Lemon, James T. "Household Consumption in Eighteenth-Century America and Its Relationship to Production and Trade: The Situation among Farmers in Southeastern Pennsylvania." *Agricultural History* 41 (January 1967) : 59–70. Important for its pioneer use of wills and inventories for food research in the United States.

Lévi-Strauss, Claude. "Le triangle culinaire." *L'Arc* 26 (1965) : 19–29; "The Culinary Triangle." *Partisan Review* 33 (Fall 1966) : 586–95. Analyzing cooking methods, the author constructs a triangle of which the points are "cru," "cuit," and "pourri," with an interior triangle formed by the methods of frying, smoking, and boiling, with discussion of the intermediate forms between the points.

Lincoln, Waldo. *American Cookery Books 1742–1860.* Revised and enlarged by Eleanor Lowenstein. Worcester, Mass.: American Antiquarian Society, 1954. A holding list of American imprints containing recipes, providing the scholar with an indication of the regional cookbooks that appeared in print before the Civil War, plus some indication of the impact of food reforms and taboos on cookbook editors (homeopathic, hydropathic, temperance, and total abstinence cookbooks) .

Lucas, Anthony T. "Irish Food Before the Potato." *Gwerin* 3 (1960–62) : 1–36. A thoroughly documented study of Irish diet before the eighteenth century, by the director of the National Museum of Ireland.

Nordland, Odd. *Brewing and Beer Traditions in Norway. The Social Anthropological Background of the Brewing Industry.* Oslo: Universitetsforlaget, 1969. Model introduction to domestic brewing, its history, technology, and vocabulary.

Richards, Audrey I. *Land, Labour and Diet in Northern Rhodesia: An Economic Study of the Bemba Tribe.* London: Oxford University Press, 1939. One of the model ethnographies of diet. See especially "Food and Drink," pp. 44–108, and "The Production of Food," pp. 228–351.

Root, Waverly. *The Food of France.* New York: Vintage Books, 1966. A readable, popular account, both historical and descriptive, of the culinary provinces of France, divided on the basis of the three materials used for cooking: butter, fat, and oil.

Simoons, Frederick J. *Eat Not This Flesh: Food Avoidances in the Old World.* Madison, Wisconsin: University of Wisconsin Press, 1963. A basic anthropological study of food taboos and their sociological and psychological meaning.

Sorre, Max. "La géographie de l'alimentation." *Annales de géographie* 61: 184–99. Reprinted in Philip L. Wagner and Marvin W. Mikesell, eds., *Readings in Cultural Geography*. Chicago: University of Chicago Press, 1962. "The Geography of Diet," pp. 445–56. Deals with the relation of diet to environment, climate, ecology, religion, and traditional production techniques. Important, among other reasons, for its use of the term "dietary regime," by which Sorre means the ensemble of foods and their preparation that sustains a human group throughout the year.

Vicaire, Georges. *Bibliographie Gastronomique: A Bibliography of Books Appertaining to Food and Drink and Related Subjects, From the Beginning of Printing to 1890*. Paris, 1890. Reprint. London: Derek Verschoyle Academic and Bibliographical Publications, Ltd., 1954. With Introduction by André L. Simon.

Wiegelmann, Günter. *Alltags- und Festspeisen: Wandel und gegenwärtige Stellung*. Marburg: N. G. Elwert Verlag, 1967. Atlas der deutschen Volkskunde, Neue Folge, Beiheft 1. Ranks at the very top of the best European historical and ethnological studies of regional diet. The bibliography (pp. 245–61) is the most useful compiled thus far on European dietary studies.

Wright, Lawrence. *Home Fires Burning: The History of Domestic Heating and Cooking*. London: Routledge and Kegan Paul, 1964. Particularly good on open-hearth cookery and the changes that were brought to the kitchen by the "iron monster," the kitchen range.

Yoder, Don. "Historical Sources for American Foodways Research and Plans for an American Foodways Archive." *Ethnologia Scandinavica* 2 (1971): 41–55. Discusses printed, manuscript, and iconographic source materials and illustrates their value by applying them to acculturation problems in Pennsylvania German cookery research. An expanded version, with illustrations, appeared in *Pennsylvania Folklife* 20 (Spring 1971): 16–29.

FOLK ARTS
16 FOLK DRAMA
Roger D. Abrahams

Drama in folk communities has been little discussed in the folklore literature, primarily because it has not often been regarded as a folk genre. Further, even when it has been so designated, it has commonly been discussed as one of a number of performance-types in festivals or rituals. This is where it would remain, were it not for the fact that drama does have certain characteristics that other festival amusements do not, and many of these were developed in sophisticated theatrical forms.

Because of this imprecision of generic definition, scholarly treatments of folk drama have generally been carried out as part of some larger argument. The strongest of these scholarly traditions, the myth-ritual argument, relates specific folk dramas to seasonal ritual patterns; well-known examples are Francis M. Cornford's and Gilbert Murray's treatments of Greek dramatic traditions and James G. Frazer's earlier overview in *The Golden Bough*. The Cornford and Murray works represent one important segment of this scholarly tradition, the study of folk drama to trace how certain of the great dramatic traditions developed. The recent studies by O. B. Hardison and C. L. Barber follow in this direction, focusing on British folk, popular, and high art plays. Frazer's relating of fertility ritual, festival, and drama is carried on by a number of British scholars like Violet Alford and Margaret Dean-Smith. E. K. Chambers's work, *The Medieval Stage,* is a combination of these approaches.

Certain traditional plays have provoked a good deal of scholarly comment, like the Mexican *Pastorela,* the German *Schauspielen,* and the British *mummers play.* The last, for instance, has been the subject of at least ten major articles and full-length books by R. J. E. Tiddy; E. K. Chambers; E. D. Cawte, Alex Helm, and N. Peacock; and Alan Gailey. These have been focused primarily on textual variation, geographical distribution, and the means by which the texts can be identified with some type of fertility ritual through establishing parallels throughout the Indo-European world in the Frazer manner. Only the recent works by Herbert Halpert and G. M. Story and by Gailey have provided much information on how the performances were put together, by whom, and for what purposes. The problems of the composition of actual playing texts is also increasingly being considered, by Alex Helm in Great Britain and by James Peacock in Indonesia, among others. It is such compositional aspects that draw attention to the real problem in treating of folk drama, for most texts that we have collected are demonstrably close to literate sources. Therefore the definition of any drama at all as a "folk" product asks for a redefinition of that central term of the discipline.

This problem cannot be considered effectively without an understanding of the nature of this activity. Drama of any sort calls for the creation of a play world by the players, generally through the use of conventional symbolic objects—masks, costumes, a special area for playing—and conventional stylized actions. Drama, in other words, is primarily recognizable as a play activity, and therefore is closely related to game, dance, and ritual. All of these call for the establishment of a play world that is recognizably removed from the real world and yet in many ways similar to it. All call for the assumption of roles by players, roles that do not conform to those played in everyday life. All demand the coordination of activities within the play world by the players according to the accepted conventions and symbolic behaviors that the players and the audience understand to be appropriate to such a traditional activity.

But drama differs from games in being concerned with providing not only a conventional conflict but a foreknown resolution to the conflict. Further, drama must establish psychic distance between performers and audience to achieve its proper aesthetic effect. In this respect, drama resembles ritual and dance. But ritual and dance call for establishing meanings primarily through symbolic movement, while in drama, movement is commonly subordinated to dialogue. Folk drama differs from other dialogue pieces only in performer-audience relationship, in mode of transmission, and most important, in vocabulary of dramatic effects. We may, for the moment, define folk drama as traditional play activity that relies primarily on dialogue to establish its meaning and that tells a story through the combination of dialogue and action, the outcome of which is known to the audience ahead of time.

In defining folk drama this way, certain recent children's "routines" would be examples of this genre, playlets like:

1: That's tough.
2: What's tough?
1: Life's tough.
2: What's life?
1: A magazine.
2: Where do you get it?
1: Down at the corner.
2: How much?
1: A dime.
2: Only got a nickel.
1: That's tough.
2: What's tough?
1: Life's tough. . . .

This routine, which may arise in the midst of any conversation among the young, calls for the sudden assumption of masks and the playing out of a little, foreknown drama through dialogue. It is true that the resolution is inconclusive, but that seems to be the very message of the piece. More resolute, and more obviously dramatic, is the children's routine parodying stage melodramas.

1: Who'll carry the mail through Death Valley?
2: I will!
1: Who are you?
2: Luke McGook.
1: Luke McGook?
2: Luke McGook.
1: But that's my name (looks menacingly).
2: But that's my name (looks menacingly).
1: But that's my name.
2: But that's my name.
1: Father!
2: Son (they embrace)!

Drama is by its nature essentially a public performance—it must be capable of being understood by the audience with a minimum of reflection. That is, drama must deal in publicly understood motives and symbols. As in other genres of art, we may distinguish, however, between three types of drama—folk, popular, and sophisticated. Folk drama exists on a village or small-group level. The performers are members of the community and therefore known to most of the audience. The dramas are given on special occasions only, most commonly a seasonal festival. Popular theater often arises from folk theater but the players are professional and the audience comes from places other than the community in which the players live. Performances may occur more often. This is the theater of the strolling players of medieval Europe that we know so well through their part in *Hamlet*. It is also the tradition of Punch and Judy, *commedia dell'arte*, and the theaters of India, described by Balwant Gargi, and of Indonesia, illuminated by James Peacock.

Drama is much more sedentary and calls for a focus more intense and thus more cerebral than folk or popular theater. Consequently, the proper milieu of sophisticated drama is the theater, while popular and folk drama can be performed anywhere. Gargi's description of the movable cart-stages in many Indian traditions is paralleled in popular traditions throughout the Indo-European world and in "village drama" in Africa.[1] The fixed stage of the sophisticated theater calls for a different performer-audience relationship than that of the folk or popular traditions. The theatergoer commonly sits in one place, and the players therefore may coordinate their activities in one direction. They are able to regard each member of the audience as an individual and may attempt to appeal to the individual's capacity to make connections, and therefore to have insights not available to a milling audience. Further, the fixed theater can count on a higher degree of concentration on the action; this situation may create an effect of greater complexity.

On the other hand, folk and popular drama must use a wide variety of techniques to focus the attention of the audience on the performance. Consequently, one encounters clowning, dancing, singing, instrumental music, bombastic speeches, and other highly stylized types of performance as part of the repertoire of effects in countryside drama.

The range of styles, in terms of subtlety, is very limited in festival drama. Indeed, the dominating moods are melodramatic or farcical. In such plays, as in most other festival activities, there is no respect for everyday reality. Indeed, festival seems to do its best to deny reality, by turning the world and its social hierarchies upside down, by having acrobats, stilt dancers, and other such performers defy

1. Cf. Leonard Doob, *Communications in Africa* (New Haven, 1961), pp. 77–78.

gravity, or by having performances given by characters whose roles are suffused with hyperbole or the ridiculous.

The mobile audience is matched, of course, by a movable performance. The audience's varied tastes may be satisfied thereby not only by having performances with a wide range of effects, but also by allowing them to see a number of different troupes. This mobility permits one group of performers to play a number of audiences, such as when groups move from one great house to another. A consequence of this kind of practice is that each performance must be short. This brevity is achieved in one of two ways—either by having a short play (such as the "Saint George and the Turk" mumming) or by enacting a story already well-known, playing only segments of it at each stopping place. This was probably the technique of the liturgical dramas performed by the guilds. Farces, too, might be played episodically, since their unity is provided by the stock characters rather than the dramatic situation.

The distinction between folk drama and other festival entertainment is one that seems to be fabricated by scholars. Folk drama, to the outside investigator, are those mimetic festival performances in which dialogue and action intermingle but in which dialogue prevails. Even here, however, it is very difficult to distinguish between drama and dance, so difficult indeed that the term dance-drama has often been substituted in academic discussions of this genre. Not only is dancing—and that other stylized kinesic activity, acrobatics—often associated with drama, but also song. For instance, the Mexican Shepherd's Play performed at Christmas always has numerous songs which punctuate the action, and in the related *Las Posadas* (The Procession to the Inn), songs predominate. Though English folk drama is not so suffused with song, it seems to have been traditional at least to end the mummings with a carol. One notable English mumming, "The Old Tup," is centered around the song of "The Derby Ram." Here is a representative version from Nottinghamshire:

The Little Tup

(The Tup Play was usually performed at Christmas time. About six men took part, and the household knew in advance that a team would be coming . . . and their arrival was eagerly awaited. First verse sung outside the house.)

> There is a little tup,
> And he's standing at your door;
> And if you'll have 'im in, Sir,
> He'll please you more and more.
> Bring 'im in, bring 'im in.

(The men are let in. Some or all have blackened faces, and the Tup (or ram) has a home-made ram's head, with a cloth or drape covering the rest of the body. He is led in, prancing, on a rope. Rest of the play is performed indoors.)

> The very first day that tup was born,
> He cut some funny capers.
> He ate a field of turnip tops.
> And fourteen tons o' 'taters.
> Bailey, Bailey, laddie-fer-lairey-aye.
>
> The wool that grew (up) on his back, Sir,
> It grew so mighty long,
> The eagles built their nests in it,
> I heard the young ones' song.
> Bailey, Bailey, laddie-fer-lairey-aye.
>
> The horns that grew up on his head,
> They grew so mighty high,
> That every time he shook 'is head,
> They rattled against the sky.
> Bailey, Bailey, laddie-fer-lairey-aye.

Leader (holding tup) : Is there a butcher in the town?

1st character: Aye! My brother Jack's a butcher.

Leader: Can 'e stick a tup?

1st character: Aye! 'E'll stick a tup, dog or devil; cut nine pounds 'o beef off a leg o' mutton all bone.

Leader: Well, if 'e's as good a pink as thee, tha'd better fetch 'im.

1st character (shouts off) : Jack! Jack! There's a job for thee.

Jack (enters) : What for?

1st character: To stick this tup.

Jack: Put your cap over 'is right left eye.

(1st character puts his cap over the tup's rump)

Jack: That's not 'is right left eye, you block 'ead!

(Jack draws knife and goes through the action of killing the Tup, which falls to the ground. All sing:)

> All the women in Derby
> Came begging for his hide,
> To make some leather "approns"
> To last them all their lives.
> Bailey, Bailey, laddie-fer-lairey-aye.
>
> All the young lads in Derby
> Came begging for his eyes
> To kick them up and down the street
> For footballs and bulls-eyes.
> Bailey, Bailey, laddie-fer-lairey-aye.
>
> All the (ringers) in Derby
> Came begging for his tail,
> To ring the Derby passing-bell
> That hangs upon the wall.
> Bailey, Bailey, laddie-fer-lairey-aye.

(This concluded the play. Cakes and ale were distributed and a collection was taken.) [2]

In point of fact, entertainments featuring dialogue and action are just one of a broad range of entertainments given license during festival times. These were variously called "holiday pleasures," "sports," "amusements," or "games." Read Baskervill has described the whole range of these activities in England:

During the Middle Ages and the Renaissance a great variety of sports and pastimes were popular with all classes. The occasion . . . likely . . . was one of the great festivals celebrated pretty generally throughout Western Europe, as those of Easter, Whitsuntide, Midsummer, or the Xmas season. . . .

Of course, such revelry was often of the most informal sort; but the general tendency was to organize it under leaders . . . [who] presided over the pastimes and often played a leading role in them. No doubt the celebrants engaged in social dancing . . . and in sports and contests of various sorts . . . . But there was a special group of entertainers representing the talent of the community. Some of these prepared a dance like the morris, or a humorous play, or perhaps even a dramatic performance drawn from a more sophisticated source. Much of the entertainment, however, seems to have been of a simpler type, consisting of comic speeches or of special dances and songs by one or two characters.[3]

The association of folk drama and festival has given rise to many theories of the genesis of drama, but they seem to have generated more heat than light. Before Frazer's world-wide excursions in *The Golden Bough,* it was argued that the drama arose *out of* the festival. After Frazer's attractive but by now disproved thesis of fertility rite survivals, folk drama along with dance and pantomime and other such entertainments was seen to be a development out of ritual.

This attitude led to many evolutionary hypotheses in regard to the stages of development of drama. For instance, Baskervill in an earlier article notes:

At least three stages can be readily distinguished; first, that of pagan ritual, still preserved in certain folk customs; second, that in which festival customs, sophisticated as a result of advancing culture and the modification of pagan festivals by the church, developed among the folk as social pastimes; third, a stage in which the diversions of the festival celebration became professionalized thru passing into the hands of village performers . . . .[4]

The problem with such an hypothesis is that we know very little of

---

2. Printed, with tune, in *Folk,* E.F.D.S. Publications 2 (October 1962) : 9–10.
3. Charles Read Baskervill, *The Elizabethan Jig and Related Song Drama* (New York, 1965; reprint) , p. 7.
4. Charles Read Baskervill, "Dramatic Elements of the Medieval Folk Festival in England," *Studies in Philology* 17 (1920) : 191.

"pagan rites" except through modern vestiges or through ancient but piecemeal accounts. Further, traditions of festivals of primitive or semiaboriginal peoples have been reported (especially from West Africa) that tend to undermine this evolutionary schema. For instance, John Messenger reports a festival tradition among the Anang of Calabar Province, Nigeria, a survival of pre-contact celebration techniques. Called the *Ekong*, the entertainments are "sanctioned by myth and guided by a spirit who is worshipped before a particular shrine." The Anang activities covered percussion music, choral singing and dancing, puppet plays, masking plays (generally satiric), stilt dancing, the carrying of a large carving of a fertility figure (a woman wrapped in the coils of a python), acrobatics, sleight-of-hand magic, and tightrope walking. The performers come from the community but they train for seven years and are paid for the performance.[5]

The existence of a tradition of this nature that is so similar to Indo-European practices seems to argue against any evolutionary theory. Rather, rite and folk drama and dance would seem to be related because they commonly arise during the same festival occasions. They rely upon the same licentious atmosphere, but they utilize it in different ways. Rite stands as the "serious" center of the festival, while drama and other amusements are the humorous counterpart of the ritual. Rituals intensify reality by emphasizing certain status relationships and by the extremely formal tone adopted. Festival sports, as noted, have no respect for reality.

Edmund R. Leach, in a brief note on the subject of ritual and license, has pointed up the major relationship of ritual and festival.

Now if we look at the general types of behaviour that we actually encounter on ritual occasions we may readily distinguish three seemingly contradictory species. On the one hand there are behaviours in which formality is increased; men adopt formal uniform, differences of status are precisely demarcated by dress and etiquette, moral rules are rigorously and ostentatiously obeyed . . . . In direct contrast we find celebrations of the Fancy Dress Party type, masquerades, revels. Here the individual, instead of emphasizing his social personality and his official status, seeks to disguise it. The world goes in a mask, the formal rules of orthodox life are forgotten.

And finally, in a few relatively rare instances, we find an extreme form of revelry in which the participants play-act at being precisely the opposite to what they really are: men act as women, women as men, Kings as beggars, servants as masters, acolytes as Bishops.[6]

5. John C. Messenger, "Anang Art, Drama, and Social Control," in *Arts, Human Behavior, and Africa,* ed. Alan P. Merriam (New York: African Studies Association, 1962), pp. 29–35.

6. Edmund R. Leach, *Rethinking Anthropology* (London, 1961), pp. 134–35.

Formality and revelry are perceived as being counterparts of the same occasion, "contrasted opposites." Both involve the assumption of roles and masks, but in the case of formality, these epitomize the usual social role and order, while in masquerade they comment ironically on it at the same time as they provide a release from everyday social restrictions.

Given this view, there is little reason to judge ritual more archaic than festival or to see drama or dance necessarily as developing from rite. They all, rather, stem from the same occasions, those transitional periods of life that are deemed special. Since the occasion provides the tone and often the subject of the celebration, it should come as no surprise that there often are similar matters discussed in both formal and masquerading performances. Since rituals are extremely formal and their performance is commonly given over to an ordained member of the priestly class, there is a greater tendency toward stability in such practice. Rituals are also more "serious." It is difficult for sophisticated (or puritanical) Westerners to imagine festivities that might burlesque the serious, so folk drama and dance, light and mocking in tone, are seen to be degenerate ritual rather than a contrasted opposite to a rite. But what little evidence we have argues that they are vitally connected. There is no reason, for instance, to see the play of "The Old Tup" as a degenerate descendant of a sacrificial rite when it continued until recently to be performed at Christmas or Easter where it stands in strangely appropriate contrast to the central rites of Christianity.[7]

By this I do not mean to argue that no folk drama has developed out of liturgical rite. On the contrary, we have abundant evidence that some of the most notable plays in the folk literature, such as the English Mystery and the Spanish Shepherd's plays, have developed out of serious, church-sponsored Christian observances. However, this seems to represent a clerical strategy to more fully engage the populace during a time when pagan survivals continued to compete with Christianity. And significantly, the plays gravitated markedly toward the subjects and the techniques of festival celebrations.

Folk drama and other festival activities are unique traditional expressive genres because they call for such a high degree of playing coordination for meaningful interaction. These play activities are organized so that communicative relationships of two different kinds are established, between the individual players and between the players and the audience. The illusion must be established that the energies of the players are directed toward their interplay when in

7. O. B. Hardison, *Christian Rite and Christian Drama in the Middle Ages* (Baltimore, 1965), pp. 1–34.

fact they are directed at the audience. This is true both of seasonal rituals, reenacted commonly by a priestly class, and of festival sports. The continuity of the tradition of the ritual is guaranteed by the formal nature of the enactment and by the heavy role-investment by the priestly group.

But this is not true of licentious festival entertainments including the dramas. Consequently, one commonly finds one person who serves as a director making sure that the performance is organized effectively and coherently. This person is usually the one who knows the piece best and who teaches the others their parts. Known as the "enseñador" in Mexico and the "captain" in the West Indies (Gargi calls him the "stage-manager"), he is the one who ensures the continuity of the tradition by recruiting new players and teaching them how to co-ordinate themselves to the total movement of the piece. Often this same person serves as the intermediary between the performance and the audience, announcing the beginning and the ending of the play. He also often serves as prompter, though in the longer plays this position may be taken by someone else.

Where folk dramas exist in peasant communities, the organizer's role most commonly is assumed by the cleverest and most outgoing man in town. This is significant not only because he must be clever enough to organize the performance and to keep it going but also because his talents often include reading and writing. This affects the plays in two ways. First, he is able to write out the play and thus to have a script for others to refer to. Further, he can write out the parts for those of his players who can read. Second, since he can read, he often goes to books as sources for his plays. Consequently, it is not unusual to find all sorts of highly sophisticated literary traditions drawn upon in folk theater. Shakespeare, for instance, has been played by strolling players in England and is still being played throughout the English Caribbean. However, this occasional use of printed or written sources has somewhat misled scholars. When scripts exist, they do not determine the totality of either action or dialogue; they are simply a guide for the performance that is more often than not de-parted from. This confusion between play-script and play has most recently been made by Juan Rael in his otherwise excellent book on the Mexican Shepherds' Play. We know from observations of such plays that there is a great deal of interpretation calling for the addi-tion of both clowning parts and serious parts. (A recent addition in the play performed in San Antonio, for instance, is the passage of a kneeling man across the floor to the place of the Holy Family—a pas-sage added because of the holy vow made by the man who per-formed it.)

This consideration of the recorded text fits into the idea of folk drama in its other aspects, since it emphasizes the spontaneous nature of wayside performances. Folk drama, and related sports, have been and continue to be the mark of festive occasions. Even though some of the old performances have been dying out recently, others continue to have a vital hold on life in connection with the seasonal passage, most observably, in Europe and the Americas in the Christmas and pre-Lenten celebrations in Winter and Easter and April Fool's Day in the spring.

Bibliography and Selected Readings

Alford, Violet. *Sword Dance and Drama*. London: Merlin Press, 1962. A geographical survey of the relating of sword dances with hero-combat and similar dramatic presentations.

Barber, C. L. *Shakespeare's Festive Comedy*. Reprint. Cleveland and New York: World Publishing, 1963. This, and Hardison's work, are the best studies of the uses of folk patterns of performance in a corpus of sophisticated drama.

Baskervill, Charles Read. *The Elizabethan Jig and Related Song Drama*. Reprint. New York: Dover Publications, 1965. An older but worthy study of a British popular form of dance-drama still close to its folk sources.

Bentley, Eric. *The Life of the Drama*. New York: Atheneum Press, 1967. This work is important for its discussion of the patterns of the dramatic forms of farce and melodrama and their relationship with the more sophisticated patterns of comedy and tragedy.

Campa, Arthur R. *El origen y la naturaleza del drama folklórico* in *Folklore Americas*. Miami: University of Miami Press, 1960. This study, which fills a whole issue of *Folklore Americas,* is unique in its breadth of description and unity of focus on the genre of folk drama.

Cawte, E. D., Alex Helm, and N. Peacock. *English Ritual Drama: A Geographical Index*. London: The Folklore Society, 1967. This remarkable book not only gives bibliographical listings for all of the play texts and reportings of the Saint George mumming but it provides a play typology based on the central action. Text examples are included.

Chambers, E. K. *The English Folk-Play*. Reprint. New York: Russell and Russell, 1964. An early survey of the traits (and their distribution) of the Saint George play, with a consideration of ritual origins and analogues.

———. *The Medieval Stage*. 2 vols. Oxford: Clarendon Press, 1913. This classic study remains useful in placing the British folk play traditions in the context of the entire range of folk and popular entertainments: minstrelry, revels, festivals, pageants, religious processions, etc.

Gailey, Alan. *Irish Folk Drama.* Cork: Mercier Press, 1969. A model for regional studies of folk drama, this little book surveys the Irish literature on mumming traditions, compares its texts with other British reportings, gives representative texts, surveys the scholarship on origins and analogues, and discusses the players' organization, when they perform, and why.

Gargi, Balwant. *Folk Theater of India.* Seattle: University of Washington, 1966. In spite of the title, this is primarily a solid study of diverse popular and classical theatrical traditions in India.

Halpert, Herbert, and G. M. Story, eds. *Christmas Mumming in Newfoundland.* Toronto: University of Toronto Press, 1969. A series of essays by folklorists and social scientists on the distribution, content, and social uses of a wide range of masking activities in Newfoundland.

Hardison, O. B. *Christian Rite and Christian Drama in the Middle Ages.* Baltimore: Johns Hopkins University Press, 1965. This work is, with Barber's, an example of the uses of folk drama in the criticism of more complex theatrical forms. Here the folk background is explored primarily in local forms of religious ritual.

Peacock, James. *The Rites of Modernization.* Chicago: University of Chicago Press, 1968. An ethnographic study of Indonesian urban neighborhood drama. It demonstrates a relationship between textual and social changes and argues that this makes the plays rites of modernization, helping to bring the audience contemporary values.

Rael, Juan B. *The Sources and Diffusion of the Mexican Shepherds' Plays.* Guadalajara: Libreria la Vogita, 1965. A full, rich study of a still active liturgical folk drama tradition.

Schmidt, Leopold. *Le Théâtre populaire européen.* Paris: G. P. Maisonneuve, 1965. A collection of texts from a wide range of traditions, with introductory materials of limited usefulness—yet the only such collection available.

Speaight, George. *The History of the English Puppet Theater.* London: G. G. Harrap, 1955. Much more than its title implies, this book surveys very competently the various forms of folk and popular theater that have influenced puppeting. The author ranges widely historically and geographically.

Tiddy, K. J. E. *The Mummers Play.* Oxford: Clarendon Press, 1923. A posthumous work, assembled from the author's notes and drafts, this was the first full-length study of the various forms of the British mumming plays.

Wittington, Robert. *English Pageantry: An Historical Outline.* 2 vols. Reprint. New York: Benjamin Blom, 1963. A gathering of sources concerning community-based pageants in Great Britain, this work is central to an understanding of the varieties of festival dramatic forms.

17 FOLK MUSIC
George List

The term folk music is often loosely applied to cover all traditional or aurally[1] transmitted music, music that is passed on by ear and performed by memory rather than by the written or printed musical score. In a specific sense the term refers to aurally transmitted music found within a society that also has art or cultivated music that is transmitted through the musical score. It is thus differentiated from the music of nonliterate people where music writing is nonexistent. Like the term folklore, the term folk music was originally applied to the traditions of the rural peasant societies of Europe. It has since been broadened to characterize all types of traditional music found in Western civilization. It is in the latter sense that it is used here.

From the scholarly point of view, genuine folk music exhibits a

---

1. Folklorists are primarily interested in verbal traditions that are passed on by word of mouth. They thus write of "oral tradition" and "oral transmission." Folk music is not transmitted by word of mouth, nor does man's oral apparatus play any part whatsoever in the performance of much of folk instrumental music. Folk music as well as verbal folklore, however, must be heard before it can be retransmitted. For this reason the term "aural" is used here rather than "oral."

number of traits in addition to that of aural transmission. One criterion frequently applied is that the origin of the melody must be unknown to its performer. Music that originally appeared in published form can be considered folk music if it has been passed on by ear and memory until the performer is no longer aware of its origin. Such music is said to have entered the "oral tradition." A second requirement applied is that the melody exist in variant forms. As it is transmitted from one individual to another and diffused from one locality to another, as performance succeeds performance, both unconscious and conscious modifications of the melody occur. Each such varied performance when captured in a recording or transcribed into musical notation is known as a "variant."

Folk melodies form part of the repertory of regional groups, of subcultures, rather than being known by entire populations. Once a traditional melody becomes known over a large area it loses its flexibility; it is no longer subject to variation. Songs such as "Alouette," "For He's a Jolly Good Fellow," or "Happy Birthday" are in most cases learned by ear. Few who sing them have learned them from a musical score. Nevertheless, these songs are congealed in form, and each rendition is almost identical. Scholars do not consider songs of this type folksongs since they lack variants. The melody and text of true folksong is in constant flux.

An exception to the above formulation must be made in the case of musical genres such as the Yugoslav heroic epic and traditional dirges sung in eastern Europe in which the rendition is an improvisation based upon a stock of melodic formulas. Since improvisation is a form of composition, one can consider the composer to be known in such cases. In these loosely organized genres it is the traditional style and content of the improvisation that places the performance within the category of folk music, not a specific strophic melody that can be recognized in variant forms.

Folk music and popular music are not synonymous terms[2] although as forms they share common traits. Popular music may or may not be transmitted by the musical score. It is often varied in performance and at times is improvisatory in nature. Popular music, however, is generally an ephemeral commercial product intended for mass consumption rather than a tradition known and practiced in a restricted area or by a subculture. City and country have always been in contact, and popular music and folk music have mutually influenced each other. Popular songs have become part of rural repertory, and rural folksongs have been brought to the city, each being modified to suit

2. In French usage, the terms *musique populaire* and *musique folklorique* seem to be interchangeable.

its new environment. Some folksongs, as those of college students, are urban in origin.

An interest in folk music as an aesthetic phenomenon or as a basis for musical composition has existed for many centuries. Early Icelandic and Polish folk melodies are preserved in notation in manuscripts of the thirteenth century. Numerous German folk melodies of the fifteenth century were noted in the *Lochamer Liederbuch*. In the eighteenth century, Haydn and Beethoven published arrangements of Scottish folksongs. Interest in folk music became intense in the latter part of the nineteenth century with the rise of nationalist movements. Composers like Smetana, Borodin, and Grieg seized upon the folk music of their countries as a means of developing a "national" musical style.

The collection of folk music was flourishing by the end of the century, but an objective, scientific approach to the study of folk music was slow to develop. In many publications, aesthetic considerations were still paramount. Compilers of collections of folksongs felt at liberty to alter the melodies to suit their particular taste.[3] Many folk melodies contain intervallic relationships not common to art music of the eighteenth and nineteenth centuries. Not recognizing the existence of musical systems other than those known to them, editors assumed these unfamiliar pitch patterns represented errors made by the untutored folksinger and therefore "corrected" them. As the developing scientific point of view exerted more and more influence on the study of folklore, collectors and students began to recognize that folk music often exhibits stylistic characteristics quite dissimilar to those of European art music. A conscious effort began to be made to reproduce the melodies in notation as objectively as possible, exactly as heard.

The study of folk music received its greatest impetus from the development of the cylinder phonograph, a mechanical means for reproducing sound. Before the advent of such equipment a transcription could be made only through listening to actual performance. Since the human ear is incapable of grasping every detail of a musical performance at first hearing, notation of a folk melody required listening to a number of renditions of the same item by the same informant. As there is usually some variation in the successive performances, the best of transcribers was able only to produce a general framework of the melody. The cylinder phonograph obviated this problem. By use of this recording device it is possible to listen to exact repetitions of the same performance and thus to make a rela-

3. Sabine Baring-Gould and H. Fleetwood Sheppard, *A Garland of Country Song* (London, 1895).

tively detailed and accurate transcription of the particular performance heard.

The cylinder phonograph was invented in 1877. By 1890 light, portable, spring-wound phonographs were available on the open market. Béla Vikár, a Hungarian scholar, was probably the first to use the cylinder phonograph in field recording in 1892. This seems to have set a precedent in eastern Europe where most early collectors utilized the phonograph in their field work. In contrast, Cecil Sharp, the most active collector of English folk music, made use of the phonograph on rare occasions only. He preferred to continue the practice of notating from actual performance. This practice was facilitated by the fact that the folk music of western Europe is less complex rhythmically and more akin in general style to art music than that of eastern Europe. In contemporary practice the scholar invariably makes acoustical recordings of the music in the field, usually with a tape recorder, and then transcribes it at his leisure in the laboratory.

While recording in the field, the collector obtains documentation of the recording. This includes data concerning the background of the informant, how he learned the music and skills required to perform it, the function served by the music in the community, and similar matters. The materials collected must then be placed in an order that will facilitate their study. The collection may remain in the hands of the individual who collected it or it may be preserved by deposit in one of the many archives that have been established for this purpose. Since methods of fieldwork and archiving are treated elsewhere in this volume,[4] they will not be discussed here.

Once the collection has been placed in good order, transcriptions must be made before a thorough analysis of the melodies can be made. Some information concerning singing styles and other performance practices can be secured by merely listening to the recordings rather than transcribing them. On the other hand, an accurate characterization of melodic style requires the comparison of detailed transcriptions of the music in question.

Transcription is an extremely difficult process requiring a well-trained ear. Much experience is also necessary before adequate results can be achieved. The transcriber is normally trained in European art music rather than in folk music. Hearing is a psychological as well as a physiological process. Unless the transcriber has trained his ear to hear objectively it is prone to reduce what is heard to patterns with which it is familiar, those of European art music, rather than those actually heard.

4. See Part 2 chap. 3, "Fieldwork: Recording Traditional Music," and Part 2, chap. 4, "Archiving."

Lady Isabel and the Elf Knight

A

Sung by Mrs. MARY SANDS
at Allanstand, N. C., Aug. 2, 1916

Pentatonic. Mode 3 (Tonic G).

1. Get down, get down, get down, says he, Pull off that fine silk gown; For it is too fine and cost - ly To rot in the salt - wa - ter sea, sea, sea, To rot in the salt - wa - ter sea.

2 Turn yourself all round and about
With your face turned toward the sea.
And she picked him up so manfully
And over'd him into the sea.

3 Pray help me out, pray help me out,
Pray help me out, says he,
And I'll take you to the old Scotland
And there I will marry thee.

4 Lie there, you false-hearted knight,
Lie there instead of me,
For you stripped me as naked as ever I was born,
But I'll take nothing from thee.

5 She jumped upon the milk-white steed
And she led the dapple grey,
And she rode back to her father's dwelling
Three long hours before day.

17–1. Musical transcription from Cecil J. Sharp, *English Folk Songs from the Southern Appalachians,* ed. Maud Karpeles (London: Oxford University Press, 1932).

The scholar's transcription of a folk melody is descriptive rather than prescriptive in purpose. It is a record of a particular performance intended for study. Unlike the violin part of a symphony, there is no need that it be read and translated into performance at sight. The transcriber may therefore offer as much detail as he feels useful as a description of the musical style. A competent and persistent transcriber can produce an amazingly detailed score. The degree of detail notated depends, however, upon the purpose of the transcription. If the desire is to study certain performance practices, it is necessary to indicate phenomena such as vocal glides, sharpening and flatting of pitch, and slight divergences in duration of pitches. Should the scholar wish only to compare general melodic outlines, much less detail need be indicated (Fig. 17–1).

Béla Bartók, the Hungarian ethnomusicologist, published a great many highly detailed transcriptions of folk melodies of eastern Europe. He apparently believed this elaboration of detail to be indispensable in the understanding of the musical styles of the region (Fig. 17–2).[5] On the other hand, in making his numerous transcriptions of English and Anglo-American folk tunes, Cecil Sharp produced rather simple and straightforward scores, offering few indications of subtleties in rhythm or meter and none of vocal glides or of pitches flatted or sharpened less than a half step.[6]

Folk music that exhibits a regular metrical pattern, as does music that accompanies the dance, presents much less difficulty in transcription than music whose free rhythmic organization is closer to that of speech. Two terms, *tempo giusto* and *parlando rubato,* are employed to describe these contrasting types of melodies. A *tempo giusto* melody can be given a regular metrical signature and the measures indicated by bar lines. A *parlando rubato* melody is often written without a metrical signature. In this case rhythmic groups may be indicated by vertical dotted lines instead of bars or bars may be used to indicate phrasing rather than measure.

The notation system in use in Western art music offers no means of indicating many of the subtleties of pitch and rhythm that the transcriber of folk music wishes to describe. In an important and pioneer work published in 1909 two German scholars, Otto Abraham and Erich M. von Hornbostel[7] offered a number of special symbols

5. See, for example, Béla Bartók and Albert B. Lord, *Serbo-Croatian Folk Songs* (New York: Columbia University Press, 1951).

6. See, for example, Cecil J. Sharp, *English Folk Songs from the Southern Appalachians,* ed. Maud Karpeles, 2 vols. (London, 1932). First ed., 1917.

7. Otto Abraham and Erich M. von Hornbostel, "Vorschläge zur Transkription exotischer Melodien," *Sammelbände der Internationalen Musikgesellschaft* 11 (1909).

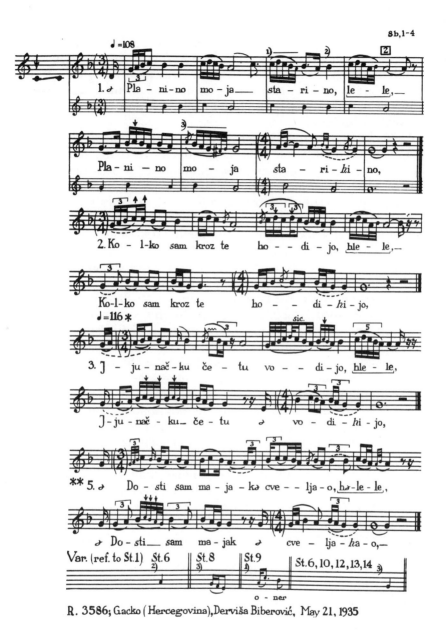

R. 3586; Gacko (Hercegovina), Derviša Biberović, May 21, 1935

17–2. Musical transcription from Béla Bartók and Albert B. Lord, *Serbo-Croatian Folk Songs* (New York: Columbia University Press, 1951).

with which to describe such phenomena. Later scholars have substituted other symbols that they found more useful and have invented further markings as needed to describe characteristics of a particular style. There is still no common agreement on methods of notation. Thus when publishing transcriptions scholars usually offer a key to the symbols utilized.

Conferences of experts in folk music were held under the auspices of UNESCO in 1949 and 1950 in an attempt to codify transcription methods. The participants in these meetings found it somewhat difficult to reach agreement, probably because of the disparity of the musical styles in which each was interested. Although the manual published as a result of these discussions, *Notation de la Musique Folklorique*,[8] is a useful guide, the methods suggested have not received general acceptance.

A number of acoustical and electronic devices are also made use of in transcription. Where pitches vary consistently from those utilized in Western art music, the system of *cents* devised by Alexander John Ellis[9] can be used as a measurement. In this system the tempered semitone, the smallest interval on the piano, is divided into one hundred equal parts. Pitches may be measured in this manner by ear through use of the simple instrument known as the *monochord* or by means of electronic devices such as the *sonoscope*.

Electronically produced graphs of melodies can also be secured through use of the *spectograph* or the *melograph*. The spectograph reproduces the overtones of a pitch as well as its fundamental, and the former must be elided to secure a melodic contour. The melograph, developed by the American musicologist and folklorist Charles Seeger,[10] produces a graph of the fundamentals only (Fig. 17–3). Melody is as much a cultural as an acoustical phenomenon. The graphs produced by the melograph offer such an abundance of detail that they must be interpreted to be of value in analysis. They are thus of more utility as a check upon the transcriber's ear than as transcriptions in their own right.

In western Europe and the United States, scale or mode is the characteristic by which melodies are most commonly classified. A scale is an abstract representation of the pitch materials found in the melody in which all pitches heard are notated upon the staff in as-

8. *Notation de la Musique Folklorique*. Recommandations du Comité d' Experts réunis par les Archives Internationales de Musique Populaire à Genève du 4 au 9 juillet 1949 et à Paris du 12 au 14 décembre 1950. Publié en 1952 avec le concours de l'U.N.E.S.C.O.

9. Alexander J. Ellis, "On the Musical Scales of Various Nations," *Journal of the Society of Arts* (1885).

10. Charles Seeger, "Toward a Universal Sound-Writing for Musicology," *Journal of the International Folk Music Council* 9 (1957) : 63–66.

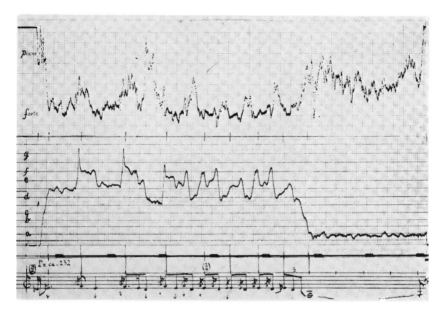

17–3. From Charles Seeger, "Prescriptive and Descriptive Music Writing," *Musical Quarterly* 44 (1958). Automatic graph (oscillogram), made by electronic-mechanical reduction written directly on paper, of Abatutsi traditional song, sung by man's voice. Excerpt of Band 16 in *Voice of the Congo* (Riverside World Folk Music Series, RLP 4002), recorded in Ruanda by Alan P. and Barbara W. Merriam, 1951–52. Upper, broken, line shows amplitude; lower, continuous, line, fundamental frequency, upon rectangular millimeter chart with ruled, semitonal staff, and with seconds marked by timer. (Reduced.)

cending or descending order. This is normally done within the compass of an octave. Scales are described by the number of different pitches found within the octave—heptatonic, seven pitches; hexatonic, six pitches; pentatonic, five pitches; and so on. The major and minor scales that form the basis of eighteenth- and nineteenth-century art music and the earlier scales utilized in the liturgy of the Catholic Church contain seven pitches and are therefore described as heptatonic scales. Folk music scales frequently contain less than seven pitches. Hexatonic scales are common in Anglo-American folk tunes, and pentatonic scales are widespread. Traditional children's tunes often exhibit scales of less than five pitches.

In the determination of the scale of a melody, one method utilized is to omit consideration of ornamental tones, those tones considered of less importance since they occur infrequently, in unstressed position, or are produced with less intensity. In the notated scale such secondary tones are omitted or indicated within parentheses or by means of smaller note heads.

A mode is a scale written in such a manner as to indicate the functions and relationships of the constituent tones. The primary function shown is that of the tonic, normally the pitch upon which the melody ends. The selection of the final tone of the melody as the basis for the organization of the mode has been characteristic of European musical theory for ten centuries. In its modern development this procedure is based upon the assumption that the differing tones of the mode exhibit various dynamic functions, all related to one tone, the tonic, which offers a final point of rest. Each mode is characterized by a particular set of interval relationships. Thus, beginning with the tonic, the major mode contains two whole tones, a semitone, three whole tones, and a semitone. The dorian mode contains a whole tone, a semitone, three whole tones, a semitone, and a whole tone.

Cecil Sharp was one of the first scholars to classify large bodies of folk melodies according to their modes. In his *English Folk-Song: Some Conclusions*,[11] he notes that many English folk tunes are cast in the medieval church modes, as, for example, the dorian or mixolydian, rather than in the major and minor modes that formed the basis of Western art music of the eighteenth and nineteenth centuries.

Although very many types of studies can be made utilizing a limited number of melodies, the achievement of general conclusions concerning a musical style normally requires the transcription and comparison of a large body of material. Such larger studies may be exami-

11. Cecil Sharp, *English Folk-Song, Some Conclusions*, 4th ed. revised (Belmont, California, 1965).

nations of the music of a particular region, as Cecil Sharp's *English Folk Songs from the Southern Appalachians*,[12] or of a particular genre, as Bertrand H. Bronson's *The Traditional Tunes of the Child Ballads*.[13]

The classification of folksong and folk instrumental music may take place on two levels. The first involves the placing of large bodies of melodies in sufficient order that an individual melody can be readily located, thus providing a finding list or melodic index. The second, and higher, level requires that the melodies be organized and classified in such a manner that genetic relationships can be traced. The emphasis here is genetic and historical, leading to the study of the process of change and evolution. By this means archetypes and tune families can be established. In both cases the problem is to arrive at groupings in which similar or related melodies will be found in proximity. The development of such a classification is extremely difficult to achieve since the interrelationships of melodies are indeed very complex.

In eastern Europe large bodies of folk music have been published in classified form. Béla Bartók's *Hungarian Folk Music*,[14] for example, contains transcriptions of 320 melodies. In this work Bartók does not use either scale or mode as a means of classification. Rather he classifies the melodies according to the number of their text lines, the number of syllables per line, the cadential pitches of each melodic line, and the compass of the melodies. Classification by means of line and syllable count had been utilized by earlier students of folk music in Hungary. Bartók's use of cadential pitches as a means of classification was adapted from the work of the Finnish scholar, Ilmari Krohn,[15] although the particular combination of methods used and their order of application is that of Bartók.

Other scholars have made use of simpler methods of classification that do not involve musical notation. These scholars have usually felt that an *incipit*, an outline of the first phrase of the melody, is sufficient for purposes of classification. Thus Sigurd Bernhard Hustvedt[16] has characterized the first phrase of Anglo-American ballad tunes by

12. See n. 6.
13. Bertrand H. Bronson, *The Traditional Tunes of the Child Ballads*, 4 vols. (Princeton, New Jersey, 1959, 1962, 1966, 1971).
14. Béla Bartók, *Hungarian Folk Music* (London, 1931).
15. Ilmari Krohn, "Welche ist die beste Methode, um Volks- und volksmässige Lieder nach ihrer melodischen (nicht textlichen) Beschaffenheit lexikalisch zu ordnen?" *Sammelbände der Internationalen Musikgesellschaft* 4 (1903): 643–60.
16. Sigurd Bernhard Hustvedt, *A Melodic Index of Child's Ballad Tunes*, Publications of the University of California at Los Angeles in Languages and Literature, Vol. 1, No. 2 (1936): 51–78.

representing the number of semitones found in the rising and falling intervals by numbers and letters. Bertrand Bronson[17] has represented the melodic outline of phrases of ballad tunes by means of numbers indicating the scale degrees of the accented pitches. A similar method is in use as an *incipit* index at the Deutsches Volksliedarchiv in Freiburg.[18] In this case the melodic outline of the first phrase is symbolized by the letter names of the accented pitches. Omitting consideration of specific scale degrees or intervals, Sirvart Poladian[19] has suggested that melodies be characterized by their general contours, "undulating," "gradually descending," and the like. This method is rather imprecise but may be useful as a general description of melody.

Bronson has combined methods used in eastern and western Europe and the United States in his large-scale study of ballad tunes utilizing computer techniques.[20] Among the means of analysis employed are compass, mode, cadential pitches of phrases, and outlines of the accented pitches of the phrases.

Analysis of large bodies of folk melodies has produced notable results. Sharp and later writers have been able to define the scalar and modal characteristics of Anglo-American folk music. Bartók's studies enabled him to establish three basic styles of Hungarian folk music, the old style, the new style, and a miscellaneous class. The examination of large bodies of Anglo-American tunes has led American scholars to attempt the description of "tune families," groups of melodies that display constant correspondences and interrelationships. Samuel Bayard[21] has described two such tune families; Bronson[22] has established tentative archetypes for the same number.

From the various studies there have developed theories concerning the origin and age of folk melodies and the forces and mechanisms that produce melodic modification. These theories are frequently based on or influenced by Darwinian evolutionary theory. Zoltan Kodály[23] believes that folk music exhibits a process of stratification

17. Bertrand H. Bronson, "Toward the Comparative Analysis of British-American Folk Tunes," *Journal of American Folklore* 72 (1959) : 165 ff.

18. Wolfgang Suppan, "The German Folksong Archive," *The Folklore and Folk Music Archivist*, Vol. 7, No. 2 (1964) : 29 ff.

19. Sirvart Poladian, "The Problem of Melodic Variation in Folk Song," *Journal of American Folklore* 55 (1942) : 204–11.

20. Bronson, "Toward the Comparative Analysis of British-American Folk Tunes," *Journal of American Folklore* 72 (1959) : 165ff.

21. Samuel Bayard, "Two Representative Families of British Tradition," *Midwest Folklore* 4 (Spring 1954) : 13 ff.

22. Bertrand H. Bronson, "Melodic Stability in Oral Tradition," *Journal of the International Folk Music Council* 3 (1951) : 50–55.

23. Zoltán Kodály, *Folk Music of Hungary* (London, 1960) .

into historical layers, the oldest of which exemplifies the most characteristic features of the ethnic or indigenous style. New styles develop constantly as derivative of the old or through the incorporation of foreign influences. George Herzog[24] is of the opinion that simplicity in melodic structure is an indication of melodic age or archaism in style. Thus the many children's songs that exhibit extremely limited scalar structures represent a primitive layer in European song.

Sharp postulates the principles underlying the evolution of folk melodies to be continuity, variation, and selection. In this scheme a strong tendency to conserve tradition is modified by variation in performance. Selection governs what is retained in tradition. Later studies by Bayard and Bronson have indicated that the principle of continuity is predominant since archaic melodic styles that can be traced back for several centuries are still found in aural tradition. According to these scholars, variation seems to be held within certain norms producing a relative stability of tradition.

The study of American Negro folk music has centered around a controversy concerning the origins of this musical style. "Survivalists" such as Melville J. Herskovits[25] have judged the basic elements of the style to be African in origin. George Pullen Jackson in his *White and Negro Spirituals*[26] attempts to prove that American Negro music is derived from Anglo-American melodies. Present opinion rests between these two poles, ascribing certain characteristics of the rhythm and certain performance practices such as responsorial singing to African influence and the general melodic and harmonic materials to the European.

We have dealt so far with the melodies themselves. Their manner of performance is also of interest. Although Charles Seeger in his article, "Singing Style,"[27] has outlined the directions that studies of performance practice can fruitfully follow, there have been few special studies of this nature. Those recently made by Alan Lomax,[28] an extremely active collector of folk music, characterize singing style by means of terms such as "tense" and "relaxed." Earlier writers have described traditional Anglo-American song performance as straightforward and undemonstrative. Thus a stanza describing a murder is sung with no more expression than one describing a journey. In both

---

24. George Herzog, "Some Primitive Layers in European Folk Song," *Bulletin of the American Musicological Society* 10–11 (1947): 11 ff.
25. Melville J. Herskovits, "Patterns of Negro Music," *Transactions of the Illinois State Academy of Science* 34 (1941): 19–23.
26. (New York, 1943).
27. Charles Seeger, "Singing Style," *Western Folklore* 17 (1958): 3–11.
28. Alan Lomax, "Folk Song Style," *American Anthropologist* 61 (1959): 927–54.

England and New England the last line of the song is often spoken rather than sung. American Negro folksong, on the other hand, has been characterized as highly expressive, shifting frequently from song to declamation. A fully adequate categorization of performance practices is yet to be devised.

There is no fixed bond between the text and the melody of a folksong. The same text may be sung to different tunes, often within the same region. There are usually more texts in the repertory than tunes. Children's taunts and play-calls are sung in Europe and the United States to much the same melody. There are many texts for the old eastern European calendric songs and dirges, but they are sung to a very limited melodic repertory. Although text and tune are thus not an indissoluble whole, they must obviously fit together. Some relationships in rhythm, accent, and caesuras have been established. Evidence also exists that melody may affect verse structure. In eastern Europe texts have usually been taken into consideration in the study of the melodies of folksongs. Although scholars in the United States have recently become more inclined to study both aspects of folksong simultaneously, melodies and texts have more frequently been examined as separate entities.

The increasing influence of ethnological theory on the study of folk music has brought to the fore an interest in the social milieu in which folk music exists and in the function of music to this milieu. Folk music is said to exhibit a clearer social function than art music. This judgment, in particular, is applicable to the music of the old European rural folk community where music played an indispensable role in the turning points of human life—childhood, marriage, and death. Here elaborate song cycles accompanied the wedding ceremony, and funerary rites involved long and complex dirges sung by professional mourners. Lullabies were and are sung to infants in both Europe and America. In the French Pyrenees there was an abundance of teaching songs that were sung to children to teach them to walk, to eat their meals, and to otherwise adapt themselves to community standards. The maturation of children was also served by play-songs, often imitations of adult activities. Chanteys and other work songs directed the energies of workers or relieved the tedium of labor.

Studies of the function of folk music are not only concerned with the role of music in society but with that of the performer of the music as well. In his *Vie musicale d'un village,* Constantin Brăiloiu[29] offers autobiographies of the individual performers and an investiga-

29. (Paris, 1960).

tion in detail of the function of their performances in a Romanian village. Other scholars have dealt with the means by which the folk musician learns his performing skills and the influences that bear upon the establishment of style preferences by audience and performer.

Social function is also evident in industrial folksongs, songs of miners, railwaymen, and textile workers. These songs have been collected and studied in both the United States and Europe. Often they are songs of protest that have been utilized in the struggles of unions and radical groups, particularly in the United States during the depression of the 1930s.

Beginning in the 1940s, folk music became very popular among middle-class youth in urban areas of the United States and Great Britain. Many have themselves taken up the performance of folk music. This movement is known as the urban folk music "revival." As public interest grew there developed a class of professional performers of folk music, entertainers who earned their living, or a portion thereof, through the performance of folk music. In a few cases these individuals came from an environment in which the music they perform was part of a local tradition. Others, with no roots in a folk environment, learned their songs from recordings of traditional performances or from each other. The folk music, thus transplanted to a new milieu and performed for a different audience, is necessarily modified to some degree and loses its full traditional character.

In the contemporary scene there has been a merging of folk and popular music styles, producing a "folk style" that is in wide use in radio, television, and film and forms the basis of thousands of performances offered in commercially issued disks. This, in turn, has affected the performance of folk music in rural areas. According to the published statements of performers of present-day folk-popular music, they now apply the term "folk" to any performance that exhibits any element linking it to a traditional folk style or embodying an element of protest.

The rapid industrialization of eastern Europe is producing similar effects. In addition, Communist governments have utilized folk music for propaganda purposes, employing trained symphony musicians to perform it. Thus folk music, like society, is undergoing a constantly increasing rate of change. Acculturative influences, where the music of one culture affects that of another, can also be seen. Asian instruments such as the sitar are now being introduced into folk-popular ensembles. As the rural folk society disappears or is transformed, an even greater variety of urban-based aural traditions will emerge that will form a fascinating basis for future studies.

Bibliography and Selected Readings

General

Herzog, George. "Song: Folk Song and the Music of Folk Song." *Standard Dictionary of Folklore, Mythology, and Legend.* Edited by Maria Leach. New York: Funk and Wagnalls, 1950. 2:1032–50. A concise but thorough discussion of the characteristics of folk music, its relation to the social context in which it is found, and the study of folk music.

Lloyd, A. L. "Folk Music." *Encyclopaedia Britannica.* 1964. 9:522–26. A later survey that considers various definitions of folk music, theories concerning its origin and development, the function of folk music in society, performance characteristics, melodic and rhythmic patterns, and folk instruments. Includes discussion of the urban folk music "revival" movement.

Various authors. Articles concerning folk music of Europe and the Americas. *Grove's Dictionary of Music and Musicians.* 8th ed. 1954. 3:182–422. Additions and corrections in 10:135–72. Includes articles on the folk music of Latin America, a region that, in general, is not considered in the above articles by Herzog and Lloyd.

Area Collections and Studies

Bartók, Béla, and Albert B. Lord. *Serbo-Croatian Folksongs.* New York: Columbia University Press, 1951. In the section concerning music Bartók offers 54 of his characteristic, highly detailed transcriptions and a concise discussion of his methods of transcribing and classifying folk melodies.

Bronson, Bertrand H. *The Traditional Tunes of the Child Ballads with their Texts.* Princeton, New Jersey: Princeton University Press, 1959–71. 4 vols. An anthology of the traditional tunes associated with ballad texts akin to those classified by Francis James Child in his *The English and Scottish Popular Ballads.* Like Child, who offers no clear exposition of his method of grouping texts, Bronson does not offer full explanation of the basis upon which he groups the tunes. He does briefly describe his method of modal classification that is derived to some extent from that of Sharp.

Courlander, Harold. *Negro Folk Music U.S.A.* New York: Columbia University Press, 1963. The most recent and comprehensive survey of the subject. Although transcriptions of music are included, the emphasis is folkloristic or anthropological rather than musicological.

Kodály, Zoltán. *Folk Music of Hungary.* Translated by Ronald Tempest and Cynthia Jolly. London: Barrie and Rockliff, 1960. Discusses the various Hungarian folk music styles with special reference to how they differ from those of the popular and Gypsy music of his country.

Sharp, Cecil J. *English Folk-Song, Some Conclusions.* London: Simpkin, 1907. One of the earliest and most provocative studies of folk music and its development. Sharp's evolutionary theories are still being debated. The work suffers, however, from Sharp's apparent lack of knowledge of folk music styles other than the English. Some of the conclusions offered have not withstood the test of time.

———. *English Folk Songs from the Southern Appalachians.* Edited by Maud Karpeles. London: Oxford University Press, 1932. Reprinted 1960, 2 vols. in one. (First ed., 1917). This collection was made when that region was still relatively isolated and represents the older white traditions. Relations with folk songs in England are emphasized.

Wilgus, D. K. *Anglo-American Folksong Scholarship Since 1898.* Brunswick, New Jersey: Rutgers University Press, 1959. Chap. 4, "The Study of Anglo-American Folksong," pp. 240–343. The discussion is primarily devoted to texts, although a summary of tune scholarship is offered, pp. 326–36. It is the most complete summary extant but is somewhat limited in its usefulness since the author is not a specialist in folk music.

18 FOLK DANCE
Joann Wheeler Kealiinohomoku

What is folk dance? How deceptively simple such a question appears.
One might reply, logically, "Folk dance is dance done by the folk."
Alan Dundes tells us that "the folk" are any group of people "who
share at least one common factor."[1] Immediately we get into trouble
if we consider a group whose common denominator is a non-folk
dance form. For example, if a classical ballet company comprises a
folk, its dance, by this logic, is folk dance. Clearly no folklorist would
find that conclusion tenable. Neither would the ballet company! The
ballet company would admit, however, that much of their chore-
ography, many of their steps, and several of their story themes are
based on or inspired by folk dance. What do *they* mean by folk dance?
They mean "national" dance and/or "racial"[2] dance, and they usually

1. Alan Dundes, *The Study of Folklore* (Englewood Cliffs, New Jersey: Prentice-
Hall, 1965) , p. 2.
2. Walter Terry, "Folk Dancing in America," *The Dance Encyclopedia*, ed.
Anatole Chujoy and P. W. Manchester (New York: Simon and Schuster, 1967;
first pub. ed., Anatole Chujoy, 1947) , pp. 370–71.

mean the "unrefined" dances of European peasants. Some would answer that folk dance for ballet is the same as that division of their art known as "character dance" or "characteristic dance,"[3] a term derived from the French and meaning dance in the characteristic style of some nonaristocratic group that has a traditional, unself-conscious, anonymously choreographed (or, even, communally derived) dance that is both distinctive and "quaint." If we follow Dundes and call a ballet company a "folk," we find that such a company does have its own lore. Indeed, a fascinating study could be made of the folklore of a ballet company. But their dance is not folk dance. Something goes amiss in the transposition of the term folklore to folk dance, because the genre does not seem to permit parallel substitution. Ballet people say their dance is not folk dance because it is innovative, self-consciously choreographed, learned and performed by known artists and professional dancers (i.e., dancers who make dance a vocation).

Let us see if the idea of "national" will delineate folk dance, and let us use Japanese dance for the test. Some of our Western dance scholars imply that this is the answer; such a well-known choreographer as Agnes DeMille includes the Azuma Kabuki Company in her chapter on contemporary folk dance companies.[4] "Travesty!" shout those in the know about Japanese dance. Though it would be admitted that there is Japanese folk dance, such as the dances performed for the Bon Odori festivals, never would such highly refined forms as Kabuki, Noh, or Gagaku be considered in the folk idiom; indeed, these are considered national treasures. It is because of such distinctions that the Indiana University "Archives of Traditional Music" had to adopt their current name over their old title of "Archives of Folk and Primitive Music"; too many national groups were offended by the idea of lumping together all of their music and dance forms under the rubric of "folk" or "primitive."

Perhaps the protesting nationality groups know what folk dance *is* if they know what it is *not*. Do they also mean a traditional, unself-conscious, anonymously choreographed (or communally derived) dance that is both distinctive and quaint and performed by peasant groups? Well, not quite. In Asia we find dance forms that, in ethno-classifications, are *not* folk dance but that are traditional as opposed to innovative, such as Gagaku, and whose choreographers are lost in the pages of time and are even imputed to be mythical beings. They would reject the idea of vocation as the criterion to divide folk and

3. Troy Kinney and Margaret West Kinney, *The Dance* (New York: Frederick A. Stokes Co., 1924), p. 165.
4. Agnes DeMille, *The Book of the Dance* (New York: Golden Press, 1963), pp. 166–71.

classic forms because often the most highly polished performers of classic dance forms do not make dance a vocation: For example, the classical dances of Java have, until recently, been performed only by the aristocracy or those attached to the royal house and they danced for pious as well as artistic motives.[5] On the other hand, throughout Asia there are traveling companies of performers who make their living from dancing. Their work is not considered a classical art, but it is considered a folk form, for example the Burmese traveling troupes. This negation of the criterion of professionalism should not disturb us. After all, we find paid craftsmen who are considered to be plying a folk art, such as the oldtime barrel and basket makers. It seems clear that dance scholars who use the criterion of professionalism to separate art from folk dance are thinking only of Western standards for the performing arts. For Asia it seems that the major distinction between folk dance and art dance is the degree of recognition and prestige awarded to the dance form by the national government. Such a distinction does not help in the United States where the government has paid scant attention to any dance form. Does this leave us in a state of confusion?

The confusion is compounded further if we question the inclusion of dance by nonliterate groups of the world. "No!" exclaim most folklorists. "Primitive dance is not folk dance." Curt Sachs, for example, claimed that folk dance fits on an evolutionary continuum, midway between primitive and civilized dance, and its presence in the contemporary world is a kind of living relic.[6] Arnold Haskell tells us the distinction is that primitive dance is communal and segregated by sex whereas folk dance is characterized by couples dancing with partners of the opposite sex.[7] For those who would imply that folk dance is on some kind of evolutionary scale there is no guide to show what caused such changes to come about, to indicate the point of transition. For those who use the division of the sexes as a criterion, they will soon find too many exceptions for a rule to be drawn. For example, English morris dances are for male dancers only, yet we find some "primitive" Tahitian dances with male and female couples.

Some suggest that the distinction is that primitive dance is ritually based, whereas folk dance is for pleasure. If that is so then we must wonder what Cecil Sharp and Violet Alford have been writing about

5. Information in a personal communication to the author from Sri Kusumobroto, director of the Dance Conservatory Krida Beksa Wirama, Tedjokusuman, Jogjakarta, Indonesia, 1968.

6. Curt Sachs, *World History of the Dance,* trans. Bessie Schönberg (New York: Bonanza Books, 1937) , p. 216.

7. Arnold Haskell, *The Wonderful World of Dance* (New York: Garden City Books, 1960) , p. 50.

in their voluminous works on weapon dances, hobbyhorse dances, and the like in England and throughout Europe. Clearly these dances are bound to ritual.

The real puzzler is to find it perfectly acceptable to include "folktales" of the Hopi or the Hawaiians, for example, as part of the provenance of folklorists, even those tales that are both serious and part of ritual. Why are not their dances, therefore, folk dances? As a matter of fact, these dance forms are generally considered proper subjects for anthropologists rather than for folklorists. This can be proved by picking at random almost any book about folk dance in the United States. Almost without exception, such books never even consider American Indian dances as folk dance. American folk dance, we are told, includes regionally developed forms that have an Old World heritage, and this means the square and round dances as they developed in rural areas. Indian dances are excluded because they do not represent the general population of the United States, and because they are usually ritually oriented.[8] Yet, ritual orientation is a criterion for "real" folk dance in England, as for example, the May Day hobbyhorse masques of rural England, mentioned above.

Curiously, folk dance experts in the United States do not include popular dance as a folk form.[9] This exclusion seems contrary to all of the criteria so far suggested. Popular dance is nonritual, nonprofessional, unself-conscious, anonymously choreographed, and usually performed by couples of the opposite sex. Conversely, by the way, there are performing companies today from Mexico, the U.S.S.R., Yugoslavia, the Philippines, and elsewhere that purport to be doing folk dance yet violate all of the suggested criteria for folk dance. The Janković sisters call this "adapted" or "paraphrased folk dance" as compared with "genuine folk dance."[10] They have no argument against adapted dances as long as they are honestly presented as such, and as long as the producers strive only to promote "the animation of folk style on the stage."[11]

Returning once again to Dundes and the problem that his all-inclusive definition of "folk" presents, we find no additional help from the model he gives for the "lore" part of that compound word "folklore." Lore, he tells us, is best explained to the beginner, not by definition, but by a listing of what it includes, and he includes non-

8. John Martin, *The Dance* (New York: Tudor Publishing, 1946), p. 26.
9. See Elizabeth Burchenal, "Folk Dances of the United States: Regional Types and Origins," *Journal of the International Music Council* 3 (1951) : 18.
10. Ljubica Janković and Danica Janković, *Summary Folk Dances* 1–6 (Belgrade: Council of Science and Culture of the Government of the F.P.R. of Yugoslavia, 1934–51), p. 31.
11. Ibid. p. 33.

verbal forms such as folk dance.[12] But what is folk dance? It does not suffice to follow the model of listing inclusions, nor even of listing what folk dance excludes. We can summarize our findings by saying that, variously, folk dance is traditional, but that not all traditional forms are folk dance; we learn that it is nonvocational, but that sometimes it is vocational; we realize that it is communal, but that this is not always so; we are instructed that it is and that it is not ritually based. We have seen that the most widespread form of recreational dance in the United States—modern popular dance—fulfills all the basic criteria, only it is not considered folk dance. Strangely, in the United States it *is* considered folk dance if a group of people perform the dances of some group other than their own, which eliminates the criterion of "national" or "racial." Also, we cannot consider the degree of competence to distinguish folk dance from some other dance form, because many folk dances are difficult to do, may require much rehearsing, and there are gifted folk dance performers who qualify as artists.

By this time we might well wash our hands of the whole affair, and say that if no one can agree on what constitutes folk dance, maybe the phenomenon is but an illusion and does not really exist. Clearly, however, no one questions seriously the existence of folk dance. The lesson is for the reader to beware of any glib conclusion of what it is.

Our task of delineating folk dance is given a new lease when we study those who have tried to remedy the problem by substituting a word for folk dance, or by analyzing the phenomenon sufficiently to subcategorize it and to discover meaningful features. For the first, we have Marshall and Jean Stearns calling jazz dance "vernacular" dance.[13] Since later we hope to show that jazz dance, as a form of popular dance, can legitimately be subsumed under the name of folk dance, we must pay particular attention to this use of the word "vernacular." For one thing, this substitution permits the Stearnses to include polished professional performers along with nonprofessional performers, who may also be gifted dancers, as we have already mentioned. Because we want to retain the term "folk dance" to show its relationship with other forms of folklife, we will not substitute the term "vernacular" but rather will use the term to help us define folk dance, as we will see.

Our second enlightenment comes from Hoerburger's subdivision of folk dance (and folk music) into what he calls a first and a second existence. By this he means that in the first existence "folk dance is

---

12. Dundes, *The Study of Folklore*, p. 3.
13. Marshall Stearns and Jean Stearns, *Jazz Dance: The Story of American Vernacular Dance.* (New York: Macmillan Co.; London: Collier-Macmillan Ltd., 1968).

an integral part of the life of a community," whereas in the second existence it is no longer a functionally integral part of the community but has become the property "only of a few interested people."[14] This is a distinction that does not directly help us to define folk dance, but it does help us to refine our understanding of folk dance in all its ramifications. For one thing, this useful dichotomy points to contrasts in the mechanisms of transmission. Dundes has already pointed out that oral transmission need not be a criterion for folklore:

[a] difficulty with the criterion of oral transmission concerns those forms of folklore depending upon body movements; that is, there is some question as to whether folk dances, games, and gestures are passed on *orally*. A child may acquire these forms by watching and participating without necessarily being instructed verbally.[15]

It would be a mistake to read this and believe that folk dancers are mute in this area of folklife. It is more accurate to say that folk dance also *depends upon* oral transmission. Seldom does formalized motor behavior occur without being part of some dramatic context, the understanding of which is passed on orally. In other words, participants in folk dance usually talk about the dance and its context, whereas they might not talk about everyday gestures that are learned by unconscious mimicry. Whenever folk dance occurs it is always part of a special occasion insofar as it requires the will to perform. In addition, folk dance standards are maintained and taught through vocal approval and disapproval of the visual results. Actual dance movements are indeed usually (but not always) transmitted through a combination of emulation and trial and error. Very often experienced performers will help the novice by physically putting him through the paces. Sometimes the master performer even manipulates the neophyte's body into the right shapes and movements.[16]

In any case, the method of transmission for first existence folk dance is comparable to an oral tradition in depending upon a one-to-one relationship between the transmitter and the receiver.

Second existence folk dance, as Hoerburger points out, is more fixed or less dynamic. It is usually excerpted from the dramatic context and is not a part of a larger complex that requires oral transmission. But insofar as it is often a recreative process through how-

14. Felix Hoerburger, "Once Again: On the Concept of 'Folk Dance,' " *Journal of the International Folk Music Council* 20 (1968) : 30–32.

15. Dundes, *The Study of Folklore,* p. 2.

16. Joann Wheeler Kealiinohomoku, "A Comparative Study of Dance as a Constellation of Motor Behaviors Among African and United States Negroes" (M.A. thesis, Northwestern University, 1965) , p. 110.

to-do-it manuals, and by mnemonic aids and notation systems used by the dance leader, actual instruction may be verbal. Thus we find a real qualitative rather than quantitative differentiation between the first and second existence folk dance—the former to be equated, in part, with survivals, and the latter to be, more or less, equated with revivals.

Hoerburger sent out a questionnaire to the members of the International Folk Music Council to see if there was any consensus on what comprised folk dance. The replies indicated an amazing range of answers.[17] Such a diversity of opinion makes it necessary to avoid a rigid definition. Clearly, we need a working definition. For practical purposes, let us define folk dance as:

a vernacular dance form performed in either its first or second existence as part of the little tradition within the great tradition of a given society. It is understood that dance is an affective mode of expression which requires both time and space. It employs motor behavior in redundant patterns which are closely linked to the definitive features of musicality.

This definition combines the contributions of the Stearnses and of Hoerburger. It also includes the concept of the little and great tradition as proposed by Redfield,[18] and it includes the useful notion of redundance as suggested by Lomax.[19]

Under the terms of this definition both social and popular dance forms, including jazz dance, can be considered folk dance. In contrast, the art and classical dance forms (known as "ethnologic dance"[20] in some of the dance literature) are not so considered.

The dances of a nonliterate society would not be included as folk dance under this definition if that society has no dichotomy between a little and a great tradition. It appears, however, that such a double tradition does exist in many nonliterate societies. For example, the ancient Hawaiian hula, as performed by initiated practitioners, is not to be considered folk dance under the terms of this definition, but the social, improvised dances performed by noninitiated people for their own pleasure at feasts and the like might well be considered

17. Felix Hoerburger, "Folk Dance Survey," *Journal of the International Folk Music Council* 17, part 1 (1965) : 7–8.

18. Robert Redfield, *The Little Community* and *Peasant Society and Culture* (Chicago and London: Phoenix Books, University of Chicago Press, 1969; first published separately, 1956) , pp. 23, 40–41.

19. Alan Lomax, "Special Features of the Sung Communication," *Essays on the Verbal and Visual Arts* (Proceedings of the American Ethnological Society's 1966 meetings, 1967) , p. 124.

20. See Walter Sorell, *The Dance Through the Ages* (New York: Grosset and Dunlap, 1967) , p. 75, and Joann Wheeler Kealiinohomoku, "An Anthropologist Looks at Ballet as a Form of Ethnic Dance," *Impulse* (1970) : 24–33.

folk dance. Or again, the formal dances of the Hopis that are per-formed by initiated society members would not be considered folk dance. But if we are willing to extend to them the notion of an in-ternal great and little tradition, the spontaneous corn-grinding dances that used to be performed might well be considered a folk form; while today the Friday and Saturday night dances in which the young people dance in couples to the music of country-western, rock, Mex-ican-type bands might now be the equivalent for recreation within a little tradition, newly developed, in relationship to the non-Indian world's great tradition.

The above definition does not include the notion of "authentic" or the idea of tradition as passed through the generations, although the usual definitions insist on the inclusion of these criteria.[21] Such dis-tinctions become meaningless when carefully considered. As long as a dance form is viable in function and is the reflection of vernacular expression it has its own intrinsic authenticity, even though it may be the product of change and innovation, or even direct creation. This is consonant with the more modern folkloristic thinking that admits to its lists of serious study such verbal forms as streetcorner jokes, children's jump rope rhymes, graffiti, and the like. Neither can any form of expression be said to have emerged without some precedent, even if the lineage is not stretched forth in a clear un-broken line of tradition. Expressive and affective behavior does not arise in a vacuum; it always develops within a cultural milieu.

HISTORY OF THE STUDY OF FOLK DANCE

In the English-speaking world, scholars from England began formal studies of folk dance long before Americans did. Three figures stand especially tall in English folk dance scholarship. They are Cecil J. Sharp, Maud Karpeles, and Violet Alford. Sharp was the first serious scholar of folk dance in England, and his studies were inspired after a great awakening of awareness within himself when he saw a morris dance in 1899.[22] Sharp founded the English Folk Dance Society in 1911. In 1932, eight years after Sharp's death, the society joined forces with the Folk Song Society, founded in 1898. During the years of World War I, Sharp and his assistant, Maud Karpeles, came to the United States to record folk music here, and once again he had a great moment of dance discovery when, in 1917, he and Karpeles discovered the Kentucky "Running Set."[23]

21. Cf. Burchenal, n. 9.
22. Maud Karpeles, *Cecil Sharp: His Life and Work* (Chicago: University of Chicago Press; London: Routledge and Kegan Paul, 1967), pp. 24–25.
23. Ibid., p. 163.

The purpose of the Folk Dance Society in England, as Sharp envisioned it, was to promote and make known English country dancing, morris dancing, and sword dancing. These purposes still form the major commitment in England. "Ironically," as Dorson put it, "the call for collecting in behalf of survival would be answered in the spirit of revival. The future lay indeed with the followers of Cecil Sharp."[24] The society is still as active as ever, and it even has a branch in the United States, under the national directorship of May Gadd, which is dedicated to preserving English folk dance and music in the United States.[25]

Violet Alford has edited a series of folk dance handbooks that represent most European nations. These handbooks follow the usual English focus, to include mostly descriptive materials, a bit of historical reconstruction, and suggestions for accurately reproducing the dances in question. They also list festivals and other occasions when folk dances can be seen by the public. The handbooks have not included any theory or methods for the scholarly study of folk dance since they are designed to assist folk dance performers. Violet Alford has also made contributions to the world of scholarship, especially with her book *Sword Dances and Drama* (1962).

The most profound folk dance scholarship is to be found in non-English-speaking countries. The monumental research and analyses of the Janković sisters of the folk dances of Yugoslavia, for example, should serve as inspiration to dance scholars from the United States, most of whom have lagged woefully. Another important contributor to dance scholarship was Rudolf Laban, who developed the system of notation known as kinetography in England and the Continent and as Labanotation in the United States. In addition to his system of movement notation, which is not universally accepted as a pragmatic answer for recording dance, Laban also made important analyses of movement-through-time that are without peer and should be digested by every folk dance researcher whether or not he does use Laban's notation system. There are other noteworthy European dance scholars such as Hoerburger of Germany and Martin and Pesovár from Hungary. It seems wise, however, to caution against accepting the evolutionary categories that are implicit in the works of most continental scholars.[26]

24. Richard M. Dorson, *The British Folklorists: A History* (Chicago: University of Chicago Press, 1968), p. 281.

25. "Folk Dance," *Dance Encyclopedia*, p. 370.

26. See György Martin, "Dance Types in Ethiopia," *Journal of the International Folk Music Council* 19 (1967): 23–27 and György Martin and Erné Pesovár, "A Structural Analysis of the Hungarian Folk Dance (A Methodological Sketch)," *Acta Ethnographica* 10 (1961): 1–40.

It must be noted that in England and throughout the Continent national governments have supported and encouraged folk dance studies (that pattern is repeated in South American countries). In England, for example, H.R.H. Princess Margaret is the patron of the English Folk Dance and Song Society. In contrast, the United States government has shown almost no interest in folk dance, with the exception of housing collections of folk research at the Smithsonian Institution in Washington, D.C. It is not surprising, actually, that the United States government has shown so little interest in folk dance. In the first place, our government has seldom supported any of the arts. In the second place, the misleading, currently popular descriptions of folk dance have not recommended many truly American folk dance forms for study. Folk dance scholarship has been promoted here and elsewhere, however, by the International Folk Music Council. As reported by Hoerburger, IFMC ran a "Congress on Dance Notation and Folk Dance Research" in Dresden in October 1957.[27]

In the United States, the bulk of folk dance research has been carried on by private or local governmental organizations, and by private persons. The results of the research and of performance are often reported in *Dance Magazine*. The single American scholar who has made an extended contribution to folk dance scholarship is Gertrude P. Kurath. She contributed some six hundred entries to *The Dictionary of Folklore, Mythology and Legend*.[28] She has also published a number of studies with theoretical implications, including the tracing of Old World dance influences in the Americas. Future folk dance scholars should also know that the greatest single collection of folk dance materials is housed in the archives of the New York Public Library under the curatorship of Genevieve Oswald.

It is noteworthy that most of the young folk dance scholars in the United States have been attracted to folk dance forms outside of the United States, such as Gypsy groups in the Balkans. On the other hand, there have been literally thousands of books produced in the United States by folk dancers and teachers, but what they consider to be the folk dance of the United States is almost exclusively square and round dance. Most of these books resemble cookbooks, that is, books giving "recipes" for reproducing the dances. At most, such books include a few pages of "background" and perhaps include a chapter of definitions with some vague theorizing. Often these pages are far too subjective or simplistic to be of much value to scholars in

27. Felix Hoerburger, "Dance Notation and Folk Dance Research," *Journal of the International Folk Music Council* 10 (1958): 63.
28. Maria Leach, ed., *The Dictionary of Folklore, Mythology and Legend*, 2 vols. (New York: Funk and Wagnalls, 1949–50).

other fields of folklife. Sometimes the information or photographs are really dissonant, such as Hall's photograph of youngsters from his classes performing a Philippine folk dance wearing pseudo-Hawaiian outfits.[29]

At the opposite extreme in the United States are those scholars who write about everything except the dance itself. For example, in the monograph *The Dance Dramas of Mexican Villages*, the dramatic texts are published in full and a few words are given about sequence of events, but there is no discussion of the dance proper.[30] Or again, Bode's otherwise admirable article "The Dance of the Conquest of Guatemala" gives the background of the dance and discusses the meaning and function of the dance, but one could finish the article with little idea about the dance itself.[31] From one extreme to the other, American scholarship in folk dance has a long way to go before developing sophisticated and inclusive methods of studying folk dance. We will return to this subject later.

EXAMPLES OF FOLK DANCE

In order to illustrate the form of folklife that we define as folk dance, it is useful to follow Hoerburger's distinction of first and second existence. In the first existence, throughout the Continent, there are survivals of old ritualistic dance dramas. This usually comes as a surprise to us on this side of the Atlantic. It is a shock to find masked dance dramas (obviously it is often impossible to draw a clear line between dance and drama), for example, in the Black Forest and in Switzerland where tradition puts the butchers in charge of masked festivals occurring before the beginning of Lent.[32] This festival seems to be a reinterpretation of an older, pre-Christian rite. Such reinterpretations, that is the reworking of the old to fit into a Christian framework, are one *modus operandi* for the continuation of a ritual. Other ceremonies seem to continue without the superimposition of a Christian rationale, such as the sword dances that are found all over the Continent and England in close association with mining operations.[33] These two examples point to another source of traditional folk dance; that is, dance in association with occupations. Another

29. J. Tillman Hall, *Dance: A Complete Guide to Social, Folk, and Square Dancing* (Belmont, Calif.: Wadsworth Publishing Co., 1963), p. 121.

30. Frances Gillmor, *The Dance Dramas of Mexican Villages*, Humanities Bulletin No. 5 (Tucson: University of Arizona, April 1943), vol. 14, no. 2.

31. Barbara Bode, "The Dance of the Conquest of Guatemala," Middle American Research Institute Publication, no. 27 (Tulane University, 1961), pp. 203–98.

32. Agnes Hostettler, "Carnival Masques and Customs of the Black Forest and Switzerland" (paper presented at the annual meeting of the American Folklore Society, Atlanta, Georgia, 9 November 1969).

33. Violet Alford, *Sword Dance and Drama* (London: Merlin Press, 1962).

major source of folk dance in the first existence are calendrical observances such as the May Day festivities. The remarkable film 'Oss 'Oss Wee 'Oss, filmed by Alan Lomax in Padstow, Cornwall, in 1958 for the English Folk Dance and Song Society documents such an event. Still another source for folk dance in the first existence is dance ritual associated with rites of passage, especially those associated with weddings and funerals.

As for folk dance in its second existence, we have already mentioned England's concern with revivals of the survivals. A somewhat similar movement has occurred elsewhere on the Continent where folk dance has been encouraged at official levels in order to promote nationalistic pride. In addition, governments have discovered that folk dance is a popular commodity for export, and a rash of folk dance companies have developed during the last two decades. The usual pattern here is government-sponsored organization of gifted dancers under the direction of a well-known choreographer. The latter coordinates and theatricalizes first existence dance into slick and attractive show pieces, in order to present a variety of forms that represent different regions of the country. Our State Department also sends dance companies abroad to perform, but they choose already existing, privately managed companies; though they pick up the tab for the tour, our government does not reward the company with further subsidization.

The folk dance situation in the United States is complex. There is such a variety of folk dancing that one must revise those pessimistic warnings that our nation is turning into a nation of spectators rather than of participators.

As far as second existence performance is concerned, recreational folk dancing in the United States is very popular. Folk dance groups, organized as a leisure-time activity, are found all over the country, especially in large cities and on college campuses. Folk dance is also an integral part of physical education programs from the elementary school through the university. First existence folk dance occurs in the United States also. For example, enclaves of groups who are trying to maintain identities with their Old World traditions have continued to dance as their ancestors did. They do not carry on seasonal or occupational rituals, as far as I know, but in the rites of passage, especially those concerned with marriage, folk dance lives on. Go to a German, Bavarian, Polish, Russian, Croatian, Greek, Italian, or Armenian wedding here in the United States, and you will find folk dances to keep your feet tapping late into the night.

Many of these enclaves of people who share a common heritage carry on their traditional social dance forms by organizing clubs, or by informal gatherings at restaurants and dance halls. Thus, to use

Milwaukee, Wisconsin, as a paradigm, a balalaika orchestra holds forth at the Balkan Inn several times a week, while Russian and Croatian dancers, and often a few Greeks, perform their dances with verve and skill. In the same city a Bavarian restaurant provides opportunity for eager dancers to wear their costumes and perform *schulplatters* or to dance to old-style polka bands. Over at the Milwaukee Jewish Community Center is a group of young people who identify with the Zionist movement by performing that hybrid called "Israeli dance" with its combination of dances derived from the Caucasus, Arab, and Yemenite worlds, plus deliberately composed dances designed to be in biblical style. Are these dance performances first or second existence? The distinction is sometimes unclear.

Still using Milwaukee as a paradigm, we find a group of teenagers of Polish ancestry practicing national dances in order to further pride in that ancestry. This group was formed as a corrective measure for young people who had felt discriminated against because of their Polish ancestry—a kind of "Polish is beautiful" movement. Step into the black ghetto of Milwaukee to see examples of jazz dance that most white Americans probably never believed existed. Go to the black churches to see religious dances that result in climactic states of disassociation.[34] Or go to the uptown neighborhoods or to the outskirts of Milwaukee, where on special occasions streets are blocked off for street dances given by neighborhood merchants who hire musicians to play for both popular dancing and beer barrel polkas. Finally, every fall in Milwaukee the International Institute and the city give an annual International Folk Festival where many of the local dance groups live out a kind of second existence by performing dances that have been arranged for the purpose of exhibition. Here are also dance performances by groups of foreign students who have banded together as a panacea against loneliness. Such international folk festivals have become popular all over the United States.

To be found in the United States are other kinds of folk dances associated with pageants and parades, dances performed by amateurs whose common bond is the pageant itself. Totally immersed in the dance preparations, these people are, in fact, creating their own genre of folk dance. We are referring here to such groups as those that perform in the annual New Year's Day Mummers' Parade in Philadelphia, and to the various groups that participate in pre-Lenten Mardi Gras celebrations in the southern section of our country.

In Kentucky, where Sharp was so stimulated, Appalachian folk dance still exists. Some of it is self-conscious and living a second exist-

34. Kealiinohomoku, "Study," pp. 95–111.

ence through dance workshops such as the annual folk dance workshops at Berea every Christmas and again in the spring for folk dancers who come from all over the country. But there are first existence dances too. If you would see this on film, view *High, Lonesome Sound,* produced in 1962 and distributed by Brandon Films. In this film you can watch descendants of Scotch-Irish settlers in a variety of dance forms, from the young man who listlessly shuffles on his front porch to the music played by his father, to the variety of religious exercises in the local churches.

In the deep South, marching bands still lead black funeral processions to the cemeteries. The mourners and sympathizers dance down the street under their black umbrellas in a manner that is reminiscent of West African processionals. You can still see black "pat juba" just as Dorothy Scarborough reported forty-five years ago.[35] Folk dance is still viable and profuse in the Sea Islands, and blacks perform a variety of music games and secular dances along with the religious ring shout. These forms, with their complex rhythms and their call and response vocal patterns, clearly show an African heritage that excites and surprises the outside viewer (as at a performance of children and their chaperone, sponsored by Mary Arnold Twining, at the African Studies Association meetings in New York in 1967). These dances are definitely folk dances of the first existence. If we admit that these viable forms are of the first existence, it is logical to think that popular dance forms that are found in the Sea Islands and are just as functionally embedded are also folk dances. Much of the diffusion and borrowings of these dance forms can be traced by following some of the black migrants to, say, Chicago. They have been bringing their dances with them since before the turn of the century, and they are still doing so.[36]

In this folk dance tour of the United States, we move west into the southwestern states where the Mexican influence becomes apparent. Of course the Spanish-Americans have much folk dancing, but their influence has entered into the dances of other groups as well. For example, after the New Mexico Santa Domingo Pueblo Indians have performed their annual all-day "Green Corn Dance" on August 4, these Indians cross the bridge from their village to a large vacant lot. There a traveling carnival pitches its concessions every year at that time, and there the Indians dance on a square wooden platform constructed for that purpose, to the music of a Mariachi band. Pueblo Indians are not noted for their love of things Mexican, unless we

35. Dorothy Scarborough, *On the Trail of Negro Folk-Songs* (Cambridge, Mass.: Harvard University Press, 1925).
36. Kealiinohomoku, "Study," pp. 90–92.

except the food, but they do love the dances and are vigorous in performing a gay *corrido*.

Throughout our entire country, especially on Saturday nights, folks get together for good, old-time square dancing. The style of the dance will vary with the locality, but it is recognizable still as that kind of dance that is considered uniquely American. When the folks get together in someone's garage in rural Indiana, and each family brings a covered dish for the midnight supper, and some of the group play fiddles, mandolins, and banjos while the others, old and young, slough off their cares and reaffirm life through rhythmic fellowship, they are carrying on a tradition in the first existence. But even in the city, urban dwellers put on their fancy duds and go to the "Y" or neighborhood church to do a little square dancing too. Foster calls the rural dance "survival" and the urban dance "revival." Still, for all participants, the functions are the same—good fun, healthful exercise, release of emotion and tension, and fellowship. Foster puts it this way:

> Wherever it is found, the American square dance has grown from its historical roots into something like nothing to be found elsewhere in the world. It has the advantage of being both a survival (in the country) and a revival (in the city) —the living, free traditions of the one combined with the enthusiasm of the other.[37]

We can follow the square dance across the Pacific to our fiftieth state, Hawaii. In Waikiki, every fall, the city sponsors a *Hoolaulea,* or street festival. In this unique state of Hawaii, the varieties of folk dances are legion, although it is not surprising that most of them are from Asia and the Pacific. But the square dancers are there too with fancy costumes and skillful callers. All dance groups are assigned platforms on Kalakaua Avenue for the *Hoolaulea.* Hour after hour they perform so that anyone walking down that avenue can see folk dances by Hawaiians, Samoans, Tongans, Filipinos, Japanese, Koreans, Okinawans, Chinese, and also Mainland-type whites performing square dances. Other groups that have formed dance clubs also dance at the *Hoolaulea,* and the dances are of European origin. For example, there may be fully costumed dance representatives of the local chapter of the Robert Burns Society.

Also in our newest state, every summer Japanese Buddhists go through the Bon Odori dances to honor their ancestors. Nearly every weekend, from the end of June to early September, under the hostship of a different temple or Young Buddhist Association, the dances

37. Damon S. Foster, *The History of Square Dancing* (Barre, Mass.: Barre Gazette, 1957) , p. 52.

move to a different location. On Wednesday and Thursday nights the dancers practice, and on Friday and Saturday nights they wear their kimonos while they dance around and around the musicians for hours on end.

If one is in the Hawaiian Islands six months after the Bon Odori dances, the Chinese communities can be viewed as they bring in the New Year with their enormous dragons and lions that are manned by several strong male dancers and are accompanied down the streets by dancing members of the Chinese athletic club amid firecrackers and much excitement.

Religious dance is an important part of the folk idiom in the United States. We have already mentioned the black churches and the Buddhist Bon Odori, which, incidentally, is performed in several locations in California and probably wherever large enough groups of Buddhists congregate. In addition to these religious dances, there are also those fundamentalist white Christian groups, such as the Holy Rollers, who express religious fervor in dance exercises. There is a somewhat similar religious movement in the Japanese cult of the Dancing Goddess, which has branches in Hawaii and in California.[38] In quite a different vein, there are the meditative dances that Frank Lloyd Wright's widow teaches at his two main studios, Taliesin East in Wisconsin and Taliesin West in Arizona—dances that are supposed to be mystic movements from ancient Babylonia and Egypt (the author studied briefly with Iovanna Lloyd Wright). Rumors and popular newspaper accounts tell of a new upsurge in witchcraft in this country. Perhaps it is time for to someone to document the kind of dances performed by the witch covens!

One of the best documented of the folk religious dance groups is the Shakers. They are now defunct in a first existence, but there is a body of noteworthy literature about them.[39] Apparently within the last year some young people in our country are trying to give a second existence to the Shakers' religious dance and crafts by living in the old Shaker communities for weeks at a time while trying to revive these arts.

Another kind of second existence is being given to American folk dance, which is both creative and commercial, via the mass medium of television, such as the tapping square dance group that performs weekly on "Western Hayride." Many of our gifted choreographers have used folk dance themes in their choreographies. In addition, many actual folk dance groups are given an opportunity to perform

38. Kay Tateishi, "Japanese Teen Inherits Title 'Goddess of Dance'," *Louisville Courier Journal,* 14 April 1968, sec. D. p. 4.

39. Sibyl R. Helm, "The Shakers," *CORD* (Committee on Research in Dance) *News* 2 (April 1970) : 27–39.

on television at the local level, and also on educational television. Sometimes they perform on national commercial television on such programs as "The Ed Sullivan Show," like the Irish jigging and reeling dancers he usually presented around Saint Patrick's Day.

But the very best and most easily accessible place to view contemporary, first existence American folk dance, as we have previously defined folk dance, is on the weekly television show "The American Bandstand," when young people from all over the country gather to compete in their own versions of the latest popular dances. Folk dancing? Most assuredly. It is a genuine American dance form with a combined Euro-Afro heritage. It is learned in three basic ways: through observation; by performing with experienced partners; and, finally, by experimentation. It functions much as other folk dances do—as catharsis, as a form of self-expression, and as a means of identification with a group, although the group is an age group rather than one based on nationality, religion, or organization. It is a slice of culture that has an internal sense of cohesion. The important thing to remember here is that even though the music may be written by a known composer, the dances are not. The dances are anonymous. Alexander Krappe says that the most "common reason for excluding popular music from the folk idiom [is] because the former is composed and the latter is 'anonymous.' "[40] Obviously this reason does not extend to the dance that accompanies popular music, unless the dance is guilty by association with the music. This association is merely fortuitous for two reasons in addition to its anonymity. The first is that popular dances are seldom expected to "go with" only one particular song; rather they form a style of dancing that is adapted through improvisation to any number of songs. Second, although popular songs are "arranged" by the performing group, the basic song is fixed on paper and is subject to copyright laws. In contrast, the accompanying dance has no such sanctions but is left entirely up to the performer. Indeed, popular dances are usually acknowledged by the older generation in negative terms only.

THE FUTURE OF FOLK DANCE STUDIES

All of the folk dance forms that we have mentioned have several things in common. They are vernacular, redundant, and part of a "little tradition." They provide the performer with a means of group identity, the individuals with a means of expression, and they give the performers both physical and emotional outlets. In all cases, folk dances in their first existence are performed primarily for the

40. Alexander H. Krappe, *The Science of Folk-Lore* (London: Methuen and Co., 1930), p. 153.

benefit of the dancers rather than for spectators. Dance is the only means of affective expression that exists in both time and space, and it is the only activity that so completely involves mind-body activity. It probably always has been, and probably always will be, the most totally satisfying activity for the largest number of people, both as participants and, vicariously, as observers.

Folk dancing in the United States is quite healthy, as we have seen. As Walter Terry noted, it is in a unique position since only in the United States could we find such an enormous variety of folk dance styles that reflect such a wide variety of backgrounds.[41] In addition, the popular appeal of folk dance seems to be growing rather than declining. This trend should increase as we come to have fewer working hours and more leisure time.

In contrast, the state of "folk dancistics" (if we can coin such a phrase to indicate the study of folk dance, after Dundes's use of "folkloristics") [42] is in very bad shape. Not only do we write mainly "cookbooks," as we have already mentioned; we have shown little inclination toward developing a rigorous scholarly analysis. In short, folk dance studies in the United States are very primitive. Writers about folk dance use four main approaches: the "how-to-do-it" manuals; the impressionistic, journalistic rhapsodies; the historic accounts and reconstructions; and the studies that tell about everything except the dance.

This unfortunate situation is compounded by nondancers who write about dance without making an effort to learn its basic terminology, thus preventing the most rudimentary communication. It is unforgivable, for example, that writers should use the words hop, jump, and leap indiscriminately to mean a generalized springing into the air. These terms have definite meanings that are not difficult to learn. Let all readers remember that a hop is a spring on one foot to the same foot, a jump is a spring using both feet simultaneously, and a leap is a spring with the weight shifting from one foot to the other. Without this simple set of distinctions verbal descriptions become meaningless. Thus in Hoffman's book on the American Indians we are faced with such impossibilities as a jump on one foot and a hop on both feet.[43] Until some effort is made to learn these basic terms, even the "cookbooks" will not provide good recipes. For accurate descriptions of basic terminology see Gertrude Kurath's entries in the Dictionary of Folklore, Mythology and Legend and Lois Ells-

41. Walter Terry, "Dance, History of," The Dance Encyclopedia, ed. Anatole Chujoy and P. W. Manchester (New York: Simon and Schuster, 1967), p. 370.

42. Dundes, The Study of Folklore, p. 3.

43. Charles Hoffman, American Indians Sing (New York: John Day Co., 1967), pp. 41–43.

feldt's *Folk Dance*. The consistent and careful use of basic terminology is a prerequisite for writing about dance.

But the main key to future folk dance studies is to go beyond descriptions of motor activities. Dance must be analyzed within its context; descriptions are incomplete unless they include the entire dance event.[44] Such context includes the historical background; it includes all the activities of nondancing participants; and of course it includes an account of sequence, visual effects, and all the emotional and aesthetic values placed on the event by the participants and the observers. The ethnoaesthetics of the group involved will help reveal the psychological aspects of the occasion and the reasons why it is or is not perpetuated. Studies of value judgments should account for individual variations and for the varieties displayed between performances. Studies must certainly include all of the symbiotic aspects of the performance such as music, the audience response, and the entire mechanisms at work from the time of transmission and learning through the recall of the performance once it is passed. In addition, all those factors that bring about changes, whether they are small or large changes, must be included. Viable folk dance includes either or both dramatic innovation and insidious change. As Maud Karpeles points out, "it is well known that traditional art forms never remain static."[45] This fact is not well enough known, and purists should heed Ljubica Janković when she states that "folk dances live in the creative process."[46]

I prefer to put this entire dance complex into a dynamic verb form and call it "dance eventing." In other words, what we need in this country are rigorous studies of folk dance eventings, and we need a willingness to learn from successful dance scholars of other nations. We must also borrow methods from scholars of other genres wherever such methods can be adapted.

The future of folk dance studies depends upon our being able to ask new questions, instead of being content to observe and record "steps" and "stylistics" only. Alan Lomax has asked exciting questions in his studies of cantrometrics and choreometrics.[47] Some of his suggested answers seem suspect and overgeneralized. Some of his data is skewed or incomplete. Nevertheless, he has raised important questions for further research, enough to keep many researchers busy for

44. For a comparable view see Robert A. Georges, "Toward an Understanding of Storytelling Events," *Journal of American Folklore* 82 (1969) : 313–28.

45. Cecil J. Sharp, *Sword Dances of Northern England* (London: Novello and Company, Ltd., 1951, rev. by Maud Karpeles) , p. 11.

46. Ljubica S. Janković, "Paradoxes in the Living Creative Process of Dance Tradition," *Ethnomusicology* 13 (January 1969) : 127.

47. Alan Lomax, *Folk Song Style and Culture* (Washington, D. C.: American Association for the Advancement of Science Publication No. 88, 1968) , pp. 222–73.

a long time. Answering some of these questions should ultimately
lead from special and unique studies to meaningful cross-cultural
studies and typologies.

There have been other valid approaches to the study of folk dance.
That venerable folklorist, Alexander Krappe, was interested in the
origins and functions of various dance types.[48] Violet Alford used
mapping to trace various correlations of sword dances with other
data throughout Europe. Ljubica Janković urges recognition of the
variations of the "same" dance from one region to another.[49] She and
her sister insist on awareness of the contribution of specific individuals
to dance style and technique, believing that in every dance group
there will be both the gifted creators and those that "carry on."[50]
Roger Abrahams also sees the need for studying the individual performer. Though he was specifically speaking about folk singers, the
principle holds true for dancers. He suggests that the comparative
analysis of idiosyncrasies will give insights into the standards for ethnoaesthetics.[51] Alan Dundes suggests that there may be similarities in
structure and form between folk dance and verbal folk forms that
will prove useful to analysis.[52] Of course, it is not surprising to hazard that such similarities exist since dance usually is associated with
songs or with a dramatic presentation. Nevertheless, this lead must
have systematic study before the intuitive judgment becomes the
concrete correlation. This can be done only when structural analyses
are made for folk dance forms.

Folk dance scholars might also take a page from the books of other
folklorists in trying to develop systems of indexes, such as a motif
index of movement and a semantic index of meanings, especially as
far as gestures are concerned.

In summary, there is much folk dancing on both first and secondary
levels of existence, but the scholarship of these dances, at least in the
United States, is in its infancy. We need, first of all, rigorous means
for description and notation; we need complete analysis of the entire
dance eventing complex; we need studies of both individual and
group ethnoaesthetics; we need to include the body of lore that surrounds a dance and a dancing group; we need to develop typologies
for cross-cultural studies; and we need to see how folk dance functions within the society in which it appears. Above all, we must study

48. Krappe, pp. 301–9.
49. Ljubica S. Janković, p. 127.
50. Ljubica and Danica Janković, p. 30.
51. Roger D. Abrahams, "Creativity, Individuality, and the Traditional Singer,"
Studies in the Literary Investigations 3 (April 1970) : 7, 12.
52. Alan Dundes, "On Game Morphology: A Study of the Structure of Non-
Verbal Folklore," *New York Folklore Quarterly* 20 (December 1964) : 275–88.

the producers as well as the product, and we must learn to ask creative questions. For example, we should try to discover why a dance form is sometimes more conservative than the function, and why, in other instances, the dance function is more conservative than the form. These questions have been asked before, but little has been done to find the answers. We should try to ascertain how other aspects of the culture, the environment and the physical qualities of the dancers, affect the dance. There is another vast area for folklorists that is relatively untouched and that concerns the lore *about* the dance performers. For example, why do dancers in the Western world, like actors, often wish one another luck by saying "Break a leg"? Why do masked dancers in many parts of the world have a belief that the mask cannot be removed from a dancer who fails to conform to certain sanctions? Such tales are known to me from both Japan and from the Hopi Indians, and there is reason to believe that they can be found elsewhere.

The primary reference for folk dance studies is the living performance. Second, an important resource is extended interviewing with individual participants. In addition, much can be gleaned from both motion and still pictures, from drawings and other art forms, from accounts in old newspapers and journals, from books and articles, and from communication with other scholars.

Walter Terry points out that there has been a renascence of interest in performing folk dance in the United States.[53] Now is the time for a revival of interest in folk dance as a subject for serious scholarship.

Bibliography and Selected Readings

Alford, Violet. *Sword Dance and Drama*. London: Merlin Press, 1962. An important study that traces this form of dance and drama throughout Europe.

———, and Rodney Gallop. *The Traditional Dance*. London: Methuen and Co., Ltd., 1935. Contains exciting description of folk dances observed in Portugal, Basque, Switzerland, Hungary, Italy, and other countries in Europe.

Como, William, ed. *Dance Magazine*. New York. Published monthly. A well-produced and lavishly illustrated magazine that several times a year includes articles of interest to folklorists.

---

53. Terry, "Folk Dancing," p. 371.

Duggan, Anne S.; Jeanette Schlottmann; and Abbie Rutledge. *Folk Dance Library.* New York: A. S. Barnes and Co., 1948. 5 vols. The five volumes deal with, respectively, teaching of folk dances, dances of Scandinavia, dances of continental Europe, dances of the British Isles, and dances of the United States and Mexico. Each unit gives background information on the area covered, information on origins of dances, and an overview of the dances included. A good educational tool.

Ellfeldt, Lois. *Folk Dance.* Dubuque, Iowa: William C. Brown Co., 1969. Contains good descriptions of basic movements and steps. Describes styles of dances of the Western world and attempts to grapple with definition and theory in the chapter "What is Folk Dance?"

Foster, Damon S. *The History of Square Dancing.* Barre, Mass.: Barre Gazette, reprinted from Proceedings of the American Antiquarian Society, 1957. This book is scholarly, entertaining, and perhaps the most complete history of its type.

Helm, Sibyl R. "The Shakers," CORD (Committee on Research in Dance) *News* 2 (April 1970) : 27–39. Surveys the literature about Shaker dance.

Hoerburger, Felix. "Dance Notation and Folk Dance Research." *Journal of the International Folk Music Council* 10 (1958) : 63. Reports on the historic Dresden conference concerned with problems of notation and research.

———. "The Study of Folk Dance and the Need for a Uniform Method of Notation." *Journal of the International Folk Music Council* 11 (1959) : 71–73. Points out reasons for studying folk dance, and notes a logical sequence of study with suggestions for basic methods of putting information about folk dance on paper.

———. "Folk Dance Survey." *Journal of the International Folk Music Council* 17 (1965) : 7–8. Explains the results of the questionnaire about folk dance which had been distributed to folklorists throughout the world.

———. "Once Again on the Concept of 'Folk Dance.' " *Journal of the International Folk Music Council* 20 (1968) : 30–32. Discusses problems in defining folk dance, and introduces the terms "first existence" and "second existence" as these terms are used in Germany.

Hutchinson, Anne. *Labanotation: The System for Recording Movement.* New York: New Directions Books, 1954. Whether or not the system of notation described in this book is used, Hutchinson's work should be studied carefully by anyone who plans to analyze body movement.

Janković, Ljubica S. "Paradoxes in the Living Creative Process of Dance Tradition." *Ethnomusicology* 13 (January 1969) : 124–28. Discusses the contradictory phenomena found in folk dances, such as the differences encountered from one region to another among dances with the same name. The article is useful, empirical, and well illustrates her thesis.

Janković, Ljubica and Danica. *Summary Folk Dances.* Belgrade: Council of Science and Culture of the Government of the F. P. R. of Yugoslavia, 1934–51. 6 vols. Folk dance collecting and analysis without peer. This stupendous set of works is a must.

Kaeppler, Adrienne L. *The Structure of Tongan Dance.* Ph.D. dissertation. Honolulu: University of Hawaii, 1967. Reproduced by University Microfilms, Inc., Ann Arbor, Mich. This study of dance, which is the result of extended field research, is a model for applying the concept of etic and emic dance analysis.

————. "Folklore as Expressed in the Dance in Tonga." *Journal of American Folklore* 80 (1967) : 160–68. Excellent example of how folklore studies of dance can contribute to the overall understanding of a culture.

Karpeles, Maud. *Cecil Sharp: His Life and Work.* Chicago: University of Chicago Press; London: Routledge and Kegan Paul, 1967. This interesting work is necessary background for anyone who plans a scholarly study of folk dance.

————, ed. *Collection of Folk Music and Other Ethnomusicological Material.* London: International Folk Music Council and Royal Anthropological Institute of Great Britain and Ireland, 1958. First published as *Manual for Folk Dance Collectors*, 1951. A kind of notes and queries, especially useful for orienting fieldworkers. Especially helpful is "The Collecting of Dances," pp. 28–32.

Kealiinohomoku, Joann Wheeler. "A Comparative Study of Dance as a Constellation of Motor Behaviors Among African and United States Negroes." M. A. thesis Northwestern University (1965). The first extensive comparative analysis of motor behavior. The observations of dance among United States blacks should be of interest to folklorists.

————. "An Anthropologist Looks at Ballet as a Form of Ethnic Dance." *Impulse* (1970) : 24–33. An attempt to clear away the muddied thinking of Western dance scholars concerning non-Western dance.

————, and Frank J. Gillis, "Special Bibliography: Gertrude Prokosch Kurath," *Ethnomusicology* 14 (1970) : 114–28. Anyone who plans to study folk dance from a scholarly point of view should be acquainted with Kurath's works.

Kennedy, Douglas. *English Folk Dancing Today and Yesterday.* London: S. Bell and Son, Ltd., 1964. A kind of memoir of dances that have been viewed by this former president of the English Folk Dance and Folk Song Society.

Krappe, Alexander H. *The Science of Folk-lore.* London: Methuen and Co., 1930. Though outdated in theory, it should be read for its probing of ideas that have not yet been fully explored. Good listings of commonly found rites and customs (pp. 270ff), many of which have dance associated with them. The chapter actually dealing with dance (pp. 301–309) is disappointing in comparison with the rest of the book, and it should be read with caution. Still, it is useful to see how Krappe approaches ancient forms and functions of dance. There is no pragmatic help from this book, for he proposes no methodology.

Kurath, Gertrude P. "Dance Notation." *Four Symposia on Folklore.* Edited by Stith Thompson. Bloomington: Indiana University Press, 1953. Pp. 35–42. Should be studied carefully by anyone wishing to do research on dance.

Laban, Rudolf. *Principles of Dance and Movement Notation.* London: Macdonald and Evans, 1956. A basic notation system for folk dance research.

Martin, György, and Erné Pesovár. "A Structural Analysis of the Hungarian Folk Dance (A Methodological Sketch)." *Acta Ethnographica* 10 (1961): 1–40. An excellent model for future folk dance studies. Analyzes functional, musical, and morphological aspects of folk dance.

Schneider, Gretchen A. *Pigeon Wings and Polkas: The Dance of the California Miners. Dance Perspectives* 39 (Winter 1969). A monograph in two parts that contains accounts of the setting and dances of the Forty-Niners. The material is drawn largely from journals, diaries, and letters. Lavishly illustrated.

Schwartz, Paul, ed. *Folk Dance Guide.* 3d ed. New York: edited and published by Paul Schwartz, 1953. Contains listings of the places in the United States where folk dance can be seen. A useful bibliography is included.

Sharp, Cecil J. *Sword Dances of Northern England.* Revised by Maud Karpeles. London: Novello and Company, Ltd., 1951. First published in 1911, this book was written for those interested in the revival of sword dancing.

———, and A. P. Oppé. *The Dance.* London: Halton and Truscott Smith, Ltd., New York: Minton, Balch and Co., 1924. A posthumously published summary and history of the dance in Europe. Sharp summarizes some of his own thinking as a result of his remarkable career.

———, and Herbert C. Macilwaine. *The Morris Book.* London: Novello and Co., Ltd., 1907. Sharp states that his goals are "not primarily for the information of the archaeologist and scholar, but to help those who might be disposed to restore a vigorous and native custom to its lapsed pre-eminence." The book is an important document of folk dance in England. Anyone interested in making scholarly studies of folk dance should familiarize himself with all of Sharp's works.

II The Methods of Folklife Study

1 FIELDWORK: COLLECTING ORAL LITERATURE
Donald A. MacDonald

The novice in the collecting game should take comfort from the thought that anyone entering the field for the first time is probably beset by the same doubts and fears. Some beginners will clearly require more preparations than others. A native of the proposed area of operations, or someone of native stock, is liable to know a good deal already—local people, local color, something of the oral tradition, the minority local language—although he must beware of thinking that he knows it all. The complete outsider is faced with more demanding preparations to familiarize himself with the area. In either event he should not allow himself to be put off completely by writings that suggest that this is a game for supermen only. Anyone who is reasonably fit and intelligent and gets on well with people can make a useful contribution—provided he has done his homework thoroughly.

Admittedly almost anyone can go into a tradition-rich area and pick up something useful, but systematic fieldwork usually begins at the desk, in the library and the archive. If the chosen area has been collected in the past, one must make oneself as familiar as possible with the results. Useful background information can also be gleaned from histories and guidebooks. Reading should of course include general theory and practice. One interested in tales should know about the Aarne-Thompson classification; the ballad hunter needs to be aware of the Anglo-American ballad types arranged by Child, Coffin, and Laws (see appended references), and so forth.

The aspiring collector should thus have acquired a good basic knowledge of how to set about his task before he enters the field. He should be aware that it is no longer sufficient to isolate a bare, undocumented text, that even when most concerned with his texts as literature he will lose much unless he is able to place them in terms of their social ambience. A truly functional situation is rarely encountered nowadays in a "modern" society. One such is vividly described by MacEdward Leach from a field trip to Jamaica.

It is, however, an unforgettable experience to hear an Anansi tale told by a good native teller of tales to an appreciative audience. Typical is the tale of "Anansi and Tiger" which I heard in the Blue Mountains of Jamaica a few years ago. Men, women and children were crowded into the small room and overflowed onto the narrow porch. Some squatted on the floor; some stood around the walls; children, black eyes wide, sat at their parents' feet; the bed in the corner was loaded with women and babies. All were silent, intent on the story-teller, Arthur Wyles. Mr. Wyles was sixty-one, his hair white and kinky like sheep's wool. His eyes were unforgettable—very large, very black, and remote, expressionless. He stood throughout the story, constantly moving about. First, he would be at one side of the room taking the part of Anansi; then he would jump quickly to the other and face back as he took the role of Tiger. His voice was whining and ingratiating as Anansi; his face took on a smirk; his words were given a wheedling twist. But when he became Tiger, he drew himself up stern and dignified and majestic; his voice was deep and powerful and his walk stately. This story ends with a fight between Tiger and Death. Mr. Wyles, voice full of excitement, arms flailing, staged the fight, blow by blow, taking the parts alternately of Tiger and of Death. When the climax was reached and Tiger delivered the knock-out blow conquering Death, the narrator over-reached himself and his clenched fist hit the door jamb a cruel blow that bloodied his knuckles. He seemed to feel nothing but went into the very realistic death throes of Brother Death. Though the audience had heard this story many times, they sat enthralled, eyes shining, audibly satisfied with the ending. Here, then, in the *telling* is the characterisation and the drama, absent in the story when merely read, now abundantly supplied.[1]

We know that such a scene was common until comparatively re-

1. MacEdward Leach, "Problems of Collecting Oral Literature," *Publications of the Modern Language Association* 77 (1962) : 336.

cently in many societies. It is interesting to compare, for instance, the testimony of Alexander Carmichael, one of Campbell of Islay's collaborators and later a distinguished collector in his own right:

The romance school has the largest following, and I go there, joining others on the way. The house of the storyteller is already full, and it is difficult to get inside and away from the cold wind and soft sleet without. But with that politeness native to the people, the stranger is pressed to come forward and occupy the seat vacated for him beside the houseman. The house is roomy and clean, if homely, with its bright peat fire in the middle of the floor. There are many present—men and women, boys and girls. All the women are seated, and most of the men. Girls are crouched between the knees of fathers or brothers or friends, while boys are perched wherever—boy-like—they can climb.

The houseman is twisting twigs of heather into ropes to hold down thatch, a neighbour crofter is twining quicken roots into cords to tie cows, while another is plaiting bent grass into baskets to hold meal . . .

The housewife is spinning, a daughter is carding, another daughter is teazing, while a third daughter, supposed to be working, is away in the background conversing in low whispers with the son of a neighbouring crofter. Neighbour wives and neighbour daughters are knitting, sewing, or embroidering. The conversation is general: the local news, the weather, the price of cattle, these leading up to higher themes—the clearing of the glens (a sore subject), the war, the parliament, the effects of the sun upon the earth and the moon upon the tides. The speaker is eagerly listened to, and is urged to tell more. But he pleads that he came to hear and not to speak, saying:—

> "A chiad sgial air fear an taighe
> Sgial go la air an aoidh."

> The first story from the host
> Story till day from the guest.

The stranger asks the houseman to tell a story, and after a pause the man complies. The tale is full of incident, action, and pathos. It is told simply yet graphically, and at times dramatically—compelling the undivided attention of the listener. At the pathetic scenes and distressful events the bosoms of the women may be seen to heave and their silent tears to fall. Truth overcomes craft, skill conquers strength, and bravery is rewarded. Occasionally a momentary excitement occurs when heat and sleep overpower a boy and he tumbles down among the people below, to be trounced out and sent home. When the story is ended it is discussed and commented upon, and the different characters praised or blamed according to their merits and the views of the critics.[2]

This kind of functional storytelling has now all but totally dis-

2. Alexander Carmichael, *Carmina Gadelica*, 2d ed. (Edinburgh and London, 1928) , 1: xxii–xxiii.

appeared in the Hebrides. But we know it existed until comparatively recently, and the same stories can still occasionally be recorded from more or less passive tradition-bearers who, through the excellence of their memory and their interest, are still able to record them, but now lack an audience.

In the case of the Jamaican situation, the collector has a clear duty to place the total situation on record as he observes it—a daunting task. In the Hebridean situation the tradition-bearer must be encouraged to fill in these details, to recreate for us this functional setting from his memory. The collector must know how to set about extracting this information. He must, then, devise for himself a pattern of questionnaires. He may write these out, if necessary, but should commit them to memory rather than reading out questions to his informant. On function, style, and ambience, an example that the trainee might profitably follow is that set out by Sean O'Sullivan.

If you can, take a photograph of each storyteller and of his home. Write down an account of his (her) life from each storyteller. Give the storyteller's geneaology, if possible.

Give an account of the setting in which the story was told. Where were stories usually told? At the fireside? At wakes? At the forge? At work in the fields? At the turf-bog? In fishing boats? How were storytellers usually induced to tell a tale? What conditions were necessary on the part of the storyteller and the audience? Describe the scene. Were certain stories favourites with both narrator and audience? Give details. Did storytellers tell only tales of their own choice, or did they comply with requests for particular tales? Did they use gestures? Describe. Were interruptions or interjections during the telling of a story resented or welcomed by the storyteller and the audience? What was the usual type of comment or interjection by a member of the audience during the course of a tale? What was said at the conclusion (in praise of the storyteller, as a comment on the tale or its characters, etc.) ? Did members of the audience learn tales so told and tell them afterwards? Were certain houses properly recognised as storytelling centres? Give an account of local ones.

What types of persons usually told tales? Men or women? Age of storytellers? Profession or occupation? Did men or women act as professional storytellers? Was it usual for travelling men or women (beggars, hucksters, etc.) to tell tales in houses where they spent a night? Did neighbours usually assemble to hear these storytellers? Did "poor scholars" act as storytellers? Did good storytellers resent the telling of tales by amateurs? Were storytelling competitions held locally?[3]

It ought to be part of every fieldworker's training and practice to have basic systematic, yet variable, question patterns of this kind at

3. Sean O'Sullivan (Ó Súilleabháin), *A Handbook of Irish Folklore* (Dublin, 1942), pp. 556–57.

his fingertips. In an interview situation these questions can help to avoid awkwardness and hesitation, and they can also yield rich results. He should also learn and carry about in his head summaries of stories, texts of songs, proverbs, riddles, and so on, to use as bait.

Recording machinery is obviously one of the very important factors. Most modern theory and practice are based on the assumption that the days of paper recording texts are now past except in the most exceptional circumstances. The advent of sophisticated machinery has taken much of the drudgery out of collecting—and, what is more important, it has also removed much of the inaccuracy. The function of paperwork should, by and large, be confined to note-taking, transcription, documentation of recordings, setting the scene, and filling in other detail that, for one reason or another, it has been found impossible to incorporate in the sound record. Granted that even the professional phonetician will usually concede the difficulty of producing a totally objectively accurate transcription, even from captive material, the case for the use of machinery in all possible situations scarcely needs stating.

While it may be possible to take down on paper from a performer the text of a song or a short stereotyped prose passage, it is almost impossible to do this in a tale, for instance, even granted the use of shorthand, without serious loss of accuracy, not to mention spontaneity and other such matters of style. Even the tape recorder cannot cope with all features of style, though it represents an immense advance on paperwork.

Many collectors have commented on the adverse effect on a storyteller when he had to be slowed down and stopped to make transcription possible. In 1860 Campbell of Islay made this note on a version of a story:

I have a third version of this written by MacLean, told by Donald MacPhie, in South Uist. The old man was very proud of it, and said it was "the HARDEST" story that the transcriber had ever heard. He told me the same.

As often happens with aged reciters, when he repeated it a second time slowly for transcribing, nearly all the curious, "impassioned, and sentimental" language was left out. This is MacLean's account, and it entirely agrees with my own experience of this man, who is next thing to a professional reciter.[4]

This seems to have been a regular experience and is, indeed, exactly what one would expect. Thus, fortunately, almost all our material from written collections, admirable though it be, must be regarded as less than totally trustworthy.

4. John Francis Campbell, *Popular Tales of the West Highlands* (Edinburgh, 1860), 1:21.

Any text worth recording is worth recording in detail, and any argument based on the cost of tape should be dismissed as irrelevant to any kind of professional work. Arguments as to the interference of machinery with the spontaneity of the recital are often overstated. If machinery can be used at all, the distraction is obviously less than in the case of dictation. In general, I have found that a good informant, who knows that he has a contribution to make, will become almost totally oblivious to the presence of the machine.

The actual choice of equipment to be used is a matter for careful consideration. Cheap machinery has no part in serious professional work. The array of choice is wide and the uninitiated should take care to consult a qualified electronics expert rather than base his judgment on the advice of a salesman. The chosen equipment should preferably be easily portable and capable of operation off either mains current or batteries. Batteries have the advantage of not using the informant's electricity, for which he has to pay. A machine with a tape speed of $7\frac{1}{2}$ inches per second will generally be found satisfactory for most purposes, either for prose or musical materials; $3\frac{3}{4}$ inches per second will give sufficiently accurate results for prose, though the higher speed is preferable. Lower speeds should generally be disregarded even when one is tempted to economize on tape or avoid interrupting the performer. The choice of microphone and the quality of tape to be used are other matters on which qualified advice should always be taken. A machine may sometimes be found to yield better results with a microphone other than the one supplied with it.

Supervised training in the use of the chosen machine is also indispensable. There can be no excuse for sloppy recording techniques or failure to exploit the best possibilities of one's equipment. Ease and fluency in the use of the controls, in checking recording and power levels, in changing tapes and batteries efficiently and with a minimum of fuss, should be acquired as soon as possible. Microphone techniques should also be practiced, and one should also get to know something of the directional properties of the chosen microphone. A practiced and unobtrusive recording technique will obviously pay dividends later in the field.

Another important item of equipment is the camera, not nearly so widely used hitherto in oral literature situations as it ought to be. The camera should, of course, be capable of taking flashlight photographs as most recording sessions are conducted indoors and often in artificial light. The use of the cine-camera for this type of work is still in its infancy, though obviously it has a most important contribution to make. Cine-film synchronized with the sound recording can supply many of the details of style that hitherto, even at best, have been all too inadequately handled by the pen, and often not at all. The expense of professional quality equipment, and the need for trained technicians, of course constitute major problems.

Most of what I have said so far has had to do with the qualifications and preparations that ideally might be expected of the novice *before* entering the field. Insofar as real collecting work is the student's aim, the most crucial point of all will obviously come when he finds himself in the field for the first time.

How the beginner should be blooded is a tricky point. I like Dorson's suggestion that beginners ought to be encouraged to make a start by prospecting for oral tradition among their own relatives—getting to know their grandparents, as it has been put.[5] Further, a good deal of useful prospecting can be done in towns and cities and not necessarily only among immigrants of country stock. Or—another of Dorson's suggestions—the novice could be encouraged to make a beginning by inquiring into the state of oral tradition among friends within his own age group. It is surprising how much oral tradition can be picked up anywhere, though the quality and genre are another matter.

Hunting in pairs or teams usually has a great deal to recommend it. Problems can be shared. Discussion is useful and stimulating. A tired member of a team can be encouraged, cajoled, or bullied into carrying on—or even, exceptionally, allowed an evening off without wrecking a prior arrangement. Help in operating recording machinery, in taking turns at knocking at strange doors, in keeping an interview from flagging by opening up new avenues of questioning: all of these are mighty assets. Besides, teamwork can prove much less expensive to the sponsoring institution, since vehicle expenses, for instance, are very much the same for an individual as for a team, and the return on investment is generally much higher in terms of results. Much more territory can be canvassed by splitting up, as convenient, to explore and record.

Any field situation is thickly strewn with imponderables: the state of tradition in a community, the number and quality of potential informants, their age and the state of their health, whether they are early or late bedders, their readiness to cooperate, the nature of their work, the season of the year, the weather, whether there are visitors or children in a house, whether it is possible to record informants undisturbed or in a genuine, manageable, informant-audience situation. These are only some of the field factors that can be expected to influence the results.

The nature of the search is of course conditioned by one's previous

5. Richard M. Dorson, *Buying the Wind* (Chicago and London, 1964) , p. 18.

knowledge or lack of knowledge of the area. If he already has some local source of contact, the beginnings at least are much simplified.

If it is completely strange territory, one of the best methods is to contact anyone whose official duties put him in regular contact with a wide cross-section of the populace. It could be the hotelkeeper, the policeman, the postman, the schoolteacher, the doctor, the local shopkeeper, the priest or minister, and so on. On the subject of clergymen I should perhaps sound a note of warning. It may be wiser to inquire of someone else as to their attitudes before approaching them. In Scotland, where many clergymen have played a distinguished part in the annals of oral tradition, others, depending on their personal brand of fundamentalist theology, have formed the vanguard of the enemy. One calls to mind Bishop Carsewell's blast in the introduction to his Gaelic translation of the Prayer Book in 1567:

> And great is the blindness and darkness of sin and ignorance and design of those who teach and write and cultivate Gaelic, that they are more desirous, and more accustomed, to compose vain, seductive, lying, worldly tales about the Tuatha Dé Danann and the Sons of Mil and the heroes and Finn MacCoul with his warriors and to cultivate and piece together much else which I will not enumerate or tell here, for the purpose of winning for themselves the vain rewards of the world, rather than write and teach and cultivate the true words of God and the pure ways of truth.

This attitude can still occasionally be found among a few of the more obscurantist fundamentalists in Gaelic Scotland. But usually any of the above-mentioned classes is more than likely to be friendly and helpful, and indeed one may even recruit a useful informant or two from their ranks.

Again, there is no one general rule for seeking out contacts. Dorson recalls how he was once forced to resort to a very blunt method:

> Wandering around the tumbledown Negro settlement of New Bethel in Michigan, without leads or contacts, I saw a fleshy, somber woman standing in the doorway of the last house on the path, and called out, "Do you know any old stories?" Sarah Hall said yes and invited me in. So I met the storytelling mother of three storytelling daughters, who was also the hoodooed ex-wife of still another narrator.[6]

One may have the luck to bump into a good informant in a shop, in a pub, on the road—almost anywhere, in fact—and indeed it can be almost anyone, so it is by no means safe to judge by appearances. There may be nothing "folksy" looking about the best informants. The prospector ought to be ready to talk to anyone who is prepared to talk to him. Exceptionally, he may be lucky enough to find some-

6. Ibid, p. 8.

one who is widely known and liked, who is himself very interested in tradition, and is prepared to spend a good deal of time helping with the work. Almost any community will turn up someone whose assistance is a veritable boon. The system of local resident collectors, so successfully employed by the Irish Folklore Commission, could well be emulated elsewhere.

Questions of how to behave and what to wear also require consideration. The best general advice is that one should act as naturally as possible: be oneself and assume neither airs nor false roles. Some care should be taken not to outrage the susceptibilities of the populace; it is self-defeating to lay oneself open to ridicule or ostracism. One should not be over- or underdressed, though here the outsider can often get away with more than the collector with local connections. Again, there is no one universal set of rules, and even apparent codes of rules can be broken without serious consequence provided this is done gracefully and through obvious interest.

If approaching a strange house alone, following up a suggestion that so-and-so living there may prove a useful source, my own practice is to go up, knock at the door, and ask "Does so-and-so live here?" or "Are you such and such?" depending on whether the appearance matches the description. Having established that this is the informant himself, or having been taken in to him, or he out to me, I generally come directly to the point. In a way the worst is already over. The short period between stopping the car and getting a response to the knock can seem an eternity, and the few yards a long way, feeling that you are very likely being scrutinized from behind a curtain and perhaps being summed up rightly or wrongly as a bloody pest of some kind, some petty official or similar menace. The formula is variable, but usually something like this: "I'll tell you why I've come. I'm looking for old stories, old songs, any kind of old traditions. I'm told that you know plenty." The first reaction is often one of relief. The potential pest at least speaks Gaelic, which is usually enough to put him on a reasonably sound footing straightaway. I am generally invited in, more or less cordially, though it sometimes takes a few more preliminary exchanges at the door. Never have I had a door closed in my face or been spoken to discourteously and rarely indeed have I not been invited in. Rather, I have been almost slain by hospitality.

It is at such a stage that reasonably wide knowledge of background can be important. I recall my own first visit some years ago to a man who lives in my own native island of North Uist, though in a part of it that was almost totally unknown to me at that time. I had been told that his father had been a fine storyteller. The son, now in his seventies, might have something to offer. I arrived at his door with a colleague who was prospecting for material culture. Our informant, who lives with his sister, answered our knock himself, and I engaged him in conversation. Yes, his father had had stories, plenty of them, but there was no interest in stories now and he could not remember any, his memory was failing. It quickly became obvious that I was getting nowhere on this tack. The old man was slightly ill at ease and would obviously be glad to retreat inside. I had noticed that his cottage was well built and in process of being beautifully thatched: "Did you thatch the house yourself? I see you use heather. We use bent-grass on our side. I was born in a thatched house myself." Interest immediately quickened. He had thatched and built the house himself. His own people had been evicted from my side of the island over a century ago in a brutal land clearance. We were quickly inside. Before we left we had got details of thatching processes and an account of traditional house building; he was a skilled mason of the old school. We had learned of the local operation within living memory of a *caraidh,* a tidal fish trap. This technique had gone out in most areas centuries before. We had gathered history of the plight of the evicted tenants. And we had also secured an excellent version of Aarne-Thompson 300 + 303, *The Dragon Slayer* compounded with *The Twins,* and a number of other fine stories, besides a text of *Duan na Ceardach,* one of the old heroic ballads. Rapport and friendship were cemented, and further visits have been very warmly welcomed and rewarding.

Seldom, except in the case of a really outstanding informant, can one get an immediate, straightforward admission of knowing much. It is more usually as above: "Yes, there were stories, there were songs. I've heard them when I was young. You should have been here forty years ago. The old people are all gone. My father had hundreds of stories." But having started this kind of train of reminiscence one is usually already halfway there. Common ground is soon established, perhaps as above, perhaps by discussion of acquaintances or relatives in common, names, genealogy, crops, cattle, weather, work; the conversation can take any of a score of turns. At the first opportunity possible I say that I am from the School of Scottish Studies in Edinburgh. The name and the sort of salvage operation we are conducting are generally known and approved of. Most of the older generation are proud of the old traditions and regret their passing. Often it is necessary to stress that we have no connection with the radio, though we do contribute occasional programs, and to assure them that we do not release or publish any material without the written consent of the informant, usually a telling point. The conversation comes back gradually to tradition: stories, songs, old techniques of doing things. At a carefully judged point I produce the bottle of whisky, which is part of the standard gear: "Would it be right for me to offer you a dram?" The response varies immensely, ranging from: "It's my friend who would offer it to me" to "No thank you. I don't touch it now. There was a time. . . ." But I have never yet found offense taken. There are few total abstainers in the Hebrides or West Highlands, even among the very religious. The offer, whether accepted or not, is usually regarded as a graceful social gesture—and if there is anything in the house, the informant is equally quick to make the gesture himself. Toasts and blessings are exchanged, and the whole household is of course included, from well-grown children upward, depending on the area. Never have I found this offer interpreted as a possible bribe or reward and never, though this is often the subject of much jocularity, have I been seriously accused of trying to make the informant drunk to loosen his tongue. Exceptionally, an informant will state frankly that he must have a good skinful before he can perform, and of course one has to oblige.

When to introduce the tape recorder—usually left in the car at first—into any given situation is a matter of judgment and timing. If the visit is the result of an agreed arrangement, it may be taken in right away. Most people are now quite accustomed to the idea of machines and, though they often elicit wondering and even ribald comment, there is usually little difficulty experienced. The setting up of the machine should be done as quickly and unobtrusively as possible. To find a suitable place for it and for the microphone can cause problems, but these can usually be solved by the exercise of a little ingenuity. Microphone and recorder should never be placed on the same hard-topped surface, a table for instance, as reverberations will affect the quality of the results.

The positioning of the microphone is vital. Too great a distance can lead to loss of presence and an irritating increase in the level of background noise picked up. A distance of about two feet will often be found ideal, granted that the informant is not distressed by such close proximity. One also has to decide whether the balance of advantage lies with a fixed or a movable microphone. A hand-held microphone will often be found to have advantages. The ability to follow the movements of the informant rather than have to pay absolutely constant attention to the recording level control can prove an asset. One must have already established whether the body of the microphone is sensitive to hand friction or not.

To allow the informant a certain amount of free and natural movement is usually vital if he is not to be distracted, though he may have to be tactfully reminded that the scraping of boots on the floor or the occasional emphatic thump at the equipment are not in the best interests of the results. If recording a group or situation entailing movement, it may be found helpful to suspend the microphone in a suitable central position or make use of the services of an assistant—either a colleague, if hunting in groups, or a member of the company who is not actually involved in the situation.

Again, it is one of the great advantages of teamwork that a colleague can operate the machine and make notes while the interviewer does the microphone work, directing it as necessary to group work, or sitting close to a single informant, holding it fairly unobtrusively. A word of warning here, however: holding a microphone unsupported can become almost incredibly cramping and exhausting, and I have often found that a very helpful trick is to rest the elbow on the arm of one's chair or on one's knee.

The ideal is to have the services of a qualified technician available in the field. It also has the advantage of giving the technician a well-earned break from laboratory work, and the opportunity of experiencing for himself the sort of recording conditions in which field-workers have to operate. Recording should be done with the minimum amount of interference possible with normal household arrangements. It is a great advantage if one can arrange, without undue artificiality, to isolate the informant in a room that is undisturbed by normal household activities. For a special set-piece recording it may be desirable to ask for the removal of clocks or such irritations as hissing pressure lamps.

These are only a few points for general guidance. Again, every situation must be treated on its merits.

How much to play back is also a matter often requiring an on-the-spot decision. It is desirable to play back at least a little to make sure that the equipment is functioning properly. Some informants, especially practiced ones, are quite happy with this practice. On the other hand, some expect, and must be conceded to have a right to expect, to hear the whole of every item immediately after it is performed. This of course can be very time-consuming, and power-consuming if batteries are being used. It can be useful, however, to give the interviewer an opportunity to listen, make notes and lists, check anything he does not understand, and later switch on again to ask further questions as necessary. It can be quite an experience, too, to watch an informant react either critically or delightedly to his own performance—and, indeed, he is often spurred on to new efforts.

I remember one man, who was particularly good on stories and historical tradition, as he was persuaded with extreme difficulty to sing one of the fine songs he knew. He had acquired a remarkably poor impression of himself as a singer and had no wish to be immortalized in this respect. When finally cajoled to make one attempt, on the promise of erasure of the recording if he was dissatisfied with it, he was startled and delighted to find that he sounded much better than he thought he would. Needless to say, he went on to sing more. This raises the point, by the way, that a new informant, while he can readily identify everyone else's voice on a tape, often finds difficulty in coming to terms with his own. A little soothing praise is occasionally necessary. Indeed it is often desirable to point out that the playback even on a good portable is mainly intended for checking purposes and may not do full justice to the quality of the performance.

Sometimes, having finished a long recording session, one finds oneself faced with playing much of it back for the approval and entertainment of the informant's household, if they have been excluded from the actual recording session. This again is an obligation not to be refused, and indeed one can sometimes find another informant in the ranks of the family in this way.

How much to play back later to other tradition-bearers or interested friends and neighbors can be a problem, and must always be subject to the informant's own approval. Normally I make it a point of doing as little of this as possible, though there are occasions when it can stimulate the memory of another potentially good source. Extreme care is always necessary, especially if the material being handled has local social connotations. This risk is illustrated in a case noted by Alan Healey: "I know of a field-worker who replayed a tape for entertainment, without realizing that it contained material highly insulting to one of the audience. In a flash the man was brandishing a bush-knife and chasing the informant and his relatives.[7]

Secret recording, done without the knowledge or permission of the informant, is never to be encouraged. Sometimes one is strongly tempted, but in all cases the performer must be the final arbiter in all questions affecting the use of his own materials. Occasionally when I have been told "Turn that off till I run through this," I have left the machine running, as the first performance can often be by far the better of the two. When the informant is finished, however, I always tell him what I have recorded and give him the option of whether to erase or not.

As distinct from the technical side, the handling of a recording session from the content point of view presents its own special problems. The necessary prerequisite of establishing rapport has already been noticed and, from the sort of general conversation I have sketched, one has become aware before setting up the equipment of some of the material the informant has to offer. Indeed, the cue for setting it up is usually some item of tradition that has been mentioned

7. Alan Healey, *Handling Unsophisticated Linguistic Informants* (Canberra, 1964) , p. 20.

in conversation. The collector takes the opportunity to say, "Now that's very interesting. Do you mind if we get that on the record?" Meanwhile he has been making mental notes or, if the conversation has ranged widely over tradition, scribbled notes as an *aide memoire*. In the latter case it is wise to ask permission first before starting to write. I have noticed that the appearance of a notebook often seems to affect an informant more than the setting up of a recorder. One often, then, starts by recording a story or a song, a more natural situation than starting off on a general interview because the performer can easily come to terms with the wish of the collector to hear an old story or song. One must make sure to listen with attention and interest to the performance, smiling, as the occasion may demand, nodding understandingly rather than saying, "Yes," "Uh-uh" —the curse of many otherwise good recordings. In the case of a song, one can be seen to beat time or sway rhythmically in sympathy. When the performance is obviously ending, avoid rushing in too quickly on the last syllables of the performer's rendering. Then the deserved words of praise, the expressions of wonder and encouragement, and now the tricky part, the interview situation.

There are two basic types of interview technique, the directive and the nondirective. Either may be used, or a combination of both. The usual beginning is, "And from whom did you hear it?" The response conditions what is to follow. The nondirective interview gives the informant his head for the time being. His first answer may be, "From my father," and from there he is allowed to go on by free association. If he pauses, one nods, says, "Yes?" and gives him a moment to go on if he so wishes. Direct questioning is avoided in this type of interview unless the informant dries up or gets on to matters that are fairly judged to be totally irrelevant. Questions that occur to the listener are scribbled down or noted mentally. If there are others present, conversation should be allowed to break out and range freely within the limits noted above; such discussion may bring out interesting new slants, or even give clues to the ability of the others as potential informants. The tape, which is one's field notebook, is of course left running all the time unless it is specifically requested that it be turned off. If other stories or songs come up, they are (if possible) recorded without a break, the only interference by the collector to plead for a brief pause when he has to turn over or change a tape. This delay can have a serious effect on spontaneous conversation. (Here, if there are two or more fieldworkers present, is a strong case for having two machines running, the one taking up from the other to avoid a break in continuity). A break is also necessary if the informant calls for playback of any item, and can deflect the whole situation into a new, though not necessarily less rewarding, orbit.

This kind of interview can be very rewarding. It should only be interrupted when talk has dried up or gone off the rails. The collector then has the choice of guiding the conversation back into better channels or turning it into the directive type of interview. This is the more usual approach and the more difficult, depending as it does on question-and-answer technique. The collector must first ask the questions that have occurred to him in the course of the free-ranging discussion, if there has been one, either to elucidate points that he wants to clear up or to explore the other possible avenues that have been hinted at but not pursued.

In any question-and-answer situation, the interviewer should be careful to pose his questions in such a way that they do not put words in the mouth of the informant. Thus one should say, "How many years ago was that?" rather than, "That would be fifty years or more ago, I suppose?" Questions should be aimed at eliciting the fullest possible range of information. They will be based on the variable patterns of mental questionnaires to which I referred earlier.

Of course the two techniques of interviewing can be interchanged at a moment's notice. In a directive interview, any tendency by the informant to go off on a relevant, free-ranging path should be encouraged.

In questions whose object is to elicit further material, as distinct from eliciting information, the range of possibilities and patterns is obviously wide. If the collector wishes to explore the full extent of the informant's repertoire, it is usually better that the first questions be as general as possible: "What other stories did your father tell?" "What are your own favorite stories?" "What other songs did your mother sing?" In this way one begins not only to build up a picture of the informant's repertoire but also, no less importantly, some idea of his personal aesthetic. Each item obtained may be followed by the new questions that suggest themselves, while the collector continues to alternate between the two types of interview.

When the informant's response to this pattern of questioning also seems to be drying up or turning into trivial channels, the collector may go on to a slightly more specific type of question: "Do you know any stories about animals that talk, about giants, about heroes (or ballads, lullabies)?" and so on, using categories that have not appeared so far. The next logical stage would be more specific still, looking for material by giving summaries of stories, or titles and verses of songs. Stories told or songs sung as bait should generally not be performed too brilliantly for fear of giving the informant a feeling of inferiority. While all this is going on the interviewer is also using what are called observation techniques, recording in his mind or his notebook matters of setting and style that cannot be got on tape. These observations, especially important in group- or audience-informant situations, should be written up as soon as possible afterward. Observation techniques may also help to give the interviewer some idea of whether he is getting accurate answers or not. If not, he may decide to change his pattern of questioning to elicit more accurate information.

The outline sketched so roughly above represents perhaps a rather idealized system. In an actual interview, the permutation of possibilities is obviously vast, and even the most ideal pattern will inevitably yield to the pressures of expediency.

Most of what has been set out above presupposes a talented informant and perfect interviewing conditions. All too often, however, one is scraping for material and wondering what question to ask next, fearing all the time that one may put the informant off completely by feeding his questions to which he is forced to answer: "I don't know," "I never heard that," "I can't really remember it." One risk is that he may pretend that he has heard such-and-such, though he does not remember it. Such situations can often present a hard and unrewarding slog, though one hesitates to give up, as a question may suddenly elicit a remarkable piece of tradition grappled up almost from the informant's subconscious. A high work rate can yield low returns. Yet even the establishment of nil returns in answer to detailed questioning and summaries can help to show statistically that a certain item does not seem to have played any important part in the tradition of a particular area.

One must be prepared, if necessary, to be firm in pursuit, though never to the point of being rude or bullying the victim. My own experience is that most people can be made to grasp our purpose if sufficient effort is put into the search, and are very willing to do their best to help. One does find oneself sometimes recording material eagerly offered that has little or no merit or relevance to the search to avoid hurting the feelings of the informant or putting him off.

In the case of a really outstanding informant, material should very seldom be rejected. Even if he offers, say, a song that is poor and not on a par with the rest of his repertoire and yet obviously likes it himself, it should be recorded. He likes it for some reason that may be discovered, and this will tell one something about his code of aesthetics. On the other hand, he may have to be reminded that some kinds of materials that he may deliberately refrain from mentioning—erotica for instance—are worth recording.

If an informant seems to resent a line of questioning, and is still not ready to respond after the purpose is explained, this line should be dropped rather than run the risk of offending him. Some informants appear very reluctant to reveal the sources of their information. One should try to reach some conclusion as to why this should be so; there may be hidden clues. Is it simply forgetfulness, the usual answer given? Could the speaker have it from a rival who is still alive? Could it be from a printed source, the informant knowing that one is interested in oral material? Or could it be that the informant feels that he is losing something, that the texts are no longer "his own" if he reveals his sources? One of my very best informants for songs was most unforthcoming in this way: "Don't I know them myself? God knows where I heard them; everyone knew them when I was young." There may well be much truth in this for a good deal of an extensive repertoire—but it is hardly likely, say, in the case of a long and complicated story. People who are at first reluctant to supply information of this kind may improve on getting to know the collector. As I have said, if a line of questioning seems to upset the informant, it should be dropped. It is better to have good material undocumented than not to have it at all. Most good informants, however, are very ready to discuss their sources. They have an immense respect for tradition and the old people who passed it on to them.

Incidentally, one of the reasons for inquiring into sources is strikingly pointed by the pedigree of a story collected in 1860 by Hector MacLean, one of Campbell of Islay's team:

From Janet Currie, Stony-Bridge, South Uist, who learnt it from her father about forty years ago. Her father died about twenty years ago, and was past eighty-five years of age. He learnt it from Eachann Mac Mhurchaidh Mhic Alasdair Dhomhnullaich, a maternal uncle of his, who died before Quebec was taken by the English, which took place 13 September 1759. This MacDonald learnt it in his youth from Neil Currie, the Bard.[8]

"Neil Currie the Bard" was Niall MacMhuirich in South Uist, one of the famous family of professional poets and historians. He was one of the last of the old class of learned bards and died in South Uist early in the eighteenth century. Thus we have an oral pedigree for a tale extending back to a man who could have had it from a manuscript source.

Perhaps it develops that a story has come from a printed source at first-, second-, or third-hand. My own practice does not usually follow that of some commentators who advise against recording such

8. J. G. McKay, "Language of Birds," *Scottish Gaelic Studies* 3 (1931) : 180.

material. In dealing with a good tradition-bearer, it can be useful to record his version of something he himself had read years ago. We can learn about the oral process if his version can be checked against the printed source. We see what kind of literary story interested an oral practitioner. And we can appreciate a well-told narrative.

One further point on interview techniques. It will often be found beneficial and illuminating to cover much the same ground with one or more other good informants in the same area. The results when compared will usually allow one to reach more objective conclusions than any that can be based on the result from one situation alone.

The rapport and friendship established in the field can and should be maintained. The first visit may have confirmed a deep-seated, though seldom expressed, belief on the part of the informant that his tradition is of value and worth preserving. If so, there will always be something special in his attitude to you from now on, and of course he should reasonably expect not to be forgotten. Return visits are almost always welcome, indeed often looked for, and usually invaluable. A good tradition-carrier, once stimulated, has almost always recollected something else to offer by the next visit. With the very best the process goes on and on. On my last of many visits to the great Angus MacLellan in South Uist, shortly before he died at the age of 97, I obtained material that I had never heard from him before. And I am convinced, despite the remarkable repertoire recorded from him by a number of collectors, that he took much with him to his grave. His astonishing sister, Mrs. Marion Campbell, who was singing songs and heroic ballads right up to the time of her death at the age of 101, had something fresh to offer every time I visited her.

Rerecording of material already collected from the same informant can also be vitally important because of the light it throws on the oral process. Indeed, in the case of a really artistic performer it is a duty to try, and try again, to do full justice to his best standards. Even if nothing further is expected, a brief return visit is a graceful gesture.

This brings one to the thorny problem of direct payments in cash to informants for services rendered. In some societies payment seems to be the expected and regular practice. In Scotland, I myself have never heard payment mentioned, a lucky thing, as anything more than the merest token, spread over our vast number of informants, would be ruinous to the departmental budget. Still one recalls that Campbell of Islay made a practice of paying informants in proportion to results. Collectors, both institutional and private, must study carefully their practice in this respect. If payment is the regular and expected pattern in their area of operations, it should be on a fair and uniformly regulated scale. The risks of selectivity, leading to local jealousies and dissensions, queering the pitch for future operations, cannot be overemphasized.

There are special cases where payment should be regarded as absolutely obligatory, namely for textual or live material used in connection with any profit-making venture. Under this head comes broadcasting, disk publication, or printing with the aim of popular sales and good returns. The duty of the collector or institution here is obvious. They are honor-bound to see to it that some part of the reward goes to the informant, and this point should be made clear to broadcasting companies and publishers. Far too often one meets the attitude—founded surely on what has been one of the most blatant fallacies underlying certain "folk" theories—that such materials, desirable and interesting though they may be, represent a flotsam carried along willy-nilly on the anonymous, amorphous tide of the "folk," having been created by an equally anonymous communal process. The individual is assumed to have played little or no part in the shaping, in the creative aspect, of tradition, and those materials are there to be creamed off by any interested collector from the "civilized" strata, to be exploited as he sees fit. Such attitudes are still all too common. A few years ago my colleague, John MacInnes, was told by a professional singer prospecting for exploitable materials at the school: "These people may have feelings but they have no rights." Needless to say, that prospector went away with a very dusty answer and no treasures.

Not much more reputable is the attitude of scholars who will edit and publish field material without troubling to obtain specific clearance from their informants. The argument is sometimes heard that the material is good, it is needed for scholarly purposes, but that its use might not readily be approved by the informant, perhaps on grounds of content, a case in point perhaps being "social dynamite" of one kind or another. Often the scholar may lose the struggle with his conscience, if indeed he puts up one at all, and go ahead and publish, in the hope, often well founded, that the facts may never come to the attention of his informant. I even suspect that it may not occur seriously to some scholars that the informant does have rights—and yet these same scholars, and the other "developers" I have mentioned, would be the first to scream if their own copyright were infringed.

The attitudes and practices outlined above either miss, or choose to ignore, the point that in most societies the outstanding tradition-bearer is a literary artist and that, even in the most tradition-rich areas, an outstanding few in every generation have probably been responsible for the greatest share in the process of creating, molding and passing on the best in oral literature. Again MacEdward Leach makes the point strikingly:

In every community, however, there are individuals who have more songs or more stories than the others and usually they sing better and tell a tale better. Although all in a folk community know the stock cures, the granny woman is the expert. Likewise, in any community you will find the best songs in the keeping of one or two individuals. Often the position is hereditary. . . . In the summer of 1960 I collected in eight little outports of Labrador. In each outport there was one outstanding singer or storyteller: Peter Letto in Launce au Clair; Andrew Roberts in Forteau; George Trim in Englishtown; Ned Odell in Pinware. So I have found in Jamaica, in Cape Breton, in Virginia. We need a detailed study of this matter—the continuing tradition of the scop, the filid, the makar, the poet, and we need fuller information from present-day collectors about these superior informants. We need answers to questions like these: Where did they get their songs? Why do they cling to them? Is there a family tradition? Do they ever deliberately change a song, or tune, or story? I, for one, am quite convinced that new songs and stories, new groupings of material, variations, selective changes— all the processes by which folk literature improves—are due directly or indirectly to those few individuals in each culture. It is these who make an oral literature more complex, who extend it by borrowing from their fellows across the borders. Every fieldworker in anthropology who has the slightest understanding of literature knows that literary artists exist in every preliterate community, that they are recognized as such by the community, and that, moreover, fictional and semihistorical narratives are told for the sheer delight of telling them. That presupposes, of course, an audience willing to listen and able to evaluate and appreciate.[9]

Even one serious visit to a tradition-rich area ought to be enough to convince any reasonable observer that the "folk" are people—as much individuals as people anywhere—and that the best tradition-bearers are truly remarkable and talented individuals. These men and women who have given so freely of their time, their enthusiasm, and their unique and remarkable artistry and scholarship seem to me entitled to the same sort of consideration, courtesy, and respect as the literary artist and scholar anywhere.

In a largely undocumented minority culture, these people are not only our artists and historians, they are also the live books and manuscripts that enshrine the materials and much of the scholarship. The approach of the collector to this situation may be selective or eclectic; both are valid. What I do resent is the imputation, so often met with, that wide collecting over the spectrum of a culture always represents "ragbag collecting" and is necessarily unscholarly.

9. Leach, p. 338.

It could well be argued from the other side that a narrow-fronted approach can be irresponsible. If I may use a simile, the ultraspecialist who stumbles on a new and remarkable source of tradition, asks for the story of the Dragon Slayer, gets it, and goes on his way rejoicing without probing further is like a scholar finding a unique manuscript, tearing out the one text that interests him, and throwing the rest away.

My own practice is to try to achieve a balance between the two. This can be appallingly difficult. Like anyone else, I have my own special interests and an undoubted right to exercise value-judgments. Within the department my work is mainly concerned with tales. And yet what is one to do about the old man up the road who is known to be a source for heroic ballads, who has not been collected, and who may well be dead before a specialist can be got to come and record him? The answer seems to me to be clear. One owes a duty to this man, this society, these materials, indeed to scholarship. I must record him.

The choice is seldom so clear cut, and collecting work so often develops into a tricky exercise in balancing one's conscience. There is scarcely a trip from which one does not come back with a sense of elation for something recorded, something rescued from oblivion. Yet equally one always comes back with the burden of opportunities missed.

A few years ago in Barra, Thorkild and Anelise Knudsen and I were recording waulking songs from a group of women in Earsary led by Mary Morrison, a performer of outstanding caliber. Waulking, the fulling of heavy, home-woven cloth by kneading and thumping it rhythmically on a board (to the accompaniment of special choral songs), had been dead as a functional process in most parts of Barra for something like forty years. The nucleus of our group had taken part in the real thing, and women had continued to meet for years afterward to sing the songs, sometimes in a contrived setting. Some members of this group had previously been rehearsed and recorded by a number of collectors, including our own people from the School of Scottish Studies. This time conditions seemed ideal; the group had had a good deal of practice together and were all physically fit, including the human dynamo Mary Morrison, despite her eighty-odd years. We brought them together in a natural setting, Mary's thatched cottage in Earsary. The atmosphere was conducive. We had first-rate equipment. The group was set down to board and cloth, and the session began. From the beginning the session was obviously an outstanding success. The rhythm, the movement, the singing became more and more vigorous and insistent until the whole situation was transformed; it achieved a pitch, a mood, in which we were all caught up. The energy, the singing, the whole action, as a completely integrated team, of these middle-aged and elderly women, inspired and driven on as they were by the example of their leader, exhilarated all of us. It was no longer a staged performance. They were totally involved again in the real process. Within moments we the observers learned more about function in labor songs than we could have in a lifetime of scholarship. I had to quell a wild impulse to throw the microphone away. I shall never forget those integrated, precise, intense, flying hands. Nor shall I ever be able properly to describe them. Here was style, here was function, here was an artistically total fact.

Some of the sound recordings made that night are of stunning quality, but they cannot possibly hope to convey the whole situation to anyone who was not actually there. How often have we wished since that it could have been filmed. The possibilities of filming are actually being investigated by the school at the moment, but it may be impossible now to recreate that setting to the full. The women are that little bit older. They have not been practicing; Mary Morrison herself has been unwell. Something beautiful may be beyond recovery.

There are times when one wearies of it all and wishes to retreat into a sane backwater, away from the crises, the adjustments, the constant preoccupation with decay and death, even the occasional frustration and boredom. And yet, the best moments one would never exchange—to have met such people, to have thrilled with them, laughed and sorrowed and been moved with them and lived with them, and to have put something of their unique heritage on record, has been indeed a privilege.

For my last example I go across to Ireland. Between 1923 and 1931 J. H. Delargy had taken down a magnificent collection of traditions from Seán Ó Conaill, of Cillrialaig, County Kerry. Delargy says:

When, at last, my work was done, and the last tale was written down, my old friend turned to me and said: "I suppose you will bring out a book of these stories some day. I have told you now all the tales I can remember, and I am glad that they have been written. I hope that they will shorten the night for those who read them or hear them being read, and let them not forget me in their prayers, nor the old people from whom I myself learned them.[10]

A month later Seán Ó Conaill was dead. Anyone who is not moved by Seán Ó Conaill's colophon ought not to be collecting oral literature.

10. J. H. Delargy, "The Gaelic Story-Teller," *Proceedings of the British Academy* 31 (1945) : 186.

Bibliography and Selected Readings

Burne, Charlotte S. *The Handbook of Folklore*. London, 1914. A considerably expanded edition of Gomme's handbook, designed for overseas collectors in the Empire, such as "missionaries, travellers, settlers, and others whose lot is cast among uncivilized or half civilized populations abroad." This edition reflects the anthropological bias of the late Victorian folklorists.

Campbell, John Francis. *Popular Tales of the West Highlands*. 4 vols. Edinburgh, 1860–62. The Introduction (I: ix–xxxii), "The Fairy-Egg and What Came Out of It," recounts the field impressions of one of the earliest and most skillful collectors in Britain who uncovered a glorious cache of wonder tales in the Highlands and Hebrides. (Reprinted in Richard M. Dorson, ed., *Peasant Customs and Savage Myths*. Chicago, University of Chicago Press, 1968 [2: 655–72].)

Dorson, Richard M. "Introduction: Collecting Oral Folklore in the United States." *Buying the Wind*. Chicago: University of Chicago Press, 1964. Pp. 1–20. Suggestions for field collecting techniques based on the author's trips to northern Michigan, Negro communities in the south and north, and the Maine coast.

Gardner, Emelyn E. *Folklore from the Schoharie Hills, New York*. Ann Arbor: University of Michigan Press, 1937. Chap. 1, pp. 1–8, gives a compact but richly informative account of the author's field experiences in allaying the suspicions of this isolated hill people of German and Scotch-Irish ancestry.

Goldstein, Kenneth G. *A Guide for Field Workers in Folklore*. Hatboro, Penna., and London: Folklore Associates and Herbert Jenkins, 1964. The only book-length treatise in English on the problems, preparations, field behavior, and minutiae of the field trip. Too detailed for the casual collector.

Gomme, George L. *The Handbook of Folklore*. London, 1890. The first book-length collector's guide in English, a slender but lucid questionnaire directed at the county squire, parson, and schoolmaster and their wives and mirroring the concern with surviving custom and belief of English folklorists.

Leach, MacEdward. "Problems of Collecting Oral Literature." *Publications of the Modern Language Association* 77 (1962): 335–40. A personal statement by an experienced collector in Canada and the West Indies of the need to collect the cultural matrix, the personality and attitudes of the tradition-bearer, and a variety of genres in order to understand the folk esthetic. He distinguishes the folk aesthetic from the aesthetic of sophisticated art.

Lomax, John. *Adventures of a Ballad Hunter*. New York: Macmillan, 1947. The autobiographical narrative of a Texas banker who spent much of his life collecting and publishing cowboy and Negro folksongs. Unlike his son Alan, who shared many of these adventures, John was no scholar or theoretician, but this readable account of his fortunes and misfortunes in the field has lessons for every folklorist.

O'Sullivan, Sean (O Súilleabháin, Seán). *A Handbook of Irish Folklore.* The Educational Company of Ireland, Ltd., 1942. The exhaustive questionnaire based on materials already collected by the Irish Folklore Commission and used by the fieldworkers of the commission for further depth interviews. Every conceivable aspect of folklife is included, even to traditions about sneezing and traveling.

2 FIELDWORK: RECORDING MATERIAL CULTURE
Warren E. Roberts

The importance of fieldwork and recording in the area of traditional material culture cannot be too highly stressed. Several generations of folklorists have warned that folkloristic items are disappearing without leaving a trace behind. This warning is, if anything, more applicable today than ever before, especially in connection with material culture. More and more traditional artifacts and techniques are outmoded by accelerating technological changes. Those displaced are soon cast away and forgotten. In the United States, the spread of cities and highways continually engulfs farms and farm buildings, and the bulldozer buries valuable material and data. Elsewhere, when large reservoirs and artificial dams are constructed, responsible governmental agencies work with archeologists to uncover and register aboriginal material; and yet the traditional material culture of contemporary inhabitants is usually destroyed without a backward glance. In recent years there has been an increased interest in architectural preservation. Many individuals and organizations have rescued fine old buildings and even large groups of buildings from the wrecker's ball, and these buildings have often been restored and preserved for the future. Nearly always, however, the preservationists have saved examples of academic architecture, the mansions of the wealthy, while few have spoken out in favor of preserving examples of the traditional architecture of the common people. Surely there is a desperate need for competent fieldworkers to collect and record traditional material culture. The Industrial Revolution spelled the doom of most folk crafts and the traditional ways of life associated with them. Modern urban life threatens to obliterate much of what has persisted into the present.

The importance of fieldwork and recording in the area of traditional material culture needs stressing also because so little work of this sort has been done in Great Britain and the United States. This fact has been underlined in other sections of this work and need not be treated here. We need, however, recordings of many different kinds. Ideally, all aspects of the traditional ways of life of a given area should be recorded. Only in this way can one comprehend the true function and significance of the various interrelated parts. As an example, the tools used in harvesting, the customs of cooperative labor involved in harvesting, the beliefs associated with harvesting, the harvest festivals, the songs sung while harvesting and at the festivals, and the place of harvest time in the entire seasonal round of life all need to be studied together along with many other associated items in order to see their true significance. One could hardly isolate harvest songs, for instance, and study them outside their context without missing a great deal of their meaning. At the same time, it must be admitted that a study of all aspects of the traditional ways of life of even a small geographical area is immensely time-consuming and would involve the cooperative efforts of a number of specialists, for it is the rare fieldworker who is equally competent in, let us say, recording the techniques of a folk craft and the music of a fiddle tune. In actual practice, therefore, fieldworkers tend to concentrate on one subject or a group of closely related ones without ignoring the remainder, and fieldwork of this sort can be extremely fruitful. Even when one concentrates on one specific subject, however, the recording must be done in detail and in depth, as will be pointed out below.

Before one begins actual fieldwork, a considerable amount of preparation must be done. The exact preparation will, of course, vary from one collecting subject to another and from one geographical locality to another, but some generalized suggestions can be made. First of all, the prospective recorder must gather as much information as he can about the area in which he is going to work and about the subject he is going to record. As for the area in which he is going to record, one can talk with other collectors who have worked in the area or with someone who lives in or has lived in the area and read what written sources are available. In addition to any earlier collections or other folkloristic sources, local histories, guidebooks, and the like may prove useful, though one must be careful not to go out with preconceived notions that might influence his approach or lead him to ignore some data. Formulating a thesis and going out in the field to test it is a useful device for some types of collecting. By and large, there has been so little accurate fieldwork done with traditional material culture that it is necessary to do the basic recording before formulating theses.

The prospective recorder must also find out as much as he can about the subject he plans to record before he ventures out into the field. If he intends to concentrate upon a specific folk craft, for example, he must have some general information about that craft so that he will know, in a broad way, what to look for, so that he can ask meaningful questions, and so that he can attempt to gather all pertinent information. In interviewing a craftsman, for instance, one can hardly expect him to volunteer all pertinent information about his craft. One must question him about such topics as where he gets his raw materials, what the sources of his designs are, and where he has learned his craft. At the same time, a craftsman will usually talk much more freely to a person who has some knowledge of the craft than he will to a person who professes or shows complete ignorance of the craft. In this connection it often proves helpful to prepare a collecting guide in advance to insure that the recorder will not overlook some important type of information while in the field. One may become so engrossed in taking notes, making sketches, measuring, and photographing that only later does he realize that he has forgotten to investigate some aspects of his subject. A preliminary collecting guide should always be subject to revision as work in the field progresses and as the recorder gains more knowledge of his subject, and the guide should never be referred to so frequently that the informant gets the impression that he is being asked a number of cut-and-dried questions to be entered on a form. Still, a well-prepared and intelligently used guide can be a definite assistance to the recorder.

Before actually setting out to record, one should, if at all possible, obtain both contacts and leads. A contact is, normally, a person who lives in the area where recording is to be done and who is familiar with the area. He may or may not have information on the subject the recorder is looking for, but he can often suggest other people who do have useful information. When the recorder approaches an informant, he can say, "So-and-so told me that you might be able to help me," and the informant is then much more likely to be cooperative than otherwise. A lead is a person who actually has information or who possesses an item of interest. Other collectors and government, agricultural, and forestry agencies are possible sources of contacts and leads.

The recorder of material culture also needs a certain amount of equipment, varying with the work he intends to do, besides a reliable form of transportation. Under normal circumstances the fieldworker does not collect actual artifacts in the course of trips, although the occasion may arise when he can purchase some items either for himself or for some sponsoring institution. Instead, he accumulates photographs, measurements, and other data. He must, therefore, have a reliable camera and be familiar with it. It is at best discouraging to return from a long field trip to find that one has either poor quality photographs or none at all due to a malfunctioning camera or some human error. The exact type of camera equipment one uses will be dictated by the work he intends to do. A motion picture camera would prove useful if craftsmen at work are to be studied, but a still camera is adequate for most collecting. A camera equipped with extra lenses is certainly desirable. A wide-angle lens can be used to advantage in photographing the interior of a house or a craftsman's workshop, while a telephoto lens, for example, may be needed to take a picture of the details of the roof construction of a barn. If one expects to take some photographs in dark interiors, and some craftsmen's workshops are poorly lighted, flash equipment or very fast film is needed. The decision as to whether to use color film or black and white again depends on the subjects sought. If one is likely to photograph gaily painted barn decorations, for instance, color film is a necessity, but unless colors are important, black and white film is to be preferred, for it is more versatile and does not fade over the years as color films tend to do, especially when not properly stored. Some fieldworkers are able to carry two cameras with them when collecting, one loaded with color film and one with black and white film, using either as the circumstances dictate. Whatever photographic equipment is decided on, the prospective fieldworker will do well to take a roll of photographs and have them developed before setting out on his trip to be sure that his equipment is functioning properly and that he knows how to use it. When actually in the field, it is well to use the camera liberally, for film is a negligible investment compared to the time and expense of most field trips.

Since measurements are important data, measuring devices appropriate to the task must be taken into the field. For architectural work a fifty-foot steel tape and a six-foot folding wood rule are most useful. For investigating a craft, a six-foot rule may be adequate. With it one can measure a workshop or a tool equally well. It is also useful to have a clearly marked rule, preferably with alternating black and white solid rectangles marking the inches, that can be placed beside a small item to be photographed so that the marking on the rule will appear in the print. In this way the size of the item is clearly indicated without recourse to separate notes.

For some types of fieldwork a tape recorder is also a valuable tool. In recording data on processes, to be discussed below, a great deal of oral information must be gleaned. When one is talking with a craftsman about his work, for example, and how, when, and where he learned it, a tape recorder is obviously far more useful than a notebook. At the same time, of course, the fieldworker must bear in mind that some informants will hesitate to talk freely when faced with a tape recorder. Many informants can record a set or memorized performance such as a folksong with comparative ease. It is another matter, however, to have them talk clearly and easily into a microphone when they are searching their memories for details about their craft. The fieldworker must use his own judgment in this matter with each informant, balancing the ease of recording and the desirability of having the informant's own words on tape as against the possibility that the informant may be embarrassed and hesitant about speaking into a microphone.

Maps are needed both to help one find his way and to record the exact location of an item such as a house in case it is necessary to revisit it or so that someone else can find it. In the United States, U. S. Geological survey maps are invaluable for they are of such a scale and in such detail that they give the actual location of each house and barn in the countryside, identifying them by small squares. They need to be supplemented only in one way: they do not always give the local names of rural roads, and one will nearly always be given directions in this manner. Hence a local map giving these names is very valuable. A compass may be necessary, not that one is apt to get lost without it, but so that one can indicate the direction a building faces or so that the relationships between the various buildings on a farm can be given. Binoculars can save time in helping one decide whether to walk a long distance across a field to a remote barn, for instance. Finally, I personally carry a snake-bite kit with me in warm weather, for snakes love old houses and barns. I have never had to use it, but I usually feel better for having it when I tramp through the high weeds surrounding an abandoned barn.

There are two general kinds of recording that the fieldworker in material culture may collect. One involves recording data on artifacts, be they as large as a barn or as small as a thimble, while the other involves recording descriptions of processes such as the way a blacksmith makes a hinge or a farmer plows a field. The range of artifacts that may be recorded is so great that it is probably better to discuss one subject in detail rather than to attempt to generalize. Recording data on a house can be taken as an example with the hope that it will also give some insight into the problems of recording data on other artifacts. Recordings for a house can be of three kinds: measured plans, photographs, and sketches. Each has its own uses, and they can supplement one another.

Ideally, the data to be recorded on a building should be so complete that the building could be reproduced down to the last detail in case it were destroyed. Recording this much data on even an average house, however, would require many days of work. From a practical standpoint, the type of research that is being undertaken can dictate the amount of detail to be recorded. One must always bear in mind, however, that other workers may make use of one's recordings and that each generation of folklorists has tended to be critical of the preceding generation because it has not included enough detail in its recordings. It is certainly wiser to err on the side of being too detailed than to err in recording too little detail.

Measured plans cannot, of course, be completed in the field, but the measurements can be made and recorded on a rough plan, later to be transferred to a scaled plan. A floor plan for each floor should be made, giving the location and dimensions of such features as room partitions, doors, windows, fireplaces, stairways, and the like. A scaled elevation for each of the four sides of the house should also be made, showing the location and dimensions of doors, windows, exterior chimneys, and so on. A practical problem arises with heights such as the height of the ridgepole above the ground or the height of the chimney above the roof. Ladders to allow one to actually measure heights are usually not available, and owners are understandably reluctant to have strangers clambering around on their roofs. The recorder can always measure up six feet and then hold his rule above his head thus gaining a measured height of twelve feet. The remaining height can usually be estimated reasonably accurately. If the building is made of brick or if it has horizontal siding regularly applied, it is possible to determine the size of each course and count the number of courses, thus assuring reasonable accuracy.

Photographs and sketches can usually supplement one another. In most instances a photograph is preferable because it is not only more accurate but also takes far less time to obtain. Photographs should be taken of all four sides of the exterior as well as of interior details such as the foundation, doors, windows, and trim. Inside the house, one should try to photograph typical details such as doors, moldings, fireplaces, staircases, and the like. It is often necessary to sketch features that cannot be photographed either because one cannot get into a position to take a picture or because there is insufficient light. In many ways, J. F. Kelly's *Early Domestic Architecture of Connecticut* can serve as a guide to the fieldworker who is recording data on houses. First of all, Kelly gives excellent photographs and measured drawings that can serve as models. The thoroughness with which Kelly treats the various aspects of architecture is noteworthy. One can also profit by following Kelly's outline that includes such subjects as the house frame, roof framing, masonry, the outside covering, windows, front entrances, interior woodwork, paneling, mantels, cupboards, the stairs, moldings, and hardware.

In addition to measurements, photographs, and sketches, one should record other data of various kinds. The placement of the house in relationship to other buildings, roads, and features of terrain such as streams and springs can be shown by a rough sketch. Any information that the owner or people living nearby can give about the history of the building such as date of construction, name of builder, and names of past owners should be noted down. Moreover, any evidence from the building itself that might aid in determining its age should be recorded. Unfortunately, evidence of this sort is not always immediately apparent and takes considerable experience to evaluate properly, but some indications of the type of evidence that can be useful in this connection can be given.

First of all, one must always be aware of the fact that material in a house may not be contemporaneous with the building of the house. Materials may have been salvaged from earlier buildings and used in the construction, and many changes may have been made in the house after it was built so that material much newer than the house may be found in it. Kelly reports on the basis of his experience in Connecticut, "Rooms were panelled, ceilings plastered, fireplaces reduced in size, stairs rebuilt, mantels introduced, and entrances changed or added during the years after the original house-building."[1] Often the evidence that can be gleaned from the house itself, however, is the only source of dating that one can use.

One source of evidence involves the way in which timbers and boards have been cut. The telltale marks of the broadax indicate that a timber has been hewn, while the straight saw marks left by the up-and-down blade of a water-driven sawmill differ noticeably from the curved saw marks of the modern circular saw. One needs, of course, to examine timbers exposed in the basement or attic or to examine the bottom sides of floorboards seen in the basement and the like, for the marks of broadax or saw have been removed by plan-

1. J. F. Kelly, *Early Domestic Architecture of Connecticut* (New Haven, 1924), pp. v–vi.

ing in most finished parts of a house. On places where many coats of paint or long wear has not obscured them, one can often find the somewhat irregular marks of the hand plane or the faintly rippled surface left by a power-driven modern planing mill. Unpainted closet shelves and the backs of closet doors are good places to examine for plane marks. Masonry can also be examined for evidence of age. The use of concrete, for example, indicates modern work. Uncut field-stone can be used in any period, but if cut stone has been used, one can distinguish between stone that has been shaped or "picked" by hand and that sawed with modern machinery. If brick has been used, one can distinguish old, hand-made bricks from factory-made bricks be-cause the hand-made bricks are more uneven and irregular and show greater variation in color. In older masonry work, too, clay was often used in place of mortar, especially where it would not be exposed to rain such as in a chimney built in the center of a house. If plaster has broken loose any place, or if it is possible to examine the back side of plastering either in a closet or a basement stairway, some indi-cations as to age may be obtained. If animal hair is used in the plaster itself it is an evidence of age. Older lath will either be rived, usually from oak, or sawed in broad sheets and then spread out accordion fashion by being split partially through. Sawed lath that is regular in size and shape indicates modern construction. Windows and doors should also be examined. Old window glass was thinner than modern glass and filled with streaks and bubbles. Very old glass often shows a metallic iridescence. In general, too, the smaller the panes are, the older the window is. Modern window frames are more complicated than older ones, for in older work the upper sash was fixed and only the lower sash could be raised. While it is usually difficult to examine the actual construction of the window sash, it is possible to see how doors were constructed. Older doors were often of the "board and batten" type in which vertical boards are held together by means of two or three horizontal boards nailed across the back. A more com-plicated form of door construction in which panels are set into a frame was often used also in earlier houses. The same type of door is still manufactured today, though hand-made doors can usually be recognized because the tenons of the rails pass completely through the stiles. Wedges were usually driven in beside the outer end of the tenon, and wooden pegs were driven through the entire joint. Nails and hardware should also be examined. There are three general types of nails. The earliest is the hand-wrought nail that can be recognized by its irregularity. The head of the most common type is large and usually shows the marks of the blacksmith's hammer while the shank of the nail is square in cross-section and tapers unevenly to a point. But nails in use throughout most of the nineteenth century are much more regular in appearance. The head of the most common type is rectangular, and the shank is rectangular and tapers towards a blunt point on two sides only. Wire nails have been used mainly in the twentieth century. They have round heads and round shanks that taper very abruptly to a point. (Anyone attempting to establish dates of construction on the basis of the type of nail used should consult Lee H. Nelson's "Nail Chronology as an aid to Dating Old Buildings," American Association for State and Local History Technical Leaflet 15.) It is usually possible to recognize hand-wrought door hinges and latches that are the earliest type. Cast-iron hinges and latches replaced hand-wrought ones, replaced in their turn by modern steel ones. Sometimes hardware of solid brass was used in earlier houses, especially in such an important place as the front door, while much modern hardware is brass-plated steel. If it is possible to remove a wood screw, one can usually tell whether it is a modern, machine-made screw by its general smoothness and its point. Old screws that were hand-made are very irregular and early machine-made screws are blunt.

Another type of recording involves processes such as those involved in various crafts. Here, again, statements that could apply to all processes are so generalized that it is better to indicate some of the steps in recording data about a single craft such as cabinetmaking. Here there are various types of information to be recorded about such topics as materials used, tools and their use, designs and their sources, and the craftsman and his customers. After the fieldworker has had the opportunity to visit the cabinetmaker and become acquainted with him, he can begin recording information. A natural preliminary step is to ask for biographical information, stressing especially the ways in which the cabinetmaker learned his craft. Whenever possible, the fieldworker should try to find out as much as he can about changes that have occurred in the course of time that the informant remembers or that he has heard about from older craftsmen.

The materials the cabinetmaker uses are, of course, mainly wood. The fieldworker should try to find out where the cabinetmaker gets his wood of different kinds, how he seasons it, and why he uses different kinds of wood for different purposes. Information should also be recorded about the other kinds of materials the cabinetmaker may use such as hardware, glue, and finishing materials like varnish and lacquer.

Detailed information on the tools of the cabinetmaker and their use may require a number of visits. Unless the craftsman has a great deal of free time at his disposal and can demonstrate how each tool is used, the fieldworker will simply have to try to be present when the tools are being used in the normal course of the craftsman's work. A wise preliminary step would be to make a measured floor plan of the workshop showing the location of work benches, stationary tools, storage areas, and the like. If possible, an inventory of the tools should be made giving the craftsman's name for each tool and any information he may be able to give as to its age, where he got it, and how often he uses it. When time permits, each tool should be measured and photographed. As the occasion arises when the craftsman is actually using his tools, as many photographs as possible should be taken. If a motion picture camera is available, it should be used to show the tools in use. Any explanations that the craftsman can give as to why he uses certain tools in certain ways should likewise be recorded. Mercer's *Ancient Carpenters' Tools* is an excellent source to use for general information in this regard.[2]

Gathering detailed information on the designs or plans the cabinetmaker follows in building his furniture is a time-consuming but vital task. One should undoubtedly begin by locating, photographing, and measuring as many of the craftsman's products as can be found. This will entail visiting his customers and getting their permission to examine the furniture the craftsman has made for them. The owners of the furniture and the cabinetmaker himself may be able to supply information about the dates when the furniture was made.

A second step would involve an investigation of the sources of the craftsman's designs or plans. As time permits, the fieldworker should talk with the cabinetmaker and record any information he can give as to which designs he has drawn up himself and which he has acquired in a traditional way either from those from whom he learned his craft or from other craftsmen. One must bear in mind that information from the craftsman himself must be treated with some caution, though it must be recorded in detail. A craftsman who has been making a certain type of chair for many decades may firmly believe that he designed the chair himself in the first place, whereas in actual fact it may be a reasonably exact replica of chairs made by earlier craftsmen. The cabinetmaker may also be able to give information concerning changes he has made in designs over a period of time and the reasons why he has made these changes. Many cabinetmakers also have in their shops detailed plans, sketches, and full-sized patterns made of heavy paper, cardboard, or thin wood for parts or entire pieces of furniture. These can be photographed or copied in other ways, and the craftsman may be able to tell where he obtained them. The fieldworker should not overlook the possibility that some of the cabinetmakers' designs may have come from books and magazines or that some of his designs may have been influenced by printed sources.

2. Henry C. Mercer, *Ancient Carpenters' Tools* (Doylestown, Pa., 1929).

If it is at all possible, the fieldworker should attempt to document the influences on the cabinetmaker's designs by investigating the tradition in which he is working. For the sake of simplicity, let us assume that the cabinetmaker has learned his trade from his father. Any pieces of furniture made by his father that can be located should be photographed and measured so that comparisons can be made. Moreover, the furniture made by other cabinetmakers in the area whose work the informant may be familiar with should also be investigated.

Finally, the fieldworker should try to discover whether or not the cabinetmaker knows and uses a general or traditional principle of design or knows an inherited rule of thumb that he follows in making new designs. As an example, let us assume that the cabinetmaker has been asked to make a chest of drawers unlike those he has made in the past. How does he determine the general proportions, i.e., width, height, and depth, assuming that these have not been specified by the purchaser? How high are the legs or the base? Since all the drawers are usually not the same size in a chest, how does he decide what the height of each drawer is? How thick is the top and what size should be the moldings under the top and elsewhere on the piece? It may well be, of course, that the cabinetmaker will answer queries of this sort by saying, "I've always done it that way," or "That wouldn't look right," and be unable to give any further information. He may, however, know the rule of thumb that, in a chest of drawers, the height of each drawer should be less than the one below it by an amount equal to the size of the piece of wood separating them. (As a simple illustration, take a chest with four drawers: if the strip of wood between drawers is one inch in height and the bottom drawer is seven inches in height, the next drawer should be six inches in height, the next five inches, and the top drawer four inches.)

Information about the craftsman and his customers should also be obtained, for it is a subject that has been almost totally neglected in the past. Some of this information can be gleaned from the cabinetmaker himself, but his customers should also be interviewed if it is at all possible. Some points to be investigated in this connection include: to what extent have the customers determined the designs and specifications of furniture the cabinetmaker has made; how do his customers regard his furniture in comparison with that of other craftsmen or that made in factories; how has furniture made by the craftsman in years gone by held up in actual use; does the craftsman regard his customers as friends and acquaintances whom he is happy to oblige or are they thought of in more impersonal terms; and is the craftsman admired for his skill and considered an important person in the community? It may be well to stress once again the importance of detailed recording of this kind. Traditional crafts that are of great antiquity are on the point of disappearing. They represent an important part of a traditional way of life that is also being submerged by a new and different way. The few craftsmen who still carry on their crafts should be studied as thoroughly as possible while there is still time.

In addition to the work that he carries out in the field, the student of material culture must consider how best to store and file his accumulated records. Much will depend, of course, upon how extensive his fieldwork is, how many different types of material he is recording, and other factors, but in general some sort of file or archive will be necessary. Two general principles should guide the person who is trying to decide how to organize his recorded data: the material should be easily accessible, and related materials should be kept together. It is beyond the purpose of this paper to describe how a large archive for an entire state, for example, should be set up, although many of the ideas that apply to a small collection can apply also to a large archive.

First of all, the data—photographs, drawings, measurements, transcriptions of tape recordings, or other notes regarding one item or one craftsman—should be placed in a large envelope or folder. The way in which these envelopes or folders is arranged in sequence will vary according to the subject. At least three methods can be cited. If the fieldworker is recording many different kinds of material, the arrangement should probably be based upon the kinds of material. For example, his file might contain a section on architecture, another on agriculture, a third on crafts, and so on. If the fieldworker is concentrating on one subject, architecture, let us say, it is probable that a geographical arrangement will prove most satisfactory. With this system, all the buildings recorded in one township, for example, can be filed together. If, on the other hand, craftsmen are being visited and interviewed, it is quite likely that an alphabetical arrangement based upon the informants' names will be most useful. Whatever basic scheme is used, a system of cross-referencing should also be considered. If the system is based upon the kinds of material investigated, some type of geographical cross-reference should be developed, as well as an alphabetical list of names of informants or of the owners of the material investigated. For a geographical cross-reference it may be possible to use a map or some arrangement of file cards may be worked out, while for personal names a file card system is obviously best. If, on the other hand, the basic filing system is a geographical one, a cross-reference index for subject matter and another for personal names should be used. As an example, let us assume that architecture is being recorded and that the folders containing data on the individual buildings are filed according to their geographical location. A separate file of cards covering the different kinds of buildings—dwelling house, barn, smokehouse, and so on—keyed to the main file should be developed together with another file of cards listing alphabetically the owners' names. Finally, if the basic system depends upon the owners' or informants' names, separate cross-reference indexes should be drawn up for the geographical location and the type of material. In any case, it is wise to keep a map on hand giving the location where fieldwork has been done as an aid in planning one's work and laying out future field trips.

Bibliography and Selected Readings

Evans, G. Ewart. *Ask the Fellows Who Cut the Hay.* London: Faber, 1956. An excellent book concerned with the recording of oral tradition in East Anglia. Ewart Evans's other books, *The Horse in the Furrow,* London: Faber, 1960, and *The Pattern Under the Plough,* London: Faber, 1966 are also very valuable.

Fenton, Alexander. "An Approach to Folk Life Studies." *Keystone Folklore Quarterly* 12 (1967) : 5–21. Contains practical suggestions for fieldwork in material culture based upon the author's experiences in Scotland.

Higgs, J. W. Y. *Folk Life Collection and Classification.* London: The Museum's Association, 1963. Reproduces in condensed form the classification scheme used at the Museum of English Rural Life and gives sample questionnaires.

Jenkins, J. G. "Field-Work and Documentation in Folk-Life Studies." *The Journal of the Royal Anthropological Institute* 90 (1960): 250–71. Valuable information based upon the author's own fieldwork in England and Wales.

————, ed. *Studies in Folk Life.* London: Routledge and Kegan Paul, Ltd., 1969. Contains a series of twenty essays presented to Dr. I. C. Peate. The essays are by European scholars and cover material, linguistic, and social aspects of folk life.

————, ed. *Traditional Tools and Equipment.* Transactions of the Museum Assistants' Group, No. 5. London, 1965. Contains brief articles by several different scholars with emphasis on collection and classification.

Owens, T. M. "The Recording of Past Social Conditions." *Folk Life* 4 (1966) : 85–89. Deals with the use of the tape recorder to collect oral data on a wide range of social topics.

Peate, Iorwerth C. *Folk Museums.* Cardiff: University of Wales Press, 1948. A description of folk museums in Europe and of the Welsh Folk Museum at St. Fagans.

————, ed. *Gwerin.* Vols. 1–3 (1956–61). Contains numerous articles relating to folk collections. The successor to *Gwerin* is *Folk Life* (edited by

J. Geraint Jenkins), published annually by the Society for Folk Life
Studies.

Scottish Studies. School of Scottish Studies, University of Edinburgh, 1957–. A
bi-annual journal devoted to Scottish folklore and folklife.

Ulster Folklife. Ulster Folk Museum; Dublin. A quarterly journal dealing
with folklife studies of northern Ireland.

The handbooks of folk museums such as the Welsh Folk Museum, The
Museum of English Rural Life, the Luton Museum, the City of Gloucester
Museum, and the Castle Museum, York, are useful for information on the
collections of those museums.

3 FIELDWORK: RECORDING TRADITIONAL MUSIC
George List

Fieldwork is the means utilized in securing the raw data upon which studies of folk music are based. Much folk music is recorded by amateurs who are moved to do so by their esthetic appreciation of the music or through their interest in the cultural group that performs this music. There are also those whose principal purpose in collecting is to secure materials for the issuance of albums of recordings. The utility of such recordings in the study of folk music depends to a great extent upon the degree of background information that accompanies the recordings and upon the accuracy of such information.

In general, field collections made by the scholar who will himself study and publish the music collected are of greater value than those made by others. The scholar is conversant with the methods commonly employed in the study of folk music. He is therefore cognizant of the types of recordings that will be of greatest value in the particular study he has in mind and what background information will be pertinent to such studies. Of even greater importance is the fact that the scholar-collector is a trained scientific investigator. As such he endeavors to maintain at all times as high a degree of objectivity and accuracy in his work as possible. The need for accuracy is widely recognized, as indicated in the following instructions concerning notating song texts found in a Russian guide to collectors: "The basic requirements demanded for scientific recording should be strictly carried out, above all—accuracy. No omissions, changes or additions to the text are admissible."[1]

In addition to his formal training, the scholar-collector probably has had previous experience in fieldwork. He thus has developed through actual experience not only the techniques of recording and interviewing necessary to success in this complex activity but also the ability to make valid judgments as to what he should or should not record, thus conserving time and energy. All field situations differ one from another. The collector may find it impossible to secure recordings and documentation sufficient for his planned study. Or he may find himself mining a vein so rich that it is beyond his capacity to properly work it with the time and recording tape at his disposal. In the latter case he is continually faced with the necessity of making judgments as to the course he should pursue.

Ideally, each musical performance should be recorded in its entirety. In some regions this presents little difficulty since the genres performed are relatively short. Elsewhere, performances may exceed the recording time offered by a single tape roll. Should the collector be recording a single informant, possibly this individual may be able to stop at a particular point until the tape is replaced and then continue. If the actual performance of a lengthy ceremony is being recorded this is usually not feasible. Under such circumstances the collector is frequently faced with the necessity of deciding with some rapidity when he will record and when he will not.

Institutions that sponsor field collection by their staff members solve such problems by sending out expeditions of more than one individual and equipped with more than one recorder. The field expeditions of the Institute for Dialect and Folklore Research at Uppsala, Sweden, consist of a collector and a technician who travel in a small bus equipped with two racked tape recorders. The bus is parked in front of the home of an informant. The collector then goes into the house carrying a microphone attached to a long cord that issues from the bus. The technician remains in the bus, operates the equipment, monitors the recording, and switches the microphone

1. P. G. Bogatyrev et al., eds., *Russkoe narodne tvorčestvo* [Russian Folklore] (Moscow, 1966). From chapter on field collecting by Erna V. Pomeranceva; p. 335, translated by Barbara Krader for George List.

from the input of one recorder to the other before the first tape is exhausted. In this manner recording can continue without pause.

Most field recording, however, is done by individuals. The skilled field recorder therefore necessarily develops an almost automatic ability to adjust the volume control of his recorder as circumstances require. Should he record a group rather than an individual performer, he records a short section as a test of balance and recording level before taping the entire performance. He must also be conversant with various tricks of the trade that permit him to secure good recordings under various difficult circumstances. In moving the microphone and informants to secure balance, he avoids sound-reflecting surfaces. Should there be a high level of extraneous noise, he shields the microphone with a trumpet of soft material, places the microphone closer to the informant, and records at low level. If the informant accompanies his song by playing an instrument, the collector secures proper balance by hanging the microphone from the ceiling immediately in front of and above the informant's head.

The skilled collector has also developed a competency in the techniques of interview. Two types of interviewing techniques are recognized, the directive and the nondirective.[2] In directed interviews, a specific line of inquiry is pursued. The interviewer may utilize a previously prepared questionnaire or he may question the informant in a less formal manner. In nondirective interviews, a preliminary question or two are posed and the informant is then allowed to follow his own line of thought or interest. Each type of interviewing offers specific advantages. Directive interview is the most efficient method of quickly acquiring desired information. In nondirective interview, on the other hand, the informant, through the free flow of his related experiences, may provide the collector with leads concerning useful directions of inquiry of which the collector could have no knowledge in advance. For this reason many collectors use nondirective interviews in work with informants preliminary to a recording session. Interviews during the following recording session are then generally limited to direct questioning.

In actual practice both methods are employed, to some extent at least, in all interviewing. The collector who utilizes only the method of direct interview, who slavishly follows a questionnaire or a specific line of questioning without permitting digressions on the part of his informant, is likely to miss a good deal of useful information that

2. For a detailed discussion of these two types of interview techniques see Kenneth S. Goldstein, *A Guide for Field Workers in Folklore* (Hatboro, Penn., 1964), pp. 108–12.

otherwise could have been secured. The experienced interviewer permits his informant to deviate from the line of questioning being pursued when this seems useful. The following, taken from the author's own field experience, will serve to illustrate this point:

I was engaged in fieldwork on the Hopi Indian Reservation in northern Arizona where I was recording kachina dance songs. These songs are sung during the dance ceremony by a group of men. The songs are usually composed for the occasion by individual Hopi men. One is not permitted to record during the actual ceremony, but a few individuals were willing to sing the songs for me. One of these men referred me to an elderly Hopi known for his ability as a composer. He had become a Christian and no longer participated in the dance ceremonies.

This Hopi rather grudgingly sang for me several songs he had composed some years in the past. Singing the songs apparently awakened unpleasant memories, and he launched into a series of complaints concerning the lot of the Hopi composer: there was never sufficient rehearsal; the songs were never sung as the composer conceived them, the group constantly modifying the tune to suit their taste; and so on.

I gave him free rein and listened. At one point he complained of the performing group's insistence on composing the "middle part" of the song, as though the composer were not competent to do this himself.

When the man had exhausted his complaints I returned to the matter of the "middle part" that interested me very much. I had a rather large collection of recordings of Hopi kachina dance songs made by other collectors. Some had been made as early as 1903. In none of these recordings, nor in those that I had made on the reservation myself, was there a section that could be described as a "middle part."

Upon further interrogation I discovered that the "middle part" was omitted when kachina dance songs were sung in other than ceremonial circumstances as, for example, by adults to children. It had therefore been omitted in performances for collectors. However, this "middle part," which consists of a very short section of new material plus repetition of all or part of the principal section of the song, is ceremonially the most important aspect of the kachina dance song. It was thus through a chance remark of an informant that I became cognizant of the full structure of the kachina dance song. Following this incident I instructed my informants to duplicate ceremonial practice in their renditions. By this means I was able to secure the first recordings ever made of complete kachina dance songs.

The collector goes into the field with a goal in mind. His goal may be fairly precise. He may wish to collect a particular genre as performed under given circumstances in a specific region. Or his goal may be more general, the collection of the folk music of a fairly homogeneous group living in a particular geographic area. Whatever his goal, he spends much time in preparing for the planned fieldwork. He reads widely concerning the history, customs, and geography of the region he will visit. Certain information that he gleans from these sources may have considerable bearing upon the success of his expedition. He may find, for example, that there are seasons of the year when heavy rains make travel extremely difficult and that he should, if possible, avoid engaging in fieldwork during these periods. In further preparation he reads existent publications concerning the folk music of the region or cultural group he will visit and seeks out individuals who have previously collected there to secure further information and advice. He listens to music previously recorded in the area when it is available.

Should the fieldworker not possess some competency in the dialect or language that his informants will speak, he attempts to gain some skill in it before entering the field. Many collectors develop a repertory of songs and instrumental pieces that they may expect to hear performed. Through the knowledge of this repertory the collector is able to draw out his informants by asking if they know and can perform a particular item.

In the early days of field collection, scholars often notated by hand the music performed, not wishing to make use of the relatively inefficient recording devices of the period. Now that portable tape recorders of excellent quality are available, this practice has been discontinued. Music is acoustically recorded in the field and transcribed later under laboratory conditions.

In preparation for his expedition the collector secures that type of recording equipment that is most suitable to the conditions under which he will work. A portable tape recorder that can be operated either by batteries or electricity is usually the most advantageous. He may need a transformer if line supply is to be utilized. Should the region to be visited be hot or humid, he selects a type of recording tape appropriate to these climate conditions. He may further protect his recordings by sealing the tape rolls in metal cans. He also equips himself with a reliable camera with which to photograph his informants, the dances and ceremonies in which the music he records plays a part, and the cultural milieu in general. Should he not have had previous experience with any of the equipment selected, he becomes familiar with its operation before leaving for the field.

No matter how thorough his preparation, the collector may find it difficult, if not impossible, to reach the goal he has set himself. The information that led him to engage in this particular investigation may be inaccurate in one aspect or another. The genre he seeks to record may no longer be performed or it may exist in oral tradition in fragmentary form only. The experienced collector is therefore ready, when necessary, to adapt his goals to the objective situation. Should he expend his energy in the attempt to reach possibly unattainable goals, he may not recognize, and therefore not be in a position to take advantage of, opportunities to collect other materials of equal interest. Again, an illustration from the author's own field experience may prove useful:

During fieldwork among the Negroes of the Atlantic coastal region of Colombia, South America, I was endeavoring to secure recordings of the *cumbiamba,* an ensemble that accompanies the local folk dances. I had arrived one morning by jeep at the town of Mahates where such an ensemble had been known to exist. Unfortunately, I soon learned that the leader of the group, who played the indispensable *caña de millo,* had recently left Mahates and the ensemble was therefore unable to play for me. One of the players informed me that the absent leader had been taught to play the *caña de millo* by a man who lived in the not-too-distant village of Evitar. I could inquire there.

No Evitar appeared on my map of the province. My driver, however, finally found the muddy road that led to but not through this little village. I was delighted to find that Evitar did have a *cumbiamba,* but my joy was short-lived. Three brothers had played the *caña de millo.* One brother had left the village, a second had just died, and the third brother refused to perform since he was *en luto* (in mourning) for his deceased brother.

It was now two o'clock in the afternoon. Further quest for a *cumbiamba* was impractical on that day. I made my way to the one store in the village. Here I secured information concerning the types of songs sung in the village and the individuals who could sing them for me. The palm-thatched school-house was made available to me. Here, from four o'clock until nearly midnight, I recorded lullabies, children's game songs, worksongs, songs sung at the *velorio* (the death vigil) , and others.

The folk music tradition of this isolated little village proved to be so rich and so typical of the region that I returned to it several times. Eventually, I secured materials sufficient to document the entire musical life of the village of Evitar.

Once the collector reaches the region in which he will work, he is faced with the problem of locating informants who are able and willing to offer him the materials he is seeking. There are many means of making contacts with informants. Names of individuals to contact may have been secured in advance from collectors who have previously worked in the area. Local contacts are made with individuals who are likely to have a wide acquaintance—ministers, priests, schoolteachers, or newspaper editors. The collector frequents places where people gather—taverns, marketplaces, and barber shops.[3] Once he has secured one or two informants, they may lead him to others.

3. See Richard M. Dorson, *Buying the Wind* (Chicago, 1964) , pp. 6–7, for a discussion of means of contacting informants.

Should the collector not have sufficient command of the language or dialect spoken by his informants to successfully communicate with them, he must find an intermediary to assist him. The intermediary or translator follows the collector's instructions, carries on interview either by means of a previously prepared questionnaire or by conveying the collector's questions to the informants, translating the latter's replies. When the collector works through an intermediary, misunderstandings usually arise. For this reason the preferred procedure is to record all interviews as well as music. The accuracy of translations by the intermediary can then be checked later with the assistance of other individuals familiar with the language.

Collector-informant relationships are obviously of the utmost importance. The collector's task is to establish as great a rapport as possible with each informant. Some informants are suspicious of the collector's motives and may be reluctant to cooperate. Utilizing his previously acquired knowledge of local custom, the collector couches his approach in a manner calculated to overcome the informant's suspicions or objections.

Other informants may be eager and even anxious to record for the collector but may place little premium on accuracy and may considerably exercise their imaginations during interview. When the collector has doubts concerning the trustworthiness of his informant, he does not display his doubts outwardly. Rather, he depends upon means other than direct interrogation in checking the accuracy of what he has recorded or noted. He asks the same question of other informants and compares answers, or he asks other informants to comment on his understanding of certain points; in doing so he does not indicate the source of his information.

Field recordings of folk music are of little value unless accompanied by full documentation. The minimal information that is usually secured for each recorded item may be described as the four "w's," "where," "when," "who," and "what." Where was the recording made and when? Who performed the item recorded and what was performed?

This is the bare bones of documentation. Much more background information is needed for a study in any depth. In enlarging their knowledge of "who" and "what," some collectors prefer to note the information by hand, others find it more convenient to record all documentation on tape. In the latter case all proper names or unusual words are spelled out or noted separately. No matter which method is employed, hand notation or tape recording, sufficient information is recorded before or immediately after each musical performance to permit its ready identification.

Among the items of information usually secured concerning informants are place of birth, age, sex, occupation, present residence, and places of former habitation. The informant is queried concerning his ethnic background and that of his family and immediate relatives. Other questions may be asked to ascertain whether or not the informant is fully representative of the cultural group whose music will be the subject of study. In Yugoslavia, for example, there are many linguistic groups. Should an Albanian or a Macedonian sing a Serbian song, the performance may differ in some particulars from that of a Serb.

The name or title of each item performed is noted. If alternative titles exist, they are also given. In the case of a song, the first line may also be noted. All instruments recorded are identified. The genre or type of each item recorded is also noted—that it is a ballad, a work song, a skipping-rope song, a fiddle tune accompanying a particular dance, and so on.

Texts of the songs recorded form an important basis of study. If the language in which the songs are sung is familiar to the collector, he may be able to transcribe the texts himself. Nevertheless, he will listen to the recordings carefully before leaving the area in order that he may secure assistance from his informants if any of the words sung are not intelligible to him. Should the collector not have command of the language or dialect in which the songs are sung, he endeavors to secure the text in the original language and a translation of the text into his language. For this he calls upon his intermediary or seeks the assistance of another bilingual person who is familiar with the area in which the songs have been recorded.

When a musical instrument is played, it is measured, described, and photographed. The informant is queried concerning the techniques of playing the instruments. If the informant made the instrument, or if it was made locally, he is asked to describe the process of fabrication and to list the materials from which it is constructed.

Should the music performed form part of a particular custom or ceremony, a full description of this larger activity is secured. The collector observes the ceremony himself, if at all possible, and records his observations. If the music forms part of a game or dance, the collector, within his ability, describes the figures, steps, or other activities involved.

The scholar-collector is also interested in securing data that is of value in certain specialized studies such as the categorization of repertories, the degree and kinds of social participation in folk music performance in the community or region, the methods of transmission of music and performing skills, the variations which arise from performance to performance, and the esthetic judgments of the community concerning folk music repertory and style of performance. For these purposes the collector attempts to secure a full representation of the genre or genres in which he is interested. He asks several informants to offer a list of those items known to them and questions them concerning the names used locally to identify the types or genres into which they fall. He then inquires concerning the type of participation exhibited in each case. Is the type or genre under consideration usually performed by one individual or by a group? If the latter, what is the usual number of participants? If instrumental performance is involved, what is the usual instrument employed? If a group performance, are the same number and type of instruments utilized in each case or is practice flexible in this regard? Further, is there a type or genre that is sung only by men or only by women? only by children? only by agricultural workers? Do differing social classes have special repertories? Are some performers professionals, that is, are they paid for their services in goods or money? If so, what type of music do they perform, under what circumstances? From what social class or classes do these performers come?

For the purpose of the study of transmission of folk music, information is secured concerning when and where the informant learned the item performed and from whom. If he plays a musical instrument, he is asked how he learned to play it. From whom did he learn to play the instrument? Is he self-taught? Whose playing did he observe and imitate?

Two performances of the same song or instrumental piece are rarely alike, whether performed by the same informant or by different informants. As a means of studying this variation, more than one performance of the same item is recorded from the same informant, preferably on different days. Performances of the same item by other informants are also recorded.

Certain questions are commonly asked as a means of securing aesthetic judgments. Which items in an informant's repertory are his favorites and why? Which performers in the area are most highly considered? Why? Is it the quality of their voice, their retentive memory, or their technical skill that is admired? Are there individuals who frequently perform but whose performance is in general held in low esteem? Having secured answers to these questions from several informants, the collector records both the highly rated and the poorly rated performers. Through the analysis of these materials the scholar is able to arrive at some conclusions concerning the aesthetic judgments of the community.

Bibliography and Selected Readings

Dorson, Richard M. *Buying the Wind.* Chicago: University of Chicago Press, 1964. Introduction: "Collecting Oral Folklore in the United States," pp. 1–20. A very readable exposition of the problems of fieldwork, illustrated by the experiences of the author in collecting in various areas of the United States.

Goldstein, Kenneth S. *A Guide for Field Workers in Folklore.* Hatboro, Penna.: Folklore Associates, 1964. A thorough, anthropologically oriented survey of field problems and methods based on the author's extensive fieldwork in the eastern United States and in Scotland, and also on the literature. Discusses observation versus interview methods in collecting.

Karpeles, Maud, ed. *The Collection of Folk Music and Other Ethnomusicological Materials, a Manual for Field Workers.* London: International Folk Music Council and the Royal Anthropological Institution of Great Britain and Ireland, 1958. A concise work that offers practical advice concerning field methods including the recording of dance. Excellent discussion of the use of recorders, motion picture cameras, and the making of sound film. Although there has been much improvement in the equipment available for use in the field since this manual was published, the comments in this regard are still generally applicable.

List, George. "Documenting Field Recordings." *The Folklore and Folk Music Archivist* 3, 3 (1960). An outline of data to be secured in the field for the documentation of recordings with special reference to that data needed when the recordings are deposited in an archive.

Thompson, Stith, ed. *Four Symposia on Folklore.* Bloomington: Indiana University Press, 1953. Chap. 1, "The Collecting of Folklore," pp. 1–88. A transcription of a stimulating discussion session of the Midcentury International Folklore Conference held at Indiana University 21 July through 4 August, 1950, with distinguished participants from various areas of the world.

4 ARCHIVING
George List

The contemporary scene is characterized by an increase in industrialization and urbanization of all societies and the development of rapid
means of communication and transportation. This cannot but affect
the stability of cultural traditions, causing them to be modified or
discarded and thus disappear. The folklore archive serves to record
these traditions as an aid to the study of cultural history and as a
means of interpreting cultural change.

The term "archive" is applied to more than one type of repository
of records. It is most frequently applied to a repository of those
records of a public or private institution that are judged worthy of
preservation for reference or research purposes. Government documentary archives of this type are found in most nations, the first such
archive being established in France in 1790.[1] The folklore archive
differs in many respects from the documentary archive. The folklore

1. For a discussion of the history and development of governmental documentary
archives see T. R. Schellenberg, *Modern Archives, Principles and Techniques*
(Chicago: University of Chicago Press, 1956) , pp. 3–8.

archive preserves in one form or another traditions and skills passed on by memory, the documentary archive materials disseminated in written, typed, or printed form. The folklore archive secures its materials from a variety of sources, the documentary archive from one source only.

The following outline, representing the system of classification utilized by the Institute for Dialect and Folklore Research at Uppsala, Sweden,[2] will serve to illustrate the possible scope of materials of interest to a folklore archive:

A. Settlement and dwelling
B. Livelihood and household support
C. Communication and trade
D. The community
E. Human life
F. Nature
G. Folk medicine
H. Time and division of time
I. Principles and rules of popular belief and practice
J. Myths
K. Historical tradition
L. Individual thoughts and memories
M. Popular oral literature
N. Music
O. Athletics, dramatics, playing, dancing
P. Pastimes, card games, betting, casting lots, toys
Q. Architecture
R. Special ethnic units
S. Swedish culture in other countries
T. Traditions about foreign countries and people
U. Additional

This classification system is also in use in modified form by the Irish Folklore Commission in Dublin.[3]

In the widest sense, then, a folklore archive is concerned with all forms of human thought and endeavor insofar as these are remembered in popular tradition. Nevertheless, not all of the varied traditions characteristic of Western culture are customarily found within the institution known as the folklore archive. The traditions of a purely physical nature, baskets, pots, tools, the artifacts of a culture, are more usually stored and displayed in museums than in folklore

2. For the detail under each heading see Manne Eriksson, "Indexing Materials in the Institute for Dialect and Folklore Research at Uppsala, Sweden," *The Folklore and Folk Music Archivist*, vol. 4, no. 1 (Spring 1961) : 2.

3. See Caoimhín Ó Danachair, "The Irish Folklore Commission," *The Folklore and Folk Music Archivist*, vol. 4, no. 1 (Spring 1961) : 1.

archives. When verbal or musical folklore has been transcribed and published, it is more frequently to be found in a library than in an archive. The materials most commonly found in folklore archives are, then, unpublished verbal and musical folklore in the form of manuscripts or acoustical recordings. This statement, of course, is true only in a general sense. There is much overlapping. Photographs of folk objects, of informants, of folk dance may be found in the museum, the library, or the folklore archive. The archive itself may form part of a library or museum. Folklore archives vary enormously in their content and their institutional affiliation.

Since folklore is a relatively young discipline, folklore archives are generally of recent origin. Usually archives have had their beginnings as accumulations of materials collected by individual scholars; as they grew by accretion, they were finally made the basis of a formally organized archive. In Finland such collections were in existence as early as 1835. The Folklore Archive of the Finnish Literature Society, the first folklore archive to be established, became an entity in 1888.[4]

National or regional folklore archives are concerned with the traditions of the people of a particular geographic area. With the development of anthropological studies, interest arose in the traditions of non-European peoples. These traditions were initially collected by missionaries and traders and then by expeditions organized for this express purpose. The collections secured were deposited in museums or research institutes sponsored by governments or universities. National or regional archives were first established in areas of northwestern Europe as a reaction to strong forces, usually foreign in origin, that threatened the native heritage of language and traditions. In this development nationalism was a strong motivating force. On the other hand, it was the highly industrialized and imperialistic nations of Middle Europe that first developed non-European collections that were made primarily in their colonies.

With the invention of the cylinder phonograph toward the end of the nineteenth century, it became possible to record acoustically dialects and verbal and musical traditions. Special repositories for recordings were soon developed. The earliest such archive to be established was the Phonogramm-Archiv of the Austrian Academy of Sciences.[5] The founding of similar archives in Paris, Berlin, and London fol-

4. For information concerning the development of the Finnish Folklore archive see Jouko Hautala and Urpo Vento, "The Folklore Archives of the Finnish Literature Society," *The Folklore and Folk Music Archivist*, vol. 8, no. 2 (Winter 1965–66) : 39–53.

5. See Walter Graf, "The Phonogrammarchiv der österreichischen Akademie der Wissenschaften in Vienna," *The Folklore and Folk Music Archivist*, vol. 4, no 4 (Winter 1961) : 1, 3.

lowed soon after. In North America, collections of recordings were accumulated early in the century at anthropological institutes in Washington, New York, Chicago, and Ottawa, but the first formally established archive of sound recordings, the Archive of Folksong at the Library of Congress,[6] did not come into existence until 1928.

Since World War II there has been a great development of repositories of folklore. Archives of one type or another now exist in every European country, in Egypt and Israel, in Brazil, Canada, Chile, and Venezuela. Almost without exception, these institutions receive direct state support. In the United States there are now some twenty folklore archives. The majority have been established at state universities. Only one, the Archive of Folksong at the Library of Congress, is supported by the federal government.

There has been further specialization. Certain archives are restricted in their coverage to a particular genre, as the Northern Institute for Folk Literature in Copenhagen[7] whose primary concern is folktales and legends of Scandinavia and adjacent areas. Others restrict their collections to the folklore of specific linguistic-cultural groups. Of this character is the Franco-American Folklore Archive at Laval University in Quebec. An archive that limits its interest to a particular genre among a specific linguistic-cultural group is the German Folk Song Archive in Freiburg, Germany.[8]

In general, folklore archives have similar functions and face similar problems. Archives seek to secure accurately identified and representative collections of the type of folklore with which they are concerned; they attempt to preserve these collections for posterity; and they catalogue and index the collections to make them accessible for research.

To be useful in folklore studies it is necessary that the materials collected be properly documented, that is, accurate data must be available concerning date and place of collection, the name and background of the informant or informants, how and when the informant acquired the item collected, and so forth. The archive therefore endeavors to advise and instruct collectors by one means or another to assist them in identifying various types of folklore and in securing the needed documentation.

When possible, archives utilize paid collectors. These collectors

6. See Rae Korson, "The Archive of Folk Song in the Library of Congress," *The Folklore and Folk Music Archivist,* vol. 2, no. 1 (Spring 1959) : 1; vol. 2, no. 2 (Summer 1959) : 1–2.

7. See L. Bødker, "Nordic Folklore Reports, 1958–59," *ARV, Journal of Scandinavian Folklore* 14 (Uppsala, 1958) : 163–64.

8. See Wolfgang Suppan, "The German Folksong Archive," *The Folklore and Folk Music Archivist,* vol. 7, no. 2 (Spring 1964) : 29–40.

may be staff members of the archive or individuals who devote full time to collecting. Such persons receive training from the archive they represent and are often provided with written instructions concerning procedures to be followed. The Irish Folklore Commission in Dublin, for example, has published a manual for the use of its collectors.[9]

Part-time collectors are also used extensively. In some cases they receive remuneration; in others, the archive depends upon their interest and enthusiasm. The Swedish Institute for Dialect and Folklore Research at Uppsala sends students of the University of Uppsala to collect in their own parishes. Local collectors are also utilized, people of various professions and social classes, clergymen, teachers, farmers, lumbermen, and others.[10] To aid these field workers the institute has compiled some 250 questionnaires for use in collecting. The Irish Folklore Commission has also issued a large number of questionnaires for use by its field collectors.[11]

The Finnish Folklore Archive has sponsored annual collecting contests during which emphasis has been placed on the collection of a particular type of folklore. Thousands of individuals have participated in these contests, and business concerns have offered prizes. In one contest teachers throughout the nation asked their pupils to describe in writing every game they customarily played. Through these contests a network of over a thousand collectors was developed. The collecting of this network of interested individuals has been guided by extensive correspondence, published questionnaires, and by means of a periodical issued for this purpose.[12]

With the exception of work done during the 1930s under the auspices of the Works Progress Administration,[13] the pattern of paid field collecting has not been followed in the United States. Much collecting has been done under foundation grants or under the sponsorship of the larger academic institutions. The funds provided, however, have usually covered only the expenses of fieldwork and have not been conceived as payment for services rendered. Such collecting has been carried on as a necessary aspect of the research of a particular scholar; it has rarely been specifically designed to develop acces-

9. Seán Ó Súilleabháin, *A Handbook of Irish Folklore*, Educational Company of Ireland, Ltd., for the Folklore of Ireland Society (Dublin, 1942).

10. See Folke Hedblom, "The Institute for Dialect and Folklore Research at Uppsala, Sweden," *The Folklore and Folk Music Archivist*, vol. 3; no. 4 (Winter 1961) : 1–2.

11. See "The Irish Folklore Commission, A Sample Questionnaire," *The Folklore and Folk Music Archivist*, vol. 4, no. 2 (Summer 1961) : 2, 4.

12. *Kansantieto*, Finnish Literature Society, Helsinki.

13. Under the sponsorship of the Folk-Song and Folklore Department, Federal Service Bureau, Works Progress Administration.

sions for deposit in a particular archive. Although the materials collected may eventually be deposited in an archive, this may occur after rather than before their publication.

Nevertheless, directed collecting of folklore has been carried on in a number of areas in the United States through means not involving payment of the collectors. Collecting of Child ballads in Virginia has been sponsored by the Virginia Folklore Society, which was founded in 1913 for this express purpose.[14] Through press releases, lectures, printed circulars, and the formation of ballad clubs in various schools and colleges in the state, the interest of many individuals was aroused and the society acquired a corps of devoted collectors. The materials collected were deposited in an office provided for this purpose at the University of Virginia and formed the basis of several scholarly publications.[15]

The collecting program at the University of Arizona is of a more recent origin, beginning in 1946.[16] This program has been sponsored by an interdepartmental committee of faculty members. Contacts have been made through principals of public schools with teachers and community clubs, and many collections have been received and deposited in the archive created for this purpose at the university.

Directed collecting by students in college folklore classes has been a frequently utilized means of securing materials for archives in the United States. Students often have better entrée to the circles of their own acquaintances and relatives than might be obtained by a professional collector not known in the area or among the group in question. The students are given explicit instructions of the type of materials to seek and their proper identification, often in mimeographed form. Among the institutions where faculty members have guided students in folklore classes in such field collecting are Albany State Teachers College in New York, Murray State College in Kentucky, and Michigan State University at East Lansing.[17]

In a library, books dealing with similar subjects are shelved adja-

14. For a history of the Virginia Folklore Society see Arthur Kyle Davis, ed., *Folk-Songs of Virginia* (Durham, N. C.: Duke University Press, 1948), pp. xxvii–xxxv.

15. Ibid.; and under the same editorship, *Traditional Ballads of Virginia* (Cambridge, Mass., 1929); *More Traditional Ballads of Virginia* (Chapel Hill: University of North Carolina Press, 1960).

16. See Frances Gillmor, "The University of Arizona Folklore Archive," *The Folklore and Folk Music Archivist*, vol. 2, no. 1 (Spring 1959): 2.

17. For discussions of directed student collecting see Louis C. Jones, "The Farmers' Museum Folklore Archive," *The Folklore and Folk Music Archivist*, vol. 2, no. 2 (Summer 1959): 2; remarks by Herbert Halpert in *Four Symposia on Folklore*, edited by Stith Thompson, Folklore Series No. 8 (Bloomington: Indiana University Press, 1953), p. 102; and Richard M. Dorson, "The Michigan State University Folklore Archive," *Midwest Folklore* 5 (Spring 1955): 51–59.

cent to one another to permit browsing. Should a book be lost, another copy can usually be purchased. In a folklore archive each item in storage is often unique and irreplaceable. Browsing is therefore not usually permitted. For this reason, like items need not be shelved adjacent to each other. Rather, they are stored in whatever manner is most convenient. Materials of like shape and size are placed together rather than next to those of like content. They are also stored in a manner that will best insure their preservation. Phonograph disks, for example, must be shelved in vertical position with frequent dividers for support. Otherwise the disks will exert undue pressure one upon the other and warping will ensue. Extreme temperatures, excessive humidity, dust, mildew, and other factors cause deterioration of the paper of manuscripts, the wax and plastic of recordings, and the wood and leather of folk objects. The environment in which these materials are stored must therefore be controlled for proper preservation. This is accomplished by the use of air-conditioning and, in some cases, by storing materials in sealed containers.

The following two examples will indicate the variety of methods used in shelving manuscripts. At the Swedish Institute for Dialect and Folklore Research at Uppsala, the paid collectors are provided with standard sheets upon which to record folklore and dialect. When the filled sheets are returned to the institute, they are filed in large envelopes. Each envelope contains only one type of folklore. These envelopes are filed in geographic order according to the provinces of Sweden and, within the provinces, according to the name of the collector, in alphabetical order. At the Irish Folklore Commission, the collectors are given notebooks, and these notebooks when returned are bound into volumes according to the name of the collector, in chronological order of receipt. Thus the Swedish materials are stored primarily according to the province of their origin and the Irish materials primarily according to the name of the collector. In both cases elaborate and detailed card indexes are made of the individual items found in the sheets or notebooks, and it is necessary to refer to these card indexes in order to locate a specific item.

Thus it is that the indexes or catalogues of the materials in storage are the keys to the accessibility of these materials for research. These indexes take many forms, depending upon the type of materials indexed and the research interests of the particular archive. One obvious requirement is that each such index, no matter what other function it may serve, also act as a shelf or finding index, that is, that it indicate exactly where each item indexed may be found in the archive.

Indexes are organized in numerical or alphabetical order, or according to a specific outline. Numerical indexes are normally shelf lists indicating the location in storage of items of the same size and shape—for example, 5-inch rolls of recording tape or 2 x 2 color slides. Shelf lists serve primarily as a means of making an inventory of the holdings of the archive. Alphabetical indexes commonly list items by the names of the collectors, the names of the informants, or according to geographic location.

Indexes in outline form may be organized according to languages or dialects or according to geographic-cultural areas. Linguistic indexes or classifications differ from archive to archive and are usually organized in regional form. No accepted international classification of languages or dialects is in wide use. Two geographic-cultural outlines of international scope are in use in the United States, that of the Human Relations Area Files[18] and the *Atlas for Anthropology*.[19] In both the world is divided into geographic areas and subdivided primarily according to cultural groups.

Other indexes in use present classification systems applied to particular genres of folklore. Such indexes require considerable skill in their application. Of this character is *The Types of Folktale*,[20] originally developed by the Finnish scholar Antti Aarne and later expanded by the American scholar Stith Thompson.

Archives of folk music utilize various means for classifying the transcriptions made of melodies. At the German Folksong Archive in Freiburg, the basis of classification is an *incipit* consisting of the first line of the melody. The aspects of the *incipits* classified are primarily the stressed pitches in the melody, ambitus or range, and meter.[21] In eastern Europe (Bratislava, Ljubljana, Zagreb, Budapest, etc.), punch cards and computer equipment are extensively utilized in developing indexes of melodies.

With few exceptions, established archives offer their research facilities to visiting scholars. Many will answer inquiries and will furnish materials to the research scholar by mail for a fee. There are many small folklore archives, often the outgrowth of the activities of a single interested scholar, that can offer only a minimum of assistance due to lack of funds and facilities. In the majority of cases, the materials in the archive are utilized in research by staff members.

18. George P. Murdock, *Outline of World Cultures* (New Haven, Conn.: Human Relations Area Files Press, 1958).

19. Robert F. Spencer and Elden Johnson, *Atlas for Anthropology* (Dubuque, Iowa: M. C. Brown Co., 1960).

20. Antti Aarne, *Verzeichnis der Märchentypen* (Helsinki, 1910), Folklore Fellows Communications 3; revision and expansion by Stith Thompson, *The Types of the Folktale* (Helsinki: Folklore Fellows Communications 74, 1928); further revision by Thompson under the same title (Helsinki: Folklore Fellows Communications 184, 1961).

21. Suppan, pp. 35–39.

The resultant studies are published by the institution in question or in scholarly journals. Archives of sound recordings frequently issue disk albums of materials selected from their holdings, accompanied by brochures describing the contents of the album.

Bibliography and Selected Readings

Eriksson, Manne. "Indexing Materials in the Institute for Dialect and Folklore Research at Uppsala, Sweden." *The Folklore and Folk Music Archivist* 4 (1961). Describes the methods used in this institute in classifying and storing materials secured through questionnaires distributed to fieldworkers. Included is a list of the main headings used in the systematic or subject index and sample catalogue cards.

The Folklore and Folk Music Archivist. Vols. 1–10 (1958–68). A journal devoted to the collection, documentation, indexing, and cataloguing of folklore and folk music. Vol. 10, No. 3 contains a cumulative index to all ten volumes.

"The Irish Folklore Commission: A Sample Questionnaire." *The Folklore and Folk Music Archivist* 4 (1961). A questionnaire concerning tinkers used by fieldworkers of the Irish Folklore Commission.

James, Thelma G. "Problems of Archiving." *The Folklore and Folk Music Archivist* 1 (1958). A discussion of the difficulties involved in standardizing classification systems utilized by archives with special reference to classifying song texts, folktales, proverbs, riddles, and superstitions.

List, George. "Archiving Sound Recordings." *Phonetica* 6 (1961): 18–31. Contains detailed recommendations concerning the storage, preservation, and documentation of sound recordings, the protection of the rights of collectors and informants, and indexing methods. Based primarily upon the author's experience as director of the Indiana University Archives of Traditional Music.

Thompson, Stith, ed. *Four Symposia on Folklore*. Bloomington: Indiana University Press, 1953. Chapter 2, "Archiving Folklore," pp. 89–154. A transcription of a stimulating discussion session of the joint meetings of the Midcentury International Folklore Conference and the International Folk Music Council held in 1950 with distinguished participants from various areas of the world.

5 THE USE OF PRINTED SOURCES
Richard M. Dorson

The folklorist obtains his primary data in three basic ways: through fieldwork, from archives, and by way of printed sources. Ideally, he would himself record every item he uses, but such a practice is possible only for limited ethnographies; nor can he visit all the archives of the world to consult the field material gathered by others. His chief resource for broad comparative studies must be printed sources.

A printed source is a publication in which folk traditions have found lodging more or less accidentally and casually. Writers and journalists usually do not know they are publishing folklore. Field collections, of course, are printed, but they are not printed sources in the technical sense that the folklorist must determine the relationship of the printed text to an oral tradition. The traveler, the novelist, the newspaper editor, and the diarist may all note customs and legends they have observed and heard, but they feel no obligation, and presumably lack the technique, to record them verbatim. The story-book compiler, the antiquarian, and the local historian may gather in many intriguing traditional matters that they themselves have culled from earlier printed sources, and so their works may be used, if cautiously, by the folklorist.

The most compelling reason the folklorist must supplement field-collected and field-observed reports with printed sources is that the concept of fieldwork dates only from the early nineteenth century. To provide historical antecedents for contemporary specimens of oral and material culture, he must comb earlier records. Then he faces the question of how to locate, identify, and evaluate the quality of folklore in the vast labyrinth of printed words.

One query is always asked concerning the relationship of the spoken to the printed text: "What happens to the oral tradition when it gets written down and put in a book? Does it not come to an end?" The answer is no. The narrator, the singer, and the craftsman keep on in their traditional ways whether or not their words and works have been brought to the attention of sophisticated audiences. Few of the thousands of streams of oral and craft tradition are ever sluiced off into print in any case. Then, too, printed and oral texts do not necessarily compete with each other but may act in conjunction, in a mutually stimulating camaraderie. The publication by the Grimms of the *Household Tales* did not inhibit the telling of Märchen, but other forces, notably the replacement of agrarian by industrialized society, dried up the old fairy tales.

CATEGORIES OF PRINTED SOURCES

All kinds of publications, from trash for the masses to literary masterpieces, may prove to be repositories for folklore. Where does the folklorist start to look? He can begin with the great story collections that have become, or once were, household treasures, such as the *Arabian Nights, Aesop's Fables,* the *Panchatantra,* and the *Gesta Romanorum.* These must be classed as literary productions, in the form in which we receive them, since their various compilers and translators have polished the narratives whose oral counterparts still sometimes surface in the field.

A related source is cheap booklets and pamphlets filled with entertaining stories and songs, which enjoyed a vogue in the seventeenth and eighteenth centuries when chapmen and peddlers hawked chapbooks and songsters. Often their contents were based on well-known folktales and ballads. Some of these ephemeral and flimsy productions fell into the hands of antiquarian scholars like John Ashton and George Laurence Gomme, who republished them in sturdier nineteenth-century editions. In his scholarly edition of chapbook legends of the English strong hero Tom Hickathrift, Gomme traced the close intertwining of verbal and subliterary variants. Another English antiquary and bibliophile, James Orchard Halliwell-Phillips, specialized in rescuing and reissuing fugitive jestbooks. A comparable publication to the English chapbook was the American almanac, called by the literary historian Moses Coit Tyler "the pack-horse of American letters." Intended for the practical use of farmers, the almanac blossomed forth in colonial times beyond tables of weather predictions and planting tips to carry drolleries, facetiae, anecdotes, and rhymes. Benjamin Franklin turned *Poor Richard's Almanac* into a vehicle for his own vein of proverbial wisdom and both drew from and contributed to circulating proverbs. How full of folk belief is the long file of Robert Thomas's *The Old Farmer's Almanac*, which commenced in 1793, was demonstrated by the eminent Harvard scholar George Lyman Kittredge in his ingenious study, *The Old Farmer and His Almanack* (1904). By the early decades of the nineteenth century, almanacs were responding to new currents of American humor and carrying jokes about stereotyped comic characters. A whole series from 1835 to 1856 dealt with the tall-tale adventures, scrapes, and exploits in the backwoods and foreign countries of Davy Crockett. How much of the Crockett almanac legends is folk and how much is literary remains a question, but evidently the almanac-makers built upon an active oral cycle of frontier yarns. Probably the closest relationship of oral to printed text is the broadsheet or broadside ballad, composed and crudely printed by sensation-peddling balladmongers in the vein of the old traditional ballads. Often the broadside ballads themselves entered the song repertoires of folksingers.

Many publications that contain some folklore do not necessarily bear a close relation to oral sources, and folk items are scattered over miles of print. Newspapers and magazines are the main reading fare of modern man, and inevitably some will catch folk materials. Zealous folklorists and literary scholars have identified certain rewarding serials and extrapolated their folklore. *Notes and Queries*, founded by the namer of "folk-lore," William John Thoms, naturally included many folkloristic nuggets, some of which Thoms gathered together in a little book he titled *Choice Notes from 'Notes and Queries': Folk-Lore* (1859). In *The Gentleman's Magazine Library*, the active Victorian folklorist George Laurence Gomme prepared substantial volumes of articles he selected and classified from the files of the *Gentleman's Magazine*, 1731 to 1868. He titled these cullings *Manners and Customs*; *Dialect, Proverbs and Word-Lore*; *Popular Superstitions*; and *English Traditions and Foreign Customs* (1883–85). In his introduction to the volume on superstitions, Gomme states his conviction that the "force of traditional superstition" is only really understood through its continual reiteration in the pages of publications like the *Gentleman's Magazine*. Examples of witchcraft recur regularly in the gentlemanly notes of the periodical, even as late as 1827, reported by a correspondent who believes that this will very likely not be the final instance:

On the 11th April, 1827, at the Monmouth Assizes, William Watkins, and three others, were indicted and found guilty of an assault upon Mary Nicholas, a decrepit old woman, upwards of ninety, which they had committed under a belief, prevalent in that neighbourhood, that she was a witch. The old woman deposed to the prisoners and others having seized her, and beaten her with thorns and briars, for the purpose of, as in days of yore, drawing blood; and they also attempted to force her into a pool, for the purpose of trying the efficacy of the water ordeal.

A witness proved the prisoners having taken the old woman to a lane where three cattle had died, and charged her with being the author of their death; and then, taking her to a stable where there was a colt, made her repeat several times, "God bless the colt!" They afterwards stripped her naked, and searched her, in order to find her teat, which they declared they had found, upon their discovering a wart or wen upon her head.

This in all probability, is the latest instance to be met with of English credulity as to the existence of this surprizing art, and it may be questionable whether it will not be the last.[1]

Commenting on this last assertion, Gomme in an appended note cites comparable evidence of surviving witch belief in a Scottish newspaper of 1884. Printed sources reveal the continuity of these dark, subterranean folk notions, which are dredged up by antiquaries and observers who half-believed in what they related. "Thus the very literary forms of these relics of the past are instructive lessons to the Folklorist of to-day."[2]

English folklorists undertook a systematic identification of folk traditions from printed sources in the series *County Folk-Lore, Printed Extracts,* sponsored by the Folk-Lore Society. Several different hands took part in this enterprise, the most active being Mrs. Eliza Gutch, who did volumes for Yorkshire and Lincolnshire. In a concise prefatory statement to the first volume, for Gloucestershire (1892), Edwin Sidney Hartland, one of the "Great Team" of English folklorists, explains with his customary clarity the principles of this kind of investigation.

As a starting-point for the work of collection it is desirable to know what has already been recorded. . . . It is with this view that a beginning has been attempted with the Folk-lore of Gloucestershire in the extracts printed

---

1. *The Gentleman's Magazine Library: Popular Superstitions*, edited by George Laurence Gomme (London, 1884), p. 250.
2. Ibid., pp. vi–vii.

in the following pages from Rudder's *History of Gloucestershire,* Atkyns' *Ancient and Present State of Glocestershire,* and the first four volumes of *Gloucestershire Notes and Queries* . . . as an indication of the kind of literary work remaining to be done, and a foundation for the more difficult, but more useful and far more interesting, task of collection from the lips and the hands of those who still repeat in speech and practice the traditions they have received from their fathers.[3]

Hartland quickly adds that various other printed sources, which he enumerates, could also be examined, and that the extracts from these sources are of unequal value, some indeed of little worth because of their vagueness and errant opinions. But in sum they covered the range of English folklore. The Table of Contents for the second number, edited for Suffolk by Lady Eveline Camilla Gurdon (1893), lists the topics Agricultural Myths, Ancient Omens, Birth Customs, Cure Charms, Death Omens, Fairies (or Frairies and Pharisees), Folk Tales, Funeral Customs, Games, Harvest Customs, Legends, Love Charms and Tests, Miscellaneous Customs, Miscellaneous Omens, Nursery Rhymes, Proverbs and Similes, Sleep Charms, Weather Myths, Well Worship, and Witchcraft. The longest of these sections is the cure charms, legends, and omens. Only two "folk tales" were included, from the *Ipswich Journal* for 1877 and 1878, but they were prizes in the lean store of English Märchen, "Cap o' Rushes" (Cinderella) and "Tom Tit Tot" (Rumpelstiltskin), both reproduced in dialect as "Told by an old servant to the writer when a child."

In view of the sparse fieldwork done in England, these county volumes added considerably to the store of visible British traditions, and the printed extracts conformed closely in general themes to the field collections, which also were done on a county basis.

Newspapers present an even more formidable wilderness than periodicals for the folklorist to traverse, and yet some paths have been laid out. American literary scholars in the 1930s excavated buried treasures of antebellum humor from forgotten files of daily newspapers and of specialized weeklies catering to sportsmen and bon vivants, like the New York *Spirit of the Times* and the Boston *Yankee Blade.* The stories they reprinted showed a clear influence from oral yarn-spinning. One consequence of this research was the realization that all the American newspapers of the 1825–55 period, during the first flush of nationalism and up until the clamor of sectional strife, were close to the grass roots and many were filled with folk humor

3. *County Folk-Lore, Printed Extracts, No. 1,* edited by Edwin Sidney Hartland. Published for the Folk-Lore Society by D. Nutt, 1892. Publications of the Folk-Lore Society (1895), 37:4–5.

and supernatural oddities. But how to get at them? Poring over pages of newsprint day by day can fatigue the most ardent folklore researcher, although some scholars have done just that. The present writer recalls his good fortune at discovering in the University of Vermont Library a comprehensive index to the *Burlington Free Press* (Vermont) compiled by workers on the Federal Writers Project. This index contained such categories as "Humor," "Stories," and "Anecdotes," and pointed to a mine of humorous folktales. Since the advent of the national wire services, newspapers have grown further away from folk sources, but they still trap a good deal of floating tradition. Examples are printed in the department "Folklore in the News," in *Western Folklore,* from clippings sent in by alert folklorists. Newsclipping services might prove useful in ferreting out kinds of folklore identifiable by key phrases, such as Paul Bunyan, and on this basis I accumulated a considerable body of journalistic allusions to the lumberjack hero, subsequently published in three serial articles in *Western Folklore* under the title "Paul Bunyan in the News." These newsclippings yielded a whole new perspective on this largely spurious folk hero. If folklorists like myself had once been intent on demolishing his claim to legendary status, they can now explore his symbolic role in the mass culture. Paul Bunyan has come to represent any grotesquely oversized object or action.

Local history offers another hunting ground for folk traditions in print. While less highly esteemed than national history, and often written by amateur antiquarians, town and county histories are apt to contain folkloric matter that the professional historian would disregard. The small town is itself a folk community with its own word-of-mouth annals revolving about rumor-laden events, odd characters, witches of olden time, haunted houses, and curious incidents imbedded in place names. Autobiographies, memoirs, and reminiscences of individuals with a country background may furnish unexpected yields of personally observed folk usage and belief. The Scottish writer and geologist Hugh Miller devoted sizable parts of his retrospections, *My Schools and Schoolmasters,* to legends of his home town of Cromarty high on the northern coast, to Highland storytelling, to sea lore, and to the traditions of stone masons. In *The Jonny-Cake Letters,* Thomas Robinson Hazard reminisced chattily about the Narragansett country of southern Rhode Island and strung together a seemingly endless series of local anecdotes. The literature of travel constitutes a fertile cache of manners and customs, for the traveler to distant parts particularly notices and describes for his home audience the strange behavior patterns he encounters. While the travel writer lacks the techniques and detachment of the trained ethnographer, and may indeed mislead the unwary reader, he does provide a kind of documentation to be checked with other evidence. Marco Polo initiated the literary genre of the odyssey to remote and exotic climes where the traveler reports on fabulous wonders.

Literature itself must be regarded as a bountiful printed source of folklore. A distinction needs to be made between the folkstuff employed for artistic purposes by novelists, dramatists, and poets and folk matter in the other sources we have been describing. Folklore in literature may be consistently transmuted from its oral form. The difference can become one of kind rather than degree. A folktale or folksong lodged in a newspaper or a local journal may be a blurred and inexact transcript of the original verbal text, but it does not radically depart from that text. A creative writer may introduce and develop characters and motivation, scenes and tensions, that change the structure and nature of the tradition. Hawthorne was always on the lookout for the local legend he could develop into a story with a "deep moral."

There are many ways in which a writer may employ folk materials. A revealing study was made by the folklorist Arthur Palmer Hudson, who wrote to a number of southern authors asking them where they had obtained the ballads inserted into their fiction. They responded that they had (1) used traditional ballads actually heard in their home environment, (2) composed entire ballads or expanded oral fragments, and (3) reprinted ballad texts from the published collection of Francis James Child. Sometimes folklore provides bits of local color setting, and sometimes it supplies the heart of the narrative. Still again, oral literature may be refined and polished by one or more bards until it achieves the status of art literature, as with the Homeric folk epics. Consequently we cannot offer any easy generalizations about the relation of folklore to literature, except to say that literature is indeed an invaluable, if ambiguous, source for the folklorist. Greater and lesser authors have often, if unwittingly, taken on the function of the field collector and participant observer and shown extraordinary alertness and sensitivity to folk culture. This role is not to be wondered at since master storytellers like Boccaccio, Chaucer, Sholom Aleichem, Tagore, and Mark Twain could be expected to listen sympathetically to folk storytellers. Dickens was so alert to the proverb containing a quotation ("Everyone to his own taste, as the old woman said when she kissed the cow") that this form of proverbial utterance is called a Wellerism, after Sam Weller in *The Pickwick Papers,* into whose mouth Dickens placed such sayings.

Sometimes the artist becomes to a degree a conscious folklorist. William Butler Yeats assembled two volumes of Irish fairy legends from earlier collectors and writers, and then set out himself, with

Lady Gregory, to record oral tales and beliefs in the Gaelic tongue. *The Celtic Twilight* is his collector's logbook, and his subsequent writing was powerfully influenced by the peasant idiom. After the publication of his first Uncle Remus book, Joel Chandler Harris found himself quoted as an authority on folklore. He joined the Chicago Folklore Society, and entered into discussions about the diffusion of folktales, supporting the Africanist theory of American Negro folktale origins. Lafcadio Hearn deliberately sought out Shinto and Buddhist legends as a means of penetrating the mind and soul of traditional Japan.

Walter Scott well exemplifies the mixing of literary and folkloric interests. He wrote historical novels, but documented them with sober notes about traditions and antiquities; he collected Border ballads, but completed and altered them to enhance their poetry; he wrote a scholarly treatise on *Demonology and Witchcraft* (1830), and corresponded for a while with Jacob Grimm, but let the relationship lapse when it became too pedantic. As an example of how famous writers know and relate folktales among themselves, we find Scott at his home in Abbotsford in 1817, telling Washington Irving, another romancer fond of local legendry, the story of "The King of the Cats," suggested by a grave tabby sitting attentively in a chair by the fire. Irving recounts the scene in his vignette on "Abbotsford" in *The Crayon Miscellany*:

> He [Scott] went on to tell a little story about a gude man who was returning to his cottage one night, when, in a lonely out-of-the-way place, he met with a funeral procession of cats all in mourning, bearing one of their race to the grave in a coffin covered with a black velvet pall. The worthy man, astonished and half frightened at so strange a pageant, hastened home and told what he had seen to his wife and children. Scarce had he finished, when a great black cat that sat beside the fire raised himself up, exclaimed, 'Then I am King of the Cats!' and vanished up the chimney. The funeral seen by the gude man was one of the cat dynasty.[4]

"The King of the Cats" is an international folktale, told by Plutarch about the death of Pan, collected in northern and western Europe, and reported from Texas Negroes. It remains an enigmatic tale, and perhaps that is why it appealed not only to Scott and Irving but to such other authors as Robert Southey, Percy Bysshe Shelley, and Stephen Vincent Benet.

Contemporary African literature bears a close relationship to folklore sources, and indeed offers us case studies of how unwritten traditions pass into literary form. The highly acclaimed novel of Chinua

---

4. Quoted in Arthur Palmer Hudson, "Some Versions of 'The King of the Cats'," *Southern Folklore Quarterly* 17 (1953) : 225–31.

Achebe, *Things Fall Apart* (1958), written in English by an Ibo of Nigeria educated at Oxford, illustrates this process. It is a poetic ethnography, written simply and eloquently, about village life before and during the coming of the white man. Chapters are episodic scenes, threaded together on the trials of Okonkwo, a strong hero suggestive of Heroic Age champions. Every episode is filled with custom, ritual, and animistic belief and references to music, dance, song, and tales, sometimes with full texts. Almost every speech contains proverbs, for among the Ibo "proverbs are the palm-oil with which words are eaten." The preparation of food, the building of huts, and the planting of yams are described with lucid accuracy. Yet if the novel is ethnographic, it is also artistic. Its point is not the "pacification of the primitive tribes of the lower Niger," the ironic title of a British colonial official's projected book with which Achebe ends his own novel. Instead, for once, the viewpoint is that of the native, loyal to his own culture, accepting its blows, as when he leaves his clan and his village for seven years of exile because of an accidental death caused by his exploding gun, or when by tribal decree he kills his own adopted son. Okonkwo swallows the bitter pills believing that he will win the status rewards of his clan. Then these rewards are challenged by the white man's God and government; Okonkwo kills a government man and hangs himself. This conflict of his spirit could never be understood without a full and faithful picture of the tribal folkways.

A TYPOLOGY OF FOLKLORE IN PRINTED SOURCES

Accepting the value of printed sources, we must make some distinctions among them. They are vastly uneven and bear many different relations to oral tradition. Some general relationships may be suggested here in a typological scheme ranging from close-to-oral to remote-from-oral printed sources.

The first category may be called *close replicas of oral texts*. In this group anecdotes, proverbs, beliefs, and other genres are set down without attempt at embellishment or alteration. Since the journalist, traveler, novelist, or other recorder is recalling his text from memory or perhaps rough notes, he presents a paraphrase. For a short superstition or saying or rhyme, he may indeed give a verbatim text. The folklorist can judge the approximation of the printed item to oral tradition by comparing it with field-collected analogues. A good illustration is afforded in the popular American tall tale of "The Lucky Shot" (Type 1890), which enters into printed sources from early in the nineteenth century up to the present, as well as in field collections up until today. Below appear a printed and an oral version, the first from the *The Farmer's Almanack* of 1809, and the second told to me in 1942 by "Slick" MacQuoid in Wilton, Maine.

Wonderful Story related by George Howell, *a mighty Hunter, and known in that part of the country where he lived by the name of* the Vermont Nimrod.

"I WAS once," said he, "passing down the banks of the Hudson in search of game, and suddenly heard a crackling on the opposite bank. Looking across the river, I saw a stately Buck, and instantly drew up and let fly at him. That very moment a huge sturgeon leapt from the river in the direction of my piece. The ball went through him, and passed on. I flung down my gun, threw off my coat and hat, and swam for the floating fish, which mounting, I towed to the bank and went to see what more my shot had done for me. I found that the ball had passed through the heart of the deer, and struck in a hollow tree beyond; where the honey was running out like a river! I sprung round to find something to stop the hole with, and caught hold of a white rabbit. It squeaked just like a stuck pig; so I thrash'd it away from me in a passion at the disappointment, and it went with such force that it killed three cock partridges and a woodcock."!!!

SLICK MACQUOID'S STORY

Best shot I ever heard about was told me by a guide from Moosehead. Coming home at dusk he saw a partridge sitting on the limb of a birch. He fired, and five partridge fell down off the branch. He picked them up, stuffed them in his back pocket, and walked down the bank of the stream a ways, where he found a deer had been frightened by the report and jumped off the bank into the mud, where she stuck up to her haunches. After slitting her throat he tied her legs to his gun, loaded her on his shoulders, and started to cross the stream on a log. But the load made his footing unsteady, and he slipped into the water. After floundering around for his gun, the deer and the partridges, he climbed up the other side of the bank, but he was so wet he thought he would wring his clothes out. Five fish fell out of them when he did. So he loaded the partridges, the deer and the fish— now that's quite a load on your back—and he had to give his suspenders a hoist. A button popped off and killed a rabbit forty feet behind him.

The almanac version is so like the collected version that it could qualify as a told tale. Indeed it gives more verisimilitude than Slick's rendering since George Howell is quoted directly, where Slick repeats the guide's whopper in indirect quotation.

A second grouping may be labeled *elaborations and revisions of oral texts.* Here the core of folklore is still plainly recognizable, but extra, nontraditional episodes have been added.

In his short story titled "How Sharp Snaffles Got His Capital and Wife," the prolific southern novelist William Gilmore Simms makes use of "The Lucky Shot," combined with other recognizable tall tales, "The Man Carried through the Air by Geese" (Type 1881) and

"How the Man Came out of a Tree Stump" by grasping a bear's tail (Type 1900). Further, he clearly testifies to his familiarity with oral yarn-spinning by using the frame device of the story within a story. A group of Tennessee mountaineers engages in matching whoppers, in a contest presided over by "The Big Lie," whose duty it is to see that no one tells the truth. But Simms is a man of letters, not a collector of folklore, and he imposes the standard plot of "Boy meets girl, boy loses girl, boy gets girl" on the folktale. Sharp Snaffles courts a mountain lass whose father rejects him because of his lack of capital. Sharp goes off hunting, and through his lucky accidents ends up with much game. Now a man of capital, his suit prospers.

The borderline between a tradition-dominated and an invention-dominated piece is crossed in the third category, *literary invention based on oral folklore*. Folk themes and folk style stimulate the writer to embark on his own imaginative flight. On a first reading, Thomas Bang Thorpe's classic story of the old southwest, "The Big Bear of Arkansas," seems like an epic hunting yarn transcribed by an adept reporter. There is the frame situation, with the Arkansas chararter, Jim Doggett, regaling a steamboat crowd with his vernacular speech and brags; there are some preliminary tall tales about the lush soil and fat turkeys of Arkansas familiar in oral circulation (Baughman, Motif X1265*(b), "Large turkey"; X1402, "Lie: the fast-growing vine"), with which Jim awes and softens up his incredulous auditors for his climatic adventure. This is Jim's pursuit of a giant "b'ar" who miraculously eludes all hunters until, as Jim put it, the time came for its end. Such a hunt again seems to fall into the pattern of many traditional Münchausen-type folktales, keyed to such honored motifs as X955 (a), "Remarkable killing of bear," and X1110, "Wonderful hunt." Yet as we scrutinize Jim Doggett's carefully detailed, suspenseful saga we realize that it is far too richly embroidered for any typical tall tale. The folk theme of the mighty hunter and his formidable prey has launched Thorpe into a grander, universal theme of myth and literature, the hero's quest for and death struggle with the monster, exemplified in the grapples between Apollo and Python, Theseus and Medusa, Beowulf and Grendel, Ahab and Moby Dick.

In a fourth division, *literary invention based on literary folklore*, we have moved far away from folk sources, although the composition may elaborate a plot well known in tradition. Washington Irving's story of "The Devil and Tom Walker" is such a piece. Editors of folklore journals have published an article praising it as a fine specimen of the oral folktale set down with a minimum of change.[5] No

5. Sara P. Rodes, "Washington Irving's Use of Traditional Folklore," *Southern Folklore Quarterly* 19 (1956) : 143–53, and *New York Folklore Quarterly* 13 (1957) : 3–15.

field collector would ever support such an assertion. Irving's production is highly polished, witty, sophisticated, and lengthy. Its action hinges on the compact between a greedy mortal and the devil. Walker sells his soul to Satan for Kidd's treasure, starts a loan office in Boston, prospers through usury, joins a church, and seems to have outsmarted the fiend, until one day he mentions the devil by name without his Bible handy, and is whisked off in a trice. The whole treatment of the tale is ironical and tongue-in-cheek, in Irving's light vein, which is quite contrary to the lean, fragmentary style of folk anecdotes about the devil. Such legends and jokes tell of the devil's appearance and disappearance, and of his being outwitted in literal contracts with mortals. But the devil, and particularly the victorious devil, is not a conspicuous figure in American folk narrative. The Faustian theme has its own powerful literary tradition, based on medieval legends, and this is the ancestry for Irving's sketch. We know that Irving read deeply in German Gothic literature and legendry and visited Germany in search of further materials. He himself said that he utilized popular traditions in print as foundations for fictional writings. In this way he transplanted the literary legend of Peter Klaus from the Harz Mountains in Germany to the Catskill Mountains in New York as a setting for Rip Van Winkle. Even had Irving wished to levy upon field-collected tales, they were not available in the early nineteenth century, and the sources upon which he drew were already rewritten.

The technique of identifying folklore in printed sources and the investigation into literary uses of folk materials are large and complicated subjects that can only be introduced here. Sooner or later they must engage the attention of every practicing folklorist.

Bibliography and Selected Readings

Collections

Ashton, John. *Chapbooks of the Eighteenth Century*. London, 1882. Reproductions of the popular English chapbooks that formed a bridge between folk and literary traditions.

Blair, Walter, and Franklin J. Meine, eds. *Half Horse Half Alligator. The Growth of the Mike Fink Legend*. Chicago: University of Chicago Press, 1956. Legends of Mike Fink, hero of Mississippi and Ohio River keelboatmen in the 1820s, reprinted from giftbook annuals, almanacs, newspapers, and local histories.

Briggs, Katharine M. *A Dictionary of British Folk Tales*. 4 vols. London: Routledge and Kegan Paul; and Bloomington: Indiana University Press, 1970–71. A systematic anthology of British traditional narratives culled largely from fugitive publications, and greatly enlarging the known stock of English folktales.

Dorson, Richard M., ed. *America Begins.* New York: Pantheon, 1950. Reprinted Bloomington: Indiana University Press, 1971. A selection of passages from early colonial writings running largely to the folklore of remarkable providences, witchcraft, natural wonders, and Indian beliefs. Folk motifs not identified.

———, ed. *Davy Crockett, American Comic Legend.* New York: Rockland Editions, 1939. Selections from the Crockett almanacs of 1835–56, which carried legendary and comical exploits of the backwoods hunter and Tennessee congressman.

———. *Jonathan Draws the Long Bow.* Cambridge, Mass.: Harvard University Press, 1946. New England popular tales and legends culled from newspapers, periodicals, town histories, and literary works. Some narratives are summarized and some are given in full. Folk motifs identified in the index of Ernest W. Baughman, *Type and Motif-Index of the Folktales of England and North America* (The Hague: Mouton, 1966).

Masterson, James, *Tall Tales from Arkansaw.* Boston: Chapman and Grime, 1942. Reprintings of humor from a variety of publications, including the New York *Spirit of the Times,* about Arkansas folk characters. Folk and subliterary materials are intermingled. Well-documented, but folk motifs are not identified.

Moore, Arthur K. "Specimens of the Folktales from Some Antebellum Newspapers of Louisiana." *Louisiana Historical Quarterly* 32 (1949) : 723–58. Journalistic, tradition-based tale texts of frontier humor identified by Aarne-Thompson numbers.

Taylor, Archer, and Bartlett J. Whiting. *A Dictionary of American Proverbs and Proverbial Phrases, 1820–1880.* Cambridge, Mass.: Harvard University Press, 1958. A standard reference work on proverbs found in the works of nineteenth-century American authors who are used as literary sources.

6 FOLK ATLAS MAPPING
Robert Wildhaber

INTRODUCTION: HISTORY AND AIM

Much of what I have to say about mapping seems to hold good only
for European countries and their folk cultures, and probably is applicable to the North American situation only to a certain extent. Folklore—and, in a broader sense, folklife too—was, and to some extent
still is, fundamentally a philological-historical discipline. It has been
affiliated with the history of literature and language of the respective
European countries (Germanistics, Anglistics, Scandinavistics, Slavis-
tics) or with geography, but it has become a "department" in its own
right only in some universities and only in recent years. As a section of
philological-historical sciences it made use of the same methods as
these, that is, it was philologically and historically oriented. This was
one of the possible ways—and not a bad one at that—as long as the
problems had to do with folklore in its narrow sense. To give an
example: of Märchen it might be interesting to know about the motif,
its sources and historical background, its development and change
in different regions, its adaptions to various cultures and regions;

and yet the fact that it is told in one village and not in a neighboring village is not of great importance in studying the Märchen itself. Historical value and, in some cases, psychological considerations (*Vöelkerpsychologie*) are determining factors for the study of a Märchen. But we must not overlook that the geographical method for the solution of pure folklore problems was initiated and strongly stressed by Kaarle Krohn in 1926[1] when he wrote his famous essay, "Die folkloristische Arbeitsmethode," and, by doing so, founded what is generally called the "Finnish School." In France, the impetus was given by Jean Brunhes with his book *La géographie humaine; essai de classification positive; principes et exemples* (Paris 1912). P. Deffontaines gave a practical application of this method in his work, *Géographie humaine de la France* (1920). In the same year the Spanish philologist R. Menéndez Pidal published an essay, "Sobre geografía folklórica. Ensayo de un método," in which he tried out the mapping method to show, clearly and convincingly, the development of two Spanish romances. Menéndez Pidal gives distribution patterns of the regional variants, considering both literary themes and stylistic particularities, and by doing so is able to point out archaic and progressive zones, centers of irradiation, and lines of expansion. One sees the philological point of view giving way before the urge to understand the biological laws of a folk culture; folklore and folklife are no longer mere springs of philology but independent disciplines answering questions that cannot be satisfactorily solved by other disciplines. For Germany, one of the leading works displaying this new tendency was that written by Hermann Aubin, Theodor Frings, and Josef Müller, *Kulturströmungen und Kulturprovinzen in den Rheinlanden: Geschichte, Sprache, Volkskunde*. The title itself indicates that cultural trends and culture provinces in the Rhenish regions are influenced by historic, linguistic, and folklife factors. Fritz Krueger's book, *Géographie des traditions populaires en France* (1950), belongs to the same category. In Ireland, the influence of Estyn E. Evans, professor in the Department of Geography at Queen's University in Belfast, in mapping folklife elements is to be seen both in northern Ireland and in Eire.[2] When we read the title of Anna Birgitta Rooth's essay, "Tradition Areas in Eurasia," we are reminded of the famous books by Waldemar Liungman about "Traditionswanderungen" that treat the spreading of folk-cultural facts along traditional geographical lines. The same idea is made use of by

1. Many years before Krohn had written "Die geographische Verbreitung estnischer Lieder, durch eine Karte erläutert," *Fennia* 5, no. 13 (1892).
2. As an example, Caoimhín Ó Danachair, "Some Distribution Patterns in Irish Folk Life," *Béaloideas* 25 (1957): 108–23.

Arnold van Gennep in his masterwork, *Manuel de folklore français contemporain.*

In all the titles mentioned above we see this new trend in geographical thinking. Even when maps are used, they still seem to be used haphazardly—one might be inclined to say by chance, not systematically—as a means in themselves, or as a means for pursuing a complex end. In a way, Wilhelm Mannhardt may be called a forerunner of this method. When he was working on his *Wald- und Feldkulte,* he realized that many problems might be solved only by asking questions that aimed at a specified answer. So he sent out questionnaires in 1865 to roughly two thousand correspondents in Germany, Austria, Switzerland, Hungary, and some other countries. These questionnaires contained about thirty questions concerning agrarian usages and customs especially during harvest time. Only 2 percent of these questionnaires came back with answers. Mannhardt was not satisfied with this result and decided to travel about himself to obtain the desired information. In essence we have adumbrated here two different mapping systems: by correspondence and by "exploration." Mannhardt himself did not intend to do any mapping, but he used a new method to get more and more reliable first-hand information about the area spread of the topics he had in mind. This system certainly is questionable and arbitrary, because too much is left to chance in finding the right places and the right persons from which to get information.

Actual systematic mapping began with the language atlases of linguistic departments. Since their aims are different, they cannot be regarded as folklife atlases; only in rare cases do they combine *Wörter und Sachen* (words and things). The idea of a modern folklife atlas seems first to have been mentioned and discussed by Wilhelm Pessler, who was originally a geographer. The idea to which he devoted his life is shown in his dissertation, "Das altsächsische Bauernhaus in seiner geographischen Verbreitung" ("The Geographical Distribution of the Old-Saxon Peasant House"). His theories are best set forth in an article, "Die geographische Methode in der Volkskunde," and in the book *Deutsche Volkstumgeographie.* His aim was not quite what we understand by folklife, but rather signified *Volkstum* (national characteristics) as a whole: geography, race, and cultural influences, according to then-current political tendencies in Germany (1931). He also made a sample atlas himself: *Volkstumsatlas von Niedersachsen* (1933).

The modern geographical method in folklife may be called a representation of items by cartographical means and therefore a way of looking at these items in their regional surroundings and location, and of drawing those conclusions that can safely be drawn. One point must be absolutely clear: a map is always an auxiliary means and not an aim in itself; it is not the finished result, but it can be an ideal instrument for research work. In a way, an atlas has the same function as a collection of nicely classified and neatly filled source materials. What you should see in well-drawn maps are cultural areas (*Kulturräume*) and cultural frontiers (*Kulturgrenzen*), that is, you may see indicated the specialties of a folk-group or of a region, or the influences from and connections with other groups and regions. Why these areas are as they are, why some frontier lines have become effective for folklife items and others have not, will not be shown by the map. From this point on it is up to you to use comparative methods, to find help in archives and historical sources, or to try other approaches. Still, a map must not necessarily be static; it will be so in many cases, but by means of helpful symbols and a commentary with additional annotations the map can show dynamically the historical development of a given item. Much depends upon the dexterity of the map-planner and map-designer.

TECHNIQUE AND METHOD

It will be best to distinguish three stages:

a. Collecting of material;
b. Preliminary steps before publication;
c. Publication.

COLLECTING OF MATERIAL

Let us take for granted that you know the regions in which to collect and the problems you want to be mapped, and that financial difficulties have been overcome. The most important question then is whether the collecting should be done by correspondence or by "explorers" (trained folklife collectors, doing the collecting personally), or with the help of both systems. To a certain extent the system depends on whether a "big-area atlas" (*Grossraum-Atlas*) or a "small-area atlas" (*Kleinraum-Atlas*) is needed. They differ because of the simple practical reasons of time, personnel, and money. With correspondents (that is, by sending out questionnaires) it is possible to receive answers from a high density of places at comparatively small cost. A native correspondent, if he wishes, can check his answers by contacting his neighbors and other inhabitants of his village; in doing so he is more valuable than a trained collector. But he may not understand all the questions; he may not be interested in some questions, and may not even answer them; he may have religious and political prejudices. Also, the choice of places to investigate is more or less a matter of chance. Most certainly, with different correspondents not all answers will have the same reliability for the whole map, and the possibility of an objective comparison is reduced as soon as an answer demands neither a "Yes" nor a "No" but a differentiation. With explorators (fieldworkers trained for folk atlas research) the question of time and money becomes fairly important, but otherwise they offer considerable advantages. They are trained in the same way, they operate in the same manner in all places, and therefore all their questions and answers should have the same quality. The explorator will have to find the right informants himself, at the places that have been selected, before he starts collecting. He will always be able to change his questions a bit and adapt them to the standard of his informant; he will be able to seek out other informants, should that prove necessary. And, most important of all, should he hear of items and facts in places nearby that have not been selected for collecting because they did not seem worthwhile, he may quickly make up his mind to visit such places and find new items, if luck is with him. There is also a psychological fact that should be taken into consideration: villagers may object to answering written questionnaires and yet enjoy being asked questions in person.

The crucial matter is the setting up of the questionnaire. Questions must be selected whose answers will clearly help interpret folklife phenomena. These answers may serve to make visible cultural areas. Contacts are necessary with neighboring regions and countries; they may show that some item is on the point of dying out or of gaining expansive new strength. Questions that in all probability will be answered in the same way throughout the whole region of the atlas might as well be left out. Then, the number of questions to be asked should also be considered; the time and the patience of informants are not to be misused. One will also need to consider which questions can be usefully turned into maps. At the moment there is a lively discussion going on as to whether a European (or national) atlas of legends *(Sagen)* will yield results.[3]

The usual type of a question seeks to ascertain if one or several items occur at a given place. As a rule, "occurrence" signifies a traditional or group occurrence and not an isolated instance. The maps

3. See Klaus Beitl, "Die Sagen vom Nachtvolk. Untersuchung eines alpinen Sagentypus," *International Congress for Folk-Narrative Research in Athens. Lectures and Reports* 5 (1965): 14–21; Gerda Grober-Glück, "Aufhocker und Aufhocken nach den Sammlungen des *Atlas der deutschen Volkskunde,*" *Rheinisches Jahrbuch für Volkskunde* 15/16 (1965): 117–43; Jaromír Jech, "Variabilität der Sagen und einige Fragen der Katalogisierung," *Acta Ethnographica* 13 (1964): 107–10; W. Van Nespen, "De cartografische verwerking van het vlaamse sagenmateriaal," *Volkskunde* 64 (1963): 186–89; Matthias Zender, "Volkssage und Kulturraumforschung," *Fabula* 9 (1967): 303–12.

formed by these questions show the occurrence of an item within a given area, but little is said about the relation of this respective item as a cultural good to the culture-bearer (*Kulturträger*). The ideal statement would enable the map-reader to know the frequency factor of this item: to know whether only specialized groups are the bearers of the folklore (peasants in opposition to workers, Catholics to Protestants, younger people to the older generation); to know whether a belief is still firmly valid or only casually referred to; to know if one has to do with a declining and retrograde or a progressive and active movement.

The questionnaire should be published, not only because it has to be sent to the correspondents or to be given to the explorators, but because it is important for any scholar to see what was asked and thus to obtain an idea of the aim and tendency of the atlas. Sometimes not all questions and their answers can or will be published, but in these cases the scholar should be informed that he can consult material about these items in the archives.

Another point of great importance concerns the uniform distribution of the places to be explored within an area. There may be reasons why special places, which otherwise would not be needed to compose an equal pattern of distribution, need to be taken into account, for instance to represent areas far away from traffic routes, or isolated mountainous settlements. A modern atlas will not only show peasant villages but both smaller and larger towns. In countries where there are minority groups—even if they live in one or two settlements only—they should certainly not be overlooked. There may be very old settlements or new communities, or places where all inhabitants more or less are workers, craftsmen, miners, fishermen, herdsmen, and so on. In other words, all ethnic, social, linguistic minorities, and special cases should be explored.

Should you employ the correspondent system, you must find out first the right persons to whom to send the questionnaire. They may be located with the help of a clergyman or a priest, a doctor, a teacher, or a mayor. If one prefers the explorator system, he has to be careful to find explorators sufficiently trained to discuss intelligently with their informants agriculture and cattle-breeding, household work and craftsmanship. The explorators must know how to handle people, especially when they encounter sensitive problems of religion and political affiliation. A good explorator should be phonetically trained, should be able to speak and understand the dialect of the area, and should also be able to assist a farmer in his work if called upon to do so, because by so doing he facilitates contact. Trial surveys with the atlas-planner are highly recommended as a means of adjusting mis-

understandings before the start and to enable the explorator to surmise the length of time a given survey may take. An explorator
usually will have to find his informants in a village. He will take them
from different professional and age groups; he will ask men, women,
and sometimes children. For each informant the explorator should
put down in a minute book personal dates and facts (age, schooling,
periods of residence in the community, profession, social position).

As for the answers to questions, a differentiation should be made
between primary material (direct answers), secondary material (answers that are not given immediately but require time for reflection),
and spontaneous material (statements not given as answers to questions but made casually in the course of a discussion, which often
prove highly useful in leading to facts that otherwise would be overlooked).

PRELIMINARY STEPS BEFORE PUBLICATION

After all the material of all correspondents and explorators has come
in and been checked (and perhaps sent back for additional information), registered, and filed, the mapping of one question can begin.
Let us take as an example the mapping of a seasonal custom. One
reads all the answers through to obtain an idea of how the main
lines and areas may emerge. Then one analyzes the custom and
dissects it into its various elements. Not all of them may yield a satisfactory map or can be well-represented cartographically; some elements can be discussed only in the commentary. It is essential to
make a proper choice of symbols for the map; the principal and most
important facts of an item must be recognized at first glance, so that
"areas", "frontiers", and "lines" can be made out clearly. A map
should not be overcharged and overcrowded with too many symbols
and signs; sometimes it is better to join two or more elements together in one symbol and distinguish them by small additional signs
within the symbol. Minor details should not be overvalued by allowing them an extra symbol. Apart from the frequency of occurrence,
other factors (historical, sociological, psychological, of intensity) may
be expressed by additional small signs, to indicate, for instance, whether they are obsolete, recent, rare, or progressive. A map that simply
reports whether or not a certain item occurs at the explored place
needs only two symbols—let us say a circle and a point. Should several
factors be represented in one map, one may take the plain geo-
metrical, fundamental symbols (line, circle, triangle, square, rec-
tangle) and vary them by filling them partly or fully with black or
various colors. One may also combine the fundamental symbols. But
in all cases the symbols must be chosen in such a way that they will
not lose intelligibility when they are printed in a smaller scale.

A point of discussion always is whether the area-system or the point-system will produce a better map. Maps are meant for research work and not as "posters," so one had better decide from a scholarly point of view and not from an esthetic one. The point-system, roughly speaking, seems to be the only accurate, precise way of giving specific facts; this system shows each statement at the very place to which it applies. The area-system generalizes from a smaller or larger number of local statements grouped together as an area unit (perhaps marked with horizontal or vertical lines and surrounded by a frontier line), including also those places for which no statement has been given in the documentary files. Certainly, the area-system is justified, when 100 percent of the places are explored, or when a region is so uniform in its population distribution that it is possible to draw generalizing conclusions (as in a large, flat region, but not in regions with many small valleys and mountains). In what is called *Kleinkammer-Gebiete* ("small chamber-regions"), the point-system is to be preferred.

The written commentary, which may reach the size of a small monograph, will, on the whole, refrain from interpreting the facts. Interpretation will be left to the scholar using the maps. The commentary should refer to all relevant archive documents, pertinent passages from printed sources, and the so-called spontaneous data. Then there should be as complete a bibliography as possible, perhaps supplemented with drawings, diagrams, and photographs. The introduction must contain a "statement of accounts" explaining what questions from the whole material have been framed from the data, and why and with what points in mind the keys, signs, and symbols have been chosen. Linguistic additions may prove useful.

PUBLICATION

Let us take for granted that you have found a wonderful benefactor to finance the atlas project, a publisher willing to take over the task, and an editor madly in love with his work. Some small questions still remain. First of all, the scale: in Europe, neighboring countries try to use scales easily assimilated and those that can easily be transposed, since some of the newer atlases already have in mind assimiliation in a proposed all-European atlas. For a folklife atlas it is very useful to include some basic maps about political frontiers, geological and climatic conditions, nature of the soil, railways, streets, languages, religions, historical development, occupations of the population, towns, industries. All these maps may help in an understanding of a culture area as well as in depicting the growth or diminution of folk-life items. It must then be decided whether the single folklife maps should be printed on strong paper or as transparent overlays to make it possible to put one or two on top of a basic map. In a few cases, especially when one is dealing with material culture (e.g., types of houses, forms of ploughs, tools), an explanatory drawing at the side of the map can show at once what might otherwise demand an extensive description.

THE NATIONAL ATLASES[4]

The usual conception of a national atlas is the mapping of one political country, but there are cases in which an atlas, because of ethnic or linguistic reasons, reaches across political frontiers. When this is done nowadays, as with the Swedish and the Dutch atlases, the institutes of the countries involved collaborate. The first German (prewar) atlas included all German-speaking areas and countries in Europe, while the present German atlas is restricted to Germany. There are also plans for atlases that will include only part of a political country, if this portion differs linguistically and culturally from other regions of the country, or if intrapolitical reasons are strong enough.

ATLAS DER DEUTSCHEN VOLKSKUNDE (ADV)

We must distinguish between two series of the ADV. The first, and the oldest, folklife atlas existing was planned before 1930. The idea was to give an exhaustive geographical inventory of all folk aspects of all Germans; that is to say, all German-speaking areas in Europe would be covered regardless of political boundaries. (Truly a large-area atlas!). Five questionnaires were sent out to correspondents in the period from 1930 to 1935. The fifth questionnaire included questions concerning the color of eyes and hair and the form of noses, because the editors (or the political leaders behind them) were convinced they would be able to map a characterology of the German *Volk* (*Volks-Charakterkunde*). In 1937, the Nazi regime took over the organization of the atlas; all former members of the Atlas-Comité were dismissed, and the new editors sent out no further questionnaires but began immediately with the printing of the maps. From 1937 to 1939 six fascicles appeared, each with twenty maps. No introduction and no commentaries were ever published, hence now it is fairly difficult to read and interpret these maps. From 1940 on, all work on the atlas stopped. Not until 1954 was Matthias Zender commissioned to undertake a new series. His problem was how to continue. The original questionnaire material had not been destroyed in the war and gave a completely uniform collection of the status of about 1930 (collected by correspondents, certainly, and therefore not always fully

4. This chapter was finished at the beginning of 1967 and gives the status of the national atlases at that time. But each survey of this kind has to stop at a given moment, although the work on atlases continues.

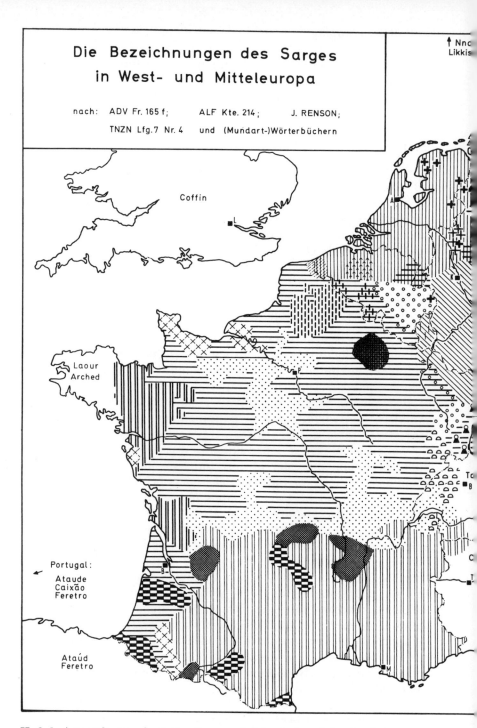

II–6–1. A sample map from the German folklore atlas giving local names for coffins in central and western Europe. From Heinrich L. Cox, *Die Bezeichnungen des Sarges im Kontinental-Westgermanischen.* Supplement 2 to Matthias Zender, *Atlas der deutschen Volkskunde,* new series. Marburg, 1967.

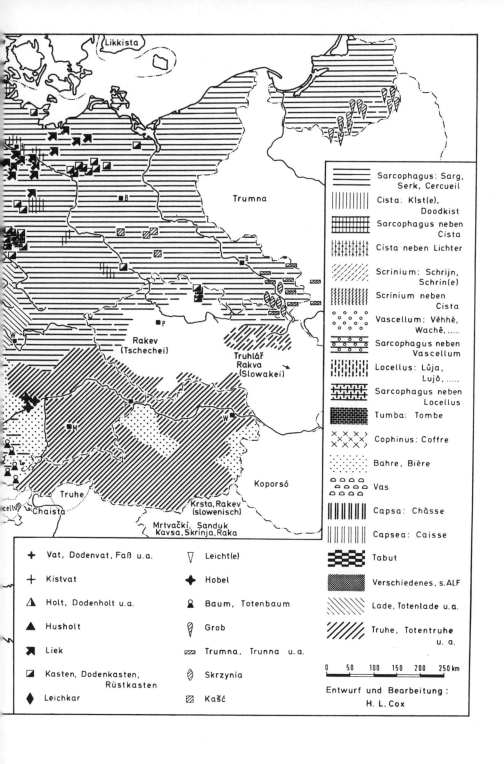

Likkista

Trumna

Rakev
(Tschechei)

Truhlář
Rakva
(Slowakei)

Koporsó

Truhe

Chaista

cellum

Krsta, Rakev
(slowenisch)

Mrtvački, Sanduk
Kavsa, Skrinja, Raka

Sarcophagus: Sarg, Serk, Cercueil	
Cista: Kist(e), Doodkist	
Sarcophagus neben Cista	
Cista neben Lichter	
Scrinium: Schrijn, Schrin(e)	
Scrinium neben Cista	
Vascellum: Vêhhê, Wachê, ...	
Sarcophagus neben Vascellum	
Locellus: Lûja, Lujô, ...	
Sarcophagus neben Locellus	
Tumba: Tombe	
Cophinus: Coffre	
Bahre, Bière	
Vas	
Capsa: Châsse	
Capsea: Caisse	
Tabut	
Verschiedenes, s. ALF	
Lade, Totenlade u.a.	
Truhe, Totentruhe u. a.	

+ Vat, Dodenvat, Faß u.a.

✛ Kistvat

△ Holt, Dodenholt u.a.

▲ Husholt

✈ Liek

◪ Kasten, Dodenkasten, Rüstkasten

◆ Leichkar

▽ Leicht(e)

✦ Hobel

♟ Baum, Totenbaum

⬗ Grob

▱ Trumna, Trunna u. a.

⬙ Skrzynia

◩ Kašć

0   50   100   150   200   250 km

Entwurf und Bearbeitung:
H. L. Cox

reliable, but still representing a wealth of material possessed by no other country). If Zender wanted to start a new collection, it would mean taking into consideration the results of the war, including fundamentally changed situations, industrialization everywhere, and new settlements of refugees. It was evident that new maps could not be compared with the maps of the first series. In the end he decided to use the material of the original questionnaires, therefore making his atlas, in a way, a historical atlas, showing the status of 1930 in all its contrasts with the present. As material culture was not represented at all in the old atlas, Zender intended to carry out a completely new investigation by explorers for this aspect of folk culture to reflect the situation roughly between 1960 and 1970. Parts of the results of this new inventory were to be published in special monographs. The first fascicle of the new series appeared in 1959, containing twelve maps and an exceedingly good commentary. Up to 1967, four fascicles have been published, all with first-rate commentaries. The maps treat some highly interesting questions: division of labor between men and women in agricultural duties, popular veneration of saints, objects placed in coffins and graves at burials, wakes and funeral banquets, customs at marriage and baptism, second-sight and prophesying, belief in nightmares, and similar conceptions.

ATLAS DER SCHWEIZERISCHEN VOLKSKUNDE (ASV)

The material for this mapping was collected in two different inquiries. The first was sent to correspondents, but absolutely unsystematically. It was meant more or less as an initial survey about what might be done afterward, since virtually no preliminary studies existed. The second inquiry was made with the help of eight explorators intimate with the regions and dialects of the four languages spoken in Switzerland. The questionnaire contained 150 questions, partly subdivided. Of the 3,000 political "units" (*Gemeinden*) in Switzerland, 400 were chosen in such a way as to represent the Swiss diversity in languages and geography, i.e., mountainous parts, rural regions, industrial regions, alpine culture. For each place an explorator needed about three days on an average. The collecting was done in the years 1937 to 1942 and publication began in 1949. Up to 1967 twelve fascicles have appeared, with sixteen more planned. For each fascicle a commentary is added giving many details and a wealth of information taken from archives and books. Though the Swiss atlas covers many fields of folklife, some parts have been omitted purposely, such as house-research and settlements, folksong, folk drama, and oral tradition (jests, anecdotes, legends, fairy tales).

ÖESTERREICHISCHER VOLKSKUNDEATLAS (ÖVA)

This atlas differs from the others in its conception of collecting and editing. First there is the material that was brought together in the questionnaires of the first German atlas (as of 1930). Then, after the foundation of the Austrian atlas in 1953, questionnaires were sent out to all school authorities, who passed them on to schoolteachers to be answered and filled out. Finally there exist private collections initiated by certain scholars for specific problems. These scholars have been asked to draw up maps for their special fields and to write the supporting commentaries. The maps in themselves may be very good, but the disadvantage is that they cannot be compared with each other, as the several scholars brought their material together in quite different ways, not covering all "lands" of Austria with the same reliability, and with datings from different times and years. So the material of the maps is disparate, although this fault may be corrected, to a certain extent, in the commentaries. The first fascicle, edited in 1959 by Ernst Burgstaller and A. Helbok in Linz, contained thirteen maps, covering such disparate subjects as German dialects in Austria, pastries and breads for festival days, terms for servants, wreaths for Advent, and strangely enough, reverse paintings on glass. The editorship meanwhile was turned over to Richard Wolfram, who published the second fascicle in 1965 in Vienna. Material culture is represented by types of barns and of baking-ovens, by the baking of bread and the household distilling of brandy. There are also several maps concerning customs, for instance Christmas celebrations.

POLSKI ATLAS ETNOGRAFICZNY

In 1958 Gajek, as editor of the atlas, brought out an "experimental trial issue" with seventeen maps and a small commentary, as a prelude for discussion to decide the final system of mapping. The task presents enormous difficulties, since after the war Polish frontiers were considerably altered, millions of the population having migrated and settled in other regions. The Polish atlas tries to do something new; it seeks to determine the culture elements acquired by the new settlers, to show the elements they brought with them, and finally to map the results of adaptation. Explorators had done the fieldwork, based on four material-culture questionnaires about cattle breeding, agriculture, economic functions of buildings, and house-types. The maps try out the different systems: by areas, by points, by using one or more colors. For the net system Poland was divided by a screen into equal squares, and in each square a village was selected that seemed to be characteristic. The density of population is not taken

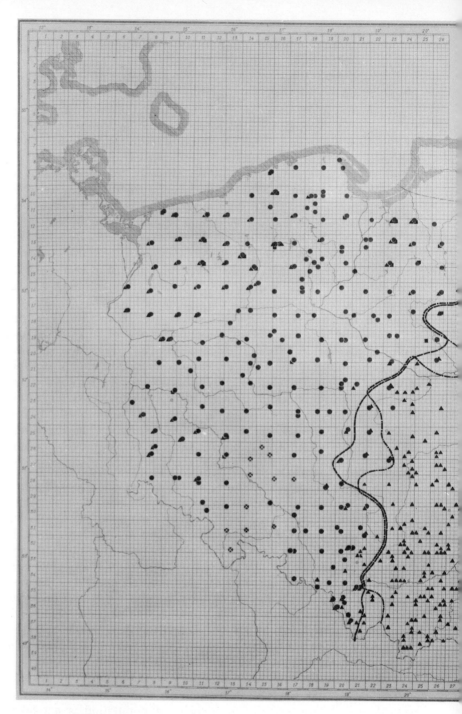

II–6–2. A sample map from the Polish folklore atlas showing types and distribution of flails. From Józef Gajek, *Polski Atlas Etnograficzny*. 2 vols., Warsaw, 1964–65.

LAS ETNOGRAFICZNY

Zeszyt próbny

Skala 1:2 000 000

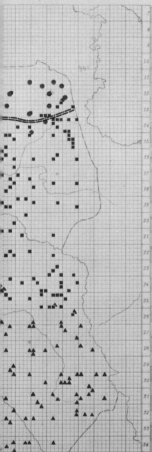

Mapa 9

FORMY CEPÓW

Występowanie trzech głównych form cepów na podstawie badań terenowych w 1953 i 1954 r. oraz dawniejszych danych.
(zasięgi z 1953 i 1954 r.)

Opracowanie
J. GAJEK i Z. STASZCZAKÓWNA

Kwestionariusz nr 1 (1953)

Rozdział X. 5. Opisać i narysować z podaniem rozmiarów cep względnie cepy, o ile we wsi występuje więcej niż jeden typ czy odmiana. Przy opisie i rysunku zwrócić uwagę na: a) proporcje poszczególnych części; b) kształt nasieć i otworów na bijaku i dzierżaku; c) na przekrój podłużny i poprzeczny bijaka (okrągły, prostokątny, macugowaty, prosty itp.; d) na kształt i sposób umocowania oraz materiał wiązań. Inwentarz dzierżak z bijakiem. 7. W wypadku, gdy we wsi występuje kilka odmian lub typów cepów, należy zapisać: a) który typ (odmiana) jest bardziej gospodarny, który używany jest rzadziej; b) który uważany jest we wsi za dawniejszy, a który pojawił się za pamięci ludzkiej. 8. Na Ziemiach Odzyskanych stwierdzić: a) jaki typ cepu zastali osiedleńcy w danej wsi; b) jaki typ, odmianę przywieźli ze sobą i skąd?

Kwestionariusz nr 2 (1954)

Rozdział VIII. 5. Dokładnie opisać w jaki sposób kapica jest umieszczona na dzierżaku (rysunek) i stwierdzić, czy zawsze kapica obraca się na dzierżaku. Ponieważ kilka zrealizowanych odpowiedzi dopuszcza taką możliwość, należy tę sprawę dokładnie ustalić.

Objaśnienia

A. Cepy kapicowe

1 — Cepy z dwoma kapicami ze skóry (kapica na dzierżaku jest stosunkowo szerokim i miękkim pasem skóry).

2 — Cepy ze skórzaną kapicą na bijaku, z drewnianym pałączkiem na dzierżaku.

3 — Cepy ze skórzaną kapicą na bijaku, ze skórzanym (z bykowca) pałączkiem na dzierżaku.

B. Cepy gąsewkowe

— Cepy gąsewkowe, przy których bijak z dzierżakiem łączy skórzany pierścień (gąsew) przywiązany do dzierżaka i bijaka skórzanymi trokami.

C. Zasięgi niektórych innych cech cepów

1   1a — Pojedyncze zacięcie dzierżaków.
   1b — Okrągły, rzadziej wieloboczny przekrój bijaków lekkich.

2   2a — Podwójne zacięcia dzierżaków.
   2b — Przekroje czworokątne lub owalne bijaków ciężkich.

3   — Najdalszy zachodni, zwarty zasięg dzierżaków z pojedynczym zacięciem i lekkim bijakiem — jak rys. 1a i 1b.

4   — Najdalszy wschodni, zwarty zasięg dzierżaków z podwójnym zacięciem i ciężkim bijakiem — jak rys. 2a i 2b.

UWAGA. Nie uwzględniono na mapie przeniesień tych elementów po II wojnie światowej.

D. Występowanie dwu lub więcej form danego wytworu w jednej wsi

— Znak górny, niepełny oznacza, że dana forma wytworu jest we wsi uboczna, rzadsza.

— Znak dolny, niepełny oznacza, że zjawisko jest tu we wsi nowsze, przybyło z falą osadniczą po II wojnie światowej.

UWAGA. Mapę opracowano na podstawie badań terenowych w 357 wsiach stałej sieci PAE, w oparciu o kwestionariusze nr 1 (1953), nr 2 (1954) oraz naniesiono na mapę dane z 378 wsi na podstawie literatury i niedrukowanych zbiorów materiałów: Archiwum Atlasu Kultury Ludowej w Polsce, Archiwum Polskiego Towarzystwa Ludoznawczego we Wrocławiu, Archiwum Pracowni Atlasu i Słownika Gwar Polskich Zakładu Językoznawstwa PAN pod kier. prof. K. Nitschą, Seminarium Etnografii Słowian U.J., Zakładu Etnografii w Warszawie; materiały: J. Gajka, M. Gładysza, K. Moszyńskiego, R. Reinfussa i.

into account. Only the sections of the squares are numbered, no place names being given.

A prewar Polish atlas had been published by Kazimierz Moszyński in Kraków in three volumes, 1934–36, containing thirty maps. But modern Poland is so completely different from its prewar condition that it was necessary to start a new atlas.

ATLAS ÖVER SVENSK FOLKKULTUR

The first volume of the Swedish atlas illustrating "material and social culture" was published in 1957 under the editorship of Sigurd Erixon and Eerik Laid. It contains twenty-four main maps and forty-four smaller ones. Geographically, it covers not only Sweden but also the Swedish population in Finland. The collecting was done by correspondents and explorators, with the material historically limited to the time between 1850 and 1900; present-day situations and conditions are deliberately not shown. The maps only intend to reproduce the occurrence of an item; the social functions of this item and the attitude of man toward it are left to the commentary. Three further volumes are planned to illustrate folklore (legends, beliefs, annual feasts), popular language (proverbs, riddles), and place names.

VOLKSKUNDE-ATLAS VOOR NEDERLAND EN VLAAMS-BELGIË

In this atlas, edited by P. J. Meertens and M. De Meyer, we again have a close collaboration between two countries, the Netherlands and Belgian Flanders, both having the same language and the same culture. The collecting was done by correspondents interrogating on all fields of folklife: folk belief, popular science, year-cycle, house life, community life, handicrafts, professions. Two fascicles, each with ten maps and accompanied by commentaries, were published in 1959 and 1965. The first fascicle was especially interesting, because it tried out the problematic experiment of mapping belief-questions: will-o'-the-wisp (jack-o'-lantern), recognition of witches, werewolf, "burning man," the Wild Hunt. To some extent the second fascicle follows along the same lines: folk medicine, bogies for children, rituals to obtain fine weather.

ETNOLOŠKI ATLAS JUGOSLAVIJE

The Yugoslav folk atlas is edited by Branimir Bratanić and others. Since questionnaires for collectors had been set up, and some trial surveys made, it was possible to publish in 1963 eight trial maps (*pokusne karte*), showing distribution of yokes, manners of threshing, tools for threshing, village meeting places, annual bonfires, masquerades. The task for the editor and the explorators is not easy, since the questionnaires had to be written in Slovenian, Croatian, Serbian, and Macedonian. The atlas also must take into consideration all minority groups in regions of mixed ethnic population.

PREPARATIONS FOR ATLASES UNDER WAY

Some publications from first reports, in Denmark, Finland, Hungary, the Soviet Union, and Italy (Friuli and Sardinia), are now available. A current aim is to draw up a European folklife atlas. Definite steps toward this goal were taken at a conference in Zagreb in 1966.[5] All those present were of the opinion that it would be best to start with three items, for which sufficient preliminary work (maps, monographs, articles) seems to have been published in most of the European countries: ploughing tools, threshing, and bonfires. For further maps the plans include: other agricultural tools (hoes, sickles, scythes), house-building, the question of succession by inheritance, and winter customs.

Finally, a special type of new international atlas deserves mention: the international atlas of clerical history (*Kirchenhistorischer Atlas*), decided upon in 1960. Each country will contribute its own maps. Austria made the beginning in 1966 when the first fascicle appeared (two from Austria are planned). It contains twelve maps, some dealing with folklife matters such as religious orders, pilgrimages, and veneration of the saints.[6]

Bibliography and Selected Readings

Barabás, Jenó. *Kartográfiai módszer a néprajzban.* Budapest, 1963. Methods in folklore—atlases looked at generally from the political standpoint of the author. In Hungarian, with a short summary in German.

Bjerrum, Anders. "Atlas der dänischen Volskultur." *Folk-Liv* 5 (1941): 113–23. The plan for a Danish folklife atlas.

Campbell, Åke. "Notes on a Swedish Contribution to the *Folk Culture Atlas of Europe.*" *Laos* 1 (1951): 111–20.

Driver, Harold E. *Indians of North America.* Chicago: University of Chicago Press, 1961. Thirty-eight maps give areas and distribution patterns of ethnological items.

Erixon, Sigurd. "Die Frage der kartographischen Darstellung vom Standpunkt der nordischen Ethnologie in Schweden aus betrachtet." *Folk-Liv* 1 (1937): 168–80. Presentation of the leading ideas for the Swedish atlas.

5. Branimir Bratanić, "Internationale Arbeitskonferenz über die ethnologische Kartographie," *Ethnologia Europaea* 1 (1967): 75–77; Reinhard Peesch, "Internationale Arbeitskonferenz über ethnologische Kartographie in Zagreb, 8–10. Februar 1966," *Demos* 7 (1966): 371–72.

6. *Kirchenhistorischer Atlas von Österreich* (Wien: Wiener Dom-Verlag, 1966).

Hotzenköcherle, Rudolf. *Einführung in den Sprachatlas der deutschen Schweiz.* 2 vols. Bern: Francke, 1962. Vol. A: *Zur Methodologie der Kleinraumatlanten.* Vol. B: *Fragebuch, Transkriptionsschlüssel, Aufnahmeprotokolle.* A very good handbook for a linguistic atlas, with practical hints for folklife atlases too.

Kretschmer, Ingrid. *Die thematische Karte als wissenschaftliche Aussageform der Volkskunde. Eine Untersuchung zur volkskundlichen Kartographie.* Forschungen zur deutschen Landeskunde, 153. Bad Godesberg: Bundesanstalt für Landeskunde und Raumforschung, 1965. A critical survey of the existing European atlases (mostly of the Germanic area), stresses description of the symbols in the presentation of a map.

Kurath, Hans. *A Word Geography of the Eastern United States.* Ann Arbor: University of Michigan Press, 1949. Materials collected for a linguistic atlas of the United States and Canada. Isoglosses in areas, but also maps with point-systems.

Menéndez Pidal, Ramón. "Sobre geografía folklórica. Ensayo de un método." *Revista de filología española* 7 (1920) : 229–338.

Ó Danachair, Caoimhín. "Some Distribution Patterns in Irish Folk Life." *Béaloideas* 25 (1957) : 108–23.

Perusini, Gaetano. "L'atlante Storico-linguistico-etnografico Del Friuli-Venezia Giulia." *Alpes Orientales* 4 (1966) : 117–26. Plan for an atlas (historical, linguistical, and folklife) of northeastern Italy.

Röhr, Erich. *Die Volkstumskarte.* Leipzig, 1939. Concerning the first series of the *Atlas der deutschen Volkskunde*: the political ideas represented in the book may now be looked at from an historical distance.

Schlenger, Herbert. *Methodische und technische Grundlagen des Atlas der deutschen Volkskunde.* Deutsche Forschung, 27. Berlin, 1934. A matter-of-fact description of the first series of the *Atlas der deutschen Volkskunde.*

Varagnac, André. "La méthode cartographique dans le folklore." *Revue de Folklore français* 3 (1932) : 224–33.

Weiss, Richard. *Einführung in den Atlas der schweizerischen Volkskunde.* Basel: Schweizerische Gesellschaft für Volkskunde, 1950. A valuable handbook for the Swiss atlas, treating all problems concerning a small-area atlas.

Wiegelmann, Günter. "Der 'Atlas der deutschen Volkskunde' als Quelle für die Agrargeschichte." *Zeitschrift für Agrargeschichte und Agrarsoziologie* 12 (1964) : 164–80. Atlas-maps as sources for an agrarian history, presented in a superior manner.

———. "Reliktzonen und moderne Gebiete in der bäuerlichen Sachkultur der Neuzeit." *Kulturraumprobleme aus Ostmitteleuropa und Asien.* Pp. 23–36. Kiel Universität Geographisches Institut. Schriften, vol. 23. Kiel, 1964. Agrarian relic and innovation areas are made visible through maps.

7 THE USE OF ARTIFACTS AND FOLK ART IN THE FOLK MUSEUM

J. Geraint Jenkins

To many, a folk museum is merely a place where the tools and implements of past centuries are shown to an interested public. The word *folk* in itself seems to breed a strange reaction, conjuring up a picture of woolen-stockinged, black-cloaked, brogue-shod women chasing fairies through the glens and men with bells around their knees dancing merrily on the village green. But even if the more enlightened section of the community has gone beyond that picture of primitive life, far too many still tend to regard *the folk* as hewers of wood and drawers of water, who cling to antiquated customs, live in primitive thatched houses, and speak a broad dialect. Nothing could be further from the truth, for the folk include all levels of society—the village squire living in his mansion as well as the weaver in his one-room cottage, the dame of high degree as well as the milkmaid, the yeoman farmer as well as the ploughman. The word *folk* signifies the complete way of life of the community; it concerns every stratum of the community. Undoubtedly the squirearchy played a vitally important part in the development of community life, and in our study of the folk we would be disregarding an essential ingredient of society if we were to forget it.

In the Welsh Folk Museum at Saint Fagans, near Cardiff, a section of the museum is given over to the life and habits of the aristocratic classes of Wales. In 1947, the National Museum of Wales was presented with an Elizabethan manor house of many rooms, surrounded by high walls and formal gardens, with fishponds, mulberry grove, and stable block. The manor has been furnished in a style that befitted the aristocracy of Wales and includes fine furniture, much of it imported from the European continent, expensive tapestries, and a large, well-equipped kitchen. In order to depict the life of every stratum of the community a museum must therefore include material associated with the aristocracy as well as material relating to the peasant classes.

What the student of folklife is not concerned with, except as they affect the daily life of the people, are the political crises, the diplomatic intrigues, and the prominent personages of the past that quite properly find their place in the usual history books. Our chief aim is to study ordinary people as they constitute the overwhelming proportion of every community. Our duty is to collect the tools and implements that they used, and to record details of their life, their skills, their homes, their fields, their customs, their speech, and their leisure activities. The student of folklife searches for the key to the world of ordinary people; he attempts to throw light on their astonishingly ill-documented day-to-day life. It was the prophet Esdras who said, "It was not in our minds to be curious of the high things, but of such as pass by us daily." That is the theme of folklife studies.

Folklife is a new approach to the investigation and understanding of human social organization. It aims to coordinate the information resulting from other disciplines, but there is also the added task of investigating and recording aspects of human society that hitherto have been beyond the scope of those individual studies. "We lose too much if we stand on the narrow ground of only one discipline—local history, say, as it is generally understood—and it is clear that we should use any method that is useful in understanding, recording and illuminating the material that is just going under."[1] Folklife is therefore an holistic approach to the study of an organic community, and it will live down "the doubtful overtones of the word *folk* because it offers a very valuable method of studying a society at this point in history."[2]

1. G. E. Evans, "Folk Life Studies in East Anglia" in J. G. Jenkins, ed., *Studies in Folk Life* (London, 1969), p. 37.
2. Ibid., p. 36.

During the nineteenth century, the antiquarian movement flourished in the British Isles, and local societies known variously as philosophical societies, literary societies, antiquarian societies, and museum societies were established in great number throughout the country to cater to the new interest in antiquities. One of the most important functions of these societies was to rescue the material remains of earlier centuries, and to most antiquaries this meant the collection of prehistoric and proto-historic objects that were obtained through excavation of early sites. Excavation was more often than not unscientific, and the stone, metal, and pottery objects excavated were sometimes cleaned, presented to the society's museum, and shown there in a forest of ebonized glass cases without any documentation at all. The museums were cabinets of curiosities, and few attempts were made to study in any great detail the material obtained by museums. There was naturally some scientific work, but only on isolated articles that had a value of their own. During the present century, archeology has developed phenomenally, and although the amateur excavator and the antiquarian still have a part to play in archeological work, great care is taken to insure that a site is clearly documented and the material from it clearly dated and labeled. There is, in most cases, an attempt to place the object in evolutionary sequence and to discover the cultural contacts associated with the item. In addition, scholars are studying the typology of material, its provenance and dating, while a collection of excavated objects may provide the raw materials for historians to study the ways of life connected with those objects.

Folklife studies have suffered greatly from a one-sided, archeological approach and for a long time were regarded merely as an appendage to archeology. In the nineteenth century "bygones" of post-medieval times were collected and immediately banished to a dark corner of a museum, where a case display was usually arranged under the title "Local Bygones." In most cases no attempt at all was made to explain the design and social significance of those locally collected objects. The old generation of museum curators tended to regard the objects in their care as exhibition pieces only, not as a basis for scientific study. They rejected folklife material, on the ground that in order to gain a place in a museum an object must have intrinsic value. If it was not a work of art or an artifact closely associated with some historical occasion, then it must be an object of universal curiosity. Curators were loath to harbor among their collections objects that, apart from their connection with a local culture, might be completely worthless. "The same problem had arisen at an earlier stage, when the supporters of systematic archeology sought to gain admission for their potsherds and fragments."[3] Curiously enough, the admission of systematic archeology as an important subject in the study of past civilizations and cultures did not ease the entrance of folklife studies, and some of its fiercest opponents were to be found amongst archeologists themselves. "Rubbish is rubbish, even if it is old rubbish," Sophus Muller, the archeologist director of the National Museum of Denmark, is said to have remarked when told of a scheme to found a folk museum.[4]

The same was true in Great Britain; indeed, folklife studies are not yet fully recognized as an academic discipline in this country. Folklife material is far too often referred to as "bygones" and still regarded as an appendage to archeology. In prehistoric archeology, the object is all the student possesses in his interpretation of prehistory, but the student of folklife has far more. He has oral tradition, custom and belief, dialect, and the persistence of age-old techniques to help him in his work. The very word "bygones" denotes a wrong attitude to the subject, for in folklife studies we are concerned with the study of man as a cultural being, with "his mental, spiritual and material struggle towards civilization."[5] Such a struggle will not tolerate any arbitrary amputation in time or approach. One wonders why a nineteenth-century carpenter's brace should be described by some museums as "a bygone," while a Bronze Age pot is not, for surely both are elements in man's struggle for ever greater efficiency. One wonders too how a nineteenth-century cooper's inside shave can be termed "a bygone," while if the same tool were to be excavated from a Roman site it is no longer "a bygone" but an archeological specimen, and it is certainly not "a bygone" when it is seen in constant use in a cooper's shop in the nearest brewery.[6] The case for folklife studies may therefore be restated to say that it is not merely concerned with the collection of material objects. Such a collection is useless unless the student is prepared to go further and discover the social organization, the economic conditions, and the lore and culture associated with these objects. The material objects in a folk collection should contribute to a clearer understanding of the community that is being studied; collection is not an end in itself, but merely the means of reaching the people to whom these material objects had the meaning of everyday things. As Albert Sandvig, the creator of the Norwegian Folk Museum at Lillehammer, wrote of his museum in 1907, "It is a collection of homes into which one can enter and go

3. Sigurd Erixon, "Editorial," *Folk-Liv* 1 (1937) : 6.

4. As quoted by J. W. Y. Higgs, *Folk Life Collection and Classification* (London, 1963) , p. 18.

5. I. C. Peate, "The Study of Folk Life," *Gwerin* 2 (1959) : 98.

6. J. G. Jenkins, *Traditional Country Craftsmen* (London, 1965) , pp. 91–95.

II–7–1. Coracle maker and fishermen at Cenarth on the River Teim, 1938. All of the photographs accompanying this chapter are furnished by the author.

straight to the people that lived there thus learning to know their way of life, their tastes and their work; the fashioning and furnishing of a home depict the people themselves."[7]

The tools of agriculture, craft, and industry are only a means of reaching the people that used those tools. For example, coracles that are still used on three Welsh rivers are rather uninteresting canvas-covered fishing crafts with hazel frameworks, ash seats, and carrying straps of leather or twisted withy. As students of folklife, we are concerned with their construction, which varies greatly from one region to another; with the variety of local names for the parts of a coracle, with the methods of using coracles, and with the equipment for fishing salmon on Welsh rivers. We are concerned with tracing the evolution of this unique fishing craft, with the details of its construction, and with the customs connected with it. Above all, we are concerned with the men that row coracles and with their place in the local community, and with fishery bylaws that limit their use on many rivers. In speaking of the Pacific, Malinowski has stressed that "the cultural reality of a canoe can not be brought home to a student, by placing a perfect specimen before him. To understand a canoe fully, the student would need to know the rules concerning its ownership, how and by what people it was sailed; the ceremonies associated with its construction and use and particularly the emotional attitude of the craftsman to his craft, which he surrounds with an atmosphere of romance, built up of tradition and of personal experience."[8]

Hence the folklife scholar interests himself not only in the objects produced by the inhabitants of a country, not only in their homes, their fields and workshops, but with the whole tradition, the life that gave existence to those material things. At the Welsh Folk Museum there is exhibited a straw basket together with a piece of cow horn and a bone awl that were used in making it. The basket itself is a thing of beauty, but the tools as such are completely valueless.[9] Nevertheless, their value can be greatly increased when something of the background to the whole craft of lip work is discovered: that tradition has dictated the bone awl must be from a horse's hind leg, that the straw used must be unbrushed, unthreshed winter wheat, and that the bramble for tying the straw rolls must be cut in the forests and not from hedgerows. It is even more important to know something of the life of the community in which the craftsman who made the basket lived and worked. In Wales today there is only one craftsman who still makes lip work baskets. He is a stonemason and smallholder

7. Gjessing Thale, *The Sandvig Collections* (Oslo, 1949 ed.) , p. 7.
8. Bronislaw Malinowski, *Argonauts of the Western Pacific* (London, 1922) , p. 12.
9. Jenkins, *Craftsmen*, pp. 142–44.

II–7–2. A Cardiganshire lip-worker using wheat straw and split bramble
to make baskets.

who lives in a remote croft on a hillside in central Cardiganshire. But from the point of view of traditional craftsmanship he is something far more than a manipulator of straw and bramble stalks, for he represents a tradition that is dying: the tradition of the amateur, part-time craftsman who contributed substantially to the cultural heritage of Wales. It is the tradition that gave us love spoons, patchwork quilts, knitting sheaths, stay busks, and decorated lace bobbins. They were produced by members of an isolated community where entertainment was at a premium and who practiced some creative craft in their spare time.

It has been argued that scholars who are concerned with folklife should not study material that is already fully documented in books, patent rights, and records of manufacturers. No museum, they contend, should collect those artifacts. Those that support this view argue, for example, that steam threshing equipment is not worthy of note because it is already fully documented in patent specifications, trade catalogues, and other sources. These sources may give the full technical specifications for tools and machinery, but they cannot tell us about systems of farm cooperation, the division of labor on threshing day, and the processes of decision whereby each farmer living in a close community picked out a particular day for threshing. Documents cannot ·describe regional differences in terminology. Yet all these aspects of threshing should be of as much concern to the student of folklife as the design and construction of threshing equipment.

The objects in a folk collection should do two things. First, they should give a clear picture of the life of a community; they should express the personality of the region or nation that a museum serves. Second, the collection should provide a clear picture of the development of human society throughout the ages in the area that the museum serves.

Folklife is concerned with the study of those elements, be they social, material, or linguistic, that distinguish one community from the other. Whether the British student of folklife carry out his work in Inverness or Cornwall, in Norfolk or Pembrokeshire, what he is really concerned with are those features that distinguish one region from the other. He is not concerned with the mass media of the twentieth century, with television and its influences, with the type of semidetached suburban dwelling that is basically similar in all quarters of these islands; he is not concerned with the flat tones of a standardized language. These great standardizing influences have tended to make all parts of the country similar in outlook and sense of values, for no longer does the countryman look toward his own village or locality for the means of life. Today, the products of the industrial districts are within reach of even the remotest farmhouse in the hills; newspapers and television are constantly encouraging the countryman to buy goods and articles that are exactly the same in all quarters of the globe. The character of community life is becoming so standardized that the various regions of Britian are rapidly losing their identity. Until recent times, every locality in Britain had its own range of agricultural tools—ploughs, shovels, carts, and seed drills; every locality had its own distinctive architecture, its own dialect variation, and its own peculiar brand of social organization, custom, and spiritual culture. It was this variety that gave each region its character and personality. Just as the features of an individual, the complexion, color of hair, accent and voice, and many other elements as well, all add up to give that individual his distinct personality, so too do the features of a region, the cultural landscape, architecture, dialects, and other aspects add up to make that region's personality. Folklife studies seek to trace the personality of the various regions of the world expressed in material culture. In the domestic architecture of Wales, regional variation ranges from the half-timbered cottages of the east borderland and the well-forested valleys of mid-Wales, to the moorland long houses that afforded shelter for man and beast under the same roof, and from the trim, whitewashed, thatched cottages of the Vale of Glamorgan to the mud-walled cottages of Llŷn and the massive stone-walled farmhouses of north Pembrokeshire. Agriculture vehicles varied, from the wheelcar of the Radnorshire forest to the long carts of Pembrokeshire, and from the slide cars of north Carmarthenshire to the elegant, four-wheeled bow wagons of Glamorgan. It is the duty of the folk museum both in its collection and its research to record the personality of local communities. Its collection of material objects should exemplify the ingrained tradition of the region that it serves.

Man's development as a cultural being has been a continuous process, and no arbitrary dateline at the beginning or end of that time scale may be laid down. Such a dateline was recommended in a memorandum prepared by sixteen fellows of the Royal Anthropological Institute in 1949. They presented the case for the establishment of a Museum of English Life and Traditions, which was virtually a folk museum for England.[10] Under the heading "Scope of Proposed Museum," the memorandum states, "Only objects of later date than the accession of Henry VII should be accepted for inclusion in the collections, objects of earlier date being considered to come within the scope of archeology." This amputation of time makes

10. Royal Anthropological Institute. *A Scheme for the Development of a Museum of English Life and Traditions* (London, 1949) , p. 5.

little sense when one considers that the origin of most cultural elements dates back long before 1485.

Take the wheel. At a very early date, spoked wheels replaced disk wheels on certain types of vehicles, and even in the second century B.C., a Chinese document describes in detail the techniques of constructing a multispoke wheel.[11] This technique differs only very slightly from that adopted by wheelwrights in modern Britain. Already in Iron Age times the inhabitants of the British Isles were conversant with all the techniques of wheelwrighting, which were to remain basically unchanged for the next two thousand years. Are we to disregard these early developments, or is it our duty to trace the wheelwrights' art only from the last quarter of the fifteenth century, a period when the techniques of wheelwrighting had reached the lowest ebb of degeneration?[12] It may be stated that since human development is a continuous process, folklife collections cannot be limited to post-medieval material. As R. H. Buchanan points out with reference to Ireland, ". . . one may still see implements such as the gowlgob or the graffan which may well have been familiar to our neolithic ancestors; their continued use makes it impractical for us to confine our view within any fixed chronological limits."[13] Eighteenth- and nineteenth-century material often cannot be understood without reference to its medieval and even prehistoric antecedents. Conversely, much of the material the archeologist excavates can be interpreted only when compared with its post-medieval counterpart. "It is only through the known we can comprehend the unknown, only by a study of the present we can understand the past," says R. B. Dixon, "and archeological investigations must be largely barren if pursued in isolation and independent of ethnology.[14]

At the other extreme, some scholars insist that a museum concerned with collecting folklife objects should not consider material made after 1900. Others give the beginning of the so-called Industrial Revolution as the end of the ethnographer's period. This limitation of the subject to a preindustrial era makes very little sense in the face of the persistence of ancient traditions, already discussed. After all, a student of folklife is concerned with man himself and seeks objective knowledge of the material associated with his everyday life. To do this he can never ignore present-day phenomena. "History never ceases to be made; we are never at the end of time, but always

11. J. Needham and R. A. Salaman, "The Wheelwright's Art in Ancient China" (Ms., 1957).

12. J. G. Jenkins, *The English Farm Wagon* (Reading, 1961), pp. 22–32.

13. R. H. Buchanan, "Geography and Folklife," *Folklife* 1 (1963): 10.

14. R. B. Dixon, "Some Aspects of North American Archeology," *American Anthropologist n.s.* 15 (1913): 565.

II–7–3. A long house dating from the sixteenth century, as restored at the Welsh Folk Museum.

in the middle of it. With every economic, social or industrial change, there goes a way of life; a whole world of habit, incident, thought and terminology, the memory and savour of which can be preserved only if recovered from the lips of those who lived in it and through it."[15] The student of folklife, therefore, depends not on documented and excavated evidence alone, but on oral tradition, on the social customs, on the dialects and terminology that have persisted to this day, unswamped as yet by the great standardizing influences of the twentieth century.

It has been said that a museum's task is threefold: collection, preservation, and presentation. Collection consists of far more than the haphazard assembling of objects. Preservation consists of far more than the immersing of wooden objects in a woodworm killer and rusty iron in acid. Presentation too consists of something far beyond arranging a shop window display in an immaculate glass case. In addition, a fourth task, that of study and research, is essential in a folk museum. This task must be carried out continuously by the curator, for a collection of three-dimensional objects is valueless unless the curator is willing to search for an intimate knowledge of the background to his collections. Objects collected by a museum on their own may be trivialities, but if the whole background to these objects —social, economic, natural and geographical—is studied, then those objects may begin to have some significance. For example, Higgs cites the case of a handful of "small pebbles used by a shepherd in Baxhall for counting sheep."[16] Any museum curator would be right to regard them with profound suspicion, and sooner or later they would be quietly disposed of. Supposing, however, that the person who collected them had been given them by a shepherd at the end of a counting and had taken the time and trouble to find out and record the whole story as it is found in Ewart Evans's classic of Suffolk life. The unimportant-looking pebbles would then have far greater significance when it is known that in Suffolk sheep were counted by the score. When a shepherd was counting his sheep, he placed a hurdle so that only two sheep could run through at the same time. As each pair went through, he would say to himself "Yew and yar partner, yew and yar partner" ten times over. At the end of each ten he would drop a tally stone in his pocket, and the number of stones at the end represented the number of score of sheep.[17] Far too often it was be-

15. *Libraries, Museums and Art Galleries: A Report of the Advisory Council on Education in Scotland* (1957), p. 90.

16. Higgs, *Folk Life Collection*, p. 37.

17. George Ewart Evans, *Ask the Fellows Who Cut the Hay* (London: Faber and Faber, 1956), pp. 51–52.

lieved that once an object made its appearance behind glass in a museum gallery, that that was the end of the story. It should not be the end, it may be suggested, but the beginning. In a folk collection the objects exhibited are only a part of the community's life, be it a contemporary society or one of a few thousand years ago.

Collecting is one of the main functions of a folk museum, and great care has to be taken in the choice and selection of material to be collected. No museum, however large it may be, can ever hope to collect all the material that should be preserved, and the curator must be trained to make a value judgment of what is significant. Again this cannot be done without a great deal of basic research and fieldwork, and ideally a detailed survey of the region that the museum serves should be made before a single object is collected. In establishing an open-air museum, for example, before a single stone is transported, the curator should know exactly what type of house or building is required, of what date, from what district, and how that house fits into the over-all plan for the museum. The early nineteenth-century cottage from Caernarvonshire at the Welsh Folk Museum has few architectural merits; it is plain and unornamented, but the cottage is typical of the quarrying district of north Wales. There may have been better houses in the district; there may have been older ones displaying more sophisticated taste and architectural design. But the function of an open-air museum is not to collect the unusual but to emphasize the typical in an attempt to preserve a picture of the life of a nation or region in miniature. In designing a folk museum, therefore, it is essential to choose very carefully the example that should be presented; this can only be done after a full-scale survey of the region has been carried out.

In the field of agrarian tools and implements, for example, no museum can ever hope to collect more than a tiny proportion of the devices that the inventive ability of man has designed over the centuries in order to ease his labors and increase the efficiency of his farm. This process of adoption has gone on from the dawn of civilization to the present day, and the curator is faced with the well-nigh-impossible task of selecting and preserving a small proportion of these tools and implements. Patent office records show that between 1650 and 1850 there were patented 203 root pulpers, 278 grain screens, 770 threshing machines, 1,020 ploughs, and 1,125 reaping machines. In addition, there must have been thousands of implements, covering all farm processes from milking cattle to winnowing grain and from crushing clods to bird-scaring, that were never patented. Indeed, it is safe to say that only a tiny proportion of the implements in use in the countryside were ever patented.

There are a large number of things that a museum cannot collect, due to their size or for some other reason. Buildings and workshops worthy of preservation should be kept *in situ*.

A museum also has its duty to the general public; it must exhibit its collections. The primary purpose of a folk museum is not to show things that are unique; neither is it to show gems of architectural history, although such features as the evolution of building techniques and the history of technology may be illustrated in the exhibit of a folk museum. We are not dealing with unique curios of great intrinsic value but with buildings, domestic furniture and equipment, craft tools and agricultural equipment, and objects that are often valueless if removed from the people that used them.

The whole concept of a folk museum is to take the visitor out of his present-day environment and straight to the people that lived in some bygone age. If the purpose of a folk museum is to create a picture of national or regional personality, if the re-erected buildings are to have the atmosphere and character of the original, then there are two things that should not be done. First, no labels at all should be visible in a re-erected building and, ideally, there should be no barriers, ropes, or plate glass to prevent visitors from entering certain parts of the house. Once those are added, the visitor is immediately conscious that he is looking at a piece of museum technique, and by no stretch of the imagination can he picture the inhabitants of the house that has been so carefully prepared to capture his imagination. The visitor then cannot go straight to the people that lived there, to learn of their way of life, their taste, and their work. After all, that is the sole purpose of the re-erection. Second, there should be no explanatory display case of any kind in a re-erected building. The kind of exhibition that explains techniques, distribution, and evolution should be limited to a formal museum gallery and should not appear in a re-erected building.

One of the main duties of a museum is to give the public a new awareness of things previously taken for granted. They may be stimulated to search further for knowledge, to realize that they inherit a long, complex tradition. A museum must never neglect to bridge the gap between past and present, between the ordinary and the extraordinary. To a museum official a collection of Iron Age tools or of medieval pottery may be significant, but what do they mean to the ordinary visitor? Far too often, in museum work the contemporary scene is neglected; but this may be the only point of contact between curator and visitor. A collection of Iron Age turned ware is far more significant when it is realized that the products of over two thousand years ago are not dissimilar to those produced by turners' shops in recent years. Roman tools become far more

II–7–4. A Caernarvonshire cottage of 1762 before removal to the Welsh Folk Museum.

meaningful when compared with those of modern times. In research work, too, the contemporary scene must not be neglected, for ancient traditions and methods may still persist in the most unexpected places. No European community is totally unaffected in part or in whole by industrialization, but in all those communities evidence of the persistence of traditional life has remained to this day. We have to concern ourselves with that pattern, where it is strong and where it is weak. Quite often, highly industrialized communities still possess their living traditional culture, and folklife studies are not limited to rural communities. Donald McKelvie carried out a detailed survey of living traditions in modern Bradford and notes ". . . once we penetrate below the surface of life in a modern city, into the houses of its poor, into its markets and cheap eating houses and workmen's hostels, the traditions we may previously have thought of as surviving only in isolated areas beyond the spoiling influence of our cities, do indeed and perhaps in new forms live on vigorously in the heart of our cities."[18] In many cases, the only places where prestandardized material and customs persist are in those highly industrialized and urbanized societies that are seemingly of no interest to the student of folklife. In the field of traditional crafts and industries, coopering is limited to industrial, urban districts; clogmaking persists in such places as Huddersfield and Halifax, tanning in Warrington and Leeds, and chair-making in High Wycombe. We can never ignore the present day in our search for the history of man.

The pioneers of the folk movement were the Swedes, and all scholars in the field of folklife study owe much to Scandinavia in general and Sweden in particular.[19] As far back as 1630, King Gustav II gave his approval to the appointment of a Royal Custodian of Antiquities, while later in the century Olaf Rudbeck of the University of Uppsala attempted to show the greatness of Sweden by writing a number of works in which he attempted to prove that the sources of an European culture were to be found in the north. The imperialistic period in Swedish history was followed by eighteenth-century rationalism, when Sweden's natural, historical, and industrial resources were investigated in some detail. The large number of houses built at this time give an excellent picture of eighteenth-century Sweden. After the period of rationalism came a century of romanticism expressing itself in a national movement aimed at strengthening Swedish culture. Music and poetry drew the attention of the public toward the history and characteristics of the Swedish

18. Donald McKelvie, "Aspects of Oral Tradition and Belief in an Industrial Region," *Folk Life* 1 (1963) : 77–96.

19. A great deal of the following information has been extracted from Matt Rehnberg, *The Nordiska Museet and Skansen* (1957), p. 9 *et seq.*

people. Local historical societies turned their attention to investigating and preserving local antiquities. These societies were the background to the foundation of local or provincial archeological museums, the earliest of which was founded in 1867. By 1870 interest in Swedish dialect had increased phenomenally and special societies had been organized in the university for the investigation of local languages and oral traditions. A young ex-Army officer and language reader, Artur Hazelius (1833–1901), became interested in the varieties of spoken Swedish and in Swedish history and began collecting material objects to illustrate the life and culture of his people. As a result of his work he opened the Nordiska Museet in Stockholm in 1873. In 1880 work commenced on the vast building that now houses the collection. But Hazelius soon realized that such a collection exhibited between the four walls of a museum was inadequate, and he looked upon the Northern Museum as only a part of the scheme. In 1891 the second part, known as Skansen, was opened. Artur Hazelius, scholar and patriot, laid the basis of the folk museum, the pattern of which has been copied in other countries throughout the world.

The museum consists of two parts. First, there is a building for the systematic display of the materials of life and culture, where the emphasis is on the evolution and distribution of types, the development of styles, and other characteristics. Second, the folk museum contains an open-air section where dwelling houses, craft workshops, and public buildings that reflect traditional life are re-erected. The Nordiska Museet, with its systematic displays, and Skansen, created in rolling park land near Stockholm, remain a permanent memorial to Hazelius's vision.

Sweden now has eight hundred and more folk museums, ranging from small local museums consisting perhaps of a single farmhouse or workshop to the large Kulturen ar Lund, which is primarily a town museum located on four acres in the heart of that ancient city.

Sweden's example as a pioneer of folk museums was soon followed by other Scandinavian nations. In addition to numerous local or regional museums in Norway, for instance, there are two national collections, the Norsk Museum Bygdøy near Oslo and the famous Sandvig collection at Lillehammer, established as early as 1887. Writing of the establishment of this outstanding museum, the current guide to the museum says:

One summer day in 1887 a young man came driving into Lillehammer. He came from the north of the valley and there he sat as proud as a monarch on a sack of hay atop a load of old rubbish. The young man was Anders Sandvig, a dentist, 25 years old, home from one of his travels in Gudbrand Valley, where twice a year he practised at the various farms and posting stations. In this way the Scandinavian collections were founded. After collecting a vast amount of material, including six houses, which were re-erected in his garden, Sandvig finally managed to persuade the town authorities of Lillehammer to purchase his collections and Maihaugen [May Hill] was chosen as the site of the new museum which was opened in 1904. "As I see it," said Sandvig, "Maihaugen when complete is to be a collection of homes, into which one can enter and go straight to the people that lived there, thus learning to know their way of life, their tastes and their work: the fashioning and furnishings of a home depict the people themselves."

Anders Sandvig, the Norwegian pioneer, lived to see his dream come true, for Maihaugen with its farmsteads, churches, craft workshops, and cottages built on a hillside at Lillehammer is a monument to the industry and vision of the country dentist.

In Denmark, Frilandsmuseet near Copenhagen was founded in 1901 and occupies a site of one hundred acres. "We have tried," Kai Uldall, the late director of Frilandsmuseet, wrote in a letter, "to divide the museum up into areas of natural Danish landscape, where necessary adjusting the cover of the land to suit the district as a background to the houses . . . ." The buildings are erected in geographical order, so that a trip through the park is in the nature of a short trip through Denmark. Frilandsmuseet is primarily a rural museum. By contrast, Den Gamle By (the Old Town) at Aarhus is a town museum, founded in 1909, which has within its boundaries merchants' mansions, artisans' cottages, craft workshops, a school, a burgomaster's residence, and even a brewery. Like Sweden and Norway, Denmark also possesses numerous local folk museums such as the Fünen county museum and the Tonder county museum as well as specialized museums such as the Landbrigmuseet of Agriculture at Copenhagen and the Hans Anderson Museum at Odense. By 1920 many other European nations had established a network of local, regional, and national folk museums, and some, like the Finnish museums and those of the Netherlands, were of outstanding quality.

In Great Britain, the folk museum movement took root slowly. Although Ulster and Wales have their large and rapidly developing folk museums, neither England, Scotland, nor Ireland possess national institutions concerned with folk life. Nevertheless, a certain amount of progress has been made, either through the work of private individuals or municipal authorities.

Of the private museums, the outstanding example is the Highland Folk Museum at Kingussie in Scotland, founded by Isabel Grant in 1936. The museum was almost completely financed by Dr. Grant, who re-erected three cottages and a mill on three acres of land. In 1955, the museum was taken over and administered by three Scottish universities, but it has made few developments in recent years. In Scotland there are a number of small local folk museums such as the Glenesk Folk Museum and the Angus Folk Museum, which are the result of the energies of dedicated local people, while the National Museum of Antiquities of Scotland devotes its folklife section to the collecting of material and information relating to Scottish life. There is, however, no full-scale national folk museum in Scotland.

Another pioneer of the folk museum movement in Britain was J. L. Kirk of Pickering, Yorkshire, a noted antiquary who was an assiduous collector of material. Unfortunately, he made few attempts to document his vast collections, and when he died a great deal of the information on the history of the material he collected was lost. In 1935 the City of York obtained the Kirk collection as the basis for its Castle Museum. This is one of the most entertaining showplaces in Britain, with re-erected streets, period rooms, and craft workshops presented to the public in a most attractive manner. Much of the collection is undocumented, and the museum can add little to the scientific knowledge on the development of man in the region that the museum serves.

Museums financed by local authorities, which set out to illustrate the way of life of a city or region, vary tremendously in size and quality. Many do not employ folklife specialists, and folklife material is usually relegated to a room or even a case or two of "local bygones." In such museums, the curators consider the specimen rather than the community that produced those specimens. There are a number of specialized local folk museums such as Shibden Hall in Halifax, Kirkstall Abbey in Leeds, the Newarke houses in Leicester, Bishop Hooper's lodging in Gloucester, and Blaise Castle in Bristol that are concerned with local folklife. The latest development in the field has been the establishment of the open-air museum for the north of England near the city of Durham, which will be mainly concerned with the creation of an industrial folk museum, representing the ingrained tradition of that area.

The Welsh Folk Museum at Saint Fagans, near Cardiff, with its Elizabethan mansion, farmhouses, chapel, cottages, tannery, woollen mill, toll gate house, cockpit, and working craftsmen, is the oldest of the national folk museums. It combines the functions of a remarkable tourist attraction, representing the traditions of the Welsh nation, and that of a research institute, concerned with studying all aspects of Welsh linguistics, folktales, musicology, and material culture. The Ulster Folk Museum at Holyrood, near Belfast, has grown rapidly within the last ten years and contains a manor house, cottages, farmhouses, and mill, re-erected in beautiful surroundings on the south shore of Belfast Lough. In England no progress has been made with the long-overdue establishment of a national folk collection, although the Museum of English Rural Life at the University of Reading has an extensive collection of material relating to agriculture, rural crafts, and domestic life. There are no plans at Reading to develop an open-air museum, and the collection is of necessity a research collection.

Bibliography and Selected Readings

Allen, D. "Folk Museum at Home and Abroad." *Proceedings of the Scottish Anthropological and Folklore Society* 5 (1956) : 91–121. Briefly describes folk museums in Great Britain, Scandinavia, and North America. Illustrated with photographs.

Evans, E. Estyn. "Folklife Studies in Northern Ireland." *Journal of the Folklore Institute* 2 (1965) : 355–63. The Ulster Folk Museum.

Fenton, Alexander. "Material Culture as an Aid to Local History Studies in Scotland." *Journal of the Folklore Institute* 2 (1965) : 326–39.

Jenkins, J. Geraint, ed. *Studies in Folk Life. Essays in Honour of Iorwerth C. Peate.* London: Routledge and Kegan Paul, 1969. A Festschrift to the longtime curator of the Welsh Folk Museum, in which twenty British and European material culture specialists write on the distribution, history, and ethnology of such topics as brass manufacturing, peat-cutting, turf and sod houses, and plough teams. Photographs and text figures.

Peate, Iorwerth. "The Welsh Folk Museum." *Journal of the Folklore Institute* 2 (1965) : 314–16.

Rasmussen, H., ed. *Dansk Folkemuseum and Frilandmuseet, History and Activities.* Copenhagen: Gyldendal, 1966. Articles by curators and scholars on the staff of these two major institutions devoted to Danish folklife give a conspectus of their operations and museum techniques.

Winchester, A. *The Antiques Treasury of Furniture and Other Decorative Arts at Winterthur, Williamsburg, Sturbridge, Ford Museum, Cooperstown, Deerfield, and Shelburne.* New York: Dutton, 1959. A lavishly illustrated pictorial survey of those museums in the United States that most closely approximate the folk museums of Scandinavia, namely, Old Sturbridge Village and the Farmers' Museum, as well as more distantly related museums.

8 THE CULTURAL GEOGRAPHER AND FOLKLIFE RESEARCH
E. Estyn Evans

Folklife study can be undertaken wherever there are folk, and its field is therefore *ecumene*, the occupied earth. By definition, this is also the field of cultural geography, and since both are concerned with certain aspects of human culture the differences between the two disciplines lie not so much in content as in approach. Folklife, to be sure, is concerned only with the traditional elements of culture, but since folk-tradition is not systematic, folklife studies cannot dispense with the evidence to be gleaned from other lines of study. Nor, as we shall see, can the cultural geographer afford to neglect the folk elements in regional cultures. It is suggested that cooperation between the two disciplines would enrich them both. What then is the approach of cultural geography; and how, it may be asked, does it fit into the general scheme of geographical studies?

Throughout Europe, and at least in the younger universities of North America, especially in the large state universities, geography is well established as an academic discipline, but the emphasis has been mainly on physical and urban economic geography, which pose more obvious problems than cultural geography and bring more immediate rewards in the contemporary world. Yet the larger problem of the interrelations between the total way of life and the environment has been a central theme in geography since the subject emerged as the mother of sciences in classical Ionia. Arab writers and Renaissance scholars turned their attention to this problem, but it was not until the nineteenth century that general laws, based on the accumulated data derived from world-wide explorations, could be formulated. It was a French geographer, P. Vidal de la Blache, reacting against the determinism of the German scholar Friedrich Ratzel, who first put forward what is still the most acceptable view of the man-habitat relationship. He envisaged human societies not as the puppets of their environments, blindly submitting to the forces of nature, but as partners in a joint enterprise, molding environments in their own image. He referred to the organized complex of techniques and customs that distinguish one human group or society from another as the *genre de vie*. For the cultural geographer the *genre de vie*—hardly to be translated by the hackneyed "way of life"—is an index of the extent to which the possibilities offered by any environment are utilized.

For most parts of the world the concept of natural environment is an abstraction. We have to deal with cultural landscapes, envisaged as the product of human effort and aspirations modifying and adapting to, but not dictated by, particular environments. The man-made features of a landscape, whether nomad's tent or skyscraper, forest trail or parkway, totem pole or temple, are cultural phenomena, and they are proper objects of study for ethnographers, architectural historians, engineers, and so on, but if we consider them as components of landscape we are practicing cultural geography. This concern with areal differentiation leads to the detailed study of small regions; and this is one of the first points of contact between the geographer and the student of folklife. The geographer's purpose is to portray the personality of regions and to try to explain how and why one region differs from another in its *genre de vie*. For the folklorist, in Europe anyhow, the driving force has often been devotion to a particular region, language, or national group: one may instance the inspired efforts of the Folklore Commission of the Irish Republic or of many of the national groups that emerged in Europe after the 1914–18 war. Both for the geographer and the folklorist there is the added stimulus provided by the feasibility, in a small area of the earth's surface, of personal observation, collection, and fieldwork. If this involvement carries with it the dangers of parochialism or a narrow nationalism, the comparative method of the geographer, who wants to know why one region differs from another, is a useful corrective. The student of folklife, too, seeking cultural origins, is forced to take into account other regions and other times. In any event there need be no contradiction between intensive research on a local scale and a universal outlook: international reputations can be built on studies of real situations in local environments.

All cultural landscapes are the product of time. Even for the lands of old civilization and long-recorded history in the sub-tropical belts of the world, the prehistoric ages are far longer than the historic. For large parts of the world, recorded history is no more than a few centuries old at most. Even so, it rarely chronicles the folkways of mankind. "History", wrote J. H. Fabre, "celebrates the battle-fields whereon we meet our death, but scorns to speak of the ploughed fields whereby we thrive: it knows the names of the king's bastards, but cannot tell us the origin of wheat."[1] Yet, century after century, men who left no documents behind them wrote their runes on the land in ploughed furrows and embossed it with the mounds that mark their burials (barrows) and their settlements (tells). An Irish triad lists the track of a spade in the ground as one of three things that last forever. Prehistoric remains, of course, can be explored by archeological methods, but until recently prehistorians have been more concerned with the relics of priests and kings than with folk-cultural remains. And only indirectly can excavated material throw light on the nonmaterial aspects of folk culture.

The geographer, then, seeking to interpret the cultural landscape, readily turns to ethnographic material and folklore for assistance in identifying the distinctive artifacts and beliefs that have left their mark on the landscape. Ideally, he studies these survivals in the field, measuring them against observed environmental realities. Folklore and folk music no less than material culture are ecologically linked in many intimate ways with the various regions of the earth. Of course there are international folktales and mythological themes, just as certain artifacts have a world-wide distribution, but even here some local color is often imparted by regional adaptation. Martha Wolfenstein has shown how the version of Jack and the Beanstalk that is told in North Carolina takes on a regional flavor and reveals a suppression of magical elements and a characteristic American emphasis on masculine prowess and practical accomplishments.[2] To take a more familiar example, the hell that Christianity borrowed from the nomads of the Arabian desert was a burning torment, but in the mythology of the Scandinavian northlands it was a frozen waste. Of course the Scandinavian hell changed its temperature with the coming of Christi-

1. J. H. Fabre, *The Wonders of Instinct* (London, 1918) , p. 291.
2. Martha Wolfenstein, "Jack and the Beanstalk: An American Version," in *Childhood in Contemporary Culture,* edited by Margaret Mead and Martha Wolfenstein (Chicago, 1955) .

anity, but in other ways the pagan traditions left their mark on the customs of Christendom. Thus the historic taboo on the eating of horseflesh in northern Europe probably reflects a reaction to its use in sacrificial feasts in pre-Christian times. Pagan deities, on the other hand, seem to have been translated directly into local saints. Cultural borrowings and adjustments in historic and prehistoric times are factors of which the cultural geographer must take account. His primary concern, however, is not with the processes of diffusion but with the accommodation of its products to regional environments.

To illustrate our theme, we may consider folk architecture in the form of its most universal expression, the house. Vidal de la Blache described the traditional house as one of the faithful signs of the mentality of the inhabitants,[3] embodying the spirit of a region in the values attached to it as well as in its materials and methods of construction. Some societies are house-proud, so that the house becomes a prestige-symbol, while others attach little importance to the house but may, like the French people, lavish care on cooking and attach great value to food. These varying cultural values can often be related to environmental and economic opportunities. It is clear that environment colors house construction, for example, through the necessary use, until quite recent times, of local building materials because of the limitations of means of transporting heavy materials. The local climate, too, influences the structure of the house, its ability to cope with heavy rains, snow, or high winds. The traditional house tends to acquire prestige in proportion to its size and durability, for example where stone or long-lasting varieties of massive timbers such as oak and cedar are used in its construction. The great longhouses of the Nootka of British Columbia would hardly be conceivable without the availability of gigantic, straight-grained cedars, and the associated culture-traits of lavish display and conspicuous waste would be unthinkable without the abundance of nature. If it were not leading us out of the field of folk culture, we might discuss the not-dissimilar values of the mass-producing industrialized societies of North America.

Very different are the dwellings of the pastoral nomad in the steppes of the Old World. The tent of skin, cloth, or felt must be portable and of restricted size, and it is the nomad's immemorial philosophy not to lay up treasure on earth. His wealth is in his sons and other livestock, and in portable trinkets. The tent, with its framework of light radial supports, tends to be circular in ground plan, and this is an advantage in regions where strong winds blow over open plains. The economical use of the restricted living space is formalized in its well-defined functional and ritual allocation: thus

3. P. Vidal de la Blache, *Principes de géographie humaine* (Paris, 1922), p. 167.

it is customary among the Mongols for the left hand side of the tent to be reserved for women folk. On the other hand, the long straight timbers of the forested regions of the world naturally lead to the erection of rectangular houses by their occupants, whether they live in the Rain Forests, the deciduous woods of the temperate belt, or the coniferous forests of high latitudes, and this shape results in a linear disposition of furnishings and functions. In Europe north of the Alps the rectangular longhouse has been traditional for over 5,000 years, but in prehistoric times some marginal areas such as Ireland also had circular houses—constructed either of stone or of light timbers—and it is interesting to notice that Neolithic grave monuments, which in western Europe were typically built of great stones (megaliths), tend to fall into two groups: round chambers covered by round barrows and rectangular chambers covered by long barrows. It seems very likely that the abodes of the dead that survive as conspicuous features of "Atlantic" cultural landscapes were modeled on the homes of the living, which have almost entirely disappeared.

In the Mediterranean region the stone dwelling house has been characteristic since prehistoric times, the prevailing type, rectangular in plan, having evolved from a timber prototype. In this environment, where forests have long been degraded, the peasant uses stone for many purposes where wood is normally employed, not only for walls but also for roofs. This is related to the prevalence of soft limestone that when freshly quarried can be worked and carved in any direction with cutting tools but that becomes so durable that buildings last for centuries and even millennia. Such was the prestige attaching to the Greek style of temple architecture—a prestige partly deriving from a superb quality of workmanship that has withstood the ravages of time—that public buildings in all parts of the Western world have imitated it; and in New England, for example, Greek Revival houses, reverting to wood and copying functionless details of timber construction that had been petrified for over two and a half millennia, were very fashionable in the early nineteenth century. In nearly all parts of the Mediterranean region, a simple form of the rectangular stone house is found. Yet in certain parts of the region circular stone buildings of more ancient origin, with corbeled, beehive roofs, have persisted, notably the *trulli* of Apulia in southeast Italy. Elsewhere, circular or oval, dry-stone corbeled buildings constructed of fieldstone serve as outhouses and field shelters, or as shepherds' huts as on Mount Ida in Crete. They have the advantage of relative ease of construction, and they continue to be built because they are adequate for their purpose. And, despite the Mediterranean addiction to stone, wherever occupation extends into large stretches of stoneless lowlands, one finds local house-types—admittedly rapidly disappearing under modern conditions—that range from the thatched mud house of the Camargue, with northern gable hipped against the Mistral, to the round and oval reed houses of the Roman Campania, which Erixon has described.[4] In these examples adaptation to environment is clearly demonstrated.

Vernacular building in the British Isles, which has long been a subject of interest to architectural historians and descriptive topographical writers, has in recent years attracted the attention of students of folklife and cultural geographers. Using as criteria such facts as ground plans, elevation, building materials, and forms and methods of roofing, many regional styles can be distinguished. These change slowly through time in response to new fashions and new building materials, but in England and Wales throughout the ages traditional rural houses tend to fall into a distributional pattern comprising three main zones: the Highland Zone in Wales and North England, the lowlands southeast of a line from the Humber to the Isle of Wight, and the intermediate lowlands centered on the English Midlands.[5] In medieval times, for example, when farmhouses were timber-framed for the most part, one finds the cruck-framed house in the Highlands, the box-framed in the southeast, and a mixture in the intermediate zone running from the flanks of the Pennines through the Welsh marches to southwestern England. Not only do the styles intermingle in the middle zone, but hybridization also takes place, and certain novelties in framing techniques can be identified from Lancashire to Wessex. In other aspects of culture, too, the middle zone can be shown to be one of innovation. In a valuable study by Margaret Hodgen of the role of diffusion in British economic history,[6] this zone emerges as one where cross-fertilization led to repeated technological advances in the centuries preceding the Industrial Revolution. Regional environmental factors such as the presence of coal and iron, of water power and good river communications, were also at work at this time, but another factor stressed by Miss Hodgen was social inheritance from a line of innovating forebears who were peasants and part-time craftsmen in areas of marginal agriculture from Yorkshire to Devon.

4. Sigurd Erixon, "Some Primitive Constructions and Types of Lay-out," *Folkliv* 1 (1937) : 124–55.
5. This is a refinement of the division into Highland and Lowland zones first recognized by the geographer Sir H. J. Mackinder, *Britain and the British Seas* (Oxford, 1906) , and developed by the archeologist Sir Cyril Fox, *The Personality of Britain* (Cardiff, 1932) . See June A. Sheppard, "Vernacular Buildings in England and Wales," *Transactions of the Institute of British Geographers* 40 (London, 1966) : 21–37.
6. Margaret T. Hodgen, *Change and History*, Viking Fund Publications in Anthropology, no. 18 (New York, 1952) .

In the late Neolithic and early metal periods, some fifty centuries ago, the southern sector of this middle zone was culturally outstanding. The location of Stonehenge in the area where natural bridges of dry chalk facilitated communication between east and west is significant, and H. J. Fleure pointed out long ago that its "blue stones" (derived from Pembrokeshire) show that its cultural links were partly with the Highland Zone.[7] It may well be concluded, if and when the current, lively discussions between archeologists and astronomers as to the refinements and purposes of Stonehenge are resolved, that this highly sophisticated monument, devised as a means of determining the seasons and perhaps of predicting eclipses, was the product not primarily of an intrusive élite but of hybridization among peasant peoples of high intelligence.

The varieties of timber house construction in western Europe are of interest also to students of North American folk culture. There is a growing interest among ethnographers and geographers in the cultural antecedents of the various European groups who made the Atlantic crossing in the seventeenth and eighteenth century. The forerunners of the Switzer barn, which was to make a striking contribution to the cultural landscape of a belt of country stretching westward from the Delaware through Ohio to Indiana, are not in doubt, but there is less certainty about the derivation of early house-types in the Old West, partly because there seems to have been a good deal of cultural cross-fertilization in southeast Pennsylvania. Distributional studies of the various types of half-timbered construction, however, both in England and in Germany, can be expected to throw light on the precise homelands of various groups of immigrants, concerning which there is little precise documentary information. More attention has been given to the variants of log-house construction in North America and in Europe. In America the interest sprang from a sentimental attachment to the log cabin as a symbol of democracy. Increasingly, students of folklife and cultural geography are taking part in investigations, and important contributions have been made by geographer Fred Kniffen, who pioneered the study of folk housing in Louisiana, and his student, folklorist Henry Glassie.[8] In 1939 Harold R. Shurtleff explored the "log cabin myth," which, since the political campaign of 1840, has associated the log house with the early colonial English settlements.[9] He championed a

7. H. J. Fleure. "Folklore and Culture Contacts," *Bulletin of the John Ryland Library* 23 (1939) : 5.

8. Fred Kniffen, "North American Folk Housing," *Annals of the Association of American Geographers* 55 (1965) : 549–77; Fred Kniffen and Henry Glassie, "Building in Wood in the Eastern United States," *Geographical Review* 56 (1966) : 40–66.

9. H. R. Shurtleff, *The Log Cabin Myth*, edited by S. E. Morison (Cambridge, Mass., 1939) .

Swedish origin for the American log cabin, but Thomas J. Wertenbaker had previously championed a German origin,[10] and since then
its German antecedents have been established, though the American
habit of leaving interstices between the hewn logs finds its nearest
parallel today in Bohemia. The methods of "chinking" the gaps with
mud, stones, or slivers of wood deserve attention: the effect produced
in some parts of the Old West was one of horizontal black-and-white
half-timbering.

It is well known that a major contribution to the backwoods
culture of the Old West was made by the Scotch-Irish who took over
the log cabin from their German neighbors in Pennsylvania and
adapted it to their needs, apparently clinging to it while other settlers
for the most part abandoned it in favor of framed houses. The cruck-
framed house and its derivatives in upland Britain and in northern
Ireland was limited for constructional reasons both as to its width
and its height. The Scotch-Irish had been accustomed in North
Ireland, where the woods had been largely destroyed, to live in houses
of mud or stones—or a mixture of both—with the main room, the
kitchen-living room (often occupying the whole house) measuring
about 15 by 21 feet internally. The house was never more than one
room wide and was single-storied, probably with a half-loft, though
it sometimes had a full loft and was in this case a story and a half
high. Over much of the country it was the custom to have two doors,
facing each other about halfway along the front and back, and the
doors were invariably provided with additional half-doors. The
chimney, attached to the inside of the gable wall, was provided with
a canopy or brace (breast) of mud and wattle. The open hearth was
the focus of the house, and the space in front of it was kept clear of
furniture, which was lined along the walls. This living room was
frequently also the bedroom—at least of the farmer and his wife—
and at night it would sometimes shelter some of the livestock as well.
Cattle were the mainstay of the farm, and the crops were oats, some
barley, flax, and potatoes. The cattle were fed for part of the year
on common, free-range grazing.[11]

The Scotch-Irish, exchanging their stony fields for the forests of
Pennsylvania, found that they could reproduce most of the features
of their old homes by adopting and adapting the German log house.
Their first shelters were rough log cabins or pole-shacks made of un-
trimmed logs and roughly thatched, but they were replaced by
shingled houses of hewn hardwood logs, with interstices filled with

10. Thomas J. Wertenbaker, *The Founding of American Civilization: The Middle Colonies* (New York, 1938), p. 303.
11. E. E. Evans, *Irish Folk Ways* (London, 1957), chaps. 3–5.

more familiar materials, stone and clay. There is to my mind a strong Scotch-Irish flavor about the statement quoted from Tennessee, that "the man who can make mud which will stick between the logs even if thrown from a distance is as proud as the man who is an expert with the broadaxe."[12] Moreover, the mud chinking, like the Irish house, was often limewashed. The type of log house that Henry Glassie believes to have been especially associated with the Scotch-Irish was a one-and-a-half storied building measuring internally about 16 by 22 feet. It had a dry-stone gable chimney, originally often of mud and wattle (cats-and-clay), but for safety's sake it was built externally. It had two opposite doors and evidently the half-door was known, though it is not clear from descriptions whether it was of Irish type.[13] This type of house is found particularly along the eastern face of the Alleghanies, in the Blue Ridge country and in Kentucky. In all log houses the size of the log "pen"—the constructional unit—was of course limited by the size of the timbers and the problem of handling them, but when it is said that some log houses were forty feet long and that the log house adopted by the English settlers moving in from tidewater tended to be about sixteen feet square, it will be realized that cultural antecedents must be partly responsible for the various types of log houses in North America. Another distinguishing feature of the Scotch-Irish log house was the particular variety of corner fastening adopted. This was the half-dovetail, a simplified modification of the full dovetail cornering, which is all but confined to southeastern Pennsylvania. "Half-dovetail corner timbering is found on houses and all other buildings commonly from the north-eastern Alleghanies of West Virginia, along the North Carolina-Tennessee Blue Ridge and through the Tennessee Valley, from where it spread into the Deep South, into the upland areas of Arkansas and Missouri, and northward through Kentucky into southern Ohio, Indiana and Illinois."[14]

Not only did the log house provide the large living room that served to meet nearly all the family's needs, but it was furnished with familiar gear: wall-shelves, corner cupboards, folding tables, and the simple apparatus of open-hearth cooking—crane, pot-hooks, iron pots, flesh-fork, frying pan, and griddle. The log house, moreover, was associated with a simple economy in which, as in Ulster, the free-

12. Henry H. Glassie, "Southern Mountain Houses: A Study in American Folk Culture," (M.A. thesis, State College of New York at Oneonta, 1965), p. 73. See also the same author's *Pattern in the Material Folk Culture of the Eastern United States* (Philadelphia, 1969).

13. W. F. Dunaway, *The Scotch-Irish of Colonial Pennsylvania* (Chapel Hill, 1944), p. 185.

14. Glassie, "Southern Mountain Houses," p. 51.

range grazing of cattle was supplemented by a spring-sown cereal, in this case Indian corn, which like the Irish corn (oats) was food for man and beast. Habits of cooking and eating and drinking suffered little change. The conditions of frontier life also favored the survival of superstitions, charms, and herbal cures. The American pioneer, like the peasant of the Old World Atlantic fringe, had few material resources and expressed his emotional needs in media requiring little equipment beyond personal gifts such as dexterity of voice and hand, in song and oratory and the music of the fiddle. In such arts all folk are potentially equal, one man is likely to be as good as the next, and a democratic spirit is in the air.

So far we have been concerned with traditional house-types as distinctive elements in cultural landscapes, without reference to the patterns of settlement. In one region the farmhouses may be scattered, in others they are grouped in nucleations, such as hamlets and villages, which may vary in size and form. The study of these variations, which is the subject of a branch of cultural geography known as settlement geography, is as relevant to folklife studies as it is to cultural geography, for they directly affect living habits and attitudes to the land. At first sight there might seem to be compelling environmental controls governing patterns of rural settlement. For example, it has been argued that limited sources of water, as in the Mediterranean lands, forced man to congregate around springs. But in other areas where water is just as scarce, scattered settlement prevails, and conversely nucleation is frequently found where there is an abundant and well-distributed water supply. Clearly we cannot speak of direct environmental control of settlement patterns. Nor does the ethnic factor invoked by August Meitzen offer a satisfactory alternative explanation.[15] European regions that he described as having inherited the Celtic Einzelhof (single-farm) system can be shown to have had nucleated hamlets until quite recent times. But Meitzen also related types of settlement to methods of land use and field-systems, and this has proved to be a more valuable approach. The environment operates through the economy that its topography and soil will support, but the economy may vary according to the cultural level and technological equipment of the users. A system of land-use and settlement, once it is established in a region, will tend to override minor differences in the physical environment to give rise to a characteristic cultural landscape. Thus the single farms of Ireland occur even in areas of fissured limestone where water for man and beast has to be carried. The two extremes of peasant land-use, livestock husbandry on the one hand and intensive polyculture on the other, involve con-

15. August Meitzen, *Siedelung und Agrarwesen* (Berlin, 1895) .

stant attention on the spot to animals or crops, and both tend to be associated with the single farm. On the other hand, the compact village implies, in origin, some form of communal enterprise devoted to a limited range of staple crops. The nucleated hamlet or village appears to be the settlement norm among food-producing communities the world over. In most of Europe north of the Alps, the classic type was the three-field village, adapted to areas of brown forest soil fertile enough for two of the three open-fields to be kept under rotating crops, one spring-sown, another autumn-sown, while the third was fallow. On *a priori* grounds we should expect nucleation to be older than the isolated settlement: indeed, the evidence from surviving hunters and gatherers shows that living and squatting in "bands" goes back to that cultural stage. We know also that, in the Scandinavian countries for example, the predominant single farms have resulted from the deliberate break-up of historic village communities in recent centuries, though as a settlement form the Einzelhof can be traced back archeologically to the pre-Roman Iron Age, and, with derivative hamlets produced by subdivision, has remained typical of the poorer parts of the northlands and of the Atlantic fringes of Europe. The small open-fields or in-fields of these hamlets could be kept in permanent production because of the plentiful supply of fertilizers from livestock and from the seashore. In general, peasant arts and crafts are more richly developed in the agricultural villages than in the more pastoral single farms and hamlets. For them the small two-wheeled cart suffices, whereas the elaborate four-wheeled wagon has been characteristic of the village system. Similarly, the corpus of folklore in each region, serving as a bolster to established ways and as an educative device, is a reflection of the cultural landscape. In the Mediterranean lands, where strongly nucleated settlements have been characteristic since prehistoric times, communities are attached to their localities, and many customs and beliefs are related to the rivalries between neighboring communities. Along the Atlantic fringe, on the other hand, the rivalries and attendant beliefs have to do with kin-groups.

A more complex environment is found in the Alpine belt of Europe, where the mountain topography provides a great range of local climates and emphasizes seasonal changes, and where transhumance enriches the solid contributions of the permanent settlements—in good-quality woodwork and husbandry—with the skills and lore of the pastoral life. Long summer days spent in the isolation of the high pastures help to conserve traditional ways and support the crafts of spinning, weaving, and embroidery. Long winters in the valley homes are occupied with wood carving and related skills in metalwork that are as old as the prehistoric Swiss lake dwellings. Whereas in Switzerland the pastoral life revolves around the milk cow, in the southern Carpathians, where movement over greater distances is required, sheep support a different range of folk arts, illustrated in the decorated sheepskin coat. In both environments, isolation in mountain refuges has enabled old languages, dialects, and a wealth of folklore to survive.

In the nonmaterial aspects of folklife such as traditional beliefs, superstitions, proverbs, and weather lore, while there is much that relates to regional environments, there are also, leaving aside the universals, transmitted elements that can be studied by mapping their geographical distribution. Here the geographer is equipped to make a special contribution to ethnography through his professional interest in cartographic techniques. While some students have been reluctant to use distribution maps because of the risk of drawing erroneous conclusions from incomplete data, others, notably adherents of the hyperdiffusionist school, have not been so inhibited. Erroneous conclusions have been reached by the innocent use (or preached by the conscious abuse) of symbols so grossly exaggerated in size that, on a small-scale map, the vast distance between, let us say, Easter Island and the coast of South America is almost annihilated by a couple of symbols, and the incautious reader concludes that prehistoric contact between them (across more than two thousand miles of ocean) is thereby proven. On a regional scale the distribution of elements of folklife, including folklore, has been most fully mapped in parts of Europe, notably in the Swiss Volkskunde Atlas.

Probably the element of folklore that most closely reflects direct regional observation and experience is weather lore, and here the geographer (qua climatologist) is trained to assist in interpretation. Of course there are many frankly superstitious prognostications based on sympathetic magic such as bonfires, bell-ringing, or the symbolism of numbers, but others enshrine the orally-transmitted experience of ancestral generations. If they do not accord with regional weather records, it is sometimes because they are of great antiquity and relate to older climates and calendars. Indeed, the popular protest against the calendar reform of 1583 was largely because of the high esteem accorded to weather sayings and the well-founded fears that they would lose their value.[16] In general, it may be assumed that those prognostications that persist are the ones that have proved useful. The prediction of a fine day from a red sunset is said to be as popular in Japan as it is in Britain.

16. K. Sinnhuber, "On the Relations of Folklore and Geography," *Folk-Lore* 68 (1957) : 385.

We have said that the accommodation to regional environments of diffused ideas and skills is a matter of interest to the cultural geographer. The adjustment is a two-way process, provided the gap between the two cultures is not excessive. Living as we do in a world of increasing contacts, we tend to regard rapid cultural change as a phenomenon of industrial civilization, forgetting that cultural contacts in the past have often brought about more fundamental changes. Languages, for example, may change fairly quickly if they do not possess written records and institutional formulas, or at least are not consecrated in the memorable phrases of heroic epics.[17] Such phases of cultural change are likely to be reflected in folklore, and they may also result in innovations in material culture, thanks to the interpenetration of native and intrusive ideas. But the deep-rooted elements of native culture are surprisingly tenacious: their mysteries impress themselves on newcomers who will, in adopting them, give them new interpretations.

We may illustrate the antiquity and vitality of indigenous cultural elements by reference to some Irish folk practices. Many customs associated with water, fire, stones, and with native trees, flowers, and shrubs seem to have originated with the clearing and burning of the forests for agriculture and the associated erection of megalithic tombs in the third millennium B.C. It has been shown by the study of fossil-pollens preserved in the bogs that the shrubs that are venerated are those that flourished as weeds in the forest clearings, following the footsteps of man: hazel, holly, rowan, and whitethorn.[18] The creamy blossoms of whitethorn and rowan are associated in popular belief with a full flow of milk. Similarly, a number of yellow flowers, which first flourished as weeds in association with man's earliest husbandry, have been regarded as bringing luck to butter-making: the golden mayflower still figures in May Day ceremonies. The lone-standing whitethorn or maybush—the fairy thorn—is surrounded by superstitions that have been respected by native Roman Catholic and immigrant Protestant alike. We need feel no surprise at the suggestion of survivals through fifty centuries. We recall that von Sydow believed that some international folktales were diffused through western Europe with the megalithic culture.[19] In Ireland, indeed, where an insular setting, peripheral location, and a diversified environment provide ideal conditions for cultural survivals, some elements in the

17. Fleure, "Folklore and Culture Contacts," p. 13.
18. Evans, *Irish Folk Ways*, p. 297.
19. Carl W. von Sydow, "Folktale Studies in Philology: Some Points of View," *Selected Papers on Folklore*, edited by Laurits Bϕdker (Copenhagen, 1948), pp. 189–219.

persistent "Elder Faiths" may well be of premegalithic antiquity and derive from the primary layer of mesolithic culture.

Maire MacNeill has shown that the great pilgrimage to Croagh Patrick in County Mayo, which attracts thousands of the faithful on the last Sunday in July, probably had its origin in the pagan first-fruits festival of Lughnasa.[20] Out of a total of 95 assemblies that are held (or were held until recently) on Irish hilltops at about the beginning of August, no less than 78 have no recognized connections with religious observance. Lughnasa (the festival of Lugh, a Celtic god) is linked in legend with one of the prehistoric invasions of Ireland, but there is little doubt that just as it owes its present popularity and survival-value to the patronage of Christianity, so the Celtic festival was adapted to older native traditions. Culture-contact from time to time, far from killing old customs, has thus stimulated and renovated them.

To sum up, the cultural geographer looks on man and nature as completely interacting phenomena. He sees different responses arising at various times in the infinitely varied regions of the earth, and he sees culture contacts as well as survivals as complicating factors in those responses. If he cannot afford to neglect the unwritten folk elements in the *genre de vie*, the student of folklife in turn can profit from the geographer's approach to the total personality of a region.[21]

Bibliography and Selected Readings

Balfour, Henry. "The Geographical Study of Folklore." *Folk-Lore* 35 (1924) : 16–25. This article is a pioneer discussion of the use of distribution maps ("dispersal-maps") as tools for the study of folklife, taking an example from the protective disguises given children to avoid the evil eye.

Buchanan, Ronald H. "Geography and Folk Life." *Folk Life* 1 (1963) : 5–15. One of the very few articles in the English language on the subject discussed in this chapter.

De la Blache, P. Vidal. *Principles de géographie humaine.* Paris: Colin, 1922. Translated by Millicent T. Bingham as *Principles of Human Geography.* New York, 1926. Includes a useful discussion of *genres de vie.*

Erixon, Sigurd. "Regional European Ethnology." *Folk-Liv* 1 (1937) : 89–108.

20. Maire MacNeill, *The Festival of Lughnasa* (Oxford, 1962) , chap. 6.
21. The author has tried to illustrate this approach in his study of the *Mourne Country* (Dundalk, 1951; revised, 1967) .

———. "West European Connections and Cultural Relations." Folkliv 2 (1938) : 137–72. Both of these articles illustrate the comprehensive approach of one of the pioneers of modern folklife studies and the founder of the international journal *Folkliv* (1937).

Eskerbod, A. "Folk Society and Western Civilization." *Folkliv* 17/18 (1953–54) : 53–60. A brief introduction to European folk cultures.

Evans, E. Estyn. *Irish Folk Ways*. London: Routledge and Kegan Paul, 1957. Largely a description of Irish folk material culture and related lore, this work also contains chapters on festivals, fairs, weddings and wakes, and old superstitions (*pishrogues*). Numerous text illustrations and photographs.

———. "The Atlantic Ends of Europe." *The Advancement of Science* 15 (1958) : 54–64.

———. "The Peasant and the Past." *The Advancement of Science* 17 (1960) : 293–302.

———. "Culture and Land Use in the Old West of North America." *Festgabe für Gottfried Pfeifer: Heidelberger Studien zur Kulturgeographie* 15 (1966) : 72–80.

———. "The Scotch-Irish: Their Cultural Adaptation and Heritage in the American Old West." In *Essays in Scotch-Irish History*, edited by E. R. R. Green. London: Routledge and Kegan Paul, 1969. While mainly concerned with Ireland, the author discusses its folk relations with the other Atlantic ends of Europe and in the last two articles traces its influence in colonial North America.

Fleure, Herbert J. *Some Problems of Society and Environment*. Institute of British Geographers, Publication No. 12. London, 1947.

———. *A Natural History of Man in Britain*. London: Collins, 1951. Revised ed., 1959. Fleure's writings are illuminated by the breadth of vision of a natural scientist who moved into fields of cultural geography, anthropology, archeology, and ethnology.

Forde, C. Daryll. *Habitat, Economy and Society*. London 1934. University Paperback, 1963. A world-wide survey with abundant illustrations and useful discussions of interrelationships.

Glassie, Henry. *Pattern in the Material Folk Culture of the Eastern United States*. Philadelphia: University of Pennsylvania Press, 1969. As the title implies, Glassie is concerned with regional types, particularly of folk architecture. Contains admirable sketches and a useful bibliography that covers European origins.

Kniffen, Fred. "Folk Housing: Key to Diffusion." *Annals of American Geographers* 55 (1965) : 549–77.

———, and Henry Glassie. "Building in Wood in the Eastern United States of America." *Geographical Review* 56 (1966) : 40–66. This article illustrates the productive cooperation of a cultural geographer and a folklorist.

Leighly, John, ed. *Land and Life: Selections from the Writings of Carol Ortwin Sauer*. Berkeley: University of California Press, 1963. Contains some masterly essays by the greatest of American cultural geographers.

Pezzler, W. "Die Geographische Methode in der Volkskunde." *Anthropos* 27 (1932) : 707–42. An early contribution to the distributional study of folklife.

Sheppard, June A. "Vernacular Buildings in England and Wales." *Transactions, Institute of British Geographers* 40 (1966) : 21–37. A demonstration of the usefulness of type-mapping for an understanding of environmental relationships.

Sinnhuber, Karl A. "On the Relations of Folklore and Geography." *Folk-Lore* 68 (1957) : 385–404. Contains many examples of interrelations drawn from central Europe.

Wagner, P. L., and M. W. Mikesell. *Readings in Cultural Geography.* Chicago: University of Chicago Press, 1962. A collection of essays by diverse authors discussing the methodology and findings of cultural geographers.

Weiss, Richard. *Volkskunde der Schweiz.* Zurich: E. Retsch, 1946. An account of the work of one of the most enterprising groups of folklife students in Europe.

CONTRIBUTORS

ROGER D. ABRAHAMS is Professor of English and Anthropology and
director of the African and Afro-American Research Institute at
the University of Texas at Austin.

LINDA DÉGH is Professor of Folklore at Indiana University and editor
of *Indiana Folklore.*

RICHARD M. DORSON is Distinguished Professor of History and Folklore and director of the Folklore Institute at Indiana University.

ALAN DUNDES is Professor of Anthropology and Folklore at the University of California at Berkeley and graduate adviser of the M.A.
program in Folklore.

E. ESTYN EVANS is Professor Emeritus and formerly Director of the
Institute of Irish Studies at Queen's University, Belfast.

ROBERT A. GEORGES is Associate Professor of English and Folklore
and vice-chairman of the Folklore and Mythology Group at the
University of California at Los Angeles.

HENRY GLASSIE is Assistant Professor of Folklore at Indiana University.

J. GERAINT JENKINS is Keeper of the Welsh Folk Museum, Saint Fagans
Castle, Cardiff.

JOANN WHEELER KEALIINOHOMOKU is Assistant Professor of Anthropology at Northern Arizona University, Flagstaff.

GEORGE LIST is Professor of Folklore and director of the Archives of
Traditional Music at Indiana University.

DONALD A. MACDONALD is on the staff of the School of Scottish
Studies, the University of Edinburgh.

JOHN C. MESSENGER is Professor of Anthropology at The Ohio State
University.

FELIX J. OINAS is Professor of Slavic Languages and Literatures and
of Uralic and Altaic Studies and fellow of the Folklore Institute
at Indiana University.

W. Edson Richmond is Professor of English and Folklore at Indiana University.

Warren E. Roberts is Professor of Folklore at Indiana University.

Robert J. Smith is Assistant Professor of Anthropology at the University of Kansas.

Robert Wildhaber was longtime director of the Museum für Völkerkunde in Basel, Switzerland, and is editor of the *International Folklore Bibliography*.

Don Yoder is Associate Professor of Religious Thought and member of the Graduate Department of Folklore and Folklife at the University of Pennsylvania.

INDEX